Organizational Behavior Version 1.0

By

Talya Bauer and Berrin Erdogan

S-28776-BW-2

9 780982 043066

Organizational Behavior Version 1.0

Talya Bauer and Berrin Erdogan

Published by:

Flat World Knowledge, Inc.
1111 19th St NW, Suite 1180
Washington, DC 20036

Brief Contents

About the Authors
Acknowledgments
Dedications
Preface

Chapter 1	Organizational Behavior
Chapter 2	Managing Demographic and Cultural Diversity
Chapter 3	Understanding People at Work: Individual Differences and Perception
Chapter 4	Individual Attitudes and Behaviors
Chapter 5	Theories of Motivation
Chapter 6	Designing a Motivating Work Environment
Chapter 7	Managing Stress and Emotions
Chapter 8	Communication
Chapter 9	Managing Groups and Teams
Chapter 10	Conflict and Negotiations
Chapter 11	Making Decisions
Chapter 12	Leading People Within Organizations
Chapter 13	Power and Politics
Chapter 14	Organizational Structure and Change
Chapter 15	Organizational Culture

Index

Contents

About the Authors 1

Acknowledgments 2

Dedications 3

Preface 4

Chapter 1 Organizational Behavior 7

- Understanding Organizational Behavior 8
- Understanding Your Learning Style 13
- Understanding How OB Research Is Done 15
- Trends and Changes 17
- Conclusion 22
- Exercises 22
- Endnotes 23

Chapter 2 Managing Demographic and Cultural Diversity 25

- Demographic Diversity 27
- Cultural Diversity 38
- The Role of Ethics and National Culture 44
- Conclusion 45
- Exercises 46
- Endnotes 47

Chapter 3 Understanding People at Work: Individual Differences and Perception 49

- The Interactionist Perspective: The Role of Fit 50
- Individual Differences: Values and Personality 52
- Perception 60
- The Role of Ethics and National Culture 66
- Conclusion 68
- Exercises 69
- Endnotes 70

Chapter 4 Individual Attitudes and Behaviors 73

- Work Attitudes 74
- Work Behaviors 78
- The Role of Ethics and National Culture 84
- Conclusion 85
- Exercises 86
- Endnotes 87

Chapter 5 Theories of Motivation 89

Need-Based Theories of Motivation 91
Process-Based Theories 96
The Role of Ethics and National Culture 105
Conclusion 107
Exercises 107
Endnotes 109

Chapter 6 Designing a Motivating Work Environment 111

Motivating Employees Through Job Design 112
Motivating Employees Through Goal Setting 118
Motivating Employees Through Performance Appraisals 122
Motivating Employees Through Performance Incentives 126
The Role of Ethics and National Culture 129
Conclusion 131
Exercises 131
Endnotes 133

Chapter 7 Managing Stress and Emotions 135

What Is Stress? 136
Avoiding and Managing Stress 143
What Are Emotions? 149
Emotions at Work 151
The Role of Ethics and National Culture 155
Conclusion 156
Exercises 156
Endnotes 159

Chapter 8 Communication 161

Understanding Communication 162
Communication Barriers 165
Different Types of Communication and Channels 172
The Role of Ethics and National Culture 182
Conclusion 185
Exercises 186
Endnotes 187

Chapter 9 Managing Groups and Teams 189

Group Dynamics 190
Understanding Team Design Characteristics 197
Management of Teams 204
Barriers to Effective Teams 207
The Role of Ethics and National Culture 209
Conclusion 210

Exercises 211
Endnotes 212

Chapter 10 Conflict and Negotiations 215

Understanding Conflict 216
Causes and Outcomes of Conflict 220
Conflict Management 223
Negotiations 227
The Role of Ethics and National Culture 235
Conclusion 236
Exercises 237
Endnotes 239

Chapter 11 Making Decisions 241

Understanding Decision Making 242
Faulty Decision Making 250
Decision Making in Groups 253
The Role of Ethics and National Culture 258
Conclusion 259
Exercises 260
Endnotes 263

Chapter 12 Leading People Within Organizations 265

Who Is a Leader? Trait Approaches to Leadership 267
What Do Leaders Do? Behavioral Approaches to Leadership 271
What Is the Role of the Context? Contingency Approaches to Leadership 274
What's New? Contemporary Approaches to Leadership 280
The Role of Ethics and National Culture 288
Conclusion 290
Exercises 290
Endnotes 292

Chapter 13 Power and Politics 295

The Basics of Power 296
The Power to Influence 300
Organizational Politics 308
Understanding Social Networks 311
The Role of Ethics and National Culture 313
Conclusion 314
Exercises 315
Endnotes 319

Chapter 14 Organizational Structure and Change 321

Organizational Structure 323
Organizational Change 329

The Role of Ethics and National Culture 339
Conclusion 341
Exercises 341
Endnotes 342

Chapter 15 Organizational Culture 343

Understanding Organizational Culture 344
Characteristics of Organizational Culture 347
Creating and Maintaining Organizational Culture 352
Creating Culture Change 361
The Role of Ethics and National Culture 364
Conclusion 365
Exercises 365
Endnotes 369

Index 371

About the Authors

TALYA BAUER

Talya Bauer (Ph.D., 1994, Purdue University) is the Gerry and Marilyn Cameron Professor of Management at Portland State University. Dr. Bauer is an award-winning teacher who specializes in teaching organizational behavior, management, power and influence, and negotiations, as well as training and development at the graduate and undergraduate level. She conducts research about relationships at work. More specifically, she works in the areas of leadership, selection, and new employee onboarding, which has resulted in dozens of journal publications. She has acted as a consultant for a variety of government, Fortune 1000, and start-up organizations. Dr. Bauer is involved in professional organizations and conferences at the national level, such as serving on the Human Resource Management Executive Committee of the Academy of Management and SIOP Program Chair and member-at-large for SIOP. She is the editor of *Journal of Management* and is on the editorial boards for the *Journal of Applied Psychology* and *Industrial and Organizational Psychology: Perspectives on Science and Practices*, was recognized as one of the most published authors of the 1990s, and is a Fellow of SIOP and APS.

BERRIN ERDOGAN

Berrin Erdogan (Ph.D., 2002, University of Illinois at Chicago) is the Express Employment Professionals Endowed Professor at Portland State University. Dr. Erdogan is an award-winning teacher who teaches management, organizational behavior, and human resources management. Her research interests focus on individual attachment to organizations through fairness, leader-subordinate relations, contextual factors such as organizational culture, and person-organization fit. Her work has been published in journals such as *Academy of Management Journal*, *Journal of Applied Psychology*, and *Personnel Psychology*. She has conducted managerial seminars on the topics of motivation, organizational justice, performance appraisals, and training and development, and has worked as a corporate trainer. She serves on the editorial boards of *Journal of Applied Psychology*, *Journal of Management*, *Journal of Organizational Behavior*, and *Personnel Psychology*.

Acknowledgments

We want to thank Margaret Lannamann and Brett Guidry for doing such a great job keeping all the balls in the air, and Jeff Shelstad and Eric Frank for having the vision and persistence to bring Flat World Knowledge into being, and their faith in us as among the first Flat World Knowledge authors. Many thanks to Andrea Meyer, Sharon Koch, Pamela Tierney, Dean Scott Dawson, and Portland State University for supporting our work.

We would also like to thank the following colleagues whose comprehensive feedback and suggestions for improving the material helped make this a better text:

Cheryl Adkins, Longwood University

Sid Barsuk, Governors State University

Carrie Blair, College of Charleston

Pamela Buckle Henning, Adelphi University

Claudia Cogliser, Texas Tech

Leslie Connell, University of Central Florida

Donald Dahlin, The University of South Dakota

Deborah Good, University of Pittsburgh

Gideon Falk, Purdue University, Calumet

David Futrell, Butler University

Bruce Gillies, California Lutheran University

Michael Hadani, Long Island University, CW Post Campus

Jeff Haldeman, Webster University

Kathy Harris, Northwestern Oklahoma State University

Kelly Kilcrease, University of New Hampshire, Manchester

Antoinette S. Knechtges, Eastern Michigan University

Michael Komos, Benedictine University

Damian Lonsdale, University of South Dakota

Don McCormick, California State University, Northridge

Janet Moen, The University of North Dakota

Lorrie Mowry, McCook Community College

Peter Nowak, Boston College, Boston University, Suffolk University

Samuel Rabinowitz, Rutgers University

Gary Renz, Webster University

Brenda Riddick, California State University, Dominguez Hills

Laura Riolli, California State University, Sacramento

Mark Schwiesow, Marquette University

Leslie Shore, Metropolitan State University

Valarie Spiser-Albert, University of Texas at San Antonio

Christy Weer, Salisbury University

Marilyn Wesner, George Washington University

Jim Woodrum, University of Wisconsin-Madison

The authors also appreciate the efforts of those instructors who have contributed to the project with their work on supplementary materials. Deborah Good from the University of Pittsburgh developed the Student Quizzes and the Test Item File, and Frank Markham from Mesa State College, along with his wife Marylin, created the PowerPoint slide presentation.

In addition, two instructors assisted the development of this material by using it in their classrooms. Their input, along with their students' feedback, has provided us with valuable feedback and confirmation that the material is effective in the classroom:

Pamela Henning, Adelphi University School of Business

Jim Woodrum, University of Wisconsin School of Business

The cadre of copy editors, graphics designers, and technical designers involved in this first-of-its-kind global publishing project also garner our heartfelt thanks. Finally, this book would not have the incredible value and meaning it does without the support and interest of the faculty and students who have commented on early iterations, and will serve to make this 'their book' in the many years to come.

Dedications

TALYA BAUER

This book is dedicated to Jo Ann and Frank Bauer, who fueled my desire to learn, read, and write and to my husband, Horst, and our children, Nicholas and Alexander, who are carrying on the tradition.

BERRIN ERDOGAN

This book is dedicated to my parents, Ilhan and Fulda Erdogan, who were my role models and first introduction to life in academia. I also dedicate this book to my husband, Emre, and our son, Devin, for their love and support.

Preface

To love what you do and feel that it matters—how could anything be more fun?
- Katherine Graham

This quote sums up how we feel about teaching. What could be better than teaching? It is fun, at times exciting, and it really matters. And one of the best courses in the world to teach is Organizational Behavior. Together we have been teaching for over twenty-nine years and have taught thousands of students at the undergraduate, master's, and doctoral levels. Our teaching styles are different, but we share some common values when it comes to teaching, including the beliefs that:

- Organizational Behavior matters
- Evidence-based research is the foundation of Organizational Behavior
- Different students learn in different ways
- There is no substitute for hands-on learning
- Learning the language of OB helps you be more effective in the workplace
- Technology can greatly enhance learning
- Flexibility in teaching delivery allows for student success

NOT "JUST ANOTHER" TEXTBOOK

When we thought about writing a textbook, we knew we didn't want to write "just another" OB book. Enter Flat World Knowledge. Their model solves many of the common challenges faculty and students face when it comes to textbooks. Here are a few that have always bothered us and that Flat World has solved:

- *"I had to buy the whole book, but my teacher didn't use the XYZ chapter."* This isn't a problem with our book because faculty can rearrange chapters as well as add and delete them.
- *"Textbooks are too expensive!"* Textbooks have traditionally been very expensive and the business model of traditional publishing firms has been a huge part of those costs. With our book, students get to choose how to read the material in a number of inexpensive formats ranging from online viewing, black-and-white or color books, audio chapters, or printable PDFs.
- *"New editions come out too quickly and don't really change."* The reason that new editions come out is because used books don't make money for the publishers, but new ones do. With our book, you can change editions when you want and when you think enough is different to warrant the change.

Our journey in creating this book has been a long one. After we wrote the first draft of this book, each chapter went through multiple reviews and revisions, as well as beta tests with real students before this textbook made its way to you. A truly virtual team of authors, copy editors, managing editors, graphic designers, technology gurus, and publishing experts worked together to create something that has never been done before.

WHAT WILL YOU SEE?

Our book emphasizes *active learning*, *meaningful examples*, and *tools* you can use today or put into your OB Toolbox for the years to come. How did we do this?

- We wrote opening cases that bring the topics to life.
- We included learning objectives, key takeaways, and discussion questions for every section of each chapter.
- We created OB Toolboxes with information you can use today.
- We wrote a section on cross-cultural implications for every chapter.
- We also wrote a section on ethical implications for every chapter.
- We included original ethical dilemmas, individual exercises, and group exercises for every chapter.
- For faculty, we have comprehensive PowerPoint slides, a rich test bank, and an extensive author-written Instructor's Manual to enrich teaching.

HOW ARE INSTRUCTORS SUPPORTED?

- A summary of IdeaCasts listed at the beginning of the manual
- Discussion questions for the opening cases
- Answers to the discussion questions throughout the book
- End-of-chapter materials
    - Ethical dilemmas
    - Individual exercises
    - Group exercises
- Solutions to the end-of-chapter materials
- Bonus material
- Further reading suggestions

So welcome to the **textbook revolution**—we are happy to have you on the Bauer and Erdogan's *Organizational Behavior* team! Given that *Organizational Behavior* is an important management course, our objective in developing this material was to provide students and instructors with a solid and comprehensive foundation on *Organizational Behavior* that is accessible and fun. Each of the fifteen chapters is comprehensive but succinct, and action-oriented whether you are just starting out in the world of work or if you are an experienced manager. Moreover, the book and supplements have been written in a direct and active style that we hope students and instructors find both readily accessible and relevant.

THANK YOU FOR JOINING THE REVOLUTION

In reading Bauer and Erdogan, you are quietly **joining the revolution** that is otherwise known as Flat World Knowledge, our partner and publisher. For this we thank you. The people at Flat World Knowledge and your author team share a common vision about the future of management education that is based on *powerful but fun and simple-to-use teaching and learning tools*. Moreover, Flat World Knowledge gives you—you the student and you the instructor—the power to choose. Our fifteen chapters are written using a "modular" format with self-contained sections that can be reorganized, deleted, "added to," and even edited at the sentence level. Using our build-a-book platform, you can easily customize your book to suit your needs and those of your students.

Only with Flat World Knowledge learning platforms do you have the power to choose what your *Organizational Behavior* book looks like, when and how you access your *Organizational Behavior* material, what you use and don't use, when it will be changed, how much you pay for it, and what other study vehicles you leverage. These innovative study vehicles range from book podcasts, flash cards, and peer discussion groups organized in social network formats. Nowhere on the planet can this combination of user-friendliness, user choice, and leading edge technologies be found for business education and learning.

We hope you find Organizational Behavior *to be informative, accessible, and fun!*

CHAPTER 1
Organizational Behavior

LEARNING OBJECTIVES

After reading this chapter, you should be able to understand and articulate answers to the following questions:

1. What is organizational behavior (OB)?
2. Why does organizational behavior matter?
3. How can I maximize my learning in this course?
4. What research methods are used to study organizational behavior?
5. What challenges and opportunities exist for OB?

Employees Come First at Wegmans

This Wegmans is located in Germantown, Maryland.

Source: http://www.flickr.com/photos/mdu2boy/60626190/in/photostream/.

Ever since *Fortune* magazine created its list of the 100 Best Companies to Work For, Wegmans has consistently remained within its ranks. In 2007, Wegmans was given the Food Network's award as the nation's top supermarket. Wegmans is a thriving grocery store chain based in Rochester, New York, that grew to 71 stores across Maryland, New Jersey, New York, Pennsylvania, and Virginia by 2008. Wegmans is a family-run business. Daniel Wegman, the current CEO, is the grandson of the company's cofounder. Daniel's daughter Colleen Wegman is president of the company. The *Fortune* magazine ranking came as a surprise to many in the grocery industry, as Wegmans is characterized by low profit margins, low-paying and tedious jobs, and demanding customer interactions.

There are many reasons that Wegmans has such loyal workers and a turnover rate of only 8% for their 35,000 employees (compared to the industry average, which is closer to 50%). They utilize job sharing and a compressed workweek and also offer telecommuting for some employees. Ultimately, Wegmans created an environment that shows employees they matter. The company motto is "Employees first. Customers second" is based on the belief that when employees feel cared for, they will in turn show concern for the customers they serve. In response to the 2008 ranking as the third best company in the United States to work for, CEO Danny Wegman said, "Every one of our employees and customers should stand up and take a bow, because together they make Wegmans a special place."

Wegmans has also consistently brought innovations to a fairly traditional industry. For example, Wegmans launched a Web site for its stores in 1996 with specifics on health and recipes and other helpful information for its customers. Many have called the experience at Wegmans "Food Theater." With sales of organic foods in the United States soaring to $17 billion, Wegmans supermarkets started its own 50-acre organic research farm. Its goal is to develop best practices in terms of health and efficiency and to share those practices with the hundreds of farmers that supply their stores with fresh fruits and vegetables.

Wegmans is demonstrating that being both socially and environmentally responsible can increase employee loyalty, growth, and profits, creating a win–win situation for the organization, important stakeholders such as employees and customers, and the communities where they are located.

Sources: Based on information contained in Ezzedeen, S. R., Hyde, C. M., & Laurin, K. R. (2006). Is strategic human resource management socially responsible? The case of Wegmans Food Markets, Inc. Employee Responsibility and Rights Journal, 18, 295–307; Niedt, B. (2008, January 22). Wegmans no. 3 on Fortune's "Best companies to work for" list. The Post-Standard; Borden, M., Chu, J., Fishman, C., Prospero, M. A., & Sacks, D. (2008, September 11). 50 ways to green your business. Fast Company. Retrieved January 27, 2008, from http://www.fastcompany.com/magazine/120/50-ways-to-green-your-business_5.html; 100 best companies to work for. (2008). Retrieved January 27, 2008, from the Fortune Web site: http://money.cnn.com/magazines/fortune/bestcompanies/2008/snapshots/3.html.

1. UNDERSTANDING ORGANIZATIONAL BEHAVIOR

LEARNING OBJECTIVES

1. **Learn about the layout of this book.**
2. **Understand what organizational behavior is.**
3. **Understand why organizational behavior matters.**
4. **Learn about OB Toolboxes in this book.**

1.1 About This Book

The people make the place.

- *Benjamin Schneider, Fellow of the Academy of Management*

This book is all about people, especially people at work. As evidenced in the opening case, we will share many examples of people making their workplaces work. People can make work an exciting, fun, and productive place to be, or they can make it a routine, boring, and ineffective place where everyone dreads to go. Steve Jobs, cofounder, chairman, and CEO of Apple Inc. attributes the innovations at Apple, which include the iPod, MacBook, and iPhone, to people, noting, "Innovation has nothing to do with how many R&D dollars you have....It's not about money. It's about the people you have, how you're led, and how much you get it."[1] This became a sore point with investors in early 2009 when Jobs took a medical leave of absence. Many wonder if Apple will be as successful without him at the helm, and Apple stock plunged upon worries about his health.[2]

Mary Kay Ash, founder of Mary Kay Inc., a billion-dollar cosmetics company, makes a similar point, saying, "People are definitely a company's greatest asset. It doesn't make any difference whether the product is cars or cosmetics. A company is only as good as the people it keeps."[3]

Just like people, organizations come in many shapes and sizes. We understand that the career path you will take may include a variety of different organizations. In addition, we know that each student reading this book has a unique set of personal and work-related experiences, capabilities, and career goals. On average, a person working in the United States will change jobs 10 times in 20 years.[4] In order to succeed in this type of career situation, individuals need to be armed with the tools necessary to be lifelong learners. So, this book will not be about giving you all the answers to every situation you may encounter when you start your first job or as you continue up the career ladder. Instead, this book will give you the vocabulary, framework, and critical thinking skills necessary for you to diagnose situations, ask tough questions, evaluate the answers you receive, and act in an effective and ethical manner regardless of situational characteristics.

Throughout this book, when we refer to organizations, we will include examples that may apply to diverse organizations such as publicly held, for-profit organizations like Google and American Airlines, privately owned businesses such as S. C. Johnson & Son Inc. (makers of Windex glass cleaner) and Mars Inc. (makers of Snickers and M&Ms), and not-for-profit organizations such as the Sierra Club or Mercy Corps, and nongovernmental organizations (NGOs) such as Doctors Without Borders and the International Red Cross. We will also refer to both small and large corporations. You will see examples from Fortune 500 organizations such as Intel Corporation or Home Depot Inc., as well as small start-up organizations. Keep in mind that some of the small organizations of today may become large organizations in the future. For example, in 1998, eBay Inc. had only 29 employees and $47.4 million in income, but by 2008 they had grown to 11,000 employees and over $7 billion in revenue.[5] Regardless of the size or type of organization you may work for, people are the common denominator of how work is accomplished within organizations.

Together, we will examine people at work both as individuals and within work groups and how they impact and are impacted by the organizations where they work. Before we can understand these three levels of organizational behavior, we need to agree on a definition of organizational behavior.

FIGURE 1.2

Steve Jobs is known for developing innovative products by hiring the right people for the job and fostering a culture of hard work and creativity.

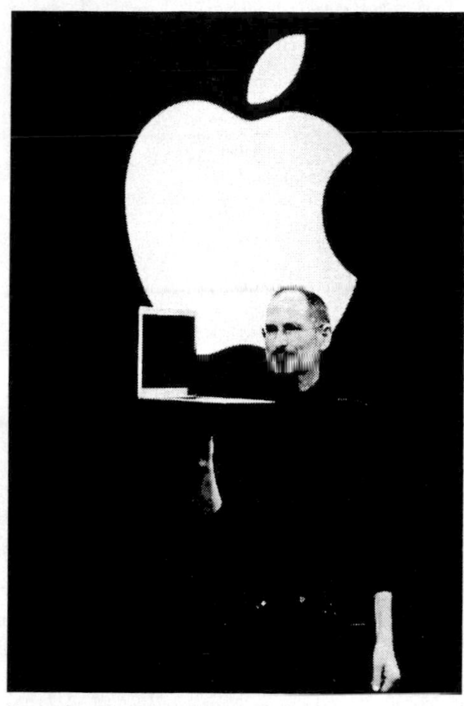

Source: http://en.wikipedia.org/wiki/Image:SteveJobsMacbookAir.JPG.

1.2 What Is Organizational Behavior?

Organizational behavior (OB) is defined as the systematic study and application of knowledge about how individuals and groups act within the organizations where they work. As you will see throughout this book, definitions are important. They are important because they tell us what something is as well as what it is not. For example, we will not be addressing childhood development in this course—that concept is often covered in psychology—but we might draw on research about twins raised apart to understand whether job attitudes are affected by genetics.

organizational behavior (OB)

The systematic study and application of knowledge about how individuals and groups act within the organizations where they work.

OB draws from other disciplines to create a unique field. As you read this book, you will most likely recognize OB's roots in other disciplines. For example, when we review topics such as personality and motivation, we will again review studies from the field of psychology. The topic of team processes relies heavily on the field of sociology. In the chapter relating to decision making, you will come across the influence of economics. When we study power and influence in organizations, we borrow heavily from political sciences. Even medical science contributes to the field of organizational behavior, particularly to the study of stress and its effects on individuals.

FIGURE 1.3

OB spans topics related from the individual to the organization.

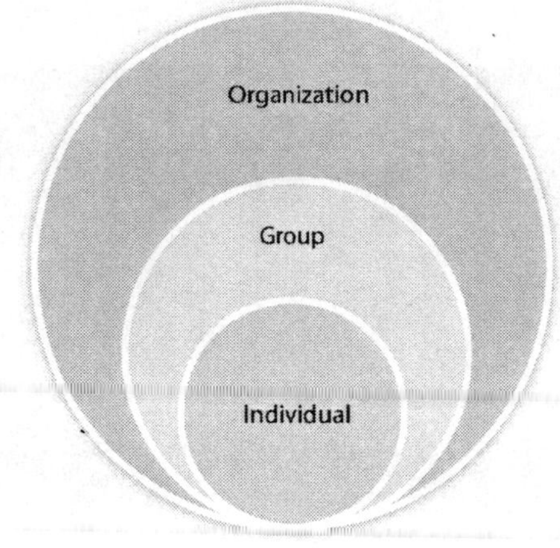

Those who study organizational behavior—which now includes you—are interested in several outcomes such as work attitudes (e.g., job satisfaction and organizational commitment) as well as job performance (e.g., customer service and counterproductive work behaviors). A distinction is made in OB regarding which level of the organization is being studied at any given time. There are three key **levels of analysis** in OB. They are examining the individual, the group, and the organization. For example, if I want to understand my boss's personality, I would be examining the individual level of analysis. If we want to know about how my manager's personality affects my team, I am examining things at the team level. But, if I want to understand how my organization's culture affects my boss's behavior, I would be interested in the organizational level of analysis.

levels of analysis

In OB, includes examining the individual, the group, and the organization.

1.3 Why Organizational Behavior Matters

OB matters at three critical levels. It matters because it is all about **things you care** about. OB can help you become a more engaged organizational member. Getting along with others, getting a great job, lowering your stress level, making more effective decisions, and working effectively within a team...these are all great things, and OB addresses them!

It matters because **employers care** about OB. A recent survey by the National Association of Colleges and Employers (NACE) asked employers which skills are the most important for them when evaluating job candidates, and OB topics topped the list.[6] The following were the top five personal qualities/skills:

1. Communication skills (verbal and written)
2. Honesty/integrity
3. Interpersonal skills (relates well to others)
4. Motivation/initiative
5. Strong work ethic

These are all things we will cover in OB.

Finally, it matters because **organizations care** about OB. The best companies in the world understand that the people make the place. How do we know this? Well, we know that organizations that value their employees are more profitable than those that do not.[7] Research shows that successful organizations have a number of things in common, such as providing employment security, engaging in selective hiring, utilizing self-managed teams, being decentralized, paying well, training employees, reducing status differences, and sharing information.[8] For example, every Whole Foods store has an open compensation policy in which salaries (including bonuses) are listed for all employees. There is also a salary cap that limits the maximum cash compensation paid to anyone in the organization, such as a CEO, in a given year to 19 times the companywide annual average salary of all full-time employees. What this means is that if the average employee makes $30,000 per year, the highest potential pay for their CEO would be $570,000, which is a lot of money but pales in comparison to salaries such as Steve Jobs of Apple at $14.6 million or the highest paid CEO in 2007, Larry Ellison of Oracle, at $192.9 million.[9] Research shows that organizations that are considered healthier and more effective have strong OB characteristics throughout them such as role clarity, information sharing, and performance feedback. Unfortunately, research shows that most organizations are unhealthy, with 50% of respondents saying that their organizations do not engage in effective OB practices.[10]

In the rest of this chapter, we will build on how you can use this book by adding tools to your OB Toolbox in each section of the book as well as assessing your own learning style. In addition, it is important to understand the research methods used to define OB, so we will also review those. Finally, you will see what challenges and opportunities businesses are facing and how OB can help overcome these challenges.

1.4 Adding to Your OB Toolbox

Your OB Toolbox

OB Toolboxes appear throughout this book. They indicate a tool that you can try out today to help you develop your OB skills.

Throughout the book, you will see many OB Toolbox features. Our goal in writing this book is to create something useful for you to use now and as you progress through your career. Sometimes we will focus on tools you can use today. Other times we will focus on things you may want to think about that may help you later. As you progress, you may discover some OB tools that are particularly relevant to you while others are not as appropriate at the moment. That's great—keep those that have value to you. You can always go back and pick up tools later on if they don't seem applicable right now.

The important thing to keep in mind is that the more tools and skills you have, the higher the quality of your interactions with others will be and the more valuable you will become to organizations that compete for top talent.[11] It is not surprising that, on average, the greater the level of education you have, the more money you will make. In 2006, those who had a college degree made 62% more money than those who had a high school degree.[12] Organizations value and pay for skills as the next figure shows.

FIGURE 1.4

Education and training have financial payoffs as illustrated by these unemployment and earnings for workers 25 and older.

Education & Training Pays, 2006

Unemployment & earnings for workers 25 & older by educational attainment; earnings for full-time wage and salary workers

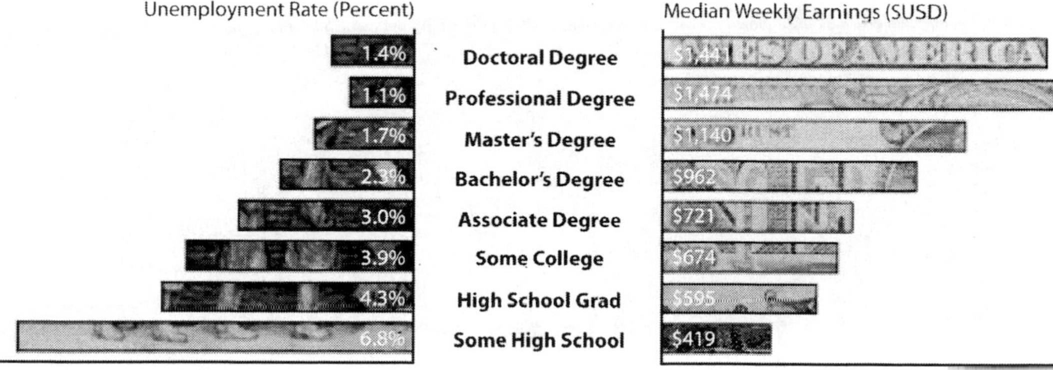

Source: U.S. Bureau of Labor Statistics, http://www.bls.gov.

Tom Peters is a management expert who talks about the concept of individuals thinking of themselves as a brand to be managed. Further, he recommends that individuals manage themselves like free agents.[13] The following OB Toolbox includes several ideas for being effective in keeping up your skill set.

Your OB Toolbox: Skill Survival Kit

- *Keep your skills fresh.* Consider revolutionizing your portfolio of skills at least every 6 years.
- *Master something.* Competence in many skills is important, but excelling at something will set you apart.
- *Embrace ambiguity.* Many people fear the unknown. They like things to be predictable. Unfortunately, the only certainty in life is that things will change. Instead of running from this truth, embrace the situation as a great opportunity.
- *Network.* The term has been overused to the point of sounding like a cliché, but networking works. This doesn't mean that having 200 connections on MySpace, LinkedIn, or Facebook makes you more effective than someone who has 50, but it does mean that getting to know people is a good thing in ways you can't even imagine now.
- *Appreciate new technology.* This doesn't mean you should get and use every new gadget that comes out on the market, but it does mean you need to keep up on what the new technologies are and how they may affect you and the business you are in.

Source: Adapted from ideas in Peters, T. (2007). Brand you survival kit. Fast Company. Retrieved July 1, 2008, from http://www.fastcompany.com/magazine/83/playbook.html.

journaling

The process of writing out thoughts and emotions on a regular basis.

A key step in building your OB skills and filling your toolbox is to learn the language of OB. Once you understand a concept, you are better able to recognize it. Once you recognize these concepts in real-world events and understand that you have choices in how you will react, you can better manage yourself and others. An effective tool you can start today is **journaling**, which helps you chart your progress as you learn new skills. For more on this, see the OB Toolbox below.

OB Toolbox: Journaling as a Developmental Tool

- *What exactly is journaling?* Journaling refers to the process of writing out thoughts and emotions on a regular basis.
- *Why is journaling a good idea?* Journaling is an effective way to record how you are feeling from day to day. It can be a more objective way to view trends in your thoughts and emotions so you are not simply relying on your memory of past events, which can be inaccurate. Simply getting your thoughts and ideas down has been shown to have health benefits as well such as lowering the writer's blood pressure, heart rate, and decreasing stress levels.
- *How do I get started?* The first step is to get a journal or create a computer file where you can add new entries on a regular basis. Set a goal for how many minutes per day you want to write and stick to it. Experts say at least 10 minutes a day is needed to see benefits, with 20 minutes being ideal. The quality of what you write is also important. Write your thoughts down clearly and specifically while also conveying your emotions in your writing. After you have been writing for at least a week, go back and examine what you have written. Do you see patterns in your interactions with others? Do you see things you like and things you'd like to change about yourself? If so, great! These are the things you can work on and reflect on. Over time, you will also be able to track changes in yourself, which can be motivating as well.

Sources: Created based on ideas and information in Bromley, K. (1993). Journaling: Engagements in reading, writing, and thinking. New York: Scholastic; Caruso, D., & Salovey, P. (2004). The emotionally intelligent manager: How to develop and use the four key emotional skills of leadership. San Francisco: Jossey-Bass; Scott, E. (2008). The benefits of journaling for stress management. Retrieved January 27, 2008, from About.com: http://stress.about.com/od/generaltechniques/p/profilejournal.htm.

1.5 Isn't OB Just Common Sense?

As teachers we have heard this question many times. The answer, as you might have guessed, is *no—OB is not just common sense.* As we noted earlier, OB is the systematic study and application of knowledge about how individuals and groups act within the organizations where they work. *Systematic* is an important word in this definition. It is easy to think we understand something if it makes sense, but research on decision making shows that this can easily lead to faulty conclusions because our memories fail us. We tend to notice certain things and ignore others, and the specific manner in which information is framed can affect the choices we make. Therefore, it is important to rule out alternative explanations one by one rather than to assume we know about human behavior just because we are humans! Go ahead and take the following quiz and see how many of the 10 questions you get right. If you miss a few, you will see that OB isn't just common sense. If you get them all right, you are way ahead of the game!

Putting Common Sense to the Test

Please answer the following 10 questions by noting whether you believe the sentence is *true* or *false*.

1. Brainstorming in a group is more effective than brainstorming alone. _____
2. The first 5 minutes of a negotiation are just a warm-up to the actual negotiation and don't matter much. _____
3. The best way to help someone reach their goals is to tell them to do their best. _____
4. If you pay someone to do a task they routinely enjoy, they'll do it even more often in the future. _____
5. Pay is a major determinant of how hard someone will work. _____
6. If a person fails the first time, they try harder the next time. _____
7. People perform better if goals are easier. _____
8. Most people within organizations make effective decisions. _____
9. Positive people are more likely to withdraw from their jobs when they are dissatisfied. _____
10. Teams with one smart person outperform teams in which everyone is average in intelligence. _____

You may check your answers with your instructor.

KEY TAKEAWAY

This book is about people at work. Organizations come in many shapes and sizes. Organizational behavior is the systematic study and application of knowledge about how individuals and groups act within the organizations where they work. OB matters for your career, and successful companies tend to employ effective OB practices. The OB Toolboxes throughout this book are useful in increasing your OB skills now and in the future.

EXERCISES

1. Which type of organizations did you have the most experience with? How did that affect your understanding of the issues in this chapter?
2. Which skills do you think are the most important ones for being an effective employee?
3. What are the three key levels of analysis for OB?
4. Have you ever used journaling before? If so, were your experiences positive? Do you think you will use journaling as a tool in the future?
5. How do you plan on using the OB Toolboxes in this book? Creating a plan now can help to make you more effective throughout the term.

2. UNDERSTANDING YOUR LEARNING STYLE

LEARNING OBJECTIVES

1. **Understand different dimensions of learning styles.**
2. **Diagnose your own learning style.**
3. **Explore strategies for working with your preferred learning style.**

2.1 Learning Styles

In order to maximize your learning in this course and in any learning situation, it's important to understand what type of learner you are. Some people learn better by seeing information. For example, if you notice that you retain more information by reading and seeing diagrams and flow charts, you may be a **visual learner**. If you primarily learn by listening to others such as in lectures, conversations, and videos, you may be an **auditory learner**. Finally, if you have a preference for actually doing things and learning from trial and error, you may be a **kinesthetic learner**. If you are unaware of what your primary learning style is, take a moment to diagnose it at the Web site listed below.

visual learner

One who processes information most effectively by looking at words and diagrams.

auditory learner

One who processes information most effectively by listening or talking.

kinesthetic learner

One who processes information most effectively by actively engaging with the material.

What Is Your Learning Style?

Take the following online learning style quiz to find out what type of learner you are:

http://www.vark-learn.com/english/page.asp?p=questionnaire

Now that you have established which type of learner you are, let's go through some recommendations for your style. Here are some learning recommendations.[14]

- If you are a *visual learner*,
  - draw pictures and diagrams to help you understand;
  - take careful notes during class so you can refer back to them later on;
  - summarize the main points of what you learn using charts.
- If you are an *auditory learner*,
  - join study groups so you can discuss your questions and ideas and hear responses;

- write down any oral instructions you hear in class right away;
- consider taping lectures if your professor says it is OK and view online lectures on topics you are interested in.

- If you are a *kinesthetic learner*,
  - schedule your homework and study sessions so you can take breaks and move around between reading your notes or chapters;
  - take good notes during class—this will force you to pay attention and process information even when you feel like you are "getting it";
  - don't sign up for long once-a-week classes—they normally require too much sitting and listening time.

For various reasons, using flash cards seems to help with all three learning styles. For example, for an auditory learner, saying the answers aloud when using flash cards helps to solidify concepts. For a visual learner, seeing the answers written down on the flash card can be helpful. And for the kinesthetic learner, the act of creating and organizing flash cards helps the concepts stick.

FIGURE 1.5

While individuals tend to have a dominant, or primary, learning style, being able to adapt to different learning situations is a big plus, so anytime you get a chance to learn in a new way, grab it. The more you practice, the better you will become at learning to process information in different ways.

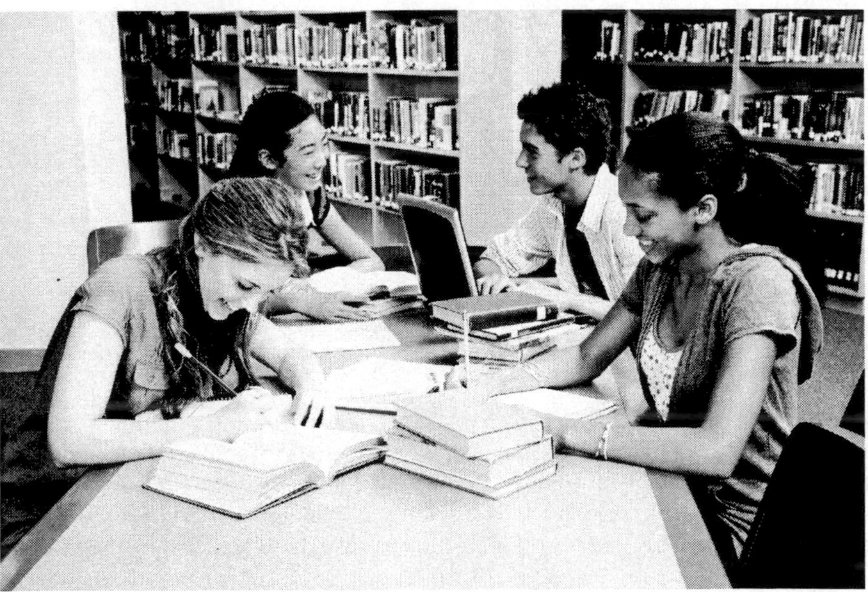

KEY TAKEAWAY

People tend to have a preferred learning style. Visual learners see things to learn them. Auditory learners hear things to learn them. Kinesthetic learners do things to learn them.

EXERCISES

1. Were you surprised by your primary learning style? Why or why not?
2. How does your learning style affect the kinds of classes you take?
3. Try out a few of the suggestions for your learning style over the next week and see how they work.
4. Now that you've learned more about your own learning style, are there some things you might consider doing to expand on your other styles? If so, what steps might you take to do this?

3. UNDERSTANDING HOW OB RESEARCH IS DONE

LEARNING OBJECTIVES

1. Learn the terminology of research.
2. Understand the different types of OB research methods used.

3.1 OB Research Methods

OB researchers have many tools they use to discover how individuals, groups, and organizations behave. Researchers have working **hypotheses** based on their own observations, readings on the subject, and information from individuals within organizations. Based on these ideas, they set out to understand the relationships among different **variables**. There are a number of different research methods that researchers use, and we will discuss a few of these below. Imagine that your manager has asked you to find out if setting goals will help to make the employees at your company more productive. We will cover the different ways you could use research methods to answer this question, impress your boss, and hopefully get a promotion.

hypotheses

Tentative guesses or hunches for an expected observation, phenomenon, or scientific problem that can be tested.

variables

Entities that can take on different values.

Surveys

Surveys are one of the primary methods management researchers use to learn about OB. A basic survey involves asking individuals to respond to a number of questions. The questions can be open-ended or close-ended. An example of an open-ended question that could be used to address your manager's question would be to ask employees how they feel about goal setting in relation to productivity, then summarize your findings. This might work if you have a small organization, but open-ended surveys can be time consuming to summarize and hard to interpret at a glance. You could get more specific by asking employees a series of close-ended questions in which you supply the response key, such as a rating of 1 to 5. Today it is easy to create online surveys that quickly compile the results automatically. There are even several free survey tools available online such as http://freeonlinesurveys.com/ and http://www.surveygizmo.com/, or you can use paper-and-pencil surveys.

surveys

Research tools used to elicit respondents' reactions to specific questions.

Sample Survey About the Effectiveness of Goal Setting

Instructions: We would like to gather your opinions about different aspects of work. Please answer the following three questions using the scale below:

Response Scale:

1=Strongly disagree

2=Disagree

3=Neither agree nor disagree

4=Agree

5=Strongly agree

Setting goals at work helps me to focus	1	2	3	4	5
Goal setting is effective in improving performance	1	2	3	4	5
I get more done when I use goal setting	1	2	3	4	5

FIGURE 1.6

Researchers may even use a handheld device to randomly or systematically survey participants about key aspects of their day to get a more dynamic view. This is called time sampling.

Regardless of the method you choose to collect your information, the next step is to look at the average of the responses to the questions and see how the responses stack up. But this still wouldn't really answer the question your boss asked, which is whether using goal setting would help employees be more effective on the job. To do this, you would want to conduct a field study.

Field Studies

field studies

Research conducted in actual organizations. They may include observation, interviews, surveys, or experiments.

experimental design

A study having a group that receives a treatment and a comparison group that receives no treatment.

control group

A group that does not receive any experimental manipulation so it can be compared to a treatment group.

treatment group

A group that receives experimental manipulation.

Field studies are also effective ways to learn about what is truly going on within organizations. There are survey field studies like the one above, but more compelling evidence comes from field studies that employ an **experimental design**. Here you would assign half the employees at your company to the goal setting condition and the other half to the **control group** condition. The control group wouldn't get any information on goal setting but the **treatment group** would. If you found that the treatment group was more effective than the control group, you could tell your boss that goal setting works.

Laboratory Studies

lab study

Research conducted under controlled conditions and may include observation, interviews, surveys, or experiments.

OB researchers are often interested in basic research questions such as "Can we show that goal setting increases performance on a simple task?" This is how research on goal setting started, and it is also how we can establish the conditions under which it works more or less effectively. Again, to address this, researchers may conduct a **lab study** in which one group is assigned one condition and the other group is assigned the control condition (generally the control condition involves no change at all). You may even have been involved in a lab study during your time at your university. One of the most important concepts to understand with lab studies is that they give the researcher a great deal of control over the environment they are studying but do so in a less "realistic" way, since they are not studying real employees in real work settings. For example, in a lab study, a researcher could simulate hiring and firing employees to see if firing some employees affected the goal-setting behavior of the remaining employees. While this wouldn't be legal or ethical to do in a real organization, it could be a compelling lab study. At the same time, however, firing someone in a lab setting does not necessarily carry the same consequences as it would in real life.

Case Studies

case studies

In-depth descriptions of a single industry or company.

generalizability

The likelihood that findings in a given study would be found in another setting or study.

Case studies are in-depth descriptions of a single industry or company. Case writers typically employ a systematic approach to gathering data and explaining an event or situation in great detail. The benefits of case studies are that they provide rich information for drawing conclusions about the circumstances and people involved in the topics studied. The downside is that it is sometimes difficult to **generalize** what worked in a single situation at a single organization to other situations and organizations.

Meta-Analysis

meta-analysis

The process of summarizing research findings from studies on related topics.

Meta-analysis is a technique used by researchers to summarize what other researchers have found on a given topic. This analysis is based on taking observed correlations from multiple studies, weighting them by the number of observations in each study, and finding out if, overall, the effect holds or not. For example, what is the average relationship between job satisfaction and performance? Research shows that, looking across 300 studies, the relationship is moderately strong.[15] This is useful information because for years people had thought that the relationship did not exist, but when all the studies to date were examined together, the original beliefs about the satisfaction–performance relationship deteriorated. The advantage of meta-analysis is that it gives a more definitive answer to a question than a single study ever could. The downside is that meta-analysis is only possible if sufficient research has been done on the topic in question.

3.2 Measurement Issues in OB

reliability

The consistency of measurement.

validity

The truth of the measurement.

Another important thing to understand is the difference between **reliability** and **validity**. Imagine you own a trucking company. A major component in trucking is managing the weight of different cargo. If you had a scale that gave you the same weight three times, we would say that was a very reliable scale. But, if it turns out the weights given are in kilograms instead of pounds, it would not be a valid measure if you charge for delivery by the pound.

Finally, much of management research addresses **correlations** between two concepts rather than actual **causation**. Correlation simply means that two things co-vary. For example, it would be inaccurate to assume that because 99% of the people who died this year also drank water, consuming water kills people. Yet many people claim their product caused a positive outcome when, in fact, the data do not support their claim any more than the water example. This brings up something that confuses even seasoned researchers. When you have only one observation it is called a **datum**. When you use the word **data**, it refers to multiple observations, so it is always plural.

correlation

Measures the strength of the relationship between two variables.

causation

The act of making something happen.

datum

The term that refers to a single observation.

data

The term used to describe multiple observations and is always plural (as if you were using the word *numbers*).

KEY TAKEAWAY

OB researchers test hypotheses using different methods such as surveys, field studies, case studies, and meta-analyses. Reliability refers to consistency of the measurement while validity refers to the underlying truth of the measurement. It is important to recognize the difference between correlation and causation.

EXERCISES

1. Create a hypothesis about people at work. Now that you have one in mind, which method do you think would be most effective in helping you test your hypothesis?
2. Have you used any of the OB research methods before? If not, what can you do to become more familiar with them?
3. Give an example of a reliable measure.
4. Give an example of a valid measure.
5. How can you know if a relationship is causal or correlational?

4. TRENDS AND CHANGES

LEARNING OBJECTIVES

1. **Understand current challenges for OB.**
2. **Understand current opportunities for OB.**

4.1 Challenges and Opportunities

There are many trends within the workplace and around the globe that have and will continue to affect the workplace and your career. We are sure you have noticed many of these trends simply by reading newspaper headlines. We will highlight some of these trends along with the challenges and opportunities they present for students of organizational behavior.

Ethical Challenges

Business ethics refers to applying ethical principles to situations that arise at work. It feels like it's been one ethical scandal after the other. Enron Corp., AIG, Tyco International, WorldCom, and Halliburton Energy Services have all been examples of what can be described in terms ranging from poor judgment to outright illegal behavior. The immediate response by government has been the Sarbanes-Oxley Act, which went into effect in 2002. This act consists of 11 different requirements aimed at greater accountability, which companies must comply with in terms of financial reporting. And while there may be some benefit to businesses from complying with these rules,[16] few see this as the long-term solution to dealing with unethical behavior. The challenge is to continue to think about business ethics on a day-to-day basis and institute cultures that support ethical decision making. The opportunity for organizations to be on the forefront of ethical thinking and actions is wide open. OB research finds that the most important determinant of whether a company acts ethically is not necessarily related to the policies and rules regarding ethical conduct but instead whether it has a culture of consistently ethical behavior and if leaders are committed to this ethical behavior.[17]

OB Toolbox: Take an Ethics-at-Work Audit

- *Do you integrate ethics into your day-to-day decisions at work?* It's easy to think about ethics as something big that you either have or don't have, but the reality is that ethical decisions are made or not made each and every day.
- *Do you take the "front page" test when making important decisions at work?* Thinking about how you would feel if the decisions you are making at work showed up on the front page of your local newspaper can help you avoid engaging in questionable behavior.
- *Do you role model ethics at work?* Seeing others engage in unethical behavior is the start of a slippery slope when it comes to ethics. Consider the decisions you are making and how they are consistent or inconsistent with how you would like to be seen by others.
- *Do you consider if rewards are distributed ethically at work?* Situations in which there are "haves" and "have nots" are breeding grounds of unethical behavior. Maintaining pay equity can help keep everyone more honest.
- *Have you held a "risk brainstorm" at work?* If you ask those around you if they see any situations that are challenging ethical behavior, you can uncover some seriously risky situations and avoid them.

Sources: Adapted from ideas in Callahan, D. (2004). The cheating culture: Why more Americans are doing wrong to get ahead. New York: Harcourt Books; Toffler, B. L. (2003). Five ways to jump-start your company's ethics. Fast Company. Retrieved May 4, 2008, from http://www.fastcompany.com/magazine/75/5ways.html; Trevino, L. K., Weaver, G. R., & Reynolds, S. J. (2006). Behavioral ethics in organizations: A review. Journal of Management, 32, 951–990.

Lack of Employee Engagement

employee engagement

A person who is fully involved in and enthusiastic about their work is engaged.

Studies suggest that fostering engagement, a concept related to passion, in employees has a significant impact on the corporate bottom line. Gallup, for instance, has been on the forefront of measuring the impact of what is called employee engagement. **Employee engagement** is a concept that is generally viewed as managing discretionary effort, that is, when employees have choices, they will act in a way that furthers their organization's interests. An engaged employee is a person who is fully involved in and enthusiastic about their work.[18] The consulting firm BlessingWhite offers this description of engagement and its value: "Engaged employees are not just committed. They are not just passionate or proud. They have a line-of-sight on their own future and on the organization's mission and goals. They are 'enthused' and 'in gear' using their talents and discretionary effort to make a difference in their employer's quest for sustainable business success."[19]

Engaged employees are those who are performing at the top of their abilities and happy about it. According to statistics that Gallup has drawn from 300,000 companies in its database, 75%–80% of employees are either "disengaged" or "actively disengaged."[20]

That's an enormous waste of potential. Consider Gallup's estimation of the impact if 100% of an organization's employees were fully engaged:

- Customers would be 70% more loyal.
- Turnover would drop by 70%.
- Profits would jump by 40%.

Job satisfaction studies in the United States routinely show job satisfaction ratings of 50%–60%. But one recent study by Harris Interactive of nearly 8,000 American workers went a step further.[21] What did the researchers find?

- Only 20% feel very passionate about their jobs.
- Less than 15% agree that they feel strongly energized by their work.
- Only 31% (strongly or moderately) believe that their employer inspires the best in them.

It is clear that engagement is both a challenge and an opportunity for OB.

Technology

Technology has transformed the way work gets done and has created many great opportunities. The nexus of increasing personal computing power, the Internet, as well as nanotechnology are allowing things to be created that weren't even imaginable 50 years ago. And the rate of technological change is not expected to slow down anytime soon. Gordon Moore, a cofounder of Intel Corp., shocked the world in 1975 with what is now termed Moore's Law, which states that computing power doubles every 2 years. This explains why a 4-year-old computer can barely keep up with the latest video game you have purchased. As computers get faster, new software is written to capitalize on the increased computing power. We are also more connected by technology than ever before. It is now possible to send and receive e-mails or text messages with your coworkers and customers regardless of where in the world you are. Over 100 million adults in the United States use e-mail regularly (at least once a day)[22] and Internet users around the world send an estimated 60 billion e-mails every day,[23] making e-mail the second most popular medium of communication worldwide, second only to voice. Technology has also brought a great deal of challenges to individuals and organizations alike. To combat the overuse of e-mail, companies such as Intel have instituted "no e-mail Fridays," in which all communication is done via other communication channels. The technology trend contains challenges for organizational behavior.

FIGURE 1.7

A consequence of greater connectivity is the potential for more work–family spillover and conflict.

Flattening World

Thomas Friedman's book *The World Is Flat: A Brief History of the Twenty-First Century* makes the point that the Internet has "flattened" the world and created an environment in which there is a more level playing field in terms of access to information. This access to information has led to an increase in innovation, as knowledge can be shared instantly across time zones and cultures. It has also created intense competition, as the speed of business is growing faster and faster all the time. In his book *Wikinomics*, Don Tapscott notes that mass collaboration has changed the way work gets done, how products are created, and the ability of people to work together without ever meeting.

There are few barriers to information today, which has created huge opportunities around the globe. Marc Andreessen, cofounder of Netscape Communications Corporation, notes, "Today, the most profound thing to me is the fact that a 14-year-old in Romania or Bangalore or the Soviet Union or Vietnam has all the information, all the tools, all the software easily available to apply knowledge however they want."[24] Of course, information by itself is not as important as having the right information at the right time. A major challenge for individuals in the flattened world is learning how to evaluate the quality of the information they find. For tips on how to evaluate the quality of information, see the OB Toolbox below.

OB Toolbox: Tips for Evaluating the Quality of Information

Here is a resource to refer to when evaluating information you find on the Web:

- http://guides.library.jhu.edu/evaluatinginformation

Sustainability and Green Business Practices

The primary role of for-profit companies is to generate shareholder wealth. More recently, the concept of the **triple bottom line** has been gaining popularity. Those subscribing to the triple bottom line believe that beyond economic viability, businesses need to perform well socially and environmentally. While some organizations have embraced the concepts underlying the triple bottom line, businesses are also undergoing a great deal of "greenwashing," which refers to the marketing of products or processes as green to gain customers without truly engaging in sustainable business practices. **Sustainable business practices** are those that meet the present needs without compromising the needs of future generations. The challenge is to reconcile the accountability that publicly owned firms have in generating wealth for their shareholders while attending to the triple bottom line. On the other hand, organizations also have an opportunity to leverage a proactive stance toward innovative processes that can result in even greater profits for their products. For example, sales of the Toyota Prius, which combines combustion engine efficiency with hybrid electric technology, have been dramatic and have helped propel Toyota to record market share and profits. An unlikely leader in the sustainability movement is Wal-Mart. Wal-Mart hired Adam Werbach, the former president of the Sierra Club, to help train 1.3 million North American Wal-Mart employees about sustainability. Wal-Mart has also been pressuring suppliers to produce compact fluorescent lightbulbs with less mercury and has slashed the resources needed in packaging by requiring all suppliers to make packages smaller.[25] In the future, increasing interdependence between businesses, governmental agencies, and NGOs is bound to effect change throughout the economy.[26]

FIGURE 1.8

Social responsibility is not just something organizations do at the price of profits. It can also lead to superior results. Environmentally Neutral Design (END) has designed a shoe that reduces the amount of material needed so it costs less to produce and is the lightest performance shoe on the market.

Source: Used with permission of END.

triple bottom line

Evaluating organizations against three performance criteria including economic, social, and environmental viability.

sustainable business practices

Practices that meet the current needs of businesses without compromising the needs of future generations.

Aging Workforce and the Millennial Generation

You have probably heard that the American workforce is aging. Over the next 30 years, 76 million baby boomers will retire, but there will only be 46 million new workers from Generations X and Y entering the labor force. This demographic trend creates both challenges and opportunities for organizations.

The aging trend has been predicted for decades. "The number of U.S. workers over the age of 40 has increased significantly over the past 30 years. By 2010, more than 51% of the workforce will be 40 or older, up almost 20% over 30 years. At the same time, the portion of the workforce aged 25 to 39 will decline by nearly 3%. The number of workers aged 55 and older will grow from 13% of the labor force in 2000 to 20% in 2020."[27] There will be record numbers of retirements. Aging workforces can create great opportunities for industries such as health care, but it can also mean great challenges lie ahead as entire industries related to basic infrastructure face massive retirement projections. For example, everything from air traffic controllers to truck drivers are predicted to be in huge demand as thousands of retiring workers leave these industries at roughly the same time.[28]

FIGURE 1.9 Percentage of Labor Force by Age Group for 2004 and Projections for 2014

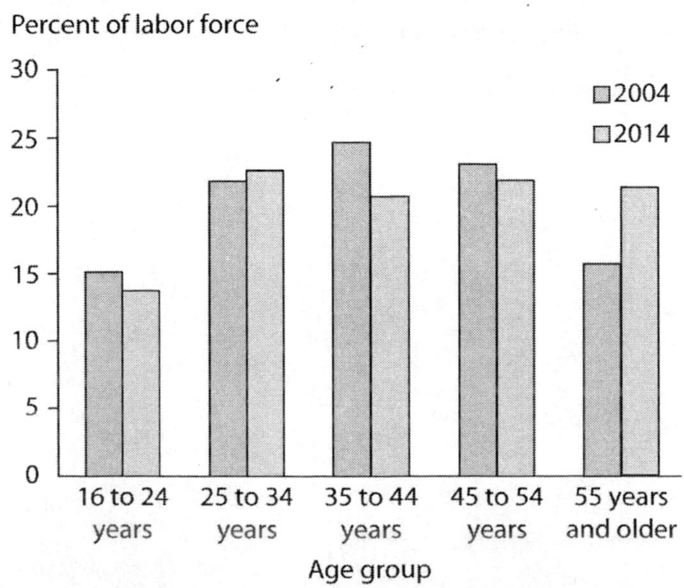

Source: U.S. Department of Labor, Bureau of Labor Statistics Occupational Outlook Handbook 2006–2007 edition. Retrieved October 15, 2007, from http://www.bls.gov/oco/images/ocotjc03.gif.

The Millennial Generation (which includes those born between 1980 and 2000) differs from previous generations in terms of technology and multitasking as a way of life. Having never known anything different, this population has technology embedded in their lives. In addition, they value teamwork, feedback, and challenging work that allows them to develop new skills. If you are in this generation or know those who are, you know there is an expectation of immediate interaction.[29] The challenge for organizational behavior is to keep individuals from different generations communicating effectively and managing people across generational lines despite different values placed on teamwork, organizational rewards, work–life balance, and desired levels of instruction.

The Global Marketplace for Staffing: Outsourcing

Outsourcing has become a way of life for many organizations—especially those based in the United States that are outsourcing to other countries where labor is relatively inexpensive. *Outsourcing* refers to having someone outside the formal ongoing organization doing work previously handled in-house. This practice can involve temporary employees, consultants, or even offshoring workers. **Offshoring** means sending jobs previously done in one country to another country. Nowhere is there more outsourcing and offshoring than in the software technology industry. A survey of software developers revealed that 94% outsource project work, and when they offshore, the work most frequently goes to India, Singapore, Russia, and China.[30] Microsoft has been expanding their use of employees in Canada for a variety of reasons such as closer proximity to Microsoft's headquarters in Seattle, Washington, as well as similarity of language and time zones. Across industries, more than 80% of boards of directors in the United States have considered offshore outsourcing.[31] Charles Handy, author of *The Age of Paradox*, coined the term *shamrock organization*, which is an organization comprising one-third regular employees, one-third temporary employees, and one-third consultants and contractors. He predicts that this is where organizations are headed in the future. The darker side of the changing trend in organization composition revolves around potential unemployment issues as companies move toward a shamrock layout. Fortunately, this shift also presents an opportunity for organizations to staff more flexibly and for employees to consider the tradeoffs between consistent, full-time work within a single organization versus the changing nature of work as a temporary employee, contract worker, or consultant—especially while developing a career in a new industry, in which increased exposure to various organizations can help an individual get up to speed in a short amount of time. The challenge for organizational behavior is managing teams consisting of different nationalities separated not only by culture and language but also in time and space.

FIGURE 1.10

A shamrock organization includes an equal number of regular employees, temporary employees, and consultants and contractors.

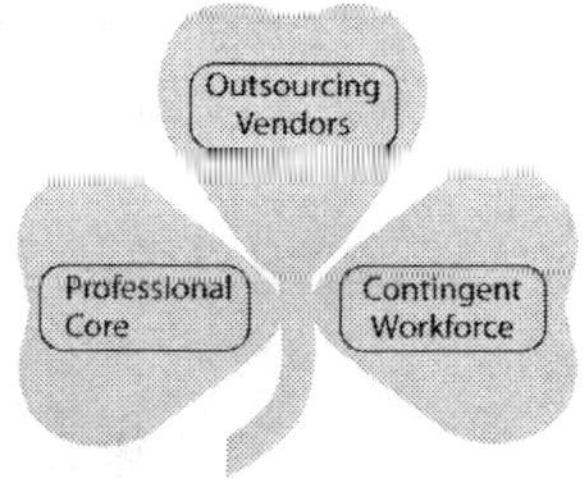

outsourcing

An organization asking an outside organization to perform functions that could have been performed by itself.

offshoring

Refers to some or all of a business process being moved from one country to another country.

KEY TAKEAWAY

Trends include ethical challenges, rapid technological change, a flattening world, sustainable business practices, demographic trends, and the global marketplace. A number of trends will influence the way work gets done today and in the future. Understanding organizational behavior will help you anticipate and adapt to these changes as a lifelong learner.

EXERCISES

1. Share an ethical dilemma you have observed at work or school to someone in your class. What do you think should have been done differently and why?
2. How has technology and the flattening world affected you in the last 10 years? Please share examples of this.
3. Do you think the sustainability movement in business is a trend that's here to stay or a business fad? Why or why not?
4. Do you see the aging (and retiring) workforce as an opportunity or a threat for businesses? How do you think this will affect your career?

5. CONCLUSION

This chapter is designed to familiarize you with the concept of organizational behavior. We have covered methods organizations might use to address issues related to the way people behave at work. In addition, you should now be familiar with the large number of factors, both within an individual and within the environment, that may influence a person's behaviors and attitudes. In the coming years, society is likely to see a major shift in the way organizations function, resulting from rapid technological advances, social awareness, and cultural blending. OB studies hope to enhance an organization's ability to cope with these issues and create an environment that is mutually beneficial to the company as well as its employees.

6. EXERCISES

INDIVIDUAL EXERCISE

Create an Action Plan for Developing Your OB Skills

1. Hopefully you have already completed reading this chapter. If not, wait until you've done so to complete this individual exercise.
2. If you have not done so already, please take the learning styles survey at http://www.vark-learn.com/english/page.asp?p=questionnaire.
3. In addition, please be sure you have reviewed the table of contents for this organizational behavior textbook.
4. What themes do you see? How do you think these topics affect your interactions with others? How might your learning style affect how you'll approach this course? Have you ever considered journaling as a technique for self-improvement and reflection?
5. Now, write down five action steps that you plan to take as you work through this book. Refer to these steps throughout the term and modify them as needed.

GROUP EXERCISE

Best Job–Worst Job

1. Please think about the best and worst jobs you have ever had. If you have never had a job, think of a school project instead. What made the job or project great or horrible?
2. Now get into a small group of students and share your experience with them. Listen to what others are saying and see if you see any themes emerge. For example, what are the most common features of the best jobs? What are the most common features of the worst jobs?

ENDNOTES

1. Kirkpatrick, D. (1998). The second coming of Apple. *Fortune, 138,* 90.
2. Parloff, R. (2008, January 22). Why the SEC is probing Steve Jobs. *Money.* Retrieved January 28, 2009, from http://money.cnn.com/2009/01/22/technology/stevejobs_disclosure.fortune/?postversion=2009012216.
3. Retrieved June 4, 2008, from http://www.litera.co.uk/t/NDk1MDA/.
4. U.S. Bureau of Labor Statistics. (2005). Retrieved December 8, 2005, from the U.S. Bureau of Labor Statistics Web site: http://www.bls.gov/nls/nlsfaqs.htm#anch5.
5. Gibson, E. (2008, March). Meg Whitman's 10th anniversary as CEO of eBay. *Fast Company,* 25.
6. NACE 2007 Job Outlook Survey. Retrieved July 26, 2008, from the National Association of Colleges and Employers (NACE) Web site: http://www.naceweb.org/press/quick.htm#qualities.
7. Huselid, M. A. (1995). The impact of human resource management practices on turnover, productivity, and corporate financial performance. *Academy of Management Journal, 38,* 635-672; Pfeffer, J. (1998). *The human equation: Building profits by putting people first.* Boston: Harvard Business School Press; Pfeffer, J., & Veiga, J. F. (1999). Putting people first for organizational success. *Academy of Management Executive, 13,* 37–48; Welbourne, T., & Andrews, A. (1996). Predicting performance of Initial Public Offering firms: Should HRM be in the equation? *Academy of Management Journal, 39,* 910–911.
8. Pfeffer, J., & Veiga, J. F. (1999). Putting people first for organizational success. *Academy of Management Exec-* [illegible]
9. Elmer-DeWitt, P. (2008, May 2). Top-paid CEOs: Steve Jobs drops from no. 1 to no. 120. *Fortune.* Retrieved July 26, 2008, from CNNMoney.com: http://apple20.blogs.fortune.cnn.com/2008/05/02/top-paid-ceos-steve-jobs-drops-from-no-1-to-no-120/.
10. Aguirre, D. M., Howell, L. W., Kletter, D. B., & Neilson, G. L. (2005). A global check-up: Diagnosing the health of today's organizations (online report). Retrieved July 25, 2008, from the Booz & Company Web site: http://www.orgdna.com/downloads/GlobalCheckUp-OrgHealthNov2005.pdf.
11. Michaels, E., Handfield-Jones, H., & Axelrod, B. (2001). *The war for talent.* Boston: Harvard Business School Publishing.
12. U.S. Bureau of Labor Statistics.
13. Peters, T. (1997). The brand called you. *Fast Company.* Retrieved July 1, 2008, from http://www.fastcompany.com/magazine/10/brandyou.html; Peters, T. (2004). Brand you survival kit. *Fast Company.* Retrieved July 1, 2008, from http://www.fastcompany.com/magazine/83/playbook.html.
14. Adapted from recommendations by Jennifer Yeh at San Francisco State University. Retrieved June 1, 2008, from the Center for the Enhancement of Teaching, San Francisco State University: http://oct.sfsu.edu/introduction/learningstyles/index.html.
15. Judge, T. A., Thoresen, C. J., Bono, J. E., & Patton, G. K. (2001). The job satisfaction-job performance relationship: A qualitative and quantitative review. *Psychological Bulletin, 127,* 376–407.
16. Wagner, S., & Dittmar, L. (2006, April). The unexpected benefits of Sarbanes-Oxley. *Harvard Business Review, 84,* 133–140.
17. Driscoll, K., & McKee, M. (2007). Restorying a culture of ethical and spiritual values: A role for leader storytelling. *Journal of Business Ethics, 73,* 205–217.
18. Employee engagement. Retrieved September 12, 2008, from Gallup Web site: http://www.gallup.com/consulting/52/Employee-Engagement.aspx.
19. BlessingWhite. (2008, April). 2008 Employee engagement report. Retrieved May 15, 2008, from the BlessingWhite Inc. Web site: http://www.blessingwhite.com/eee__report.asp.
20. Gallup Press. (2006, October 12). Gallup study: Engaged employees inspire company innovation. *Gallup Management Journal.* Retrieved October 29, 2008, from http://gmj.gallup.com/content/24880/Gallup-Study-Engaged-Employees-Inspire-Company.aspx.
21. Zinkewicz, P. (2005, April 11). Satisfaction (not) guaranteed. Retrieved October 29, 2008, from the Age Wave Web site: http://www.agewave.com/media_files/rough.html.
22. Taylor, C. (2002, June 10). 12 Steps for email addicts. *Time.com.* Retrieved October 14, 2008, from http://www.time.com/time/magazine/article/0,9171,1002621,00.html.
23. CNET UK. (2006, April 26). 60 billion emails sent daily worldwide. Retrieved July 26, 2008, from the CNET UK Web site: http://www.cnet.co.uk/misc/print/0,39030763,49265163,00.htm.
24. Friedman, T. L. (2005, April 3). It's a flat world, after all. *New York Times.* Retrieved June 1, 2008, from http://www.nytimes.com/2005/04/03/magazine/03DOMINANCE.html.
25. Fetterman, W. (2006). Wal-Mart grows "green" strategies. *USA Today.* Retrieved June 1, 2008, from http://www.usatoday.com/money/industries/retail/2006-09-24-wal-mart-cover-usat_x.htm; Sacks, D. (2007, December 19). Working with the enemy. *Fast Company.* Retrieved June 1, 2008, from http://[illegible]/working-with-the-enemy.html.
26. Campbell, J. L. (2007). Why would corporations behave in socially responsible ways? An institutional theory of corporate social responsibility. *Academy of Management Review, 32,* 946–967; Etzion, D. (2007). Research on organizations and the natural environment, 1992–present: A review. *Journal of Management, 33,* 637–664.
27. Mosner, E., Spiezle, C., & Emerman, J. (2003). The convergence of the aging workforce and accessible technology: The implications for commerce, business, and policy (Microsoft white paper). Retrieved June 1, 2008, from the Microsoft Web site: http://www.microsoft.com/enable/aging/convergence.aspx.
28. Ewart, H. (2008, April 29). Female truckies needed amid driver shortage. Retrieved June 1, 2008, from the ABC News Web site: http://www.abc.net.au/news/stories/2008/04/29/2229837.htm; Watson, B. (2008, January 30). Aviation. Retrieved June 1, 2008, from the MSNBC Web site: http://www.msnbc.msn.com/id/22917202/.
29. Oblinger, D. (2003). Boomers, Genexers and Millennials: Understanding the new students. *Educause Review.* Retrieved June 2, 2008, from http://net.educause.edu/ir/library/pdf/ERM0342.pdf.
30. McGee, M. K. (2007, October 2). Canada wants to become the next India for U.S. software companies. *Information Week.* Retrieved May 22, 2008, from http://www.informationweek.com/news/management/showArticle.jhtml?articleID=202200301.
31. Diana, A. (2003, November 12). Outsourcing by the numbers. *TechNewsWorld.* Retrieved May 22, 2008, from http://www.technewsworld.com/story/32114.html?welcome=1211412779&welcome=1211478843.

CHAPTER 2
Managing Demographic and Cultural Diversity

LEARNING OBJECTIVES

After reading this chapter, you should be able to do the following:

1. Understand what constitutes diversity.
2. Explain the benefits of managing diversity.
3. Describe challenges of managing a workforce with diverse demographics.
4. Describe the challenges of managing a multicultural workforce.
5. Understand diversity and ethics.
6. Understand cross-cultural issues regarding diversity.

Managing Diversity at IBM

IBM operates in over 170 countries, including this office in Tokyo, Japan. The diversity of IBM employees makes effective management of diversity a key business priority.

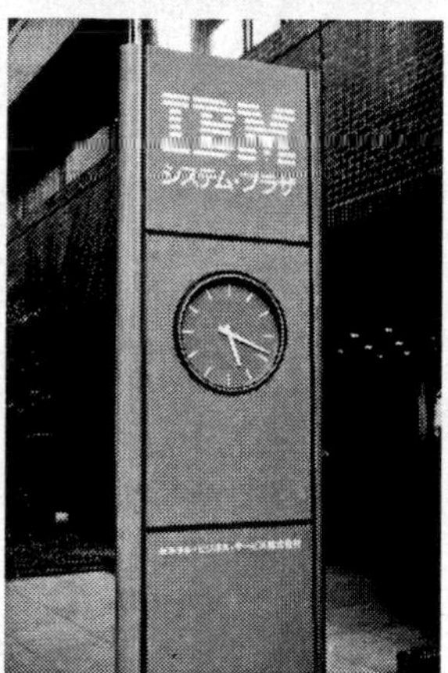

Source: http://commons.wikimedia.org/wiki/Image:IBM.jpg.

When you are a company that operates in over 170 countries with a workforce of over 350,000 employees, understanding and managing diversity effectively is not optional—it is a key business priority. A company that employs individuals and sells products worldwide needs to understand the diverse groups of people that make up the world.

Starting from its early history in the United States, IBM Corporation has been a pioneer in valuing and appreciating its diverse workforce. In 1935, almost 30 years before the Equal Pay Act guaranteed pay equality between the sexes, then IBM President Thomas Watson promised women equal pay for equal work. In 1943, the company had its first female vice president. Again, 30 years before the Family and Medical Leave Act (FMLA) granted women unpaid leave for the birth of a child, IBM offered the same benefit to female employees, extending it to 1 year in the 1960s and to 3 years in 1988. In fact, the company has been ranked in the top 10 on the *Working Mother* magazine's 100 Best Companies list in 2007 and has been on the list every year since its inception in 1986.

IBM has always been a leader in diversity management. Yet, the way diversity was managed was primarily to ignore differences and provide equal employment opportunities. This changed when Louis Gerstner became the CEO in 1993. Gerstner was surprised at the low level of diversity in the senior ranks of the company. For all the effort being made to promote diversity, the company still had what he perceived a masculine culture. In 1995, he created eight diversity task forces around demographic groups such as women and men, as well as Asians, African Americans, LBGT (lesbian, bisexual, gay, transgender) individuals, Hispanics, Native Americans, and employees with disabilities. These task forces consisted of senior-level, well-respected executives and higher level managers, and members were charged with gaining an understanding of how to make each constituency feel more welcome and at home at IBM. Each task force conducted a series of meetings and surveyed thousands of employees to arrive at the key factors concerning each particular group. For example, the presence of a male-dominated culture, lack of networking opportunities, and work–life management challenges topped the list of concerns for women. Asian employees were most concerned about stereotyping, lack of networking, and limited employee development plans. African American employee concerns included retention, lack of networking, and limited training opportunities. Armed with a list of priorities, the company launched a number of key programs and initiatives to address these issues. As an example, employees looking for a mentor could use the company's Web site to locate one willing to provide guidance and advice. What is probably most unique about this approach is that the company acted on each concern whether it was based on reality or perception. They realized that some women were concerned that they would have to give up leading a balanced life if they wanted to be promoted to higher management, whereas about 70% of the women in higher levels actually had children, indicating that perceptual barriers can also act as a barrier to employee aspirations. IBM management chose to deal with this particular issue by communicating better with employees as well as through enhancing their networking program.

Today, the company excels in its recruiting efforts to increase the diversity of its pool of candidates. One of the biggest hurdles facing diversity at IBM is the limited minority representation in fields such as computer sciences and engineering. For example, only 4% of students graduating with a degree in computer sciences are Hispanic. To tackle this issue, IBM partners with colleges to increase recruitment of Hispanics to these programs. In a program named EXITE (Exploring Interest in Technology and Engineering), they bring middle school female students together for a weeklong program where they learn math and science in a fun atmosphere from IBM's female engineers. To date, over 3,000 girls have gone through this program.

What was the result of all these programs? IBM tracks results through global surveys around the world and identifies which programs have been successful and which issues no longer are viewed as problems. These programs were instrumental in more than tripling the number of female executives worldwide as well as doubling the number of minority executives. The number of LBGT executives increased sevenfold, and executives with disabilities tripled. With growing emerging markets and women and minorities representing a $1.3 trillion market, IBM's culture of respecting and appreciating diversity is likely to be a source of competitive advantage.

Sources: Based on information from Ferris, M. (2004, Fall). What everyone said couldn't be done: Create a global women's strategy for IBM. The Diversity Factor, 12(4), 37–42; IBM hosts second annual Hispanic education day (2007, December–January). Hispanic Engineer, 21(2), 11; Lee, A. M. D. (2008, March). The power of many: Diversity's competitive advantage. Incentive, 182(3), 16–21; Thomas, D. A. (2004, September). Diversity as strategy. Harvard Business Review, 82(9), 98–108.

Around the world, the workforce is becoming diverse. In 2007, women constituted 46% of the workforce in the United States. In the same year, 11% of the workforce was African American, 14% were of Hispanic origin, and 5% were Asian.[1] Employees continue to work beyond retirement, introducing age diversity to the workforce. Regardless of your gender, race, and age, it seems that you will need to work with, communicate with, and understand people different from you at school as well as at work. Understanding cultures different from your own is also becoming increasingly important due to the globalization of business. In the United States, 16% of domestic employees were foreign born, indicating that even those of us who are not directly involved in international business may benefit from developing an appreciation for the differences and similarities between cultures.[2] In this chapter, we will examine particular benefits and challenges of managing a diverse workforce and discuss ways in which you can increase your effectiveness when working with diversity.

As we discuss differing environments faced by employees with different demographic traits, we primarily concentrate on the legal environment in the United States. Please note that the way in which demographic diversity is treated legally and socially varies around the globe. For example, countries such as Canada and the United Kingdom have their own versions of equal employment legislation. Moreover, how women, employees of different races, older employees, employees with disabilities, and employees of different religions are viewed and treated shows much variation based on the societal context.

1. DEMOGRAPHIC DIVERSITY

LEARNING OBJECTIVES

1. **Explain the benefits of managing diversity effectively.**
2. **Explain the challenges of diversity management.**
3. **Describe the unique environment facing employees with specific traits such as gender, race, religion, physical disabilities, age, and sexual orientation.**

Diversity refers to the ways in which people are similar or different from each other. It may be defined by any characteristic that varies within a particular work unit such as gender, race, age, education, tenure, or functional background (such as being an engineer versus being an accountant). Even though diversity may occur with respect to any characteristic, our focus will be on diversity with respect to demographic, relatively stable, and visible characteristics: specifically gender, race, age, religion, physical abilities, and sexual orientation. Understanding how these characteristics shape organizational behavior is important. While many organizations publicly rave about the benefits of diversity, many find it challenging to manage diversity effectively. This is evidenced by the number of complaints filed with the Equal Employment Opportunity Commission (EEOC) regarding discrimination. In the United States, the Age Discrimination Act of 1975 and Title VII of the Civil Rights Act of 1964 outlaw discrimination based on age, gender, race, national origin, or religion. The 1990 Americans with Disabilities Act prohibits discrimination of otherwise capable employees based on physical or mental disabilities. In 2008, over 95,000 individuals filed a complaint claiming that they were discriminated based on these protected characteristics. Of course, this number represents only the most extreme instances in which victims must have received visibly discriminatory treatment to justify filing a complaint. It is reasonable to assume that many instances of discrimination go unreported because they are more subtle and employees may not even be aware of inconsistencies such as pay discrimination. Before the passing of antidiscrimination laws in the United States, many forms of discrimination were socially acceptable. This acceptance of certain discrimination practices is more likely to be seen in countries without similar employment laws. It seems that there is room for improvement when it comes to benefiting from diversity, understanding its pitfalls, and creating a work environment where people feel appreciated for their contributions regardless of who they are.

diversity

The ways in which people are similar or different from each other.

1.1 Benefits of Diversity

What is the business case for diversity? Having a diverse workforce and managing it effectively have the potential to bring about a number of benefits to organizations.

Higher Creativity in Decision Making

An important potential benefit of having a diverse workforce is the ability to make higher quality decisions. In a diverse work team, people will have different opinions and perspectives. In these teams, individuals are more likely to consider more alternatives and think outside the box when making decisions. When thinking about a problem, team members may identify novel solutions. Research shows that diverse teams tend to make higher quality decisions.[3] Therefore, having a diverse workforce may have a direct impact on a company's bottom line by increasing creativity in decision making.

FIGURE 2.2

Research shows that diverse teams tend to make higher quality decisions.

© 2010 Jupiterimages Corporation

Better Understanding and Service of Customers

A company with a diverse workforce may create products or services that appeal to a broader customer base. For example, PepsiCo Inc. planned and executed a successful diversification effort in the recent past. The company was able to increase the percentage of women and ethnic minorities in many levels of the company, including management. The company points out that in 2004, about 1% of the company's 8% revenue growth came from products that were inspired by the diversity efforts, such as guacamole-flavored Doritos chips and wasabi-flavored snacks. Similarly, Harley-Davidson Motor Company is pursuing diversification of employees at all levels because the company realizes that they need to reach beyond their traditional customer group to stay competitive.[4] Wal-Mart Stores Inc. heavily advertises in Hispanic neighborhoods between Christmas and The Epiphany because the company understands that Hispanics tend to exchange gifts on that day as well.[5] A company with a diverse workforce may understand the needs of particular groups of customers better, and customers may feel more at ease when they are dealing with a company that understands their needs.

More Satisfied Workforce

When employees feel that they are fairly treated, they tend to be more satisfied. On the other hand, when employees perceive that they are being discriminated against, they tend to be less attached to the company, less satisfied with their jobs, and experience more stress at work.[6] Organizations where employees are satisfied often have lower turnover.

Higher Stock Prices

Companies that do a better job of managing a diverse workforce are often rewarded in the stock market, indicating that investors use this information to judge how well a company is being managed. For example, companies that receive an award from the U.S. Department of Labor for their diversity management programs show increases in the stock price in the days following the announcement. Conversely, companies that announce settlements for discrimination lawsuits often show a decline in stock prices afterward.[7]

Lower Litigation Expenses

Companies doing a particularly bad job in diversity management face costly litigations. When an employee or a group of employees feel that the company is violating EEOC laws, they may file a complaint. The EEOC acts as a mediator between the company and the person, and the company may choose to settle the case outside the court. If no settlement is reached, the EEOC may sue the company on behalf of the complainant or may provide the injured party with a right-to-sue letter. Regardless of the outcome, these lawsuits are expensive and include attorney fees as well as the cost of the settlement or judgment, which may reach millions of dollars. The resulting poor publicity also has a cost to the company. For example, in 1999, the Coca-Cola Company faced a race discrimination lawsuit claiming that the company discriminated against African Americans in promotions. The company settled for a record $192.5 million.[8] In 2004, the clothing retailer Abercrombie & Fitch faced a race discrimination lawsuit that led to a $40 million settlement and over $7 million in legal fees. The company had constructed a primarily Caucasian image and was accused of discriminating against Hispanic and African American job candidates, steering these applicants to jobs in the back of the store. As part of the settlement, the company agreed to diversify its workforce and catalog, change its image to promote diversity, and stop recruiting employees primarily from college fraternities and sororities.[9] In 2007, the new African American district attorney of New Orleans, Eddie Jordan, was accused of firing 35 Caucasian employees and replacing them with African American employees. In the resulting reverse-discrimination lawsuit, the office was found liable for $3.7 million, leading Jordan to step down from his office in the hopes of preventing the assets of the office from being seized.[10] As you can see, effective management of diversity can lead to big cost savings by decreasing the probability of facing costly and embarrassing lawsuits.

Higher Company Performance

As a result of all these potential benefits, companies that manage diversity more effectively tend to outperform others. Research shows that in companies pursuing a growth strategy, there was a positive relationship between racial diversity of the company and firm performance.[11] Companies ranked in the Diversity 50 list created by *DiversityInc* magazine performed better than their counterparts.[12] And, in a survey of 500 large companies, those with the largest percentage of female executives performed better than those with the smallest percentage of female executives.[13]

1.2 Challenges of Diversity

If managing diversity effectively has the potential to increase company performance, increase creativity, and create a more satisfied workforce, why aren't all companies doing a better job of encouraging diversity? Despite all the potential advantages, there are also a number of challenges associated with increased levels of diversity in the workforce.

Similarity-Attraction Phenomenon

One of the commonly observed phenomena in human interactions is the tendency for individuals to be attracted to similar individuals.[14] Research shows that individuals communicate less frequently with those who are perceived as different from themselves.[15] They are also more likely to experience emotional conflict with people who differ with respect to race, age, and gender.[16] Individuals who are different from their team members are more likely to report perceptions of unfairness and feel that their contributions are ignored.[17]

The **similarity-attraction phenomenon** may explain some of the potentially unfair treatment based on demographic traits. If a hiring manager chooses someone who is racially similar over a more qualified candidate from a different race, the decision will be ineffective and unfair. In other words, similarity-attraction may prevent some highly qualified women, minorities, or persons with disabilities from being hired. Of course, the same tendency may prevent highly qualified Caucasian and male candidates from being hired as well, but given that Caucasian males are more likely to hold powerful management positions in today's U.S.-based organizations, similarity-attraction may affect women and minorities to a greater extent. Even when candidates from minority or underrepresented groups are hired, they may receive different treatment within the organization. For example, research shows that one way in which employees may get ahead within organizations is through being mentored by a knowledgeable and powerful mentor. Yet, when the company does not have a formal mentoring program in which people are assigned a specific mentor, people are more likely to develop a mentoring relationship with someone who is similar to them in demographic traits.[18] This means that those who are not selected as protégés will not be able to benefit from the support and advice that would further their careers. Similarity-attraction may even affect the treatment people receive daily. If the company CEO constantly invites a male employee to play golf with him while a female employee never receives the invitation, the male employee may have a serious advantage when important decisions are made.

similarity-attraction phenomenon

The tendency to be more attracted to individuals who are similar to us.

Why are we more attracted to those who share our demographic attributes? Demographic traits are part of what makes up **surface-level diversity**. Surface-level diversity includes traits that are highly visible to us and those around us, such as race, gender, and age. Researchers believe that people pay attention to surface diversity because they are assumed to be related to **deep-level diversity**, which includes values, beliefs, and attitudes. We want to interact with those who share our values and attitudes, but when we meet people for the first time, we have no way of knowing whether they share similar values. As a result, we tend to use surface-level diversity to make judgments about deep-level diversity. Research shows that surface-level traits affect our interactions with other people early in our acquaintance with them, but as we get to know people, the influence of surface-level traits is replaced by deep-level traits such as similarity in values and attitudes.[19] Age, race, and gender dissimilarity are also stronger predictors of employee turnover during the first few weeks or months within a company. It seems that people who are different from others may feel isolated during their early tenure when they are dissimilar to the rest of the team, but these effects tend to disappear as people stay longer and get to know other employees.

surface-level diversity

Traits that are highly visible to us and those around us, such as race, gender, and age.

deep-level diversity

Diversity in values, beliefs, and attitudes.

As you may see, while similarity-attraction may put some employees at a disadvantage, it is a tendency that can be managed by organizations. By paying attention to employees early in their tenure, having formal mentoring programs in which people are assigned mentors, and training managers to be aware of the similarity-attraction tendency, organizations can go a long way in dealing with potential diversity challenges.

FIGURE 2.3

Individuals often initially judge others based on surface-level diversity. Over time, this effect tends to fade and is replaced by deep-level traits such as similarity in values and attitudes.

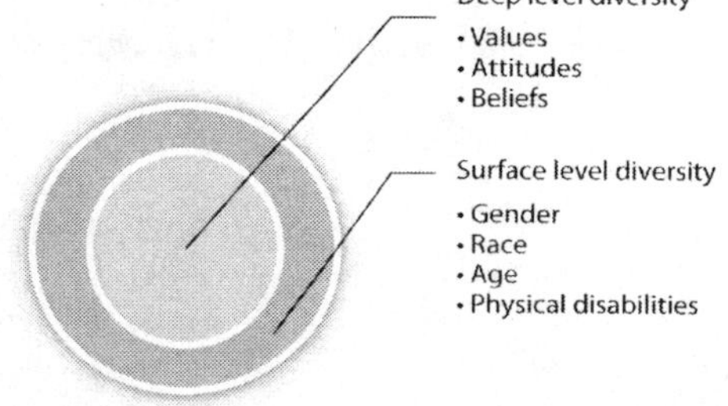

Faultlines

A **faultline** is an attribute along which a group is split into subgroups. For example, in a group with three female and three male members, gender may act as a faultline because the female members may see themselves as separate from the male members. Now imagine that the female members of the same team are all over 50 years old and the male members are all younger than 25. In this case, age and gender combine to further divide the group into two subgroups. Teams that are divided by faultlines experience a number of difficulties. For example, members of the different subgroups may avoid communicating with each other, reducing the overall cohesiveness of the team. Research shows that these types of teams make less effective decisions and are less creative.[20] Faultlines are more likely to emerge in diverse teams, but not all diverse teams have faultlines. Going back to our example, if the team has three male and three female members, but if two of the female members are older and one of the male members is also older, then the composition of the team will have much different effects on the team's processes. In this case, age could be a bridging characteristic that brings together people divided across gender.

faultline

An attribute along which a group is split into subgroups.

Research shows that even groups that have strong faultlines can perform well if they establish certain norms. When members of subgroups debate the decision topic among themselves before having a general group discussion, there seems to be less communication during the meeting on pros and cons of different alternatives. Having a norm stating that members should not discuss the issue under consideration before the actual meeting may be useful in increasing decision effectiveness.[21]

FIGURE 2.4

The group on the left will likely suffer a strong faultline due to the lack of common ground. The group to the right will likely only suffer a weak faultline because the men and women of the different groups will likely identify with each other.

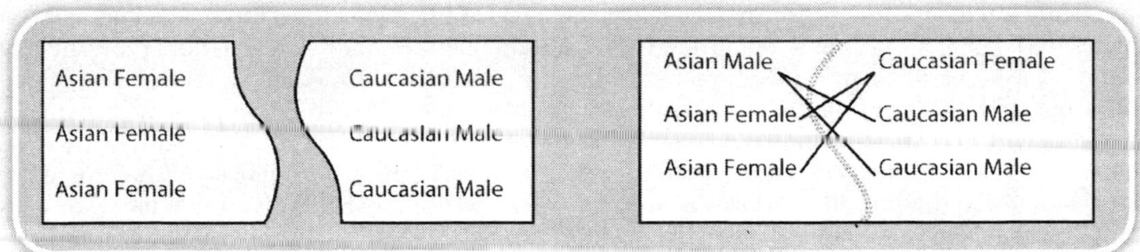

Stereotypes

stereotypes

Generalizations about a particular group of people.

An important challenge of managing a diverse workforce is the possibility that stereotypes about different groups could lead to unfair decision making. **Stereotypes** are generalizations about a particular group of people. The assumption that women are more relationship oriented, while men are more assertive, is an example of a stereotype. The problem with stereotypes is that people often use them to make decisions about a particular individual without actually verifying whether the assumption holds for the person in question. As a result, stereotypes often lead to unfair and inaccurate decision making. For example, a hiring manager holding the stereotype mentioned above may prefer a male candidate for a management position over a well-qualified female candidate. The assumption would be that management positions require assertiveness and the male candidate would be more assertive than the female candidate. Being aware of these stereotypes is the first step to preventing them from affecting decision making.

1.3 Specific Diversity Issues

Different demographic groups face unique work environments and varying challenges in the workplace. In this section, we will review the particular challenges associated with managing gender, race, religion, physical ability, and sexual orientation diversity in the workplace.

Gender Diversity in the Workplace

In the United States, two important pieces of legislation prohibit gender discrimination at work. The Equal Pay Act (1963) prohibits discrimination in pay based on gender. Title VII of the Civil Rights Act (1964) prohibits discrimination in all employment-related decisions based on gender. Despite the existence of strong legislation, women and men often face different treatment at work. The earnings gap and the glass ceiling are two of the key problems women may experience in the workplace.

Earnings Gap

An often publicized issue women face at work is the earnings gap. The median earnings of women who worked full time in 2008 was 79% of men working full time.[22] There are many potential explanations for the earnings gap that is often reported in the popular media. One explanation is that women are more likely to have gaps in their résumés because they are more likely to take time off to have children. Women are still the primary caregiver for young children in many families and career gaps tend to affect earnings potential because it prevents employees from accumulating job tenure. Another potential explanation is that women are less likely to pursue high-paying occupations such as engineering and business.

In fact, research shows that men and women have somewhat different preferences in job attributes, with women valuing characteristics such as good hours, an easy commute, interpersonal relationships, helping others, and opportunities to make friends more than men do. In turn, men seem to value promotion opportunities, freedom, challenge, leadership, and power more than women do.[23] These differences are relatively small, but they could explain some of the earnings gap. Finally, negotiation differences among women are often cited as a potential reason for the earnings gap. In general, women are less likely to initiate negotiations.[24] Moreover, when they actually negotiate, they achieve less favorable outcomes compared to men.[25] Laboratory studies show that female candidates who negotiated were more likely to be penalized for their attempts to negotiate and male evaluators expressed an unwillingness to work with a female who negotiated.[26] The differences in the tendency to negotiate and success in negotiating are important factors contributing to the earnings gap. According to one estimate, as much as 34% of the differences between women's and men's pay can be explained by their starting salaries.[27] When differences in negotiation skills or tendencies affect starting salaries, they tend to have a large impact over the course of years.

If the earnings gap could be traced only to résumé gaps, choice of different occupations, or differences in negotiation behavior, the salary difference might be viewed as legitimate. Yet, these factors fail to completely account for gender differences in pay, and lawsuits about gender discrimination in pay abound. In these lawsuits, stereotypes or prejudices about women seem to be the main culprit. In fact, according to a Gallup poll, women are over twelve times more likely than men to perceive gender-based discrimination in the workplace.[28] For example, Wal-Mart Stores Inc. was recently sued for alleged gender-discrimination in pay. One of the people who initiated the lawsuit was a female assistant manager who found out that a male assistant manager with similar qualifications was making $10,000 more per year. When she approached the store manager, she was told that the male manager had a "wife and kids to support." She was then asked to submit a household budget to justify a raise.[29] Such explicit discrimination, while less frequent, contributes to creating an unfair work environment.

Glass Ceiling

Another issue that provides a challenge for women in the workforce is the so-called **glass ceiling**. While women may be represented in lower level positions, they are less likely to be seen in higher management and executive suites of companies. In fact, while women constitute close to one-half of the workforce, men are four times more likely to reach the highest levels of organizations.[30] In 2008, only twelve of the Fortune 500 companies had female CEOs, including Xerox Corporation, PepsiCo, Kraft Foods Inc., and Avon Products Inc. The absence of women in leadership is unfortunate, particularly in light of studies that show the leadership performance of female leaders is comparable to, and in some dimensions such as transformational or change-oriented leadership, superior to, the performance of male leaders.[31]

glass ceiling

The situation that some qualified employees are prevented from advancing to higher level positions due to factors such as discrimination. Glass ceiling is often encountered by women and minorities.

One explanation for the glass ceiling is the gender-based stereotypes favoring men in managerial positions. Traditionally, men have been viewed as more assertive and confident than women, while women have been viewed as more passive and submissive. Studies show that these particular stereotypes are still prevalent among male college students, which may mean that these stereotypes may be perpetuated among the next generation of managers.[32] Assumptions such as these are problematic for women's advancement because stereotypes associated with men are characteristics often associated with being a manager. Stereotypes are also found to influence how managers view male versus female employees' work accomplishments. For example, when men and women work together in a team on a "masculine" task such as working on an investment portfolio and it is not clear to management which member has done what, managers are more likely to attribute the team's success to the male employees and give less credit to the female employees.[33] It seems that in addition to working hard and contributing to the team, female employees should pay extra attention to ensure that their contributions are known to decision makers.

There are many organizations making the effort to make work environments more welcoming to men and women. For example, IBM is reaching out to female middle school students to get them interested in science, hoping to increase female presence in the field of engineering.[34] Companies such as IBM, Booz Allen Hamilton Inc., Ernst & Young Global Ltd., and General Mills Inc. top the 100 Best Companies list created by *Working Mother* magazine by providing flexible work arrangements to balance work and family demands. In addition, these companies provide employees of both sexes with learning, development, and networking opportunities.[35]

FIGURE 2.5

Ursula Burns became president of Xerox Corporation in 2007. She is responsible for the company's global R&D, engineering, manufacturing, and marketing.

Used by permission of Xerox Corporation.

Race Diversity in the Workplace

Race is another demographic characteristic that is under legal protection in the United States. Title VII of the Civil Rights Act (1964) prohibits race discrimination in all employment-related decisions. Yet race discrimination still exists in organizations. In a Korn-Ferry/Columbia University study of 280 minority managers earning more than $100,000, 60% of the respondents reported that they had seen discrimination in their work assignments and 45% have been the target of racial or cultural jokes. The fact that such discrimination exists even at higher levels in organizations is noteworthy.[36] In a different study of over 5,500 workers, only 32% reported that their company did a good job hiring and promoting minorities.[37] One estimate suggests that when compared to Caucasian employees, African

Americans are four times more likely and Hispanics are three times more likely to experience discrimination.[38]

Ethnic minorities experience both an earnings gap and a glass ceiling. In 2008, for every dollar a Caucasian male employee made, African American males made around 79 cents while Hispanic employees made 64 cents.[39] Among Fortune 500 companies, only three (American Express Company, Aetna Inc., and Darden Restaurants Inc.) have African American CEOs. It is interesting that while ethnic minorities face these challenges, the demographic trends are such that by 2042, Caucasians are estimated to constitute less than one-half of the population in the United States. This demographic shift has already taken place in some parts of the United States such as the Los Angeles area where only 30% of the population is Caucasian.[40]

Unfortunately, discrimination against ethnic minorities still occurs. One study conducted by Harvard University researchers found that when Chicago-area companies were sent fictitious résumés containing identical background information, résumés with "Caucasian" sounding names (such as Emily and Greg) were more likely to get callbacks compared to résumés with African American sounding names (such as Jamal and Lakisha).[41]

Studies indicate that ethnic minorities are less likely to experience a satisfying work environment. One study found that African Americans were more likely to be absent from work compared to Caucasians, but this trend existed only in organizations viewed as not valuing diversity.[42] Similarly, among African Americans, the perception that the organization did not value diversity was related to higher levels of turnover.[43] Another study found differences in the sales performance of Hispanic and Caucasian employees, but again this difference disappeared when the organization was viewed as valuing diversity.[44] It seems that the *perception* that the organization does not value diversity is a fundamental explanation for why ethnic minorities may feel alienated from coworkers. Creating a fair work environment where diversity is valued and appreciated seems to be the key.

Organizations often make news headlines for alleged or actual race discrimination, but there are many stories involving complete turnarounds, suggesting that conscious planning and motivation to improve may make organizations friendlier to all races. One such success story is Denny's Corporation. In 1991, Denny's restaurants settled a $54 million race discrimination lawsuit. In 10 years, the company was able to change the situation completely. Now, women and minorities make up half of their board and almost half of their management team. The company started by hiring a chief diversity officer who reported directly to the CEO. The company implemented a diversity-training program, extended recruitment efforts to diverse colleges, and increased the number of minority-owned franchises. At the same time, customer satisfaction among African Americans increased from 30% to 80%.[45]

Age Diversity in the Workplace

FIGURE 2.6

Older employees tend to be reliable and committed employees who often perform at comparable or higher levels than younger workers.

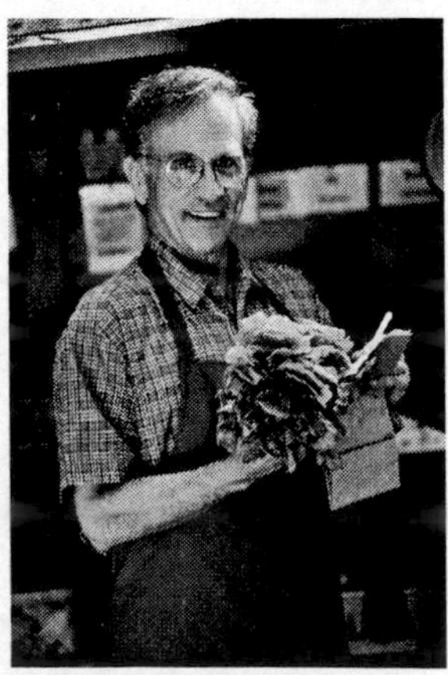

© 2010 Jupiterimages Corporation

The workforce is rapidly aging. By 2015, those who are 55 and older are estimated to constitute 20% of the workforce in the United States. The same trend seems to be occurring elsewhere in the world. In the European Union, employees over 50 years of age are projected to increase by 25% in the next 25 years.[46] According to International Labor Organization (ILO), out of the world's working population, the largest group is those between 40 and 44 years old. In contrast, the largest segment in 1980 was the 20- to 24-year-old group.[47] In other words, age diversity at work will grow in the future.

What happens to work performance as employees get older? Research shows that age is correlated with a number of positive workplace behaviors, including higher levels of citizenship behaviors such as volunteering, higher compliance with safety rules, lower work injuries, lower counterproductive behaviors, and lower rates of tardiness or absenteeism.[48] As people get older, they are also less likely to want to quit their job when they are dissatisfied at work.[49]

Despite their positive workplace behaviors, employees who are older often have to deal with age-related stereotypes at work. For example, a review of a large number of studies showed that those between 17 and 29 years of age tend to rate older employees more negatively, while younger employees were viewed as more qualified and having higher potential.[50] However, these stereotypes have been largely refuted by research. Another review showed that stereotypes about older employees—they perform on a lower level, they are less able to handle stress, or their performance declines with age—are simply inaccurate.[51] The problem with these stereotypes is that they may discourage older workers from remaining in the workforce or may act as a barrier to their being hired in the first place.

In the United States, age discrimination is prohibited by the Age Discrimination in Employment Act of 1967, which made it illegal for organizations to discriminate against employees over 40 years of age. Still, age discrimination is prevalent in workplaces. For example, while not admitting wrongdoing, Honeywell International Inc. recently settled an age discrimination lawsuit for $2.15 million. A group of older sales representatives were laid off during company reorganization while younger employees with less experience were kept in their positions.[52] Older employees may also face discrimination because some jobs have a perceived "correct age." This was probably the reason behind the lawsuit

International Creative Management Inc. faced against 150 TV writers. The lawsuit claimed that the talent agency systematically prevented older workers from getting jobs at major networks.[53]

FIGURE 2.7

In many family-owned businesses, different generations work together.

What are the challenges of managing age diversity beyond the management of stereotypes? Age diversity within a team can actually lead to higher team performance. In a simulation, teams with higher age diversity were able to think of different possibilities and diverse actions, leading to higher performance for the teams.[54] At the same time, managing a team with age diversity may be challenging because different age groups seem to have different opinions about what is fair treatment, leading to different perceptions of organizational justice.[55] Age diversity also means that the workforce will consist of employees from different generations. Some organizations are noticing a generation gap and noting implications for the management of employees. For example, the pharmaceutical company Novo Nordisk Inc. noticed that baby boomers (those born between 1946 and 1964) were competitive and preferred individual feedback on performance, while Generation Y workers (born between 1979 and 1994) were more team oriented. This difference led one regional manager to start each performance feedback e-mail with recognition of team performance, which was later followed by feedback on individual performance. Similarly, Lockheed Martin Corporation noticed that employees from different generations had different learning styles, with older employees preferring PowerPoint presentations and younger employees preferring more interactive learning.[56] Paying attention to such differences and tailoring various aspects of management to the particular employees in question may lead to more effective management of an age-diverse workforce.

Religious Diversity in the Workplace

In the United States, employers are prohibited from using religion in employment decisions based on Title VII of the Civil Rights Act of 1964. Moreover, employees are required to make reasonable accommodations to ensure that employees can practice their beliefs unless doing so provides an unreasonable hardship on the employer.[57] After September 11, cases involving religion and particularly those involving Muslim employees have been on the rise.[58] Religious discrimination often occurs because the religion necessitates modifying the employee's schedule. For example, devout Muslim employees may want to pray five times a day with each prayer lasting 5 to 10 minutes. Some Jewish employees may want to take off Yom Kippur and Rosh Hashanah, although these days are not recognized as holidays in the United States. These situations pit employers' concerns for productivity against employees' desires to fulfill religious obligations.

Accommodating someone's religious preferences may also require companies to relax their dress code to take into account religious practices such as wearing a turban for Sikhs or covering one's hair with a scarf for Muslim women. In these cases, what matters most is that the company makes a good faith attempt to accommodate the employee. For example, in a recent lawsuit that was decided in favor of Costco Wholesale Corporation, the retailer was accused of religious discrimination. A cashier who belonged to the Church of Body Modification, which is a church with about 1,000 members worldwide, wanted to be able to display her tattoos and facial piercings, which was against the dress code of Costco. Costco wanted to accommodate the employee by asking the individual to cover the piercings with skin-colored Band-Aids, which the employee refused. This is likely the primary reason why the case was decided in favor of Costco.[59]

Employees with Disabilities in the Workplace

Employees with a wide range of physical and mental disabilities are part of the workforce. In 2008 alone, over 19,000 cases of discrimination based on disabilities have been filed with the EEOC. The Americans with Disabilities Act of 1990 (ADA) prohibits discrimination in employment against individuals with physical as well as mental disabilities if these individuals are otherwise qualified to do their jobs with or without reasonable accommodation. For example, an organization may receive a job application from a hearing impaired candidate whose job responsibilities will include talking over the phone. With the help of a telephone amplifier, which costs around $50, the employee will be able to perform the job; therefore, the company cannot use the hearing impairment as a reason not to hire the person, again, as long as the employee is otherwise qualified. In 2008, the largest groups of complaints were cases based on discrimination related to disabilities or illnesses such as cancer, depression, diabetes, hearing impairment, manic-depressive disorder, and orthopedic impairments, among others.[60] Particularly employees suffering from illnesses that last for a long time and require ongoing care seem to be at a disadvantage, because they are more likely to be stereotyped, locked into dead-end jobs, and employed in jobs that require substantially lower skills and qualifications than they possess. They also are more likely to quit their jobs.[61]

What can organizations do to create a better work environment for employees with disabilities? One legal requirement is that, when an employee brings up a disability, the organization should consider reasonable accommodations. This may include modifying the employee's schedule and reassigning some nonessential job functions. Organizations that offer flexible work hours may also make it easier for employees with disabilities to be more effective. Finally, supportive relationships with others seem to be the key for making these employees feel at home. Particularly, having an understanding boss and an effective relationship with supervisors are particularly important for employees with disabilities. Because the visible differences between individuals may act as an initial barrier against developing rapport, employees with disabilities and their managers may benefit from being proactive in relationship development.[62]

Sexual Orientation Diversity in the Workplace

Lesbian, bisexual, gay, and transgender (LBGT) employees in the workplace face a number of challenges and barriers to employment. There is currently no federal law in the United States prohibiting discrimination based on sexual orientation, but as of 2008, 20 states as well as the District of Columbia had laws prohibiting discrimination in employment based on sexual orientation.[63]

Research shows that one of the most important issues relating to sexual orientation is the disclosure of sexual identity in the workplace. According to one estimate, up to one-third of lesbian, gay, and bisexual employees do not disclose their sexual orientation at work. Employees may fear the reactions of their managers and coworkers, leading to keeping their sexual identity a secret. In reality though, it seems that disclosing sexual orientation is not the key to explaining work attitudes of these employees—it is whether or not they are *afraid* to disclose their sexual identity. In other words, those employees who fear that full disclosure would lead to negative reactions experience lower job satisfaction, reduced organizational commitment, and higher intentions to leave their jobs.[64] Creating an environment where all employees feel welcome and respected regardless of their sexual orientation is the key to maintaining a positive work environment.

How can organizations show their respect for diversity in sexual orientation? Some companies start by creating a written statement that the organization will not tolerate discrimination based on sexual orientation. They may have workshops addressing issues relating to sexual orientation and facilitate and create networking opportunities for lesbian and gay employees. Perhaps the most powerful way in which companies show respect for sexual orientation diversity is by extending benefits to the partners of same-sex couples. In fact, more than half of Fortune 500 companies currently offer health benefits to domestic partners of same-sex couples. Research shows that in companies that have these types of programs, discrimination based on sexual orientation is less frequent, and the job satisfaction and commitment levels are higher.[65]

OB Toolbox: I think I am being asked illegal interview questions. What can I do?

In the United States, demographic characteristics such as race, gender, national origin, age, and disability status are protected by law. Yet according to a survey of 4,000 job seekers, about one-third of job applicants have been asked illegal interview questions. How can you answer such questions?

Here are some options.

- *Refuse to answer.* You may point out that the question is illegal and refuse to answer. Of course, this may cost you the job offer, because you are likely to seem confrontational and aggressive.
- *Answer shortly.* Instead of giving a full answer to a question such as "are you married," you could answer the question briefly and change the subject. In many cases, the interviewer may be trying to initiate small talk and may be unaware that the question is potentially illegal.
- *Answer the intent.* Sometimes, the illegal question hides a legitimate concern. When you are being asked where you are from, the potential employer might be concerned that you do not have a work permit. Addressing the issue in your answer may be better than answering the question you are being asked.
- *Walk away from the interview.* If you feel that the intent of the question is discriminatory, and if you feel that you would rather not work at a company that would ask such questions, you can always walk away from the interview. If you feel that you are being discriminated against, you may also want to talk to a lawyer later on.

Sources: Cottle, M. (1999, April 25). Too personal at the interview. New York Times, p. 10; Thomas, J. (1999, July–August). Beware of illegal interview questions. Women in Business, 51(4), 14.

1.4 Suggestions for Managing Demographic Diversity

What can organizations do to manage diversity more effectively? In this section, we review research findings and the best practices from different companies to create a list of suggestions for organizations.

Build a Culture of Respecting Diversity

In the most successful companies, diversity management is not the responsibility of the human resource department. Starting from top management and including the lowest levels in the hierarchy, each person understands the importance of respecting others. If this respect is not part of an organization's culture, no amount of diversity training or other programs are likely to be effective. In fact, in the most successful companies, diversity is viewed as everyone's responsibility. The United Parcel Service of America Inc. (UPS), the international shipping company, refuses to hire a diversity officer, underlining that it is not one person's job. Companies with a strong culture—where people have a sense of shared values, loyalty to the organization is rewarded, and team performance is celebrated—enable employees with vastly different demographics and backgrounds to feel a sense of belonging.[66]

FIGURE 2.8

UPS operates in 200 countries, including Italy where a boat is carrying packages on the Canal Grande in Venice. At UPS, 58% of all senior officers are women or minorities.

Source: http://en.wikipedia.org/wiki/Image:Venezia0750UPS.jpg.

Make Managers Accountable for Diversity

People are more likely to pay attention to aspects of performance that are measured. In successful companies, diversity metrics are carefully tracked. For example, in PepsiCo, during the tenure of former CEO Steve Reinemund, half of all new hires had to be either women or minorities. Bonuses of managers partly depended on whether they had met their diversity-related goals.[67] When managers are evaluated and rewarded based on how effective they are in diversity management, they are more likely to show commitment to diversity that in turn affects the diversity climate in the rest of the organization.

Diversity Training Programs

Many companies provide employees and managers with training programs relating to diversity. However, not all diversity programs are equally successful. You may expect that more successful programs are those that occur in companies where a culture of diversity exists. A study of over 700 companies found that programs with a higher perceived success rate were those that occurred in companies where top management believed in the importance of diversity, where there were explicit rewards for increasing diversity of the company, and where managers were required to attend the diversity training programs.[68]

Review Recruitment Practices

Companies may want to increase diversity by targeting a pool that is more diverse. There are many minority professional groups such as the National Black MBA Association or the Chinese Software Professionals Association. By building relations with these occupational groups, organizations may attract a more diverse group of candidates to choose from. The auditing company Ernst & Young Global Ltd. increases diversity of job candidates by mentoring undergraduate students.[69] Companies may also benefit from reviewing their employment advertising to ensure that diversity is important at all levels of the company.[70]

Affirmative Action Programs

Policies designed to recruit, promote, train, and retain employees belonging to a protected class are referred to as **affirmative action**. Based on Executive order 11246 (1965), federal contractors are required to use affirmative action programs. In addition, the federal government, many state and local governments, and the U.S. military are required to have affirmative action plans. An organization may also be using affirmative action as a result of a court order or due to a past history of discrimination. Affirmative action programs are among the most controversial methods in diversity management because some people believe that they lead to an unfair advantage for minority members.

affirmative action

Policies designed to recruit, promote, train, and retain employees belonging to a protected class.

In many cases, the negative perceptions about affirmative action can be explained by misunderstandings relating to what such antidiscrimination policies entail. Moreover, affirmative action means different things to different people and therefore it is inaccurate to discuss affirmative action as a uniform package.

Four groups of programs can be viewed as part of affirmative action programs:[71]

1. **Simple elimination of discrimination**. These programs are the least controversial and are received favorably by employees.
2. **Targeted recruitment**. These affirmative action plans involve ensuring that the candidate pool is diverse. These programs are also viewed as fair by most employees.
3. **Tie-breaker**. In these programs, if all other characteristics are equal, then preference may be given to a minority candidate. In fact, these programs are not widely used and their use needs to be justified by organizations. In other words, organizations need to have very specific reasons for why they are using this type of affirmative action, such as past illegal discrimination. Otherwise, their use may be illegal and lead to reverse discrimination. These programs are viewed as less fair by employees.
4. **Preferential treatment**. These programs involve hiring a less-qualified minority candidate. Strong preferential treatment programs are illegal in most cases.

It is plausible that people who are against affirmative action programs may have unverified assumptions about the type of affirmative action program the company is using. Informing employees about the specifics of how affirmative action is being used may be a good way of dealing with any negative attitudes. In fact, a review of the past literature revealed that when specifics of affirmative action are not clearly defined, observers seem to draw their own conclusions about the particulars of the programs.[72]

In addition to employee reactions to affirmative action, there is some research indicating that affirmative action programs may lead to stigmatization of the perceived beneficiaries. For example, in companies using affirmative action, coworkers of new hires may make the assumption that the new hire was chosen due to gender or race as opposed to having the necessary qualifications. These effects may even occur in the new hires themselves, who may have doubts about the fact that they were chosen because they were the best candidate for the position. Research also shows that giving coworkers information about the qualifications and performance of the new hire eliminates these potentially negative effects of affirmative action programs.[73]

OB Toolbox: Dealing with Being Different

At any time in your career, you may find yourself in a situation in which you are different from those around you. Maybe you are the only male in an organization where most of your colleagues and managers are females. Maybe you are older than all your colleagues. How do you deal with the challenges of being different?

- *Invest in building effective relationships*. Early in a relationship, people are more attracted to those who are demographically similar to them. This means that your colleagues or manager may never get to find out how smart, fun, or hardworking you are if you have limited interactions with them. Create opportunities to talk to them. Be sure to point out areas of commonality.
- *Choose your mentor carefully*. Mentors may help you make sense of the organization's culture, give you career-related advice, and help you feel like you belong. That said, how powerful and knowledgeable your mentor is also matters. You may be more attracted to someone at your same level and who is similar to you, but you may have more to learn from someone who is more experienced, knowledgeable, and powerful than you are.
- *Investigate company resources*. Many companies offer networking opportunities and interest groups for women, ethnic minorities, and employees with disabilities among others. Check out what resources are available through your company.
- *Know your rights*. You should know that harassment based on protected characteristics such as gender, race, age, or disabilities, as well as discrimination based on these traits are illegal in the United States. If you face harassment or discrimination, you may want to notify your manager or your company's HR department.

KEY TAKEAWAY

Organizations managing diversity effectively benefit from diversity because they achieve higher creativity, better customer service, higher job satisfaction, higher stock prices, and lower litigation expenses. At the same time, managing a diverse workforce is challenging for several key reasons. Employees are more likely to associate with those who are similar to them early in a relationship, the distribution of demographic traits could create faultlines within a group, and stereotypes may act as barriers to advancement and fair treatment of employees. Demographic traits such as gender, race, age, religion, disabilities, and sexual orientation each face unique challenges. Organizations can manage demographic diversity more effectively by building a culture of respect, making managers accountable for diversity, creating diversity-training programs, reviewing recruitment practices, and under some conditions, utilizing affirmative action programs.

EXERCISES

1. What does it mean for a company to manage diversity effectively? How would you know if a company is doing a good job of managing diversity?
2. What are the benefits of effective diversity management?
3. How can organizations deal with the "similarity attraction" phenomenon [illegible] problems this tendency can cause?
4. What is the earnings gap? Who does it affect? What are the reasons behind the earnings gap?
5. Do you think that laws and regulations are successful in eliminating discrimination in the workplace? Why or why not?

2. CULTURAL DIVERSITY

LEARNING OBJECTIVES

1. Explain what culture is.
2. Define the four dimensions of culture that are part of Hofstede's framework.
3. Describe some ways in which national culture affects organizational behavior.

FIGURE 2.9

Due to increased globalization of businesses, understanding the role of culture for organizational behavior may provide you with a competitive advantage in your career.

© 2010 Jupiterimages Corporation

culture

The values, beliefs, and customs that exist in a society.

expatriate

Someone who is temporarily assigned to a position in a foreign country.

Culture refers to values, beliefs, and customs that exist in a society. In the United States, the workforce is becoming increasingly multicultural, with close to 16% of all employees being born outside the country. In addition, the world of work is becoming increasingly international. The world is going through a transformation in which China, India, and Brazil are emerging as major players in world economics. Companies are realizing that doing international business provides access to raw materials, resources, and a wider customer base. For many companies, international business is where most of the profits lie, such as for Intel Corporation, where 70% of all revenues come from outside the United States. International companies are also becoming major players within the United States. For example, China's Lenovo acquired IBM's personal computer business and became the world's third largest computer manufacturer.[74] As a result of these trends, understanding the role of national culture for organizational behavior may provide you with a competitive advantage in your career. In fact, sometime in your career, you may find yourself working as an expatriate. An **expatriate** is someone who is temporarily assigned to a position in a foreign country. Such an experience may be invaluable for your career and challenge you to increase your understanding and appreciation of differences across cultures.

How do cultures differ from each other? If you have ever visited a country different from your own, you probably have stories to tell about what aspects of the culture were different and which were similar. Maybe you have noticed that in many parts of the United States people routinely greet strangers with a smile when they step into an elevator or see them on the street, but the same behavior of saying hello and smiling at strangers would be considered odd in many parts of Europe. In India and other parts of Asia, traffic flows with rules of its own, with people disobeying red lights, stopping and loading passengers in highways, or honking continuously for no apparent reason. In fact, when it comes to culture, we are like fish in the sea: We may not realize how culture is shaping our behavior until we leave our own and go someplace else. Cultural differences may shape how people dress, how they act, how they form relationships, how they address each other, what they eat, and many other aspects of daily life. Of course, talking about national cultures does not mean that national cultures are uniform. In many countries, it is possible to talk about the existence of cultures based on region or geography. For example, in the United States, the southern, eastern, western, and midwestern regions of the country are associated with slightly different values.

Thinking about hundreds of different ways in which cultures may differ is not very practical when you are trying to understand how culture affects work behaviors. For this reason, the work of Geert Hofstede, a Dutch social scientist, is an important contribution to the literature. Hofstede studied IBM employees in 66 countries and showed that four dimensions of national culture explain an important source of variation among cultures. Research also shows that cultural variation with respect to these four dimensions influence employee job behaviors, attitudes, well-being, motivation, leadership, negotiations, and many other aspects of organizational behavior.[75]

FIGURE 2.10

Hofstede's culture framework is a useful tool to understand the systematic differences across cultures.

Individualism Cultures in which people define themselves as individuals and form looser ties with their groups.	**Collectivism** Cultures where people have stronger bonds to their groups and group membership forms a person's self identity.
• USA • Australia • UK • Canada • Hungary	• Guatemala • Ecuador • Indonesia • Pakistan • China
Low Power Distance A society that views an unequal distribution of power as relatively unacceptable.	**High Power Distance** A society that views an unequal distribution of power as relatively acceptable.
• Austria • Denmark • Israel • Ireland • New Zealand	• Malaysia • Slovakia • Philippines • Russia • Mexico
Low Uncertainty Avoidance Cultures in which people are comfortable in unpredictable situations and have high tolerance for ambiguity.	**High Uncertainty Avoidance** Cultures in which people prefer predictable situations and have low tolerance for ambiguity.
• Denmark • Jamaica • Singapore • China • Sweden	• Belgium • El Salvador • Greece • Guatemala • Portugal
Masculinity Cultures in which people value achievement and competitiveness, as well as acquisition of money and other material objects.	**Femininity** Cultures in which people value maintaining good relationships, caring for the weak, and quality of life.
• Slovakia • Japan • Hungary • Austria • Venezuela	• Norway • Netherlands • Sweden • Costa Rica • Chile

Source: Adapted from information in Geert Hofstede cultural dimensions. Retrieved November 12, 2008, from http://www.geert-hofstede.com/hofstede_dimensions.php.

2.1 Individualism-Collectivism

individualistic cultures

Cultures in which people define themselves as individuals and form looser ties with their groups.

collectivistic cultures

Cultures where people have stronger bonds to their groups, and group membership forms a person's self identity.

Individualistic cultures are cultures in which people define themselves as an individual and form looser ties with their groups. These cultures value autonomy and independence of the person, self-reliance, and creativity. Countries such as the United States, United Kingdom, and Australia are examples of individualistic cultures. In contrast, **collectivistic cultures** are cultures where people have stronger bonds to their groups and group membership forms a person's self identity. Asian countries such as China and Japan, as well as countries in Latin America are higher in collectivism.

In collectivistic cultures, people define themselves as part of a group. In fact, this may be one way to detect people's individualism-collectivism level. When individualists are asked a question such as "Who are you? Tell me about yourself," they are more likely to talk about their likes and dislikes, personal goals, or accomplishments. When collectivists are asked the same question, they are more likely to define themselves in relation to others, such as "I am Chinese" or "I am the daughter of a doctor and a homemaker. I have two brothers." In other words, in collectivistic cultures, self identity is shaped to a stronger extent by group memberships.[76]

In collectivistic societies, family bonds are more influential in people's daily lives. While individualists often refer to their nuclear family when thinking about their families, collectivists are more likely to define family in a broader sense, including cousins, uncles, aunts, and second cousins. Family members are more involved in each others' lives. For example, in societies such as Iran, Greece, and Turkey, extended family members may see each other several times a week. In many collectivistic societies, the language reflects the level of interaction among extended family members such that there may be different words used to refer to maternal versus paternal grandparents, aunts, or uncles. In addition to interacting with each other more often, family members have a strong sense of obligation toward each other. For example, children often expect to live with their parents until they get married. In collectivistic countries such as Thailand, Japan, and India, choosing a career or finding a spouse are all family affairs. In these cultures, family members feel accountable for each others' behavior such that one person's misbehavior may be a cause of shame for the rest of the family.[77] Understanding the importance of family in collectivistic cultures is critical to understanding their work behaviors. For example, one multinational oil company in Mexico was suffering from low productivity. When the situation was investigated, it became clear that the new manager of the subsidiary had gotten rid of a monthly fiesta for company employees and their families under the assumption that it was a waste of time and money. Employees had interpreted this to mean that the company no longer cared about their families.[78] In India, companies such as Intel organize "take your parents to work day" and involve parents in recruitment efforts, understanding the role of parents in the career and job choices of prospective employees.[79]

Collectivists are more attached to their groups and have more permanent attachments to these groups. Conversely, individualists attempt to change groups more often and have weaker bonds to them. It is important to recognize that to collectivists the entire human universe is not considered to be their in-group. In other words, collectivists draw sharper distinctions between the groups they belong to and those they do not belong to. They may be nice and friendly to their in-group members while acting much more competitively and aggressively toward out-group members. This tendency has important work implications. While individualists may evaluate the performance of their colleagues more accurately, collectivists are more likely to be generous when evaluating their in-group members. Freeborders, a software company based in San Francisco, California, found that even though it was against company policy, Chinese employees were routinely sharing salary information with their coworkers. This situation led them to change their pay system by standardizing pay at job levels and then giving raises after more frequent appraisals.[80]

Collectivistic sociéties emphasize conformity to the group. The Japanese saying "the nail that sticks up gets hammered down" illustrates that being different from the group is undesirable. In these cultures, disobeying or disagreeing with one's group is difficult and people may find it hard to say no to their colleagues or friends. Instead of saying no, which would be interpreted as rebellion or at least be considered rude, they may use indirect ways of disagreeing, such as saying "I have to think about this" or "this would be difficult." Such indirect communication prevents the other party from losing face but may cause misunderstandings in international communications with cultures that have a more direct style. Collectivist cultures may have a greater preference for team-based rewards as opposed to individual-based rewards. For example, in one study, more than 75% of the subjects in Philippines viewed team-based pay as fair, while less than 50% of the U.S.-based subjects viewed team-based rewards as fair.[81]

2.2 Power Distance

Power distance refers to the degree to which the society views an unequal distribution of power as acceptable. Simply put, some cultures are more egalitarian than others. In low power distance cultures, egalitarianism is the norm. In high power distance cultures, people occupying more powerful positions such as managers, teachers, or those who are older are viewed as more powerful and deserving of a higher level of respect. High power distance cultures are hierarchical cultures where everyone has their place. Powerful people are supposed to act powerful, while those in inferior positions are expected to show respect. For example, Thailand is a high power distance culture and, starting from childhood, people learn to recognize who is superior, equal, or inferior to them. When passing people who are more powerful, individuals are expected to bow, and the more powerful the person, the deeper the bow would be.[82] Managers in high power distance cultures are treated with a higher degree of respect, which may surprise those in lower power distance cultures. A Citibank manager in Saudi Arabia was surprised when employees stood up every time he passed by.[83] Similarly, in Turkey, students in elementary and high schools greet their teacher by standing up every time the teacher walks into the classroom. In these cultures, referring to a manager or a teacher with their first name would be extremely rude. High power distance within a culture may easily cause misunderstandings with those from low power distance societies. For example, the limp handshake someone from India may give or a job candidate from Chad who is looking at the floor throughout the interview are in fact showing their respect, but these behaviors may be interpreted as indicating a lack of confidence or even disrespect in low power distance cultures.

power distance

The degree to which the society views an unequal distribution of power as acceptable.

One of the most important ways in which power distance is manifested in the workplace is that in high power distance cultures, employees are unlikely to question the power and authority of their manager, and conformity to the manager will be expected. Managers in these cultures may be more used to an authoritarian style with lower levels of participative leadership demonstrated. People will be more submissive to their superiors and may take orders without questioning the manager.[84] In these cultures, people may feel uncomfortable when they are asked to participate in decision making. For example, peers are much less likely to be involved in hiring decisions in high power distance cultures. Instead, these cultures seem to prefer paternalistic leaders—leaders who are authoritarian but make decisions while showing a high level of concern toward employees as if they were family members.[85]

2.3 Uncertainty Avoidance

Uncertainty avoidance refers to the degree to which people feel threatened by ambiguous, risky, or unstructured situations. Cultures high in uncertainty avoidance prefer predictable situations and have low tolerance for ambiguity. Employees in these cultures expect a clear set of instructions and clarity in expectations. Therefore, there will be a greater level of creating procedures to deal with problems and writing out expected behaviors in manuals.

uncertainty avoidance

The degree to which people feel threatened by ambiguous, risky, or unstructured situations.

Cultures high in uncertainty avoidance prefer to avoid risky situations and attempt to reduce uncertainty. For example, one study showed that when hiring new employees, companies in high uncertainty avoidance cultures are likely to use a larger number of tests, conduct a larger number of interviews, and use a fixed list of interview questions.[86] Employment contracts tend to be more popular in cultures higher in uncertainty avoidance compared to cultures low in uncertainty avoidance.[87] The level of change-oriented leadership seems to be lower in cultures higher in uncertainty avoidance.[88] Companies operating in high uncertainty avoidance cultures also tend to avoid risky endeavors such as entering foreign target markets unless the target market is very large.[89]

Germany is an example of a high uncertainty avoidance culture where people prefer structure in their lives and rely on rules and procedures to manage situations. Similarly, Greece is a culture relatively high in uncertainty avoidance, and Greek employees working in hierarchical and rule-oriented companies report lower levels of stress.[90] In contrast, cultures such as Iran and Russia are lower in uncertainty avoidance, and companies in these regions do not have rule-oriented cultures. When they create rules, they also selectively enforce rules and make a number of exceptions to them. In fact, rules may be viewed as constraining. Uncertainty avoidance may influence the type of organizations employees are attracted to. Japan's uncertainty avoidance is associated with valuing job security, while in uncertainty-avoidant Latin American cultures, many job candidates prefer the stability of bigger and well-known companies with established career paths.

2.4 Masculinity–Femininity

masculine cultures

Cultures that value achievement, competitiveness, and acquisition of money and other material objects.

feminine cultures

Cultures that value maintaining good relationships, caring for the weak, and emphasizing quality of life.

Masculine cultures are cultures that value achievement, competitiveness, and acquisition of money and other material objects. Japan and Hungary are examples of masculine cultures. Masculine cultures are also characterized by a separation of gender roles. In these cultures, men are more likely to be assertive and competitive compared to women. In contrast, **feminine cultures** are cultures that value maintaining good relationships, caring for the weak, and emphasizing quality of life. In these cultures, values are not separated by gender, and both women and men share the values of maintaining good relationships. Sweden and the Netherlands are examples of feminine cultures. The level of masculinity inherent in the culture has implications for the behavior of individuals as well as organizations. For example, in masculine cultures, the ratio of CEO pay to other management-level employees tends to be higher, indicating that these cultures are more likely to reward CEOs with higher levels of pay as opposed to other types of rewards.[91] The femininity of a culture affects many work practices, such as the level of work/life balance. In cultures high in femininity such as Norway and Sweden, work arrangements such as telecommuting seem to be more popular compared to cultures higher in masculinity like Italy and the United Kingdom.

OB Toolbox: Prepare Yourself for a Global Career

With the globalizing economy, boundaries with respect to careers are also blurring. How can you prepare yourself for a career that crosses national boundaries?

- *Learn a language.* If you already know that you want to live in China after you finish school, now may be the time to start learning the language. It is true that business is often conducted in English, but it is becoming increasingly ethnocentric to speak only one language while many in the rest of the world can speak two or more. For example, only 9% of those living in the United States can speak their native language plus another language fluently, as opposed to 53% of Europeans.[92] Plus, even if business is conducted in English, your adaptation to a different society, making friends, and leading a satisfying life will be much easier if you can speak the language.
- *Immerse yourself in different cultures.* Visit different cultures. This does not mean visiting five countries in 5 days. Plan on spending more time in one locale, and get to know, observe, and understand the culture.
- *Develop an openness to different experiences.* Be open to different cuisines, different languages, and different norms of working and living. If you feel very strongly that your way of living and working is the right way, you will have a hard time adjusting to a different culture.
- *Develop a strong social support network.* Once you arrive in the culture you will live in, be proactive in making friends. Being connected to people in a different culture will have an influence on your ability to adjust to living there. If you are planning on taking family members with you, their level of readiness will also influence your ability to function in a different culture.
- *Develop a sense of humor.* Adjusting to a different culture is often easier if you can laugh at yourself and the mistakes you make. If you take every mistake too personally, your stay will be less enjoyable and more frustrating.
- *Plan your return.* If you have plans to come back and work in your home country, you will need to plan your return in advance. When people leave home for a long time, they often adapt to the foreign culture they live in and may miss many elements of it when they go back home. Your old friends may have moved on, local employers may not immediately appreciate your overseas experience, and you may even find that cultural aspects of your home country may have changed in your absence. Be ready for a reverse culture shock!

2.5 Suggestions for Managing Cultural Diversity

With the increasing importance of international business as well as the culturally diverse domestic workforce, what can organizations do to manage cultural diversity?

Help Employees Build Cultural Intelligence

cultural intelligence

A person's capability to understand how a person's cultural background influences one's behavior.

Cultural intelligence is a person's capability to understand how a person's cultural background influences one's behavior. Developing cultural intelligence seems important, because the days when organizations could prepare their employees for international work simply by sending them to long seminars on a particular culture are gone. Presently, international business is not necessarily conducted between pairs of countries. A successful domestic manager is not necessarily assigned to work on a long-term assignment in China. Of course such assignments still happen, but it is more likely that the employees will continually work with others from diverse cultural backgrounds. This means employees will not necessarily have to become experts in one culture. Instead, they should have the ability to work with people from many diverse backgrounds all at the same time. For these types of assignments, employees will need to develop an awareness of overall cultural differences and learn how to recognize cultural principles that are operating in different situations. In other words, employees will need to be selected based on cultural sensitivity and understanding and trained to enhance such qualities.[93] For example, GlobeSmart by Aperian Global is an online tool that helps employees learn how to deal with people from around the world. The process starts by completing a survey about your cultural values, and then these values are compared to those of different cultures. The tool provides specific advice about interpersonal interactions with these cultures.[94]

Avoid Ethnocentrism

Ethnocentrism is the belief that one's own culture is superior to other cultures one comes across. Ethnocentrism leads organizations to adopt universal principles when doing business around the globe and may backfire. In this chapter, we highlighted research findings showing how culture affects employee expectations of work life such as work–life balance, job security, or the level of empowerment. Ignoring cultural differences, norms, and local habits may be costly for businesses and may lead to unmotivated and dissatisfied employees. Successful global companies modify their management styles, marketing, and communication campaigns to fit with the culture in which they are operating. For example, Apple Inc.'s famous PC versus Mac advertising campaign was redone in Japan and the United Kingdom using local actors. The American ads were found to be too aggressive for the Japanese culture, where direct product comparisons are rare and tend to make people uncomfortable. The new ads feature more friendly banter and are subtler than the U.S. ads. For the British market, the advertisers localized the humor.[95]

ethnocentrism

The belief that one's own culture is superior to other cultures one comes across.

Listen to Locals

When doing cross-cultural business, locals are a key source of information. To get timely and accurate feedback, companies will need to open lines of communication and actively seek feedback. For example, Convergys, a Cincinnati-based call-center company, built a cafeteria for the employees in India. During the planning phase, the Indian vice president pointed out that because Indian food is served hot and employees would expect to receive hot meals for lunch, building a cafeteria that served only sandwiches would create dissatisfied employees. By opening the lines of communication in the planning phase of the project, Convergys was alerted to this important cultural difference in time to change the plans.[96]

Recognize That Culture Changes

Cultures are not static—they evolve over the years. A piece of advice that was true 5 years ago may no longer hold true. For example, showing sensitivity to the Indian caste system may be outdated advice for those internationals doing business in India today.

Do Not Always Assume That Culture Is the Problem

When doing business internationally, failure may occur due to culture as well as other problems. Attributing all misunderstandings or failures to culture may enlarge the cultural gap and shift the blame to others. In fact, managing people who have diverse personalities or functional backgrounds may create misunderstandings that are not necessarily due to cultural differences. When marketing people from the United States interact with engineers in India, misunderstandings may be caused by the differences in perceptions between marketing and engineering employees. While familiarizing employees about culture, emphasizing the importance of interpersonal skills regardless of cultural background will be important.

KEY TAKEAWAY

With the increasing prevalence of international business as well as diversification of the domestic workforce in many countries, understanding how culture affects organizational behavior is becoming important. Individualism-collectivism, power distance, uncertainty avoidance, and masculinity–femininity are four key dimensions in which cultures vary. The position of a culture on these dimensions affects the suitable type of management style, reward systems, employee selection, and ways of motivating employees.

EXERCISES

1. What is culture? Do countries have uniform national cultures?
2. How would you describe your own home country's values on the four dimensions of culture?
3. Reflect on a time when you experienced a different culture or interacted with someone from a different culture. How did the cultural differences influence your interaction?
4. How does culture influence the proper leadership style and reward system that would be suitable for organizations?
5. Imagine that you will be sent to live in a foreign country different from your own in a month. What are the types of preparations you would benefit from doing?

3. THE ROLE OF ETHICS AND NATIONAL CULTURE

LEARNING OBJECTIVES

1. Consider the role of diversity for ethical behavior.
2. Consider the role of national culture on diversity.

3.1 Diversity and Ethics

When managing a diverse group of employees, ensuring the ethicality of organizational behavior will require special effort. This is because employees with different backgrounds or demographic traits may vary in their standards of ethics. For example, research shows that there are some gender differences when it comes to evaluating the degree of ethicality of hypothetical scenarios, with women utilizing higher standards. Men and women seem to have similar standards when judging the ethicality of monetary issues but differ on issues such as the ethicality of breaking organizational rules. Interestingly, gender differences seem to disappear as people grow older. Age is another demographic trait that influences the standards of ethics people use, with older employees being bothered more by unethical behaviors compared to younger employees. Similarly, one study showed that older respondents found some questionable negotiation behaviors such as misrepresenting information and bluffing to be more unethical compared to younger respondents.[97]

In addition to demographic diversity, cultural diversity introduces challenges to managing ethical behavior, given that cultures differ in the actions they view as ethical. Cultural differences are particularly important when doing cross-cultural business. For example, one study compared Russian and American subjects on their reactions to ethics scenarios. Americans viewed scenarios such as an auditing company sharing information regarding one client with another client as more unethical compared to how Russian subjects viewed the same scenarios.[98] A study comparing U.S., Korean, and Indian managers found differences in attitudes toward business ethics, particularly with Koreans thinking that being ethical was against the goal of being profitable. Indian and Korean subjects viewed questionable practices such as software piracy, nepotism, or the sharing of insider information as relatively more ethical compared to subjects in the United States. At the same time, Korean and Indian subjects viewed injury to the environment as more unethical compared to the U.S. subjects.[99] In other words, the ethical standards held in different societies may emphasize different behaviors as ethical or unethical.

When dealing with unethical behavior overseas, companies will need to consider the ethical context. Having internal reporting mechanisms may help, but research shows that in very high power distant societies, these mechanisms often go unused.[100] Even when a multinational company has ethical standards that are different from local standards, using the headquarters' standards in all cross-cultural interactions will not be possible or suitable. The right action often depends on the specifics of the situation and a consideration of the local culture. For example, in the 1990s, Levi-Strauss & Company found that some of its contractors in Bangladesh were using child labor consisting of children under 14 years old in its factories. One option they had was to demand that their contractors fire those children immediately. Yet, when they looked at the situation more closely, they found that it was common for young children to be employed in factories, and in many cases these children were the sole breadwinners in the family. Firing these children would have caused significant hardship for the families and could have pushed the children into more dangerous working conditions. Therefore, Levi-Strauss reached an agreement to send the children back to school while continuing to receive their wages partly from the contractor companies and partly from Levi-Strauss. The school expenses were met by Levi-

Strauss and the children were promised work when they were older. In short, the diverse ethical standards of the world's cultures make it unlikely that one approach can lead to fair outcomes in all circumstances.

3.2 Diversity Around the Globe

Demographic diversity is a fact of life in the United States. The situation is somewhat different in other parts of the world. Attitudes toward gender, race, disabilities, or sexual orientation differ around the world, and each country approaches the topic of diversity differently.

As a case in point, Japan is a relatively homogeneous society that sees the need to diversify itself. With the increasing age of the population, the country expects to lose 650,000 workers per year. At the same time, the country famously underutilizes female employees. Overt sexism is rampant, and stereotypes about female employees as unable to lead are part of the culture. While there is antidiscrimination legislation and the desire of the Japanese government to deal with this issue, women are seriously underrepresented in management. For example, while 25% of all Hewlett-Packard Development Company managers in the United States are female, in Japan this number is around 4%. Some companies such as Sanyo Electric Co. Ltd. have female CEOs, but these companies are generally considered exceptions. Because of the labor shortage, the country is attracting immigrants from South America, thereby [illegible][101]

Attitudes toward concepts such as affirmative action are also culturally determined. For example, France experiences different employment situations for employees with different backgrounds. According to one study conducted by a University of Paris professor in which fake résumés were sent to a large number of companies, even when all qualifications were the same, candidates with French-sounding names were three times more likely to get a callback compared to those with North African–sounding names. However, affirmative action is viewed as unfair in French society, leaving the situation in the hands of corporations. Some companies such as PSA Peugeot Citroën started utilizing human resource management systems in which candidate names are automatically stripped from résumés before HR professionals personally investigate them.[102] In summary, due to differences in the legal environment as well as cultural context, "managing diversity effectively" may carry a different meaning across the globe.

KEY TAKEAWAY

Ethical behavior is affected by the demographic and cultural composition of the workforce. Studies indicate that men and women, as well as younger and older employees, differ in the types of behaviors they view as ethical. Different cultures also hold different ethical standards, which become important when managing a diverse workforce or doing business within different cultures. Around the globe, diversity has a different meaning and different overtones. In addition to different legal frameworks protecting employee classes, the types of stereotypes that exist in different cultures and whether and how the society tackles prejudice against different demographic categories vary from region to region.

EXERCISES

1. Do you believe that multinational companies should have an ethics code that they enforce around the world? Why or why not?
2. How can organizations manage a workforce with diverse personal ethical values?

4. CONCLUSION

In conclusion, in this chapter we reviewed the implications of demographic and cultural diversity for organizational behavior. Management of diversity effectively promises a number of benefits for companies and may be a competitive advantage. Yet, challenges such as natural human tendencies to associate with those similar to us and using stereotypes in decision making often act as barriers to achieving this goal. By creating a work environment where people of all origins and traits feel welcome, organizations will make it possible for all employees to feel engaged with their work and remain productive members of the organization.

5. EXERCISES

ETHICAL DILEMMA

You are working for the police department of your city. When hiring employees, the department uses a physical ability test in which candidates are asked to do 30 push-ups and 25 sit-ups, as well as climb over a 4-foot wall. When candidates take this test, it seems that about 80% of the men who take the test actually pass it, while only 10% of the female candidates pass the test. Do you believe that this is a fair test? Why or why not? If you are asked to review the employee selection procedures, would you make any changes to this system? Why or why not?

INDIVIDUAL EXERCISE

A colleague of yours is being sent to India as a manager for a call center. She just told you that she feels very strongly about the following issues:

- Democratic leaders are the best leaders because they create a more satisfied workforce.
- Employees respond best to individual-based pay incentives and bonuses as tools for motivation.
- Employees should receive peer feedback about their performance level so that they can get a better sense of how well they are performing.

After doing some research on the business environment and national culture in India, how would you advise your colleague to behave? Should she try to transfer these three managerial practices to the Indian context? Why or why not?

GROUP EXERCISE

Diversity Dilemmas

Imagine that you are working in the HR department of your company. You come across the following scenarios in which your input has been sought. Discuss each scenario and propose an action plan for management.

1. Aimee is the mother of a newborn. She is very dedicated to her work but she used to stay for longer hours at work before she had her baby. Now she tries to schedule her work so that she leaves around 5:00 p.m. Her immediate manager feels that Aimee is no longer dedicated or committed to her work and is considering passing her over for a promotion. Is this decision fair?
2. Jack is a married male, while John is single. Your company has an assignment in a branch in Mexico that would last a couple of years. Management feels that John would be better for this assignment because he is single and is free to move. Is this decision fair?
3. A manager receives a request from an employee to take off a Wednesday for religious reasons. The manager did not know that this employee was particularly religious and does not believe that the leave is for religious reasons. The manager believes that the employee is going to use this day as a personal day off. Should the manager investigate the situation?
4. A sales employee has painful migraines intermittently during the work day. She would like to take short naps during the day as a preventative measure and she also needs a place where she can nap when a migraine occurs. Her immediate manager feels that this is unfair to the rest of the employees.
5. A department is looking for an entry-level cashier. One of the job applicants is a cashier with 30 years of experience as a cashier. The department manager feels that this candidate is overqualified for the job and is likely to be bored and leave the job in a short time. Instead, they want to pursue a candidate with 6 months of work experience who seems like a better fit for the position.

ENDNOTES

1. Bureau of Labor Statistics. (2007). *Employed persons by detailed occupation, gender, race, and Hispanic or Latino ethnicity*. Retrieved November 4, 2008, from the Bureau of Labor Statistics Web site: ftp://ftp.bls.gov/pub/special.requests/lf/aat11.txt.
2. Bureau of Labor Statistics. (2007). *Labor force characteristics of foreign-born workers*. Retrieved November 4, 2008, from the Bureau of Labor Statistics Web site: http://www.bls.gov/news.release/forbrn.nr0.htm.
3. McLeod, P., Lobel, S., & Cox, T. H. (1996). Ethnic diversity and creativity in small groups. *Small Group Research, 27*, 248–264.
4. Hymowitz, C. (2005, November 14). The new diversity: In a global economy, it's no longer about how many employees you have in this group and that group; It's a lot more complicated—and if you do it right, a lot more effective. *Wall Street Journal*, p. R1.
5. Slater, S. F., Weigand, R. A., & Zwirlein, T. J. (2008). The business case for commitment to diversity. *Business Horizons, 51*, 201–209.
6. Sanchez, J. I., & Brock, P. (1996). Outcomes of perceived discrimination among Hispanic employees: Is diversity management a luxury or necessity? *Academy of Management Journal, 39*, 704–719.
7. Wright, P., Ferris, S. P., Hiller, J. S., & Kroll, M. (1995). Competitiveness through management of diversity: Effects on stock price valuation. *Academy of Management Journal, 30*, 272–287.
8. [illegible] discrimination suit targets Coke bottler CCE. *Atlanta Business Chronicle*. Retrieved January 29, 2009, from http://atlanta.bizjournals.com/atlanta/stories/2003/05/05/story1.html.
9. Greenhouse, S. (2004, November 17). Abercrombie & Fitch bias case is settled. *New York Times*. Retrieved January 29, 2009, from http://www.nytimes.com/2004/11/17/national/17settle.html.
10. After $3.7 million reverse discrimination lawsuit, the New Orleans district attorney resigns. (2007, October 31). *DiversityInc Magazine*. Retrieved November 18, 2008, from http://www.diversityinc.com/public/2668.cfm.
11. Richard, O. C. (2000). Racial diversity, business strategy, and firm performance: A resource-based view. *Academy of Management Journal, 43*, 164–177.
12. Slater, S. F., Weigand, R. A., & Zwirlein, T. J. (2008). The business case for commitment to diversity. *Business Horizons, 51*, 201–209.
13. Weisul, K. (2004, January 28). The bottom line on women at the top. *Business Week Online*. Retrieved November 14, 2008, from http://www.businessweek.com/.
14. Riordan, C. M., & Shore, L. M. (1997). Demographic diversity and employee attitudes: An empirical examination of relational demography within work units. *Journal of Applied Psychology, 82*, 342–358.
15. Chatman, J. A., Polzer, J. T., Barsade, S. G., & Neale, M. A. (1998). Being different yet feeling similar: The influence of demographic composition and organizational culture on work processes and outcomes. *Administrative Science Quarterly, 43*, 749–780.
16. Jehn, K. A., Northcraft, G. B., & Neale, M. A. (1999). Why differences make a difference: A field study of diversity, conflict, and performance in workgroups. *Administrative Science Quarterly, 44*, 741–763; Pelled, L. H., Eisenhardt, K. M., & Xin, K. R. (1999). Exploring the black box: An analysis of work group diversity, conflict, and performance. *Administrative Science Quarterly, 44*, 1–28.
17. Price, K. H., Harrison, D. A., & Gavin, J. H. (2006). Withholding inputs in team contexts: Member composition, interaction processes, evaluation structure, and social loafing. *Journal of Applied Psychology, 91*, 1375–1384.
18. Dreher, G. F., & Cox, T. H. (1996). Race, gender and opportunity: A study of compensation attainment and the establishment of mentoring relationships. *Journal of Applied Psychology, 81*, 297–308.
19. Harrison, D. A., Price, K. H., Gavin, J. H., & Florey, A. T. (2002). Time, teams, and task performance: Changing effects of surface- and deep-level diversity on group functioning. *Academy of Management Journal, 45*, 1029–1045.
20. Pearsall, M. J., Ellis, A. P. J., & Evans, J. M. (2008). Unlocking the effects of gender faultlines on team creativity: Is activation the key? *Journal of Applied Psychology, 93*, 225–234; Sawyer, J. E., Houlette, M. A., & Yeagley, E. L. (2006). Decision performance and diversity structure: Comparing faultlines in convergent, crosscut, and racially homogeneous groups. *Organizational Behavior and Human Decision Processes, 99*, 1–15.
21. Sawyer, J. E., Houlette, M. A., & Yeagley, E. L. (2006). Decision performance and diversity structure: Comparing faultlines in convergent, crosscut, and racially homogeneous groups. *Organizational Behavior and Human Decision Processes, 99*, 1–15.
22. Bureau of Labor Statistics. (2008). *Usual weekly earnings*. Retrieved November 4, 2008, from the Bureau of Labor Statistics Web site: http://www.bls.gov/news.release/wkyeng.nr0.htm.
23. Konrad, A. M., Ritchie, J. E., Lieb, P., & Corrigall, E. (2000). Sex differences and similarities in job attribute preferences: A meta-analysis. *Psychological Bulletin, 126*, 593–641.
24. Babcock, L., & Laschever, S. (2003). *Women don't ask*. Princeton, NJ: Princeton University Press.
25. Stuhlmacher, A. F., & Walters, A. E. (1999). Gender differences in negotiation outcome: A meta-analysis. *Personnel Psychology, 52*, 653–677.
26. Bowles, H. R., & Babcock, L., & Lai, L. (2007). Social incentives for gender differences in the propensity to initiate negotiations: Sometimes it does hurt to ask. *Organizational Behavior and Human Decision Processes, 103*, 84–103.
27. Gerhart, B. (1990). Gender differences in current and starting salaries: The role of performance, college major, and job title. *Industrial & Labor Relations Review, 43*, 418–434.
28. Avery, D. R., McKay, P. F., & Wilson, D. C. (2008). What are the odds? How demographic similarity affects prevalence of perceived employment discrimination. *Journal of Applied Psychology, 93*, 235–249.
29. Daniels, C. (2003, July 21). Women vs. Wal-Mart. *Fortune, 148*, 78–82.
30. Umphress, E. E., Simmons, A. L., Boswell, W. R., & Triana, M. C. (2008). Managing discrimination in selection: The influence of directives from an authority and social dominance. *Journal of Applied Psychology, 93*, 982–993.
31. Eagly, A. H., Karau S. J., & Makhijani, M. G. (1995). Gender and effectiveness of leaders: A meta-analysis. *Psychological Bulletin, 117*, 125–145; Eagly, A. H., Johannesen-Schmidt, M. C., & Van Engen, M. L. (2003). *Psychological Bulletin, 129*, 569–591.
32. Duehr, E. E., & Bono, J. E. (2006). Men, women and managers: Are stereotypes finally changing? *Personnel Psychology, 59*, 815–846.
33. Heilman, M. E., & Haynes, M. C. (2005). No credit where credit is due: Attributional rationalization of women's success in male-female teams. *Journal of Applied Psychology, 90*, 905–916.
34. Thomas, D. A. (2004). Diversity as strategy. *Harvard Business Review, 82*, 98–108.
35. 2007 100 Best companies. (2007). Retrieved November 4, 2008, from the *Working Mother* Web site: http://www.workingmother.com/?service=vpage/859.
36. Allers, K. L. (2005). Won't it be grand when we don't need diversity lists? *Fortune, 152*(4), 101; Mehta, S. N., Chen, C. Y., Garcia, F., & Vella-Zarb, K. (2000). What minority employees really want. *Fortune, 142*(2), 180–184.
37. Fisher, A. (2004). How you can do better on diversity. *Fortune, 150*(10), 60.
38. Avery, D. R., McKay, P. F., Wilson, D. C., & Tonidandel, S. (2007). Unequal attendance: The relationships between race, organizational diversity cues, and absenteeism. *Personnel Psychology, 60*, 875–902.
39. Bureau of Labor Statistics. (2008). *Usual weekly earnings summary*. Retrieved November 4, 2008, from the Bureau of Labor Statistics Web site: http://www.bls.gov/news.release/wkyeng.nr0.htm.
40. Dougherty, C. (2008, August 14). Whites to lose majority status in US by 2042. *Wall Street Journal*, p. A3.
41. Bertrand, M., & Mullainathan, S. (2004). Are Emily and Greg more employable than Lakisha and Jamal? A field experiment on labor market discrimination. *American Economic Review, 94*, 991–1013.
42. Avery, D. R., McKay, P. F., Wilson, D. C., & Tonidandel, S. (2007). Unequal attendance: The relationships between race, organizational diversity cues, and absenteeism. *Personnel Psychology, 60*, 875–902.
43. McKay, P. F., Avery, D. R., Tonidandel, S., Morris, M. A., Hernandez, M., & Hebl, M. R. (2007). Racial differences in employee retention: Are diversity climate perceptions the key? *Personnel Psychology, 60*, 35–62.
44. McKay, P., Avery, D. R., & Morris, M. A. (2008). Mean racial-ethnic differences in employee sales performance: The moderating role of diversity climate. *Personnel Psychology, 61*, 349–374.
45. Speizer, I. (2004). Diversity on the menu. *Workforce Management, 83*(12), 41–45.
46. Avery, D. R., McKay, P. F., & Wilson, D. C. (2007). Engaging the aging workforce: The relationship between perceived age similarity, satisfaction with coworkers, and employee engagement. *Journal of Applied Psychology, 92*, 1542–1556.
47. International Labor Organization. (2005). *Yearly statistics*. Geneva, Switzerland: ILO.
48. Ng, T. W. H., & Feldman, D. C. (2008). The relationship of age to ten dimensions of job performance. *Journal of Applied Psychology, 93*, 392–423.
49. Hellman, C. M. (1997). Job satisfaction and intent to leave. *Journal of Social Psychology, 137*, 677–689.
50. Finkelstein, L. M., Burke, M. J., & Raju, N. S. (1995). Age discrimination in simulated employment contexts: An integrative analysis. *Journal of Applied Psychology, 80*, 652–663.
51. Posthuma, R. A., & Campion, M. A. (in press). Age stereotypes in the workplace: Common stereotypes, moderators, and future research directions. *Journal of Management*.
52. Equal Employment Opportunity Commission. (2004). Honeywell International to pay $2.15 million for age discrimination in EEOC settlement. Retrieved November 7, 2008, from the Equal Employment Opportunity Commission Web site: http://www.eeoc.gov/press/10-4-04a.html.
53. TV writers settle age discrimination lawsuit. (2008, August 20). Retrieved November 7, 2008, from International Business Times Web site: http://www.ibtimes.com/articles/20080820/tv-writers-settle-age-discrimination-lawsuit.htm.
54. Kilduff, M., Angelmar, R., & Mehra, A. (2000). Top management-team diversity and firm performance: Examining the role of cognitions. *Organization Science, 11*, 21–34.
55. Colquitt, J. A., Noe, R. A., & Jackson, C. L. (2002). Justice in teams: Antecedents and consequences of procedural justice climate. *Personnel Psychology, 55*, 83–109.
56. White, E. (2008, June 30). Age is as age does: Making the generation gap work for you. *Wall Street Journal*, p. B6.
57. Equal Employment Opportunity Commission. (2007). Religious discrimination. Retrieved November 7, 2008, from the Equal Employment Opportunity Commission Web site: http://www.eeoc.gov/types/religion.html.
58. Bazar, E. (2008, October 16). Prayer leads to work disputes. *USA Today*. Retrieved January 29, 2009, from http://www.usatoday.com/news/nation/2008-10-15-Muslim_N.htm.
59. Wellner, A. S. (2005). Costco piercing case puts a new face on the issue of wearing religious garb at work. *Workforce Management, 84*(6), 76–78.

60. Equal Employment Opportunity Commission. (2008). ADA charge data by impairments/bases-merit factor resolutions. FY 1997–FY 2007. Retrieved November 10, 2008, from the Equal Employment Opportunity Commission Web site: http://www.eeoc.gov/stats/ada-merit.html.

61. Beatty, J. E., & Joffe, R. (2006). An overlooked dimension of diversity: The career effects of chronic illness. *Organizational Dynamics, 35*, 182–195.

62. Colella, A., & Varma A. (2001). The impact of subordinate disability on leader-member exchange relationships. *Academy of Management Journal, 44*, 302–315.

63. Human Rights Campaign. (2008). Working for gay, lesbian, bisexual and transgender equal rights. Retrieved November 7, 2008, from the Human Rights Campaign Web site: http://www.hrc.org/issues/workplace/workplace_laws.asp.

64. Ragins, B. R., Singh, R., & Cornwell, J. M. (2007). Making the invisible visible: Fear and disclosure of sexual orientation at work. *Journal of Applied Psychology, 92*, 1103–1118.

65. Button, S. (2001). Organizational efforts to affirm sexual diversity: A cross-level examination. *Journal of Applied Psychology, 86*, 17–28.

66. Chatman, J. A., Polzer, J. T., Barsade, S. G., & Neale, M. A. (1998). Being different yet feeling similar: The influence of demographic composition and organizational culture on work processes and outcomes. *Administrative Science Quarterly, 43*, 749–780; Fisher, A. (2004). How you can do better on diversity. *Fortune, 150*(10), 60.

67. Yang, J. L. (2006). Pepsi's diversity push pays off. *Fortune, 154*(5), 15.

68. Rynes, S., & Rosen, B. (1995). A field survey of factors affecting the adoption and perceived success of diversity training. *Personnel Psychology, 48*, 247–270.

69. Nussenbaum, E. (2003). The lonely recruiter. *Business 2.0, 4*(9), 132.

70. Avery, D. R. (2003). Reactions to diversity in recruitment advertising: Are differences black and white? *Journal of Applied Psychology, 88*, 672–679.

71. Cropanzano, R., Slaughter, J. E., & Bachiochi, P. D. (2005). Organizational justice and black applicants' reactions to affirmative action. *Journal of Applied Psychology, 90*, 1168–1184; Kravitz, D. A. (2008). The diversity-validity dilemma: Beyond selection—The role of affirmative action. *Personnel Psychology, 61*, 173–193; Voluntary diversity plans can lead to risk. (2007). *HR Focus, 84*(6), 2.

72. Harrison, D. A., Kravitz D. A., Mayer, D. M., Leslie, L. M., & Lev-Arey D. (2006). Understanding attitudes toward affirmative action programs in employment: Summary in meta-analysis of 35 years of research. *Journal of Applied Psychology, 91*, 1013–1036.

73. Heilman, M. E., Kaplow, S. R., Amato, M. A., & Stathatos, P. (1993). When similarity is a liability: Effects of sex-based preferential selection on reactions to like-sex and different-sex others. *Journal of Applied Psychology, 78*, 917–927; Heilman, M. E., Rivero, C. J., & Brett, J. F. (1991). Skirting the competence issue: Effects of sex-based preferential selection on task choices of women and men. *Journal of Applied Psychology, 76*, 99–105; Heilman, M. E., Simon, M. C., & Repper, D. P. (1987). Internationally favored, unintentionally harmed? Impact of sex-based preferential selection on self-perceptions and self-evaluations. *Journal of Applied Psychology, 72*, 62–68; Kravitz, D. A. (2008). The diversity-validity dilemma: Beyond selection: The role of affirmative action. *Personnel Psychology, 61*, 173–193.

74. Frauenheim, E. (2005). Crossing cultures. *Workforce Management, 84*(13), 1–32.

75. Hofstede, G. (1980). Culture and organizations. *International Studies of Management & Organization, 10*(4), 15–41; Tsui, A. S., Nifadkar, S. S., & Ou, A. Y. (2007). Cross-national, cross-cultural organizational behavior research: Advances, gaps, and recommendations. *Journal of Management, 33*, 426–478.

76. Triandis, H. C., McCusker, C., & Hui, H. C. (1990). Multimethod probes on individualism and collectivism. *Journal of Personality and Social Psychology, 59*, 1006–1020.

77. Hui, H. C., & Triandis, H. C. (1986). Individualism-collectivism: A study of cross-cultural researchers. *Journal of Cross-Cultural Psychology, 17*, 225–248.

78. Raphael, T. (2001). Savvy companies build bonds with Hispanic employees. *Workforce, 80*(9), 19.

79. Frauenheim, E. (2005). Crossing cultures. *Workforce Management, 84*(13), 1–32.

80. Frauenheim, E. (2005). Crossing cultures. *Workforce Management, 84*(13), 1–32; Hui, H. C., & Triandis, H. C. (1986). Individualism-collectivism: A study of cross-cultural researchers. *Journal of Cross-Cultural Psychology, 17*, 225–248; Javidan, M., & Dastmalchian, A. (2003). Culture and leadership in Iran: The land of individual achievers, strong family ties and powerful elite. *Academy of Management Executive, 17*, 127–142; Gomez, C., Shapiro, D. L., & Kirkman, B. L. (2000). The impact of collectivism and in-group/out-group membership on the evaluation generosity of team members. *Academy of Management Journal, 43*, 1097–1106.

81. Kirkman, B. L., Gibson, B. C., & Shapiro, D. L. (2001). Exporting teams: Enhancing the implementation and effectiveness of work teams in global affiliates. *Organizational Dynamics, 30*, 12–29.

82. Pornpitakpan, C. (2000). Trade in Thailand: A three-way cultural comparison. *Business Horizons, 43*, 61–70.

83. Denison, D. R., Haaland, S., & Goelzer, P. (2004). Corporate culture and organizational effectiveness: Is Asia different from the rest of the world? *Organizational Dynamics, 33*, 98–109.

84. Kirkman, B. L., Gibson, B. C., & Shapiro, D. L. (2001). Exporting teams: Enhancing the implementation and effectiveness of work teams in global affiliates. *Organizational Dynamics, 30*, 12–29.

85. Javidan, M., & Dastmalchian, A. (2003). Culture and leadership in Iran: The land of individual achievers, strong family ties and powerful elite. *Academy of Management Executive, 17*, 127–142; Ryan, A. M., Farland, L. M., Baron, H., & Page R. (1999). An international look at selection practices: Nation and culture as explanations for variability in practice. *Personnel Psychology, 52*, 359–391.

86. Ryan, A. M., Farland, L. M., Baron, H., & Page, R. (1999). An international look at selection practices: Nation and culture as explanations for variability in practice. *Personnel Psychology, 52*, 359–391.

87. Raghuram, S., London, M., & Larsen, H. H. (2001). Flexible employment practices in Europe: Country versus culture. *International Journal of Human Resource Management, 12*, 738–753.

88. Ergeneli, A., Gohar, R., & Temirbekova, Z. (2007). Transformational leadership: Its relationship to culture value dimensions. *International Journal of Intercultural Relations, 31*, 703–724.

89. Rothaermel, F. T., Kotha, S., & Steensma, H. K. (2006). International market entry by U.S. internet firms: An empirical analysis of country risk, national culture, and market size. *Journal of Management, 32*, 56–82.

90. Joiner, A. (2001). The influence of national culture and organizational culture alignment on job stress and performance: Evidence from Greece. *Journal of Managerial Psychology, 16*, 229–243.

91. Tosi, H. L., & Greckhamer, T. (2004). Culture and CEO compensation. *Organization Science, 15*, 657–670.

92. National Virtual Translation Center. (2009). Languages in American school and universities. Retrieved January 29, 2009, from http://www.nvtc.gov/lotw/months/november/USschoollanguages.htm.

93. Earley, P. C., & Mosakowski, E. (2004). Cultural intelligence. *Harvard Business Review, 82*(10), 139–146.

94. Hamm, S. (2008, September 8). Aperian: Helping companies bridge cultures. *Business Week Online. Retrieved* January 29, 2009, from http://www.businessweek.com/technology/content/sep2008/tc2008095_508754.htm.

95. Fowler, G. A., Steinberg, B., & Patrick, A. O. (2007, March 1). Mac and PC's overseas adventures; globalizing Apple's ads meant tweaking characters, clothing and body language. *Wall Street Journal*, p. B1.

96. Fisher, A. (2005, January 24). Offshoring could boost your career. *Fortune, 151*(2), 36.

97. Deshpande, S. P. (1997). Manager's perception of proper ethical conduct: The effect of sex, age, and level of education. *Journal of Business Ethics, 16*, 79–85; Franke, G. R., Crown, D. F., & Spake, D. F. (1997). Gender differences in ethical perceptions of business practices: A social role theory perspective. *Journal of Applied Psychology, 82*, 920–934; Peterson, D., Rhoads, A., & Vaught, B. C. (2001). Ethical beliefs of business professionals: A study of gender, age, and external factors. *Journal of Business Ethics, 31*, 225–231; Volkema, R. J. (2004). Demographic, cultural, and economic predictors of perceived ethicality of negotiation behavior: A nine-country analysis. *Journal of Business Research, 57*, 69–78.

98. Beekun, R. I., Stedham, Y., Yamamura, J. H., & Barghouti, J. A. (2003). Comparing business ethics in Russia and the U.S. *International Journal of Human Resource Management, 14*, 1333–1349.

99. Christie, P. J., Kwon, I. W., Stoeberl, P. A., & Baumhart, R. (2003). A cross-cultural comparison of ethical attitudes of business managers. *Journal of Business Ethics, 46*, 263–287.

100. MacNab, B., MacLean, J., Brislin, R., Aguilera, G. M., Worthley, R., Ravlin, E., et al. (2007). Culture and ethics management: Whistle-blowing and internal reporting within a NAFTA country context. *International Journal of Cross-Cultural Management, 7*, 5–28.

101. Kelly, T. (2008). Rio de Japano. *Forbes Asia, 4*(13), 39–40; Woods, G. P. (2005, October 24). Japan's diversity problem: Women are 41% of work force but command few top posts; A "waste," says Carlos Ghosn. *Wall Street Journal*, p. B1.

102. Valla, M. (2007, January 3). France seeks path to workplace diversity: Employers, politicians wrestle with traditions that make integration a difficult process. *Wall Street Journal*, p. A2.

CHAPTER 3
Understanding People at Work: Individual Differences and Perception

LEARNING OBJECTIVES

After reading this chapter, you should be able to do the following:

1. Define personality and describe how it affects work behaviors.
2. Understand the role of values in determining work behaviors.
3. Explain the process of perception and how it affects work behaviors.
4. Understand how individual differences affect ethics.
5. Understand cross-cultural influences on individual differences and perception.

Kronos Uses Science to Match Candidates to Jobs

Devices such as these are used to help select employees at kiosks located within retail stores.

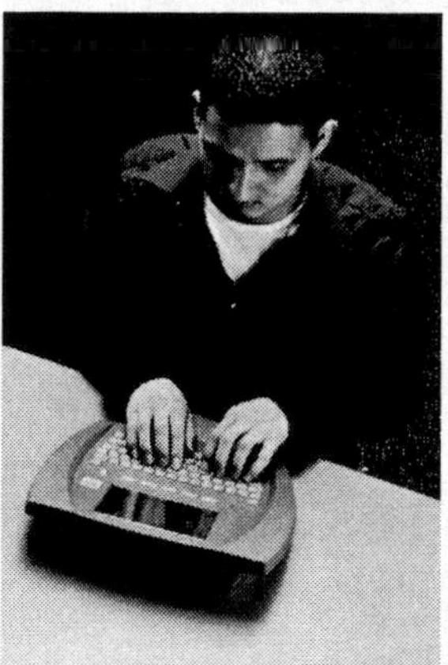

Source: Photo courtesy of Kronos, used with permission.

You are interviewing a candidate for a position as a cashier in a supermarket. You need someone polite, courteous, patient, and dependable. The candidate you are talking to seems nice. But how do you know who is the right person for the job? Will the job candidate like the job or get bored? Will they have a lot of accidents on the job or be fired for misconduct? Don't you wish you knew before hiring? One company approaches this problem scientifically, saving companies time and money on hiring hourly wage employees.

Retail employers do a lot of hiring, given their growth and high turnover rate. According to one estimate, replacing an employee who leaves in retail costs companies around $4,000. High turnover also endangers customer service. Therefore, retail employers have an incentive to screen people carefully so that they hire people with the best chance of being successful and happy on the job. Unicru, an employee selection company, developed software that quickly became a market leader in screening of hourly workers. The company was acquired by Massachusetts-based Kronos Inc. in 2006.

The idea behind the software is simple: If you have a lot of employees and keep track of your data over time, you have access to an enormous resource. By analyzing this data, you can specify the profile of the "ideal" employee. The software captures the profile of the potential high performers, and applicants are screened to assess their fit with this particular profile. More important, the profile is continuously updated as new employees are hired. As the database gets larger, the software does a better job of identifying the right people for the job.

If you applied for a job in retail, you may have already been a part of this database: The users of this system include giants such as Albertsons, Universal Studios, Costco Wholesale Corporation, Macy's, Blockbuster Inc., Target Brands Inc., and other retailers and chain restaurants. In companies such as Target or Blockbuster, applicants use a kiosk in the store to answer a list of questions and to enter their background, salary history, and other information. In other companies, such as some in the trucking industry, candidates enter the data through the Web site of the company they are applying to. The software screens people on basic criteria such as availability in scheduling as well as personality traits.

Candidates are asked to agree or disagree with statements such as "slow people irritate me" or "I don't act polite when I don't want to." After the candidates complete the questions, hiring managers are sent a report complete with a color-coded suggested course of action. Red means the candidate does not fit the job, yellow means proceed with caution, and green means the candidate can be hired on the spot. Interestingly, the company contends that faking answers to the questions of the software is not easy because it is difficult for candidates to predict the desired profile. For example, according to their research, being a successful salesman has less to do with being an extraverted and sociable person and more to do with a passion for the company's product.

Matching candidates to jobs has long been viewed as a key way of ensuring high performance and low turnover in the workplace, and advances in computer technology are making it easier and more efficient to assess candidate-job fit. Companies using such technology are cutting down the time it takes to hire people, and it is estimated that using such techniques lowers their turnover by 10%–30%.

Sources: Berta, D. (2002, February 25). Industry increases applicant screening amid labor surplus, security concerns. Nation's Restaurant News, 36(8), 4; Frauenheim, E. (2006, March 13). Unicru beefs up data in latest screening tool. Workforce Management, 85(5), 9–10; Frazier, M. (2005, April). Help wanted. Chain Store Age, 81(4), 37–39; Haaland, D. E. (2006, April 17). Safety first: Hire conscientious employees to cut down on costly workplace accidents. Nation's Restaurant News, 40(16), 22–24; Overholt, A. (2002, February). True or false? You're hiring the right people. Fast Company, 55, 108–109; Rafter, M. V. (2005, May). Unicru breaks through in the science of "smart hiring." Workforce Management, 84(5), 76–78.

Individuals bring a number of differences to work, such as unique personalities, values, emotions, and moods. When new employees enter organizations, their stable or transient characteristics affect how they behave and perform. Moreover, companies hire people with the expectation that those individuals have certain skills, abilities, personalities, and values. Therefore, it is important to understand individual characteristics that matter for employee behaviors at work.

1. THE INTERACTIONIST PERSPECTIVE: THE ROLE OF FIT

LEARNING OBJECTIVES

1. **Differentiate between person–organization and person–job fit.**
2. **Understand the relationship between person–job fit and work behaviors.**
3. **Understand the relationship between person–organization fit and work behaviors.**

Individual differences matter in the workplace. Human beings bring in their personality, physical and mental abilities, and other stable traits to work. Imagine that you are interviewing an employee who is proactive, creative, and willing to take risks. Would this person be a good job candidate? What behaviors would you expect this person to demonstrate?

The question posed above is misleading. While human beings bring their traits to work, every organization is different, and every job within the organization is also different. According to the interactionist perspective, behavior is a function of the person and the situation interacting with each other. Think about it. Would a shy person speak up in class? While a shy person may not feel like speaking, if the individual is very interested in the subject, knows the answers to the questions, and feels comfortable within the classroom environment, and if the instructor encourages participation and participation is 30% of the course grade, regardless of the level of shyness, the person may feel inclined to participate. Similarly, the behavior you may expect from someone who is proactive, creative, and willing to take risks will depend on the situation.

When hiring employees, companies are interested in assessing at least two types of fit. **Person–organization fit** refers to the degree to which a person's values, personality, goals, and other characteristics match those of the organization. **Person–job fit** is the degree to which a person's skill, knowledge, abilities, and other characteristics match the job demands. Thus, someone who is proactive and creative may be a great fit for a company in the high-tech sector that would benefit from risk-taking individuals, but may be a poor fit for a company that rewards routine and predictable behavior, such as accountants. Similarly, this person may be a great fit for a job such as a scientist, but a poor fit for a routine office job. The opening case illustrates one method of assessing person–organization and person–job fit in job applicants.

person–organization fit

The degree to which a person's values, personality, goals, and other characteristics match those of the organization.

person–job fit

The degree to which a person's skill, knowledge, abilities, and other characteristics match the job demands.

The first thing many recruiters look at is the person–job fit. This is not surprising, because person–job fit is related to a number of positive work attitudes such as satisfaction with the work environment, identification with the organization, job satisfaction, and work behaviors such as job performance. Companies are often also interested in hiring candidates who will fit into the company culture (those with high person–organization fit). When people fit into their organization, they tend to be more satisfied with their jobs, more committed to their companies, and more influential in their company, and they actually remain longer in their company.[1] One area of controversy is whether these people perform better. Some studies have found a positive relationship between person–organization fit and job performance, but this finding was not present in all studies, so it seems that fitting with a company's culture will only sometimes predict job performance.[2] It also seems that fitting in with the company culture is more important to some people than to others. For example, people who have worked in multiple companies tend to understand the impact of a company's culture better, and therefore they pay more attention to whether they will fit in with the company when making their decisions.[3] Also, when they build good relationships with their supervisors and the company, being a misfit does not seem to lead to dissatisfaction on the job.[4]

KEY TAKEAWAY

While personality traits and other individual differences are important, we need to keep in mind that behavior is jointly determined by the person and the situation. Certain situations bring out the best in people, and someone who is a poor performer in one job may turn into a star employee in a different job.

EXERCISES

1. How can a company assess person–job fit before hiring employees? What are the methods you think would be helpful?
2. How can a company determine person–organization fit before hiring employees? Which methods do you think would be helpful?
3. What can organizations do to increase person–job and person–organization fit *after* they hire employees?

2. INDIVIDUAL DIFFERENCES: VALUES AND PERSONALITY

LEARNING OBJECTIVES

1. Understand what values are.
2. Describe the link between values and individual behavior.
3. Identify the major personality traits that are relevant to organizational behavior.
4. Explain the link between personality, work behavior, and work attitudes.
5. Explain the potential pitfalls of personality testing.

2.1 Values

values

Stable life goals people have, reflecting what is most important to them.

terminal values

End states people desire in life, such as leading a prosperous life and a world at peace.

instrumental values

Views on acceptable modes of conduct, such as being honest and ethical, and being ambitious.

Values refer to stable life goals that people have, reflecting what is most important to them. Values are established throughout one's life as a result of the accumulating life experiences and tend to be relatively stable.[5] The values that are important to people tend to affect the types of decisions they make, how they perceive their environment, and their actual behaviors. Moreover, people are more likely to accept job offers when the company possesses the values people care about.[6] Value attainment is one reason why people stay in a company, and when an organization does not help them attain their values, they are more likely to decide to leave if they are dissatisfied with the job itself.[7]

What are the values people care about? There are many typologies of values. One of the most established surveys to assess individual values is the Rokeach Value Survey.[8] This survey lists 18 terminal and 18 instrumental values in alphabetical order. **Terminal values** refer to end states people desire in life, such as leading a prosperous life and a world at peace. **Instrumental values** deal with views on acceptable modes of conduct, such as being honest and ethical, and being ambitious.

According to Rokeach, values are arranged in hierarchical fashion. In other words, an accurate way of assessing someone's values is to ask them to rank the 36 values in order of importance. By comparing these values, people develop a sense of which value can be sacrificed to achieve the other, and the individual priority of each value emerges.

FIGURE 3.2 Sample Items From Rokeach (1973) Value Survey

Terminal Values	Instrumental Values
A world of beauty	Broad minded
An exciting life	Clean
Family security	Forgiving
Inner harmony	Imaginative
Self respect	Obedient

Where do values come from? Research indicates that they are shaped early in life and show stability over the course of a lifetime. Early family experiences are important influences over the dominant values. People who were raised in families with low socioeconomic status and those who experienced restrictive parenting often display conformity values when they are adults, while those who were raised by parents who were cold toward their children would likely value and desire security.[9]

Values of a generation also change and evolve in response to the historical context that the generation grows up in. Research comparing the values of different generations resulted in interesting findings. For example, Generation Xers (those born between the mid-1960s and 1980s) are more individualistic and are interested in working toward organizational goals so long as they coincide with their personal goals. This group, compared to the baby boomers (born between the 1940s and 1960s), is also less likely to see work as central to their life and more likely to desire a quick promotion.[10]

The values a person holds will affect his or her employment. For example, someone who has an orientation toward strong stimulation may pursue extreme sports and select an occupation that involves fast action and high risk, such as fire fighter, police officer, or emergency medical doctor. Someone who has a drive for achievement may more readily act as an entrepreneur. Moreover, whether individuals will be satisfied at a given job may depend on whether the job provides a way to satisfy their dominant values. Therefore, understanding employees at work requires understanding the value orientations of employees.

FIGURE 3.3

Values will affect the choices people make. For example, someone who has a strong stimulation orientation may pursue extreme sports and be drawn to risky business ventures with a high potential for payoff.

© 2010 Jupiterimages Corporation

2.2 Personality

Personality encompasses the relatively stable feelings, thoughts, and behavioral patterns a person has. Our personality differentiates us from other people, and understanding someone's personality gives us clues about how that person is likely to act and feel in a variety of situations. In order to effectively manage organizational behavior, an understanding of different employees' personalities is helpful. Having this knowledge is also useful for placing people in jobs and organizations.

personality

The relatively stable feelings, thoughts, and behavioral patterns a person has.

If personality is stable, does this mean that it does not change? You probably remember how you have changed and evolved as a result of your own life experiences, attention you received in early childhood, the style of parenting you were exposed to, successes and failures you had in high school, and other life events. In fact, our personality changes over long periods of time. For example, we tend to become more socially dominant, more conscientious (organized and dependable), and more emotionally stable between the ages of 20 and 40, whereas openness to new experiences may begin to decline during this same time.[11] In other words, even though we treat personality as relatively stable, changes occur. Moreover, even in childhood, our personality shapes who we are and has lasting consequences for us. For example, studies show that part of our career success and job satisfaction later in life can be explained by our childhood personality.[12]

Is our behavior in organizations dependent on our personality? To some extent, yes, and to some extent, no. While we will discuss the effects of personality for employee behavior, you must remember that the relationships we describe are modest correlations. For example, having a sociable and outgoing personality may encourage people to seek friends and prefer social situations. This does not mean that their personality will immediately affect their work behavior. At work, we have a job to do and a role to perform. Therefore, our behavior may be more strongly affected by what is expected of us, as opposed to how we want to behave. When people have a lot of freedom at work, their personality will become a stronger influence over their behavior.[13]

Big Five Personality Traits

How many personality traits are there? How do we even know? In every language, there are many words describing a person's personality. In fact, in the English language, more than 15,000 words describing personality have been identified. When researchers analyzed the terms describing personality characteristics, they realized that there were many words that were pointing to each dimension of personality. When these words were grouped, five dimensions seemed to emerge that explain a lot of the variation in our personalities.[14] Keep in mind that these five are not necessarily the only traits out there. There are other, specific traits that represent dimensions not captured by the Big Five. Still, understanding the main five traits gives us a good start for describing personality. A summary of the Big Five traits is presented in Figure 3.4.

FIGURE 3.4 Big Five Personality Traits

Trait	Description
Openness	Being curious, original, intellectual, creative, and open to new ideas.
Conscientiousness	Being organized, systematic, punctual, achievement oriented, and dependable.
Extraversion	Being outgoing, talkative, sociable, and enjoying social situations.
Agreeableness	Being affable, tolerant, sensitive, trusting, kind, and warm.
Neuroticism	Being anxious, irritable, temperamental, and moody.

openness

The degree to which a person is curious, original, intellectual, creative, and open to new ideas.

Openness is the degree to which a person is curious, original, intellectual, creative, and open to new ideas. People high in openness seem to thrive in situations that require being flexible and learning new things. They are highly motivated to learn new skills, and they do well in training settings.[15] They also have an advantage when they enter into a new organization. Their open-mindedness leads them to seek a lot of information and feedback about how they are doing and to build relationships, which leads to quicker adjustment to the new job.[16] When supported, they tend to be creative.[17] Open people are highly adaptable to change, and teams that experience unforeseen changes in their tasks do well if they are populated with people high in openness.[18] Compared to people low in openness, they are also more likely to start their own business.[19]

conscientiousness

The degree to which a person is organized, systematic, punctual, achievement oriented, and dependable.

Conscientiousness refers to the degree to which a person is organized, systematic, punctual, achievement oriented, and dependable. Conscientiousness is the one personality trait that uniformly predicts how high a person's performance will be, across a variety of occupations and jobs.[20] In fact, conscientiousness is the trait most desired by recruiters and results in the most success in interviews.[21] This is not a surprise, because in addition to their high performance, conscientious people have higher levels of motivation to perform, lower levels of turnover, lower levels of absenteeism, and higher levels of safety performance at work.[22] One's conscientiousness is related to career success and being satisfied with one's career over time.[23] Finally, it seems that conscientiousness is a good trait to have for entrepreneurs. Highly conscientious people are more likely to start their own business compared to those who are not conscientious, and their firms have longer survival rates.[24]

extraversion

The degree to which a person is outgoing, talkative, sociable, and enjoys being in social situations.

Extraversion is the degree to which a person is outgoing, talkative, and sociable, and enjoys being in social situations. One of the established findings is that they tend to be effective in jobs involving sales.[25] Moreover, they tend to be effective as managers and they demonstrate inspirational leadership behaviors.[26] Extraverts do well in social situations, and as a result they tend to be effective in job interviews. Part of their success comes from how they prepare for the job interview, as they are likely to use their social network.[27] Extraverts have an easier time than introverts when adjusting to a new job. They actively seek information and feedback, and build effective relationships, which helps with their adjustment.[28] Interestingly, extraverts are also found to be happier at work, which may be because of the relationships they build with the people around them and their relative ease in adjusting to a new job.[29] However, they do not necessarily perform well in all jobs, and jobs depriving them of social interaction may be a poor fit. Moreover, they are not necessarily model employees. For example, they tend to have higher levels of absenteeism at work, potentially because they may miss work to hang out with or attend to the needs of their friends.[30]

Agreeableness is the degree to which a person is nice, tolerant, sensitive, trusting, kind, and warm. In other words, people who are high in agreeableness are likeable people who get along with others. Not surprisingly, agreeable people help others at work consistently, and this helping behavior is not dependent on being in a good mood.[31] They are also less likely to retaliate when other people treat them unfairly.[32] This may reflect their ability to show empathy and give people the benefit of the doubt. Agreeable people may be a valuable addition to their teams and may be effective leaders because they create a fair environment when they are in leadership positions.[33] At the other end of the spectrum, people low in agreeableness are less likely to show these positive behaviors. Moreover, people who are not agreeable are shown to quit their jobs unexpectedly, perhaps in response to a conflict they engage with a boss or a peer.[34] If agreeable people are so nice, does this mean that we should only look for agreeable people when hiring? Some jobs may actually be a better fit for someone with a low level of agreeableness. Think about it: When hiring a lawyer, would you prefer a kind and gentle person, or a pit bull? Also, high agreeableness has a downside: Agreeable people are less likely to engage in constructive and change-oriented communication.[35] Disagreeing with the status quo may create conflict and agreeable people will likely avoid creating such conflict, missing an opportunity for constructive change.

FIGURE 3.5

Studies show that there is a relationship between being extraverted and effectiveness as a salesperson.

agreeableness

The degree to which a person is nice, tolerant, sensitive, trusting, kind, and warm.

How Accurately Can You Describe Your Big Five Personality Factors?

Go to http://www.outofservice.com/bigfive/ to see how you score on these factors.

Neuroticism refers to the degree to which a person is anxious, irritable, aggressive, temperamental, and moody. These people have a tendency to have emotional adjustment problems and experience stress and depression on a habitual basis. People very high in neuroticism experience a number of problems at work. For example, they are less likely to be someone people go to for advice and friendship.[36] In other words, they may experience relationship difficulties. They tend to be habitually unhappy in their jobs and report high intentions to leave, but they do not necessarily actually leave their jobs.[37] Being high in neuroticism seems to be harmful to one's career, as they have lower levels of career success (measured with income and occupational status achieved in one's career). Finally, if they achieve managerial jobs, they tend to create an unfair climate at work.[38]

neuroticism

The degree to which a person is anxious, irritable, aggressive, temperamental, and moody.

Myers-Briggs Type Indicator

Aside from the Big Five personality traits, perhaps the most well-known and most often used personality assessment is the Myers-Briggs Type Indicator (MBTI). Unlike the Big Five, which assesses traits, MBTI measures types. Assessments of the Big Five do not classify people as neurotic or extravert: It is all a matter of degrees. MBTI on the other hand, classifies people as one of 16 types.[39] In MBTI, people are grouped using four dimensions. Based on how a person is classified on these four dimensions, it is possible to talk about 16 unique personality types, such as ESTJ and ISTP.

MBTI was developed in 1943 by a mother–daughter team, Isabel Myers and Katherine Cook Briggs. Its objective at the time was to aid World War II veterans in identifying the occupation that would suit their personalities. Since that time, MBTI has become immensely popular, and according to one estimate, around 2.5 million people take the test annually. The survey is criticized because it relies on types as opposed to traits, but organizations who use the survey find it very useful for training and team-building purposes. More than eighty of the *Fortune* 100 companies used Myers-Briggs tests in some form. One distinguishing characteristic of this test is that it is explicitly designed for learning, not for employee selection purposes. In fact, the Myers & Briggs Foundation has strict guidelines against the use of the test for employee selection. Instead, the test is used to provide mutual understanding within the team and to gain a better understanding of the working styles of team members.[40]

FIGURE 3.6 Summary of MBTI Types

Dimension		Explanation
EI	Extraversion: Those who derive their energy from other people and objects.	Introversion: Those who derive their energy from inside.
SN	Sensing: Those who rely on their five senses to perceive the external environment.	Intuition: Those who rely on their intuition and hunches to perceive the external environment.
TF	Thinking: Those who use their logic to arrive at solutions.	Feeling: Those who use their values and ideas about what is right and wrong to arrive at solutions.
JP	Judgment: Those who are organized, systematic, and would like to have clarity and closure.	Perception: Those who are curious, open minded, and prefer to have some ambiguity.

Positive and Negative Affectivity

positive affective people

People who experience positive moods more frequently and tend to be happier at work.

negative affective people

People who experience negative moods with greater frequency, focus on the "glass half empty," and experience more anxiety and nervousness.

You may have noticed that behavior is also a function of moods. When people are in a good mood, they may be more cooperative, smile more, and act friendly. When these same people are in a bad mood, they may have a tendency to be picky, irritable, and less tolerant of different opinions. Yet, some people seem to be in a good mood most of the time, and others seem to be in a bad mood most of the time regardless of what is actually going on in their lives. This distinction is manifested by positive and negative affectivity traits. **Positive affective people** experience positive moods more frequently, whereas **negative affective people** experience negative moods with greater frequency. Negative affective people focus on the "glass half empty" and experience more anxiety and nervousness.[41] Positive affective people tend to be happier at work,[42] and their happiness spreads to the rest of the work environment. As may be expected, this personality trait sets the tone in the work atmosphere. When a team comprises mostly negative affective people, there tend to be fewer instances of helping and cooperation. Teams dominated by positive affective people experience lower levels of absenteeism.[43] When people with a lot of power are also high in positive affectivity, the work environment is affected in a positive manner and can lead to greater levels of cooperation and finding mutually agreeable solutions to problems.[44]

OB Toolbox: Help, I work with a negative person!

Employees who have high levels of neuroticism or high levels of negative affectivity may act overly negative at work, criticize others, complain about trivial things, or create an overall negative work environment. Here are some tips for how to work with them effectively.

- *Understand that you are unlikely to change someone else's personality.* Personality is relatively stable and criticizing someone's personality will not bring about change. If the behavior is truly disruptive, focus on behavior, not personality.
- *Keep an open mind.* Just because a person is constantly negative does not mean that they are not sometimes right. Listen to the feedback they are giving you.
- *Set a time limit.* If you are dealing with someone who constantly complains about things, you may want to limit these conversations to prevent them from consuming your time at work.
- *You may also empower them to act on the negatives they mention.* The next time an overly negative individual complains about something, ask that person to think of ways to change the situation and get back to you.
- *Ask for specifics.* If someone has a negative tone in general, you may want to ask for specific examples for what the problem is.

Sources: Adapted from ideas in Ferguson, J. (2006, October 31). Expert's view…on managing office moaners. Personnel Today, 29; Karcher, C. (2003, September), Working with difficult people. National Public Accountant, 39–40; Mudore, C. F. (2001, February/March). Working with difficult people. Career World, 29(5), 16–18; How to manage difficult people. (2000, May). Leadership for the Front Lines, 3–4.

Self-Monitoring

Self-monitoring refers to the extent to which a person is capable of monitoring his or her actions and appearance in social situations. In other words, people who are social monitors are social chameleons who understand what the situation demands and act accordingly, while low social monitors tend to act the way they feel.[45] High social monitors are sensitive to the types of behaviors the social environment expects from them. Their greater ability to modify their behavior according to the demands of the situation and to manage their impressions effectively is a great advantage for them.[46] In general, they tend to be more successful in their careers. They are more likely to get cross-company promotions, and even when they stay with one company, they are more likely to advance.[47] Social monitors also become the "go to" person in their company and they enjoy central positions in their social networks.[48] They are rated as higher performers, and emerge as leaders.[49] While they are effective in influencing other people and get things done by managing their impressions, this personality trait has some challenges that need to be addressed. First, when evaluating the performance of other employees, they tend to be less accurate. It seems that while trying to manage their impressions, they may avoid giving accurate feedback to their subordinates to avoid confrontations.[50] This tendency may create problems for them if they are managers. Second, high social monitors tend to experience higher levels of stress, probably caused by behaving in ways that conflict with their true feelings. In situations that demand positive emotions, they may act happy although they are not feeling happy, which puts an emotional burden on them. Finally, high social monitors tend to be less committed to their companies. They may see their jobs as a stepping-stone for greater things, which may prevent them from forming strong attachments and loyalty to their current employer.[51]

self-monitoring

The extent to which people are capable of monitoring their actions and appearance in social situations.

Proactive Personality

Proactive personality refers to a person's inclination to fix what is perceived as wrong, change the status quo, and use initiative to solve problems. Instead of waiting to be told what to do, proactive people take action to initiate meaningful change and remove the obstacles they face along the way. In general, having a proactive personality has a number of advantages for these people. For example, they tend to be more successful in their job searches.[52] They are also more successful over the course of their careers, because they use initiative and acquire greater understanding of the politics within the organization.[53] Proactive people are valuable assets to their companies because they may have higher levels of performance.[54] They adjust to their new jobs quickly because they understand the political environment better and often make friends more quickly.[55] Proactive people are eager to learn and engage in many developmental activities to improve their skills.[56] Despite all their potential, under some circumstances a proactive personality may be a liability for an individual or an organization. Imagine a person who is proactive but is perceived as being too pushy, trying to change things other people are not willing to let go, or using their initiative to make decisions that do not serve a company's best interests. Research shows that the success of proactive people depends on their understanding of a company's core values, their ability and skills to perform their jobs, and their ability to assess situational demands correctly.[57]

proactive personality

A person's inclination to fix what is perceived to be wrong, change the status quo, and use initiative to solve problems.

Self-Esteem

Self-esteem is the degree to which a person has overall positive feelings about his or herself. People with high self-esteem view themselves in a positive light, are confident, and respect themselves. On the other hand, people with low self-esteem experience high levels of self-doubt and question their self-worth. High self-esteem is related to higher levels of satisfaction with one's job and higher levels of performance on the job.[58] People with low self-esteem are attracted to situations in which they will be relatively invisible, such as large companies.[59] Managing employees with low self-esteem may be challenging at times, because negative feedback given with the intention to improve performance may be viewed as a judgment on their worth as an employee. Therefore, effectively managing employees with relatively low self-esteem requires tact and providing lots of positive feedback when discussing performance incidents.

self-esteem

The degree to which a person has overall positive feelings about oneself.

Self-Efficacy

Self-efficacy is a belief that one can perform a specific task successfully. Research shows that the belief that we can do something is a good predictor of whether we can actually do it. Self-efficacy is different from other personality traits in that it is job specific. You may have high self-efficacy in being successful academically, but low self-efficacy in relation to your ability to fix your car. At the same time, people have a certain level of generalized self-efficacy and they have the belief that whatever task or hobby they tackle, they are likely to be successful in it.

self-efficacy

A belief that one can perform a specific task successfully.

Research shows that self-efficacy at work is related to job performance.[60] This relationship is probably a result of people with high self-efficacy setting higher goals for themselves and being more committed to these goals, whereas people with low self-efficacy tend to procrastinate.[61] Academic self-efficacy is a good predictor of your GPA, whether you persist in your studies, or drop out of college.[62]

Is there a way of increasing employees' self-efficacy? Hiring people who are capable of performing their tasks and training people to increase their self-efficacy may be effective. Some people may also respond well to verbal encouragement. By showing that you believe they can be successful and effectively playing the role of a cheerleader, you may be able to increase self-efficacy. Giving people opportunities to test their skills so that they can see what they are capable of doing (or empowering them) is also a good way of increasing self-efficacy.[63]

OB Toolbox: Ways to Build Your Self-Confidence

Having high self-efficacy and self-esteem are boons to your career. People who have an overall positive view of themselves and those who have positive attitudes toward their abilities project an aura of confidence. How do you achieve higher self confidence?

- *Take a self-inventory.* What are the areas in which you lack confidence? Then consciously tackle these areas. Take part in training programs; seek opportunities to practice these skills. Confront your fears head-on.
- *Set manageable goals.* Success in challenging goals will breed self-confidence, but do not make your goals impossible to reach. If a task seems daunting, break it apart and set mini goals.
- *Find a mentor.* A mentor can point out areas in need of improvement, provide accurate feedback, and point to ways of improving yourself.
- *Don't judge yourself by your failures.* Everyone fails, and the most successful people have more failures in life. Instead of assessing your self-worth by your failures, learn from mistakes and move on.
- *Until you can feel confident, be sure to act confident.* Acting confident will influence how others treat you, which will boost your confidence level. Pay attention to how you talk and behave, and act like someone who has high confidence.
- *Know when to ignore negative advice.* If you receive negative feedback from someone who is usually negative, try to ignore it. Surrounding yourself with naysayers is not good for your self-esteem. This does not mean that you should ignore all negative feedback, but be sure to look at a person's overall attitude before making serious judgments based on that feedback.

Sources: Adapted from information in Beagrie, S. (2006, September 26). How to...build up self confidence. Personnel Today, p. 31; Beste, F. J., III. (2007, November–December). Are you an entrepreneur? In Business, 29(6), 22; Goldsmith, B. (2006, October). Building self confidence. PA Times, Education Supplement, p. 30; Kennett, M. (2006, October). The scale of confidence. Management Today, p. 40–45; Parachin, V. M. (March 2003, October). Developing dynamic self-confidence. Supervision, 64(3), 13–15.

Locus of Control

internal locus of control

The belief that a person controls their own destiny and what happens to them is their own doing.

external locus of control

The belief that things happen because of other people, luck, or a powerful being.

Locus of control deals with the degree to which people feel accountable for their own behaviors. Individuals with high **internal locus of control** believe that they control their own destiny and what happens to them is their own doing, while those with high **external locus of control** feel that things happen to them because of other people, luck, or a powerful being. Internals feel greater control over their own lives and therefore they act in ways that will increase their chances of success. For example, they take the initiative to start mentor-protégé relationships. They are more involved with their jobs. They demonstrate higher levels of motivation and have more positive experiences at work.[64] Interestingly, internal locus is also related to one's subjective well-being and happiness in life, while being high in external locus is related to a higher rate of depression.[65] The connection between internal locus of control and health is interesting, but perhaps not surprising. In fact, one study showed that having internal locus of control at the age of ten was related to a number of health outcomes, such as lower obesity and lower blood pressure later in life.[66] It is possible that internals take more responsibility for their health and adopt healthier habits, while externals may see less of a connection between how they live and their health. Internals thrive in contexts in which they have the ability to influence their own behavior. Successful entrepreneurs tend to have high levels of internal locus of control.[67]

Understand Your Locus of Control by Taking a Survey at the Following Web Site:

http://discoveryhealth.queendom.com/questions/lc_short_1.html

2.3 Personality Testing in Employee Selection

Personality is a potentially important predictor of work behavior. Matching people to jobs matters, because when people do not fit with their jobs or the company, they are more likely to leave, costing companies as much as a person's annual salary to replace them. In job interviews, companies try to assess a candidate's personality and the potential for a good match, but interviews are only as good as the people conducting them. In fact, interviewers are not particularly good at detecting the best trait that predicts performance: conscientiousness.[68] One method some companies use to improve this match and detect the people who are potentially good job candidates is personality testing. Companies such as Kronos and Hogan Assessment Systems conduct preemployment personality tests. Companies using them believe that these tests improve the effectiveness of their selection and reduce turnover. For example, Overnight Transportation in Atlanta found that using such tests reduced their on-the-job delinquency by 50%–100%.[69]

Yet, are these methods good ways of selecting employees? Experts have not yet reached an agreement on this subject and the topic is highly controversial. Some experts believe, based on data, that personality tests predict performance and other important criteria such as job satisfaction. However, we must understand that how a personality test is used influences its validity. Imagine filling out a personality test in class. You may be more likely to fill it out as honestly as you can. Then, if your instructor correlates your personality scores with your class performance, we could say that the correlation is meaningful. In employee selection, one complicating factor is that people filling out the survey do not have a strong incentive to be honest. In fact, they have a greater incentive to guess what the job requires and answer the questions to match what they think the company is looking for. As a result, the rankings of the candidates who take the test may be affected by their ability to fake. Some experts believe that this is a serious problem.[70] Others point out that even with **faking**, the tests remain valid—the scores are still related to job performance.[71] It is even possible that the ability to fake is related to a personality trait that increases success at work, such as social monitoring. This issue raises potential questions regarding whether personality tests are the most effective way of measuring candidate personality.

faking

The practice of answering questions in a way one thinks the company is looking for.

Scores are not only distorted because of some candidates faking better than others. Do we even know our own personality? Are we the best person to ask this question? How supervisors, coworkers, and customers see our personality matters more than how we see ourselves. Therefore, using self-report measures of performance may not be the best way of measuring someone's personality.[72] We all have blind areas. We may also give "aspirational" answers. If you are asked if you are honest, you may think, "Yes, I always have the intention to be honest." This response says nothing about your actual level of honesty.

There is another problem with using these tests: How good a predictor of performance is personality anyway? Based on research, not a particularly strong one. According to one estimate, personality only explains about 10%–15% of variation in job performance. Our performance at work depends on so many factors, and personality does not seem to be the key factor for performance. In fact, cognitive ability (your overall mental intelligence) is a much more powerful influence on job performance, and instead of personality tests, cognitive ability tests may do a better job of predicting who will be good performers. Personality is a better predictor of job satisfaction and other attitudes, but screening people out on the assumption that they may be unhappy at work is a challenging argument to make in the context of employee selection.

In any case, if you decide to use these tests for selection, you need to be aware of their limitations. Relying only on personality tests for selection of an employee is a bad idea, but if they are used together with other tests such as tests of cognitive abilities, better decisions may be made. The company should ensure that the test fits the job and actually predicts performance. This process is called validating the test. Before giving the test to applicants, the company could give it to existing employees to find out the traits that are most important for success in the particular company and job. Then, in the selection context, the company can pay particular attention to those traits. The company should also make sure that the test does not discriminate against people on the basis of sex, race, age, disabilities, and other legally protected characteristics. Rent-A-Center experienced legal difficulties when the test they used was found to be a violation of the Americans with Disabilities Act (ADA). The test they used for selection, the Minnesota Multiphasic Personality Inventory, was developed to diagnose severe mental illnesses and included items such as "I see things or people around me others do not see." In effect, the test served the purpose of a clinical evaluation and was discriminating against people with mental illnesses, which is a protected category under ADA.[73]

KEY TAKEAWAY

Values and personality traits are two dimensions on which people differ. Values are stable life goals. When seeking jobs, employees are more likely to accept a job that provides opportunities for value attainment, and they are more likely to remain in situations that satisfy their values. Personality comprises the stable feelings, thoughts, and behavioral patterns people have. The Big Five personality traits (openness, conscientiousness, extraversion, agreeableness, and neuroticism) are important traits that seem to be stable and can be generalized to other cultures. Other important traits for work behavior include self-efficacy, self-esteem, social monitoring, proactive personality, positive and negative affectivity, and locus of control. It is important to remember that a person's behavior depends on the match between the person and the situation. While personality is a strong influence on job attitudes, its relation to job performance is weaker. Some companies use personality testing to screen out candidates. This method has certain limitations, and companies using personality tests are advised to validate their tests and use them as a supplement to other techniques that have greater validity.

EXERCISES

1. Think about the personality traits covered in this section. Can you think of jobs or occupations that seem particularly suited to each trait? Which traits would be universally desirable across all jobs?
2. What are the unique challenges of managing employees who have low self efficacy and low self-esteem? How would you deal with this situation?
3. What are some methods that companies can use to assess employee personality?
4. Have you ever held a job where your personality did not match the demands of the job? How did you react to this situation? How were your attitudes and behaviors affected?
5. Can you think of any limitations of developing an "ideal employee" profile and looking for employees who fit that profile while hiring?

3. PERCEPTION

LEARNING OBJECTIVES

1. **Understand the influence of self in the process of perception.**
2. **Describe how we perceive visual objects and how these tendencies may affect our behavior.**
3. **Describe the biases of self-perception.**
4. **Describe the biases inherent in perception of other people.**
5. **Explain what attributions mean, how we form attributions, and their consequences for organizational behavior.**

perception

The process with which individuals detect and interpret environmental stimuli.

Our behavior is not only a function of our personality, values, and preferences, but also of the situation. We interpret our environment, formulate responses, and act accordingly. **Perception** may be defined as the process with which individuals detect and interpret environmental stimuli. What makes human perception so interesting is that we do not solely respond to the stimuli in our environment. We go beyond the information that is present in our environment, pay selective attention to some aspects of the environment, and ignore other elements that may be immediately apparent to other people. Our perception of the environment is not entirely rational. For example, have you ever noticed that while glancing at a newspaper or a news Web site, information that is interesting or important to you jumps out of the page and catches your eye? If you are a sports fan, while scrolling down the pages you may immediately see a news item describing the latest success of your team. If you are the parent of a picky eater, an advice column on toddler feeding may be the first thing you see when looking at the page. So what we see in the environment is a function of what we value, our needs, our fears, and our emotions.[74] In fact, what we see in the environment may be objectively, flat-out wrong because of our personality, values, or emotions. For example, one experiment showed that when people who were afraid of spiders were shown spiders, they inaccurately thought that the spider was moving toward them.[75] In this section, we will describe some common tendencies we engage in when perceiving objects or other people, and the consequences of such perceptions. Our coverage of biases and tendencies in perception is not exhaustive—there are many other biases and tendencies on our social perception.

3.1 Visual Perception

Our visual perception definitely goes beyond the physical information available to us. First of all, we extrapolate from the information available to us. Take a look at the following figure. The white triangle you see in the middle is not really there, but we extrapolate from the information available to us and see it there.[76]

FIGURE 3.7

Our visual perception goes beyond the information physically available. In this figure, we see the white triangle in the middle even though it is not really there.

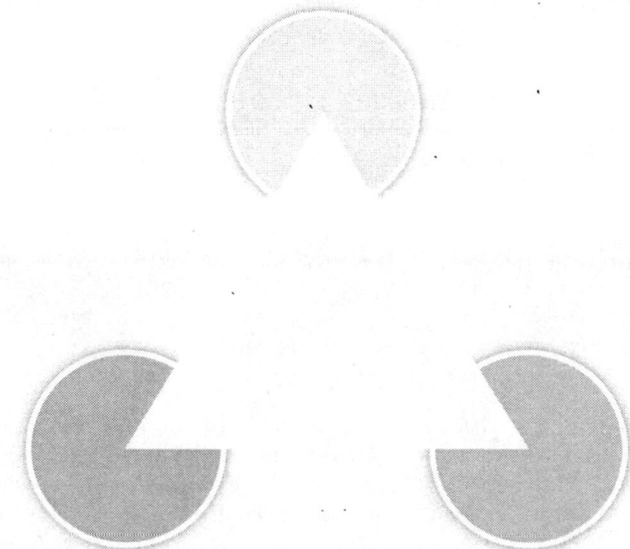

Our visual perception is often biased because we do not perceive objects in isolation. The contrast between our focus of attention and the remainder of the environment may make an object appear bigger or smaller. This principle is illustrated in the figure with circles. Which of the middle circles is bigger? To most people, the one on the left appears bigger, but this is because it is surrounded by smaller circles. The contrast between the focal object and the objects surrounding it may make an object bigger or smaller to our eye.

FIGURE 3.8

Which of the circles in the middle is bigger? At first glance, the one on the left may appear bigger, but they are in fact the same size. We compare the middle circle on the left to its surrounding circles, whereas the middle circle on the right is compared to the bigger circles surrounding it.

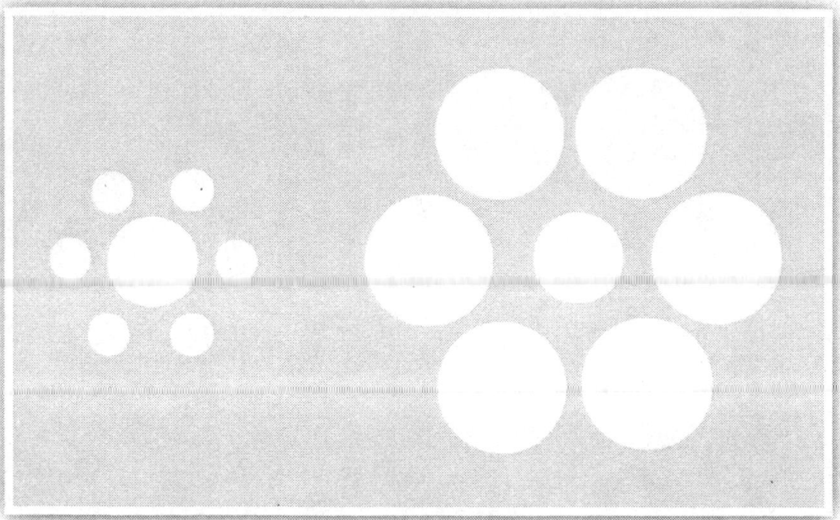

How do these tendencies influence behavior in organizations? You may have realized that the fact that our visual perception is faulty may make witness testimony faulty and biased. How do we know whether the employee you judge to be hardworking, fast, and neat is really like that? Is it really true, or are we comparing this person to other people in the immediate environment? Or let's say that you do not like one of your peers and you think that this person is constantly surfing the Web during work hours. Are you sure? Have you really seen this person surf unrelated Web sites, or is it possible that the person was surfing the web for work-related purposes? Our biased visual perception may lead to the wrong inferences about the people around us.

3.2 Self-Perception

self-enhancement bias

The tendency to overestimate our performance and capabilities and to see ourselves in a more positive light than others see us.

self-effacement bias

The tendency to underestimate our performance and capabilities, and to see events in a way that puts ourselves in a more negative light.

false consensus error

How we as human beings overestimate how similar we are to other people.

Human beings are prone to errors and biases when perceiving themselves. Moreover, the type of bias people have depends on their personality. Many people suffer from **self-enhancement bias**. This is the tendency to overestimate our performance and capabilities and see ourselves in a more positive light than others see us. People who have a narcissistic personality are particularly subject to this bias, but many others are still prone to overestimating their abilities.[77] At the same time, other people have the opposing extreme, which may be labeled as **self-effacement bias**. This is the tendency for people to underestimate their performance, undervalue capabilities, and see events in a way that puts them in a more negative light. We may expect that people with low self-esteem may be particularly prone to making this error. These tendencies have real consequences for behavior in organizations. For example, people who suffer from extreme levels of self-enhancement tendencies may not understand why they are not getting promoted or rewarded, while those who have a tendency to self-efface may project low confidence and take more blame for their failures than necessary.

When perceiving themselves, human beings are also subject to the **false consensus error**. Simply put, we overestimate how similar we are to other people.[78] We assume that whatever quirks we have are shared by a larger number of people than in reality. People who take office supplies home, tell white lies to their boss or colleagues, or take credit for other people's work to get ahead may genuinely feel that these behaviors are more common than they really are. The problem for behavior in organizations is that, when people believe that a behavior is common and normal, they may repeat the behavior more freely. Under some circumstances this may lead to a high level of unethical or even illegal behaviors.

3.3 Social Perception

How we perceive other people in our environment is also shaped by our values, emotions, feelings, and personality. Moreover, how we perceive others will shape our behavior, which in turn will shape the behavior of the person we are interacting with.

One of the factors biasing our perception is **stereotypes**. Stereotypes are generalizations based on group characteristics. For example, believing that women are more cooperative than men, or men are more assertive than women, is a stereotype. Stereotypes may be positive, negative, or neutral. Human beings have a natural tendency to categorize the information around them to make sense of their environment. What makes stereotypes potentially discriminatory and a perceptual bias is the tendency to generalize from a group to a particular individual. If the belief that men are more assertive than women leads to choosing a man over an equally (or potentially more) qualified female candidate for a position, the decision will be biased, potentially illegal, and unfair.

stereotypes

Generalizations based on a perceived group characteristic.

Stereotypes often create a situation called a **self-fulfilling prophecy**. This cycle occurs when people automatically behave as if an established stereotype is accurate, which leads to reactive behavior from the other party that confirms the stereotype.[79] If you have a stereotype such as "Asians are friendly," you are more likely to be friendly toward an Asian yourself. Because you are treating the other person better, the response you get may also be better, confirming your original belief that Asians are friendly. Of course, just the opposite is also true. Suppose you believe that "young employees are slackers." You are less likely to give a young employee high levels of responsibility or interesting and challenging assignments. The result may be that the young employee reporting to you may become increasingly bored at work and start goofing off, confirming your suspicions that young people are slackers!

self-fulfilling prophecy

This happens when an established stereotype causes one to behave in a certain way, which leads the other party to behave in a way that makes the stereotype come true.

Stereotypes persist because of a process called selective perception. **Selective perception** simply means that we pay selective attention to parts of the environment while ignoring other parts. When we observe our environment, we see what we want to see and ignore information that may seem out of place. Here is an interesting example of how selective perception leads our perception to be shaped by the context: As part of a social experiment, in 2007 the *Washington Post* newspaper arranged Joshua Bell, the internationally acclaimed violin virtuoso, to perform in a corner of the Metro station in Washington DC. The violin he was playing was worth $3.5 million, and tickets for Bell's concerts usually cost around $100. During the rush hour in which he played for 45 minutes, only one person recognized him, only a few realized that they were hearing extraordinary music, and he made only $32 in tips. When you see someone playing at the metro station, would you expect them to be extraordinary?[80]

selective perception

When we pay selective attention to parts of the environment while ignoring other parts.

Our background, expectations, and beliefs will shape which events we notice and which events we ignore. For example, the functional background of executives affects the changes they perceive in their environment.[81] Executives with a background in sales and marketing see the changes in the demand for their product, while executives with a background in information technology may more readily perceive the changes in the technology the company is using. Selective perception may perpetuate stereotypes, because we are less likely to notice events that go against our beliefs. A person who believes that men drive better than women may be more likely to notice women driving poorly than men driving poorly. As a result, a stereotype is maintained because information to the contrary may not reach our brain.

Let's say we noticed information that goes against our beliefs. What then? Unfortunately, this is no guarantee that we will modify our beliefs and prejudices. First, when we see examples that go against our stereotypes, we tend to come up with subcategories. For example, when people who believe that women are more cooperative see a female who is assertive, they may classify this person as a "career woman." Therefore, the example to the contrary does not violate the stereotype, and instead is explained as an exception to the rule.[82] Second, we may simply discount the information. In one study, people who were either in favor of or opposed to the death penalty were shown two studies, one showing benefits from the death penalty and the other discounting any benefits. People rejected the study that went against their belief as methodologically inferior and actually reinforced the belief in their original position even more.[83] In other words, trying to debunk people's beliefs or previously established opinions with data may not necessarily help.

One other perceptual tendency that may affect work behavior is that of **first impressions**. The first impressions we form about people tend to have a lasting impact. In fact, first impressions, once formed, are surprisingly resilient to contrary information. Even if people are told that the first impressions were caused by inaccurate information, people hold onto them to a certain degree. The reason is that, once we form first impressions, they become independent of the evidence that created them.[84] Any information we receive to the contrary does not serve the purpose of altering the original impression. Imagine the first day you met your colleague Anne. She treated you in a rude manner and when you asked for her help, she brushed you off. You may form the belief that she is a rude and unhelpful person. Later, you may hear that her mother is very sick and she is very stressed. In reality she may have been unusually stressed on the day you met her. If you had met her on a different day, you could have thought that she is a really nice person who is unusually stressed these days. But chances are your impression that she is rude and unhelpful will not change even when you hear about her mother. Instead, this new piece of information will be added to the first one: She is rude, unhelpful, and her mother is sick. Being aware of this tendency and consciously opening your mind to new information may protect you against some of the downsides of this bias. Also, it would be to your advantage to pay careful attention to the first impressions you create, particularly during job interviews.

FIGURE 3.9

First impressions are lasting. A job interview is one situation in which first impressions formed during the first few minutes may have consequences for your relationship with your future boss or colleagues.

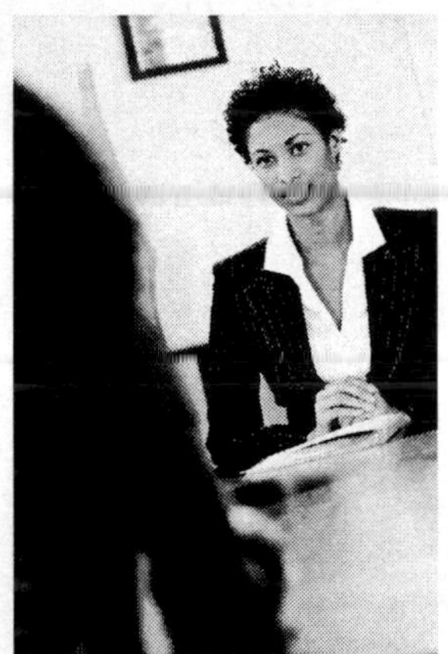

© 2010 Jupiterimages Corporation

first impressions

Initial thoughts and perceptions we form about people, which tend to be stable and resilient to contrary information.

OB Toolbox: How Can I Make a Great First Impression in the Job Interview?

A job interview is your first step to getting the job of your dreams. It is also a social interaction in which your actions during the first 5 minutes will determine the impression you make. Here are some tips to help you create a positive first impression.

- *Your first opportunity to make a great impression starts even before the interview, the moment you send your résumé.* Be sure that you send your résumé to the correct people, and spell the name of the contact person correctly! Make sure that your résumé looks professional and is free from typos and grammar problems. Have someone else read it before you hit the send button or mail it.
- *Be prepared for the interview.* Many interviews have some standard questions such as "tell me about yourself" or "why do you want to work here?" Be ready to answer these questions. Prepare answers highlighting your skills and accomplishments, and practice your message. Better yet, practice an interview with a friend. Practicing your answers will prevent you from regretting your answers or finding a better answer after the interview is over!
- *Research the company.* If you know a lot about the company and the job in question, you will come out as someone who is really interested in the job. If you ask basic questions such as "what does this company do?" you will not be taken as a serious candidate. Visit the company's Web site as well as others, and learn as much about the company and the job as you can.
- *When you are invited for an office interview, be sure to dress properly.* Like it or not, the manner you dress is a big part of the impression you make. Dress properly for the job and company in question. In many jobs, wearing professional clothes, such as a suit, is expected. In some information technology jobs, it may be more proper to wear clean and neat business casual clothes (such as khakis and a pressed shirt) as opposed to dressing formally. Do some investigation about what is suitable. Whatever the norm is, make sure that your clothes fit well and are clean and neat.
- *Be on time to the interview.* Being late will show that you either don't care about the interview or you are not very reliable. While waiting for the interview, don't forget that your interview has already started. As soon as you enter the company's parking lot, every person you see on the way or talk to may be a potential influence over the decision maker. Act professionally and treat everyone nicely.
- *During the interview, be polite.* Use correct grammar, show eagerness and enthusiasm, and watch your body language. From your handshake to your posture, your body is communicating whether you are the right person for the job!

Sources: Adapted from ideas in Bruce, C. (2007, October). Business Etiquette 101: Making a good first impression. Black Collegian, 38(1), 78–80; Evenson, R. (2007, May). Making a great first impression. Techniques, 14–17; Mather, J., & Watson, M. (2008, May 23). Perfect candidate. The Times Educational Supplement, 4789, 24–26; Messmer, M. (2007, July). 10 minutes to impress. Journal of Accountancy, 204(1), 13; Reece, T. (2006, November–December). How to wow! Career World, 35, 16–18.

3.4 Attributions

Your colleague Peter failed to meet the deadline. What do you do? Do you help him finish up his work? Do you give him the benefit of the doubt and place the blame on the difficulty of the project? Or do you think that he is irresponsible? Our behavior is a function of our perceptions. More specifically, when we observe others behave in a certain way, we ask ourselves a fundamental question: Why? Why did he fail to meet the deadline? Why did Mary get the promotion? Why did Mark help you when you needed help? The answer we give is the key to understanding our subsequent behavior. If you believe that

Mark helped you because he is a nice person, your action will be different from your response if you think that Mark helped you because your boss pressured him to.

An **attribution** is the causal explanation we give for an observed behavior. If you believe that a behavior is due to the internal characteristics of an actor, you are making an **internal attribution**. For example, let's say your classmate Erin complained a lot when completing a finance assignment. If you think that she complained because she is a negative person, you are making an internal attribution. An **external attribution** is explaining someone's behavior by referring to the situation. If you believe that Erin complained because finance homework was difficult, you are making an external attribution.

When do we make internal or external attributions? Research shows that three factors are the key to understanding what kind of attributions we make.

Consensus: Do other people behave the same way?

Distinctiveness: Does this person behave the same way across different situations?

Consistency: Does this person behave this way in different occasions in the same situation?

Let's assume that in addition to Erin, other people in the same class also complained (high consensus). Erin does not usually complain in other classes (high distinctiveness). Erin usually does not complain in finance class (low consistency). In this situation, you are likely to make an external attribution, such as thinking that finance homework is difficult. On the other hand, let's assume that Erin is the only person complaining (low consensus). Erin complains in a variety of situations (low distinctiveness), and every time she is in finance, she complains (high consistency). In this situation, you are likely to make an internal attribution such as thinking that Erin is a negative person.[85]

Interestingly though, our attributions do not always depend on the consensus, distinctiveness, and consistency we observe in a given situation. In other words, when making attributions, we do not always look at the situation objectively. For example, our overall relationship is a factor. When a manager likes a subordinate, the attributions made would be more favorable (successes are attributed to internal causes, while failures are attributed to external causes).[86] Moreover, when interpreting our own behavior, we suffer from **self-serving bias**. This is the tendency to attribute our failures to the situation while attributing our successes to internal causes.[87]

TABLE 3.1 Consensus, distinctiveness, and consistency determine the type of attribution we make in a given situation.

Consensus	Distinctiveness	Consistency	Type of attribution
High consensus	*High distinctiveness*	*Low consistency*	*External*
Everyone else behaves the same way.	This person does not usually behave this way in different situations.	This person does not usually behave this way in this situation.	
Low consensus	*Low distinctiveness*	*High consistency*	*Internal*
No one else behaves the same way.	This person usually behaves this way in different situations.	Every time this person is in this situation, he or she acts the same way.	

How we react to other people's behavior would depend on the type of attributions we make. When faced with poor performance, such as missing a deadline, we are more likely to punish the person if an internal attribution is made (such as "the person being unreliable"). In the same situation, if we make an external attribution (such as "the timeline was unreasonable"), instead of punishing the person we might extend the deadline or assign more help to the person. If we feel that someone's failure is due to external causes, we may feel empathy toward the person and even offer help.[88] On the other hand, if someone succeeds and we make an internal attribution (he worked hard), we are more likely to reward the person, whereas an external attribution (the project was easy) is less likely to yield rewards for the person in question. Therefore, understanding attributions is important to predicting subsequent behavior.

attribution

The causal explanation we give for an observed behavior.

internal attribution

Explaining someone's behavior using the internal characteristics of the actor.

external attribution

Explaining someone's behavior by referring to the situation.

consensus

The degree to which other people behave the same way as the actor.

distinctiveness

The degree to which the actor behaves the same way across different situations.

consistency

The degree to which the actor behaves the same way on different occasions in the same situation.

self-serving bias

The tendency to attribute our failures to the situation while attributing our successes to internal causes.

KEY TAKEAWAY

Perception is how we make sense of our environment in response to environmental stimuli. While perceiving our surroundings, we go beyond the objective information available to us, and our perception is affected by our values, needs, and emotions. There are many biases that affect human perception of objects, self, and others. When perceiving the physical environment, we fill in gaps and extrapolate from the available information. We also contrast physical objects to their surroundings and may perceive something as bigger, smaller, slower, or faster than it really is. In self-perception, we may commit the self-enhancement or self-effacement bias, depending on our personality. We also overestimate how much we are like other people. When perceiving others, stereotypes infect our behavior. Stereotypes may lead to self-fulfilling prophecies. Stereotypes are perpetuated because of our tendency to pay selective attention to aspects of the environment and ignore information inconsistent with our beliefs. When perceiving others, the attributions we make will determine how we respond to the situation. Understanding the perception process gives us clues to understand human behavior.

EXERCISES

1. What are the implications of contrast error for interpersonal interactions? Does this error occur only when we observe physical objects? Or have you encountered this error when perceiving behavior of others?
2. What are the problems of false consensus error? How can managers deal with this tendency?
3. Is there such a thing as a "good" stereotype? Is a "good" stereotype useful or still problematic?
4. How do we manage the fact that human beings develop stereotypes? How would you prevent stereotypes from creating unfairness in decision making?
5. Is it possible to manage the attributions other people make about our behavior? Let's assume that you have completed a project successfully. How would you maximize the chances that your manager will make an internal attribution? How would you increase the chances of an external attribution when you fail in a task?

4. THE ROLE OF ETHICS AND NATIONAL CULTURE

LEARNING OBJECTIVES

1. **Consider the role of individual differences for ethical behavior.**
2. **Consider the role of national culture on individual differences.**

4.1 Individual Differences and Ethics

Our values and personality influence how ethical we behave. Situational factors, rewards, and punishments following unethical choices as well as a company's culture are extremely important, but the role of personality and personal values should not be ignored. Research reveals that people who have an economic value orientation, that is, those who value acquiring money and wealth, tend to make more unethical choices. In terms of personality, employees with external locus of control were found to make more unethical choices.[89]

Our perceptual processes are clear influences on whether or not we behave ethically and how we respond to other people's unethical behaviors. It seems that self-enhancement bias operates for our ethical decisions as well: We tend to overestimate how ethical we are in general. Our self-ratings of ethics tend to be higher than how other people rate us. This belief can create a glaring problem: If we think that we are more ethical than we are, we will have little motivation to improve. Therefore, understanding how other people perceive our actions is important to getting a better understanding of ourselves.

How we respond to unethical behavior of others will, to a large extent, depend on the attributions we make. If we attribute responsibility to the person in question, we are more likely to punish that person. In a study on sexual harassment that occurred after a workplace romance turned sour, results showed that if we attribute responsibility to the victim, we are less likely to punish the harasser.[90] Therefore, how we make attributions in a given situation will determine how we respond to others' actions, including their unethical behaviors.

4.2 Individual Differences Around the Globe

Values that people care about vary around the world. In fact, when we refer to a country's culture, we are referring to values that distinguish one nation from others. In other words, there is systematic variance in individuals' personality and work values around the world, and this variance explains people's behavior, attitudes, preferences, and the transferability of management practices to other cultures.

When we refer to a country's values, this does not mean that everyone in a given country shares the same values. People differ within and across nations. There will always be people who care more about money and others who care more about relationships within each culture. Yet there are also national differences in the percentage of people holding each value. A researcher from Holland, Geert Hofstede, conducted a landmark study covering over 60 countries and found that countries differ in four dimensions: the extent to which they put individuals or groups first (individualism), whether the society subscribes to equality or hierarchy among people (power distance), the degree to which the society fears change (uncertainty avoidance), and the extent to which the culture emphasizes acquiring money and being successful (masculinity).[91] Knowing about the values held in a society will tell us what type of a workplace would satisfy and motivate employees.

Are personality traits universal? Researchers found that personality traits identified in Western cultures translate well to other cultures. For example, the five-factor model of personality is universal in that it explains how people differ from each other in over 70 countries. At the same time, there is variation among cultures in the dominant personality traits. In some countries, extraverts seem to be the majority, and in some countries the dominant trait is low emotional stability. For example, people from Europe and the United States are characterized by higher levels of extraversion compared to those from Asia and Africa. There are many factors explaining why some personality traits are dominant in some cultures. For example, the presence of democratic values is related to extraversion. Because democracy usually protects freedom of speech, people may feel more comfortable socializing with strangers as well as with friends, partly explaining the larger number of extraverts in democratic nations. Research also shows that in regions of the world that historically suffered from infectious diseases, extraversion and openness to experience was less dominant. Infectious diseases led people to limit social contact with strangers, explaining higher levels of introversion. Plus, to cope with infectious diseases, people developed strict habits for hygiene and the amount of spice to use in food, and deviating from these standards was bad for survival. This explains the lower levels of openness to experience in regions that experienced infectious diseases.[92]

Is basic human perception universal? It seems that there is variation around the globe in how we perceive other people as well as ourselves. One difference is the importance of the context. Studies show that when perceiving people or objects, Westerners pay more attention to the individual, while Asians pay more attention to the context. For example, in one study, when judging the emotion felt by the person, the Americans mainly looked at the face of the person in question, while the Japanese also considered the emotions of the people surrounding the focal person. In other words, the Asian subjects of the experiment derived meaning from the context as well as by looking at the person.[93]

There seems to be some variation in the perceptual biases we commit as well. For example, human beings have a tendency to self-enhance. We see ourselves in a more positive light than others do. Yet, the traits in which we self-enhance are culturally dependent. In Western cultures, people may overestimate how independent and self-reliant they are. In Asian cultures, such traits are not necessarily desirable, so they may not embellish their degree of independence. Yet, they may overestimate how cooperative and loyal to the group they are because these traits are more desirable in collectivistic cultures.[94]

Given the variation in individual differences around the globe, being sensitive to these differences will increase our managerial effectiveness when managing a diverse group of people.

Personality Around the Globe

Which nations have the highest average self-esteem? Researchers asked this question by surveying almost 17,000 individuals across 53 nations, in 28 languages.

Based on this survey, these are the top 10 nations in terms of self-reported self-esteem.

1. Serbia
2. Chile
3. Israel
4. Peru
5. Estonia
6. United States

7. Turkey
8. Mexico
9. Croatia
10. Austria

The 10 nations with the lowest self-reported self-esteem are the following:

- South Korea
- Switzerland
- Morocco
- Slovakia
- Fiji
- Taiwan
- Czech Republic
- Bangladesh
- Hong Kong
- Japan

Source: Adapted from information in Denissen, J. J. A., Penke, L., & Schmitt, D. P. (2008, July). Self-esteem reactions to social interactions: Evidence for sociometer mechanisms across days, people, and nations. Journal of Personality and Social Psychology, 95, 181–196; Hitti, M. (2005). Who's no. 1 in self-esteem? Serbia is tops, Japan ranks lowest, U.S. is no. 6 in global survey. WebMD. Retrieved November 14, 2008, from http://www.webmd.com/skin-beauty/news/20050927/whos-number-1-in-self-esteem; Schmitt, D. P., & Allik, J. (2005). The simultaneous administration of the Rosenberg self-esteem scale in 53 nationals: Culture-specific features of global self-esteem. Journal of Personality and Social Psychology, 89, 623–642.

KEY TAKEAWAY

There is a connection between how ethically we behave and our individual values, personality, and perception. Possessing values emphasizing economic well-being predicts unethical behavior. Having an external locus of control is also related to unethical decision making. We are also likely to overestimate how ethical we are, which can be a barrier against behaving ethically. Culture seems to be an influence over our values, personality traits, perceptions, attitudes, and work behaviors. Therefore, understanding individual differences requires paying careful attention to the cultural context.

EXERCISES

1. If ethical decision making depends partially on personality, what can organizations do to increase the frequency of ethical behaviors?
2. Do you think personality tests used in Western cultures in employee selection can be used in other cultures?

5. CONCLUSION

In conclusion, in this chapter we have reviewed major individual differences that affect employee attitudes and behaviors. Our values and personality explain our preferences and the situations we feel comfortable with. Personality may influence our behavior, but the importance of the context in which behavior occurs should not be neglected. Many organizations use personality tests in employee selection, but the use of such tests is controversial because of problems such as faking and low predictive value of personality for job performance. Perception is how we interpret our environment. It is a major influence over our behavior, but many systematic biases color our perception and lead to misunderstandings.

6. EXERCISES

ETHICAL DILEMMA

You are applying for the job of sales associate. You have just found out that you will be given a personality assessment as part of the application process. You feel that this job requires someone who is very high in extraversion, and someone who can handle stress well. You are relatively sociable and can cope with some stress but honestly you are not very high in either trait. The job pays well and it is a great stepping-stone to better jobs. How are you going to respond when completing the personality questions? Are you going to make an effort to represent yourself as how you truly are? If so, there is a chance that you may not get the job. How about answering the questions to fit the salesperson profile? Isn't everyone doing this to some extent anyway?

Discussion Questions

1. What are the advantages and disadvantages of completing the questions honestly?
2. What are the advantages and disadvantages of completing the questions in a way you think the company is looking for?
3. What would you really do in a situation like this?

INDIVIDUAL EXERCISE

Changing Others' Perceptions of You

How do other people perceive you? Identify one element of how others perceive you that you are interested in changing. It could be a positive perception (maybe they think you are more helpful than you really are) or a negative perception (maybe they think you don't take your studies seriously).

- What are the reasons why they formed this perception? Think about the underlying reasons.
- What have you done to contribute to the development of this perception?
- Do you think there are perceptual errors that contribute to this perception? Are they stereotyping? Are they engaging in selective perception?
- Are you sure that your perception is the accurate one? What information do you have that makes your perceptions more valid than theirs?
- Create an action plan about how you can change this perception.

GROUP EXERCISE

Selecting an Expatriate Using Personality Tests

Your department has over 50 expatriates working around the globe. One of the problems you encounter is that the people you send to other cultures for long-term (2- to 5-year) assignments have a high failure rate. They either want to return home before their assignment is complete, or they are not very successful in building relationships with the local employees. You suspect that this is because you have been sending people overseas solely because of their technical skills, which does not seem to be effective in predicting whether these people will make a successful adjustment to the local culture. Now you have decided that when selecting people to go on these assignments, personality traits should be given some weight.

1. Identify the personality traits you think might be relevant to being successful in an expatriate assignment.
2. Develop a personality test aimed at measuring these dimensions. Make sure that each dimension you want to measure is captured by at least 10 questions.
3. Exchange the test you have developed with a different team in class. Have them fill out the survey and make sure that you fill out theirs. What problems have you encountered? How would you feel if you were a candidate taking this test?
4. Do you think that prospective employees would fill out this questionnaire honestly? If not, how would you ensure that the results you get would be honest and truly reflect their personality?
5. How would you validate such a test? Describe the steps you would take.

ENDNOTES

1. Anderson, C., Spataro, S. E., & Flynn, F. J. (2008). Personality and organizational culture as determinants of influence. *Journal of Applied Psychology, 93*, 702–710; Cable, D. M., & DeRue, D. S. (2002). The convergent and discriminant validity of subjective fit perceptions. *Journal of Applied Psychology, 87*, 875–884; Caldwell, D. F., & O'Reilly, C. A. (1990). Measuring person–job fit with a profile comparison process. *Journal of Applied Psychology, 75*, 648–657; Chatman, J. A. (1991). Matching people and organizations: Selection and socialization in public accounting firms. *Administrative Science Quarterly*, 36, 459–484; Judge, T. A., & Cable, D. M. (1997). Applicant personality, organizational culture, and organization attraction. *Personnel Psychology*, 50, 359–394; Kristof-Brown, A. L., Zimmerman, R. D., & Johnson, E. C. (2005). Consequences of individuals' fit at work: A meta-analysis of person–job, person–organization, person–group, and person–supervisor fit. *Personnel Psychology*, 58, 281–342; O'Reilly, C. A., Chatman, J., & Caldwell, D. F. (1991). People and organizational culture: A profile comparison approach to assessing person–organization fit. *Academy of Management Journal, 34*, 487–516; Saks, A. M., & Ashforth, B. E. (2002). Is job search related to employment quality? It all depends on the fit. *Journal of Applied Psychology, 87*, 646–654.

2. Arthur, W., Bell, S. T., Villado, A. J., & Doverspike, D. (2006). The use of person–organization fit in employment decision making: An assessment of its criterion-related validity. *Journal of Applied Psychology, 91*, 786–801.

3. Kristof-Brown, A. L., Jansen, K. J., & Colbert, A. E. (2002). A policy-capturing study of the simultaneous effects of fit with jobs, groups, and organizations. *Journal of Applied Psychology, 87*, 985–993.

4. Erdogan, B., Kraimer, M. L., & Liden, R. C. (2004). Work value congruence and intrinsic career success. *Personnel Psychology, 57*, 305–332.

5. Lusk, E. J., & Oliver, B. L. (1974). Research Notes. American manager's personal value systems-revisited. *Academy of Management Journal, 17*(3), 549–554; Rokeach, M. (1973). *The nature of human values*. New York: Free Press.

6. Judge, T. A., & Bretz, R. D. (1992). Effects of work values on job choice decisions. *Journal of Applied Psychology, 77*, 261–271; Ravlin, E. C., & Meglino, B. M. (1987). Effect of values on perception and decision making: A study of alternative work values measures. *Journal of Applied Psychology, 72*, 666–673.

7. George, J. M., & Jones, G. R. (1996). The experience of work and turnover intentions: Interactive effects of value attainment, job satisfaction, and positive mood. *Journal of Applied Psychology, 81*, 318–325.

8. Rokeach, M. (1973). *The nature of human values*. New York: The Free Press.

9. Kasser, T., Koestner, R., & Lekes, N. (2002). Early family experiences and adult values: A 26-year prospective longitudinal study. *Personality and Social Psychology Bulletin, 28*, 826–835.

10. Smola, K. W., & Sutton, C. D. (2002). Generational differences: Revisiting generational work values for the new millennium. *Journal of Organizational Behavior, 23*, 363–382.

11. Roberts, B. W., Walton, K. E., & Viechtbauer, W. (2006). Patterns of mean-level change in personality traits across the life course: A meta-analysis of longitudinal studies. *Psychological Bulletin, 132*, 1–25.

12. Judge, T. A., & Higgins, C. A. (1999). The Big Five personality traits, general mental ability, and career success across the life span. *Personnel Psychology, 52*, 621–652; Staw, B. M., Bell, N. E., & Clausen, J. A. (1986). The dispositional approach to job attitudes: A lifetime longitudinal test. *Administrative Science Quarterly, 31*, 56–77.

13. Barrick, M. R., & Mount, M. K. (1993). Autonomy as a moderator of the relationships between the Big Five personality dimensions and job performance. *Journal of Applied Psychology, 78*, 111–118.

14. Goldberg, L. R. (1990). An alternative "description of personality": The big-five factor structure. *Journal of Personality & Social Psychology, 59*, 1216–1229.

15. Barrick, M. R., & Mount, M. K. (1991). The Big Five personality dimensions and job performance: A meta-analysis. *Personnel Psychology, 44*, 1–26; Lievens, F., Harris, M. M., Van Keer, E., & Bisqueret, C. (2003). Predicting cross-cultural training performance: The validity of personality, cognitive ability, and dimensions measured by an assessment center and a behavior description interview. *Journal of Applied Psychology, 88*, 476–489.

16. Wanberg, C. R., & Kammeyer-Mueller, J. D. (2000). Predictors and outcomes of proactivity in the socialization process. *Journal of Applied Psychology, 85*, 373–385.

17. Baer, M., & Oldham, G. R. (2006). The curvilinear relation between experienced creative time pressure and creativity: Moderating effects of openness to experience and support for creativity. *Journal of Applied Psychology, 91*, 963–970.

18. LePine, J. A. (2003). Team adaptation and postchange performance: Effects of team composition in terms of members' cognitive ability and personality. *Journal of Applied Psychology, 88*, 27–39.

19. Zhao, H., & Seibert, S. E. (2006). The Big Five personality dimensions and entrepreneurial status: A meta-analytic review. *Journal of Applied Psychology, 91*, 259–271.

20. Barrick, M. R., & Mount, M. K. (1991). The Big Five personality dimensions and job performance: A meta-analysis. *Personnel Psychology, 44*, 1–26.

21. Dunn, W. S., Mount, M. K., Barrick, M. R., & Ones, D. S. (1995). Relative importance of personality and general mental ability in managers' judgments of applicant qualifications. *Journal of Applied Psychology, 80*, 500–509; Tay, C., Ang, S., & Van Dyne, L. (2006). Personality, biographical characteristics, and job interview success: A longitudinal study of the mediating effects of interviewing self-efficacy and the moderating effects of internal locus of control. *Journal of Applied Psychology, 91*, 446–454.

22. Judge, T. A., & Ilies, R. (2002). Relationship of personality to performance motivation: A meta-analytic review. *Journal of Applied Psychology, 87*, 797–807; Judge, T. A., Martocchio, J. J., & Thoresen, C. J. (1997). Five-factor model of personality and employee absence. *Journal of Applied Psychology, 82*, 745–755; Wallace, C., & Chen, G. (2006). A multilevel integration of personality, climate, self-regulation, and performance. *Personnel Psychology, 59*, 529–557; Zimmerman, R. D. (2008). Understanding the impact of personality traits on individuals' turnover decisions: A meta-analytic path model. *Personnel Psychology, 61*, 309–348.

23. Judge, T. A., & Higgins, C. A. (1999). The Big Five personality traits, general mental ability, and career success across the life span. *Personnel Psychology, 52*, 621–652.

24. Certo, S. T., & Certo, S. C. (2005). Spotlight on entrepreneurship. *Business Horizons, 48*, 271–274; Zhao, H., & Seibert, S. E. (2006). The Big Five personality dimensions and entrepreneurial status: A meta-analytic review. *Journal of Applied Psychology, 91*, 259–271.

25. Barrick, M. R., & Mount, M. K. (1991). The Big Five personality dimensions and job performance: A meta-analysis. *Personnel Psychology, 44*, 1–26; Vinchur, A. J., Schippmann, J. S., Switzer, F. S., & Roth, P. L. (1998). A meta-analytic review of predictors of job performance for salespeople. *Journal of Applied Psychology, 83*, 586–597.

26. Bauer, T. N., Erdogan, B., Liden, R. C., & Wayne, S. J. (2006). A longitudinal study of the moderating role of extraversion: Leader-member exchange, performance, and turnover during new executive development. *Journal of Applied Psychology, 91*, 298–310; Bono, J. E., & Judge, T. A. (2004). Personality and transformational and transactional leadership: A meta-analysis. *Journal of Applied Psychology, 89*, 901–910.

27. Caldwell, D. F., & Burger, J. M. (1998). Personality characteristics of job applicants and success in screening interviews. *Personnel Psychology, 51*, 119–136; Tay, C., Ang, S., & Van Dyne, L. (2006). Personality, biographical characteristics, and job interview success: A longitudinal study of the mediating effects of interviewing self-efficacy and the moderating effects of internal locus of control. *Journal of Applied Psychology, 91*, 446–454.

28. Wanberg, C. R., & Kammeyer-Mueller, J. D. (2000). Predictors and outcomes of proactivity in the socialization process. *Journal of Applied Psychology, 85*, 373–385.

29. Judge, T. A., Heller, D., & Mount, M. K. (2002). Five-factor model of personality and job satisfaction: A meta-analysis. *Journal of Applied Psychology, 87*, 530–541.

30. Judge, T. A., Martocchio, J. J., & Thoresen, C. J. (1997). Five-factor model of personality and employee absence. *Journal of Applied Psychology, 82*, 745–755.

31. Ilies, R., Scott, B. A., & Judge, T. A. (2006). The interactive effects of personal traits and experienced states on intraindividual patterns of citizenship behavior. *Academy of Management Journal, 49*, 561–575.

32. Skarlicki, D. P., Folger, R., & Tesluk, P. (1999). Personality as a moderator in the relationship between fairness and retaliation. *Academy of Management Journal, 42*, 100–108.

33. Mayer, D., Nishii, L., Schneider, B., & Goldstein, H. (2007). The precursors and products of justice climates: Group leader antecedents and employee attitudinal consequences. *Personnel Psychology, 60*, 929–963.

34. Zimmerman, R. D. (2008). Understanding the impact of personality traits on individuals' turnover decisions: A meta-analytic path model. *Personnel Psychology, 61*, 309–348.

35. LePine, J. A., & Van Dyne, L. (2001). Voice and cooperative behavior as contrasting forms of contextual performance: Evidence of differential relationships with Big Five personality characteristics and cognitive ability. *Journal of Applied Psychology, 86*, 326–336.

36. Klein, K. J., Beng-Chong, L., Saltz, J. L., & Mayer, D. M. (2004). How do they get there? An examination of the antecedents of centrality in team networks. *Academy of Management Journal, 47*, 952–963.

37. Judge, T. A., Heller, D., & Mount, M. K. (2002). Five-factor model of personality and job satisfaction: A meta-analysis. *Journal of Applied Psychology, 87*, 530–541; Zimmerman, R. D. (2008). Understanding the impact of personality traits on individuals' turnover decisions: A meta-analytic path model. *Personnel Psychology, 61*, 309–348.

38. Mayer, D., Nishii, L., Schneider, B., & Goldstein, H. (2007). The precursors and products of justice climates: Group leader antecedents and employee attitudinal consequences. *Personnel Psychology, 60*, 929–963.

39. Carlyn, M. (1977). An assessment of the Myers-Briggs Type Indicator. *Journal of Personality Assessment, 41*, 461–473; Myers, I. B. (1962). *The Myers-Briggs Type Indicator*. Princeton, NJ: Princeton University Press.

40. Leonard, D., & Straus, S. (1997). Identifying how we think: The Myers-Briggs Type Indicator and the Hermann Brain Dominance Instrument. *Harvard Business Review, 75*(4), 114–115; Shuit, D. P. (2003). At 60, Myers-Briggs is still sorting out and identifying people's types. *Workforce Management, 82*(13), 72–74.

41. Watson, D., & Clark, L. A. (1984). Negative affectivity: The disposition to experience aversive emotional states. *Psychological Bulletin, 96*, 465–490.

42. Ilies, R., & Judge, T. A. (2003). On the heritability of job satisfaction: The mediating role of personality. *Journal of Applied Psychology, 88*, 750–759.

43. George, J. M. (1989). Mood and absence. *Journal of Applied Psychology, 74*, 317–324.

44. Anderson, C., & Thompson, L. L. (2004). Affect from the top down: How powerful individuals' positive affect shapes negotiations. *Organizational Behavior and Human Decision Processes, 95*, 125–139.

45. Snyder, M. (1974). Self-monitoring of expressive behavior. *Journal of Personality and Social Psychology, 30*, 526–537; Snyder, M. (1987). *Public appearances/public realities: The psychology of self-monitoring*. New York: Freeman.

46. Turnley, W. H., & Bolino, M. C. (2001). Achieving desired images while avoiding undesired images: Exploring the role of self-monitoring in impression management. *Journal of Applied Psychology, 86*, 351–360.

47. Day, D. V., & Schleicher, D. J. Self-monitoring at work: A motive-based perspective. *Journal of Personality*, 74, 685-714; Kilduff, M., & Day, D. V. (1994). Do chameleons get ahead? The effects of self-monitoring on managerial careers. *Academy of Management Journal, 37*, 1047–1060.

48. Mehra, A., Kilduff, M., & Brass, D. J. (2001). The social networks of high and low self-monitors: Implications for workplace performance. *Administrative Science Quarterly, 46*, 121–146.

49. Day, D. V., Schleicher, D. J., Unckless, A. L., & Hiller, N. J. (2002). Self-monitoring personality at work: A meta-analytic investigation of construct validity. *Journal of Applied Psychology, 87*, 390–401.

50. Jawahar, I. M. (2001). Attitudes, self-monitoring, and appraisal behaviors. *Journal of Applied Psychology, 86*, 875–883.

51. Day, D. V., Schleicher, D. J., Unckless, A. L., & Hiller, N. J. (2002). Self-monitoring personality at work: A meta-analytic investigation of construct validity. *Journal of Applied Psychology, 87*, 390–401.

52. Brown, D. J., Cober, R. T., Kane, K., Levy, P. E., & Shalhoop, J. (2006). Proactive personality and the successful job search: A field investigation with college graduates. *Journal of Applied Psychology, 91*, 717–726.

53. Seibert, S. E. (1999). Proactive personality and career success. *Journal of Applied Psychology, 84*, 416–427; Seibert, S. E., Kraimer, M. L., & Crant, M. J. (2001). What do proactive people do? A longitudinal model linking proactive personality and career success. *Personnel Psychology, 54*, 845–874.

54. Crant, M. J. (1995). The proactive personality scale and objective job performance among real estate agents. *Journal of Applied Psychology, 80*, 532–537.

55. Kammeyer-Mueller, J. D., & Wanberg, C. R. (2003). Unwrapping the organizational entry process: Disentangling multiple antecedents and their pathways to adjustment. *Journal of Applied Psychology, 88*, 779–794; Thompson, J. A. (2005). Proactive personality and job performance: A social capital perspective. *Journal of Applied Psychology, 90*, 1011–1017.

56. Major, D. A., Turner, J. E., & Fletcher, T. D. (2006). Linking proactive personality and the Big Five to motivation to learn and development activity. *Journal of Applied Psychology, 91*, 927–935.

57. Chan, D. (2006). Interactive effects of situational judgment effectiveness and proactive personality on work perceptions and work outcomes. *Journal of Applied Psychology, 91*, 475–481; Erdogan, B., & Bauer, T. N. (2005). Enhancing career benefits of employee proactive personality: The role of fit with jobs and organizations. *Personnel Psychology, 58*, 859–891.

58. Judge, T. A., & Bono, J. E. (2001). Relationship of core self-evaluations traits—self esteem, generalized self efficacy, locus of control, and emotional stability—with job satisfaction and job performance: A meta-analysis. *Journal of Applied Psychology, 86*, 80–92.

59. Turban, D. B., & Keon, T. L. (1993). Organizational attractiveness: An interactionist perspective. *Journal of Applied Psychology, 78*, 184–193.

60. Bauer, T. N., Bodner, T., Erdogan, B., Truxillo, D. M., & Tucker, J. S. (2007). Newcomer adjustment during organizational socialization: A meta-analytic review of antecedents, outcomes, and methods. *Journal of Applied Psychology, 92*, 707–721; Judge, T. A., Jackson, C. L., Shaw, J. C., Scott, B. A., & Rich, B. L. (2007). Self-efficacy and work-related performance: The integral role of individual differences. *Journal of Applied Psychology, 92*, 107–127; Stajkovic, A. D., & Luthans, F. (1998). Self-efficacy and work-related performance: A meta-analysis. *Psychological Bulletin, 124*, 240–261.

61. Phillips, J. M., & Gully, S. M. (1997). Role of goal orientation, ability, need for achievement, and locus of control in the self-efficacy and goal setting process. *Journal of Applied Psychology, 82*, 792–802; Steel, P. (2007). The nature of procrastination: A meta-analytic and theoretical review of quintessential self-regulatory failure. *Psychological Bulletin, 133*, 65–94; Wofford, J. C., Goodwin, V. L., & Premack, S. (1992). Meta-analysis of the antecedents of personal goal level and of the antecedents and consequences of goal commitment. *Journal of Management, 18*, 595–615.

62. Robbins, S. B., Lauver, K., Le, H., Davis, D., Langley, R., & Carlstrom, A. (2004). Do psychosocial and study skill factors predict college outcomes? A meta-analysis. *Psychological Bulletin, 130*, 261–288.

63. Ahearne, M., Mathieu, J., & Rapp, A. (2005). To empower or not to empower your sales force? An empirical examination of the influence of leadership empowerment behavior on customer satisfaction and performance. *Journal of Applied Psychology, 90*, 945–955.

64. Ng, T. W. H., Soresen, K. L., & Eby, L. T. (2006). Locus of control at work: A meta-analysis. *Journal of Organizational Behavior, 27*, 1057–1087; Reitz, H. J., & Jewell, L. N. (1979). Sex, locus of control, and job involvement: A six-country investigation. *Academy of Management Journal, 22*, 72–80; Turban, D. B., & Dougherty, T. W. (1994). Role of protégé personality in receipt of mentoring and career success. *Academy of Management Journal, 37*, 688–702.

65. Benassi, V. A., Sweeney, P. D., & Dufour, C. L. (1988). Is there a relation between locus of control orientation and depression? *Journal of Abnormal Psychology, 97*, 357–367; DeNeve, K. M., & Cooper, H. (1998). The happy personality: A meta-analysis of 137 personality traits and subjective well-being. *Psychological Bulletin, 124*, 197–229.

66. Gale, C. R., Batty, G. D., & Deary, I. J. (2008). Locus of control at age 10 years and health outcomes and behaviors at age 30 years: The 1970 British Cohort Study. *Psychosomatic Medicine, 70*, 397–403.

67. Certo, S. T., & Certo, S. C. (2005). Spotlight on entrepreneurship. *Business Horizons, 48*, 271–274.

68. Barrick, M. R., Patton, G. K., & Haugland, S. N. (2000). Accuracy of interviewer judgments of job applicant personality traits. *Personnel Psychology, 53*, 925–951.

69. Emmett, A. (2004). Snake oil or science? That's the raging debate on personality testing. *Workforce Management, 83*, 90–92; Gale, S. F. (2002). Three companies cut turnover with tests. *Workforce, 81*(4), 66–69.

70. Morgeson, F. P., Campion, M. A., Dipboye, R. L., Hollenbeck, J. R., Murphy, K., & Schmitt, N. (2007). Reconsidering the use of personality tests in personnel selection contexts. *Personnel Psychology, 60*, 683–729; Morgeson, F. P., Campion, M. A., Dipboye, R. L., Hollenbeck, J. R., Murphy, K., & Schmitt, N. (2007). Are we getting fooled again? Coming to terms with limitations in the use of personality tests for personnel selection. *Personnel Psychology, 60*, 1029–1049.

71. Barrick, M. R., & Mount, M. K. (1996). Effects of impression management and self-deception on the predictive validity of personality constructs. *Journal of Applied Psychology, 81*, 261–272; Ones, D. S., Dilchert, S., Viswesvaran, C., & Judge, T. A. (2007). In support of personality assessment in organizational settings. *Personnel Psychology, 60*, 995–1027; Ones, D. S., Viswesvaran, C., & Reiss, A. D. (1996). Role of social desirability in personality testing for personnel selection. *Journal of Applied Psychology, 81*, 660–679; Tett, R. P., & Christiansen, N. D. (2007). Personality tests at the crossroads: A response to Morgeson, Campion, Dipboye, Hollenbeck, Murphy, and Schmitt (2007). *Personnel Psychology, 60*, 967–993.

72. Mount, M. K., Barrick, M. R., & Strauss, J. P. (1994). Validity of observer ratings of the Big Five personality factors. *Journal of Applied Psychology, 79*, 272–280.

73. Heller, M. (2005). Court ruling that employer's integrity test violated ADA could open door to litigation. *Workforce Management, 84*(9), 74–77.

74. Higgins, E. T., & Bargh, J. A. (1987). Social cognition and social perception. *Annual Review of Psychology, 38*, 369–425; Keltner, D., Ellsworth, P. C., & Edwards, K. (1993). Beyond simple pessimism: Effects of sadness and anger on social perception. *Journal of Personality and Social Psychology, 64*, 740–752.

75. Riskind, J. H., Moore, R., & Bowley, L. (1995). The looming of spiders: The fearful perceptual distortion of movement and menace. *Behaviour Research and Therapy, 33*, 171.

76. Kellman, P. J., & Shipley, T. F. (1991). A theory of visual interpolation in object perception. *Cognitive Psychology, 23*, 141–221.

77. John, O. P., & Robins, R. W. (1994). Accuracy and bias in self-perception: Individual differences in self-enhancement and the role of narcissism. *Journal of Personality and Social Psychology, 66*, 206–219.

78. [illegible] *Opinion Quarterly, 40*(4), 427–448; Ross, L., Greene, D., & House, P. (1977). The "false consensus effect": An egocentric bias in social perception and attribution processes. *Journal of Experimental Social Psychology, 13*, 279–301.

79. Snyder, M., Tanke, E. D., & Berscheid, E. (1977). Social perception and interpersonal behavior: On the self-fulfilling nature of social stereotypes. *Journal of Personality and Social Psychology, 35*, 656–666.

80. Weingarten, G. (2007, April 8). Pearls before breakfast. *Washington Post*. Retrieved January 29, 2009, from http://www.washingtonpost.com/wp-dyn/content/article/2007/04/04/AR2007040401721.html.

81. Waller, M. J., Huber, G. P., & Glick, W. H. (1995). Functional background as a determinant of executives' selective perception. *Academy of Management Journal, 38*, 943–974.

82. Higgins, E. T., & Bargh, J. A. (1987). Social cognition and social perception. *Annual Review of Psychology, 38*, 369–425.

83. Lord, C. G., Ross, L., & Lepper, M. R. (1979). Biased assimilation and attitude polarization: The effects of prior theories on subsequently considered evidence. *Journal of Personality and Social Psychology, 37*, 2098–2109.

84. Ross, L., Lepper, M. R., & Hubbard, M. (1975). Perseverance in self-perception and social perception: Biased attributional processes in the debriefing paradigm. *Journal of Personality and Social Psychology, 32*, 880–892.

85. Kelley, H. H. (1967). Attribution theory in social psychology. *Nebraska Symposium on Motivation, 15*, 192–238; Kelley, H. H. (1973). The processes of causal attribution. *American Psychologist, 28*, 107–128.

86. Heneman, R. L., Greenberger, D. B., & Anonyou, C. (1989). Attributions and exchanges: The effects of interpersonal factors on the diagnosis of employee performance. *Academy of Management Journal, 32*, 466–476.

87. Malle, B. F. (2006). The actor-observer asymmetry in attribution: A (surprising) meta-analysis. *Psychological Bulletin, 132*, 895–919.

88. LePine, J. A., & Van Dyne, L. (2001). Peer responses to low performers: An attributional model of helping in the context of groups. *Academy of Management Review, 26*, 67–84.

89. Hegarty, W. H., & Sims, H. P. (1978). Some determinants of unethical decision behavior: An experiment. *Journal of Applied Psychology, 63*, 451–457; Hegarty, W. H., & Sims, H. P. (1979). Organizational philosophy, policies, and objectives related to unethical decision behavior: A laboratory experiment. *Journal of Applied Psychology, 64*, 331–338; Trevino, L. K., & Youngblood, S. A. (1990). Bad apples in bad barrels: A causal analysis of ethical decision-making behavior. *Journal of Applied Psychology, 75*, 378–385.

90. Pierce, C. A., Broberg, B. J., McClure, J. R., & Aguinis, H. (2004). Responding to sexual harassment complaints: Effects of a dissolved workplace romance on decision-making standards. *Organizational Behavior and Human Decision Processes, 95*, 66–82.

91. Hofstede, G. (2001). *Culture's consequences: Comparing values, behaviors, institutions and organizations across nations*. Thousand Oaks, CA: Sage.

92. McCrae, R. R., & Costa, P. T. (1997). Personality trait structure as a human universal. *American Psychologist, 52*, 509–516; McCrae, R. R., Terracciano, A., & 79 members of the personality profiles of cultures project (2005). *Journal of Personality and Social Psychology, 89*, 407–425; Schaller, M., & Murray, D. R. (2008). Pathogens, personality, and culture: Disease prevalence predicts worldwide variability in sociosexuality, extraversion, and openness to experience. *Journal of Personality and Social Psychology, 95*, 212–221.

93. Masuda, T., Ellsworth, P. C., Mesquita, B., Leu, J., Tanida, S., & Van de Veerdonk, E. (2008). Placing the face in context: Cultural differences in the perception of facial emotion. *Journal of Personality and Social Psychology, 94*, 365–381.

94. Sedikides, C., Gaertner, L., & Toguchi, Y. (2003). Pancultural self-enhancement. *Journal of Personality and Social Psychology, 84*, 60–79; Sedikides, C., Gaertner, L., & Vevea, J. L. (2005). Pancultural self-enhancement reloaded: A meta-analytic reply to Heine (2005). *Journal of Personality and Social Psychology, 89*, 539–551.

CHAPTER 4
Individual Attitudes and Behaviors

LEARNING OBJECTIVES

After reading this chapter, you should be able to do the following:

1. Identify the major work attitudes that affect work behaviors.
2. List the key set of behaviors that matter for organizational performance.
3. [illegible]
4. Understand cross-cultural differences in job attitudes and behaviors at work.

People Come First at SAS Institute

The SAS institute is a leader in the art of treating employees well.

© 2008. SAS Institute Inc. All rights reserved. Reproduced with permission of SAS Institute Inc., Cary, North Carolina.

Who are your best customers? Which customers are bringing you the most profits and which are the least profitable? Companies are increasingly relying on complicated data mining software to answer these and other questions. More than 90% of the top 100 companies on the *Fortune* Global 500 list are using software developed by SAS Institute Inc. for their business intelligence and analytics needs. The Cary, North Carolina, company is doing extremely well by any measure. They are the biggest privately owned software company in the world. They have over 10,000 employees worldwide, operate in over 100 countries, and reported $2.15 billion in revenue in 2007 (their 31st consecutive year of growth and profitability). The company is quick to attribute their success to the performance and loyalty of its workforce. This is directly correlated with how they treat their employees.

SAS has perfected the art of employee management. It has been ranked on *Fortune Magazine*'s best places to work list every year since the list was first published. Employees seem to genuinely enjoy working at SAS and are unusually attached to the company, resulting in a turnover rate that is less than 5% in an industry where 20% is the norm. In fact, when Google designed its own legendary campus in California, they visited the SAS campus to get ideas.

One thing SAS does well is giving its employees opportunities to work on interesting and challenging projects. The software developers have the opportunity to create cutting-edge software to be used around the world. The company makes an effort to concentrate its business in the areas of analytics, which add the most value and help organizations best analyze disparate data for decision making, creating opportunities for SAS workers to be challenged. Plus, the company removes obstacles for employees. Equipment, policies, rules, and meetings that could impede productivity are eliminated.

The company has a reputation as a pioneer when it comes to the perks it offers employees, but these perks are not given with a mentality of "offer everything but the kitchen sink." There is careful thinking and planning behind the choice of perks the company offers. SAS conducts regular employee satisfaction surveys, and any future benefits and perks offered are planned in response to the results. The company wants to eliminate stressors and dissatisfiers from people's lives. To keep employees healthy and fit, there are athletic fields, a full gym and swimming pool, and tennis, basketball, and racquetball courts on campus. Plus, the company offers free onsite health care for employees and covered dependents at their fully staffed primary medical care center, and unlimited sick leave. The company understands that employees have a life and encourages employees to work reasonable hours and then go home to their families. In fact, a famous motto in the company is, "If you are working for more than 8 hours, you are just adding bugs." SAS is truly one of the industry leaders in leveraging its treatment of people for continued business success.

Sources: Based on information from Anonymous. (2007, December 1). Doing well by being rather nice. Economist, 385(8557), 84; Cakebread, C. (2005, July). SAS...not SOS. Benefits Canada, 29(7), 18; Florida, R., & Goodnight, J. (2005, July–August). Managing for creativity. Harvard Business Review, 83(7/8), 124–131; Karlgaard, R. (2006, October 16). Who wants to be public? Forbes Asia, 2(17), 22.

1. WORK ATTITUDES

LEARNING OBJECTIVES

1. **Define "work attitudes".**
2. **Describe the relationship between attitudes and behaviors.**
3. **Define and differentiate between job satisfaction and organizational commitment.**
4. **List the factors related to job satisfaction and organizational commitment.**
5. **Describe the consequences of job satisfaction and organizational commitment.**
6. **Identify the ways in which companies can track work attitudes in the workplace.**

attitude

Our opinions, beliefs, and feelings about aspects of our environment.

job satisfaction

The feelings people have toward their jobs.

organizational commitment

The emotional attachment people have toward the company they work for.

Our behavior at work often depends on how we feel about being there. Therefore, making sense of how people behave depends on understanding their work attitudes. An **attitude** refers to our opinions, beliefs, and feelings about aspects of our environment. We have attitudes toward the food we eat, people we interact with, courses we take, and various other things. At work, two particular job attitudes have the greatest potential to influence how we behave. These are job satisfaction and organizational commitment. **Job satisfaction** refers to the feelings people have toward their job. If the number of studies conducted on job satisfaction is an indicator, job satisfaction is probably the most important job attitude. Institutions such as Gallup Inc. or the Society of Human Resource Management (SHRM) periodically conduct studies of job satisfaction to track how satisfied employees are at work. According to a recent Gallup survey, 90% of the employees surveyed said that they were at least somewhat satisfied with their jobs. The recent SHRM study revealed 40% who were very satisfied.[1] **Organizational commitment** is the emotional attachment people have toward the company they work for. There is a high degree of overlap between job satisfaction and organizational commitment, because things that make us happy with our job often make us more committed to the company as well. Companies believe that these attitudes are worth tracking because they are often associated with important outcomes such as performance, helping others, absenteeism, and turnover.

How strong is the attitude-behavior link? First of all, it depends on the attitude in question. Your attitudes toward your colleagues may influence whether you actually help them on a project, but they may not be a good predictor of whether you will quit your job. Second, it is worth noting that attitudes are more strongly related to intentions to behave in a certain way, rather than actual behaviors. When you are dissatisfied with your job, you may have the intention to leave. Whether you will actually leave is a different story! Your leaving will depend on many factors, such as availability of alternative jobs in the market, your employability in a different company, and sacrifices you have to make while changing jobs. In other words, while attitudes give us hints about how a person might behave, it is important to remember that behavior is also strongly influenced by situational constraints.

OB Toolbox: How Can You Be Happier at Work?

- *Have a positive attitude about it.* Your personality is a big part of your happiness. If you are always looking for the negative side of everything, you will find it.
- *A good fit with the job and company is important to your happiness.* This starts with knowing yourself: What do you want from the job? What do you enjoy doing? Be honest with yourself and do a self-assessment.
- *Get accurate information about the job and the company.* Ask detailed questions about what life is like in this company. Do your research: Read about the company, and use your social network to understand the company's culture.
- *Develop good relationships at work.* Make friends. Try to get a mentor. Approach a person you admire and attempt to build a relationship with this person. An experienced mentor can be a great help in navigating life at a company. Your social network can help you weather the bad days and provide you emotional and instrumental support during your time at the company as well as afterward.
- *Pay is important, but job characteristics matter more to your job satisfaction.* Don't sacrifice the job itself for a little bit more money. When choosing a job, look at the level of challenge, and the potential of the job to make you engaged.
- *Be proactive in managing organizational life.* If the job is stressful, cope with it by effective time management and having a good social network, as well as being proactive in getting to the source of stress. If you don't have enough direction, ask for it!
- *Know when to leave.* If the job makes you unhappy over an extended period of time and there is little hope of solving the problems, it may be time to look elsewhere.

1.1 What Causes Positive Work Attitudes?

What makes you satisfied with your job and develop commitment to your company? Research shows that people pay attention to several aspects of their work environment, including how they are treated, the relationships they form with colleagues and managers, and the actual work they perform. We will now summarize the factors that show consistent relations with job satisfaction and organizational commitment.

FIGURE 4.2 Factors Contributing to Job Satisfaction and Organizational Commitment

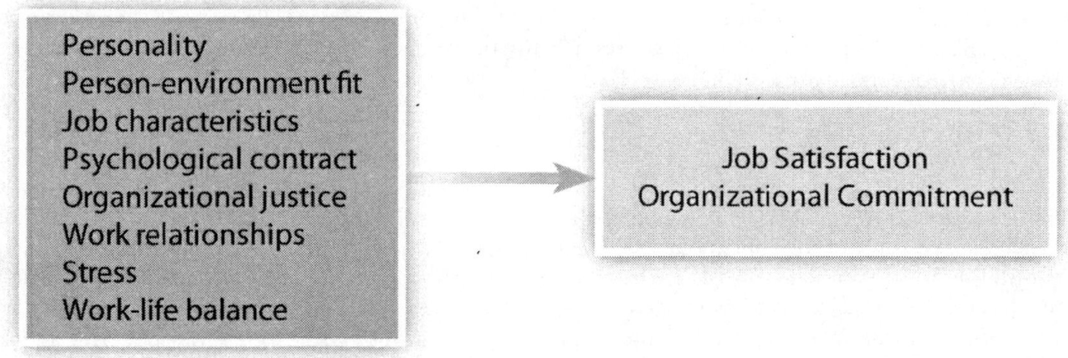

Personality

Can assessing the work environment fully explain how satisfied we are on the job? Interestingly, some experts have shown that job satisfaction is not purely environmental and is partially due to our personality. Some people have a disposition to be happy in life and at work regardless of environmental factors.

It seems that people who have a positive affective disposition (those who have a tendency to experience positive moods more often than negative moods) tend to be more satisfied with their jobs and more committed to their companies, while those who have a negative disposition tend to be less satisfied and less committed.[2] This is not surprising, as people who are determined to see the glass as half full will notice the good things in their work environment, while those with the opposite character will find more things to complain about. In addition to our affective disposition, people who have a neurotic personality (those who are moody, temperamental, critical of themselves and others) are less satisfied with their job, while those who are emotionally more stable tend to be more satisfied. Other traits such as conscientiousness, self-esteem, locus of control, and extraversion are also related to positive work attitudes.[3] Either these people are more successful in finding jobs and companies that will make them happy and build better relationships at work, which would increase their satisfaction and commitment, or they simply see their environment as more positive—whichever the case, it seems that personality is related to work attitudes.

Person–Environment Fit

The fit between what we bring to our work environment and the environmental demands influences our work attitudes. Therefore, person–job fit and person–organization fit are positively related to job satisfaction and commitment. When our abilities match job demands and our values match company values, we tend to be more satisfied with our job and more committed to the company we work for.[4]

Job Characteristics

The presence of certain characteristics on the job seems to make employees more satisfied and more committed. Using a variety of skills, having autonomy at work, receiving feedback on the job, and performing a significant task are some job characteristics that are related to satisfaction and commitment. However, the presence of these factors is not important for everyone. Some people have a high growth need. They expect their jobs to help them build new skills and improve as an employee. These people tend to be more satisfied when their jobs have these characteristics.[5]

Psychological Contract

psychological contract

An unwritten understanding about what the employee will bring to the work environment and what the company will provide in exchange.

psychological contract breach

Violation of the unwritten understanding between the employee and the organization regarding expectations.

After accepting a job, people come to work with a set of expectations. They have an understanding of their responsibilities and rights. In other words, they have a **psychological contract** with the company. A psychological contract is an unwritten understanding about what the employee will bring to the work environment and what the company will provide in exchange. When people do not get what they expect, they experience a **psychological contract breach**, which leads to low job satisfaction and commitment. Imagine that you were told before being hired that the company was family friendly and collegial. However, after a while, you realize that they expect employees to work 70 hours a week, and employees are aggressive toward each other. You are likely to experience a breach in your psychological contract and be dissatisfied. One way of preventing such problems is for companies to provide realistic job previews to their employees.[6]

Organizational Justice

A strong influence over our satisfaction level is how fairly we are treated. People pay attention to the fairness of company policies and procedures, treatment from supervisors, and pay and other rewards they receive from the company.[7]

Relationships at Work

Two strong predictors of our happiness at work and commitment to the company are our relationships with coworkers and managers. The people we interact with, their degree of compassion, our level of social acceptance in our work group, and whether we are treated with respect are all important factors surrounding our happiness at work. Research also shows that our relationship with our manager, how considerate the manager is, and whether we build a trust-based relationship with our manager are critically important to our job satisfaction and organizational commitment.[8] When our manager and upper management listen to us, care about us, and value our opinions, we tend to feel good at work. Even small actions may show employees that the management cares about them. For example, Hotel Carlton in San Francisco was recently taken over by a new management group. One of the small things the new management did created dramatic results. In response to an employee attitude survey, they replaced the old vacuum cleaners housekeepers were using and established a policy of replacing them every year. This simple act of listening to employee problems and taking action went a long way to making employees feel that the management cares about them.[9]

Stress

Not surprisingly, the amount of stress present in our job is related to our satisfaction and commitment. For example, experiencing role ambiguity (vagueness in relation to what our responsibilities are), role conflict (facing contradictory demands at work), and organizational politics, and worrying about the security of our job are all stressors that make people dissatisfied. On the other hand, not all stress is bad. Some stressors actually make us happier! For example, working under time pressure and having a high degree of responsibility are stressful, but they can also be perceived as challenges and tend to be related to high levels of satisfaction.[10]

Work–Life Balance

In the 1950s, people's work was all-consuming. Employees went to work, worked long hours, and the rest of the family accepted that work came first. As society changed, the concept of always putting work first became outdated. In modern times, more employees expect to lead balanced lives, pursue hobbies, and spend more time with their children while at the same time continuing to succeed at work. The notion of work–family conflict is one cause of job dissatisfaction. This conflict can be particularly strong for women because of the time necessary for pregnancy and giving birth, but men struggle with it as well. When work life interferes with family life, we are more stressed and unhappy with our jobs. Research shows that policies that help employees achieve a balance between their work and personal lives, such as allowing telecommuting, are related to higher job satisfaction. For example, the medical resources group of the pharmaceutical company AstraZeneca International does not have fixed working hours, and employees can work any hours they choose. Motorola's technological acceleration group also has flexible hours and can work from anywhere (home, office, or a coffee shop) at anytime.[11]

1.2 Consequences of Positive Work Attitudes

Why do we care about the job satisfaction and organizational commitment of employees? What behaviors would you expect to see from someone who has more positive work attitudes?

If you say "higher performance," you have stumbled upon one of the most controversial subjects in organizational behavior. Many studies have been devoted to understanding whether happy employees are more productive. Some studies show weak correlations between satisfaction and performance while others show higher correlations (what researchers would call "medium-sized" correlations of 0.30).[12] The correlation between commitment and performance tends to be even weaker.[13] Even with a correlation of 0.30 though, the relationship may be lower than you may have expected. Why is this so?

FIGURE 4.3

Work attitudes are often good predictors of work behavior, such as performance, citizenship behaviors, absenteeism, and turnover.

© 2010 Jupiterimages Corporation

It seems that happy workers have an inclination to be more engaged at work. They may *want* to perform better. They may be more motivated. But there are also exceptions. Think about this: Just because you want to perform, will you actually be a higher performer? Chances are that your skill level in performing the job will matter. There are also some jobs where performance depends on factors beyond an employee's control, such as the pace of the machine they are working on. Because of this reason, in professional jobs such as engineering and research, we see a higher link between work attitudes and performance, as opposed to manual jobs such as assembly line work.[14] Also, think about the alternative possibility: If you don't like your job, does this mean that you will reduce your performance? Maybe up to a certain point, but there will be factors that prevent you from reducing your performance: the fear of getting fired, the desire to get a promotion so that you can get out of the job that you dislike so much, or your professional work ethic. As a result, we should not expect a one-to-one relationship between satisfaction and performance. Still, the observed correlation between work attitudes and performance is important and has practical value.

Work attitudes are even more strongly related to organizational citizenship behaviors (behaviors that are not part of our job but are valuable to the organization, such as helping new employees or working voluntary overtime). Satisfied and committed people are absent less frequently and for shorter duration, are likely to stay with a company longer, and demonstrate less aggression at work. Just as important, people who are happy at work are happier with their lives overall. Given that we spend so much of our waking hours at work, it is no surprise that our satisfaction with our job is a big part of how satisfied we feel about life in general.[15] Finally, a satisfied workforce seems to be related to positive firm-level outcomes, such as customer satisfaction and loyalty, profitability, and safety in the workplace.[16]

1.3 Assessing Work Attitudes in the Workplace

Given that work attitudes may give us clues as to who will leave or stay, who will perform better, and who will be more engaged, tracking satisfaction and commitment levels is a helpful step for companies. If there are companywide issues that make employees unhappy and disengaged, then these issues need to be resolved. There are at least two systematic ways in which companies can track work attitudes: through **attitude surveys** and exit interviews. Companies such as KFC Corporation and Long John Silver's Inc. restaurants, the SAS Institute, Google, and others give periodic surveys to employees to track their work attitudes. Companies can get more out of these surveys if responses are held confidential. If employees become concerned that their individual responses will be shared with their immediate manager, they are less likely to respond honestly. Moreover, the success of these surveys depends on

attitude surveys

Surveys that are given to employees periodically to track their work attitudes.

the credibility of management in the eyes of employees. If management periodically collects these surveys but no action comes out of them, employees may adopt a more cynical attitude and start ignoring these surveys, hampering the success of future efforts.

exit interview

A meeting with the departing employee.

An **exit interview** involves a meeting with the departing employee. This meeting is often conducted by a member of the human resource management department. The departing employee's manager is the worst person to conduct the interview, because managers are often one of the primary reasons an employee is leaving in the first place. If conducted well, this meeting may reveal what makes employees dissatisfied at work and give management clues about areas for improvement.

KEY TAKEAWAY

Work attitudes are the feelings we have toward different aspects of the work environment. Job satisfaction and organizational commitment are two key attitudes that are the most relevant to important outcomes. Attitudes create an intention to behave in a certain way and may predict actual behavior under certain conditions. People develop positive work attitudes as a result of their personality, fit with their environment, stress levels they experience, relationships they develop, perceived fairness of their pay, company policies, interpersonal treatment, whether their psychological contract is violated, and the presence of policies addressing work–life conflict. When people have more positive work attitudes, they may have the inclination to perform better, display citizenship behaviors, and be absent less often and for shorter periods of time, and they are less likely to quit their jobs within a short period of time. When workplace attitudes are more positive, companies benefit in the form of higher safety and better customer service, as well as higher company performance.

EXERCISES

1. What is the difference between job satisfaction and organizational commitment? Which do you think would be more strongly related to performance? Which would be more strongly related to turnover?
2. Do you think making employees happier at work is a good way of motivating people? When would high satisfaction not be related to high performance?
3. In your opinion, what are the three most important factors that make people dissatisfied with their job? What are the three most important factors relating to organizational commitment?
4. How important is pay in making people attached to a company and making employees satisfied?
5. Do you think younger and older people are similar in what makes them happier at work and committed to their companies? Do you think there are male–female differences? Explain your answers.

2. WORK BEHAVIORS

LEARNING OBJECTIVES

1. **Define job performance, organizational citizenship, absenteeism, and turnover.**
2. **Explain factors associated with each type of work behavior.**

One of the important objectives of the field of organizational behavior is to understand why people behave the way they do. Which behaviors are we referring to here? We will focus on four key work behaviors: job performance, organizational citizenship behaviors, absenteeism, and turnover. These are not the only behaviors OB is concerned about, but understanding what is meant by these terms and understanding the major influences over each type of behavior will give you more clarity about analyzing the behaviors of others in the workplace. We summarize the major research findings about the causes of each type of behavior in the following figure.

FIGURE 4.4

Summary of Factors That Have the Strongest Influence Over Work Behaviors. Note: Negative relationships are indicated with (–).

Job Performance	Citizenship	Absenteeism	Turnover
General mental abilities	How we are treated at work	Health problems	Poor performance
How we are treated at work	Personality	Work/life balance issues	Positive work attitudes (–)
Stress (–)	Positive work attitudes	Positive work attitudes (–)	Stress
Positive work attitudes	Age of the employee	Age of the employee (–)	Personality
Personality			Age and tenure of the employee (–)

2.1 Job Performance

Job performance, or in-role performance, refers to the performance level on factors included in the job description. For each job, the content of job performance may differ. Measures of job performance include the quality and quantity of work performed by the employee, the accuracy and speed with which the job is performed, and the overall effectiveness of the person performing the job. In many companies, job performance determines whether a person is promoted, rewarded with pay raises, given additional responsibilities, or fired from the job. Therefore, job performance is tracked and observed in many organizations and is one of the main outcomes studied in the field of organizational behavior.

job performance

Or in-role performance refers to the performance level on factors included in the job description.

What Are the Major Predictors of Job Performance?

Under which conditions do people perform well, and what are the characteristics of high performers? These questions received a lot of research attention. It seems that the most powerful influence over our job performance is our **general mental ability**, or cognitive abilities. Our reasoning abilities, verbal and numerical skills, analytical skills, and overall intelligence level seems to be important across most situations. It seems that general mental ability starts influencing us early in life; it is strongly correlated with measures of academic success.[17] As we grow and mature, cognitive ability is also correlated with different measures of job performance.[18] General mental ability is important for job performance across different settings, but there is also variation. In jobs with high complexity, it is much more critical to have high general mental abilities. In jobs such as working in sales, management, engineering, or other professional areas, this ability is much more important, whereas for jobs involving manual labor or clerical work, the importance of high mental abilities for high performance is weaker (yet still important).

general mental ability

Or cognitive abilities, refers to our reasoning abilities, verbal and numerical skills, analytical skills, and overall intelligence level.

How we are treated within an organization is another factor determining our performance level. When we feel that we are being treated fairly by a company, have a good relationship with our manager, have a manager who is supportive and rewards high performance, and we trust the people we work with, we tend to perform better. Why? It seems that when we are treated well, we want to reciprocate. Therefore, when we are treated well, we treat the company well by performing our job more effectively.[19]

Following the quality of treatment, the *stress* we experience determines our performance level. When we experience high levels of stress, our mental energies are drained. Instead of focusing on the task at hand, we start concentrating on the stressor and become distracted trying to cope with it. Because our attention and energies are diverted to deal with stress, our performance suffers. Having role ambiguity and experiencing conflicting role demands are related to lower performance.[20] Stress that prevents us from doing our jobs does not have to be related to our experiences at work. For example, according to a survey conducted by Workplace Options, 45% of the respondents said that financial stress affects work performance. When people are in debt, are constantly worrying about mortgage or tuition payments, or are having trouble paying for essentials such as gas and food, their performance will suffer.[21]

Our *work attitudes*, specifically job satisfaction, are moderate correlates of job performance. When we are satisfied with the job, we may perform better. This relationship seems to exist in jobs with greater levels of complexity and weakens in simpler and less complicated jobs. It is possible that in less complex jobs, our performance depends more on the machinery we work with or organizational rules and regulations. In other words, people may have less leeway to reduce performance in these jobs. Also, in some jobs people do not reduce their performance even when dissatisfied. For example, among nurses there seems to be a weak correlation between satisfaction and performance. Even when they are unhappy, nurses put substantial effort into their work, likely because they feel a moral obligation to help their patients.[22]

Finally, job performance has a modest relationship with *personality*, particularly conscientiousness. People who are organized, reliable, dependable, and achievement-oriented seem to outperform others in various contexts.[23]

2.2 Organizational Citizenship Behaviors

organizational citizenship behaviors (OCB)

Voluntary behaviors employees perform to help others and benefit the organization.

While *job performance* refers to the performance of duties listed in one's job description, organizational citizenship behaviors involve performing behaviors that are more discretionary. **Organizational citizenship behaviors (OCB)** are voluntary behaviors employees perform to help others and benefit the organization. Helping a new coworker understand how things work in your company, volunteering to organize the company picnic, and providing suggestions to management about how to improve business processes are some examples of citizenship behaviors. These behaviors contribute to the smooth operation of business.

What are the major predictors of citizenship behaviors? Unlike performance, citizenship behaviors do not depend so much on one's abilities. Job performance, to a large extent, depends on our general mental abilities. When you add the education, skills, knowledge, and abilities that are needed to perform well, the role of motivation in performance becomes more limited. As a result, someone being motivated will not necessarily translate into a person performing well. For citizenship behaviors, the motivation-behavior link is clearer. We help others around us if we feel motivated to do so.

Perhaps the most important factor explaining our citizenship behaviors is *how we are treated* by the people around us. When we have a good relationship with our manager and we are supported by management staff, when we are treated fairly, when we are attached to our peers, and when we trust the people around us, we are more likely to engage in citizenship behaviors. A high-quality relationship with people we work with will mean that simply doing our job will not be enough to maintain the relationship. In a high-quality relationship, we feel the obligation to reciprocate and do extra things to help those around us.[24]

Our *personality* is yet another explanation for why we perform citizenship behaviors. Personality is a modest predictor of actual job performance but a much better predictor of citizenship. People who are conscientious, agreeable, and have positive affectivity tend to perform citizenship behaviors more often than others.[25]

Job attitudes are also moderately related to citizenship behaviors. People who are happier at work, those who are more committed to their companies, and those who have overall positive attitudes toward their work situation tend to perform citizenship behaviors more often than others. When people are unhappy, they tend to be disengaged from their jobs and rarely go beyond the minimum that is expected of them.[26]

Interestingly, age seems to be related to the frequency with which we demonstrate citizenship behaviors. People who are older are better citizens. It is possible that with age, we gain more experiences to share. It becomes easier to help others because we have more accumulated company and life experiences to draw from.[27]

FIGURE 4.5

Organizational citizenship behaviors are voluntary actions, such as helping a coworker. While outside the scope of job duties, these behaviors contribute to the effective functioning of an organization.

2.3 Absenteeism

Absenteeism refers to unscheduled absences from work. Absenteeism is costly to companies because of its unpredictable nature. When an employee has an unscheduled absence from work, companies struggle to find replacement workers at the last minute. This may involve hiring contingent workers, having other employees work overtime, or scrambling to cover for an absent coworker. The cost of absenteeism to organizations is estimated at $74 billion. According to a Mercer LLC human resource consulting study, 15% of the money spent on payroll is related to absenteeism.[28]

absenteeism

Unscheduled absences from work.

What causes absenteeism? First we need to look at the type of absenteeism. Some absenteeism is unavoidable and is related to *health reasons.* For example, reasons such as lower back pain, migraines, accidents on or off the job, or acute stress are important reasons for absenteeism.[29] Health-related absenteeism is costly, but dealing with such absenteeism by using organizational policies penalizing absenteeism is both unreasonable and unfair. A sick employee who shows up at work will infect coworkers and will not be productive. Instead, companies are finding that programs aimed at keeping workers healthy are effective in dealing with this type of absenteeism. Companies using wellness programs that educate employees about proper nutrition, help them exercise, and reward them for healthy habits are related to reduced absenteeism.[30]

Work–life balance is another common reason for absences. Staying home to care for a sick child or relative, attending the wedding of a friend or relative, or skipping work to study for an exam are all common reasons for unscheduled absences. Companies may deal with these by giving employees more flexibility in work hours. If employees can manage their own time, they are less likely to be absent. Organizations such as Lahey Clinic Foundation Inc. at Burlington, Massachusetts, find that instead of separating sick leave and paid time off, merging them is effective in dealing with unscheduled absences. When a company has "sick leave" but no other leave for social and family obligations, employees may fake being sick and use their "sick leave." Instead, having a single paid time off policy would allow workers to balance work and life, and allow companies to avoid unscheduled absences. Some companies such as IBM Corporation got rid of sick leave altogether and instead allow employees to take as much time as they need, as long as their work gets done.[31]

FIGURE 4.6

Absenteeism costs companies an estimated $74 billion annually. A common reason for absenteeism is health problems. Companies using wellness programs targeting employee health are found to reduce absenteeism.

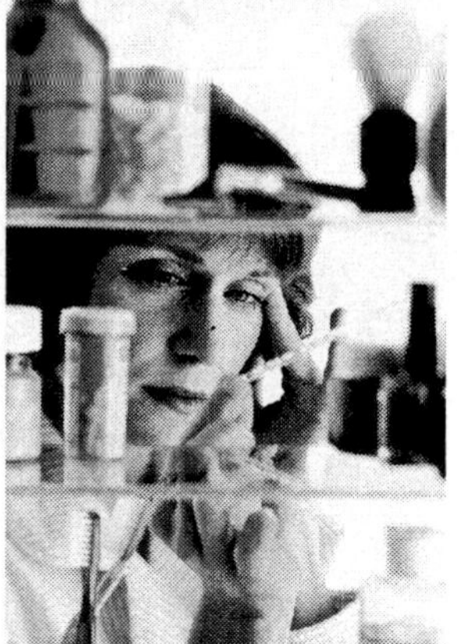

© 2010 Jupiterimages Corporation

Sometimes, absenteeism is a form of work withdrawal and can lead to resignation from the job. In other words, *poor work attitudes* lead to absenteeism. When employees are dissatisfied with their work or have low organizational commitment, they are likely to be absent more often. In other words, absenteeism is caused by the desire to avoid an unpleasant work environment in addition to related factors such as problems in job design, lack of organizational justice, extreme levels of stress, and ineffective relations with coworkers and supervisors. In this case, management may deal with absenteeism by investigating the causes of dissatisfaction and dealing with them.[32]

Are there personal factors contributing to absenteeism? Research does not reveal a consistent link between personality and absenteeism. One demographic criterion that predicts absenteeism is age. Interestingly, and counter to the stereotype that increased age would bring more health problems, research shows that age is negatively related to both frequency and duration of absenteeism. Because of reasons including higher loyalty to their company and a stronger work ethic, older employees are less likely be absent from work.[33]

OB Toolbox: Dealing with Late Coworkers

Do you have team members that are chronically late to group meetings? Are your coworkers driving you crazy because they are perpetually late? Here are some suggestions that may help.

- *Try to get to the root cause and find out what is making your coworker unhappy.* Often, lateness is an extension of dissatisfaction one feels toward the job or tasks at hand. If there are ways in which you can solve these issues, such as by giving the person more responsibility or listening to the opinions of the person and showing more respect, you can minimize lateness.
- *Make sure that lateness does not go without any negative consequences.* Do not ignore it, and do not remain silent. Mention carefully and constructively that one person's lateness slows down everyone.
- *Make an effort to schedule meetings around everyone's schedules.* When scheduling, emphasize the importance of everyone's being there on time and pick a time when everyone can comfortably attend.
- *When people are late, be sure to ask them to compensate, such as by doing extra work.* Negative consequences tend to discourage future lateness.
- *Shortly before the meeting starts, send everyone a reminder.* Yes, you are dealing with adults and they should keep their own schedules, but some people's schedules may be busier than others, and some are better at keeping track of their time. Reminders may ensure that they arrive on time.

- *Reward timeliness.* When everyone shows up on time, verbally recognize the effort everyone made to be there on time.
- *Be on time yourself!* Creating a culture of timeliness within your group requires everyone's effort, including yours.

Sources: Adapted from information in DeLonzor, D. (2005, November). Running late. HR Magazine, 50(11), 109–112; Grainge, Z. (2006, November 21). Spotlight on…lateness. Personnel Today, p. 33.

2.4 Turnover

turnover

An employee's leaving an organization.

Turnover refers to an employee leaving an organization. Employee turnover has potentially harmful consequences, such as poor customer service and poor companywide performance. When employees leave, their jobs still need to be performed by someone, so companies spend time recruiting, hiring, and training new employees, all the while suffering from lower productivity. Yet, not all turnover is bad. Turnover is particularly a problem when high-performing employees leave, while a poor performer's turnover may actually give the company a chance to improve productivity and morale.

FIGURE 4.7

Employees quit their jobs because of many reasons, including their performance level, job dissatisfaction, personality, age, and how long they have been with the company. Regardless of the reason, turnover of high-performing employees affects company performance and customer service.

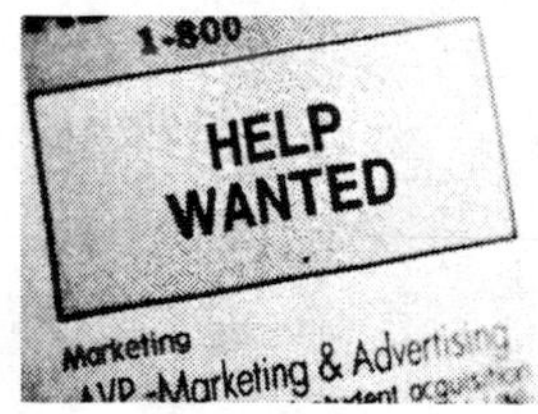

© 2010 Jupiterimages Corporation

Why do employees leave? An employee's *performance* level is an important reason. People who perform poorly are actually more likely to leave. These people may be fired or be encouraged to quit, or they may quit because of their fear of being fired. If a company has pay-for-performance systems, poor performers will find that they are not earning much, owing to their substandard performance. This pay discrepancy gives poor performers an extra incentive to leave. On the other hand, instituting a pay-for-performance system does not mean that high performers will always stay with a company. Note that high performers may find it easier to find alternative jobs, so when they are unhappy, they can afford to quit their jobs voluntarily.[34]

Work attitudes are often the primary culprit in why people leave. When workers are unhappy at work, and when they are not attached to their companies, they are more likely to leave. Loving the things they do, being happy with the opportunities for advancement within the company, and being happy about pay are all aspects of work attitudes relating to turnover. Of course, the link between work attitudes and turnover is not direct. When employees are unhappy, they might have the intention to leave and may start looking for a job, but their ability to actually leave will depend on many factors such as their employability and the condition of the job market. For this reason, when national and regional unemployment is high, many people who are unhappy will still continue to work for their current company. When the economy is doing well, people will start moving to other companies in response to being unhappy. Many companies make an effort to keep employees happy because of an understanding of the connection between employee happiness and turnover. As illustrated in the opening case, at the SAS Institute, employees enjoy amenities such as a swimming pool, child care at work, and a 35-hour workweek. The company's turnover is around 4%–5%. This percentage is a stark contrast to the industry average, which is in the range of 12%–20%.[35]

People are more likely to quit their jobs if they experience *stress* at work as well. Stressors such as role conflict and role ambiguity drain energy and motivate people to seek alternatives. For example, call-center employees experience a great deal of stress in the form of poor treatment from customers, long work hours, and constant monitoring of their every action. Companies such as EchoStar Corporation realize that one method for effectively retaining their best employees is to give employees opportunities to move to higher responsibility jobs elsewhere in the company. When a stressful job is a step toward a more desirable job, employees seem to stick around longer.[36]

There are also individual differences in whether people leave or stay. For example, *personality* is a factor in the decision to quit one's job. People who are conscientious, agreeable, and emotionally stable are less likely to quit their jobs. Many explanations are possible. People with these personality traits may perform better at work, which leads to lower quit rates. Additionally, they may have better relations with coworkers and managers, which is a factor in their retention. Whatever the reason, it seems that some people are likely to stay longer at any given job regardless of the circumstances.[37]

Whether we leave a job or stay also depends on our *age and how long we have been there*. It seems that younger employees are more likely to leave. This is not surprising, because people who are younger will have fewer responsibilities such as supporting a household or dependents. As a result, they can quit a job they don't like much more easily. Similarly, people who have been with a company for a short period of time may quit more easily. New employees experience a lot of stress at work, and there is usually not much keeping them in the company, such as established bonds to a manager or colleagues. New employees may even have ongoing job interviews with other companies when they start working; therefore, they may leave more easily. For example, Sprint Nextel Corporation found that many of their new hires were quitting within 45 days of their hiring dates. When they investigated, they found that newly hired employees were experiencing a lot of stress from avoidable problems such as unclear job descriptions or problems hooking up their computers. Sprint was able to solve the turnover problem by paying special attention to orienting new hires.[38]

OB Toolbox: Tips for Leaving Your Job Gracefully

Few people work in one company forever, and someday you may decide that your current job is no longer right for you. Here are tips on how to leave without burning any bridges.

- *Don't quit on an impulse.* We all have bad days and feel the temptation to walk away from the job right away. Yet, this is unproductive for your own career. Plan your exit in advance, look for a better job over an extended period of time, and leave when the moment is right.
- *Don't quit too often.* While trading jobs in an upward fashion is good, leaving one place and getting another job that is just like the previous one in pay, responsibilities, and position does not help you move forward in your career, and makes you look like a quitter. Companies are often wary of hiring job hoppers.
- *When you decide to leave, tell your boss first, and be nice.* Don't discuss all the things your manager may have done wrong. Explain your reasons without blaming anyone and frame it as an issue of poor job fit.
- *Do not badmouth your employer.* It is best not to bash the organization you are leaving in front of coworkers. Do not tell them how happy you are to be quitting or how much better your new job looks. There is really no point in making any remaining employees feel bad.
- *Guard your professional reputation.* You must realize that the world is a small place. People know others and tales of unprofessional behavior travel quickly to unlikely places.
- *Finish your ongoing work and don't leave your team in a bad spot.* Right before a major deadline is probably a bad time to quit. Offer to stay at least two weeks to finish your work, and to help hire and train your replacement.
- *Don't steal from the company!* Give back all office supplies, keys, ID cards, and other materials. Don't give them any reason to blemish their memory of you. Who knows…you may even want to come back one day.

Sources: Adapted from information in Challenger, J. E. (1992, November–December), How to leave your job without burning bridges. Women in Business, 44(6), 29; Daniels, C., & Vinzant, C. (2000, February 7). The joy of quitting, Fortune, 141(3), 199–202; Schroeder, J. (2005, November). Leaving your job without burning bridges. Public Relations Tactics, 12(11), 4; Woolnough, R. (2003, May 27). The right and wrong ways to leave your job. Computer Weekly, 55.

KEY TAKEAWAY

Employees demonstrate a wide variety of positive and negative behaviors at work. Among these behaviors, four are critically important and have been extensively studied in the OB literature. Job performance is a person's accomplishments of tasks listed in one's job description. A person's abilities, particularly mental abilities, are the main predictor of job performance in many occupations. How we are treated at work, the level of stress experienced at work, work attitudes, and, to a lesser extent, our personality are also factors relating to one's job performance. Citizenship behaviors are tasks helpful to the organization but are not in one's job description. Performance of citizenship behaviors is less a function of our abilities and more of motivation. How we are treated at work, personality, work attitudes, and our age are the main predictors of citizenship. Among negative behaviors, absenteeism and turnover are critically important. Health problems and work–life balance issues contribute to more absenteeism. Poor work attitudes are also related to absenteeism, and younger employees are more likely to be absent from work. Turnover is higher among low performers, people who have negative work attitudes, and those who experience a great deal of stress. Personality and youth are personal predictors of turnover.

EXERCISES

1. What is the difference between performance and organizational citizenship behaviors? How would you increase someone's performance? How would you increase citizenship behaviors?
2. Are citizenship behaviors always beneficial to the company? If not, why not? Can you think of any citizenship behaviors that employees may perform with the intention of helping a company but that may have negative consequences overall?
3. Given the factors correlated with job performance, how would you identify future high performers?
4. What are the major causes of absenteeism at work? How can companies minimize the level of absenteeism that takes place?
5. In some companies, managers are rewarded for minimizing the turnover within their department or branch. A part of their bonus is tied directly to keeping the level of turnover below a minimum. What do you think about the potential effectiveness of these programs? Do you see any downsides to such programs?

3. THE ROLE OF ETHICS AND NATIONAL CULTURE

LEARNING OBJECTIVES

1. **Consider the role of job attitudes on ethical behavior.**
2. **Consider the role of national culture on job attitudes and behaviors.**

3.1 Job Attitudes, Behaviors, and Ethics

People prefer to work in companies that have an ethical environment. Studies show that when an organization has a moral climate that values doing the right thing, people tend to be happier at work, more committed to their companies, and less likely to want to leave. In other words, in addition to increasing the frequency of ethical behaviors, the presence of an ethical climate will attach people to a company. An ethical climate is related to performing citizenship behaviors in which employees help each other and their supervisors, and perform many behaviors that are not part of their job descriptions.[39]

whistleblowers

People who report wrongdoing.

If people are happy at work and committed to the company, do they behave more ethically? This connection is not as clear. In fact, loving your job and being committed to the company may prevent you from realizing that the company is doing anything wrong. One study showed that, when people were highly committed to their company, they were less likely to recognize organizational wrongdoing and less likely to report the problem to people within the organization. **Whistleblowers**, or people who reported wrongdoing, were more likely to have moderate levels of commitment to the company. It is possible that those people who identify with a company are blind to its faults.[40]

Companies trying to prevent employees from behaving unethically face a dilemma. One way of reducing unethical behaviors is to monitor employees closely. However, when people are closely monitored through video cameras, when their e-mails are routinely read, and when their online activities are closely monitored, employees are more likely to feel that they are being treated unfairly and with little respect. Therefore, high levels of employee monitoring, while reducing the frequency of unethical behaviors, may reduce job satisfaction and commitment, as well as work performance and citizenship behaviors. Instead of monitoring and punishing employees, organizations can reduce unethical behavior by creating an ethical climate and making ethics a shared value.[41]

3.2 Job Attitudes Around the Globe

Do the same things satisfy people around the globe? Even though many of the findings regarding satisfaction are generalizable to different cultures, some research reveals that differences may also exist. In one study comparing job satisfaction in 20 countries, work–family conflict was found to lower job satisfaction only in individualistic cultures. It is possible that in collectivistic cultures, when people have to make sacrifices for work, they may compensate by forming better relations with coworkers, which prevents employees from being dissatisfied. There is also evidence that while autonomy and empowerment are valued in the United States, Mexico, and Poland, high levels of empowerment were related to lower job satisfaction in India.[42] Despite some variation, major factors that make people happy, such as being treated well and having good relations with others, are likely to generalize across cultures.

Culture also influences work behaviors. Behaviors regarded as a citizenship behavior in the United States or other Western cultures, such as helping a new coworker learn the job, may be viewed as part of a person's job performance in other cultures. Research shows that managers in cultures such as Hong Kong and Japan define job performance more broadly. For example, the willingness to tolerate less than ideal circumstances within the company without complaining was viewed as part of someone's job in Hong Kong, whereas this was viewed as more discretionary in the United States and Australia. Norms regarding absenteeism and turnover are also subject to cultural differences. One study shows that in China, absence from work because of one's illness, stress, or depression was relatively unacceptable, while in Canada, these reasons were viewed as legitimate reasons for being absent.[43]

KEY TAKEAWAY

There is a connection between a company's ethics climate, work attitudes, and citizenship behaviors demonstrated by employees. A highly committed workforce may not necessarily demonstrate higher levels of ethics, because highly committed people may be less likely to notice companywide wrongdoing and, in turn, not report them. Companies have to strike a balance between reducing unethical behaviors and maintaining a highly ethical and committed workforce. Some tactics of reducing unethical behaviors, such as close monitoring of employees, may erode trust between management and employees and lead to negative work attitudes. There are cross-cultural differences in how employee work attitudes are shaped and the work behaviors that are expected from employees. Being aware of these differences facilitates effective management of a global workforce.

EXERCISES

1. Which factors related to work attitudes in Western cultures should also be related to work attitudes in other cultures? Are there any that you think would not be important in a different culture you are familiar with?
2. Do you think people leave their jobs for the same reasons around the world? If not, explain why you think so.

4. CONCLUSION

Work attitudes are our feelings toward our company and job. Job satisfaction and organizational commitment are related to many outcomes of interest, such as absenteeism, performance, and turnover. Therefore, companies track feelings toward work and try to create more positive attitudes. The main behaviors that contribute to organizational effectiveness are job performance, citizenship behaviors, absenteeism, and turnover. These behaviors are affected by a complex blend of personality and situational factors, and factors affecting these behaviors and work attitudes will be examined in more detail in other chapters of this book.

85

5. EXERCISES

ETHICAL DILEMMA

You are a department manager in an advertising agency. The employees of the department have recently completed an attitude survey. Three employees in your department reported that they were harassed by senior people in the department and they are experiencing a hostile work environment. You do not know who these people are, but you feel that you need to do something. The surveys were filled out confidentially, and employees were assured that their identities would not be revealed to management. You feel that you can identify who they are because the person in HR who administered the survey is a friend of yours and that person can tell you the demographics of the employees, which would help you identify them.

1. Should you ask for the identity-revealing information? What are the advantages and disadvantages of finding out the identity of these people?
2. How would you handle a situation like this now and in the future?

INDIVIDUAL EXERCISE

Reading and Responding to Employee Blogs

You found out that one employee from your company has created a blog about the company. Other current and ex-employees are also posting on this blog, and the picture they are painting is less than flattering. They are talking about their gripes, such as long work hours and below-market pay, and how the company's products are not great compared to those of competitors. Worse, they are talking about the people in the company by name. There are a couple of postings mentioning you by name and calling you unfair and unreasonable.

1. What action would you take when you learn the presence of this blog? Would you take action to stop this blogger? How?
2. Would you do anything to learn the identity of the blogger? If you found out, what action would you take to have the employee disciplined?
3. What would you change within the company to deal with this situation?
4. Would you post on this blog? If so, under what name, and what comments would you post?

GROUP EXERCISE

Exit Interview Role-Play and Developing an Attitude Survey

This role-play will be played by three students. One student will be an employee from the human resources (HR) department conducting the interview, the second will be the employee who is leaving, and the third will be an observer. The HR employee and the departing employee will conduct an exit interview. At the conclusion of the interview, the observer will provide feedback to the HR employee regarding how the interview could have been improved and how the employee could have been more open.

Part 1: Role-Play

Be sure to read only the role sheet assigned to you.

Part 2

In groups of three, review the information gathered from the exit interview. Many of these problems may be affecting the rest of the employees. Develop an attitude survey to be distributed to remaining employees of this company. Develop questions based on what came out of the interview as well as other areas you feel may be important to know. Discuss how the surveys would be administered and what would be done to (a) have a high response rate and (b) ensure the accuracy of responses.

ENDNOTES

1. What keeps employees satisfied? (2007, August). *HR Focus*, pp. 10–13; Sandberg, J. (2008, April 15). For many employees, a dream job is one that isn't a nightmare. *Wall Street Journal*, p. B1.

2. Connolly, J. J., & Viswesvaran, C. (2000). The role of affectivity in job satisfaction: A meta-analysis. *Personality and Individual Differences, 29*, 265–281; Thoresen, C. J., Kaplan, S. A., Barsky, A. P., de Chermont, K., & Warren, C. R. (2003). The affective underpinnings of job perceptions and attitudes: A meta-analytic review and integration. *Psychological Bulletin, 129*, 914–945.

3. Judge, T. A., Heller, D., & Mount, M. K. (2002). Five-factor model of personality and job satisfaction: A meta-analysis. *Journal of Applied Psychology, 87*, 530–541; Judge, T. A., & Bono, J. E. (2001). Relationship of core self-evaluations traits—self esteem, generalized self efficacy, internal locus of control, and emotional stability—with job satisfaction and job performance: A meta-analysis. *Journal of Applied Psychology, 86*, 80–92; Zimmerman, R. D. (2008). Understanding the impact of personality traits on individuals' turnover decisions: A meta-analytic path model. *Personnel Psychology, 61*, 309–348.

4. Kristof-Brown, A. L., Zimmerman, R. D., & Johnson, E. C. (2005). Consequences of individuals' fit at work: A meta-analysis of person-job, person-organization, person-group, and person-supervisor fit. *Personnel Psychology, 58*, 281–342; Verquer, M. L., Beehr, T. A., & Wagner, S. H. (2003). A meta-analysis of relations between person-organization fit and work attitudes. *Journal of Vocational Behavior, 63*, 473–489.

5. Loher, B. T., Noe, R. A., Moeller, N. L., & Fitzgerald, M. P. (1985). A meta-analysis of the relation of job characteristics to job satisfaction. *Journal of Applied Psychology, 70*, 280–289; Mathieu, J. E., & Zajac, D. M. (1990). A review and meta-analysis of the antecedents, correlates, and consequences of organizational commitment. *Psychological Bulletin, 108*, 171–194.

6. Premack, S. L., & Wanous, J. P. (1985). A meta-analysis of realistic job preview experiments. *Journal of Applied Psychology, 70*, 706–719; Wanous, J. P., Poland, T. D., Premack, S. L., & Davis, K. S. (1992). The effects of met expectations on newcomer attitudes and behaviors: A review and meta-analysis. *Journal of Applied Psychology, 77*, 288–297; Zhao, H., Wayne, S. J., Glibkowski, B. C., & Bravo, J. (2007). The impact of psychological contract breach on work-related outcomes: A meta-analysis. *Personnel Psychology, 60*, 647–680.

7. Cohen-Charash, Y., & Spector, P. E. (2001). The role of justice in organizations: A meta-analysis. *Organizational Behavior and Human Decision Processes, 86*, 278–321; Colquitt, J. A., Conlon, D. E., Wesson, M. J., Porter, C. O. L. H., & Ng, K. Y. (2001). Justice at the millennium: A meta-analytic review of 25 years of organizational justice research. *Journal of Applied Psychology, 86*, 425–445; Meyer, J. P., Stanley, D. J., Herŝcivitch, L., & Topolnytsky, L. (2002). Affective, continuance, and normative commitment to the organization: A meta-analysis of antecedents, correlates, and consequences. *Journal of Vocational Behavior, 61*, 20–52.

8. Bauer, T. N., Bodner, T., Erdogan, B., Truxillo, D. M., & Tucker, J. S. (2007). Newcomer adjustment during organizational socialization: A meta-analytic review of antecedents, outcomes, and methods. *Journal of Applied Psychology*, 92, 707–721; Gerstner, C. R., & Day, D. V. (1997). Meta-analytic review of leader-member exchange theory: Correlates and construct issues. *Journal of Applied Psychology, 82*(6), 827–844; Judge, T. A., Piccolo, R. F., & Ilies, R. (2004). The forgotten ones? The validity of consideration and initiating structure in leadership research. *Journal of Applied Psychology, 89*, 36–51; Kinicki, A. J., McKee-Ryan, F. M., Schriesheim, C. A., & Carson, K. P. (2002). Assessing the construct validity of the job descriptive index: A review and meta-analysis. *Journal of Applied Psychology, 87*, 14–32; Mathieu, J. E., & Zajac, D. M. (1990). A review and meta-analysis of the antecedents, correlates, and consequences of organizational commitment. *Psychological Bulletin, 108*, 171–194; Meyer, J. P., Stanley, D. J., Herscivitch, L., & Topolnytsky, L. (2002). Affective, continuance, and normative commitment to the organization: A meta-analysis of antecedents, correlates, and consequences. *Journal of Vocational Behavior, 61*, 20–52; Rhoades, L., & Eisenberger, R. (2002). Perceived organizational support: A review of the literature. *Journal of Applied Psychology, 87*, 698–714.

9. Dvorak, P. (2007, December 17). Theory and practice: Hotelier finds happiness keeps staff checked in: Focus on morale boosts Joie de Vivre's grades from workers, guests. *Wall Street Journal*, p. B3.

10. Kinicki, A. J., McKee-Ryan, F. M., Schriesheim, C. A., & Carson, K. P. (2002). Assessing the construct validity of the job descriptive index: A review and meta–analysis. *Journal of Applied Psychology, 87*, 14–32; Meyer, J. P., Stanley, D. J., Herscivitch, L., & Topolnytsky, L. (2002). Affective, continuance, and normative commitment to the organization: A meta-analysis of antecedents, correlates, and consequences. *Journal of Vocational Behavior, 61*, 20–52; Miller, B. K., Rutherford, M. A., & Kolodinsky, R. W. (2008). Perceptions of organizational politics: A meta-analysis of outcomes. *Journal of Business and Psychology, 22*, 209–222; Podsakoff, N. P., LePine, J. A., & LePine, M. A. (2007). Differential challenge stressor-hindrance stressor relationships with job attitudes, turnover intentions, turnover, and withdrawal behavior: A meta-analysis. *Journal of Applied Psychology, 92*, 438–454.

11. Ernst Kossek, E., & Ozeki, C. (1998). Work-family conflict, policies, and the job-life satisfaction relationship: A review and directions for organizational behavior-human resources research. *Journal of Applied Psychology, 83*, 139–149; Gajendran, R. S., & Harrison, D. A. (2007). The good, the bad, and the unknown about telecommuting: Meta-analysis of psychological mediators and individual consequences. *Journal of Applied Psychology, 92*, 1524–1541; Shellenbarger, S. (2007, October 4). What makes a company a great place to work today. *Wall Street Journal*, p. D1.

12. Iaffaldano, M. T., & Muchinsky, P. M. (1985). Job satisfaction and job performance: A meta-analysis. *Psychological Bulletin, 97*, 251–273; Judge, T. A., Thoresen, C. J., Bono, J. E., & Patton, G. T. (2001). The job satisfaction—job performance relationship: A qualitative and quantitative review. *Journal of Applied Psychology, 127*, 376–407; Petty, M. M., McGee, G. W., & Cavender, J. W. (1984). A meta-analysis of the relationships between individual job satisfaction and individual performance. *Academy of Management Review, 9*, 712–721; Riketta, M. (2008). The causal relation between job attitudes and performance: A meta-analysis of panel studies. *Journal of Applied Psychology, 93*, 472–481.

13. Mathieu, J. E., & Zajac, D. M. (1990). A review and meta-analysis of the antecedents, correlates, and consequences of organizational commitment. *Psychological Bulletin, 108*, 171–194; Riketta, M. (2002). Attitudinal organizational commitment and job performance: A meta-analysis. *Journal of Organizational Behavior, 23*, 257–266; Wright, T. A., & Bonnett, D. G. (2002). The moderating effects of employee tenure on the relation between organizational commitment and job performance: A meta-analysis. *Journal of Applied Psychology, 87*, 1183–1190.

14. Riketta, M. (2002). Attitudinal organizational commitment and job performance: A meta-analysis. *Journal of Organizational Behavior, 23*, 257–266.

15. Brush, D. H., Moch, M. K., & Pooyan, A. (1987). Individual demographic differences and job satisfaction. *Journal of Occupational Behaviour, 8*, 139–156; Carsten, J. M., & Spector, P. E. (1987). Unemployment, job satisfaction, and employee turnover: A meta-analytic test of the Muchinsky model. *Journal of Applied Psychology, 72*, 374–381; Cohen, A. (1991). Career stage as a moderator of the relationships between organizational commitment and its outcomes: A meta-analysis. *Journal of Occupational Psychology, 64*, 253–268; Cohen, A. (1993). Organizational commitment and turnover: A meta-analysis. *Academy of Management Journal, 36*, 1140–1157; Cohen, A., & Hudecek, N. (1993). Organizational commitment—turnover relationship across occupational groups: A meta-analysis. *Group & Organization Management, 18*, 188–213; Fassina, N. E., Jones, D. A., & Uggerslev, K. L. (2008). Relationship clean-up time: Using meta-analysis and path analysis to clarify relationships among job satisfaction, perceived fairness, and citizenship behaviors. *Journal of Management, 34*, 161–188; Hackett, R. D. (1989). Work attitudes and employee absenteeism: A synthesis of the literature. *Journal of Occupational Psychology, 62*, 235–248; Herschcovis, M. S., Turner, N., Barling, J., Arnold, K. A., Dupre, K., E., Innes, M., et al. (2007). Predicting workplace aggression: A meta-analysis. *Journal of Applied Psychology, 92*, 228–238; Kinicki, A. J., McKee-Ryan, F. M., Schriesheim, C. A., & Carson, K. P. (2002). Assessing the construct validity of the job descriptive index: A review and meta-analysis. *Journal of Applied Psychology, 87*, 14–32; LePine, J. A., Erez, A., & Johnson, D. E. (2002). The nature and dimensionality of organizational citizenship behavior: A critical review and meta-analysis. *Journal of Applied Psychology, 87*, 52–65; Mathieu, J. E., & Zajac, D. M. (1990). A review and meta-analysis of the antecedents, correlates, and consequences of organizational commitment. *Psychological Bulletin, 108*, 171–194; Meyer, J. P., Stanley, D. J., Herscivitch, L., & Topolnytsky, L. (2002). Affective, continuance, and normative commitment to the organization: A meta-analysis of antecedents, correlates, and consequences. *Journal of Vocational Behavior, 61*, 20–52; Organ, D. W., & Ryan, K. (1995). A meta-analytic review of attitudinal and dispositional predictors of organizational citizenship behavior. *Personnel Psychology, 48*, 775–802; Randall, D. M. (1990). The consequences of organizational commitment: Methodological investigation. *Journal of Organizational Behavior, 11*, 361–378; Scott, K. D., & Taylor, G. S. (1985). An examination of conflicting findings on the relationship between job satisfaction and absenteeism: A meta-analysis. *Academy of Management Journal, 28*, 599–612; Tait, M., Padgett, M. Y., & Baldwin, T. T. (1989). Job and life satisfaction: A reevaluation of the strength of the relationship and gender effects as a function of the date of the study. *Journal of Applied Psychology, 74*, 502–507; Tett, R. P., & Meyer, J. P. (1993). Job satisfaction, organizational commitment, turnover intentions, and turnover: Path analyses based on meta-analytic findings. *Personnel Psychology, 46*, 259–293; Zimmerman, R. D. (2008). Understanding the impact of personality traits on individuals' turnover decisions: A meta-analytic path model. *Personnel Psychology, 61*, 309–348.

16. Harter, J. K., Schmidt, F. L., & Hayes, T. L. (2002). Business-unit-level relationship between employee satisfaction, employee engagement, and business outcomes: A meta-analysis. *Journal of Applied Psychology, 87*, 268–279.

17. Kuncel, N. R., Hezlett, S. A., & Ones, D. S. (2004). Academic performance, career potential, creativity, and job performance: Can one construct predict them all? *Journal of Personality and Social Psychology, 86*, 148–161.

18. Bertua, C., Anderson, N., & Salgado, J. F. (2005). The predictive validity of cognitive ability tests: A UK meta-analysis. *Journal of Occupational and Organizational Psychology, 78*, 387–409; Kuncel, N. R., Hezlett, S. A., & Ones, D. S. (2004). Academic performance, career potential, creativity, and job performance: Can one construct predict them all? *Journal of Personality and Social Psychology, 86*, 148–161; Salgado, J. F., Anderson, N., Moscoso, S., Bertua, C., de Fruyt, F., & Rolland, J. P. (2003). A meta-analytic study of general mental ability validity for different occupations in the European community. *Journal of Applied Psychology, 88*, 1068–1081; Schmidt, F. L., & Hunter, J. (2004). General mental ability of the world of work: Occupational attainment and job performance. *Journal of Personality and Social Psychology, 86*(1), 162–173; Vinchur, A. J., Schippmann, J. S., Switzer, F. S., & Roth, P. L. (1998). A meta-analytic review of predictors of job performance for salespeople. *Journal of Applied Psychology, 83*, 586–597.

19. Colquitt, J. A., Conlon, D. E., Wesson, M. J., Porter, C. O. L. H., & Ng, K. Y. (2001). Justice at the millennium: A meta-analytic review of 25 years of organizational justice research. *Journal of Applied Psychology, 86*, 425–445; Colquitt, J. A., Scott, B. A., & LePine, J. A. (2007). Trust, trustworthiness, and trust propensity; A meta-analytic test of their unique relationships with risk taking and job performance. *Journal of Applied Psychology, 92*, 909–927; Podsakoff, P. M., MacKenzie, S. B., & Bommer, W. H. (1996). Meta-analysis of the relationships between Kerr and Jermier's substitutes for leadership and employee job attitudes, role perceptions, and performance. *Journal of Applied Psychology, 81*, 380–399.

20. Gilboa, S., Shirom, A., Fried, Y., & Cooper, C. (2008). A meta-analysis of work demand stressors and job performance: Examining main and moderating effects. *Personnel Psychology, 61*, 227–271.

21. Financial stress: The latest worker risk. (2008). *HR Focus, 85*(6), 12.

22. Judge, T. A., Thoresen, C. J., Bono, J. E., & Patton, G. T. (2001). The job satisfaction—job performance relationship: A qualitative and quantitative review. *Journal of Applied Psychology, 127*, 376–407.

23. Barrick, M. R., & Mount, M. K. (1991). The Big Five personality dimensions and job performance: A meta-analysis. *Personnel Psychology, 44*, 1–26; Dudley, N. M., Orvis, K. A., Lebiecki, J. E., & Cortina, J. M. (2006). A meta-analytic investigation of conscientiousness in the prediction of job performance: Examining the intercorrelations and the incremental validity of narrow traits. *Journal of Applied Psychology, 91*, 40–57; Vinchur, A. J., Schippmann, J. S., Switzer, F. S., & Roth, P. L. (1998). A meta-analytic review of predictors of job performance for salespeople. *Journal of Applied Psychology, 83*, 586–597.

24. Cohen-Charash, Y., & Spector, P. E. (2001). The role of justice in organizations: A meta-analysis. *Organizational Behavior and Human Decision Processes, 86*, 278–321; Colquitt, J. A., Conlon, D. E., Wesson, M. J., Porter, C. O. L. H., & Ng, K. Y. (2001). Justice at the millennium: A meta-analytic review of 25 years of organizational justice research. *Journal of Applied Psychology, 86*, 425–445; Colquitt, J. A., Scott, B. A., & LePine, J. A. (2007). Trust, trustworthiness, and trust propensity: A meta-analytic test of their unique relationships with risk taking and job performance. *Journal of Applied Psychology, 92*, 909–927; Fassina, N. E., Jones, D. A., & Uggerslev, K. L. (2008). Relationship clean-up time: Using meta-analysis and path analysis to clarify relationships among job satisfaction, perceived fairness, and citizenship behaviors. *Journal of Management, 34*, 161–188; Hoffman, B. J., Blair, C. A., Meriac, J. P., & Woehr, D. J. (2007). Expanding the criterion domain? A quantitative review of the OCB literature. *Journal of Applied Psychology, 92*, 555–566; Ilies, R., Nahrgang, J. D., & Morgeson, F. P. (2007). Leader-member exchange and citizenship behaviors: A meta-analysis. *Journal of Applied Psychology, 92*, 269–277; LePine, J. A., Erez, A., & Johnson, D. E. (2002). The nature and dimensionality of organizational citizenship behavior: A critical review and meta-analysis. *Journal of Applied Psychology, 87*, 52–65; Organ, D. W., & Ryan, K. (1995). A meta-analytic review of attitudinal and dispositional predictors of organizational citizenship behavior. *Personnel Psychology, 48*, 775–802; Podsakoff, P. M., MacKenzie, S. B., & Bommer, W. H. (1996). Meta-analysis of the relationships between Kerr and Jermier's substitutes for leadership and employee job attitudes, role perceptions, and performance. *Journal of Applied Psychology, 81*, 380–399; Riketta, M., & Van Dick, R. (2005). Foci of attachment in organizations: A meta-analytic comparison of the strength and correlates of workgroup versus organizational identification and commitment. *Journal of Vocational Behavior, 67*, 490–510.

25. Borman, W. C., Penner, L. A., Allen, T. D., & Motowidlo, S. J. (2001). Personality predictors of citizenship performance. *International Journal of Selection and Assessment, 9*, 52–69; Dalal, R. S. (2005). A meta-analysis of the relationship between organizational citizenship behavior and counterproductive work behavior. *Journal of Applied Psychology, 90*, 1241–1255; Diefendorff, J. M., Brown, D. J., Kamin, A. M., & Lord, R. G. (2002). Examining the roles of job involvement and work centrality in predicting organizational citizenship behaviors and job performance. *Journal of Organizational Behavior, 23*, 93–108; Organ, D. W., & Ryan, K. (1995). A meta-analytic review of attitudinal and dispositional predictors of organizational citizenship behavior. *Personnel Psychology, 48*, 775–802.

26. Dalal, R. S. (2005). A meta-analysis of the relationship between organizational citizenship behavior and counterproductive work behavior. *Journal of Applied Psychology, 90*, 1241–1255; Diefendorff, J. M., Brown, D. J., Kamin, A. M., & Lord, R. G. (2002). Examining the roles of job involvement and work centrality in predicting organizational citizenship behaviors and job performance. *Journal of Organizational Behavior, 23*, 93–108; Hoffman, B. J., Blair, C. A., Meriac, J. P., & Woehr, D. J. (2007). Expanding the criterion domain? A quantitative review of the OCB literature. *Journal of Applied Psychology, 92*, 555–566; LePine, J. A., Erez, A., & Johnson, D. E. (2002). The nature and dimensionality of organizational citizenship behavior: A critical review and meta-analysis. *Journal of Applied Psychology, 87*, 52–65; Organ, D. W., & Ryan, K. (1995). A meta-analytic review of attitudinal and dispositional predictors of organizational citizenship behavior. *Personnel Psychology, 48*, 775–802; Riketta, M. (2002). Attitudinal organizational commitment and job performance: A meta-analysis. *Journal of Organizational Behavior, 23*, 257–266; Riketta, M., & Van Dick, R. (2005). Foci of attachment in organizations: A meta-analytic comparison of the strength and correlates of workgroup versus organizational identification and commitment. *Journal of Vocational Behavior, 67*, 490–510.

27. Ng, T. W. H., & Feldman, D. C. (2008). The relationship of age to ten dimensions of job performance. *Journal of Applied Psychology, 93*, 392–423.

28. Conlin, M. (2007, November 12). Shirking working: The war on hooky. *Business Week, 4058*, 72–75; Gale, S. F. (2003). Sickened by the cost of absenteeism, companies look for solutions. *Workforce Management, 82*(9), 72–75.

29. Farrell, D., & Stamm, C. L. (1988). Meta-analysis of the correlates of employee absence. *Human Relations, 41*, 211–227; Martocchio, J. J., Harrison, D. A., & Berkson, H. (2000). Connections between lower back pain, interventions, and absence from work: A time-based meta-analysis. *Personnel Psychology, 53*, 595–624.

30. Parks, K. M., & Steelman, L. A. (2008). *Journal of Occupational and Organizational Psychology, 13*, 58–68.

31. Cole, C. L. (2002). Sick of absenteeism? Get rid of sick days. *Workforce, 81*(9), 56–61; Conlin, M. (2007, November 12). Shirking working: The war on hooky. *Business Week, 4058*, 72–75; Baltes, B. B., Briggs, T. E., Huff, J. W., Wright, J. A., & Neuman, G. A. (1999). Flexible and compressed workweek schedules: A meta-analysis of their effects on work-related criteria. *Journal of Applied Psychology, 84*, 496–513.

32. Farrell, D., & Stamm, C. L. (1988). Meta-analysis of the correlates of employee absence. *Human Relations, 41*, 211–227; Hackett, R. D. (1989). Work attitudes and employee absenteeism: A synthesis of the literature. *Journal of Occupational Psychology, 62*, 235–248; Scott, K. D., & Taylor, G. S. (1985). An examination of conflicting findings on the relationship between job satisfaction and absenteeism: A meta-analysis. *Academy of Management Journal, 28*, 599–612.

33. Martocchio, J. J. (1989). Age-related differences in employee absenteeism: A meta-analysis. *Psychology and Aging, 4*, 409–414; Ng, T. W. H., & Feldman, D. C. (2008). The relationship of age to ten dimensions of job performance. *Journal of Applied Psychology, 93*, 392–423.

34. Williams, C. R., & Livingstone, L. P. (1994). Another look at the relationship between performance and voluntary turnover. *Academy of Management Journal, 37*, 269–298.

35. Carsten, J. M., & Spector, P. E. (1987). Unemployment, job satisfaction, and employee turnover: A meta-analytic test of the Muchinsky model. *Journal of Applied Psychology, 72*, 374–381; Cohen, A. (1991). Career stage as a moderator of the relationships between organizational commitment and its outcomes: A meta-analysis. *Journal of Occupational Psychology, 64*, 253–268; Cohen, A. (1993). Organizational commitment and turnover: A meta-analysis. *Academy of Management Journal, 36*, 1140–1157; Cohen, A., & Hudecek, N. (1993). Organizational commitment—turnover relationship across occupational groups: A meta-analysis. *Group & Organization Management, 18*, 188–213; Griffeth, R. W., Hom, P. W., & Gaertner, S. (2000). A meta-analysis of antecedents and correlates of employee turnover: Update, moderator tests, and research implications for the next millennium. *Journal of Management, 26*, 463–488; Hom, P. W., Caranikas-Walker, F., Prussia, G. E., & Griffeth, R. W. (1992). A meta-analytical structural equations analysis of a model of employee turnover. *Journal of Applied Psychology, 77*, 890–909; Karlgaard, R. (2006). Who wants to be public? *Forbes Asia, 2*(17), 22; Meyer, J. P., Stanley, D. J., Herscivitch, L., & Topolnytsky, L. (2002). Affective, continuance, and normative commitment to the organization: A meta-analysis of antecedents, correlates, and consequences. *Journal of Vocational Behavior, 61*, 20–52; Steel, R. P., & Ovalle, N. K. (1984). A review and meta-analysis of research on the relationship between behavioral intentions and employee turnover. *Journal of Applied Psychology, 69*, 673–686; Tett, R. P., & Meyer, J. P. (1993). Job satisfaction, organizational commitment, turnover intentions, and turnover: Path analyses based on meta-analytic findings. *Personnel Psychology, 46*, 259–293.

36. Badal, J. (2006, July 24). "Career path" programs help retain workers. *Wall Street Journal*, p. B1; Griffeth, R. W., Hom, P. W., & Gaertner, S. (2000). A meta-analysis of antecedents and correlates of employee turnover: Update, moderator tests, and research implications for the next millennium. *Journal of Management, 26*, 463–488; Podsakoff, N. P., LePine, J. A., & LePine, M. A. (2007). Differential challenge stressor-hindrance stressor relationships with job attitudes, turnover intentions, turnover, and withdrawal behavior: A meta-analysis. *Journal of Applied Psychology, 92*, 438–454.

37. Salgado, J. F. (2002). The Big Five personality dimensions and counterproductive behaviors. *International Journal of Selection and Assessment, 10*, 117–125; Zimmerman, R. D. (2008). Understanding the impact of personality traits on individuals' turnover decisions: A meta-analytic path model. *Personnel Psychology, 61*, 309–348.

38. Cohen, A. (1991). Career stage as a moderator of the relationships between organizational commitment and its outcomes: A meta-analysis. *Journal of Occupational Psychology, 64*, 253–268; Cohen, A. (1993). Organizational commitment and turnover: A meta-analysis. *Academy of Management Journal, 36*, 1140–1157; Ebeling, A. (2007). Corporate moneyball. *Forbes, 179*(9), 102–103.

39. Leung, A. S. M. (2008). Matching ethical work climate to in-role and extra-role behaviors in a collectivist work-setting. *Journal of Business Ethics, 79*, 43–55; Mulki, J. P., Jaramillo, F., & Locander, W. B. (2006). Effects of ethical climate and supervisory trust on salesperson's job attitudes and intentions to quit. *Journal of Personal Selling & Sales Management, 26*, 19–26; Valentine, S., Greller, M. M., & Richtermeyer, S. B. (2006). Employee job response as a function of ethical context and perceived organization support. *Journal of Business Research, 59*, 582–588.

40. Somers, M. J., & Casal, J. C. (1994). Organizational commitment and whistle-blowing: A test of the reformer and the organization man hypotheses. *Group & Organization Management, 19*, 270–284.

41. Crossen, B. R. (1993). Managing employee unethical behavior without invading individual privacy. *Journal of Business and Psychology, 8*, 227–243.

42. Robert, C., Probst, T. M., Martocchio, J. J., Drasgow, F., & Lawler, J. J. (2000). Empowerment and continuous improvement in the United States, Mexico, Poland, and India: Predicting fit on the basis of the dimensions of power distance and individualism. *Journal of Applied Psychology, 85*, 643–658; Spector, P. E., Allen, T. D., Poelmans, S. A., Lapierre, L. M., & Cooper, C. L., O'Driscoll, M., et al. (2007). Cross-national differences in relationships of work demands, job satisfaction, and turnover intentions with work-family conflict. *Personnel Psychology, 60*, 805–835.

43. Johns, G., & Xie, J. L. (1998). Perceptions of absence from work: People's Republic of China versus Canada. *Journal of Applied Psychology, 83*, 515–530; Lam, S. S. K., Hui, C., & Law, K. S. (1999). Organizational citizenship behavior: Comparing perspectives of supervisors and subordinates across four international samples. *Journal of Applied Psychology, 84*, 594–601.

CHAPTER 5
Theories of Motivation

LEARNING OBJECTIVES

After reading this chapter, you should be able to do the following:

1. Understand the role of motivation in determining employee performance.
2. Classify the basic needs of employees.
3. Describe how fairness perceptions are determined and consequences of these perceptions.
4. Understand the importance of rewards and punishments.
5. Apply motivation theories to analyze performance problems.

Motivation at Trader Joe's

Trader Joe's, the California-based grocery store, uses a unique blend of pay, recognition, autonomy, and supportive work environment to motivate its employees.

People in Hawaiian T-shirts. Delicious fresh fruits and vegetables. A place where parking is tight and aisles are tiny. A place where you will be unable to find half the things on your list but will go home satisfied. We are, of course, talking about Trader Joe's, a unique grocery store headquartered in California and located in 22 states. By selling store-brand and gourmet foods at affordable prices, this chain created a special niche for itself. Yet the helpful employees who stock the shelves and answer questions are definitely a key part of what makes this store unique and helps it achieve twice the sales of traditional supermarkets.

Shopping here is fun, and chatting with employees is a routine part of this experience. Employees are upbeat and friendly to each other and to customers. If you look lost, there is the definite offer of help. But somehow the friendliness does not seem scripted. Instead, if they see you shopping for big trays of cheese, they might casually inquire if you are having a party and then point to other selections. If they see you chasing your toddler, they are quick to tie a balloon to his wrist. When you ask them if they have any cumin, they get down on their knees to check the back of the aisle, with the attitude of helping a guest that is visiting their home. How does a company make sure its employees look like they enjoy being there to help others?

One of the keys to this puzzle is pay. Trader Joe's sells cheap organic food, but they are not "cheap" when it comes to paying their employees. Employees, including part-timers, are among the best paid in the retail industry. Full-time employees earn an average of $40,150 in their first year and also earn average annual bonuses of $950 with $6,300 in retirement contributions. Store managers' average compensation is $132,000. With these generous benefits and above-market wages and salaries, the company has no difficulty attracting qualified candidates.

But money only partially explains what energizes Trader Joe's employees. They work with people who are friendly and upbeat. The environment is collaborative, so that people fill in for each other and managers pick up the slack when the need arises, including tasks like sweeping the floors. Plus, the company promotes solely from within, making Trader Joe's one of few places in the retail industry where employees can satisfy their career aspirations. Employees are evaluated every 3 months and receive feedback about their performance.

Employees are also given autonomy on the job. They can open a product to have the customers try it and can be honest about their feelings toward different products. They receive on- and off-the job training and are intimately familiar with the products, which enables them to come up with ideas that are taken seriously by upper management. In short, employees love what they do, work with nice people who treat each other well, and are respected by the company. When employees are treated well, it is no wonder they treat their customers well on a daily basis.

Sources: Based on information in Lewis, L. (2005). Trader Joe's adventure. Chicago: Dearborn Trade; McGregor, J., Salter, C., Conley, L., Haley, F., Sacks, D., & Prospero, M. (2004). Customers first. Fast Company, 87, 79–88; Speizer, I. (2004). Shopper's special. Workforce Management, 83, 51–54.

What inspires employees to provide excellent service, market a company's products effectively, or achieve the goals set for them? Answering this question is of utmost importance if we are to understand and manage the work behavior of our peers, subordinates, and even supervisors. Put a different way, if someone is not performing well, what could be the reason?

Job performance is viewed as a function of three factors and is expressed with the equation below.[1] According to this equation, motivation, ability, and environment are the major influences over employee performance.

FIGURE 5.2

Performance is a function of the interaction between an individual's motivation, ability, and environment.

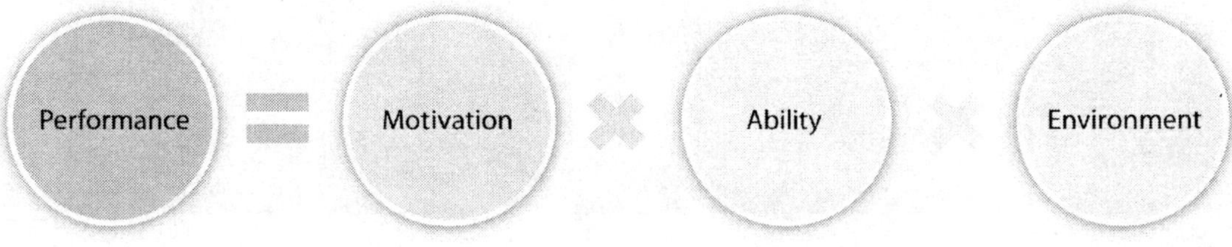

Motivation is one of the forces that lead to performance. **Motivation** is defined as the desire to achieve a goal or a certain performance level, leading to goal-directed behavior. When we refer to someone as being motivated, we mean that the person is trying hard to accomplish a certain task. Motivation is clearly important if someone is to perform well; however, it is not sufficient. **Ability**—or having the skills and knowledge required to perform the job—is also important and is sometimes the key determinant of effectiveness. Finally, **environmental** factors such as having the resources, information, and support one needs to perform well are critical to determine performance. At different times, one of these three factors may be the key to high performance. For example, for an employee sweeping the floor, motivation may be the most important factor that determines performance. In contrast, even the most motivated individual would not be able to successfully design a house without the necessary talent involved in building quality homes. Being motivated is not the same as being a high performer and is not the sole reason why people perform well, but it is nevertheless a key influence over our performance level.

motivation

The desire to achieve a goal or a certain performance level, leading to goal-directed behavior.

ability

Having the skills and knowledge required to perform the job.

environmental

External factors that affect performance.

So what motivates people? Why do some employees try to reach their targets and pursue excellence while others merely show up at work and count the hours? As with many questions involving human beings, the answer is anything but simple. Instead, there are several theories explaining the concept of motivation. We will discuss motivation theories under two categories: need-based theories and process theories.

1. NEED-BASED THEORIES OF MOTIVATION

LEARNING OBJECTIVES

1. **Explain how employees are motivated according to Maslow's hierarchy of needs.**
2. **Explain how the ERG (existence, relatedness, growth) theory addresses the limitations of Maslow's hierarchy.**
3. **Describe the differences among factors contributing to employee motivation and how these differ from factors contributing to dissatisfaction.**
4. **Describe need for achievement, power, and affiliation, and identify how these acquired needs affect work behavior.**

The earliest studies of motivation involved an examination of individual needs. Specifically, early researchers thought that employees try hard and demonstrate goal-driven behavior in order to satisfy needs. For example, an employee who is always walking around the office talking to people may have a need for companionship, and his behavior may be a way of satisfying this need. At the time, researchers developed theories to understand what people need. Four theories may be placed under this category: Maslow's hierarchy of needs, ERG theory, Herzberg's two-factor theory, and McClelland's acquired-needs theory.

1.1 Maslow's Hierarchy of Needs

Abraham Maslow is among the most prominent psychologists of the twentieth century. His hierarchy of needs is an image familiar to most business students and managers. The theory is based on a simple premise: Human beings have needs that are hierarchically ranked.[2] There are some needs that are basic to all human beings, and in their absence nothing else matters. As we satisfy these basic needs, we start looking to satisfy higher order needs. In other words, once a lower level need is satisfied, it no longer serves as a motivator.

FIGURE 5.3 Maslow's Hierarchy of Needs

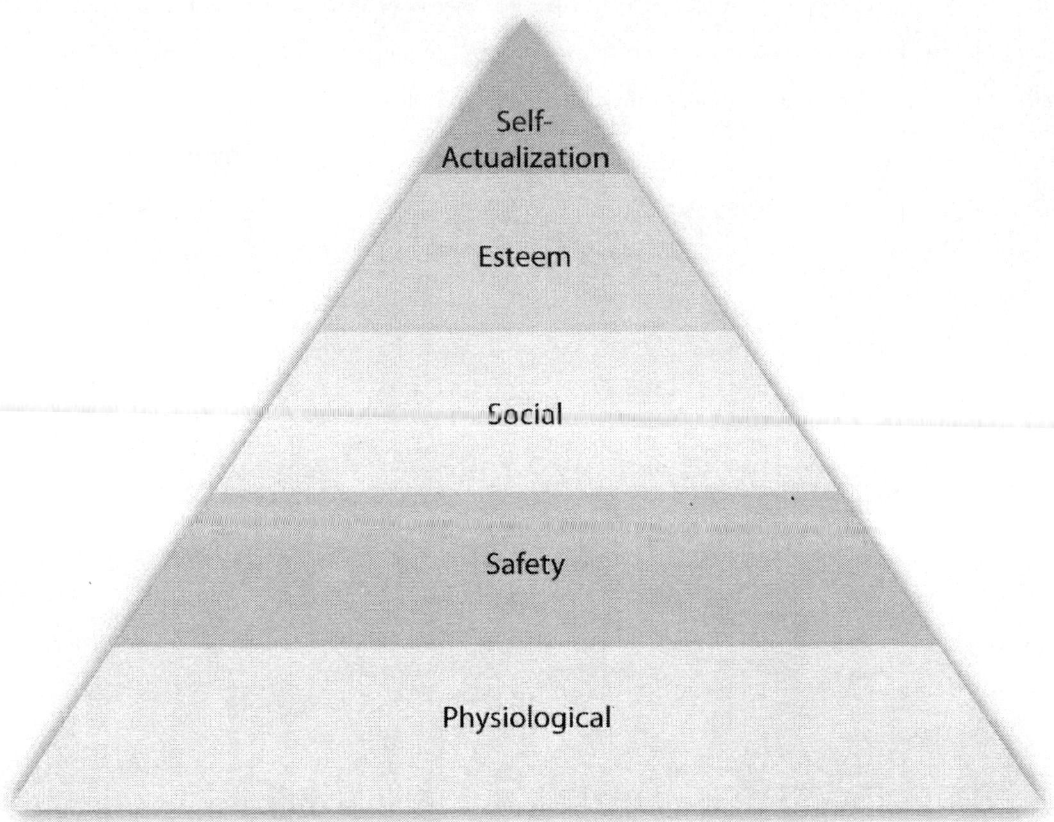

physiological needs

The need for air, food, and water.

safety need

The need to be free from danger and pain.

social needs

The needs of bonding with other human beings, being loved, and forming lasting attachments with them.

esteem needs

The desire to be respected by one's peers, feel important, and be appreciated.

self-actualization need

The need to become all you are capable of becoming.

The most basic of Maslow's needs are **physiological needs**. Physiological needs refer to the need for food, water, and other biological needs. These needs are basic because when they are lacking, the search for them may overpower all other urges. Imagine being very hungry. At that point, all your behavior may be directed at finding food. Once you eat, though, the search for food ceases and the promise of food no longer serves as a motivator. Once physiological needs are satisfied, people tend to become concerned about **safety needs**. Are they free from the threat of danger, pain, or an uncertain future? On the next level up, **social needs** refer to the need to bond with other human beings, be loved, and form lasting attachments with others. In fact, attachments, or lack of them, are associated with our health and well-being.[3] The satisfaction of social needs makes **esteem needs** more salient. Esteem need refers to the desire to be respected by one's peers, feel important, and be appreciated. Finally, at the highest level of the hierarchy, the need for **self-actualization** refers to "becoming all you are capable of becoming." This need manifests itself by the desire to acquire new skills, take on new challenges, and behave in a way that will lead to the attainment of one's life goals.

Maslow was a clinical psychologist, and his theory was not originally designed for work settings. In fact, his theory was based on his observations of individuals in clinical settings; some of the individual components of the theory found little empirical support. One criticism relates to the order in which the needs are ranked. It is possible to imagine that individuals who go hungry and are in fear of their lives might retain strong bonds to others, suggesting a different order of needs. Moreover, researchers failed to support the arguments that once a need is satisfied it no longer serves as a motivator and that only one need is dominant at a given time.[4]

Despite the lack of strong research support, Maslow's theory found obvious applications in business settings. Understanding what people need gives us clues to understanding them. The hierarchy is a systematic way of thinking about the different needs employees may have at any given point and explains different reactions they may have to similar treatment. An employee who is trying to satisfy esteem needs may feel gratified when her supervisor praises an accomplishment. However, another employee who is trying to satisfy social needs may resent being praised by upper management in front of peers if the praise sets the individual apart from the rest of the group.

How can an organization satisfy its employees' various needs? In the long run, physiological needs may be satisfied by the person's paycheck, but it is important to remember that pay may satisfy other needs such as safety and esteem as well. Providing generous benefits that include health insurance and company-sponsored retirement plans, as well as offering a measure of job security, will help satisfy safety needs. Social needs may be satisfied by having a friendly environment and providing a workplace conducive to collaboration and communication with others. Company picnics and other social get-togethers may also be helpful if the majority of employees are motivated primarily by social needs (but may cause resentment if they are not and if they have to sacrifice a Sunday afternoon for a company picnic). Providing promotion opportunities at work, recognizing a person's accomplishments verbally or through more formal reward systems, and conferring job titles that communicate to the employee that one has achieved high status within the organization are among the ways of satisfying esteem needs. Finally, self-actualization needs may be satisfied by the provision of development and growth opportunities on or off the job, as well as by work that is interesting and challenging. By making the effort to satisfy the different needs of each employee, organizations may ensure a highly motivated workforce.

1.2 ERG Theory

FIGURE 5.4

ERG theory includes existence, relatedness, and growth.

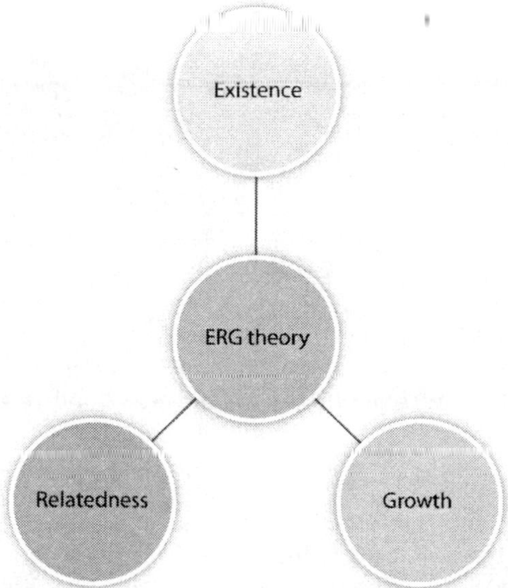

Source: Based on Alderfer, C. P. (1969). An empirical test of a new theory of human needs. Organizational Behavior and Human Performance, 4, 142–175.

ERG theory, developed by Clayton Alderfer, is a modification of Maslow's hierarchy of needs.[5] Instead of the five needs that are hierarchically organized, Alderfer proposed that basic human needs may be grouped under three categories, namely, existence, relatedness, and growth. **Existence** corresponds to Maslow's physiological and safety needs, **relatedness** corresponds to social needs, and **growth** refers to Maslow's esteem and self-actualization.

existence

A need corresponding to Maslow's physiological and safety needs.

relatedness

A need corresponding to Maslow's social needs.

growth

A need referring to Maslow's esteem and self-actualization.

ERG theory's main contribution to the literature is its relaxation of Maslow's assumptions. For example, ERG theory does not rank needs in any particular order and explicitly recognizes that more than one need may operate at a given time. Moreover, the theory has a "frustration-regression" hypothesis suggesting that individuals who are frustrated in their attempts to satisfy one need may regress to another. For example, someone who is frustrated by the growth opportunities in his job and progress toward career goals may regress to relatedness need and start spending more time socializing with coworkers. The implication of this theory is that we need to recognize the multiple needs that may be driving individuals at a given point to understand their behavior and properly motivate them.

1.3 Two-Factor Theory

Frederick Herzberg approached the question of motivation in a different way. By asking individuals what satisfies them on the job and what dissatisfies them, Herzberg came to the conclusion that aspects of the work environment that satisfy employees are very different from aspects that dissatisfy them.[6] Herzberg labeled factors causing dissatisfaction of workers as "hygiene" factors because these factors were part of the context in which the job was performed, as opposed to the job itself. **Hygiene factors**

hygiene factors

Company policies, supervision, working conditions, salary, safety, and security on the job.

included company policies, supervision, working conditions, salary, safety, and security on the job. To illustrate, imagine that you are working in an unpleasant work environment. Your office is too hot in the summer and too cold in the winter. You are being harassed and mistreated. You would certainly be miserable in such a work environment. However, if these problems were solved (your office temperature is just right and you are not harassed at all), would you be motivated? Most likely, you would take the situation for granted. In fact, many factors in our work environment are things that we miss when they are absent but take for granted if they are present.

motivators

Factors that are intrinsic to the job, such as achievement, recognition, interesting work, increased responsibilities, advancement, and growth opportunities.

In contrast, **motivators** are factors that are intrinsic to the job, such as achievement, recognition, interesting work, increased responsibilities, advancement, and growth opportunities. According to Herzberg's research, motivators are the conditions that truly encourage employees to try harder.

FIGURE 5.5

The two-factor theory of motivation includes hygiene factors and motivators.

Hygiene Factors	Motivators
• Company policy	• Achievement
• Supervision and relationships	• Recognition
• Working conditions	• Interesting work
• Salary	• Increased responsibility
• Security	• Advancement and growth

Sources: Based on Herzberg, F., Mausner, B., & Snyderman, B. (1959). The motivation to work. New York: John Wiley and Sons; Herzberg, F. (1965). The motivation to work among Finnish supervisors. Personnel Psychology, 18, 393–402.

Herzberg's research is far from being universally accepted.[7] One criticism relates to the primary research methodology employed when arriving at hygiene versus motivators. When people are asked why they are satisfied, they may attribute the causes of satisfaction to themselves, whereas when explaining what dissatisfies them, they may blame the situation. The classification of the factors as hygiene or motivator is not that simple either. For example, the theory views pay as a hygiene factor. However, pay may have symbolic value by showing employees that they are being recognized for their contributions as well as communicating that they are advancing within the company. Similarly, the quality of supervision or the types of relationships employees form with their supervisors may determine whether they are assigned interesting work, whether they are recognized for their potential, and whether they take on more responsibilities.

Despite its limitations, the theory can be a valuable aid to managers because it points out that improving the environment in which the job is performed goes only so far in motivating employees. Undoubtedly, contextual factors matter because their absence causes dissatisfaction. However, solely focusing on hygiene factors will not be enough, and managers should also enrich jobs by giving employees opportunities for challenging work, greater responsibilities, advancement opportunities, and a job in which their subordinates can feel successful.

1.4 Acquired-Needs Theory

Among the need-based approaches to motivation, David McClelland's acquired-needs theory is the one that has received the greatest amount of support. According to this theory, individuals acquire three types of needs as a result of their life experiences. These needs are the need for achievement, the need for affiliation, and the need for power. All individuals possess a combination of these needs, and the dominant needs are thought to drive employee behavior.

Thematic Apperception Test (TAT)

A test that assesses a person's dominant needs.

McClelland used a unique method called the **Thematic Apperception Test (TAT)** to assess the dominant need.[8] This method entails presenting research subjects an ambiguous picture asking them to write a story based on it. Take a look at the following picture. Who is this person? What is she doing? Why is she doing it? The story you tell about the woman in the picture would then be analyzed by trained experts. The idea is that the stories the photo evokes would reflect how the mind works and what motivates the person.

If the story you come up with contains themes of success, meeting deadlines, or coming up with brilliant ideas, you may be high in need for achievement. Those who have high **need for achievement** have a strong need to be successful. As children, they may be praised for their hard work, which forms the foundations of their persistence.[9] As adults, they are preoccupied with doing things better than they did in the past. These individuals are constantly striving to improve their performance. They relentlessly focus on goals, particularly stretch goals that are challenging in nature.[10] They are particularly suited to positions such as sales, where there are explicit goals, feedback is immediately available, and their effort often leads to success. In fact, they are more attracted to organizations that are merit-based and reward performance rather than seniority. They also do particularly well as entrepreneurs, scientists, and engineers.[11]

FIGURE 5.6

The type of story you tell by looking at this picture may give away the dominant need that motivates you.

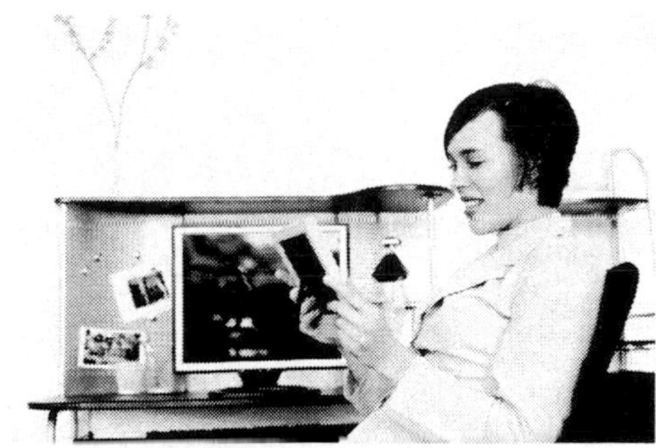

© 2010 Jupiterimages Corporation

Are individuals who are high in need for achievement effective managers? Because of their success in lower level jobs where their individual contributions matter the most, those with high need for achievement are often promoted to higher level positions.[12] However, a high need for achievement has significant disadvantages in management positions. Management involves getting work done by motivating others. When a salesperson is promoted to be a sales manager, the job description changes from actively selling to recruiting, motivating, and training salespeople. Those who are high in need for achievement may view managerial activities such as coaching, communicating, and meeting with subordinates as a waste of time and may neglect these aspects of their jobs. Moreover, those high in need for achievement enjoy doing things themselves and may find it difficult to delegate any meaningful authority to their subordinates. These individuals often micromanage, expecting others to approach tasks a particular way, and may become overbearing bosses by expecting everyone to display high levels of dedication.[13]

need for achievement

Having a strong need to be successful.

If the story you created in relation to the picture you are analyzing contains elements of making plans to be with friends or family, you may have a high need for affiliation. Individuals who have a high **need for affiliation** want to be liked and accepted by others. When given a choice, they prefer to interact with others and be with friends.[14] Their emphasis on harmonious interpersonal relationships may be an advantage in jobs and occupations requiring frequent interpersonal interaction, such as a social worker or teacher. In managerial positions, a high need for affiliation may again serve as a disadvantage because these individuals tend to be overly concerned about how they are perceived by others. They may find it difficult to perform some aspects of a manager's job such as giving employees critical feedback or disciplining poor performers. Thus, the work environment may be characterized by mediocrity and may even lead to high performers leaving the team.

need for affiliation

Wanting to be liked and accepted by others.

Finally, if your story contains elements of getting work done by influencing other people or desiring to make an impact on the organization, you may have a high need for power. Those with a high **need for power** want to influence others and control their environment. A need for power may in fact be a destructive element in relationships with colleagues if it takes the form of seeking and using power for one's own good and prestige. However, when it manifests itself in more altruistic forms such as changing the way things are done so that the work environment is more positive, or negotiating more resources for one's department, it tends to lead to positive outcomes. In fact, the need for power is viewed as an important trait for effectiveness in managerial and leadership positions.[15]

need for power

Wanting to influence others and control their environment.

McClelland's theory of acquired needs has important implications for the motivation of employees. Managers need to understand the dominant needs of their employees to be able to motivate them. While people who have a high need for achievement may respond to goals, those with a high need for power may attempt to gain influence over those they work with, and individuals high in their need for affiliation may be motivated to gain the approval of their peers and supervisors. Finally, those who have a high drive for success may experience difficulties in managerial positions, and making them aware of common pitfalls may increase their effectiveness.

KEY TAKEAWAY

Need-based theories describe motivated behavior as individuals' efforts to meet their needs. According to this perspective, the manager's job is to identify what people need and make the work environment a means of satisfying these needs. Maslow's hierarchy describes five categories of basic human needs, including physiological, safety, social, esteem, and self-actualization needs. These needs are hierarchically ranked, and as a lower level need is satisfied, it no longer serves as a motivator. ERG theory is a modification of Maslow's hierarchy, in which the five needs are collapsed into three categories (existence, relatedness, and growth). The theory recognizes that when employees are frustrated while attempting to satisfy higher level needs, they may regress. The two-factor theory differentiates between factors that make people dissatisfied on the job (hygiene factors) and factors that truly motivate employees (motivators). Finally, acquired-needs theory argues that individuals possess stable and dominant motives to achieve, acquire power, or affiliate with others. The type of need that is dominant will drive behavior. Each of these theories explains characteristics of a work environment that motivates employees. These theories paved the way to process-based theories that explain the mental calculations employees make to decide how to behave.

EXERCISES

1. Many managers assume that if an employee is not performing well, the reason must be a lack of motivation. Do you think this reasoning is accurate? What is the problem with the assumption?
2. Review Maslow's hierarchy of needs. Do you agree with the particular ranking of employee needs?
3. How can an organization satisfy employee needs that are included in Maslow's hierarchy?
4. Which motivation theory have you found to be most useful in explaining why people behave in a certain way? Why?
5. Review the hygiene and motivators in the two-factor theory of motivation. Do you agree with the distinction between hygiene factors and motivators? Are there any hygiene factors that you would consider to be motivators?
6. A friend of yours demonstrates the traits of achievement motivation: This person is competitive, requires frequent and immediate feedback, and enjoys accomplishing things and doing things better than she did before. She has recently been promoted to a managerial position and seeks your advice. What would you tell her?

2. PROCESS-BASED THEORIES

LEARNING OBJECTIVES

1. **Explain how employees evaluate the fairness of reward distributions.**
2. **Describe the three types of fairness that affect employee attitudes and behaviors.**
3. **List the three questions individuals consider when deciding whether to put forth effort at work.**
4. **Describe how managers can use learning and reinforcement principles to motivate employees.**

A separate stream of research views motivation as something more than action aimed at satisfying a need. Instead, process-based theories view motivation as a rational process. Individuals analyze their environment, develop thoughts and feelings, and react in certain ways. Process theories attempt to explain the thought processes of individuals who demonstrate motivated behavior. Under this category, we will review equity theory, expectancy theory, and reinforcement theory.

2.1 Equity Theory

Imagine that you are paid $10 an hour working as an office assistant. You have held this job for 6 months. You are very good at what you do, you come up with creative ways to make things easier around you, and you are a good colleague who is willing to help others. You stay late when necessary and are flexible if requested to change hours. Now imagine that you found out they are hiring another employee who is going to work with you, who will hold the same job title, and who will perform the same type of tasks. This particular person has more advanced computer skills, but it is unclear whether these will be used on the job. The starting pay for this person will be $14 an hour. How would you feel?

Would you be as motivated as before, going above and beyond your duties? How would you describe what you would be feeling?

If your reaction to this scenario is along the lines of "this would be unfair," your behavior may be explained using equity theory.[16] According to this theory, individuals are motivated by a sense of fairness in their interactions. Moreover, our sense of fairness is a result of the social comparisons we make. Specifically, we compare our inputs and outcomes with other people's inputs and outcomes. We perceive fairness if we believe that the input-to-outcome ratio we are bringing into the situation is similar to the input-to-outcome ratio of a comparison person, or a **referent**. Perceptions of inequity create tension within us and drive us to action that will reduce perceived inequity.

FIGURE 5.7

Equity is determined by comparing one's input-outcome ratio with the input-outcome ratio of a referent. When the two ratios are equal, equity exists.

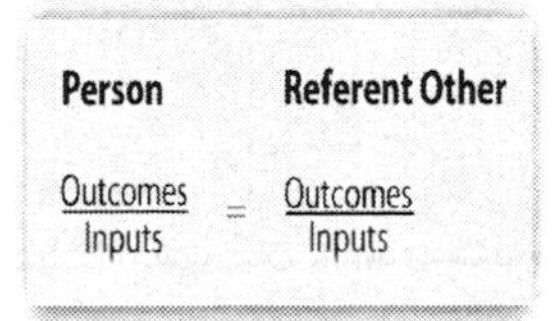

Source: Based on Adams, J. S. (1965). Inequity in social exchange. In L. Berkowitz (Ed.), Advances in experimental social psychology: Vol. 2 (pp. 267–299). New York: Academic Press.

What Are Inputs and Outcomes?

Inputs are the contributions people feel they are making to the environment. In the previous example, the person's hard work; loyalty to the organization; amount of time with the organization; and level of education, training, and skills may have been relevant inputs. Outcomes are the perceived rewards someone can receive from the situation. For the hourly wage employee in our example, the $10 an hour pay rate was a core outcome. There may also be other, more peripheral outcomes, such as acknowledgment or preferential treatment from a manager. In the prior example, however, the person may reason as follows: I have been working here for 6 months. I am loyal, and I perform well (inputs). I am paid $10 an hour for this (outcomes). The new person does not have any experience here (referent's inputs) but will be paid $14 an hour. This situation is unfair.

We should emphasize that equity perceptions develop as a result of a subjective process. Different people may look at the same situation and perceive different levels of equity. For example, another person may look at the same scenario and decide that the situation is fair because the newcomer has computer skills and the company is paying extra for those skills.

Who Is the Referent?

referent

A person we compare ourselves to in equity theory.

The referent other may be a specific person as well as a category of people. Referents should be comparable to us—otherwise the comparison is not meaningful. It would be pointless for a student worker to compare himself to the CEO of the company, given the differences in the nature of inputs and outcomes. Instead, individuals may compare themselves to someone performing similar tasks within the same organization or, in the case of a CEO, a different organization.

Reactions to Unfairness

The theory outlines several potential reactions to perceived inequity. Oftentimes, the situation may be dealt with perceptually by *altering our perceptions of our own or the referent's inputs and outcomes*. For example, we may justify the situation by downplaying our own inputs (I don't really work very hard on this job), valuing our outcomes more highly (I am gaining valuable work experience, so the situation is not that bad), distorting the other person's inputs (the new hire really is more competent than I am and deserves to be paid more), or distorting the other person's outcomes (she gets $14 an hour but will have to work with a lousy manager, so the situation is not unfair). Another option would be to *have the referent increase inputs*. If the other person brings more to the situation, getting more out of the situation would be fair. If that person can be made to work harder or work on more complicated tasks, equity would be achieved. The person experiencing a perceived inequity may also *reduce inputs or attempt to increase outcomes*. If the lower paid person puts forth less effort, the perceived inequity would be reduced. Research shows that people who perceive inequity reduce their work performance or reduce the quality of their inputs.[17] Increasing one's outcomes can be achieved through legitimate means such as negotiating a pay raise. At the same time, research shows that those feeling inequity sometimes resort to stealing to balance the scales.[18] Other options include *changing the comparison person* (e.g., others doing similar work in different organizations are paid only minimum wage) and *leaving the situation* by quitting.[19] Sometimes it may be necessary to consider taking legal action as a potential outcome of perceived inequity. For example, if an employee finds out the main reason behind a pay gap is gender related, the person may react to the situation by taking legal action because sex discrimination in pay is illegal in the United States.

TABLE 5.1 Potential Responses to Inequity

Reactions to inequity	Example
Distort perceptions	Changing one's thinking to believe that the referent actually is more skilled than previously thought
Increase referent's inputs	Encouraging the referent to work harder
Reduce own input	Deliberately putting forth less effort at work. Reducing the quality of one's work
Increase own outcomes	Negotiating a raise for oneself or using unethical ways of increasing rewards such as stealing from the company
Change referent	Comparing oneself to someone who is worse off
Leave the situation	Quitting one's job
Seek legal action	Suing the company or filing a complaint if the unfairness in question is under legal protection

Source: Based on research findings reported in Carrell, M. R., & Dittrich, J. E. (1978). Equity theory: The recent literature, methodological considerations, and new directions. Academy of Management Review, 3, 202–210; Goodman, P. S., & Friedman, A. (1971). An examination of Adams's theory of inequity. Administrative Science Quarterly, 16, 271–288; Greenberg, J. (1993). Stealing in the name of justice: Informational and interpersonal moderators of theft reactions to underpayment inequity. Organizational Behavior and Human Decision Processes, 54, 81–103; Schmidt, D. R., & Marwell, G. (1972). Withdrawal and reward reallocation as responses to inequity. Journal of Experimental Social Psychology, 8, 207–211.

Overpayment Inequity

What would you do if you felt you were over-rewarded? In other words, how would you feel if you were the new employee in our student-worker scenario? Originally, equity theory proposed that over-rewarded individuals would experience guilt and would increase their effort to restore perceptions of equity. However, research does not provide support for this argument. Instead, it seems that individuals experience less distress as a result of being over-rewarded.[20] It is not hard to imagine that individuals find perceptual ways to deal with a situation like this, such as believing they have more skills and bring more to the situation compared to the referent person. Therefore, research does not support equity theory's predictions with respect to people who are overpaid.[21]

Individual Differences in Reactions to Inequity

equity sensitivity

A personality trait that explains different reactions to inequity.

benevolents

Individuals who give without waiting to receive much in return.

entitleds

Individuals who expect to receive a lot without giving much in return.

So far, we have assumed that once people feel a situation is inequitable, they will be motivated to react. However, does inequity disturb everyone equally? Researchers have identified a personality trait that explains different reactions to inequity and named this trait as **equity sensitivity**.[22] Equity-sensitive individuals expect to maintain equitable relationships, and they experience distress when they feel they are over-rewarded or under-rewarded. At the same time, there are some individuals who are **benevolents**, those who give without waiting to receive much in return, and **entitleds**, who expect to receive substantial compensation for relatively little input. Therefore, the theory is more useful in explaining the behavior of equity-sensitive individuals, and organizations will need to pay particular attention to how these individuals view their relationships.

Fairness Beyond Equity: Procedural and Interactional Justice

distributive justice

The degree to which the outcomes received from the organization are fair.

Equity theory looks at perceived fairness as a motivator. However, the way equity theory defines fairness is limited to fairness of rewards. Starting in the 1970s, research on workplace fairness began taking a broader view of justice. Equity theory deals with outcome fairness, and therefore it is considered to be a distributive justice theory. **Distributive justice** refers to the degree to which the outcomes received from the organization are perceived to be fair. Two other types of fairness have been identified: procedural justice and interactional justice.

Let's assume that you just found out you are getting a promotion. Clearly, this is an exciting outcome and comes with a pay raise, increased responsibilities, and prestige. If you feel you deserve to be promoted, you would perceive high distributive justice (your getting the promotion is fair). However, you later found out upper management picked your name out of a hat! What would you feel? You might still like the outcome but feel that the decision-making process was unfair. If so, you are describing feelings of procedural justice. **Procedural justice** refers to the degree to which fair decision-making procedures are used to arrive at a decision. People do not care only about reward fairness. They also expect decision-making processes to be fair. In fact, research shows that employees care about the procedural justice of many organizational decisions, including layoffs, employee selection, surveillance of employees, performance appraisals, and pay decisions.[23] People also tend to care more about procedural justice in situations in which they do not get the outcome they feel they deserve.[24] If you did not get the promotion and later discovered that management chose the candidate by picking names out of a hat, how would you feel? This may be viewed as adding insult to injury. When people do not get the rewards they want, they tend to hold management responsible if procedures are not fair.[25]

FIGURE 5.8 Dimensions of Organizational Justice

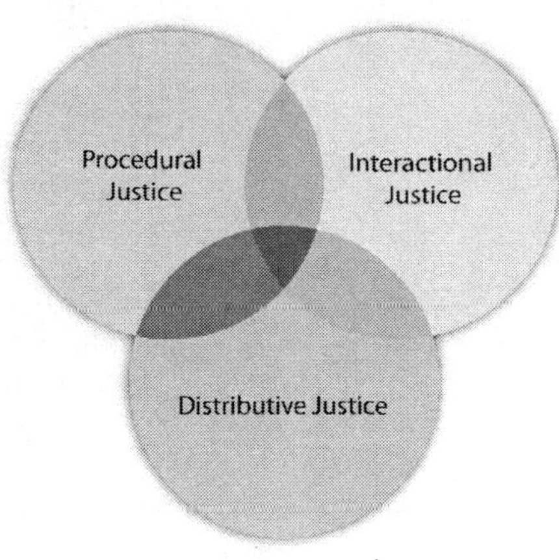

Why do employees care about procedural justice? There are three potential reasons.[26] First, people tend to believe that fairness is an end in itself and it is the right thing to do. Second, fair processes guarantee future rewards. If your name was picked out of a hat, you have no control over the process, and there is no guarantee that you will get future promotions. If the procedures are fair, you are more likely to believe that things will work out in the future. Third, fairness communicates that the organization values its employees and cares about their well-being.

procedural justice

The degree to which fair decision-making procedures are used to arrive at a decision.

Research has identified many ways of achieving procedural justice. For example, giving employees *advance notice* before laying them off, firing them, or disciplining them is perceived as fair.[27] Advance notice helps employees get ready for the changes facing them or gives them an opportunity to change their behavior before it is too late. *Allowing employees voice in decision making* is also important.[28] When designing a performance-appraisal system or implementing a reorganization, it may be a good idea to ask people for their input because it increases perceptions of fairness. Even when it is not possible to have employees participate, providing *explanations* to employees is helpful in fostering procedural justice.[29] Finally, people expect *consistency* in treatment.[30] If one person is given extra time when taking a test while another is not, individuals would perceive decision making as unfair.

Now let's imagine the moment your boss told you that you are getting a promotion. Your manager's exact words were, "Yes, we are giving you the promotion. The job is so simple that we thought even you can handle it." Now what is your reaction? The feeling of unfairness you may now feel is explained by interactional justice. **Interactional justice** refers to the degree to which people are treated with respect, kindness, and dignity in interpersonal interactions. We expect to be treated with dignity by our peers, supervisors, and customers. When the opposite happens, we feel angry. Even when faced with negative outcomes such as a pay cut, being treated with dignity and respect serves as a buffer and alleviates our stress.[31]

interactional justice

The degree to which people are treated with respect, kindness, and dignity in interpersonal interactions.

OB Toolbox: Be a Fair Person!

- *When distributing rewards, make sure you pay attention to different contribution levels of employees.* Treating everyone equally could be unfair if they participated and contributed at different levels. People who are more qualified, skilled, or those who did more than others expect to receive a greater share of rewards.
- *Sometimes you may have to disregard people's contributions to distribute certain rewards.* Some rewards or privileges may be better distributed equally (e.g., health insurance) or based on the particular employee's needs (such as unpaid leave for health reasons).
- *Pay attention to how you make decisions.* Before making a decision, ask people to give you their opinions if possible. Explain your decisions to people who are affected by it. Before implementing a change, give people advance notice. Enforce rules consistently among employees.
- *Pay attention to how you talk to people.* Treat others the way you want to be treated. Be kind, courteous, and considerate of their feelings.
- *Remember that justice is in the eye of the beholder.* Even when you feel you are being fair, others may not feel the same way, and it is *their* perception that counts. Therefore, pay attention to being perceived as fair.
- *People do not care only about their own justice level.* They also pay attention to how others are treated as well. Therefore, in addition to paying attention to how specific employees feel, creating a sense of justice in the entire organization is important.

Sources: Adapted from ideas in Colquitt, J. A. (2004). Does the justice of the one interact with the justice of the many? Reactions to procedural justice in teams. Journal of Applied Psychology, 89, 633–646; Cropanzano, R., Bowen, D. E., & Gilliland, S. W. (2007). The management of organizational justice. Academy of Management Perspectives, 21, 34–48.

Employers would benefit from paying attention to all three types of justice perceptions. In addition to being the right thing to do, paying attention to justice perceptions leads to outcomes companies care about. Injustice is directly harmful to employees' psychological health and well-being and contributes to stress.[32] High levels of justice create higher levels of employee commitment to organizations, and they are related to higher job performance, higher levels of organizational citizenship (behaviors that are not part of one's job description but help the organization in other ways, such as speaking positively about the company and helping others), and higher levels of customer satisfaction. Conversely, low levels of justice lead to retaliation and support of unionization.[33]

2.2 Expectancy Theory

According to expectancy theory, individual motivation to put forth more or less effort is determined by a rational calculation in which individuals evaluate their situation.[34] According to this theory, individuals ask themselves three questions.

FIGURE 5.9 Summary of Expectancy Theory

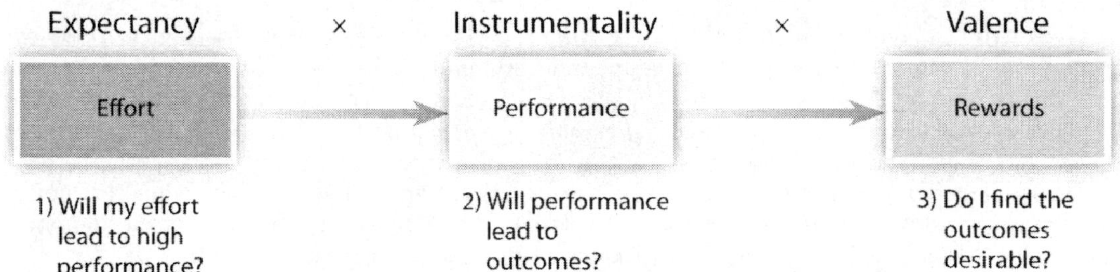

Sources: Based on Porter, L. W., & Lawler, E. E. (1968). Managerial attitudes and performance. Homewood, IL: Irwin; Vroom, V. H. (1964). Work and motivation. New York: Wiley.

expectancy

Whether the person believes that high levels of effort will lead to outcomes of interest such as performance or success.

instrumentality

The degree to which the person believes that performance is related to secondary outcomes such as rewards.

valence

The value of the rewards awaiting the person as a result of performance.

The first question is whether the person believes that high levels of effort will lead to outcomes of interest, such as performance or success. This perception is labeled **expectancy**. For example, do you believe that the effort you put forth in a class is related to performing well in that class? If you do, you are more likely to put forth effort.

The second question is the degree to which the person believes that performance is related to subsequent outcomes, such as rewards. This perception is labeled **instrumentality**. For example, do you believe that getting a good grade in the class is related to rewards such as getting a better job, or gaining approval from your instructor, or from your friends or parents? If you do, you are more likely to put forth effort.

Finally, individuals are also concerned about the value of the rewards awaiting them as a result of performance. The anticipated satisfaction that will result from an outcome is labeled **valence**. For example, do you value getting a better job, or gaining approval from your instructor, friends, or parents? If these outcomes are desirable to you, your expectancy and instrumentality is high, and you are more likely to put forth effort.

Expectancy theory is a well-accepted theory that has received a lot of research attention.[35] It is simple and intuitive. Consider the following example. Let's assume that you are working in the concession stand of a movie theater. You have been selling an average of 100 combos of popcorn and soft drinks a day. Now your manager asks you to increase this number to 300 combos a day. Would you be motivated to try to increase your numbers? Here is what you may be thinking:

- *Expectancy*: Can I do it? If I try harder, can I really achieve this number? Is there a link between how hard I try and whether I reach this goal or not? If you feel that you can achieve this number if you try, you have high expectancy.

- *Instrumentality*: What is in it for me? What is going to happen if I reach 300? What are the outcomes that will follow? Are they going to give me a 2% pay raise? Am I going to be named the salesperson of the month? Am I going to receive verbal praise from my manager? If you believe that performing well is related to certain outcomes, instrumentality is high.
- *Valence*: How do I feel about the outcomes in question? Do I feel that a 2% pay raise is desirable? Do I find being named the salesperson of the month attractive? Do I think that being praised by my manager is desirable? If your answers are yes, valence is positive. In contrast, if you find the outcomes undesirable (you definitely do not want to be named the salesperson of the month because your friends would make fun of you), valence is negative.

If your answers to all three questions are affirmative—you feel that you can do it, you will get an outcome if you do it, and you value the reward—you are more likely to be motivated to put forth more effort toward selling more combos.

As a manager, how can you motivate employees? In fact, managers can influence all three perceptions.[36]

Influencing Expectancy Perceptions

Employees may not believe that their effort leads to high performance for a multitude of reasons. First, they may not have the skills, knowledge, or abilities to successfully perform their jobs. The answer to this problem may be training employees or hiring people who are qualified for the jobs in question. Second, low levels of expectancy may be because employees may feel that something other than effort predicts performance, such as political behaviors on the part of employees. If employees believe that the work environment is not conducive to performing well (resources are lacking or roles are unclear), expectancy will also suffer. Therefore, clearing the path to performance and creating an environment in which employees do not feel restricted will be helpful. Finally, some employees may perceive little connection between their effort and performance level because they have an external locus of control, low self-esteem, or other personality traits that condition them to believe that their effort will not make a difference. In such cases, providing positive feedback and encouragement may help motivate employees.

Influencing Instrumentality Perceptions

Showing employees that their performance is rewarded is going to increase instrumentality perceptions. Therefore, the first step in influencing instrumentality is to connect pay and other rewards to performance using bonuses, award systems, and merit pay. However, this is not always sufficient, because people may not be aware of some of the rewards awaiting high performers. Publicizing any contests or award programs is needed to bring rewards to the awareness of employees. It is also important to highlight that performance, not something else, is being rewarded. For example, if a company has an employee of the month award that is rotated among employees, employees are unlikely to believe that performance is being rewarded. This type of meritless reward system may actually hamper the motivation of the highest performing employees by eroding instrumentality.

Influencing Valence

Employees are more likely to be motivated if they find the reward to be attractive. This process involves managers finding what their employees value. Desirable rewards tend to be fair and satisfy different employees' diverging needs. Ensuring high valence involves getting to know a company's employees. Talking to employees and surveying them about what rewards they find valuable are some methods to gain understanding. Finally, giving employees a choice between multiple rewards may be a good idea to increase valence.

FIGURE 5.10 Ways in Which Managers Can Influence Expectancy, Instrumentality, and Valence

Expectancy	Instrumentality	Valence
- Make sure employees have proper skills, abilities, and knowledge - Ensure that the environment facilitates performance - Provide encouragement to make people believe that their effort makes a difference	- Reward employee performance - Inform people in advance about the rewards - Try to eliminate non-performance influence over rewards	- Find rewards that are desirable to employees - Make sure that the rewards are viewed as fair - Give employees choice over rewards

2.3 Reinforcement Theory

Reinforcement theory is based on the work of Ivan Pavlov on behavioral conditioning and the later work of B. F. Skinner on operant conditioning.[37] According to reinforcement theory, behavior is a function of its outcomes. Imagine that even though no one asked you to, you stayed late and drafted a report. When the manager found out, she was ecstatic and took you out to lunch and thanked you genuinely. The consequences following your good deed were favorable, and therefore you are more likely to demonstrate similar behaviors in the future. In other words, your taking initiative was reinforced. Instead, if your manager had said nothing about it and everyone ignored the sacrifice you made, you are less likely to demonstrate similar behaviors in the future.

Reinforcement theory is based on a simple idea that may be viewed as common sense. Beginning at infancy we learn through reinforcement. If you have observed a small child discovering the environment, you will see reinforcement theory in action. When the child discovers manipulating a faucet leads to water coming out and finds this outcome pleasant, he is more likely to repeat the behavior. If he burns his hand while playing with hot water, the child is likely to stay away from the faucet in the future.

Despite the simplicity of reinforcement, how many times have you seen positive behavior ignored, or worse, negative behavior rewarded? In many organizations, this is a familiar scenario. People go above and beyond the call of duty, yet their actions are ignored or criticized. People with disruptive habits may receive no punishments because the manager is afraid of the reaction the person will give when confronted. Problem employees may even receive rewards such as promotions so they will be transferred to a different location and become someone else's problem. Moreover, it is common for people to be rewarded for the wrong kind of behavior. Steven Kerr has labeled this phenomenon "the folly of rewarding A while hoping for B."[38] For example, a company may make public statements about the importance of quality. Yet, if they choose to reward shipments on time regardless of the amount of defects contained in the shipments, employees are more likely to ignore quality and focus on hurrying the delivery process. Because people learn to repeat their behaviors based on the consequences following their prior activities, managers will need to systematically examine the consequences of employee behavior and make interventions when needed.

Reinforcement Interventions

Reinforcement theory describes four interventions to modify employee behavior. Two of these are methods of increasing the frequency of desired behaviors, while the remaining two are methods of reducing the frequency of undesired behaviors.

FIGURE 5.11 Reinforcement Methods

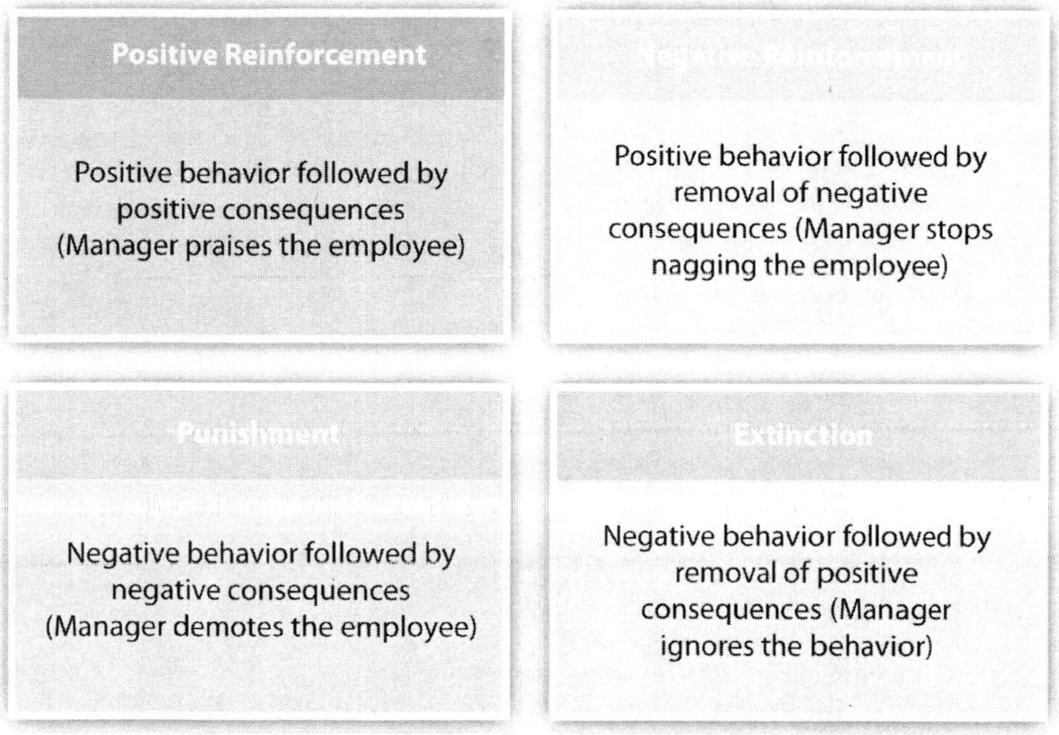

Positive Reinforcement	Negative Reinforcement
Positive behavior followed by positive consequences (Manager praises the employee)	Positive behavior followed by removal of negative consequences (Manager stops nagging the employee)

Punishment	Extinction
Negative behavior followed by negative consequences (Manager demotes the employee)	Negative behavior followed by removal of positive consequences (Manager ignores the behavior)

Positive reinforcement is a method of increasing the desired behavior.[39] Positive reinforcement involves making sure that behavior is met with positive consequences. For example, praising an employee for treating a customer respectfully is an example of positive reinforcement. If the praise immediately follows the positive behavior, the employee will see a link between the behavior and positive consequences and will be motivated to repeat similar behaviors.

positive reinforcement

Making sure that behavior is met with positive consequences.

Negative reinforcement is also used to increase the desired behavior. Negative reinforcement involves removal of unpleasant outcomes once desired behavior is demonstrated. Nagging an employee to complete a report is an example of negative reinforcement. The negative stimulus in the environment will remain present until positive behavior is demonstrated. The problem with negative reinforcement is that the negative stimulus may lead to unexpected behaviors and may fail to stimulate the desired behavior. For example, the person may start avoiding the manager to avoid being nagged.

negative reinforcement

Removal of unpleasant outcomes once desired behavior is demonstrated.

Extinction is used to decrease the frequency of negative behaviors. Extinction is the removal of rewards following negative behavior. Sometimes, negative behaviors are demonstrated because they are being inadvertently rewarded. For example, it has been shown that when people are rewarded for their unethical behaviors, they tend to demonstrate higher levels of unethical behaviors.[40] Thus, when the rewards following unwanted behaviors are removed, the frequency of future negative behaviors may be reduced. For example, if a coworker is forwarding unsolicited e-mail messages containing jokes, commenting and laughing at these jokes may be encouraging the person to keep forwarding these messages. Completely ignoring such messages may reduce their frequency.

extinction

The removal of rewards following negative behavior.

Punishment is another method of reducing the frequency of undesirable behaviors. Punishment involves presenting negative consequences following unwanted behaviors. Giving an employee a warning for consistently being late to work is an example of punishment.

punishment

Presenting negative consequences following unwanted behaviors.

Reinforcement Schedules

continuous schedule

When reinforcers follow all instances of positive behavior.

fixed-ratio schedules

Rewarding behavior after a set number of occurrences.

variable ratio

Providing the reinforcement on a random pattern.

In addition to types of reinforcements, researchers have focused their attention on schedules of reinforcement as well.[41] Reinforcement is presented on a **continuous schedule** if reinforcers follow all instances of positive behavior. An example of a continuous schedule would be giving an employee a sales commission every time he makes a sale. In many instances, continuous schedules are impractical. For example, it would be difficult to praise an employee every time he shows up to work on time. **Fixed-ratio schedules** involve providing rewards every *nth* time the right behavior is demonstrated. An example of this would be giving the employee a bonus for every tenth sale he makes. **Variable ratio** involves providing the reinforcement on a random pattern, such as praising the employee occasionally when the person shows up on time. In the case of continuous schedules, behavioral change is more temporary. Once the reward is withdrawn, the person may stop performing the desired behavior. The most durable results occur under variable ratios, but there is also some evidence that continuous schedules produce higher performance than do variable schedules.[42]

OB Toolbox: Be Effective in Your Use of Discipline

As a manager, sometimes you may have to discipline an employee to eliminate unwanted behavior. Here are some tips to make this process more effective.

- *Consider whether punishment is the most effective way to modify behavior.* Sometimes catching people in the act of doing good things and praising or rewarding them is preferable to punishing negative behavior. Instead of criticizing them for being late, consider praising them when they are on time. Carrots may be more effective than sticks. You can also make the behavior extinct by removing any rewards that follow undesirable behavior.
- *Be sure that the punishment fits the crime.* If a punishment is too harsh, both the employee in question and coworkers who will learn about the punishment will feel it is unfair. Unfair punishment may not change unwanted behavior.
- *Be consistent in your treatment of employees.* Have disciplinary procedures and apply them in the same way to everyone. It is unfair to enforce a rule for one particular employee but then give others a free pass.
- *Document the behavior in question.* If an employee is going to be disciplined, the evidence must go beyond hearsay.
- *Be timely with discipline.* When a long period of time passes between behavior and punishment, it is less effective in reducing undesired behavior because the connection between the behavior and punishment is weaker.

Sources: Adapted from ideas in Ambrose, M. L., & Kulik, C. T. (1999). Old friends, new faces: Motivation research in the 1990s. Journal of Management, 25, 231–292; Guffey, C. J., & Helms, M. M. (2001). Effective employee discipline: A case of the Internal Revenue Service. Public Personnel Management, 30, 111–128.

OB Mod

A systematic application of reinforcement theory to modify employee behaviors in the workplace.

A systematic way in which reinforcement theory principles are applied is called Organizational Behavior Modification (or **OB Mod**).[43] This is a systematic application of reinforcement theory to modify employee behaviors in the workplace. The model consists of five stages. The process starts with identifying the behavior that will be modified. Let's assume that we are interested in reducing absenteeism among employees. In step 2, we need to measure the baseline level of absenteeism. How many times a month is a particular employee absent? In step 3, the behavior's antecedents and consequences are determined. Why is this employee absent? More importantly, what is happening when the employee is absent? If the behavior is being unintentionally rewarded (e.g., the person is still getting paid or is able to avoid unpleasant assignments because someone else is doing them), we may expect these positive consequences to reinforce the absenteeism. Instead, to reduce the frequency of absenteeism, it will be necessary to think of financial or social incentives to follow positive behavior and negative consequences to follow negative behavior. In step 4, an intervention is implemented. Removing the positive consequences of negative behavior may be an effective way of dealing with the situation, or, in persistent situations, punishments may be used. Finally, in step 5 the behavior is measured periodically and maintained.

Studies examining the effectiveness of OB Mod have been supportive of the model in general. A review of the literature found that OB Mod interventions resulted in 17% improvement in performance.[44] Particularly in manufacturing settings, OB Mod was an effective way of increasing performance, although positive effects were observed in service organizations as well.

FIGURE 5.12 Stages of Organizational Behavior Modification

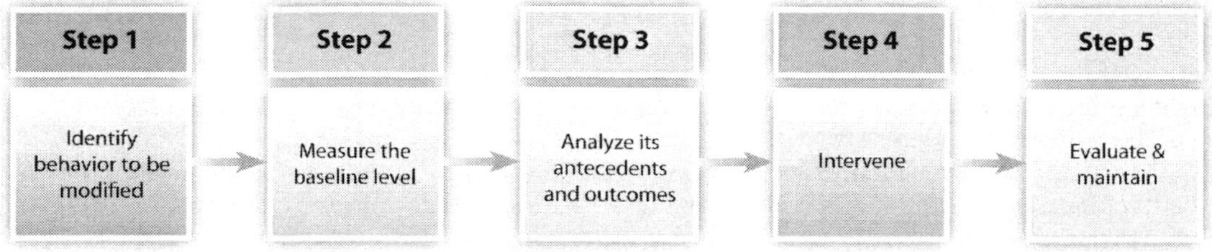

Source: Based on information presented in Stajkovic, A. D., & Luthans, F. (1997). A meta-analysis of the effects of organizational behavior modification on task performance, 1975–1995. Academy of Management Journal, 40, 1122–1149.

KEY TAKEAWAY

Process-based theories use the mental processes of employees as the key to understanding employee motivation. According to equity theory, employees are demotivated when they view reward distribution as unfair. Perceptions of fairness are shaped by the comparisons they make between their inputs and outcomes with respect to a referent's inputs and outcomes. Following equity theory, research identified two other types of fairness (procedural and interactional) that also affect worker reactions and motivation. According to expectancy theory, employees are motivated when they believe that their effort will lead to high performance (expectancy), when they believe that their performance will lead to outcomes (instrumentality), and when they find the outcomes following performance to be desirable (valence). Reinforcement theory argues that behavior is a function of its consequences. By properly tying rewards to positive behaviors, eliminating rewards following negative behaviors, and punishing negative behaviors, leaders can increase the frequency of desired behaviors. These three theories are particularly useful in designing reward systems within a company.

EXERCISES

1. Your manager tells you that the best way of ensuring fairness in reward distribution is to keep the pay a secret. How would you respond to this assertion?
2. When distributing bonuses or pay, how would you ensure perceptions of fairness?
3. What are the differences between procedural, interactional, and distributive justice? List ways in which you could increase each of these justice perceptions.
4. Using examples, explain the concepts of expectancy, instrumentality, and valence.
5. Some practitioners and researchers consider OB Mod unethical because it may be viewed as a way of manipulation. What would be your reaction to such a criticism?

3. THE ROLE OF ETHICS AND NATIONAL CULTURE

LEARNING OBJECTIVES

1. **Consider the role of motivation for ethical behavior.**
2. **Consider the role of national culture on motivation theories.**

3.1 Motivation and Ethics

What motivates individuals to behave unethically? Motivation theories have been applied to explain this interesting and important question. One theory that has been particularly successful in explaining ethical behavior is reinforcement theory. Just like any other behavior such as performance or cooperation, ethical behavior is one that is learned as a result of the consequences following one's actions. For example, in an experiment simulating the job of a sales manager, participants made a series of decisions using a computer. Partway through the simulation, subjects were informed that salespeople reporting to them were giving kickbacks to customers. Subjects in this experiment were more likely to cut the kickbacks if there was a threat of punishment to the manager. On the other hand, subjects playing the sales manager were more likely to continue giving away the kickbacks if they made a profit after providing the kickbacks.[45] In a separate study highlighting the importance of rewards and punishments, researchers found that the severity of expected punishment was the primary predictor of whether subjects reported inclination to behave unethically. In addition to the severity of the punishment, the perceived likelihood of punishment was also a major influence of ethical behavior.[46] These findings highlight the importance of rewards and punishments for motivating unethical behaviors.

There are many organizational situations in which individuals may do unethical things but then experience positive consequences such as being awarded promotions for meeting their sales quotas. For example, in many hotels, staff members routinely receive kickbacks from restaurants or bars if they refer customers to those locations.[47] Similarly, sales staff rewarded with spiffs (product-specific sales incentives) may give customers advice that goes against their own personal beliefs and in this sense act unethically.[48] As long as unethical behavior is followed by positive consequences for the person in question, we would expect unethical behavior to continue. Thus, in order to minimize the occurrence of unethical behavior (and in some instances legal problems), it seems important to examine the rewards and punishments that follow unethical behavior and remove rewards following unethical behavior while increasing the severity and likelihood of punishment.

3.2 Motivation Around the Globe

Motivation is a culturally bound topic. In other words, the factors that motivate employees in different cultures may not be equivalent. The motivation theories we cover in this chapter are likely to be culturally bound because they were developed by Western researchers and the majority of the research supporting each theory was conducted on Western subjects.

Based on the cultural context, Maslow's hierarchy of needs may require modification because the ranking of the needs may differ across cultures. For example, a study conducted in 39 countries showed that financial satisfaction was a stronger predictor of overall life satisfaction in developing nations compared to industrialized nations. In industrialized nations, satisfaction with esteem needs was a more powerful motivator than it was in developing nations.[49]

People around the world value justice and fairness. However, what is perceived as fair may be culturally dependent. Moreover, people in different cultures may react differently to perceived unfairness.[50] For example, in cross-cultural studies, it was found that participants in low power distance cultures such as the United States and Germany valued voice into the process (the opportunities for explanation and appealing a decision) more than those in high power distance cultures such as China and Mexico. At the same time, interactional justice was valued more by the Chinese subjects.[51] There is also some evidence indicating that equity (rewarding employees based on their contributions to a group) may be a culture-specific method of achieving fairness. One study shows that Japanese subjects viewed equity as less fair and equality-based distributions as more fair than did Australian subjects.[52] Similarly, subjects in different cultures varied in their inclination to distribute rewards based on subjects' need or age, and in cultures such as Japan and India, a person's need may be a relevant factor in reward distributions.[53]

KEY TAKEAWAY

Motivation theories are particularly useful for understanding why employees behave unethically. Based on reinforcement theory, people will demonstrate higher unethical behaviors if their unethical behaviors are followed by rewards or go unpunished. Similarly, according to expectancy theory, if people believe that their unethical actions will be rewarded with desirable outcomes, they are more likely to demonstrate unethical behaviors. In terms of culture, some of the motivation theories are likely to be culture-bound, whereas others may more readily apply to other cultures. Existing research shows that what is viewed as fair or unfair tends to be culturally defined.

EXERCISES

1. What is the connection between a company's reward system and the level of ethical behaviors?
2. Which of the motivation theories do you think would be more applicable to many different cultures?

4. CONCLUSION

In this chapter we have reviewed the basic motivation theories that have been developed to explain motivated behavior. Several theories view motivated behavior as attempts to satisfy needs. Based on this approach, managers would benefit from understanding what people need so that the actions of employees can be understood and managed. Other theories explain motivated behavior using the cognitive processes of employees. Employees respond to unfairness in their environment, they learn from the consequences of their actions and repeat the behaviors that lead to positive results, and they are motivated to exert effort if they see their actions will lead to outcomes that would get them desired rewards. None of these theories are complete on their own, but each theory provides us with a framework we can use to analyze, interpret, and manage employee behaviors in the workplace.

5. EXERCISES

ETHICAL DILEMMA

Companies are interested in motivating employees: Work hard, be productive, behave ethically—and stay healthy. Health care costs are rising, and employers are finding that unhealthy habits such as smoking or being overweight are costing companies big bucks.

Your company is concerned about the rising health care costs and decides to motivate employees to adopt healthy habits. Therefore, employees are given a year to quit smoking. If they do not quit by then, they are going to lose their jobs. New employees will be given nicotine tests, and the company will avoid hiring new smokers in the future. The company also wants to encourage employees to stay healthy. For this purpose, employees will get cash incentives for weight loss. If they do not meet the weight, cholesterol, and blood pressure standards to be issued by the company, they will be charged extra fees for health insurance.

Is this plan ethical? Why or why not? Can you think of alternative ways to motivate employees to adopt healthy habits?

INDIVIDUAL EXERCISE

Your company provides diversity training programs to ensure that employees realize the importance of working with a diverse workforce, are aware of the equal employment opportunity legislation, and are capable of addressing the challenges of working in a multicultural workforce. Participation in these programs is mandatory, and employees are required to take the training as many times as needed until they pass. The training program lasts one day and is usually conducted in a nice hotel outside the workplace. Employees are paid for the time they spend in the training program. You realize that employees are not really motivated to perform well in this program. During the training, they put in the minimum level of effort, and most participants fail the exam given at the conclusion of the training program and then have to retake the training.

Using expectancy and reinforcement theories, explain why they may not be motivated to perform well in the training program. Then suggest improvements in the program so that employees are motivated to understand the material, pass the exam, and apply the material in the workplace.

GROUP EXERCISE

A Reward Allocation Decision

You are in charge of allocating a $12,000 bonus to a team that recently met an important deadline. The team was in charge of designing a Web-based product for a client. The project lasted a year. There were five people in the team. Your job is to determine each person's share from the bonus.

Devin: *Project manager*. He was instrumental in securing the client, coordinating everyone's effort, and managing relationships with the client. He put in a lot of extra hours for this project. His annual salary is $80,000. He is independently wealthy, drives an expensive car, and does not have any debt. He has worked for the company for 5 years and worked for the project from the beginning.

Alice: *Technical lead*. She oversaw the technical aspects of the project. She resolved many important technical issues. During the project, while some members worked extra hours, she refused to stay at the office outside regular hours. However, she was productive during regular work hours, and she was accessible via e-mail in the evenings. Her salary is $50,000. She is a single mother and has a lot of debt. She has worked for the company for 4 years and worked for the project for 8 months.

Erin: *Graphic designer*. She was in charge of the creative aspects of the project. She experimented with many looks, and while doing that she slowed down the entire team. Brice and Carrie were mad at her because of the many mistakes she made during the project, but the look and feel of the project eventually appealed to the client, which resulted in repeat business. Her salary is $30,000. She is single and lives to party. She has worked for the company for 2 years and worked for this project from the beginning.

Brice: *Tester*. He was in charge of finding the bugs in the project and ensuring that it worked. He found many bugs, but he was not very aggressive in his testing. He misunderstood many things, and many of the bugs he found were not really bugs but his misuse of the system. He had a negative attitude toward the whole project, acted very pessimistically regarding the likelihood of success, and demoralized the team. His salary is $40,000. He has accumulated a large credit card debt. He has worked for the company for 3 years and worked for the project in the last 6 months.

Carrie: *Web developer*. She was in charge of writing the code. She was frustrated when Erin slowed down the entire project because of her experimentation. Carrie was primarily responsible for meeting the project deadline because she put in a lot of extra work hours. Her salary is $50,000. Her mother has ongoing health issues, and Carrie needs money to help her. She worked for the company for the past year and was involved in this project for 6 months.

ENDNOTES

1. Mitchell, T. R. (1982). Motivation: New directions for theory, research, and practice. *Academy of Management Review, 7,* 80–88; Porter, L. W., & Lawler, E. E. (1968). *Managerial attitudes and performance.* Homewood, IL: Dorsey Press.

2. Maslow, A. H. (1943). A theory of human motivation. *Psychological Review, 50,* 370–396; Maslow, A. H. (1954). *Motivation and personality.* New York: Harper.

3. Baumeister, R. F., & Leary, M. R. (1995). The need to belong: Desire for interpersonal attachments as a fundamental human motivation. *Psychological Bulletin, 117,* 497–529.

4. Neher, A. (1991). Maslow's theory of motivation: A critique. *Journal of Humanistic Psychology, 31,* 89–112; Rauschenberger, J., Schmitt, N., & Hunter, J. E. (1980). A test of the need hierarchy concept by a Markov model of change in need strength. *Administrative Science Quarterly, 25,* 654–670.

5. Alderfer, C. P. (1969). An empirical test of a new theory of human needs. *Organizational Behavior and Human Performance, 4,* 142–175.

6. Herzberg, F., Mausner, B., & Snyderman, B. (1959). *The motivation to work.* New York: John Wiley; Herzberg, F. (1965). The motivation to work among Finnish supervisors. *Personnel Psychology, 18,* 393–402.

7. Cummings, L. L., & Elsalmi, A. M. (1968). Empirical research on the bases and correlates of managerial motivation. *Psychological Bulletin, 70,* 127–144; House, R. J., & Wigdor, L. A. (1967). Herzberg's dual-factor theory of job satisfaction and motivation: A review of the evidence and a criticism. *Personnel Psychology, 20,* 369–389.

8. Spangler, W. D. (1992). Validity of questionnaire and TAT measures of need for achievement: Two meta-analyses. *Psychological Bulletin, 112,* 140–154.

9. Mueller, C. M., & Dweck, C. S. (1998). Praise for intelligence can undermine children's motivation and performance. *Journal of Personality and Social Psychology, 75,* 33–52.

10. Campbell, D. J. (1982). Determinants of choice of goal difficulty level: A review of situational and personality influences. *Journal of Occupational Psychology, 55,* 79–95.

11. Harrell, A. M., & Stahl, M. J. (1981). A behavioral decision theory approach for measuring McClelland's trichotomy of needs. *Journal of Applied Psychology, 66,* 242–247; Trevis, C. S., & Certo, S. C. (2005). Spotlight on entrepreneurship. *Business Horizons, 48,* 271–274; Turban, D. B., & Keon, T. L. (1993). Organizational attractiveness: An interactionist perspective. *Journal of Applied Psychology, 78,* 184–193.

12. McClelland, D. C., & Boyatzis, R. E. (1982). Leadership motive pattern and long-term success in management. *Journal of Applied Psychology, 67,* 737–743.

13. McClelland, D. C., & Burnham, D. H. (1976). Power is the great motivator. *Harvard Business Review, 25,* 159–166.

14. Wong, M. M., & Csikszentmihalyi, M. (1991). Affiliation motivation and daily experiences: Some issues on gender differences. *Journal of Personality and Social Psychology 60,* 154–164.

15. McClelland, D. C., & Burnham, D. H. (1976). Power is the great motivator. *Harvard Business Review, 25,* 159–166; Spangler, W. D., & House, R. J. (1991). Presidential effectiveness and the leadership motive profile. *Journal of Personality and Social Psychology, 60,* 439–455; Spreier, S. W. (2006). Leadership run amok. *Harvard Business Review, 84,* 72–82.

16. Adams, J. S. (1965). Inequity in social exchange. In L. Berkowitz (Ed.), *Advances in experimental social psychology* (Vol. 2, pp. 267–299). New York: Academic Press.

17. Carrell, M. R., & Dittrich, J. E. (1978). Equity theory: The recent literature, methodological considerations, and new directions. *Academy of Management Review, 3,* 202–210; Goodman, P. S., & Friedman, A. (1971). An examination of Adams' theory of inequity. *Administrative Science Quarterly, 16,* 271–288.

18. Greenberg, J. (1993). Stealing in the name of justice: Informational and interpersonal moderators of theft reactions to underpayment inequity. *Organizational Behavior and Human Decision Processes, 54,* 81–103.

19. Schmidt, D. R., & Marwell, G. (1972). Withdrawal and reward reallocation as responses to inequity. *Journal of Experimental Social Psychology, 8,* 207–211.

20. Austin, W., & Walster, E. (1974). Reactions to confirmations and disconfirmations of expectancies of equity and inequity. *Journal of Personality and Social Psychology, 30,* 208–216.

21. Evan, W. M., & Simmons, R. G. (1969). Organizational effects of inequitable rewards: Two experiments in status inconsistency. *IEEE Engineering Management Review, 1,* 95–108.

22. Huseman, R. C., Hatfield, J. D., & Miles, E. W. (1987). A new perspective on equity theory: The equity sensitivity construct. *Academy of Management Review, 12,* 222–234.

23. Alge, B. J. (2001). Effects of computer surveillance on perceptions of privacy and procedural justice. *Journal of Applied Psychology, 86,* 797–804; Bauer, T. N., Maertz, C. P., Jr., Dolen, M. R., & Campion, M. A. (1998). Longitudinal assessment of applicant reactions to employment testing and test outcome feedback. *Journal of Applied Psychology, 83,* 892–903; Kidwell, R. E. (1995). Pink slips without tears. *Academy of Management Executive, 9,* 69–70.

24. Brockner, J., & Wiesenfeld, B. M. (1996). An integrative framework for explaining reactions to decisions: Interactive effects of outcomes and procedures. *Psychological Bulletin, 120,* 189–208.

25. Brockner, J., Fishman, A. Y., Reb, J., Goldman, B., Spiegel, S., & Garden, C. (2007). Procedural fairness, outcome favorability, and judgments of an authority's responsibility. *Journal of Applied Psychology, 92,* 1657–1671.

26. Cropanzano, R., Bowen, D. E., & Gilliland, S. W. (2007). The management of organizational justice. *Academy of Management Perspectives, 21,* 34–48; Tyler, T. R. (1994). Psychological models of the justice motive: Antecedents of distributive and procedural justice. *Journal of Personality and Social Psychology, 67,* 850–863; Tyler, T., Degoey, P., & Smith, H. (1996). Understanding why the justice of group procedures matters: A test of the psychological dynamics of the group-value model. *Journal of Personality and Social Psychology, 70,* 913–930.

27. Kidwell, R. E. (1995). Pink slips without tears. *Academy of Management Executive, 9,* 69–70.

28. Alge, B. J. (2001). Effects of computer surveillance on perceptions of privacy and procedural justice. *Journal of Applied Psychology, 86,* 797–804; Kernan, M. C., & Hanges, P. J. (2002). Survivor reactions to reorganization: Antecedents and consequences of procedural, interpersonal, and informational justice. *Journal of Applied Psychology, 87,* 916–928; Lind, E. A., Kanfer, R., & Earley, C. P. (1990). Voice, control, and procedural justice: Instrumental and noninstrumental concerns in fairness judgments. *Journal of Personality and Social Psychology, 59,* 952–959.

29. Schaubroeck, J., May, D. R., & William, B. F. (1994). Procedural justice explanations and employee reactions to economic hardship: A field experiment. *Journal of Applied Psychology, 79,* 455–460.

30. Bauer, T. N., Maertz, C. P., Jr., Dolen, M. R., & Campion, M. A. (1998). Longitudinal assessment of applicant reactions to employment testing and test outcome feedback. *Journal of Applied Psychology, 83,* 892–903.

31. Greenberg, J. (2006). Losing sleep over organizational injustice: Attenuating insomniac reactions to underpayment inequity with supervisory training in interactional justice. *Journal of Applied Psychology, 91,* 58–69.

32. Greenberg, J. (2004). Managing workplace stress by promoting organizational justice. *Organizational Dynamics, 33,* 352–365; Tepper, B. J. (2001). Health consequences of organizational injustice: Tests of main and interactive effects. *Organizational Behavior and Human Decision Processes, 86,* 197–215.

33. Blader, S. L. (2007). What leads organizational members to collectivize? Injustice and identification as precursors of union certification. *Organization Science, 18,* 108–126; Cohen-Charash, Y., & Spector, P. E. (2001). The role of justice in organizations: A meta-analysis. *Organizational Behavior and Human Decision Processes, 86,* 278–321; Colquitt, J. A., Conlon, D. E., Wesson, M. J., Porter, C. O. L. H., & Ng, K. Y. (2001). Justice at the millennium: A meta-analytic review of 25 years of organizational justice research. *Journal of Applied Psychology, 86,* 425–445; Cropanzano, R., Bowen, D. E., & Gilliland, S. W. (2007). The management of organizational justice. *Academy of Management Perspectives, 21,* 34–48; Masterson, S. S. (2001). A trickle-down model of organizational justice: Relating employees' and customers' perceptions of and reactions to fairness. *Journal of Applied Psychology, 86,* 594–604; Masterson, S. S., Lewis, K., Goldman, B. M., & Taylor, S. M. (2000). Integrating justice and social exchange: The differing effects of fair procedures and treatment on work relationships. *Academy of Management Journal, 43,* 738–748; Moorman, R. H. (1991). Relationship between organizational justice and organizational citizenship behaviors: Do fairness perceptions influence employee citizenship? *Journal of Applied Psychology, 76,* 845–855; Skarlicki, D. P., & Folger, R. (1997). Retaliation in the workplace: The roles of distributive, procedural, and interactional justice. *Journal of Applied Psychology, 82,* 434–443.

34. Porter, L. W., & Lawler, E. E. (1968). *Managerial attitudes and performance.* Homewood, IL: Irwin; Vroom, V. H. (1964). *Work and motivation.* New York: Wiley.

35. Heneman, H. G., & Schwab, D. P. (1972). Evaluation of research on expectancy theory predictions of employee performance. *Psychological Bulletin, 78,* 1–9; Van Eerde, W., & Thierry, H. (1996). Vroom's expectancy models and work-related criteria: A meta-analysis. *Journal of Applied Psychology, 81,* 575–586.

36. Cook, C. W. (1980). Guidelines for managing motivation. *Business Horizons, 23,* 61–69.

37. Skinner, B. F. (1953). *Science and human behavior.* New York: Free Press.

38. Kerr, S. (1995). On the folly of rewarding A while hoping for B. *Academy of Management Executive, 9,* 7–14.

39. Beatty, R. W., & Schneier, C. E. (1975). A case for positive reinforcement. *Business Horizons, 18,* 57–66.

40. Harvey, H. W., & Sims, H. P. (1978). Some determinants of unethical decision behavior: An experiment. *Journal of Applied Psychology, 63,* 451–457.

41. Beatty, R. W., & Schneier, C. E. (1975). A case for positive reinforcement. *Business Horizons, 18,* 57–66.

42. Beatty, R. W., & Schneier, C. E. (1975). A case for positive reinforcement. *Business Horizons, 18,* 57–66; Cherrington, D. J., & Cherrington, J. O. (1974). Participation, performance, and appraisal. *Business Horizons, 17,* 35–44; Saari, L. M., & Latham, G. P. (1982). Employee reactions to continuous and variable ratio reinforcement schedules involving a monetary incentive. *Journal of Applied Psychology, 67,* 506–508; Yukl, G. A., & Latham, G. P. (1975). Consequences of reinforcement schedules and incentive magnitudes for employee performance: Problems encountered in an industrial setting. *Journal of Applied Psychology, 60,* 294–298.

43. Luthans, F., & Stajkovic, A. D. (1999). Reinforce for performance: The need to go beyond pay and even rewards. *Academy of Management Executive, 13,* 49–57.

44. Stajkovic, A. D., & Luthans, F. (1997). A meta-analysis of the effects of organizational behavior modification on task performance, 1975–1995. *Academy of Management Journal, 40,* 1122–1149.

45. Hegarty, W. H., & Sims, H. P. (1978). Some determinants of unethical decision behavior: An experiment. *Journal of Applied Psychology, 63,* 451–457.

46. Rettig, S., & Rawson, H. E. (1963). The risk hypothesis in predictive judgments of unethical behavior. *Journal of Abnormal and Social Psychology, 66,* 243–248.

47. Elliott, C. (2007). Is your bellhop on the take? *National Geographic Traveler, 24*(3), 18–20.

48. Radin, T. J., & Predmore, C. E. (2002). The myth of the salesperson: Intended and unintended consequences of product-specific sales incentives. *Journal of Business Ethics, 36,* 79–92.

49. Oishi, S., Diener, E. F., & Suh, E. M. (1999). Cross-cultural variations in predictors of life satisfaction: Perspectives from needs and values. *Personality and Social Psychology Bulletin, 25,* 980–990.

50. Erdogan, B., & Liden, R. C. (2006). Collectivism as a moderator of responses to organizational justice: Implications for leader-member exchange and ingratiation. *Journal of Organizational Behavior, 27*, 1–17; Mueller, C. W., & Wynn, T. (2000). The degree to which justice is valued in the workplace. *Social Justice Research, 13*, 1–24.

51. Brockner, J., Ackerman, G., Greenberg, J., Gelfand, M. J., Francesco, A. M., Chen, Z. X., et al. (2001). Culture and procedural justice: The influence of power distance on reactions to voice. *Journal of Experimental Social Psychology, 37*, 300–315; Tata, J. (2005). The influence of national culture on the perceived fairness of grading procedures: A comparison of the United States and China. *Journal of Psychology, 139*, 401–412.

52. Kashima, Y., Siegal, M., Tanaka, K., & Isaka, H. (1988). Universalism in lay conceptions of distributive justice: A cross-cultural examination. *International Journal of Psychology, 23*, 51–64.

53. Kashima, Y., Siegal, M., Tanaka, K., & Isaka, H. (1988). Universalism in lay conceptions of distributive justice: A cross-cultural examination. *International Journal of Psychology, 23*, 51–64; Murphy-Berman, V., Berman, J., Singh, P., Pachauri, A., & Kumar, P. (1984). Factors affecting allocation to needy and meritorious recipients: A cross-cultural comparison. *Journal of Personality and Social Psychology, 46*, 1267–1272.

CHAPTER 6

Designing a Motivating Work Environment

LEARNING OBJECTIVES

After reading this chapter, you should be able to do the following:

1. Describe the history of job design approaches.
2. Understand how to increase the motivating potential of a job.
3. Understand why goals should be SMART.
4. Set SMART goals.
5. Give performance feedback effectively.
6. Describe individual-, team-, and organization-based incentives that can be used to motivate the workforce.

Motivating Steel Workers at Nucor

Producing steel is hot and demanding work. Employees who are motivated are much more productive, as evidenced by Nucor's success.

Manufacturing steel is not a glamorous job. The industry is beset by many problems, and more than 40 steel manufacturers have filed for bankruptcy in recent years. Most young employees do not view working at a steel mill as their dream job. Yet, one company distinguished itself from all the rest by remaining profitable for over 130 quarters and by providing an over 350% return on investment to shareholders. The company is clearly doing well by every financial metric available and is the most profitable in its industry.

How do they achieve these amazing results? For one thing, every Nucor Corporation employee acts like an owner of the company. Employees are encouraged to fix the things they see as wrong and have real power on their jobs. When there is a breakdown in a plant, a supervisor does not have to ask employees to work overtime; employees volunteer for it. In fact, the company is famous for its decentralized structure and for pushing authority and responsibility down to lower levels in the hierarchy. Tasks that previously belonged to management are performed by line workers. Management listens to lower level employees and routinely implements their new ideas.

The reward system in place at Nucor is also unique, and its employees may be the highest paid steelworkers in the world. In 2005, the average Nucor employee earned $79,000, followed by a $2,000 bonus decided by the company's annual earnings and $18,000 in the form of profit sharing. At the same time, a large percentage of these earnings are based on performance. People have the opportunity to earn a lot of money if the company is doing well, and there is no upward limit to how much they can make. However, they will do much worse than their counterparts in other mills if the company does poorly. Thus, it is to everyone's advantage to help the company perform well. The same incentive system exists at all levels of the company. CEO pay is clearly tied to corporate performance. The incentive system penalizes low performers while increasing commitment to the company as well as to high performance.

Nucor's formula for success seems simple: Align company goals with employee goals and give employees real power to make things happen. The results seem to work for the company and its employees. Evidence of this successful method is that the company has one of the lowest employee turnover rates in the industry and remains one of the few remaining nonunionized environments in manufacturing.

Sources: Adapted from information in Byrnes, N., & Arndt, M. (2006, May 1). The ART of motivation. Business Week, 3982, 56–62; Foust, D. (2008, April 7). The best performers of 2008. Business Week, 4078, 51–73; Jennings, J. (2003). Ways to really motivate people: Authenticity is a huge hit with Gen X and Y. The Secured Lender, 59, 62–70; Marks, S. J. (2001). Incentives that really reward and motivate. Workforce, 80, 108–114.

What are the tools companies can use to ensure a motivated workforce? Nucor seems to have found two very useful tools to motivate its workforce: a job design incorporating empowerment, and a reward system that aligns company performance with employee rewards. In this chapter, we will cover the basic tools organizations can use to motivate workers. The tools that will be described are based on motivation principles such as expectancy theory, reinforcement theory, and need-based theories. Specifically, we cover motivating employees through job design, goal setting, performance feedback, and reward systems.

1. MOTIVATING EMPLOYEES THROUGH JOB DESIGN

LEARNING OBJECTIVES

1. **Learn about the history of job design approaches.**
2. **Consider alternatives to job specialization.**
3. **Identify job characteristics that increase motivating potential.**
4. **Learn how to empower employees.**

1.1 Importance of Job Design

Many of us assume the most important motivator at work is pay. Yet, studies point to a different factor as the major influence over worker motivation—job design. How a job is designed has a major impact on employee motivation, job satisfaction, commitment to an organization, absenteeism, and turnover.

The question of how to properly design jobs so that employees are more productive and more satisfied has received attention from managers and researchers since the beginning of the 20th century. We will review major approaches to job design starting from its early history.

1.2 Scientific Management and Job Specialization

Perhaps the earliest attempt to design jobs came during the era of scientific management. Scientific management is a philosophy based on the ideas of Frederick Taylor as presented in his 1911 book, *Principles of Scientific Management*. Taylor's book is among the most influential books of the 20th century; the ideas presented had a major influence over how work was organized in the following years. Taylor was a mechanical engineer in the manufacturing industry. He saw work being done haphazardly, with only workers in charge. He saw the inefficiencies inherent in employees' production methods and argued that a manager's job was to carefully plan the work to be performed by employees. He also believed that scientific methods could be used to increase productivity. As an example, Taylor found that instead of allowing workers to use their own shovels, as was the custom at the time, providing specially designed shovels increased productivity. Further, by providing training and specific instructions, he was able to dramatically reduce the number of laborers required to handle each job.[1]

Scientific management proposed a number of ideas that have been influential in job design in the following years. An important idea was to minimize waste by identifying the most efficient method to perform the job. Using time–motion studies, management could determine how much time each task would require and plan the tasks so that the job could be performed as efficiently as possible. Therefore, standardized job performance methods were an important element of scientific management techniques. Each job would be carefully planned in advance, and employees would be paid to perform the tasks in the way specified by management.

FIGURE 6.2

This Ford panel assembly line in Berlin, Germany, is an example of specialization. Each person on the line has a different job.

© 2010 Jupiterimages Corporation

Furthermore, job specialization was one of the major advances of this approach. **Job specialization** entails breaking down jobs into their simplest components and assigning them to employees so that each person would perform a select number of tasks in a repetitive manner. There are a number of advantages to job specialization. Breaking tasks into simple components and making them repetitive reduces the skill requirements of the jobs and decreases the effort and cost of staffing. Training times for simple, repetitive jobs tend to be shorter as well. On the other hand, from a motivational perspective, these jobs are boring and repetitive and therefore associated with negative outcomes such as absenteeism.[2] Also, job specialization is ineffective in rapidly changing environments where employees may need to modify their approach according to the demands of the situation.[3]

job specialization

Breaking down tasks to their simplest components and assigning them to employees so that each person would perform few tasks in a repetitive manner.

Today, Taylorism has a bad reputation, and it is often referred to as the "dark ages" of management when employees' social motives were ignored. Yet, it is important to recognize the fundamental change in management mentality brought about by Taylor's ideas. For the first time, managers realized their role in influencing the output levels of employees. The concept of scientific management has had a lasting impact on how work is organized. Taylor's work paved the way to automation and standardization that is virtually universal in today's workplace. Assembly lines where each worker performs simple tasks in a repetitive manner are a direct result of job specialization efforts. Job specialization eventually found its way to the service industry as well. One of the biggest innovations of the famous McDonald brothers' first fast-food restaurant was the application of scientific management principles to their operations. They divided up the tasks so that one person took the orders while someone else made the burgers, another person applied the condiments, and yet another wrapped them. With this level of efficiency, customers generally received their order within one minute.[4]

1.3 Rotation, Job Enlargement, and Enrichment

One of the early alternatives to job specialization was job rotation. **Job rotation** involves moving employees from job to job at regular intervals. When employees periodically move to different jobs, the monotonous aspects of job specialization can be relieved. For example, Maids International Inc., a company that provides cleaning services to households and businesses, utilizes job rotation so that maids cleaning the kitchen in one house would clean the bedroom in a different one.[5] Using this technique, among others, the company is able to reduce its turnover level. In a supermarket study, cashiers were rotated to work in different departments. As a result of the rotation, employees' stress levels were reduced, as measured by their blood pressure. Moreover, they experienced less pain in their neck and shoulders.[6]

job rotation

Moving employees from job to job at regular intervals.

Job rotation has a number of advantages for organizations. It is an effective way for employees to acquire new skills and in turn for organizations to increase the overall skill level of their employees.[7] When workers move to different positions, they are cross-trained to perform different tasks, thereby increasing the flexibility of managers to assign employees to different parts of the organization when needed. In addition, job rotation is a way to transfer knowledge between departments.[8] Rotation may also have the benefit of reducing employee boredom, depending on the nature of the jobs the employee is performing at a given time. From the employee standpoint, rotation is a benefit, because they acquire new skills that keep them marketable in the long run.

Is rotation used only at lower levels of an organization? Anecdotal evidence suggests that companies successfully rotate high-level employees to train managers and increase innovation in the company. For example, Nokia uses rotation at all levels, such as assigning lawyers to act as country managers or moving network engineers to handset design. This approach is thought to bring a fresh perspective to old problems.[9] Wipro Ltd., India's information technology giant that employs about 80,000 workers, uses a 3-year plan to groom future leaders of the company by rotating them through different jobs.[10]

job enlargement

Expanding the tasks performed by employees to add more variety.

Job enlargement refers to expanding the tasks performed by employees to add more variety. By giving employees several different tasks to be performed, as opposed to limiting their activities to a small number of tasks, organizations hope to reduce boredom and monotony as well as utilize human resources more effectively. Job enlargement may have similar benefits to job rotation, because it may also involve teaching employees multiple tasks. Research indicates that when jobs are enlarged, employees view themselves as being capable of performing a broader set of tasks.[11] There is some evidence that job enlargement is beneficial, because it is positively related to employee satisfaction and higher quality customer services, and it increases the chances of catching mistakes.[12] At the same time, the effects of job enlargement may depend on the *type* of enlargement. For example, job enlargement consisting of adding tasks that are very simple in nature had negative consequences on employee satisfaction with the job and resulted in fewer errors being caught. Alternatively, giving employees more tasks that require them to be knowledgeable in different areas seemed to have more positive effects.[13]

job enrichment

A job redesign technique allowing workers more control over how they perform their own tasks.

Job enrichment is a job redesign technique that allows workers more control over how they perform their own tasks. This approach allows employees to take on more responsibility. As an alternative to job specialization, companies using job enrichment may experience positive outcomes, such as reduced turnover, increased productivity, and reduced absences.[14] This may be because employees who have the authority and responsibility over their work can be more efficient, eliminate unnecessary tasks, take shortcuts, and increase their overall performance. At the same time, there is evidence that job enrichment may sometimes cause dissatisfaction among certain employees.[15] The reason may be that employees who are given additional autonomy and responsibility may expect greater levels of pay or other types of compensation, and if this expectation is not met they may feel frustrated. One more thing to remember is that job enrichment is not suitable for everyone.[16] Not all employees desire to have control over how they work, and if they do not have this desire, they may become frustrated with an enriched job.

1.4 Job Characteristics Model

job characteristics model

Five core job dimensions, leading to three critical psychological states, which lead to work-related outcomes.

The **job characteristics model** is one of the most influential attempts to design jobs with increased motivational properties.[17] Proposed by Hackman and Oldham, the model describes five core job dimensions leading to three critical psychological states, resulting in work-related outcomes.

FIGURE 6.3

The Job Characteristics Model has five core job dimensions.

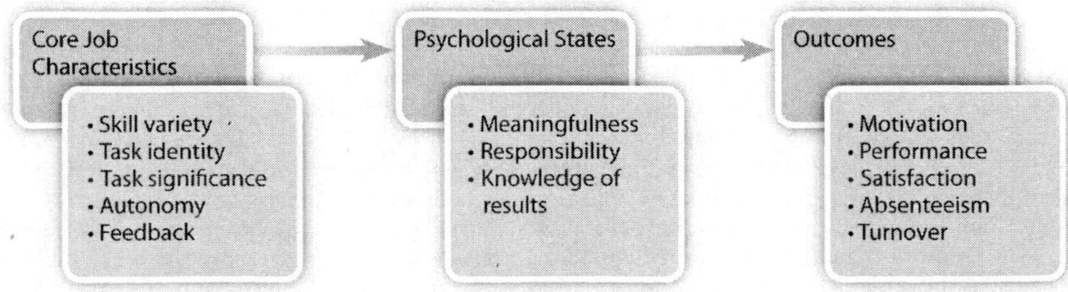

Source: Adapted from Hackman, J. R., & Oldham, G. R. (1975). Development of the job diagnostic survey. Journal of Applied Psychology, 60, 159–170.

skill variety

The extent to which the job requires a person to utilize multiple high-level skills.

Skill variety refers to the extent to which the job requires a person to utilize multiple high-level skills. A car wash employee whose job consists of directing customers into the automated car wash demonstrates low levels of skill variety, whereas a car wash employee who acts as a cashier, maintains carwash equipment, and manages the inventory of chemicals demonstrates high skill variety.

Task identity refers to the degree to which a person is in charge of completing an identifiable piece of work from start to finish. A Web designer who designs parts of a Web site will have low task identity, because the work blends in with other Web designers' work; in the end it will be hard for any one person to claim responsibility for the final output. The Web master who designs an entire Web site will have high task identity.

task identity

The degree to which a person is in charge of completing an identifiable piece of work from start to finish.

Task significance refers to whether a person's job substantially affects other people's work, health, or well-being. A janitor who cleans the floors at an office building may find the job low in significance, thinking it is not a very important job. However, janitors cleaning the floors at a hospital may see their role as essential in helping patients get better. When they feel that their tasks are significant, employees tend to feel that they are making an impact on their environment, and their feelings of self-worth are boosted.[18]

task significance

Whether a person's job substantially affects other people's work, health, or well-being.

Autonomy is the degree to which a person has the freedom to decide how to perform his or her tasks. As an example, an instructor who is required to follow a predetermined textbook, covering a given list of topics using a specified list of classroom activities, has low autonomy. On the other hand, an instructor who is free to choose the textbook, design the course content, and use any relevant materials when delivering lectures has higher levels of autonomy. Autonomy increases motivation at work, but it also has other benefits. Giving employees autonomy at work is a key to individual as well as company success, because autonomous employees are free to choose how to do their jobs and therefore can be more effective. They are also less likely to adopt a "this is not my job" approach to their work environment and instead be proactive (do what needs to be done without waiting to be told what to do) and creative.[19] The consequence of this resourcefulness can be higher company performance. For example, a Cornell University study shows that small businesses that gave employees autonomy grew four times more than those that did not.[20] Giving employees autonomy is also a great way to train them on the job. For example, Gucci's CEO Robert Polet points to the level of autonomy he was given while working at Unilever PLC as a key to his development of leadership talents.[21] Autonomy can arise from workplace features, such as telecommuting, company structure, organizational climate, and leadership style.[22]

autonomy

The degree to which people have the freedom to decide how to perform their tasks.

Feedback refers to the degree to which people learn how effective they are being at work. Feedback at work may come from other people, such as supervisors, peers, subordinates, and customers, or it may come from the job itself. A salesperson who gives presentations to potential clients but is not informed of the clients' decisions, has low feedback at work. If this person receives notification that a sale was made based on the presentation, feedback will be high.

feedback

The degree to which people learn how effective they are being at work.

The relationship between feedback and job performance is more controversial. In other words, the mere presence of feedback is not sufficient for employees to feel motivated to perform better. In fact, a review of this literature shows that in about one-third of the cases, feedback was detrimental to performance.[23] In addition to whether feedback is present, the sign of feedback (positive or negative), whether the person is ready to receive the feedback, and the manner in which feedback was given will all determine whether employees feel motivated or demotivated as a result of feedback.

According to the job characteristics model, the presence of these five core job dimensions leads employees to experience three psychological states: They view their work as *meaningful*, they feel *responsible* for the outcomes, and they acquire *knowledge of results*. These three psychological states in turn are related to positive outcomes such as overall job satisfaction, internal motivation, higher performance, and lower absenteeism and turnover.[24] Research shows that out of these three psychological states, experienced meaningfulness is the most important for employee attitudes and behaviors, and it is the key mechanism through which the five core job dimensions operate.

Are all five job characteristics equally valuable for employees? Hackman and Oldham's model proposes that the five characteristics will not have uniform effects. Instead, they proposed the following formula to calculate the motivating potential of a given job:[25]

EQUATION 6.1

$$\text{MPS} = ((\text{Skill Variety} + \text{Task Identity} + \text{Task Significance}) \div 3) \times \text{Autonomy} \times \text{Feedback}$$

According to this formula, autonomy and feedback are the more important elements in deciding motivating potential compared to skill variety, task identity, or task significance. Moreover, note how the job characteristics interact with each other in this model. If someone's job is completely lacking in autonomy (or feedback), regardless of levels of variety, identity, and significance, the motivating potential score will be very low.

Note that the five job characteristics are not objective features of a job. Two employees working in the same job may have very different perceptions regarding how much skill variety, task identity, task significance, autonomy, or feedback the job affords. In other words, motivating potential is in the eye of the beholder. This is both good and bad news. The bad news is that even though a manager may design a job that is supposed to motivate employees, some employees may not find the job to be motivational.

The good news is that sometimes it is possible to increase employee motivation by helping employees change their perspective about the job. For example, employees laying bricks at a construction site may feel their jobs are low in significance, but by pointing out that they are building a home for others, their perceptions about their job may be changed.

growth need strength

The degree to which a person has higher order needs, such as self-esteem and self-actualization.

Do all employees expect to have a job that has a high motivating potential? Research has shown that the desire for the five core job characteristics is not universal. One factor that affects how much of these characteristics people want or need is **growth need strength**. Growth need strength describes the degree to which a person has higher order needs, such as self-esteem and self-actualization. When an employee's expectation from his job includes such higher order needs, employees will have high-growth need strength, whereas those who expect their job to pay the bills and satisfy more basic needs will have low-growth need strength. Not surprisingly, research shows that those with high-growth need strength respond more favorably to jobs with a high motivating potential.[26] It also seems that an employee's career stage influences how important the five dimensions are. For example, when employees are new to an organization, task significance is a positive influence over job satisfaction, but autonomy may be a negative influence.[27]

OB Toolbox: Increase the Feedback You Receive: Seek It!

- *If you are not receiving enough feedback on the job, it is better to seek it instead of trying to guess how you are doing.* Consider seeking regular feedback from your boss. This also has the added benefit of signaling to the manager that you care about your performance and want to be successful.
- *Be genuine in your desire to learn.* When seeking feedback, your aim should be improving yourself as opposed to creating the impression that you are a motivated employee. If your manager thinks that you are managing impressions rather than genuinely trying to improve your performance, seeking feedback may hurt you.
- *Develop a good relationship with your manager.* This has the benefit of giving you more feedback in the first place. It also has the upside of making it easier to ask direct questions about your own performance.
- *Consider finding trustworthy peers who can share information with you regarding your performance.* Your manager is not the only helpful source of feedback.
- *Be gracious when you receive feedback.* If you automatically go on the defensive the first time you receive negative feedback, there may not be a next time. Remember, even if receiving feedback, positive or negative, feels uncomfortable, it is a gift. You can improve your performance using feedback, and people giving negative feedback probably feel they are risking your good will by being honest. Be thankful and appreciative when you receive any feedback and do not try to convince the person that it is inaccurate (unless there are factual mistakes).

Sources: Adapted from ideas in Jackman, J. M., & Strober, M. H. (2003, April). Fear of feedback. Harvard Business Review, 81(4), 101–107; Wing, L., Xu, H., Snape, E. (2007). Feedback-seeking behavior and leader-member exchange: Do supervisor-attributed motives matter? Academy of Management Journal, 50, 348–363; Lee, H. E., Park, H. S., Lee, T. S., & Lee, D. W. (2007). Relationships between LMX and subordinates' feedback-seeking behaviors. Social Behavior & Personality: An International Journal, 35, 659–674.

1.5 Empowerment

empowerment

The removal of conditions that make a person powerless.

One of the contemporary approaches to motivating employees through job design is empowerment. The concept of empowerment extends the idea of autonomy. **Empowerment** may be defined as the removal of conditions that make a person powerless.[28] The idea behind empowerment is that employees have the ability to make decisions and perform their jobs effectively if management removes certain barriers. Thus, instead of dictating roles, companies should create an environment where employees thrive, feel motivated, and have discretion to make decisions about the content and context of their jobs. Employees who feel empowered believe that their work is meaningful. They tend to feel that they are capable of performing their jobs effectively, have the ability to influence how the company operates, and can perform their jobs in any way they see fit, without close supervision and other interference. These liberties enable employees to feel powerful.[29] In cases of very high levels of empowerment, employees decide what tasks to perform and how to perform them, in a sense managing themselves.

structural empowerment

The aspects of the work environment that give employees discretion and autonomy, and enable them to do their jobs effectively.

Research has distinguished between *structural* elements of empowerment and *felt* empowerment. **Structural empowerment** refers to the aspects of the work environment that give employees discretion, autonomy, and the ability to do their jobs effectively. The idea is that the presence of certain structural factors helps empower people, but in the end empowerment is a perception. The following figure demonstrates the relationship between structural and felt empowerment. For example, at Harley-Davidson Motor Company, employees have the authority to stop the production line if they see a blemish on the product.[30] Leadership style is another influence over experienced empowerment.[31] If the manager is controlling, micromanaging, and bossy, chances are that empowerment will not be possible. A company's structure has a role in determining empowerment as well. Factories organized around teams, such as the Saturn plant of General Motors Corporation, can still empower employees, despite the presence of a traditional hierarchy.[32] Access to information is often mentioned as a key factor in empowering employees. If employees are not given information to make an informed decision, empowerment attempts will fail. Therefore, the relationship between access to information and empowerment is well established. Finally, empowering individual employees cannot occur in a bubble, but instead depends on creating a climate of empowerment throughout the entire organization.[33]

FIGURE 6.4

The empowerment process starts with structure that leads to felt empowerment.

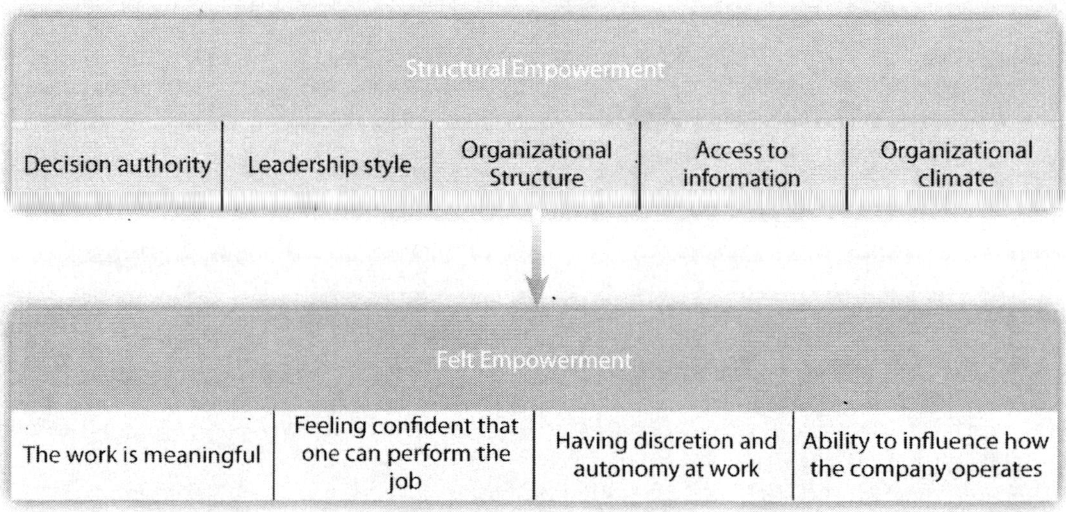

Source: Based on the ideas in Seibert, S. E., Silver, S. R., & Randolph, W. A. (2004). Taking empowerment to the next level: A multiple-level model of empowerment, performance, and satisfaction. Academy of Management Journal, 47, 332–349; Spreitzer, G. M. (1995). Psychological empowerment in the workplace: Dimensions, measurement, and validation. Academy of Management Journal, 38, 1442–1465; Spreitzer, G. M. (1996). Social structural characteristics of psychological empowerment. Academy of Management Journal, 39, 483–504.

Empowerment of employees tends to be beneficial for organizations, because it is related to outcomes such as employee innovativeness, managerial effectiveness, employee commitment to the organization, customer satisfaction, job performance, and behaviors that benefit the company and other employees.[34] At the same time, empowerment may not necessarily be suitable for all employees. Those individuals with low growth strength or low achievement need may not benefit as strongly from empowerment. Moreover, the idea of empowerment is not always easy to implement, because some managers may feel threatened when subordinates are empowered. If employees do not feel ready for empowerment, they may also worry about the increased responsibility and accountability. Therefore, preparing employees for empowerment by carefully selecting and training them is important to the success of empowerment interventions.

OB Toolbox: Tips for Empowering Employees

- *Change the company structure so that employees have more power on their jobs.* If jobs are strongly controlled by organizational procedures or if every little decision needs to be approved by a superior, employees are unlikely to feel empowered. Give them discretion at work.
- *Provide employees with access to information about things that affect their work.* When employees have the information they need to do their jobs well and understand company goals, priorities, and strategy, they are in a better position to feel empowered.
- *Make sure that employees know how to perform their jobs.* This involves selecting the right people as well as investing in continued training and development.

- *Do not take away employee power.* If someone makes a decision, let it stand unless it threatens the entire company. If management undoes decisions made by employees on a regular basis, employees will not believe in the sincerity of the empowerment initiative.
- *Instill a climate of empowerment in which managers do not routinely step in and take over.* Instead, believe in the power of employees to make the most accurate decisions, as long as they are equipped with the relevant facts and resources.

Sources: Adapted from ideas in Forrester, R. (2000). Empowerment: Rejuvenating a potent idea. Academy of Management Executive, 14, 67–79; Spreitzer, G. M. (1996). Social structural characteristics of psychological empowerment. Academy of Management Journal, 39, 483–504.

KEY TAKEAWAY

Job specialization is the earliest approach to job design, originally described by the work of Frederick Taylor. Job specialization is efficient but leads to boredom and monotony. Early alternatives to job specialization include job rotation, job enlargement, and job enrichment. Research shows that there are five job components that increase the motivating potential of a job: Skill variety, task identity, task significance, autonomy, and feedback. Finally, empowerment is a contemporary way of motivating employees through job design. These approaches increase worker motivation and have the potential to increase performance.

EXERCISES

1. Is job rotation primarily suitable to lower level employees, or is it possible to use it at higher levels in the organization?
2. What is the difference between job enlargement and job enrichment? Which of these approaches is more useful in dealing with the boredom and monotony of job specialization?
3. Consider a job you held in the past. Analyze the job using the framework of the job characteristics model.
4. Does a job with a high motivating potential motivate all employees? Under which conditions is the model less successful in motivating employees?
5. How would you increase the empowerment levels of employees?

2. MOTIVATING EMPLOYEES THROUGH GOAL SETTING

LEARNING OBJECTIVES

1. **Describe why goal setting motivates employees.**
2. **Identify characteristics of a goal that make it effective.**
3. **Identify limitations of goals.**
4. **Understand how to tie individual goals to strategic goals.**

2.1 Goal-Setting Theory

Goal-setting theory[35] is one of the most influential and practical theories of motivation. In fact, in a survey of organizational behavior scholars, it has been rated as the most important (out of 73 theories).[36] The theory has been supported in over 1,000 studies with employees ranging from blue-collar workers to research-and-development employees, and there is strong support that setting goals is related to performance improvements.[37] According to one estimate, goal setting improves performance at least 10%–25%.[38] Based on this evidence, thousands of companies around the world are using goal setting in some form, including Coca Cola Company, PricewaterhouseCoopers International Ltd., Nike Inc., Intel Corporation, and Microsoft Corporation, to name a few.

2.2 Setting SMART Goals

Are you motivated simply because you have set a goal? The mere presence of a goal does not motivate individuals. Think about New Year's resolutions that you made but failed to keep. Maybe you decided that you should lose some weight but then never put a concrete plan in action. Maybe you decided that you would read more but didn't. Why did your goal fail?

Accumulating research evidence indicates that effective goals are SMART. A **SMART goal** is a goal that is specific, measurable, aggressive, realistic, and time-bound.

FIGURE 6.5

SMART goals help people achieve results.

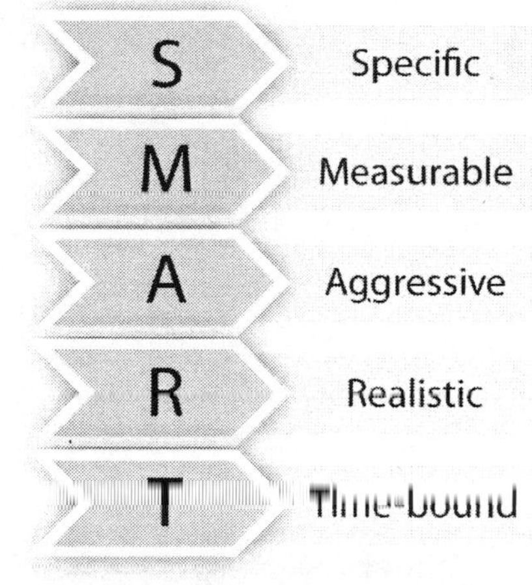

Specific and Measurable

Effective goals are specific and measurable. For example, "increasing sales to a region by 10%" is a specific goal, whereas deciding to "delight customers" is not specific or measurable. When goals are specific, performance tends to be higher.[39] Why? If goals are not specific and measurable, how would you know whether you have reached the goal? A wide distribution of performance levels could potentially be acceptable. For the same reason, "doing your best" is not an effective goal, because it is not measurable and does not give you a specific target.

Certain aspects of performance are easier to quantify. For example, it is relatively easy to set specific goals for productivity, sales, number of defects, or turnover rates. However, not everything that is easy to measure should be measured. Moreover, some of the most important elements of someone's performance may not be easily quantifiable (such as employee or customer satisfaction). So how do you set specific and measurable goals for these soft targets? Even though some effort will be involved, metrics such as satisfaction can and should be quantified. For example, you could design a survey for employees and customers to track satisfaction ratings from year to year.

SMART goal

A goal that is ***s***pecific, ***m***easurable, ***a***ggressive, ***r***ealistic, and ***t***ime-bound.

Aggressive

This may sound counterintuitive, but effective goals are difficult, not easy. Aggressive goals are also called stretch goals. According to a Hay Group study, one factor that distinguishes companies that are ranked as "Most Admired Companies" in *Fortune* magazine is that they set more difficult goals.[40] People with difficult goals outperform those with easier goals.[41] Why? Easy goals do not provide a challenge. When goals are aggressive and require people to work harder or smarter, performance tends to be dramatically higher. Research shows that people who have a high level of self-efficacy and people who have a high need for achievement tend to set more difficult goals for themselves.[42]

Realistic

While goals should be difficult, they should also be based in reality. In other words, if a goal is viewed as impossible to reach, it will not have any motivational value. In fact, setting impossible goals and then punishing people for not reaching these goals is cruel and will demotivate employees.

Time-Bound

The goal should contain a statement regarding when the proposed performance level will be reached. For example, "increasing sales to a region by 10%" is not a time-bound goal, because there is no time limit. Adding a limiter such as "by December of the current fiscal year" gives employees a sense of time urgency.

Here is a sample SMART goal: Wal-Mart Stores Inc. recently set a goal to eliminate 25% of the solid waste from U.S. stores by the year 2009. This goal meets all the conditions of being SMART (as long as 25% is a difficult yet realistic goal).[43] Even though it seems like a simple concept, in reality many goals that are set within organizations may not be SMART. For example, Microsoft recently conducted an audit of its goal setting and performance review system and found that only about 40% of the goals were specific and measurable.[44]

2.3 Why Do SMART Goals Motivate?

FIGURE 6.6

SMART goals motivate for a variety of reasons.

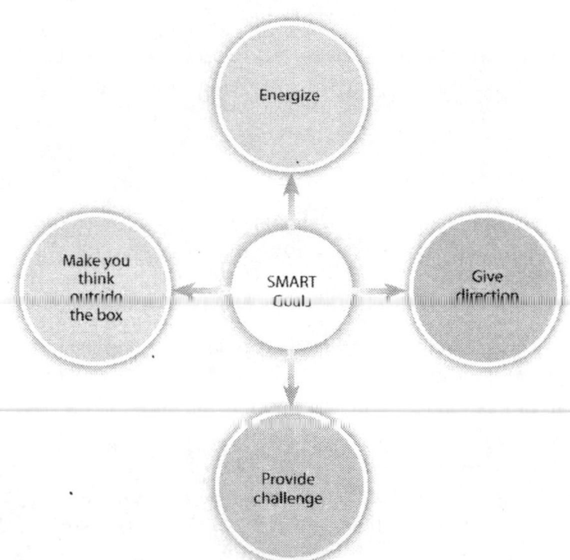

Sources: Based on information contained in Latham, G. P. (2004). The motivational benefits of goal-setting. Academy of Management Executive, 18, 126–129; Seijts, G. H., & Latham, G. P. (2005). Learning versus performance goals: When should each be used? Academy of Management Executive, 19, 124–131; Shaw, K. N. (2004). Changing the goal-setting process at Microsoft. Academy of Management Executive, 18, 139–142.

There are at least four reasons why goals motivate.[45] First, goals give us direction. When you have a goal of reducing shipment of defective products by 5% by September, you know that you should direct your energy toward defects. The goal tells you what to focus on. For this reason, goals should be set carefully. Giving employees goals that are not aligned with company goals will be a problem, because goals will direct employees' energies to a certain end. Second, goals energize people and tell them not to stop until the goal is accomplished. If you set goals for yourself such as "I will have a break from reading this textbook when I finish reading this section," you will not give up until you reach the end of the section. Even if you feel tired along the way, having this specific goal will urge you to move forward. Third, having a goal provides a challenge. When people have goals and proceed to reach them, they feel a sense of accomplishment. Finally, SMART goals urge people to think outside the box and rethink how they are working. If the goal is not very difficult, it only motivates people to work faster or longer. If a goal is substantially difficult, merely working faster or longer will not get you the results. Instead, you will need to rethink the way you usually work and devise a creative way of working. It has been argued that this method resulted in designers and engineers in Japan inventing the bullet train. Having a goal that went beyond the speed capabilities of traditional trains prevented engineers from making minor improvements and inspired them to come up with a radically different concept.[46]

2.4 When Are Goals More Effective?

Even when goals are SMART, they are not always equally effective. Sometimes, goal setting produces more dramatic effects compared to other methods. At least three conditions that contribute to effectiveness have been identified.[47]

Feedback

To be more effective, employees should receive feedback on the progress they are making toward goal accomplishment. Providing employees with quantitative figures about their sales, defects, or other metrics is useful for feedback purposes.

Ability

Employees should have the skills, knowledge, and abilities to reach their goals. In fact, when employees are lacking the necessary abilities, setting specific outcome goals has been shown to lead to lower levels of performance.[48] People are likely to feel helpless when they lack the abilities to reach a goal, and furthermore, having specific outcome goals prevents them from focusing on learning activities. In these situations, setting goals about learning may be a better idea. For example, instead of setting a goal related to increasing sales, the goal could be identifying three methods of getting better acquainted with customers.

Goal Commitment

SMART goals are more likely to be effective if employees are committed to the goal.[49] As a testament to the importance of goal commitment, Microsoft actually calls employee goals "commitments."[50] **Goal commitment** refers to the degree to which a person is dedicated to reaching the goal. What makes people dedicated or committed to a goal? It has been proposed that making goals public may increase commitment to the goal, because it creates accountability to peers. When individuals have a supportive and trust-based relationship with managers, goal commitment tends to be higher. When employees participate in goal setting, goal commitment may be higher. Last, but not least, rewarding people for their goal accomplishment may increase commitment to future goals.[51]

goal commitment

The degree to which a person is dedicated to reaching the goal.

2.5 Are There Downsides to Goal Setting?

As with any management technique, there may be some downsides to goal setting.[52] First, as mentioned earlier, setting goals for specific outcomes may hamper employee performance if employees are lacking skills and abilities needed to reach the goals. In these situations, setting goals for behaviors and learning may be more effective than setting goals for outcomes. Second, goal setting may prevent employees from adapting and changing their behaviors in response to unforeseen threats. For example, one study found that when teams had difficult goals and employees within the team had high levels of performance expectations, teams had difficulty adapting to unforeseen circumstances.[53] Third, goals focus employee attention on the activities that are measured. This focus may lead to sacrificing other important elements of performance. If goals are set for production numbers, quality may suffer. As a result, it is important to set goals touching on all critical aspects of performance. Finally, an aggressive pursuit of goals may lead to unethical behaviors. If employees are rewarded for goal accomplishment but there are no rewards for coming very close to reaching the goal, employees may be tempted to cheat.

FIGURE 6.7 Potential Downsides of Goal Setting

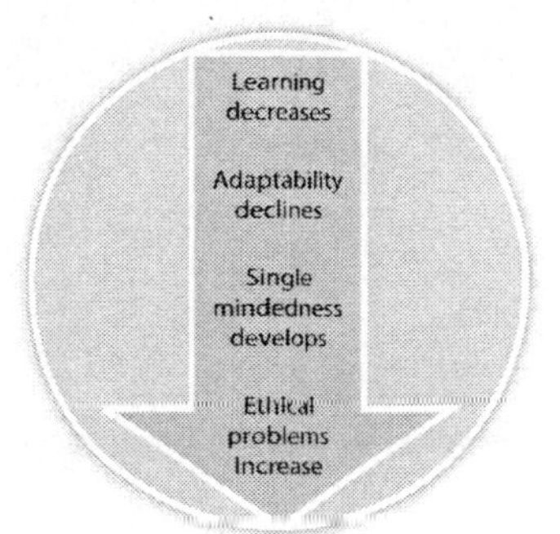

Sources: Based on LePine, J. A. (2005). Adaptation of teams in response to unforeseen change: Effects of goal difficulty and team composition in terms of cognitive ability and goal orientation. Journal of Applied Psychology, 90, 1153–1167; Locke, E. A. (2004). Linking goals to monetary incentives. Academy of Management Executive, 18, 130–133; Pritchard, R. D., Roth, P. L., Jones, S. D., Galgay, P. J., & Watson, M. D. (1988). Designing a goal-setting system to enhance performance: A practical guide. Organizational Dynamics, 17, 69–78; Seijts, G. H., & Latham, G. P. (2005). Learning versus performance goals: When should each be used? Academy of Management Executive, 19, 124–131.

2.6 Ensuring Goal Alignment Through Management by Objectives (MBO)

Goals direct employee attention toward a common end. Therefore, it is crucial for individual goals to support team goals and team goals to support company goals. A systematic approach to ensure that individual and organizational goals are aligned is **Management by Objectives (MBO)**. First suggested by Peter Drucker,[54] MBO involves the following process:

1. Setting companywide goals derived from corporate strategy
2. Determining team- and department-level goals
3. Collaboratively setting individual-level goals that are aligned with corporate strategy
4. Developing an action plan
5. Periodically reviewing performance and revising goals

A review of the literature shows that 68 out of the 70 studies conducted on this topic displayed performance gains as a result of MBO implementation.[55] It also seems that top management commitment to the process is the key to successful implementation of MBO programs.[56] Even though formal MBO programs have fallen out of favor since the 1980s, the idea of linking employee goals to corporate-wide goals is a powerful idea that benefits organizations.

Management by Objectives (MBO)

Setting companywide goals derived from corporate strategy, determining team- and department-level goals, collaboratively setting individual-level goals that are aligned with corporate strategy, developing an action plan, and periodically reviewing performance and revising goals.

KEY TAKEAWAY

Goal-setting theory is one of the most influential theories of motivation. In order to motivate employees, goals should be SMART (specific, measurable, aggressive, realistic, and time-bound). SMART goals motivate employees because they energize behavior, give it direction, provide a challenge, force employees to think outside the box, and devise new and novel methods of performing. Goals are more effective in motivating employees when employees receive feedback on their accomplishments, have the ability to perform, and are committed to goals. Poorly derived goals have the downsides of hampering learning, preventing adaptability, causing a single-minded pursuit of goals at the exclusion of other activities, and encouraging unethical behavior. Companies tie individual goals to company goals using management by objectives.

EXERCISES

1. Give an example of a SMART goal.
2. If a manager tells you to "sell as much as you can," is this goal likely to be effective? Why or why not?
3. How would you ensure that employees are committed to the goals set for them?
4. A company is interested in increasing customer loyalty. Using the MBO approach, what would be the department- and individual-level goals supporting this organization-wide goal?
5. Discuss an experience you have had with goals. Explain how goal setting affected motivation and performance.

3. MOTIVATING EMPLOYEES THROUGH PERFORMANCE APPRAISALS

LEARNING OBJECTIVES

1. **Understand why companies use performance appraisals.**
2. **Describe basic characteristics of performance appraisals.**
3. **List the characteristics of an effective performance appraisal.**
4. **Compare the advantages and disadvantages of relative versus absolute appraisals.**
5. **Learn how to conduct a performance appraisal meeting.**
6. **Understand the biases inherent in performance appraisals.**

3.1 What Is a Performance Appraisal?

performance appraisal

A process in which a rater or raters evaluate the performance of another employee.

When employees have goals, they tend to be more motivated if they also receive feedback about their progress. Feedback may occur throughout the workday, but many organizations also have a formal, companywide process of providing feedback to employees, called the **performance appraisal**. A performance appraisal is a process in which a rater or raters evaluate the performance of an employee. More specifically, during a performance appraisal period, rater(s) observe, interact with, and evaluate a person's performance. Then, when it is time for a performance appraisal, these observations are documented on a form. The rater usually conducts a meeting with the employee to communicate performance feedback. During the meeting, the employee is evaluated with respect to success in achieving last year's goals, and new goals are set for the next performance appraisal period.

Even though performance appraisals can be quite effective in motivating employees and resolving performance problems, in reality, only a small number of organizations use the performance appraisal process to its full potential. In many companies, a performance appraisal takes the form of a bureaucratic activity that is mutually despised by employees and managers. The problems a poor appraisal process can create may be so severe that many experts, including the founder of the total quality movement, Edward Deming, have recommended abolishing appraisals altogether.[57] On the other hand, creating and executing an effective appraisal system actually leads to higher levels of trust in management.[58] Therefore, identifying ways of increasing appraisal effectiveness is important.

Giving employees feedback is not synonymous with conducting a performance appraisal, because employees may (and should) receive frequent feedback. The most effective feedback immediately follows high or low performance. Therefore, waiting for a formal process to give feedback would be misguided. A formal appraisal is often conducted once a year, even though there are some organizations that conduct them more frequently. For example, there are advantages to conducting quarterly appraisals, such as allowing managers to revise goals more quickly in the face of changing environmental demands.[59] Conducting appraisals once a year has the advantage of being more convenient for managers and for effectively tying performance to annual pay raises or bonuses.

3.2 What Is the Purpose of a Performance Appraisal?

Performance appraisals can be important tools to give employees feedback and aid in their development. Yet feedback is only one reason why companies perform appraisals. In many companies, appraisals are used to distribute rewards such as bonuses, annual pay raises, and promotions. They may also be used to document termination of employees. Research shows that performance appraisals tend to be viewed as more effective when companies tie them to reward decisions and to terminate lower performers.[60] This is not surprising in light of motivation theories such as reinforcement theory, which indicates that behavior that is rewarded is repeated. Tying appraisal results to rewards may lead to the perception that performance is rewarded. However, if performance appraisal ratings are not accurate, it is possible for appraisals to be a major cause of reward unfairness.

3.3 Who Is the Rater?

Traditionally, the rater has been the supervisor. Supervisors have more at stake when an employee is not performing well and they have access to greater resources that can be used to improve performance. However, relying solely on supervisors may lead to a biased appraisal system. Many aspects of a person's performance may remain hidden from managers, particularly in team-based settings or organizations where supervisors do not work in the same physical setting as the employees. Therefore, organizations are introducing additional raters into the system, such as peers, customers, and subordinates. As organizations become more flat, introducing more perspectives may provide richer feedback to employees in question. Organizations using supervisors, peers, subordinates, and sometimes even customers are using **360-degree feedback**. In this system, feedback is gathered from all these sources, and shared with the employee for developmental purposes. It is important to note that 360-degree appraisals are not often used in determining pay or promotion decisions and instead are treated as feedback tools. Using 360-degree feedback in reward decisions may be problematic, because individuals may avoid giving objective feedback if it means causing a peer to lose a bonus. Since not all feedback will necessarily be positive, if competition or jealousy exists among peers, some feedback may be retaliatory and too negative. Keeping these problems in mind, organizations may benefit from using only supervisor ratings in reward decisions and using feedback from other sources for developmental purposes.[61]

360-degree feedback

A system where feedback is gathered from supervisors, peers, subordinates, and sometimes even customers.

3.4 What Makes an Effective Appraisal System?

What are the characteristics of an effective appraisal system? Research identified at least three characteristics of appraisals that increase the perception that they are fair. These characteristics include adequate notice, fair hearing, and judgment based on evidence. **Adequate notice** involves letting employees know what criteria will be used during the appraisal. Unfortunately, in many companies the first time employees see the appraisal form may be when they are being evaluated. Therefore, they may be rated low on something they didn't understand was part of their performance. **Fair hearing** means ensuring that there is two-way communication during the appraisal process and the employee's side of the story is heard. **Judgment based on evidence** involves documenting performance problems and using factual evidence as opposed to personal opinions when rating performance.[62]

adequate notice

Letting employees know what criteria will be used during the appraisal.

fair hearing

Ensuring that there is two-way communication during the appraisal process and the employee's side of the story is heard.

judgment based on evidence

Documenting performance problems and using factual evidence.

3.5 Absolute Rating versus Relative Ranking Appraisals

As a student, would you rather be evaluated with respect to some objective criteria? For example, you could get an A if you correctly answer 90% of the questions in the exam, but would get a B if you answered only 80%. We are calling this type of appraisal an absolute rating because the grade you get depends only on your performance with respect to the objective criteria. The alternative to this approach is relative ranking. In this system, you would get an A if you are one of the top 10% of the students in class, but you would get a B if you are between 10% and 20%. In a relative ranking system, your rating depends on how your objective performance (test grade) compares with the rest of the students' grades in your class.

If you say you would prefer an absolute rating, you are not alone. Research shows that ranking systems are often viewed more negatively by employees. However, many major corporations such as General Electric Company (GE), Intel, and Yahoo! Inc. are using relative rankings and truly believe in its advantages. For example, Jack Welch, the former CEO of General Electric, instituted a forced ranking system at GE in which 20% of employees would be in the top category, 70% would be in the middle, and 10% would be at the bottom rank. Employees who are repeatedly ranked at the lowest rank would be terminated. Relative rankings may create a culture of performance by making it clear that low performance is not tolerated; however, there are several downsides to rankings. First, these systems carry the danger of a potential lawsuit. Organizations such as Ford Motor Company and Microsoft faced lawsuits involving relative rankings, because employees who were older, female, or minority members were systematically being ranked in the lowest category with little justification. Second, relative rankings are also not consistent with creating a team spirit and may create a competitive, cutthroat environment. Enron Corporation was an organization that used relative rankings to its detriment. Third, relative systems have limited value in giving employees concrete feedback about what to do next year to get a better ranking. Despite their limitations, using them for a few years may help the organization become more performance-oriented and eliminate stagnation by weeding out some employees with persistent performance problems. As long as these systems fit with the company culture, are not used in a rigid manner, and are used for a short period of time, they may be beneficial to the organization.[63]

3.6 Conducting the Appraisal Meeting

FIGURE 6.8

A performance appraisal meeting serves as a medium through which the rater gives positive and negative feedback to the ratee, helps the ratee solve performance problems, and recognizes effective performance.

© 2010 Jupiterimages Corporation

A performance appraisal meeting is the most important component of a performance appraisal. After the rater uses the company's appraisal form to evaluate the performance of the ratee, both sides meet to discuss positive and negative instances of performance. Thus, the meeting serves as the key medium through which the rater gives feedback to the ratee. The goal of providing performance feedback is to help the ratee solve performance problems and to motivate the employee to change behavior. Conducting this meeting is often stressful for both parties, and training managers in providing performance feedback may be useful to deal with the stress of the managers as well as creating a more positive experience for both parties.[64]

In the most effective meetings, feedback is presented in a constructive manner. Instead of criticizing the person, the focus should be on discussing the performance problems and aiding the employee in resolving these problems. By moving the focus of the conversation from the person to the behaviors, employee defensiveness may be reduced. When the supervisor is constructive, employees develop a more positive view of the appraisal system. Another approach to increasing the effectiveness of appraisal meetings is to increase employee participation. When employees have the opportunity to present their side of the story, they react more positively to the appraisal process and feel that the system is fair. Finally, supervisors should be knowledgeable about the employee's performance. When it becomes clear that the person doing the evaluation has little understanding of the job being performed by the employee, reactions tend to be more negative.[65]

OB Toolbox: Conducting an Effective Performance Appraisal Meeting

Before the meeting

- *Ask the person to complete a self-appraisal.* This is a great way of making sure that employees become active participants in the process and get their voice heard.
- *Complete the performance appraisal form.* Document your rating using many examples. Have more examples handy.
- *Avoid recency bias.* Be sure that your review covers the entire year's performance, not just recent events.
- *Handle the logistics.* Be sure that you devote sufficient time to each meeting. If you schedule appraisals back to back, you may lose your energy in later meetings. Be sure that the physical location is conducive to a private conversation.

During the meeting

- *Be sure to recognize effective performance.* Give specific praise.

- *Do not start the meeting with a criticism.* Starting with positive instances of performance helps establish a better mood and shows that you recognize what the employee is doing right.
- *Give employees lots of opportunities to talk.* Ask them about their greatest accomplishments, as well as opportunities for improvement. If they touch on an area you wanted to cover, provide your thoughts.
- *Show empathy and support.* Remember: your job as a manager is to help the person solve performance problems. Identify areas where you can help.
- *Set goals and create an action plan.* The outcome of the meeting should be a written agreement about what the employee will do in the near future and how the manager will help.

After the meeting

- *Continue to give the employee periodic and frequent feedback.* Effective feedback immediately follows key incidents of performance. Do not wait until the next appraisal to discuss important issues.
- *Follow through on the goals that were set.* Provide continuous support to the employee to help him or her achieve the goals.

Sources: Make employee appraisals more productive. (2007, September). HR Focus, 84(9), 1, 11–15; Ryan, L. (2007, January 17). Coping with performance review anxiety. Business Week Online, 6; Stone, D. L. (1984). The effects of feedback sequence and expertise of the rater on perceived feedback accuracy. Personnel Psychology, 37, 487–506; Sulkowicz, K. (2007, September 10). Straight talk at review time. Business Week, 16.

3.7 Managing Potential Bias in Performance Appraisals

Performance appraisal is by nature a subjective event. Unless the performance appraisal is purely relying on objective criteria such as sales, it requires one or more human beings to observe and evaluate another and arrive at a consensus. Raters, intentionally or unintentionally, make mistakes or exhibit biases. These biases trickle down into the appraisal system and can affect other decisions that are based on appraisals, such as pay and promotion. Therefore, being aware of these tendencies is the first step to managing their influence over the appraisal system.

Liking

A performance appraisal does not occur between strangers. The rater and ratee have an existing relationship. If they like or dislike each other, these feelings may bias the ratings. For example, research shows that regardless of their objective performance levels, managers give employees they have a good relationship with higher ratings.[66] It is possible that sometimes liking is not a bias and a manager likes an employee *because* of high performance levels.[67] Still, for some managers, liking someone may mean ignoring the faults of the person and selectively remembering the positive things that person has done. One way of dealing with this problem may be journaling. By recording positive and negative performance incidents throughout the year for each employee, managers may recall each employee's performance more accurately.[68]

Leniency

One of the common problems in appraisals is that managers give employees ratings higher than warranted. There may be many reasons for this, such as the desire to avoid confrontation with the employee, having a very agreeable personality, the desire to avoid hurting the chances of the employee to get a bonus, the desire to motivate employees by giving them high ratings, or liking the employee as a person. Regardless of the reason, leniency is a problem because it makes ratings relatively useless for determining raises, bonuses, or promotions. At the same time, leniency makes it harder for employees to change their behaviors. One way of dealing with this problem could be using relative rankings or at least giving managers a suggested distribution. If managers are asked to grade on a curve, they may end up being less lenient. Moreover, making managers accountable for the ratings they give may be a good idea. For example, if managers are evaluated based on how well they recognize different levels of performance, they may be less tempted to be lenient in appraisals.[69]

Stereotypes

One of the factors that create bias in appraisals is the stereotypes that raters may have regarding the gender, race, age or another characteristic of the person being rated. Beliefs about different groups may be generalized to the person in question even though they may have little basis in reality. For example, research shows that women in stereotypically male jobs were rated lower than women in stereotypically female jobs. Similarly, attractive women were rated higher if they held nonmanagement jobs, but they were rated lower if they held management jobs. When factors that have no bearing on one's job performance are used to evaluate the person, employees, overall, will be demoralized, the appraisals will lose their effectiveness, and the company may face costly lawsuits.[70] Understanding the importance of eliminating stereotypes from performance appraisals and training managers to accurately observe and evaluate performance may be beneficial in limiting exposure to this type of bias.

KEY TAKEAWAY

Performance appraisals involve observing and measuring an employee's performance during an appraisal period, recording these observations, communicating results to the employee, and recognizing high performance while devising ways of improving deficiencies. Most appraisals are conducted by the supervisor, but there are many advantages to using 360-degree appraisals. Appraisals that are more effective give employees adequate notice, fair hearing, and judgment based on evidence. Some companies use relative rankings in which employees are compared to each other, but this system is not suitable to all companies. A performance appraisal meeting should be planned and executed carefully, with the supervisor demonstrating empathy and supportiveness. There are intentional and unintentional biases inherent in appraisals and being aware of them, increasing rater accountability, and training managers may be useful in dealing with some of them.

EXERCISES

1. What are the disadvantages of using only supervisors as the rater? What are the disadvantages of using peers, subordinates, and customers as raters?
2. Do you believe that self-appraisals are valid? Why would it be helpful to add self-appraisals to the appraisal process? Can you think of any downsides to using them?
3. Why do some managers intentionally give an employee a higher rating than deserved? What are the disadvantages of biased ratings? How could this tendency be prevented?
4. Some recommend that performance appraisals be abolished altogether. What do you think about this approach? What are the downsides of eliminating appraisals altogether?
5. If your objective is to minimize the effects of rater biases, what type of appraisal system would you design?

4. MOTIVATING EMPLOYEES THROUGH PERFORMANCE INCENTIVES

LEARNING OBJECTIVES

1. **Learn the importance of financial and nonfinancial incentives to motivate employees.**
2. **Understand the benefits of different types of incentive systems, such as piece rate and merit pay.**
3. **Learn why nonfinancial incentives can be effective motivators.**
4. **Understand the tradeoffs involved in rewarding individual, group, and organizational performance.**

4.1 Performance Incentives

Perhaps the most tangible way in which companies put motivation theories into action is by instituting incentive systems. Incentives are reward systems that tie pay to performance. There are many incentives used by companies, some tying pay to individual performance and some to companywide performance. Pay-for-performance plans are very common among organizations. For example, according to one estimate, 80% of all American companies have merit pay, and the majority of Fortune 1000 companies use incentives.[71] Using incentives to increase performance is a very old idea. For example, Napoleon promised 12,000 francs to whoever found a way to preserve food for the army. The winner of the prize was Nicolas Appert, who developed a method of canning food.[72] Research shows that companies using pay-for-performance systems actually achieve higher productivity, profits, and customer service. These systems are more effective than praise or recognition in increasing retention of higher performing employees by creating higher levels of commitment to the company.[73] Moreover, employees report higher levels of pay satisfaction under pay-for-performance systems.[74]

At the same time, many downsides of incentives exist. For example, it has been argued that incentives may create a risk-averse environment that diminishes creativity. This may happen if employees are rewarded for doing things in a certain way, and taking risks may negatively affect their paycheck. Moreover, research shows that incentives tend to focus employee energy to goal-directed efforts, and behaviors such as helping team members or being a good citizen of the company may be neglected.[75] Despite their limitations, financial incentives may be considered powerful motivators if they are used properly and if they are aligned with companywide objectives. The most frequently used incentives are listed as follows.

Piece Rate Systems

piece rate incentives

Payment to employees made on the basis of their individual output.

Under **piece rate incentives**, employees are paid on the basis of individual output they produce. For example, a manufacturer may pay employees based on the number of purses sewn or number of doors installed in a day. In the agricultural sector, fruit pickers are often paid based on the amount of fruit they pick. These systems are suitable when employee output is easily observable or quantifiable and when output is directly correlated with employee effort. Piece rate systems are also used in white-collar jobs such as check-proofing in banks. These plans may encourage employees to work very fast, but may [illegible] might be more effective. Today, increases in employee monitoring technology are making it possible to correctly measure and observe individual output. For example, technology can track the number of tickets an employee sells or the number of customer complaints resolved, allowing a basis for employee pay incentives.[76] Piece rate systems can be very effective in increasing worker productivity. For example, Safelite AutoGlass, a nationwide installer of auto glass, moved to a piece rate system instead of paying workers by the hour. This change led to an average productivity gain of 20% per employee.[77]

Individual Bonuses

bonuses

One-time rewards that follow specific accomplishments of employees.

Bonuses are one-time rewards that follow specific accomplishments of employees. For example, an employee who reaches the quarterly goals set for her may be rewarded with a lump sum bonus. Employee motivation resulting from a bonus is generally related to the degree of advanced knowledge regarding bonus specifics.

Merit Pay

merit pay

Giving employees a permanent pay raise based on past performance.

In contrast to bonuses, **merit pay** involves giving employees a permanent pay raise based on past performance. Often the company's performance appraisal system is used to determine performance levels and the employees are awarded a raise, such as a 2% increase in pay. One potential problem with merit pay is that employees come to expect pay increases. In companies that give annual merit raises without a different raise for increases in cost of living, merit pay ends up serving as a cost-of-living adjustment and creates a sense of entitlement on the part of employees, with even low performers expecting them. Thus, making merit pay more effective depends on making it truly dependent on performance and designing a relatively objective appraisal system.

Sales Commissions

In many companies, the paycheck of sales employees is a combination of a base salary and commissions. **Sales commissions** involve rewarding sales employees with a percentage of sales volume or profits generated. Sales commissions should be designed carefully to be consistent with company objectives. For example, employees who are heavily rewarded with commissions may neglect customers who have a low probability of making a quick purchase. If only sales volume (as opposed to profitability) is rewarded, employees may start discounting merchandise too heavily, or start neglecting existing customers who require a lot of attention.[78] Therefore, the blend of straight salary and commissions needs to be managed carefully.

FIGURE 6.9

Properly designed sales commissions are widely used to motivate sales employees. The blend of straight salary and commissions should be carefully balanced to achieve optimum sales volume, profitability, and customer satisfaction.

sales commissions

Rewarding sales employees with a percentage of sales volume or profits generated.

Awards

Some companies manage to create effective incentive systems on a small budget while downplaying the importance of large bonuses. It is possible to motivate employees through awards, plaques, or other symbolic methods of recognition to the degree these methods convey sincere appreciation for employee contributions. For example, Yum! Brands Inc., the parent company of brands such as KFC and Pizza Hut, recognizes employees who go above and beyond job expectations through creative awards such as the seat belt award (a seat belt on a plaque), symbolizing the roller-coaster-like, fast-moving nature of the industry. Other awards include things such as a plush toy shaped like a jalapeño pepper. Hewlett-Packard Development Company LP has the golden banana award, which came about when a manager wanted to reward an employee who solved an important problem on the spot and handed him a banana lying around the office. Later, the golden banana award became an award bestowed on the most innovative employees.[79] Another alternative way of recognizing employee accomplishments is awarding gift cards. These methods are more effective if employees have a choice among alternatives (such as between restaurants, or between a restaurant or a retailer). The advantage of gift cards over pay is that instead of paying for life's necessities such as mortgage or college, employees can enjoy the gift of going out to dinner, going on a vacation to a fun place, or acquiring a cool gadget they may not have purchased with their own money. Thus, these awards may help create a sense of commitment to the company by creating positive experiences that are attributed to the company.

FIGURE 6.10

Plaques and other recognition awards may motivate employees if these awards fit with the company culture and if they reflect a sincere appreciation of employee accomplishments.

Team Bonuses

In situations in which employees should cooperate with each other and isolating employee performance is more difficult, companies are increasingly resorting to tying employee pay to team performance. For example, in 2007, Wal-Mart gave bonuses to around 80% of their associates based on store performance. If employees have a reasonable ability to influence their team's performance level, these programs may be effective.

Gainsharing

Gainsharing is a companywide program in which employees are rewarded for performance gains compared to past performance. These gains may take the form of reducing labor costs compared to estimates or reducing overall costs compared to past years' figures. These improvements are achieved through employee suggestions and participation in management through employee committees. For example, Premium Standard Farms LLC, a meat processing plant, instituted a gainsharing program in which employee-initiated changes in production processes led to a savings of $300,000 a month. The bonuses were close to $1,000 per person. These programs can be successful if the payout formula is generous, employees can truly participate in the management of the company, and if employees are able to communicate and execute their ideas.[80]

gainsharing

A companywide program in which employees are rewarded for performance gains compared to past performance.

Profit Sharing

Profit sharing programs involve sharing a percentage of company profits with all employees. These programs are companywide incentives and are not very effective in tying employee pay to individual effort, because each employee will have a limited role in influencing company profitability. At the same time, these programs may be more effective in creating loyalty and commitment to the company by recognizing all employees for their contributions throughout the year.

profit sharing

Programs involving sharing a percentage of company profits with all employees.

Stock Options

A **stock option** gives an employee the right, but not the obligation, to purchase company stocks at a predetermined price. For example, a company would commit to sell company stock to employees or managers 2 years in the future at $30 per share. If the company's actual stock price in 2 years is $60, employees would make a profit by exercising their options at $30 and then selling them in the stock market. The purpose of stock options is to align company and employee interests by making employees owners. However, options are not very useful for this purpose, because employees tend to sell the stock instead of holding onto it. In the past, options were given to a wide variety of employees, including CEOs, high performers, and in some companies all employees. For example, Starbucks Corporation was among companies that offered stock to a large number of associates. Options remain popular in start-up companies that find it difficult to offer competitive salaries to employees. In fact, many employees in high-tech companies such as Microsoft and Cisco Systems Inc. became millionaires by cashing in stock options after these companies went public. In recent years, stock option use has declined. One reason for this is the changes in options accounting. Before 2005, companies did not have to report options as an expense. After the changes in accounting rules, it became more expensive for companies to offer options. Moreover, options are less attractive or motivational for employees when the stock market is going down, because the cost of exercising their options may be higher than the market value of the shares. Because of these and other problems, some companies started granting employees actual stock or using other incentives. For example, PepsiCo Inc. replaced parts of the stock options program with a cash incentive program and gave managers the choice of getting stock options coupled with restricted stocks.[81]

stock option

Giving an employee the right, but not the obligation, to purchase company stocks at a predetermined price.

KEY TAKEAWAY

Companies use a wide variety of incentives to reward performance. This is consistent with motivation theories showing that rewarded behavior is repeated. Piece rate, individual bonuses, merit pay, and sales commissions tie pay to individual performance. Team bonuses are at the department level, whereas gainsharing, profit sharing, and stock options tie pay to company performance. While these systems may be effective, people tend to demonstrate behavior that is being rewarded and may neglect other elements of their performance. Therefore, reward systems should be designed carefully and should be tied to a company's strategic objectives.

EXERCISES

1. Have you ever been rewarded under any of the incentive systems described in this chapter? What was your experience with them?
2. What are the advantages and disadvantages of bonuses compared to merit pay? Which one would you use if you were a manager at a company?
3. What are the advantages of using awards as opposed to cash as an incentive?
4. How effective are stock options in motivating employees? Why do companies offer them?
5. Which of the incentive systems in this section do the best job of tying pay to individual performance? Which ones do the worst job?

5. THE ROLE OF ETHICS AND NATIONAL CULTURE

LEARNING OBJECTIVES

1. **Consider the role of job design, goals, and reward systems in ethical behavior.**
2. **Consider the role of national culture on job design, goals, and reward systems.**

5.1 Designing a Motivating Work Environment and Ethics

The design components of an organization's internal environment, such as the presence of goal setting, performance appraisals, and the use of incentive-based reward systems, have a direct connection with the level of ethical or unethical behaviors demonstrated within a company. Although a large number of companies successfully use goal setting and rewarding employees based on goal accomplishment, there is an unintended consequence to using goals: Goal setting may lead to unethical behaviors on the part of employees. When goal accomplishment is rewarded, and when rewards are desirable, employees will have two basic options: Work hard to reach the goals, or cheat.

The connection between goal setting and unethical behaviors has been well documented. For example, teachers rewarded for their students' success were more likely to cheat by giving the answers to students. Sanitation workers on an incentive scheme were more likely to take their trucks to the landfill with loads exceeding legal limits.[82] Salespeople working on commissions may push customers to make a purchase beyond their budget. At higher levels within companies, a CEO's method of payment has been related to the ethical behaviors of companies. For example, when a large percentage of a CEO pay package consists of stock options, companies are more likely to misrepresent the financial situation of the company, particularly when the CEO is also the head of the board of directors.[83]

This does not mean that goal setting always causes unethical behavior. People who behave unethically tend to constitute a small percentage of the workforce. However, for this small percentage, goal setting and incentives act as motivation to behave unethically. The tendency to behave unethically under these systems also increases when goals are not met, but instead, employees come close to reaching them, particularly when they are competing against each other to receive the rewards.[84] There are several ways companies can reduce the temptation to behave unethically. Specifically rewarding ethical behavior within the company is related to lower levels of unethical behaviors.[85] Also, instead of only rewarding people who reach a high goal and not giving anything to those who come close, companies may consider creating multiple levels of goals and distribute rewards corresponding to the goal that is achieved.[86] Enforcing an ethical code of conduct and withholding rewards from those who are not demonstrating ethical behaviors are other ways of preventing goal setting from leading to unethical behaviors.

5.2 Designing a Motivating Work Environment Around the Globe

The effectiveness of methods such as job design, goal setting, performance appraisals, and the use of incentives is likely to be culturally determined. For example, research conducted in Western countries suggests that empowering employees is an effective method of motivating them. However, not all employees around the world respond favorably to concepts such as autonomy or empowerment. For example, it has been noted that the use of self-managing teams, a method of increasing employee empowerment in the workplace, is difficult to execute in Mexican companies because of the traditionally paternalistic and hierarchical nature of many Mexican organizations. In such a context, employees may not be willing or ready to take responsibility for individual action, while managers may be unwilling to share real power with employees.[87] Researchers also found in a four-country study that while employees in the United States, Mexico, and Poland responded positively to empowerment, Indian employees were actually less satisfied when they were empowered.[88] In other words, we may expect both greater levels of difficulty and potentially different reactions to empowerment depending on the cultural context.

Are all employees around the globe motivated by goal setting? Even though there is limited research in this area, existing findings point to some differences. For example, we know that American employees respond negatively to goals when these goals are perceived to be extremely difficult. However, Chinese employees actually were most motivated when the goals were very difficult. This may be because Chinese employees believe that their performance depends on their effort, and therefore, they are able to respond to goals that are very difficult with very high effort. On the other hand, there is some evidence that while specific goals motivate Western salespeople, in China goals low in specificity were more motivational.[89]

How about performance appraisals? You may predict that concepts such as 360-degree appraisal are not suitable to all cultures. The 360-degree appraisals require a climate of openness and social equality in the workplace. Therefore, countries high in power distance and authoritarianism may respond negatively to appraisal systems where lower level employees give performance feedback to their managers. Likewise, in cultures high in collectivism, using peer appraisals may not be as effective, because employees might be hesitant to give accurate performance feedback to their colleagues with the fear that negative feedback may damage interpersonal relationships.

KEY TAKEAWAY

Goal setting and reward systems influence the level of ethics in the work environment. When employees come close to reaching their goals but fall short, they are more likely to behave unethically. The type of incentive system used in a company may generate unethical behaviors. Moreover, job design, goal setting, performance appraisals, and incentives should be designed while considering the national culture context, because they may not be universally valid.

EXERCISES

1. Do you have any experience with goal setting leading to unethical behaviors?
2. Many observers and employees are concerned about the spread between CEO pay and average employee pay. Is it ethical for CEOs to be paid so much more than other employees? Under which conditions would it be unethical?
3. How would you determine whether a certain incentive scheme or a type of performance appraisal could be transferred to a different culture?

6. CONCLUSION

In this chapter, we reviewed specific methods with which companies attempt to motivate their workforce. Designing jobs to increase their motivating potential, empowering employees, setting goals, evaluating performance using performance appraisals, and tying employee pay to individual, group, or organizational performance using incentive systems are methods through which motivation theories are put into action. Even though these methods seem to have advantages, every method could have unintended consequences, and therefore, application of each method should be planned and executed with an eye to organizational fairness.

7. EXERCISES

ETHICAL DILEMMA

James is about to conduct a performance appraisal for Maria. Maria has exhibited some performance problems in the past 6 months. She has been coming in late and leaving early, and she missed two important deadlines. At the same time, she is a very likeable and nice person who gets along well with others in the office. James also knows that Maria has a significant amount of debt and getting a bonus after this appraisal would really help her. James does not want to jeopardize his relationship with her and he does not want to prevent her from getting the bonus. Therefore, he is considering giving her a "good" rating in the appraisal. What would be your advice to James regarding this situation?

INDIVIDUAL EXERCISE

- A call center is using the metric of average time per call when rewarding employees. In order to keep their average time low, employees are hanging up on customers when they think that the call will take too long to answer.
- In a department store, salespeople are rewarded based on their sales volume. The problem is that they are giving substantial discounts and pressuring customers to make unnecessary purchases.
- All employees at a factory are receiving a large bonus if there are no reported injuries for 6 months. As a result, some employees are hiding their injuries so that they do not cause others to lose their bonus.

What are the reasons for the negative consequences of these bonus schemes? Modify these schemes to solve the problems.

GROUP EXERCISE

Performance Appraisal Role Play

This role play will involve three students. One student will be the supervisor and the second will be the subordinate. The supervisor and the subordinate will conduct a formal performance appraisal interview. The third role is of an observer who should provide feedback to both parties regarding how they could have improved their effectiveness.

Be sure to read only the role sheet assigned to you by your professor.

ENDNOTES

1. Taylor, F. W. (1911). Principles of scientific management. *American Magazine, 71*, 570–581. Wilson, F. M. (1999). Rationalization and rationality 1: From the founding fathers to eugenics. *Organizational Behaviour: A Critical Introduction*. Oxford, UK: Oxford University Press.

2. Campion, M. A., & Thayer, P. W. (1987). Job design: Approaches, outcomes, and trade-offs. *Organizational Dynamics, 15*, 66–78.

3. Wilson, F. M. (1999). Rationalization and rationality 1: From the founding fathers to eugenics. *Organizational Behaviour: A Critical Introduction*. Oxford, UK: Oxford University Press.

4. Spake, A. (2001). How McNuggets changed the world. *U.S. News & World Report, 130*(3), 54; Business heroes: Ray Kroc. (2005, Winter). *Business Strategy Review, 16*, 47–48.

5. Denton, D. K. (1994). …I hate this job. *Business Horizons, 37*, 46–52.

6. Rissen, D., Melin, B., Sandsjo, L., Dohns, I., & Lundberg, U. (2002). Psychophysiological stress reactions, trapezius muscle activity, and neck and shoulder pain among female cashiers before and after introduction of job rotation. *Work & Stress, 16*, 127–137.

7. Campion, M. A., Cheraskin, L., & Stevens, M. J. (1994). Career-related antecedents and outcomes of job rotation. *Academy of Management Journal, 37*, 1518–1542.

8. Kane, A. A., Argote, L., & Levine, J. M. (2005). Knowledge transfer between groups via personnel rotation: Effects of social identity and knowledge quality. *Organizational* [illegible]

9. Wylie, I. (2003, May). Calling for a renewable future. *Fast Company, 70*, 46–48.

10. Ramamurti, R. (2001). Wipro's chairman Azim Premji on building a world-class Indian company. *Academy of Management Executive, 15*, 13–19.

11. Parker, S. K. (1998). Enhancing role breadth self-efficacy: The roles of job enrichment and other organizational interventions. *Journal of Applied Psychology, 83*, 835–852.

12. Campion, M. A., & McClelland, C. L. (1991). Interdisciplinary examination of the costs and benefits of enlarged jobs: A job design quasi-experiment. *Journal of Applied Psychology, 76*, 186–198.

13. Campion, M. A., & McClelland, C. L. (1993). Follow-up and extension of the interdisciplinary costs and benefits of enlarged jobs. *Journal of Applied Psychology, 78*, 339–351.

14. McEvoy, G. M., & Cascio, W. F. (1985). Strategies for reducing employee turnover. *Journal of Applied Psychology, 70*, 342–353; Locke, E. A., Sirota, D., & Wolfson, A. D. (1976). An experimental case study of the successes and failures of job enrichment in a government agency. *Journal of Applied Psychology, 61*, 701–711.

15. Locke, E. A., Sirota, D., & Wolfson, A. D. (1976). An experimental case study of the successes and failures of job enrichment in a government agency. *Journal of Applied Psychology, 61*, 701–711.

16. Cherrington, D. J., & Lynn, E. J. (1980). The desire for an enriched job as a moderator of the enrichment-satisfaction relationship. *Organizational Behavior and Human Performance, 25*, 139–159; Hulin, C. L., & Blood, M. R. (1968). Job enlargement, individual differences, and worker responses. *Psychological Bulletin, 69*, 41–55.

17. Hackman, J. R., & Oldham, G. R. (1975). Development of the job diagnostic survey. *Journal of Applied Psychology, 60*, 159–170.

18. Grant, A. M. (2008). The significance of task significance: Job performance effects, relational mechanisms, and boundary conditions. *Journal of Applied Psychology, 93*, 108–124.

19. Morgeson, F. P., Delaney-Klinger, K., & Hemingway, M. A. (2005). The importance of job autonomy, cognitive ability, and job-related skill for predicting role breadth and job performance. *Journal of Applied Psychology, 90*, 399–406; Parker, S. K., Wall, T. D., & Jackson, P. R. (1997). "That's not my job": Developing flexible employee work orientations. *Academy of Management Journal, 40*, 899–929; Parker, S. K., Williams, H. M., & Turner, N. (2006). Modeling the antecedents of proactive behavior at work. *Journal of Applied Psychology, 91*, 636–652; Zhou, J. (1998). Feedback valence, feedback style, task autonomy, and achievement orientation: Interactive effects on creative performance. *Journal of Applied Psychology, 83*, 261–276.

20. Davermann, M. (2006, July). HR = Higher revenues? *FSB: Fortune Small Business, 16*, 80–81.

21. Gumbel, P. (2008). Galvanizing Gucci. *Fortune, 157*(1), 80–88.

22. Gajendran, R. S., & Harrison, D. A. (2007). The good, the bad, and the unknown about telecommuting. Meta-analysis of psychological mediators and individual consequences. *Journal of Applied Psychology, 92*, 1524–1541; Garnier, G. H. (1982). Context and decision making autonomy in the foreign affiliates of U.S. multinational corporations. *Academy of Management Journal, 25*, 893–908; Lyon, H. L., & Ivancevich, J. M. (1974). An exploratory investigation of organizational climate and job satisfaction in a hospital. *Academy of Management Journal, 17*, 635–648; Parker, S. K. (2003). Longitudinal effects of lean production on employee outcomes and the mediating role of work characteristics. *Journal of Applied Psychology, 88*, 620–634.

23. Kluger, A. N., & DeNisi, A. (1996). The effects of feedback interventions on performance: A historical review, a meta-analysis, and a preliminary feedback intervention theory. *Psychological Bulletin, 119*, 254–284.

24. Brass, D. J. (1985). Technology and the structuring of jobs: Employee satisfaction, performance, and influence. *Organizational Behavior and Human Decision Processes, 35*, 216–240; Humphrey, S. E., Nahrgang, J. D., & Morgeson, F. P. (2007). Integrating motivational, social, and contextual work design features: A meta-analytic summary and theoretical extension of the work design literature. *Journal of Applied Psychology, 92*, 1332–1356; Johns, G., Xie, J. L., & Fang, Y. (1992). Mediating and moderating effects in job design. *Journal of Management, 18*, 657–676; Renn, R. W., & Vandenberg, R. J. (1995), The critical psychological states: An underrepresented component in job characteristics model research. *Journal of Management, 21*, 279–303.

25. Based on Hackman, J. R., & Oldham, G. R. (1975). Development of the job diagnostic survey. *Journal of Applied Psychology, 60*, 159–170.

26. Arnold, H. J., & House, R. J. (1980). Methodological and substantive extensions to the job characteristics model of motivation. *Organizational Behavior and Human Performance, 25*, 161–183; Hackman, J. R., & Lawler, E. E. (1971). Employee reactions to job characteristics. *Journal of Applied Psychology, 55*, 259–286; Hackman, J. R., & Oldham, G. R. (1975). Development of the job diagnostic survey. *Journal of Applied Psychology, 60*, 159–170; Oldham, G. R., Hackman, J. R., & Pearce, J. L. (1976). Conditions under which employees respond positively to enriched work. *Journal of Applied Psychology, 61*, 395–403.

27. Katz, R. (1978). Job longevity as a situational factor in job satisfaction. *Administrative Science Quarterly, 23*, 204–223.

28. Conger, J. A., & Kanungo, R. N. (1988). The empowerment process: Integrating theory and practice. *Academy of Management Review, 13*, 471–482.

29. Spreitzer, G. M. (1995). Psychological empowerment in the workplace: Dimensions, measurement, and validation. *Academy of Management Journal, 38*, 1442–1465; Thomas, K. W., & Velthouse, B. A. (1990). Cognitive elements of empowerment: An "interpretive" model of intrinsic task motivation. *Academy of Management Review, 15*, 666–681.

30. Lustgarten, A. (2004). Harley-Davidson. *Fortune, 149*(1), 76.

31. Kark, R., Shamir, B., & Chen, G. (2003). The two faces of transformational leadership: Empowerment and dependency. *Journal of Applied Psychology, 88*, 246–255.

32. Ford, R. C., & Fottler, M. D. (1995). Empowerment: A matter of degree. *Academy of Management Executive, 9*, 21–23.

33. Seibert, S. E., Silver, S. R., & Randolph, W. A. (2004). Taking empowerment to the next level: A multiple-level model of empowerment, performance, and satisfaction. *Academy of Management Journal, 47*, 332–349.

34. Ahearne, M., Mathieu, J., & Rapp, A. (2005). To empower or not to empower your sales force? An empirical examination of the influence of leadership empowerment behavior on customer satisfaction and performance. *Journal of Applied Psychology, 90*, 945–955; Alge, B. J., Ballinger, G. A., Tangirala, S., & Oakley, J. L. (2006). Information privacy in organizations: Empowering creative and extrarole performance. *Journal of Applied Psychology, 91*, 221–232; Chen, G., Kirkman, B. L., Kanfer, R., Allen, D., & Rosen, B. (2007). A multilevel study of leadership, empowerment, and performance in teams. *Journal of Applied Psychology, 92*, 331–346; Liden, R. C., Wayne, S. J., & Sparrowe, R. T. (2000). An examination of the mediating role of psychological empowerment on the relations between the job, interpersonal relationships, and work outcomes. *Journal of Applied Psychology, 85*, 407–416; Spreitzer, G. M. (1995). Psychological empowerment in the workplace: Dimensions, measurement, and validation. *Academy of Management Journal, 38*, 1442–1465.

35. Locke, E. A., & Latham, G. P. (1990). *A theory of goal setting & task performance*. Englewood Cliffs, NJ: Prentice Hall.

36. Miner, J. B. (2003). The rated importance, scientific validity, and practical usefulness of organizational behavior theories. *Academy of Management Learning and Education, 2*, 250–268.

37. Ivancevich, J. M., & McMahon, J. T. (1982). The effects of goal setting, external feedback, and self-generated feedback on outcome variables: A field experiment. *Academy of Management Journal, 25*, 359–372; Latham, G. P., & Locke, E. A. (2006). Enhancing the benefits and overcoming the pitfalls of goal setting. *Organizational Dynamics, 35*, 332–340; Umstot, D. D., Bell, C. H., & Mitchell, T. R. (1976). Effects of job enrichment and task goals on satisfaction and productivity: Implications for job design. *Journal of Applied Psychology, 61*, 379–394.

38. Pritchard, R. D., Roth, P. L., Jones, S. D., Galgay, P. J., & Watson, M. D. (1988). Designing a goal-setting system to enhance performance: A practical guide. *Organizational Dynamics, 17*, 69–78.

39. Tubbs, M. E. (1986). Goal setting: A meta-analytic examination of the empirical evidence. *Journal of Applied Psychology, 71*, 474–483.

40. Stein, N. (2000). Measuring people power. *Fortune, 142*(7), 186.

41. Mento, A. J., Steel, R. P., & Karren, R. J. (1987). A meta-analytic study of the effects of goal-setting on task performance: 1966–1984. *Organizational Behavior and Human Decision Processes, 39*, 52–83; Phillips, J. M., & Gully, S. M. (1997). Role of goal orientation, ability, need for achievement, and locus of control in the self-efficacy and goal-setting process. *Journal of Applied Psychology, 82*, 792–802; Tubbs, M. E. (1986). Goal setting: A meta-analytic examination of the empirical evidence. *Journal of Applied Psychology, 71*, 474–483; Yukl, G. A., & Latham, G. P. (1978). Interrelationships among employee participation, individual differences, goal difficulty, goal acceptance, goal instrumentality, and performance. *Personnel Psychology, 31*, 305–323.

42. Phillips, J. M., & Gully, S. M. (1997). Role of goal orientation, ability, need for achievement, and locus of control in the self-efficacy and goal-setting process.

43. Heath, D., & Heath, C. (2008, February). Make goals not resolutions. *Fast Company, 122*, 58–59.

44. Shaw, K. N. (2004). Changing the goal-setting process at Microsoft. *Academy of Management Executive, 18*, 139–142.

45. Latham, G. P. (2004). The motivational benefits of goal-setting. *Academy of Management Executive, 18*, 126–129; Seijts, G. H., & Latham, G. P. (2005). Learning versus performance goals: When should each be used? *Academy of Management Executive, 19*, 124–131; Shaw, K. N. (2004). Changing the goal-setting process at Microsoft. *Academy of Management Executive, 18*, 139–142.

46. Kerr, S., & Landauer, S. (2004). Using stretch goals to promote organizational effectiveness and personal growth: General Electric and Goldman Sachs. *Academy of Management Executive, 18*, 134–138.

47. Latham, G. P. (2004). The motivational benefits of goal-setting. *Academy of Management Executive, 18*, 126–129; Latham, G. P., & Locke, E. A. (2006). Enhancing the

benefits and overcoming the pitfalls of goal setting. *Organizational Dynamics, 35,* 332–340.

48. Seijts, G. H., & Latham, G. P. (2005). Learning versus performance goals: When should each be used? *Academy of Management Executive, 19,* 124–131.

49. Donovan, J. J., & Radosevich, D. J. (1998). The moderating role of goal commitment on the goal difficulty-performance relationship: A meta-analytic review and critical reanalysis. *Journal of Applied Psychology, 83,* 308–315; Klein, H. J., Wesson. M. J., Hollenbeck, J. R., & Alge, B. J. (1999). Goal commitment and the goal-setting process: Conceptual clarification and empirical synthesis. *Journal of Applied Psychology, 84,* 885–896; Wofford, J. C., Goodwin, V. L., & Premack, S. (1993). Meta-analysis of the antecedents of personal goal level and of the antecedents and consequences of goal commitment. *Journal of Management, 18,* 595–615.

50. Shaw, K. N. (2004). Changing the goal-setting process at Microsoft. *Academy of Management Executive, 18,* 139–142.

51. Klein, H. J., & Kim, J. S. (1998). A field study of the influence of situational constraints, leader-member exchange, and goal commitment on performance. *Academy of Management Journal, 41,* 88–95; Latham, G. P. (2004). The motivational benefits of goal-setting. *Academy of Management Executive, 18,* 126–129; Pritchard, R. D., Roth, P. L., Jones, S. D., Galgay, P. J., & Watson, M. D. (1988). Designing a goal-setting system to enhance performance: A practical guide. *Organizational Dynamics, 17,* 69–78.

52. Locke, E. A. (2004). Linking goals to monetary incentives. *Academy of Management Executive, 18,* 130–133; Pritchard, R. D., Roth, P. L., Jones, S. D., Galgay, P. J., & Watson, M. D. (1988). Designing a goal-setting system to enhance performance: A practical guide. *Organizational Dynamics, 17,* 69–78; Seijts, G. H., & Latham, G. P. (2005). Learning versus performance goals: When should each be used? *Academy of Management Executive, 19,* 124–131.

53. LePine, J. A. (2005). Adaptation of teams in response to unforeseen change: Effects of goal difficulty and team composition in terms of cognitive ability and goal orientation. *Journal of Applied Psychology, 90,* 1153–1167.

54. Greenwood, R. G. (1981). Management by objectives: As developed by Peter Drucker, assisted by Harold Smiddy. *Academy of Management Review, 6,* 225–230; Muczyk, J. P., & Reimann, B. C. (1989). MBO as a complement to effective leadership. *Academy of Management Executive, 3,* 131–138; Reif, W. E., & Bassford, G. (1975). What MBO really is: Results require a complete program. *Business Horizons, 16,* 23–30.

55. Rodgers, R., & Hunter, J. E. (1991). Impact of management by objectives on organizational productivity. *Journal of Applied Psychology, 76,* 322–336.

56. Rodgers, R., Hunter, J. E., & Rogers, D. L. (1993). Influence of top management commitment on management program success. *Journal of Applied Psychology, 78,* 151–155.

57. Carson, P. P., & Carson, K. D. (1993). Deming versus traditional management theorists on goal setting: Can both be right? *Business Horizons, 36*(5), 79–84.

58. Mayer, R. C., & Davis, J. H. (1999). The effect of the performance appraisal system on trust for management: A field quasi-experiment. *Journal of Applied Psychology, 84,* 123–136.

59. Odiorne, G. S. (1990, July–August). The trend toward the quarterly performance review. *Business Horizons,* 38–41.

60. Lawler, E. E., III. (2003). Reward practices and performance management system effectiveness. *Organizational Dynamics, 32*(4), 396–404.

61. Toegel, G., & Conger, J. A. (2003). 360-Degree assessment: Time for reinvention. *Academy of Management Learning and Education, 2,* 297–311.

62. Taylor, M. S., Tracy, K. B., Renard, M. K., Harrison, J. K., & Carroll, S. J. (1995). Due process in performance appraisal: A quasi-experiment in procedural justice. *Administrative Science Quarterly, 40,* 495–523.

63. Boyle, M. (2001). Performance reviews: Perilous curves ahead. *Fortune, 143*(11), 187–188; Lawler, E. E., III. (2003). Reward practices and performance management system effectiveness. *Organizational Dynamics, 32* (4), 396–404; McGregor, J. (2006, January 9). The struggle to measure performance. *Business Week,* 26–28.

64. Davis, B. L., & Mount, M. K. (1984). Effectiveness of performance appraisal training using computer assisted instruction and behavior modeling. *Personnel Psychology, 37,* 439–452.

65. Cawley, B. D., Keeping, L. M., & Levy, P. E. (1998). Participation in the performance appraisal process and employee reactions: A meta-analytic review of field investigations. *Journal of Applied Psychology, 83,* 615–633; Cederblom, D. (1982). The performance appraisal interview: A review, implications, and suggestions. *Academy of Management Review, 7,* 219–227; Burke, R. J., Weitzel, W., & Weir, T. (1978). Characteristics of effective employee performance review and development interviews: Replication and extension. *Personnel Psychology, 31,* 903–919.

66. Duarte, N. T., Goodson, J. R., & Klich, N. R. (1994). Effects of dyadic quality and duration on performance appraisal. *Academy of Management Journal, 37,* 499–521.

67. Varma, A., DeNisi, A. S., & Peters, L. H. (1996). Interpersonal affect and performance appraisal: A field study. *Personnel Psychology, 49,* 341–360.

68. DeNisi, A. S., Robbins, T., & Cafferty, T. P. (1989). Organization of information used for performance appraisals: Role of diary-keeping. *Journal of Applied Psychology, 74,* 124–129.

69. Bernardin, H. J., Cooke, D. K., & Villanova, P. (2000). Conscientiousness and agreeableness as predictors of rating leniency. *Journal of Applied Psychology, 85,* 232–236; Jawahar, I. M., & Williams, C. R. (1997). Where all the children are above average: The performance appraisal purpose effect. *Personnel Psychology, 50,* 905–926; Longenecker, C. O. (1989, November–December). Truth or consequences: Politics and performance appraisals. *Business Horizons,* 76–82.

70. Heilman, M. E., & Stopeck, M. H. (1985). Being attractive, advantage or disadvantage? Performance-based evaluations and recommended personnel actions as a function of appearance, sex, and job type. *Organizational Behavior and Human Decision Processes, 35,* 202–215; Lyness, K. S., & Heilman, M. E. (2006). When fit is fundamental: Performance evaluations and promotions of upper-level female and male managers. *Journal of Applied Psychology, 91,* 777–785.

71. Luthans, F., & Stajkovic, A. D. (1999). Reinforce for performance: The need to go beyond pay and even rewards. *Academy of Management Executive, 13,* 49–57.

72. Vision quest: Contests throughout history. (2008, May). *Fast Company,* 44–45.

73. Cadsby, C. B., Song, F., & Tapon, F. (2007). Sorting and incentive effects of pay for performance: An experimental investigation. *Academy of Management Journal, 50,* 387–405; Peterson, S. J., & Luthans, F. (2006). The impact of financial and nonfinancial incentives on business-unit outcomes over time. *Journal of Applied Psychology, 91,* 156–165; Salamin, A., & Hom, P. W. (2005). In search of the elusive U-shaped performance-turnover relationship: Are high performing Swiss bankers more liable to quit? *Journal of Applied Psychology, 90,* 1204–1216.

74. Heneman, R. L., Greenberger, D. B., & Strasser, S. (1988). The relationship between pay-for-performance perceptions and pay satisfaction. *Personnel Psychology, 41,* 745–759.

75. Breen, B. (2004, December). The 6 myths of creativity. *Fast Company,* 75–78; Deckop, J. R., Mengel, R., & Cirka, C. C. (1999). Getting more than you pay for: Organizational citizenship behavior and pay for performance plans. *Academy of Management Journal, 42,* 420–428; Wright, P. M., George, J. M., Farnsworth, S. R., & McMahan, G. C. (1993). Productivity and extra-role behavior: The effects of goals and incentives on spontaneous helping. *Journal of Applied Psychology, 78,* 374–381.

76. Conlin, M. (2002, February 25). The software says you're just average. *Business Week,* 126.

77. Koretz, G. (1997, February 17). Truly tying pay to performance. *Business Week,* 25.

78. Sales incentive plans: 10 essentials. (2006, November 17). *Business Week Online,* 18. Retrieved on November 23, 2008, from http://businessweek.mobi/detail.jsp?key=3435&rc=as&p=1&pv=1.

79. Nelson, B. (2009). Secrets of successful employee recognition. Retrieved November 23, 2008, from http://www.qualitydigest.com/aug/nelson.html; Sittenfeld, C. (2004, January). Great job! Here's a seat belt! *Fast Company,* 29.

80. Balu, R., & Kirchenbaum, J. (2000, December). Bonuses aren't just for bosses. *Fast Company, 41,* 74–76; Collins, D., Hatcher, L., & Ross, T. L. (1993). The decision to implement gainsharing: The role of work climate, expected outcomes, and union status. *Personnel Psychology, 46,* 77–104; Imberman, W. (1996, January–February). Gainsharing: A lemon or lemonade? *Business Horizons, 39,* 36.

81. Brandes, P., Dharwadkar, R., Lemesis, G. V., & Heisler, W. J. (2003, February). Effective employee stock option design: Reconciling stakeholder, strategic, and motivational factors. *Academy of Management Executive, 17,* 77–93; Rafter, M. V. (2004, September). As the age of options wanes, companies settle on new incentive plans. *Workforce Management, 83,* 64–67; Marquez, J. (2005, September). Firms replacing stock options with restricted shares face a tough sell to employees. *Workforce Management, 84,* 71–73.

82. Pfeffer, J. (2004). Sins of commission. *Business 2.0, 5*(4), 56.

83. Harris, J., & Bromiley, P. (2007). Incentives to cheat: The influence of executive compensation and firm performance on financial misrepresentation. *Organization Science, 18,* 350–367; Priem, R. L., Coombs, J. E., & Gilley, K. M. (2006). Do CEO stock options prevent or promote fraudulent financial reporting? *Academy of Management Journal, 49,* 483–500.

84. Bellizzi, J. A. (1995). Committing and supervising unethical sales force behavior: The effects of victim gender, victim status, and sales force motivational techniques. *Journal of Personal Selling & Sales Management, 15,* 1–15; Schweitzer, M. E., Ordonez, L., & Douma, B. (2004). Goal setting as a motivator of unethical behavior. *Academy of Management Journal, 47,* 422–432.

85. Trevino, L. K., & Youngblood, S. A. (1990). Bad apples in bad barrels: A causal analysis of ethical decision-making behavior. *Journal of Applied Psychology, 75,* 378–385.

86. Locke, E. A. (2004). Linking goals to monetary incentives. *Academy of Management Executive, 18,* 130–133.

87. Nicholls, C. E., Lane, H. W., & Brechu, M. B. (1999). Taking self-managed teams to Mexico. *Academy of Management Executive, 13*(3), 15–25.

88. Robert, C., Probst, T. M., Martocchio, J. J., Drasgow, F., & Lawler, J. J. (2000). Empowerment and continuous improvement in the United States, Mexico, Poland, and India: Predicting fit on the basis of the dimensions of power distance and individualism. *Journal of Applied Psychology, 85,* 643–658.

89. Fang, E., Palmatier, R. W., & Evans, K. R. (2004). Goal-setting paradoxes? Trade-offs between working hard and working smart: The United States versus China. *Journal of the Academy of Marketing Science, 32,* 188–202.

CHAPTER 7
Managing Stress and Emotions

LEARNING OBJECTIVES

After reading this chapter, you should be able to do the following:

1. Understand the stress cycle.
2. Recognize the sources of stress for employees.
3. Recognize the outcomes of stress.
4. Understand how to manage stress in organizational contexts.
5. Understand the role emotions play for attitudes and behaviors at work.
6. Learn about emotional labor and how to manage it.
7. Understand how emotions can affect perceptions of what is ethical.
8. Understand cross-cultural differences in stressors.

Getting Emotional at American Express

As the American Express case illustrates, selling life insurance can be both an emotional and stressful job.

© 2010 Jupiterimages Corporation

Death and money can be emotional topics. Sales reps at American Express Company's life insurance division had to deal with both these issues when selling life insurance, and they were starting to feel the strain of working with such volatile emotional materials every day. Part of the problem representatives faced seemed like an unavoidable side effect of selling life insurance. Many potential clients were responding fearfully to the sales representatives' calls. Others turned their fears into anger. They replied to the representatives' questions suspiciously or treated them as untrustworthy.

The sales force at American Express believed in the value of their work, but over time, customers' negative emotions began to erode employee morale. Sales of policies slowed. Management insisted that the representatives ignore their customers' feelings and focus on making sales. The representatives' more aggressive sales tactics seemed only to increase their clients' negative emotional responses, which kicked off the cycle of suffering again. It was apparent something had to change.

In an effort to understand the barriers between customers and sales representatives, a team led by Kate Cannon, a former American Express staffer and mental-health administrator, used a technique called emotional resonance to identify employees' feelings about their work. Looking at the problem from an emotional point of view yielded dramatic insights about clients, sales representatives, and managers alike.

The first step she took was to acknowledge that the clients' negative emotions were barriers to life insurance sales. Cannon explained, "People reported all kinds of emotional issues—fear, suspicion, powerlessness, and distrust—involved in buying life insurance." Clients' negative emotions, in turn, had sparked negative feelings among some American Express life insurance sales representatives, including feelings of incompetence, dread, untruthfulness, shame, and even humiliation. Management's focus on sales had created an emotional disconnect between the sales reps' work and their true personalities. Cannon discovered that sales representatives who did not acknowledge their clients' distress felt dishonest. The emotional gap between their words and their true feelings only increased their distress.

Cannon also found some good news. Sales representatives who looked at their job from the customer's point of view were flourishing. Their feelings and their words were in harmony. Clients trusted them. The trust between these more openly emotional sales representatives and their clients led to greater sales and job satisfaction. To see if emotional skills training could increase job satisfaction and sales among other members of the team, Cannon instituted a course in emotional awareness for a test group of American Express life insurance sales representatives. The goal of the course was to help employees recognize and manage their feelings. The results of the study proved the value of emotional clarity. Coping skills, as measured on standardized psychological tests, improved for the representatives who took Cannon's course.

The emotional awareness training program had significant impact on American Express's bottom line. Over time, as Cannon's team expanded their emotion-based program, American Express life insurance sales rose by tens of millions of dollars. American Express's exercise in emotional awareness shows that companies can profit when feelings are recognized and consciously managed. Employees whose work aligns with their true emotions make more believable corporate ambassadors. The positive use of emotion can benefit a company internally as well. According to a Gallup poll of over 2 million employees, the majority of workers rated a caring boss higher than increased salary or benefits. In the words of career expert and columnist Maureen Moriarity, "Good moods are good for business."

Sources: Schwartz, T. (2008, September 11). How do you feel? Fast Company. Retrieved January 28, 2009, from http://www.fastcompany.com/magazine/35/emotion.html?page=0%2C2; Kirkwood, G., & Ward, C. (2002, May 5). Ch...Ch...Ch...Changes. Paper presented at FMA Ideation; Moriarty, M. (2007, June 7). Workplace coach: Don't underestimate emotional intelligence. Seattle Post-Intelligencer. Retrieved July 1, 2008, from http://seattlepi.nwsource.com/business/318345_workcoach04.html

1. WHAT IS STRESS?

LEARNING OBJECTIVES

1. **Learn about the General Adaptation Syndrome.**
2. **Learn what stressors are.**
3. **Understand the outcomes of stress.**
4. **Understand individual differences in experienced stress.**

Gravity. Mass. Magnetism. These words come from the physical sciences. And so does the term *stress.* In its original form, the word *stress* relates to the amount of force applied to a given area. A steel bar stacked with bricks is being stressed in ways that can be measured using mathematical formulas. In human terms, psychiatrist Peter Panzarino notes, "Stress is simply a fact of nature—forces from the outside world affecting the individual."[1] The professional, personal, and environmental pressures of modern life exert their forces on us every day. Some of these pressures are good. Others can wear us down over time.

Stress is defined by psychologists as the body's reaction to a change that requires a physical, mental, or emotional adjustment or response.[2] Stress is an inevitable feature of life. It is the force that gets us out of bed in the morning, motivates us at the gym, and inspires us to work.

stress

The body's reaction to a change that requires a physical, mental, or emotional adjustment or response.

As you will see in the sections below, stress is a given factor in our lives. We may not be able to avoid stress completely, but we can change how we respond to stress, which is a major benefit. Our ability to recognize, manage, and maximize our response to stress can turn an emotional or physical problem into a resource.

Researchers use polling to measure the effects of stress at work. The results have been eye-opening. According to a 2001 Gallup poll, 80% of American workers report that they feel workplace stress at least some of the time.[3] Another survey found that 65% of workers reported job stress as an issue for them, and almost as many employees ended the day exhibiting physical effects of stress, including neck pain, aching muscles, and insomnia. It is clear that many individuals are stressed at work.

1.1 The Stress Process

Our basic human functions, breathing, blinking, heartbeat, digestion, and other unconscious actions, are controlled by our lower brains. Just outside this portion of the brain is the semiconscious limbic system, which plays a large part in human emotions. Within this system is an area known as the **amygdala**. The amygdala is responsible for, among other things, stimulating fear responses. Unfortunately, the amygdala cannot distinguish between meeting a 10:00 a.m. marketing deadline and escaping a burning building.

amygdala

The area of the limbic system that controls fear type responses.

Human brains respond to outside threats to our safety with a message to our bodies to engage in a "fight-or-flight" response.[4] Our bodies prepare for these scenarios with an increased heart rate, shallow breathing, and wide-eyed focus. Even digestion and other functions are stopped in preparation for the fight-or-flight response. While these traits allowed our ancestors to flee the scene of their impending doom or engage in a physical battle for survival, most crises at work are not as dramatic as this.

Hans Selye, one of the founders of the American Institute of Stress, spent his life examining the human body's response to stress. As an endocrinologist who studied the effects of adrenaline and other hormones on the body, Selye believed that unmanaged stress could create physical diseases such as ulcers and high blood pressure, and psychological illnesses such as depression. He hypothesized that stress played a general role in disease by exhausting the body's immune system and termed this the **General Adaptation Syndrome (GAS)**.[5]

General Adaptation Syndrome (GAS)

Hans Selye's hypothesis that stress plays a general role in disease by exhausting the body's immune system.

FIGURE 7.2

In Selye's GAS model, stress affects an individual in three steps: alarm, resistance, and exhaustion.

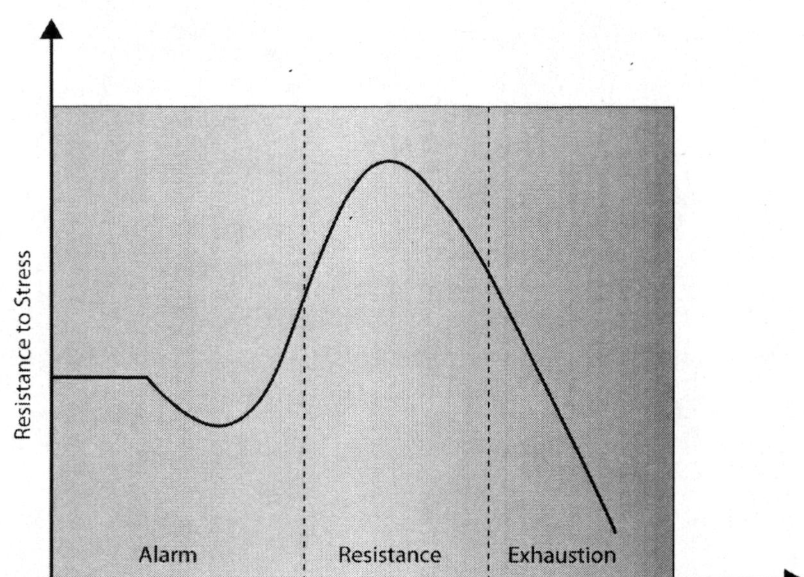

In the **alarm phase** of stress, an outside stressor jolts the individual, insisting that something must be done. It may help to think of this as the fight-or-flight moment in the individual's experience. If the response is sufficient, the body will return to its resting state after having successfully dealt with the source of stress.

alarm phase

When an outside stressor jolts the individual, insisting that something must be done.

resistance phase

When the body begins to release cortisol and draws on fats and sugar to find a way to adjust to the demands of stress.

In the **resistance phase**, the body begins to release cortisol and draws on reserves of fats and sugars to find a way to adjust to the demands of stress. This reaction works well for short periods of time, but it is only a temporary fix. Individuals forced to endure the stress of cold and hunger may find a way to adjust to lower temperatures and less food. While it is possible for the body to "adapt" to such stresses, the situation cannot continue. The body is drawing on its reserves, like a hospital using backup generators after a power failure. It can continue to function by shutting down unnecessary items like large overhead lights, elevators, televisions, and most computers, but it cannot proceed in that state forever.

exhaustion phase

When the body has depleted its stores of sugars and fats, and the prolonged release of cortisol has caused the stressor to significantly weaken the individual.

In the **exhaustion phase**, the body has depleted its stores of sugars and fats, and the prolonged release of cortisol has caused the stressor to significantly weaken the individual. Disease results from the body's weakened state, leading to death in the most extreme cases. This eventual depletion is why we're more likely to reach for foods rich in fat or sugar, caffeine, or other quick fixes that give us energy when we are stressed. Selye referred to stress that led to disease as *distress* and stress that was enjoyable or healing as *eustress*.

1.2 Workplace Stressors

stressors

Events or contexts that cause a stress reaction by elevating levels of adrenaline and forcing a physical or mental response.

Stressors are events or contexts that cause a stress reaction by elevating levels of adrenaline and forcing a physical or mental response. The key to remember about stressors is that they aren't necessarily a bad thing. The saying "the straw that broke the camel's back" applies to stressors. Having a few stressors in our lives may not be a problem, but because stress is cumulative, having many stressors day after day can cause a buildup that becomes a problem. The American Psychological Association surveys American adults about their stresses annually. Topping the list of stressful issues are money, work, and housing.[6] But in essence, we could say that all three issues come back to the workplace. How much we earn determines the kind of housing we can afford, and when job security is questionable, home life is generally affected as well.

Understanding what can potentially cause stress can help avoid negative consequences. Now we will examine the major stressors in the workplace.

A major category of workplace stressors are role demands. In other words, some jobs and some work contexts are more potentially stressful than others.

Role Demands

Role ambiguity refers to vagueness in relation to what our responsibilities are. If you have started a new job and felt unclear about what you were expected to do, you have experienced role ambiguity. Having high role ambiguity is related to higher emotional exhaustion, more thoughts of leaving an organization, and lowered job attitudes and performance.[7] **Role conflict** refers to facing contradictory demands at work. For example, your manager may want you to increase customer satisfaction and cut costs, while you feel that satisfying customers inevitably increases costs. In this case, you are experiencing role conflict because satisfying one demand makes it unlikely to satisfy the other. **Role overload** is defined as having insufficient time and resources to complete a job. When an organization downsizes, the remaining employees will have to complete the tasks that were previously performed by the laid-off workers, which often leads to role overload. Like role ambiguity, both role conflict and role overload have been shown to hurt performance and lower job attitudes; however, research shows that role ambiguity is the strongest predictor of poor performance.[8] Research on new employees also shows that role ambiguity is a key aspect of their adjustment, and that when role ambiguity is high, new employees struggle to fit into the new organization.[9]

FIGURE 7.3

George Lucas, one of the most successful filmmakers of all time, found making *The Empire Strikes Back* stressful both personally and financially. Those who worked with him on those early *Star Wars* films describe him as fully engrossed in the process, which led to role overload and work–family conflict. Following the making of that film, Lucas said he was "burnt out" and didn't want to make any more *Star Wars* films.

Source: http://en.wikipedia.org/wiki/Image:George_Lucas,_Pasadena.jpg.

Information Overload

Messages reach us in countless ways every day. Some are societal—advertisements that we may hear or see in the course of our day. Others are professional—e-mails, memos, voice mails, and conversations from our colleagues. Others are personal—messages and conversations from our loved ones and friends. Add these together and it's easy to see how we may be receiving more information than we can take in. This state of imbalance is known as **information overload**, which can be defined as "occurring when the information processing demands on an individual's time to perform interactions and internal calculations exceed the supply or capacity of time available for such processing."[10] Role overload has been made much more salient because of the ease at which we can get abundant information from Web search engines and the numerous e-mail and text messages we receive each day.[11] Other research shows that working in such a fragmented fashion significantly impacts efficiency, creativity, and mental acuity.[12]

role ambiguity

Vagueness in relation to our job responsibilities.

role conflict

Facing contradictory demands at work.

role overload

Having insufficient time and resources to complete one's job.

information overload

Information processing demands that exceed the supply or capacity of time available for such processing.

Top 10 Stressful Jobs

As you can see, some of these jobs are stressful due to high emotional labor (customer service), physical demands (miner), time pressures (journalist), or all three (police officer).

1. Inner city high school teacher
2. Police officer
3. Miner
4. Air traffic controller
5. Medical intern
6. Stockbroker
7. Journalist
8. Customer service or complaint worker
9. Secretary
10. Waiter

Source: Tolison, B. (2008, April 7). Top ten most stressful jobs. Health. Retrieved January 28, 2009, from the WCTV News Web site: http://www.wctv.tv/news/headlines/17373899.html.

Work–Family Conflict

Work–family conflict occurs when the demands from work and family are negatively affecting one another.[13] Specifically, work and family demands on a person may be incompatible with each other such that work interferes with family life and family demands interfere with work life. This stressor has steadily increased in prevalence, as work has become more demanding and technology has allowed employees to work from home and be connected to the job around the clock. In fact, a recent census showed that 28% of the American workforce works more than 40 hours per week, creating an unavoidable spillover from work to family life.[14] Moreover, the fact that more households have dual-earning families in which both adults work means household and childcare duties are no longer the sole responsibility of a stay-at-home parent. This trend only compounds stress from the workplace by leading to the spillover of family responsibilities (such as a sick child or elderly parent) to work life. Research

work–family conflict

When the demands from one's work and family are negatively affecting one another.

shows that individuals who have stress in one area of their life tend to have greater stress in other parts of their lives, which can create a situation of escalating stressors.[15]

Work–family conflict has been shown to be related to lower job and life satisfaction. Interestingly, it seems that work–family conflict is slightly more problematic for women than men.[16] Organizations that are able to help their employees achieve greater work–life balance are seen as more attractive than those that do not.[17] Organizations can help employees maintain work–life balance by using organizational practices such as flexibility in scheduling as well as individual practices such as having supervisors who are supportive and considerate of employees' family life.[18]

Life Changes

Stress can result from positive and negative life changes. The Holmes-Rahe scale ascribes different stress values to life events ranging from the death of one's spouse to receiving a ticket for a minor traffic violation. The values are based on incidences of illness and death in the 12 months after each event. On the Holmes-Rahe scale, the death of a spouse receives a stress rating of 100, getting married is seen as a midway stressful event, with a rating of 50, and losing one's job is rated as 47. These numbers are relative values that allow us to understand the impact of different life events on our stress levels and their ability to impact our health and well-being.[19] Again, because stressors are cumulative, higher scores on the stress inventory mean you are more prone to suffering negative consequences of stress than someone with a lower score.

OB Toolbox: How Stressed Are You?

Read each of the events listed below. Give yourself the number of points next to any event that has occurred in your life in the last *2 years*. There are no right or wrong answers. The aim is just to identify which of these events you have experienced.

Sample Items: Life Events Stress Inventory

Life event	Stress points	Life event	Stress points
Death of spouse	100	Foreclosure of mortgage or loan	30
Divorce	73	Change in responsibilities at work	29
Marital separation	65	Son or daughter leaving home	29
Jail term	63	Trouble with in-laws	29
Death of close family member	63	Outstanding personal achievement	28
Personal injury or illness	53	Begin or end school	26
Marriage	50	Change in living location/condition	25
Fired or laid off at work	47	Trouble with supervisor	23
Marital reconciliation	45	Change in work hours or conditions	20
Retirement	45	Change in schools	20
Pregnancy	40	Change in social activities	18
Change in financial state	38	Change in eating habits	15
Death of close friend	37	Vacation	13
Change to different line of work	36	Minor violations of the law	11

Scoring:

- If you scored fewer than 150 stress points, you have a 30% chance of developing a stress-related illness in the near future.
- If you scored between 150 and 299 stress points, you have a 50% chance of developing a stress-related illness in the near future.
- If you scored over 300 stress points, you have an 80% chance of developing a stress-related illness in the near future.

The happy events in this list such as getting married or an outstanding personal achievement illustrate how eustress, or "good stress," can also tax a body as much as the stressors that constitute the traditionally negative category of distress. (The prefix *eu-* in the word *eustress* means "good" or "well," much like the *eu-* in *euphoria.*) Stressors can also occur in trends. For example, during 2007, nearly 1.3 million U.S. housing properties were subject to foreclosure activity, up 79% from 2006.

Source: Adapted from Holmes, T. H., & Rahe, R. H. (1967). The social readjustment rating scale. Journal of Psychosomatic Research, 11, 213–218.

Downsizing

A study commissioned by the U.S. Department of Labor to examine over 3,600 companies from 1980 to 1994 found that manufacturing firms accounted for the greatest incidence of major downsizings. The average percentage of firms by industry that downsized more than 5% of their workforces across the 15-year period of the study was manufacturing (25%), retail (17%), and service (15%). A total of 59% of the companies studied fired at least 5% of their employees at least once during the 15-year period, and 33% of the companies downsized more than 15% of their workforce at least once during the period. Furthermore, during the recessions in 1985 to 1986 and 1990 to 1991, more than 25% of all firms, regardless of size, cut their workforce by more than 5%.[20] In the United States, major layoffs in many sectors in 2008 and 2009 were stressful even for those who retained their jobs.

The loss of a job can be a particularly stressful event, as you can see by its high score on the life stressors scale. It can also lead to other stressful events, such as financial problems, which can add to a person's stress score. Research shows that downsizing and job insecurity (worrying about downsizing) is related to greater stress, alcohol use, and lower performance and creativity.[21] For example, a study of over 1,200 Finnish workers found that past downsizing or expectations of future downsizing was related to greater psychological strain and absence.[22] In another study of creativity and downsizing, researchers found that creativity and most creativity-supporting aspects of the perceived work environment declined significantly during the downsizing.[23] Those who experience layoffs but have their self-integrity affirmed through other means are less susceptible to negative outcomes.[24]

1.3 Outcomes of Stress

The outcomes of stress are categorized into physiological and psychological and work outcomes.

Physiological

Stress manifests itself internally as nervousness, tension, headaches, anger, irritability, and fatigue. Stress can also have outward manifestations. Dr. Dean Ornish, author of *Stress, Diet and Your Heart*, says that stress is related to aging.[25] Chronic stress causes the body to secrete hormones such as cortisol, which tend to make our complexion blemished and cause wrinkles. Harvard psychologist Ted Grossbart, author of *Skin Deep*, says, "Tens of millions of Americans suffer from skin diseases that flare up only when they're upset."[26] These skin problems include itching, profuse sweating, warts, hives, acne, and psoriasis. For example, Roger Smith, the former CEO of General Motors Corporation, was featured in a *Fortune* article that began, "His normally ruddy face is covered with a red rash, a painless but disfiguring problem which Smith says his doctor attributes 99% to stress."[27]

The human body responds to outside calls to action by pumping more blood through our system, breathing in a more shallow fashion, and gazing wide-eyed at the world. To accomplish this feat, our bodies shut down our immune systems. From a biological point of view, it's a smart strategic move—but only in the short term. The idea can be seen as your body wanting to escape an imminent threat, so that there is still some kind of body around to get sick later. But in the long term, a body under constant stress can suppress its immune system too much, leading to health problems such as high blood pressure, ulcers, and being overly susceptible to illnesses such as the common cold.

The link between heart attacks and stress, while easy to assume, has been harder to prove. The American Heart Association notes that research has yet to link the two conclusively. Regardless, it is clear that individuals under stress engage in behaviors that can lead to heart disease such as eating fatty foods, smoking, or failing to exercise.

Psychological

Depression and anxiety are two psychological outcomes of unchecked stress, which are as dangerous to our mental health and welfare as heart disease, high blood pressure, and strokes. The Harris poll found that 11% of respondents said their stress was accompanied by a sense of depression. "Persistent or chronic stress has the potential to put vulnerable individuals at a substantially increased risk of depression, anxiety, and many other emotional difficulties," notes Mayo Clinic psychiatrist Daniel Hall-Flavin. Scientists have noted that changes in brain function—especially in the areas of the hypothalamus and the pituitary gland—may play a key role in stress-induced emotional problems.[28]

Work Outcomes

Stress is related to worse job attitudes, higher turnover, and decreases in job performance in terms of both in-role performance and organizational citizenship behaviors.[29] Research also shows that stressed individuals have lower organizational commitment than those who are less stressed.[30] Interestingly, job challenge has been found to be related to higher performance, perhaps with some individuals rising to the challenge.[31] The key is to keep challenges in the optimal zone for stress—the activation stage—and to avoid the exhaustion stage.[32]

FIGURE 7.4

Individuals who are able to find the right balance between work that is too challenging and work that is not challenging enough see increases in performance.

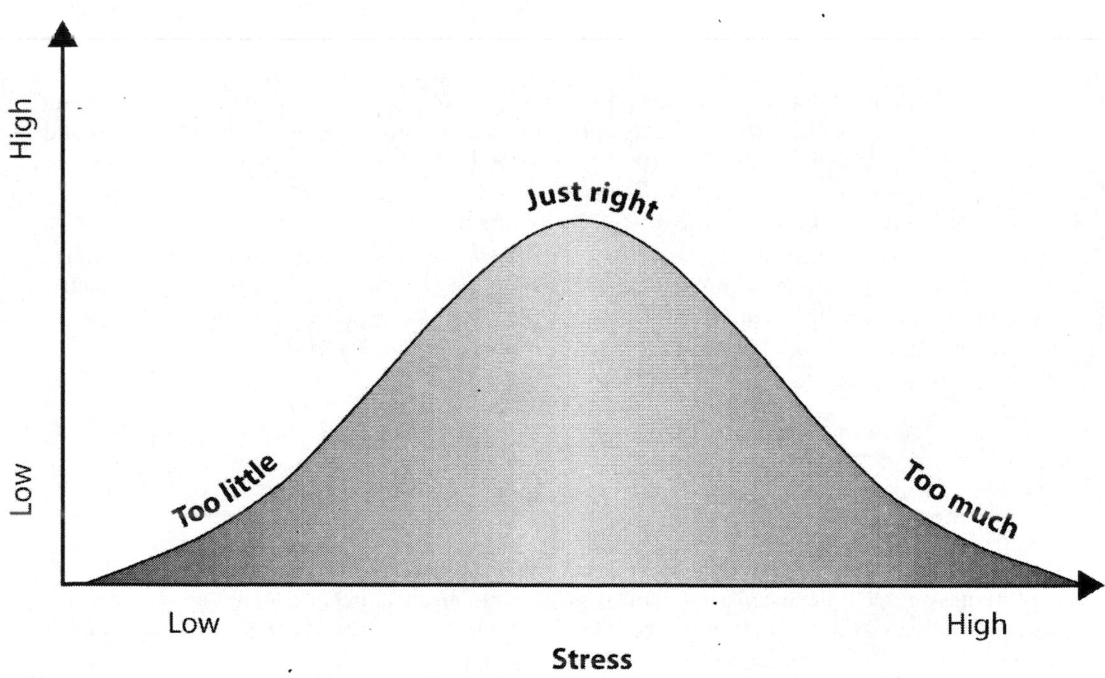

1.4 Individual Differences in Experienced Stress

type A personalities

People who display high levels of speed/impatience, job involvement, and hard-driving competitiveness.

type B personalities

People who tend to be calmer than Type A people, and tend to think through situations as opposed to reacting emotionally.

How we handle stress varies by individual, and part of that issue has to do with our personality type. **Type A personalities**, as defined by the Jenkins Activity Survey,[33] display high levels of speed/impatience, job involvement, and hard-driving competitiveness. If you think back to Selye's General Adaptation Syndrome, in which unchecked stress can lead to illness over time, it's easy to see how the fast-paced, adrenaline-pumping lifestyle of a Type A person can lead to increased stress, and research supports this view.[34] Studies show that the hostility and hyper-reactive portion of the Type A personality is a major concern in terms of stress and negative organizational outcomes.[35]

Type B personalities, by contrast, are calmer by nature. They think through situations as opposed to reacting emotionally. Their fight-or-flight and stress levels are lower as a result. Our personalities are the outcome of our life experiences and, to some degree, our genetics. Some researchers believe that mothers who experience a great deal of stress during pregnancy introduce their unborn babies to high levels of the stress-related hormone cortisol in utero, predisposing their babies to a stressful life from birth.[36]

Men and women also handle stress differently. Researchers at Yale University discovered estrogen may heighten women's response to stress and their tendency to depression as a result.[37] Still, others believe that women's stronger social networks allow them to process stress more effectively than men.[38] So while women may become depressed more often than men, women may also have better tools for countering emotion-related stress than their male counterparts.

OB Toolbox: To Cry or Not to Cry? That Is the Question...

As we all know, stress can build up. Advice that's often given is to "let it all out" with something like a cathartic "good cry." But research shows that crying may not be as helpful as the adage would lead us to believe. In reviewing scientific studies done on crying and health, Ad Vingerhoets and Jan Scheirs found that the studies "yielded little evidence in support of the hypothesis that shedding tears improves mood or health directly, be it in the short or in the long run." Another study found that venting actually increased the negative effects of negative emotion.[39]

Instead, laughter may be the better remedy. Crying may actually intensify the negative feelings, because crying is a social signal not only to others but to yourself. "You might think, 'I didn't think it was bothering me that much, but look at how I'm crying—I must really be upset,'" says Susan Labott of the University of Toledo. The crying may make the feelings more intense. Labott and Randall Martin of Northern Illinois University at Dekalb surveyed 715 men and women and found that at comparable stress levels, criers were more depressed, anxious, hostile, and tired than those who wept less. Those who used humor were the most successful at combating stress. So, if you're looking for a cathartic release, opt for humor instead: Try to find something funny in your stressful predicament.

Sources: Vingerhoets, A. J. J. M., & Scheirs, J. G. M. (2001). Crying and health. In A. J. J. M. Vingerhoets & R. R. Cornelius (Eds.), Adult crying: A biopsychosocial approach (pp. 227–247). East Sussex, UK: Brunner-Routledge; Martin, R., & Susan L. (1991). Mood following emotional crying: Effects of the situation. Journal of Research in Personality, [illegible] http://www.nlpanchorpoint.com/BolstadCrying1481.pdf

KEY TAKEAWAY

Stress is prevalent in today's workplaces. The General Adaptation Syndrome consists of alarm, resistance, and eventually exhaustion if the stress goes on for too long. Time pressure is a major stressor. Outcomes of stress include both psychological and physiological problems as well as work outcomes. Individuals with Type B personalities are less prone to stress. In addition, individuals with social support experience less stress.

EXERCISES

1. We've just seen how the three phases of the General Adaptation Syndrome (GAS) can play out in terms of physical stresses such as cold and hunger. Can you imagine how the three categories of this model might apply to work stress as well?
2. List two situations in which a prolonged work challenge might cause an individual to reach the second and third stage of GAS.
3. What can individuals do to help manage their time better? What works for you?
4. What symptoms of stress have you seen in yourself or your peers?

2. AVOIDING AND MANAGING STRESS

LEARNING OBJECTIVES

1. **Understand what individuals can do to manage their own stress.**
2. **Understand what organizations can do to help their employees avoid and manage stress.**

2.1 Individual Approaches to Managing Stress

The Corporate Athlete

Luckily, there are several ways to manage stress. One way is to harness stress's ability to improve our performance. Jack Groppel was working as a professor of kinesiology and bioengineering at the University of Illinois when he became interested in applying the principles of athletic performance to workplace performance. Could eating better, exercising more, and developing a positive attitude turn distress into eustress? Groppel's answer was yes. If professionals trained their minds and bodies to perform at peak levels through better nutrition, focused training, and positive action, Groppel said, they could become "corporate athletes" working at optimal physical, emotional, and mental levels.

The "corporate athlete" approach to stress is a proactive (action first) rather than a reactive (response-driven) approach. While an overdose of stress can cause some individuals to stop exercising, eat less nutritional foods, and develop a sense of hopelessness, corporate athletes ward off the potentially overwhelming feelings of stress by developing strong bodies and minds that embrace challenges, as opposed to being overwhelmed by them.

Flow

flow

A state of consciousness in which a person is totally absorbed in an activity.

Turning stress into fuel for corporate athleticism is one way of transforming a potential enemy into a workplace ally. Another way to transform stress is by breaking challenges into smaller parts, and embracing the ones that give us joy. In doing so, we can enter a state much like that of a child at play, fully focused on the task at hand, losing track of everything except our genuine connection to the challenge before us. This concept of total engagement in one's work, or in other activities, is called **flow**. The term *flow* was coined by psychologist Mihaly Csikszentmihalyi and is defined as a state of consciousness in which a person is totally absorbed in an activity. We've all experienced flow: It's the state of mind in which you feel strong, alert, and in effortless control.

FIGURE 7.5

A key to flow is engaging at work, yet research shows that most managers do not feel they are engaged in purposeful work.

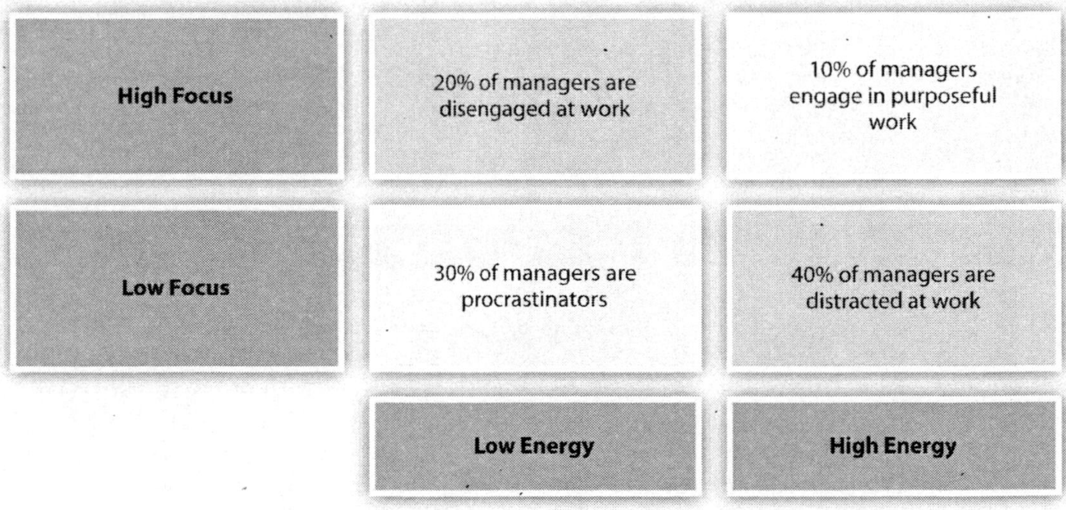

Sources: Adapted from information in Bruch, H., & Ghoshal, S. (2002, February). Beware the busy manager. Harvard Business Review, 80, 62–69; Schiuma, G., Mason, S., & Kennerley, M. (2007). Assessing energy within organizations. Measuring Business Excellence, 11, 69–78.

According to this way of thinking, the most pleasurable way for a person to work is in harmony with his or her true interests. Work is seen as more similar to playing games than most activities adults do. This is because work consists of tasks, puzzles, surprises, and potentially rewarding challenges. By breaking down a busy workday into smaller pieces, individuals can shift from the "stress" of work to a more engaged state of flow.

Designing Work That Flows

Keep in mind that work that flows includes the following:

- *Challenge*: the task is reachable but requires a stretch
- *Meaningfulness*: the task is worthwhile or important
- *Competence*: the task uses skills that you have
- *Choice*: you have some say in the task and how it's carried out[40]

Corporate athleticism and flow are two concepts that can help you cope with stress. Next, let us focus more on exactly how individual lifestyle choices affect our stress levels. Eating well, exercising, getting enough sleep, and employing time management techniques are all things we can affect that can decrease our feelings of stress.

Diet

Greasy foods often make a person feel tired. Why? Because it takes the body longer to digest fats, which means the body is diverting blood from the brain and making you feel sluggish. Eating big, heavy meals in the middle of the day may actually slow us down, because the body will be pumping blood to the stomach, away from the brain. A better choice for lunch might be fish, such as wild salmon. Fish keeps you alert because of its effect on two important brain chemicals—dopamine and norepinephrine—which produce a feeling of alertness, increased concentration, and faster reaction times.[41]

FIGURE 7.6

Eating healthy foods such as fresh fruits and vegetables is a key to stress management.

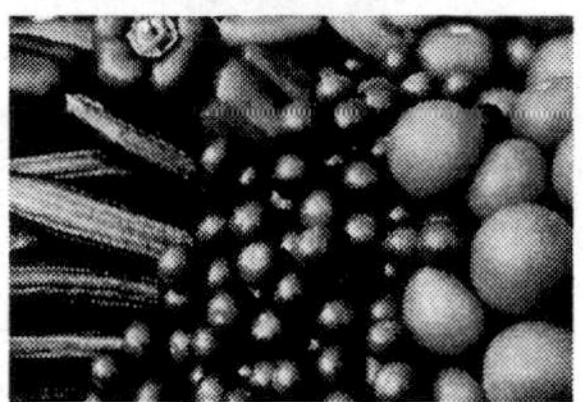

Exercise

Exercise is another strategy for managing stress. The best kind of break to take may be a physically active one. Research has shown that physically active breaks lead to enhanced mental concentration and decreased mental fatigue. One study, conducted by Belgian researchers, examined the effect of breaks on workers in a large manufacturing company. One half of the workers were told to rest during their breaks. The other half did mild calisthenics. Afterward, each group was given a battery of tests. The group who had done the mild calisthenics scored far better on all measures of memory, decision-making ability, eye–hand coordination, and fine motor control.[42]

Strange as it may seem, exercise gives us more energy. How energetic we feel depends on our maximum oxygen capacity (the total amount of oxygen we utilize from the air we breathe). The more oxygen we absorb in each breath, the more energy and stamina we will have. Yoga and meditation are other physical activities that are helpful in managing stress. Regular exercise increases our body's ability to draw more oxygen out of the air we breathe. Therefore, taking physically active breaks may be helpful in combating stress.

Sleep

It is a vicious cycle. Stress can make it hard to sleep. Not sleeping makes it harder to focus on work in general, as well as on specific tasks. Tired folks are more likely to lose their temper, upping the stress level of others. American insomnia is a stress-related epidemic—one-third of adults claim to have trouble sleeping and 37% admit to actually having fallen asleep while driving in the past year.[43]

The work–life crunch experienced by many Americans makes a good night's sleep seem out of reach. According to the journal *Sleep*, workers who suffer from insomnia are more likely to miss work due to exhaustion. These missed days ultimately cost employers thousands of dollars per person in missed productivity each year, which can total over $100 billion across all industries.[44] As you might imagine, a person who misses work due to exhaustion will return to work to find an even more stressful workload. This cycle can easily increase the stress level of a work team as well as the overtired individual.

Create a Social Support Network

A consistent finding is that those individuals who have a strong social support network are less stressed than those who do not.[45] Research finds that social support can buffer the effects of stress.[46] Individuals can help build up social support by encouraging a team atmosphere in which coworkers support one another. Just being able to talk with and listen to others, either with coworkers at work or with friends and family at home, can help decrease stress levels.

Time Management

Time management is defined as the development of tools or techniques that help to make us more productive when we work. Effective time management is a major factor in reducing stress, because it decreases much of the pressure we feel. With information and role overload it is easy to fall into bad habits of simply reacting to unexpected situations. Time management techniques include prioritizing, manageable organization, and keeping a schedule such as a paper or electronic organizing tool. Just like any new skill, developing time management takes conscious effort, but the gains might be worthwhile if your stress level is reduced.

time management

Defined as the development of tools or techniques that help to make us more productive when we work.

Listen Up and Learn More

Check out this interview with *Fast Company* and Tony Wright, CEO of RescueTime, who has created a tool to evaluate your productivity using data from your computer.

http://www.fastcompany.com/1569600/see-how-much-tme-you-are-wasting-rescuetime

This software is available at http://www.RescueTime.com/ and is currently free to use.

This is an example of output from a RescueTime user.

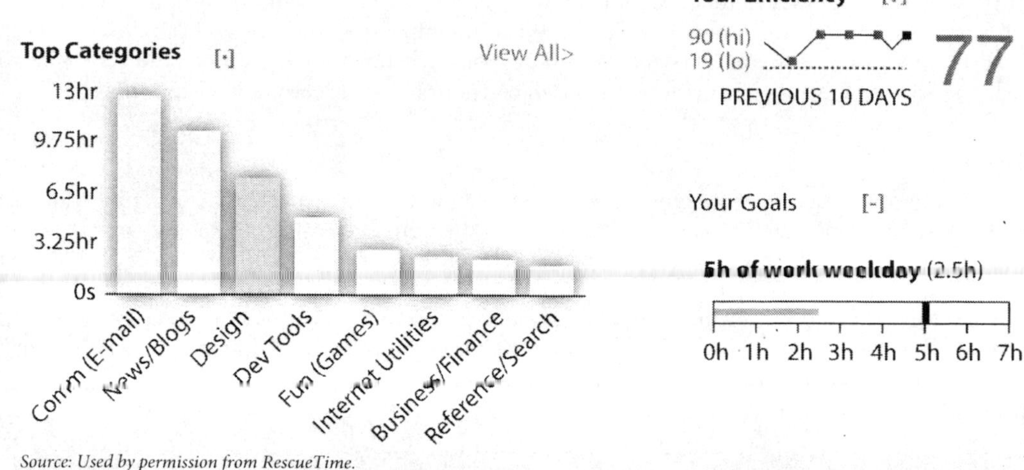

Source: Used by permission from RescueTime.

2.2 Organizational Approaches to Managing Stress

Stress-related issues cost businesses billions of dollars per year in absenteeism, accidents, and lost productivity.[47] As a result, managing employee stress is an important concern for organizations as well as individuals. For example, Renault, the French automaker, invites consultants to train their 2,100 supervisors to avoid the outcomes of negative stress for themselves and their subordinates. IBM Corporation encourages its worldwide employees to take an online stress assessment that helps them create action plans based on their results. Even organizations such as General Electric Company (GE) that are known for a "winner takes all" mentality are seeing the need to reduce stress. Lately, GE has brought in comedians to lighten up the workplace atmosphere, and those receiving low performance ratings are no longer called the "bottom 10s" but are now referred to as the "less effectives."[48] Organizations can take many steps to helping employees with stress, including having more clear expectations of them, creating jobs where employees have autonomy and control, and creating a fair work environment. Finally, larger organizations normally utilize outside resources to help employees get professional help when needed.

Make Expectations Clear

One way to reduce stress is to state your expectations clearly. Workers who have clear descriptions of their jobs experience less stress than those whose jobs are ill defined.[49] The same thing goes for individual tasks. Can you imagine the benefits of working in a place where every assignment was clear and employees were content and focused on their work? It would be a great place to work as a manager, too. Stress can be contagious, but as we've seen above, this kind of happiness can be contagious, too. Creating clear expectations doesn't have to be a top–down event. Managers may be unaware that their directives are increasing their subordinates' stress by upping their confusion. In this case, a gentle conversation that steers a project in a clearer direction can be a simple but powerful way to reduce stress. In the interest of reducing stress on all sides, it's important to frame situations as opportunities for solutions as opposed to sources of anger.

Give Employees Autonomy

Giving employees a sense of autonomy is another thing that organizations can do to help relieve stress.[50] It has long been known that one of the most stressful things that individuals deal with is a lack of control over their environment. Research shows that individuals who feel a greater sense of control at work deal with stress more effectively both in the United States and in Hong Kong.[51] Similarly, in a study of American and French employees, researchers found that the negative effects of emotional labor were much less for those employees with the autonomy to customize their work environment and customer service encounters.[52] Employees' stress levels are likely to be related to the degree that organizations can build autonomy and support into jobs.

Create Fair Work Environments

Work environments that are unfair and unpredictable have been labeled "toxic workplaces." A toxic workplace is one in which a company does not value its employees or treat them fairly.[53] Statistically, organizations that value employees are more profitable than those that do not.[54] Research shows that working in an environment that is seen as fair helps to buffer the effects of stress.[55] This reduced stress may be because employees feel a greater sense of status and self-esteem or due to a greater sense of trust within the organization. These findings hold for outcomes individuals receive as well as the process for distributing those outcomes.[56] Whatever the case, it is clear that organizations have many reasons to create work environments characterized by fairness, including lower stress levels for employees. In fact, one study showed that training supervisors to be more interpersonally sensitive even helped nurses feel less stressed about a pay cut.[57]

Supervisor Support: Work-Family Conflict Survey

Think of your current or most recent supervisor and rate each of the following items in terms of this person's behavior toward you.

Answer the following questions using 1 = not at all, 2 = somewhat, 3 = fully agree

1. _____ My supervisor is willing to listen to my problems in juggling work and nonwork life.
2. _____ My supervisor takes the time to learn about my personal needs.
3. _____ My supervisor makes me feel comfortable talking to him or her about my conflicts between work and nonwork.
4. _____ My supervisor and I can talk effectively to solve conflicts between work and nonwork issues.
5. _____ I can depend on my supervisor to help me with scheduling conflicts if I need it.
6. _____ I can rely on my supervisor to make sure my work responsibilities are handled when I have unanticipated nonwork demands.
7. _____ My supervisor works effectively with workers to creatively solve conflicts between work and nonwork.
8. _____ My supervisor is a good role model for work and nonwork balance.
9. _____ My supervisor demonstrates effective behaviors in how to juggle work and nonwork balance.
10. _____ My supervisor demonstrates how a person can jointly be successful on and off the job.
11. _____ My supervisor thinks about how the work in my department can be organized to jointly benefit employees and the company.
12. _____ My supervisor asks for suggestions to make it easier for employees to balance work and nonwork demands.
13. _____ My supervisor is creative in reallocating job duties to help my department work better as a team.
14. _____ My supervisor is able to manage the department as a whole team to enable everyone's needs to be met.

Add up all your ratings to see how your supervisor stacks up.

Score total = _______________

Scoring:

- A score of 14 to 23 indicates low levels of supervisor support.
- A score of 24 to 33 indicates average levels of supervisor support.
- A score of 34 to 42 indicates high levels of supervisor support.

Adapted from Hammer, L. B., Kossek, E. E., Yragui, N. L., Bodner, T. E., & Hanson, G. C. (in press). Development and validation of a multidimensional measure of family supportive supervisor behaviors (FSSB). Journal of Management. DOI: 10.1177/0149206308328510. Used by permission of Sage Publications.

Telecommuting

FIGURE 7.8

Telecommuting helps employees avoid traffic jams like this one.

© 2010 Jupiterimages Corporation

telecommuting

Working remotely such as from home or from a coffee shop for some portion of the workweek.

Telecommuting refers to working remotely. For example, some employees work from home, a remote satellite office, or from a coffee shop for some portion of the workweek. Being able to work away from the office is one option that can decrease stress for some employees. Of course, while an estimated 45 million individuals telecommute each year, telecommuting is not for everyone.[58] At Merrill Lynch & Co. Inc., those who are interested in telecommuting are put through a rigorous training program that includes 2 weeks in one of their three home office simulation labs in Florida, New Jersey, or Manhattan to see if telecommuting is a good fit for the employee. Employees must also submit photos of their home office and a work plan. AT&T Inc. estimates that nearly 55% of its U.S.-based managers telecommute at some point in the week, and this method is also popular with managers around the world.[59] A recent survey found that 43% of government workers now telecommute at least part time. This trend has been growing in reaction to a law passed by the U.S. Congress in 2000 requiring federal agencies to offer working from home as an option.[60] Merrill Lynch has seen higher productivity, less stress, lower turnover, and higher job satisfaction for those who telecommute.[61] A recent meta-analysis of all the studies of telecommuting (12,883 employees) confirmed researcher findings that the higher autonomy of working from home resulted in lower work-family conflict for these employees. Even more encouraging were the findings of higher job satisfaction, better performance, and lower stress as well.[62] Of course, telecommuting can also cause potential stress. The keys to successful telecommuting arrangements are to match the right employees with the right jobs to the right environments. If any variable is not within a reasonable range, such as having a dog that barks all day when the employee is at home, productivity will suffer.

Employee Sabbaticals

sabbaticals

Paid time off from a normal work routine.

Sabbaticals (paid time off from the normal routine at work) have long been a sacred ritual practiced by universities to help faculty stay current, work on large research projects, and recharge every 5 to 8 years. However, many companies such as Genentech Inc., Container Store Inc., and eBay Inc. are now in the practice of granting paid sabbaticals to their employees. While 11% of large companies offer paid sabbaticals and 29% offer unpaid sabbaticals, 16% of small companies and 21% of medium-sized companies do the same.[63] For example, at PricewaterhouseCoopers International Ltd., you can apply for a sabbatical after just 2 years on the job if you agree to stay with the company for at least 1 year following your break. Time off ranges from 3 to 6 months and entails either a personal growth plan or one for social services where you help others.[64]

Employee Assistance Programs

Employee Assistance Programs (EAPs)

Often offered to workers as an adjunct to a company-provided health care plan.

There are times when life outside work causes stress in ways that will impact our lives at work and beyond. These situations may include the death of a loved one, serious illness, drug and alcohol dependencies, depression, or legal or financial problems that are impinging on our work lives. Although treating such stressors is beyond the scope of an organization or a manager, many companies offer their employees outside sources of emotional counseling. **Employee Assistance Programs (EAPs)** are often offered to workers as an adjunct to a company-provided health care plan. Small companies in particular use outside employee assistance programs, because they don't have the needed expertise in-house. As their name implies, EAPs offer help in dealing with crises in the workplace and beyond. EAPs are often used to help workers who have substance abuse problems.

KEY TAKEAWAY

There are many individual and organizational approaches to decreasing stress and avoiding negative outcomes. Individuals can control their diet, exercise, and sleep routines; build a social support network; and practice better time management. Organizations can help make expectations clear, give employees autonomy, create fair work environments, consider telecommuting, give employee sabbaticals, and utilize employee assistance programs.

EXERCISES

1. Have you ever been in a state of "flow" as described in this section? If so, what was special about this time?
2. Whose responsibility do you think it is to deal with employee stress—the employee or the organization? Why?
3. Do you think most organizations are fair or unfair? Explain your answer.
4. Have you ever considered telecommuting? What do you think would be the pros and cons for you personally?

3. WHAT ARE EMOTIONS?

LEARNING OBJECTIVES

1. Understand what defines emotions.
2. Identify the different types of emotions people experience.
3. Understand emotion contagion.

3.1 Types of Emotions

Financial analysts measure the value of a company in terms of profits and stock. For employees, however, the value of a job is also emotional. The root of the word *emotion* comes from a French term meaning "to stir up." And that's a great place to begin our investigation of emotions at work. More formally, an **emotion** is defined as a short, intense feeling resulting from some event. Not everyone reacts to the same situation in the same way. For example, a manager's way of speaking can cause one person to feel motivated, another to feel angry, and a third to feel sad. Emotions can influence whether a person is receptive to advice, whether they quit a job, and how they perform individually or on a team.[65] Of course, as you know, emotions can be positive or negative.

emotion

Feeling that occurs quickly and profoundly in response to an event that is desired (positive) or undesired (negative).

Positive emotions such as joy, love, and surprise result from our reaction to desired events. In the workplace, these events may include achieving a goal or receiving praise from a superior. Individuals experiencing a positive emotion may feel peaceful, content, and calm. A positive feeling generates a sensation of having something you didn't have before. As a result, it may cause you to feel fulfilled and satisfied. Positive feelings have been shown to dispose a person to optimism, and a positive emotional state can make difficult challenges feel more achievable.[66] This is because being positive can lead to upward positive spirals where your good mood brings about positive outcomes, thereby reinforcing the good mood.[67]

positive emotions

Emotions such as joy, love, and surprise can result from desired events.

Emotions are also useful for creative tasks, because positive individuals tend to be more creative and open to new ideas. In addition to helping with employee creativity, companies such as Microsoft Corporation often want to understand which features of their products produce not just high ratings for usability but also high emotional ratings. Individuals with strong positive emotional reactions are more likely to use their product and recommend it to others.[68] This is something Apple Inc. has been known for doing well, as their products tend to evoke strong positive emotions and loyalty from their users.

FIGURE 7.9

Research shows that acting positive at work can actually help you become happier over time, as emotions can be influenced by actions.

FIGURE 7.10

By creating products that users feel an emotional reaction to, Apple has revolutionized the way music is experienced.

Source: http://en.wikipedia.org/wiki/Image:IPod_Line.png.

Negative emotions such as anger, fear, and sadness can result from undesired events. In the workplace, these events may include not having your opinions heard, a lack of control over your day-to-day environment, and unpleasant interactions with colleagues, customers, and superiors. Negative emotions play a role in the conflict process, with those who can manage their negative emotions finding themselves in fewer conflicts than those who do not.

The unwanted side effects of negative emotions at work are easy to see: An angry colleague is left alone to work through the anger; a jealous colleague is excluded from office gossip, which is also the source of important office news. But you may be surprised to learn that negative emotions can help a company's productivity in some cases. Anger at another company's success, for example, can spark a burst of positive effort on behalf of a competitor. Jealousy about another division's sales figures may inspire a rival division to work harder. While negative emotions can be destructive in the workplace, they can inspire bursts of valuable individual action to change situations that aren't working the way they should.[69] The key is to promote the positive emotions and work to manage the negative ones so they don't spread throughout the organization and become the norm.

negative emotions

Emotions such as anger, fear, and sadness can result from undesired events.

3.2 Emotional Contagion

Both positive and negative emotions can be contagious, with the spillover of negative emotions lasting longer than positive emotions.[70] As you may have experienced in the past, contagion can be especially salient in a team setting. Research shows that emotions are contagious and that team members affect one another even after accounting for team performance.[71] One explanation for negative emotions' tendency to linger may be a stronger connection to the fight-or-flight situations people experience. Anger, fear, and suspicion are intentionally unpleasant messages urging us to take action immediately. And to make sure we get the message, these emotions stick around.

Research shows that some people are more susceptible to emotional contagion than others.[72] But in general, when the boss is happy, the staff is happy.[73] We can also imagine how negative emotions can be transferred. Imagine you're working behind the counter at a fast-food restaurant. Your mood is fine, until a customer argues with you about an order. You argue back. The customer leaves in a huff. Your anger emotions continue, turning into negative feelings that last throughout the day. As you might guess, you are more likely to make mistakes and find ordinary challenges annoying when you're experiencing negative emotions. Unchecked, your negative emotions can spread to those around you. A negative interaction with one customer can spill over onto interactions with another customer.[74]

OB Toolbox: Practice Changing Your Emotions

Olympic athletes train for peak performance by stimulating their brains to believe they've just run a record race. You can do the same thing to experience different moods. By providing your brain with the external stimulus of happiness or sadness, you can create those feelings. Give it a try!

It's best to practice this when you are feeling relatively calm. To give yourself a neutral starting point, close your eyes and breathe in slowly. Now, release your breath. Open your eyes and smile wide. Allow your eyes to crinkle. Now smile a bit more.

The changes you have consciously made to your expression are signaling your body that a positive event has taken place. How does this affect you emotionally?

Answer these questions to find out:

Do you feel more or less energetic as you smile? More or less calm? More or less optimistic? How does the feeling resulting from your physical changes compare with your feelings a moment before?

Now, let's try the opposite: Close your eyes and breathe in and out slowly, as detailed above, to clear your "emotional slate." Then open your eyes. Pull down the corners of your mouth. Open your eyes wide. You have just signaled to your body that something negative has taken place.

Note your feelings using the list above. How do these feelings compare with your feelings of "intentional happiness"?

Now consider this: Dr. Aston Trice of Mary Baldwin College in Virginia found that humor has mood-altering effects. Subjects were given a frustrating task. Then, one-half were shown cartoons. Those who had seen the cartoons overcame their frustration and attacked a new test with renewed enthusiasm and confidence, compared to those subjects who hadn't had the humorous interlude.[75]

KEY TAKEAWAY

Emotions serve many purposes and affect people at work. There are positive and negative emotions, and both can be helpful at motivating us to work harder. Emotions are malleable and they can also be contagious.

EXERCISES

1. How easy do you think it is to "manage" one's emotions?
2. Which types of emotions are most socially accepted in the workplace? Why do you think this is?
3. What are factors that affect your emotions?
4. Share an example of either positive or negative emotional contagion. How did it start and stop?
5. What do you do, if anything, to try to change how you are feeling? How effective are your strategies?

4. EMOTIONS AT WORK

LEARNING OBJECTIVES

1. **Understand Affective Events Theory.**
2. **Understand the influence of emotions on attitudes and behaviors at work.**
3. **Learn what emotional labor is and how it affects individuals.**
4. **Learn what emotional intelligence is.**

4.1 Emotions Affect Attitudes and Behaviors at Work

Emotions shape an individual's belief about the value of a job, a company, or a team. Emotions also affect behaviors at work. Research shows that individuals within your own inner circle are better able to recognize and understand your emotions.[76]

So, what is the connection between emotions, attitudes, and behaviors at work? This connection may be explained using a theory named **Affective Events Theory (AET)**. Researchers Howard Weiss and Russell Cropanzano studied the effect of six major kinds of emotions in the workplace: anger, fear, joy, love, sadness, and surprise.[77] Their theory argues that specific events on the job cause different kinds of people to feel different emotions. These emotions, in turn, inspire actions that can benefit or impede others at work.[78]

Affective Events Theory (AET)

A theory that explores how events on the job cause different kinds of people to feel different emotions.

FIGURE 7.11

According to Affective Events Theory, six emotions are affected by events at work.

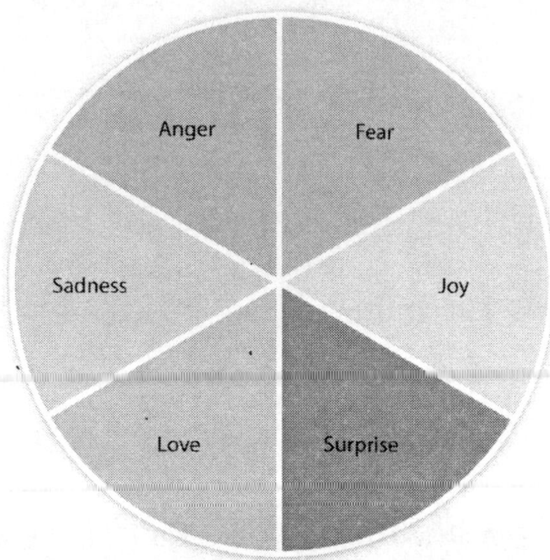

affect-driven behavior

Behavior that occurs when emotions trigger you to respond in a particular way.

For example, imagine that a coworker unexpectedly delivers your morning coffee to your desk. As a result of this pleasant, if unexpected experience, you may feel happy and surprised. If that coworker is your boss, you might feel proud as well. Studies have found that the positive feelings resulting from work experience may inspire you to do something you hadn't planned to do before. For instance, you might volunteer to help a colleague on a project you weren't planning to work on before. Your action would be an **affect-driven behavior**.[79] Alternatively, if you were unfairly reprimanded by your manager, the negative emotions you experience may cause you to withdraw from work or to act mean toward a coworker. Over time, these tiny moments of emotion on the job can influence a person's job satisfaction. Although company perks and promotions can contribute to a person's happiness at work, satisfaction is not simply a result of this kind of "outside-in" reward system. Job satisfaction in the AET model comes from the inside-in—from the combination of an individual's personality, small emotional experiences at work over time, beliefs, and affect-driven behaviors.

burnout

Ongoing negative emotional state resulting from dissatisfaction.

Jobs that are high in negative emotion can lead to frustration and **burnout**—an ongoing negative emotional state resulting from dissatisfaction.[80] Depression, anxiety, anger, physical illness, increased drug and alcohol use, and insomnia can result from frustration and burnout, with frustration being somewhat more active and burnout more passive. The effects of both conditions can impact coworkers, customers, and clients as anger boils over and is expressed in one's interactions with others.[81]

4.2 Emotional Labor

Negative emotions are common among workers in service industries. Individuals who work in manufacturing rarely meet their customers face-to-face. If they're in a bad mood, the customer would not know. Service jobs are just the opposite. Part of a service employee's job is appearing a certain way in the eyes of the public. Individuals in service industries are professional helpers. As such, they are expected to be upbeat, friendly, and polite at all times, which can be exhausting to accomplish in the long run.

persona

A professional role that involves acting out potentially artificial feelings as part of a job.

Humans are emotional creatures by nature. In the course of a day, we experience many emotions. Think about your day thus far. Can you identify times when you were happy to deal with other people and times that you wanted to be left alone? Now imagine trying to hide all the emotions you've felt today for 8 hours or more at work. That's what cashiers, school teachers, massage therapists, fire fighters, and librarians, among other professionals, are asked to do. As individuals, they may be feeling sad, angry, or fearful, but at work, their job title trumps their individual identity. The result is a **persona**—a professional role that involves acting out feelings that may not be real as part of their job.

emotional labor

The regulation of feelings and expressions for organizational purposes.

Emotional labor refers to the regulation of feelings and expressions for organizational purposes.[82] Three major levels of emotional labor have been identified.[83]

1. **Surface acting** requires an individual to exhibit physical signs, such as smiling, that reflect emotions customers want to experience. A children's hairdresser cutting the hair of a crying toddler may smile and act sympathetic without actually feeling so. In this case, the person is engaged in surface acting.
2. **Deep acting** takes surface acting one step further. This time, instead of faking an emotion that a customer may want to see, an employee will actively try to experience the emotion they are displaying. This genuine attempt at empathy helps align the emotions one is experiencing with the emotions one is displaying. The children's hairdresser may empathize with the toddler by imagining how stressful it must be for one so little to be constrained in a chair and be in an unfamiliar environment, and the hairdresser may genuinely begin to feel sad for the child.
3. **Genuine acting** occurs when individuals are asked to display emotions that are aligned with their own. If a job requires genuine acting, less emotional labor is required because the actions are consistent with true feelings.

surface acting

Behavior requiring individuals to exhibit physical signs, such as smiles, that reflect emotions they don't feel.

deep acting

Behavior requiring an individual to pretend to experience emotions they don't feel.

genuine acting

Behavior requiring an individual to display emotions aligned with their own.

FIGURE 7.12

When it comes to acting, the closer to the middle of the circle that your actions are, the less emotional labor your job demands. The further away, the more emotional labor the job demands.

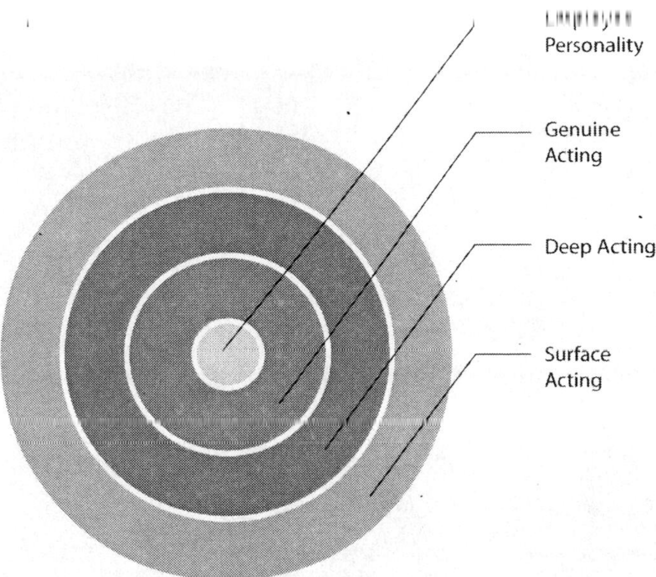

Research shows that surface acting is related to higher levels of stress and fewer felt positive emotions, while deep acting may lead to less stress.[84] Emotional labor is particularly common in service industries that are also characterized by relatively low pay, which creates the added potentials for stress and feelings of being treated unfairly.[85] In a study of 285 hotel employees, researchers found that emotional labor was vital because so many employee-customer interactions involve individuals dealing with emotionally charged issues.[86] Emotional laborers are required to display specific emotions as part of their jobs. Sometimes, these are emotions that the worker already feels. In that case, the strain of the emotional labor is minimal. For example, a funeral director is generally expected to display sympathy for a family's loss, and in the case of a family member suffering an untimely death, this emotion may be genuine. But for people whose jobs require them to be professionally polite and cheerful, such as flight attendants, or to be serious and authoritative, such as police officers, the work of wearing one's "game face" can have effects that outlast the working day. To combat this, taking breaks can help surface actors to cope more effectively.[87] In addition, researchers have found that greater autonomy is related to less strain for service workers in the United States as well as France.[88]

Cognitive dissonance is a term that refers to a mismatch among emotions, attitudes, beliefs, and behavior, for example, believing that you should always be polite to a customer regardless of personal feelings, yet having just been rude to one. You'll experience discomfort or stress unless you find a way to alleviate the dissonance. You can reduce the personal conflict by changing your behavior (trying harder to act polite), changing your belief (maybe it's OK to be a little less polite sometimes), or by adding a new fact that changes the importance of the previous facts (such as you will otherwise be laid off the next day). Although acting positive can make a person feel positive, emotional labor that involves a large degree of emotional or cognitive dissonance can be grueling, sometimes leading to negative health effects.[89]

cognitive dissonance

A term that refers to a mismatch among emotions, attitudes, beliefs, and behavior.

4.3 Emotional Intelligence

emotional intelligence

How people can understand each other more completely by becoming more aware of their own and others' emotions.

self-awareness

This exists when you are able to accurately perceive, evaluate, and display appropriate emotions.

self-management

This exists when you are able to direct your emotions in a positive way when needed.

social awareness

This exists when you are able to understand how others feel.

relationship management

This exists when you are able to help others manage their own emotions and truly establish supportive relationships with others.

One way to manage the effects of emotional labor is by increasing your awareness of the gaps between real emotions and emotions that are required by your professional persona. "What am I feeling? And what do others feel?" These questions form the heart of **emotional intelligence**. The term was coined by psychologists Peter Salovey and John Mayer and was popularized by psychologist Daniel Goleman in a book of the same name. Emotional intelligence looks at how people can understand each other more completely by developing an increased awareness of their own and others' emotions.[90]

There are four building blocks involved in developing a high level of emotional intelligence. **Self-awareness** exists when you are able to accurately perceive, evaluate, and display appropriate emotions. **Self-management** exists when you are able to direct your emotions in a positive way when needed. **Social awareness** exists when you are able to understand how others feel. **Relationship management** exists when you are able to help others manage their own emotions and truly establish supportive relationships with others.[91]

FIGURE 7.13

The four steps of emotional intelligence build upon one another.

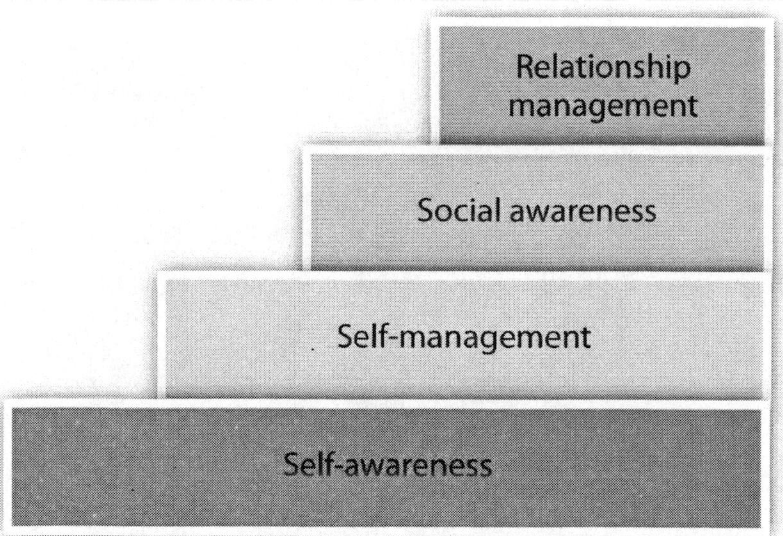

In the workplace, emotional intelligence can be used to form harmonious teams by taking advantage of the talents of every member. To accomplish this, colleagues well versed in emotional intelligence can look for opportunities to motivate themselves and inspire others to work together.[92] Chief among the emotions that helped create a successful team, Goleman learned, was empathy—the ability to put oneself in another's shoes, whether that individual has achieved a major triumph or fallen short of personal goals.[93] Those high in emotional intelligence have been found to have higher self-efficacy in coping with adversity, perceive situations as challenges rather than threats, and have higher life satisfaction, which can all help lower stress levels.[94]

KEY TAKEAWAY

Emotions affect attitudes and behaviors at work. Affective Events Theory can help explain these relationships. Emotional labor is higher when one is asked to act in a way that is inconsistent with personal feelings. Surface acting requires a high level of emotional labor. Emotional intelligence refers to understanding how others are reacting to our emotions.

EXERCISES

1. What is the worst job you have ever had (or class project if you haven't worked)? Did the job require emotional labor? If so, how did you deal with it?
2. Research shows that acting "happy" when you are not can be exhausting. Why do you think that is? Have you ever felt that way? What can you do to lessen these feelings?
3. How important do you think emotional intelligence is at work? Why?

5. THE ROLE OF ETHICS AND NATIONAL CULTURE

LEARNING OBJECTIVES

1. **Consider the role of ethics and emotion.**
2. **Consider the role of national culture on stress.**

5.1 Emotions and Ethics

We have seen before how a gap between our true feelings and the feelings we display at work can cause distress. What happens when there is a gap between our feelings and our true beliefs?

Joshua Greene is a philosopher and neuroscientist who uses magnetic imaging of the brain to show how our minds and bodies react to difficult questions. In one example, Greene asked a group of subjects to consider a situation in which a trolley is racing down a track, about to kill five people. The subjects have the ability to steer the trolley onto another track, where it will kill only one person. Most agree this feels like the right thing to do—the best of possible evils.

Greene then asks his subject to consider the same situation with one major shift: In this case, to save the five bystanders the subject must push a large man in front of the trolley to stop it in its tracks.

This time, Greene's subjects felt the sacrifice was emotionally wrong. Greene's research shows that the difference between his subjects' valuations of life in these cases was that the second was more emotional. The thought of pushing someone to his death, understandably, had brought up strong feelings among the group. If humans were computers, one person's death might be seen as "less bad" than the death of five. But human decisions are based on emotion. It was considered emotionally—and therefore, morally—unacceptable to push the man in front of the trolley to save five others.

Greene's magnetic images of his subject's brains showed that while considering the second scenario, people were using more of their brains. Greene writes, "These differences in emotional engagement affect people's judgments."[95]

Emotions are a powerful force in work and life. They are spontaneous and unpredictable elements of human beings that separate us from machines, and in some moments, from one another. By learning to identify and maximize the uses of our emotions at work, we can more appropriately respond to emotional situations.

5.2 Lack of Leisure Time and Stress Around the Globe

As economist Steven Landsburg notes, "Compared with Europeans, Americans are more likely to be employed and more likely to work longer hours—employed Americans put in about 3 hours more per week than employed Frenchmen. Most important, Americans take fewer (and shorter) vacations."[96] That is, if they take a vacation at all. A recent poll showed that 40% of Americans do not plan to take a vacation within the next year.[97]

Juliet Schor, a senior lecturer in economics and director of women's studies at Harvard University, adds to the portrait of the overworked American with a shocking statistic on Americans' free time. According to Schor's book, *The Overworked American: The Unexpected Decline of Leisure*, Americans have 16.5 hours per week of leisure time after their work and household obligations are fulfilled.[98] This is a huge concern, as research has established that recovery is a key to well-being and that the lack of recovery can lead to health concerns associated with stress.[99] Even more challenged for leisure time are some Japanese employees, working an average of 236 more hours per year than their American counterparts and 500 more hours than employees in France or Germany.[100] Leisure and recovery are key aspects to remaining healthy throughout one's lifetime.

While Europeans normally plan on taking the month of August off, Americans do not have a similar ritual. PricewaterhouseCoopers became so concerned that they have instituted a 10-day shutdown as a winter break and a 5-day shutdown around July 4 so that everyone takes that time off without feeling peer pressure to work through vacations.

KEY TAKEAWAY

Emotions play a role in shaping what we feel is ethical and what is not. Leisure time is important for avoiding the exhaustion phase of the stress cycle. Countries vary a great deal in how many hours the average worker puts in at work, with Japan working the most hours, followed by those in the United States.

EXERCISES

1. Explain a time when you have seen emotions help someone to be *more* ethical than they might have otherwise been.
2. Explain a time when you have seen emotions help someone to be *less* ethical than they might have otherwise been.
3. Why do you think some countries have so much vacation time compared to others? In your opinion, is this a problem or not? Why?

6. CONCLUSION

Stress is a major concern for individuals and organizations. Exhaustion is the outcome of prolonged stress. Individuals and organizations can take many approaches to lessening the negative health and work outcomes associated with being overstressed. Emotions play a role in organizational life. Understanding these emotions helps individuals to manage them. Emotional labor can be taxing on individuals, while emotional intelligence may help individuals cope with the emotional demands of their jobs.

7. EXERCISES

ETHICAL DILEMMA

You work at a paper supply company that employs fifty people. A coworker, Karen, is not your favorite person to work with. She is often late to work, can be unprofessional with coworkers, and isn't someone you can routinely count on to go above and beyond her job duties. Last week you even noticed that her breath smelled like alcohol when you spoke to her about some last-minute orders that needed to be filled. But, you don't like to rock the boat and you don't like to be disloyal to your coworkers, so you didn't say anything. However, David Chan just approached you and asked whether you smelled alcohol on Karen's breath last Thursday. You are surprised and ask him why. David mentions that he heard some gossip and wants to confirm if it is true or not.

What will you do?

1. Should you admit you smelled alcohol on Karen's breath last week? Why or why not?
2. What are the implications of each course of action?
3. Would you change your answer if, instead of working at a paper supply company, you worked as a nurse?

INDIVIDUAL EXERCISE

Time Management Quiz

Please answer true or false for each of the statements according to how you currently manage your time.

1. True or false: I sort my mail when it comes in, open it, place it in a folder, and deal with it when I am ready to.
2. True or false: I do what my boss asks me to do immediately.
3. True or false: I don't take breaks because they waste time.
4. True or false: I answer the phone when it rings regardless of what I am doing.
5. True or false: I check my e-mails as soon as they arrive.
6. True or false: I create a "to do" list at the start of every day.
7. True or false: I do my "heavy thinking" at the end of the day when things have calmed down.
8. True or false: I don't like to take vacations because making up the work is always too stressful.
9. True or false: Multitasking helps me be more effective at work.
10. True or false: I don't have to organize my office, since I always know where things are.

GROUP EXERCISE

Time Management Analysis

Create List 1:

List 10 activities you did at work (or at school) yesterday.

Create List 2:

List 5 things you think are key to doing your job well (or doing well in school).

Compare Lists:

Now, look at both lists and write down which items from List 1 relate to List 2.

Place each activity from List 1 on the following grid.

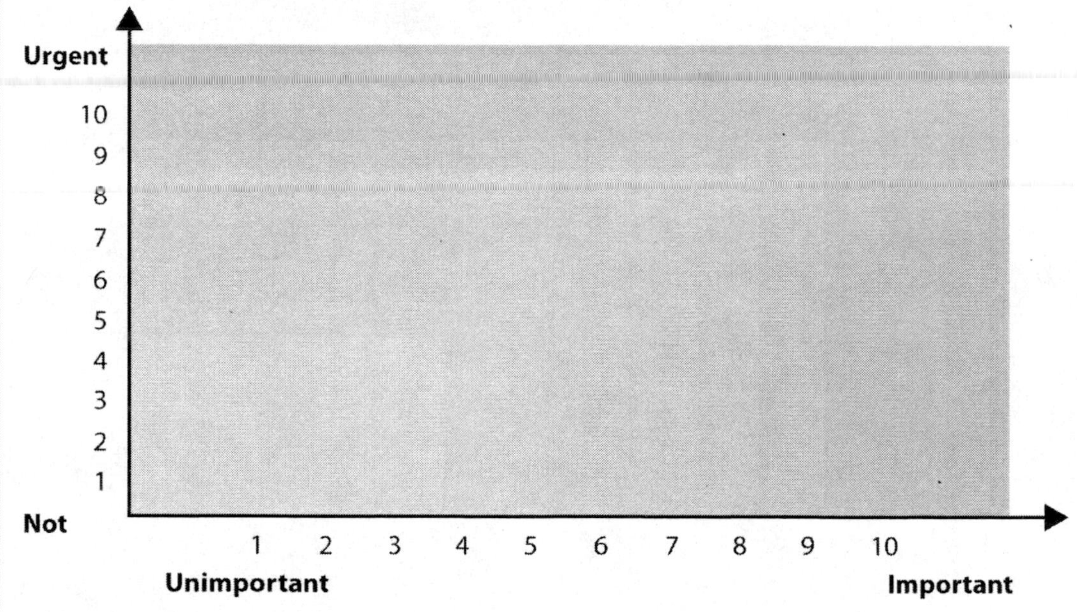

Group Discussion

Now, as a group, discuss the following questions:

1. What trends in your time management style did you notice?
2. How much of your "work" time is being spent on things that are directly related to doing well in your work or at school?
3. What works well for you in terms of time management?
4. What steps could you take to improve your time management?
5. How could your group help one another with time management?

ENDNOTES

1. Panzarino, P. (2008, February 15). Stress. Retrieved from Medicinenet.com. Retrieved May 21, 2008, from http://www.medicinenet.com/stress/article.htm.
2. Dyer, K. A. (2006). Definition of stress. Retrieved May 21, 2008, from About.com: http://dying.about.com/od/glossary/g/stress_distress.htm.
3. Kersten, D. (2002, November 12). Get a grip on job stress. *USA Today*. Retrieved May 21, 2008, from http://www.usatoday.com/money/jobcenter/workplace/stressmanagement/2002-11-12-job-stress_x.htm.
4. Cannon, W. (1915). *Bodily changes in pain, hunger, fear and rage: An account of recent researches into the function of emotional excitement*. New York: D. Appleton.
5. Selye, H. (1946). The general adaptation syndrome and the diseases of adaptation. *Journal of Clinical Endocrinology, 6*, 117; Selye, H. (1976). *Stress of life* (Rev. ed.). New York: McGraw-Hill.
6. American Psychological Association. (2007, October 24). Stress a major health problem in the U.S., warns APA. Retrieved May 21, 2008, from the American Psychological Association Web site: http://www.apa.org/releases/stressproblem.html.
7. Fisher, C. D., & Gittelson, R. (1983). A meta-analysis of the correlates of role conflict and role ambiguity. *Journal of Applied Psychology, 68*, 320–333; Jackson, S. E., & Shuler, R. S. (1985). A meta-analysis and conceptual critique of research on role ambiguity and role conflict in work settings. *Organizational Behavior and Human Decision Processes, 36*, 16–78; Örtqvist, D., & Wincent, J. (2006). Prominent consequences of role stress: A meta-analytic review. *International Journal of Stress Management, 13*, 399–422.
8. Gilboa, S., Shirom, A., Fried, Y., & Cooper, C. (2008). A meta-analysis of work demand stressors and job performance: Examining main and moderating effects. *Personnel Psychology, 61*, 227–271; Tubre, T. C., & Collins, J. M. (2000). Jackson and Schuler (1985) Revisited: A meta-analysis of the relationships between role ambiguity, role conflict, and performance. *Journal of Management, 26*, 155–169.
9. Bauer, T. N., Bodner, T., Erdogan, B., Truxillo, D. M., & Tucker, J. S. (2007). Newcomer adjustment during organizational socialization: A meta-analytic review of antecedents, outcomes, and methods. *Journal of Applied Psychology, 92*, 707–721.
10. Schick, A. G., Gordon, L. A., & Haka, S. (1990). Information overload: A temporal approach. *Accounting, organizations, and society, 15*, 199–220.
11. Definition of information overload available at *PCMag.com*. Retrieved May 21, 2008, from http://www.pcmag.com/encyclopedia_term/0,2542,t=information+overload&i=44950,00.asp; Additional information can be found in Dawley, D. D., & Anthony, W. P. (2003). User perceptions of e-mail at work. *Journal of Business and Technical Communication, 17*, 170–200.
12. Based on Overholt, A. (2001, February). Intel's got (too much) mail. *Fast Company*. Retrieved May 22, 2008, from http://www.fastcompany.com/online/44/intel.html and http://blogs.intel.com/it/2006/10/information_overload.php.
13. Netemeyer, R. G., Boles, J. S., & McMurrian, R. (1996). Development and validation of work–family conflict and family–work conflict scales. *Journal of Applied Psychology, 81*, 400–410.
14. U.S. Census Bureau. (2004). Labor Day 2004. Retrieved May 22, 2008, from the U.S. Census Bureau Web site: http://www.census.gov/press-release/www/releases/archives/facts_for_features_special_editions/002264.html.
15. Allen, T. D., Herst, D. E. L., Bruck, C. S., & Sutton, M. (2000). Consequences associated with work-to-family conflict: A review and agenda for future research. *Journal of Occupational Health Psychology, 5*, 278–308; Ford, M. T., Heinen, B. A., & Langkamer, K. L. (2007). Work and family satisfaction and conflict: A meta-analysis of cross-domain relations. *Journal of Applied Psychology, 92*, 57–80; Frone, M. R., Russell, R., & Cooper, M. L. (1992). Antecedents and outcomes of work–family conflict: Testing a model of the work–family interface. *Journal of Applied Psychology, 77*, 65–78; Hammer, L. B., Bauer, T. N., & Grandey, A. A. (2003). Work–family conflict and work–related withdrawal behaviors. *Journal of Business & Psychology, 17*, 419–436.
16. Kossek, E. E., & Ozeki, C. (1998). Work–family conflict, policies, and the job–life satisfaction relationship: A review and directions for organizational behavior–human resources research. *Journal of Applied Psychology, 83*, 139–149.
17. Barnett, R. C., & Hall, D. T. (2001). How to use reduced hours to win the war for talent. *Organizational Dynamics, 29*, 192–210; Greenhaus, J. H., & Powell, G. (2006). When work and family are allies: A theory of work–family enrichment. *Academy of Management Review, 31*, 72–92.
18. Thomas, L. T., & Ganster, D. C. (1995). Impact of family-supportive work variables on work–family conflict and strain: A control perspective. *Journal of Applied Psychology, 80*, 6–15.
19. Fontana, D. (1989). *Managing stress*. Published by the British Psychology Society and Routledge.
20. Slocum, J. W., Morris, J. R., Cascio, W. F., & Young, C. E. (1999). Downsizing after all these years: Questions and answers about who did it, how many did it, and who benefited from it. *Organizational Dynamics, 27*, 78–88.
21. Moore, S., Grunberg, L., & Greenberg, E. (2004). Repeated downsizing contact: The effects of similar and dissimilar layoff experiences on work and well-being outcomes. *Journal of Occupational Health Psychology, 9*, 247–257; Probst, T. M., Stewart, S. M., Gruys, M. L., & Tierney, B. W. (2007). Productivity, counterproductivity and creativity: The ups and downs of job insecurity. *Journal of Occupational and Organizational Psychology, 80*, 479–497; Sikora, P., Moore, S., Greenberg, E., & Grunberg, L. (2008). Downsizing and alcohol use: A cross-lagged longitudinal examination of the spillover hypothesis. *Work & Stress, 22*, 51–68.
22. Kalimo, R., Taris, T. W., & Schaufeli, W. B. (2003). The effects of past and anticipated future downsizing on survivor well-being: An Equity perspective. *Journal of Occupational Health Psychology, 8*, 91–109.
23. Amabile, T. M., & Conti, R. (1999). Changes in the work environment for creativity during downsizing. *Academy of Management Journal, 42*, 630–640.
24. Wiesenfeld, B. M., Brockner, J., Petzall, B., Wolf, R., & Bailey, J. (2001). Stress and coping among layoff survivors: A self-affirmation analysis. *Anxiety, Stress & Coping: An International Journal, 14*, 15–34.
25. Ornish, D. (1984). *Stress, diet and your heart*. New York: Signet.
26. Grossbart, T. (1992). *Skin deep*. New Mexico: Health Press.
27. Taylor, A. (1987, August 3). The biggest bosses. *Fortune*. Retrieved May 23, 2008, from http://money.cnn.com/magazines/fortune/fortune_archive/1987/08/03/69388/index.htm.
28. Mayo Clinic Staff. (2008, February 26). Chronic stress: Can it cause depression? Retrieved May 23, 2008, from the Mayo Clinic Web site: http://www.mayoclinic.com/health/stress/AN01286.
29. Mayo Clinic Staff. (2008, February 26). Chronic stress: Can it cause depression? Retrieved May 23, 2008, from the Mayo Clinic Web site. http://www.mayoclinic.com/health/stress/AN01286; Gilboa, S., Shiron, A., Fried, Y., & Cooper, C. (2008). A meta-analysis of work demand stressors and job performance: Examining main and moderating effects. *Personnel Psychology, 61*, 227–271; Podsakoff, N. P., LePine, J. A., & LePine, M. A. (2007). Differential challenge stressor-hindrance stressor relationships with job attitudes, turnover intentions, turnover, and withdrawal behavior: A meta-analysis. *Journal of Applied Psychology, 92*, 438–454.
30. Cropanzano, R., Rupp, D. E., & Byrne, Z. S. (2003). The relationship of emotional exhaustion to work attitudes, job performance, and organizational citizenship behaviors. *Journal of Applied Psychology, 88*, 160–169.
31. Podsakoff, N. P., LePine, J. A., & LePine, M. A. (2007). Differential challenge stressor-hindrance stressor relationships with job attitudes, turnover intentions, turnover, and withdrawal behavior: A meta-analysis. *Journal of Applied Psychology, 92*, 438–454.
32. Quick, J. C., Quick, J. D., Nelson, D. L., & Hurrell, J. J. (1997). *Preventative stress management in organizations*. Washington, DC: American Psychological Association.
33. Jenkins, C. D., Zyzanski, S., & Rosenman, R. (1979). *Jenkins activity survey manual*. New York: Psychological Corporation.
34. Spector, P. E., & O'Connell, B. J. (1994). The contribution of personality traits, negative affectivity, locus of control and Type A to the subsequent reports of job stressors and job strains. *Journal of Occupational and Organizational Psychology, 67*, 1–11.
35. Ganster, D. C. (1986). Type A behavior and occupational stress. *Journal of Organizational Behavior Management, 8*, 61–84.
36. BBC News. (2007, January 26). Stress "harms brain in the womb." Retrieved May 23, 2008, from http://news.bbc.co.uk/2/hi/health/6298909.stm.
37. Weaver, J. (2004, January 21). Estrogen makes the brain more vulnerable to stress. *Yale University Medical News*. Retrieved May 23, 2008, from http://www.eurekalert.org/pub_releases/2004-01/yu-emt012104.php.
38. Personality types impact on response to stress. (n.d.). Retrieved June 5, 2008, from the Discovery Health Web site: http://health.discovery.com/centers/stress/articles/pnstress/pnstress.html.
39. Brown, S. P., Westbrook, R. A., & Challagalla, G. (2005). Good cope, bad cope: Adaptive and maladaptive coping strategies following a critical negative work event. *Journal of Applied Psychology, 90*, 792–798.
40. Csikszentmihalyi, C. (1997). *Finding flow: The psychology of engagement with everyday life*. New York: Basic Books.
41. Wurtman, J. (1988). *Managing your mind and mood through food*. New York: Harper Perennial.
42. Miller, P. M. (1986). *Hilton head executive stamina program*. New York: Rawson Associates.
43. Tumminello, L. (2007, November 5). The National Sleep Foundation's *State of the States Report on Drowsy Driving* finds fatigued driving to be under-recognized and underreported. Retrieved May 23, 2008, from the National Sleep Foundation Web site: http://www.drowsydriving.org/site/c.lqLPIROCKtF/b.3568679/.
44. For additional resources, go to the National Sleep Foundation Web site: http://www.nationalsleepfoundation.org.
45. Halbesleben, J. R. B. (2006). Sources of social support and burnout: A meta-analytic test of the conservation of resources model. *Journal of Applied Psychology, 91*, 1134–1145.
46. Van Yperfen, N. W., & Hagedoorn, M. (2003). Do high job demands increase intrinsic motivation or fatigue or both? The role of job control and job social support. *Academy of Management Journal, 46*, 339–348.
47. Hobson, C., Kesic, D., Rosetti, D., Delunas, L., & Hobson, N. (2004, September). Motivating employee commitment with empathy and support during stressful life events. *International Journal of Management* website. Retrieved January 21, 2008 from http://findarticles.com/p/articles/mi_qa5440/is_200409/ai_n21362646?tag=content;col1.
48. Dispatches from the war on stress: Business begins to reckon with the enormous costs of workplace angst. (2007, August 6). *Business Week*. Retrieved May 23, 2008, from http://www.businessweek.com/magazine/content/07_32/b4045061.htm?campaign_id=rss_null.
49. Jackson, S. E., & Schuler, R. S. (1985). A meta-analysis and conceptual critique of research on role ambiguity and role conflict in work settings. *Organizational Behavior and Human Decision Processes, 36*, 16–78; Sauter S. L., Murphy L. R., & Hurrell J. J., Jr. (1990). Prevention of work-related psychological disorders. *American Psychologist, 45*, 1146–1158.
50. Kossek, E. E., Lautschb, B. A., & Eaton, S. C. (2006). Telecommuting, control, and boundary management: Correlates of policy use and practice, job control, and work–family effectiveness. *Journal of Vocational Behavior, 68*, 347–367.

51. Schaubroeck, J., Lam, S. S. K., & Xie, J. L. (2000). Collective efficacy versus self-efficacy in coping responses to stressors and control: A cross-cultural study. *Journal of Applied Psychology, 85*, 512–525.

52. Grandey, A. A., Fisk, G. M., & Steiner, D. D. (2005). Must "service with a smile" be stressful? The moderating role of personal control for American and French employees. *Journal of Applied Psychology, 90*, 893–904.

53. Webber, A. M. (1998). Danger: Toxic company. *Fast Company*. Retrieved June 1, 2008, from http://www.fastcompany.com/magazine/19/toxic.html?page=0%2C1.

54. Huselid, M. A. (1995). The impact of human resource management practices on turnover, productivity, and corporate financial performance. *Academy of Management Journal, 38*, 635–672; Pfeffer, J. (1998). *The human equation: Building profits by putting people first*. Boston: Harvard Business School Press; Pfeffer, J., & Veiga, J. F. (1999). Putting people first for organizational success. *Academy of Management Executive, 13*, 37–48; Welbourne, T., & Andrews, A. (1996). Predicting performance of Initial Public Offering firms: Should HRM be in the equation? *Academy of Management Journal, 39*, 910–911.

55. Judge, T. A., & Colquitt, J. A. (2004). Organizational justice and stress: The mediating role of work-family conflict. *Journal of Applied Psychology, 89*, 395–404.

56. Greenberg, J. (2004). Stress fairness to fare no stress: Managing workplace stress by promoting organizational justice. *Organizational Dynamics, 33*, 352–365.

57. Greenberg, J. (2006). Losing sleep over organizational justice: Attenuating insomniac reactions to underpayment inequity with supervisory training in interactional justice. *Journal of Applied Psychology, 91*, 58–69.

58. WorldatWork. (2006). *Telework trendlines for 2006* (Report). Retrieved June 1, 2008, from the WorldatWork Web site: http://www.workingfromanywhere.org/news/trendlines_2006.pdf.

59. AT&T. (2004). Remote working increasing across enterprises, according to global survey of senior executives. Retrieved June 1, 2008, from the AT&T Web site: http://www.business.att.com/enterprise/resource_item/Insights/Press_Release/20041201-1/download=yes&year=2004/; Wells, S. J. (1997, August 17). For stay-home workers, speed bumps on the telecommute. *New York Times*, p. 17.

60. Gross, G. (2008, March 6). Survey: More U.S. government employees teleworking. *InfoWorld*. Retrieved June 1, 2008, from http://www.infoworld.com/article/06/03/06/76150_HNtelework_1.html?BUSINESS%20ANALYTICS.

61. Chadderdon, L. (2007). Merrill Lynch works—at home. *Fast Company*. Retrieved June 1, 2008, from http://www.fastcompany.com/magazine/14/homework.html.

62. Gajendran, R. S., & Harrison, D. A. (2007). The good, the bad, and the unknown about telecommuting: Meta-analysis of psychological mediators and individual consequences. *Journal of Applied Psychology, 92*, 1524–1541.

63. Schwartz, S. K. (1999, November 15). The corporate sabbatical. *CNNMoney.com*. Retrieved June 1, 2008, from http://money.cnn.com/1999/11/15/life/q_sabbatical/.

64. Sahadi, J. (2006, June 13). The corporate sabbatical isn't just a pipe dream at a significant minority of companies. *CNNMoney.com*. Retrieved June 1, 2008, from http://money.cnn.com/2006/06/13/commentary/everyday/sahadi/index.htm.

65. Cole, M. S., Walter, F., & Bruch, H. (2008). Affective mechanisms linking dysfunctional behavior to performance in work teams: A moderated mediation study. *Journal of Applied Psychology, 93*, 945–958; George, J. M, & Jones, G. R. (1996). The experience of work and turnover intentions: Interactive effects of value attainment, job satisfaction, and positive mood. *Journal of Applied Psychology, 81*, 318–325; Gino, F., & Schweitzer, M. E. (2008). Blinded by anger or feeling the love: How emotions influence advice taking. *Journal of Applied Psychology, 93*, 1165–1173.

66. Kirby, L. (2001). *Personality, physiology and performance: The effects of optimism on task engagement*. Retrieved June 1, 2008, from University of Pennsylvania, Positive Psychology Center Web site: http://www.ppc.sas.upenn.edu/institute2001shortsummaries.htm#LK.

67. Frederickson, B. L., & Joiner, T. (2002). Emotions trigger upward spirals toward emotional well-being. *Psychological Science, 13*, 172–175.

68. Weler, M. H. (2008). Microsoft gets emotional with business software upgrade. *Information Week*. Retrieved June 1, 2008, from http://www.informationweek.com/news/windows/microsoft_news/showArticle.jhtml?articleID=206903128.

69. Jordan, P. J., Lawrence, S. A., & Troth, A. C. (2006). Emotions and coping with conflict: An introduction. *Journal of Management and Organization, 12*, 98–100.

70. Linguistics may be clue to emotions, according to Penn State research. (2005, January 24). Retrieved June 1, 2008, from the *ScienceDaily* Web site: http://www.sciencedaily.com_/releases/2005/01/050123213111.htm.

71. Ilies, R., Wagner, D. T., & Morgeson, F. P. (2007). Explaining affective linkages in teams: Individual differences in susceptibility to contagion and individualism-collectivism. *Journal of Applied Psychology, 92*, 1140–1148.

72. Papousek, I., Freudenthaler, H. H., & Schulter, D. (2008). The interplay of perceiving and regulating emotions in becoming infected with positive and negative moods. *Personality and Individual Differences, 45*, 463–467.

73. Bono, J. E., & Ilies, R. (2006). Charisma, positive emotions and mood contagion. *Leadership Quarterly, 17*, 317–334.

74. Pugh, S. D. (2001). Service with a smile: Emotional contagion in the service encounter. *Academy of Management Journal, 44*, 1018–1027; Hareli, S., & Rafaeli, A. (2007). Emotion cycles: On the social influence of emotion in organizations. *Research in Organizational Behavior, 28*, 35–59.

75. Colino, S. (2006, May 30). That look—it's catching. *Washington Post*, p. HE01.

76. Elfenbein, H. A., & Ambady, N. (2002). Is there an in-group advantage in emotion recognition? *Psychological Bulletin, 128*, 243–249.

77. Weiss, H. M., & Cropanzano, R. (1996). Affective events theory: A theoretical discussion of the structure, causes and consequences of affective experiences at work. *Research in Organizational Behavior, 18*, 1–74.

78. Fisher, C. D. (2002). Real-time affect at work: A neglected phenomenon in organizational behaviour. *Australian Journal of Management, 27*, 1–10.

79. Fisher, C. D. (2002). Real-time affect at work: A neglected phenomenon in organizational behaviour. *Australian Journal of Management, 27*, 1–10.

80. Lee, R. T., & Ashforth, B. E. (1996). A meta-analytic examination of the correlates of three dimensions of job burnout. *Journal of Applied Psychology, 81*, 123–133; Maslach, C. (1982). *Burnout: The cost of caring*. Englewood Cliffs, NJ: Prentice Hall; Maslach, C., & Jackson, S. E. (1981). The measurement of experienced burnout. *Journal of Occupational Behavior, 2*, 99–113.

81. Lewandowski, C. A. (2003, December 1). Organizational factors contributing to worker frustration: The precursor to burnout. *Journal of Sociology & Social Welfare*, 30, 175–185.

82. Grandey, A. (2000). Emotional regulations in the workplace: A new way to conceptualize emotional labor. *Journal of Occupational Health Psychology, 5*, 95–110.

83. Hochschild, A. (1983). *The managed heart*. Berkeley, CA: University of California Press.

84. Beal, D. J., Trougakos, J. P., Weiss, H. M., & Green, S. G. (2006). Episodic processes in emotional labor: Perceptions of affective delivery and regulation strategies. *Journal of Applied Psychology, 91*, 1053–1065; Grandey, A. A. (2003). When "the show must go on": Surface acting and deep acting as determinants of emotional exhaustion and peer-rated service delivery. *Academy of Management Journal, 46*, 86–96.

85. Glomb, T. M., Kammeyer-Mueller, J. D., & Rotundo, M. (2004). Emotional labor demands and compensating wage differentials. *Journal of Applied Psychology, 89*, 700–714; Rupp, D. E., & Sharmin, S. (2006). When customers lash out: The effects of customer interactional injustice on emotional labor and the mediating role of discrete emotions. *Journal of Applied Psychology, 91*, 971–978.

86. Chu, K. (2002). *The effects of emotional labor on employee work outcomes*. Unpublished doctoral dissertation, Virginia Polytechnic Institute and State University.

87. Beal, D. J., Green, S. G., & Weiss, H. (2008). Making the break count: An episodic examination of recovery activities, emotional experiences, and positive affective displays. *Academy of Management Journal, 51*, 131–146.

88. Grandey, A. A., Fisk, G. M., & Steiner, D. D. (2005). Must "service with a smile" be stressful? The moderating role of personal control for American and French employees. *Journal of Applied Psychology, 90*, 893–904.

89. Zapf, D. (2006). On the positive and negative effects of emotion work in organizations. *European Journal of Work and Organizational Psychology, 15*, 1–28.

90. Carmeli, A. (2003). The relationship between emotional intelligence and work attitudes, behavior and outcomes: An examination among senior managers. *Journal of Managerial Psychology, 18*, 788–813.

91. Elfenbein, H. A., & Ambady, N. (2002). Predicting workplace outcomes from the ability to eavesdrop on feelings. *Journal of Applied Psychology, 87*, 963–971; Weisinger, H. (1998). *Emotional intelligence at work*. San Francisco: Jossey-Bass.

92. Goleman, D. (1995). *Emotional intelligence*. New York: Bantam Books.

93. Goleman, D. (1998). *Working with emotional intelligence*. New York: Bantam Books.

94. Law, K. S., Wong, C., & Song, L. J. (2004). The construct and criterion validity of emotional intelligence and its potential utility for management studies. *Journal of Applied Psychology, 89*, 483–496; Mikolajczak, M., & Luminet, O. (2008). Trait emotional intelligence and the cognitive appraisal of stressful events: An exploratory study. *Personality and Individual Differences, 44*, 1445–1453.

95. Greene, J., Sommerville, R. B., Nystrom, L. E., Darley, J. M., & Cohen, J. D. (2001, September). An MRI investigation of emotional engagement in moral judgment. *Science*, 2105–2108.

96. Landsburg, S. (2006, May 23). Why Europeans work less than Americans. *Forbes*. Retrieved June 1, 2008, from http://www.forbes.com/2006/05/20/steven-landsburg-labor_cx_sl_06work_0523landsburg.html.

97. Egan, T. (2006). The rise of the shrinking-vacation syndrome. *New York Times*. Retrieved June 1, 2008, from http://travel2.nytimes.com/2006/08/20/us/20vacation.html.

98. Schor, J. B. (1993). *The overworked American: The unexpected decline of leisure*. New York: Basic Books.

99. Sonnentag, S., & Zijlstra, F. R. H. (2006). Job characteristics and off-job activities as predictors of need for recovery, well-being, and fatigue. *Journal of Applied Psychology, 91*, 330–350.

100. Nishiyama K., & Johnson, J. (2006). Karoshi—death from overwork: Occupational health consequences of Japanese production management. *The Fordism of Ford and Modern Management: Fordism and Post-Fordism. Volume 1* [e-book]. An Elgar Reference Collection, 462–478.

CHAPTER 8
Communication

LEARNING OBJECTIVES

After reading this chapter, you should be able to do the following:

1. Understand the communication process.
2. Compare and contrast different types of communication.
3. Compare and contrast different communication channels.
4. Understand and learn to overcome barriers to effective communication.
5. Understand the role listening plays in communication.
6. Learn how ethics can play a role in how messages are communicated as well as how they are perceived.
7. Learn how verbal and nonverbal communication can carry different meanings among cultures.

You've Got Mail...and You're Fired!

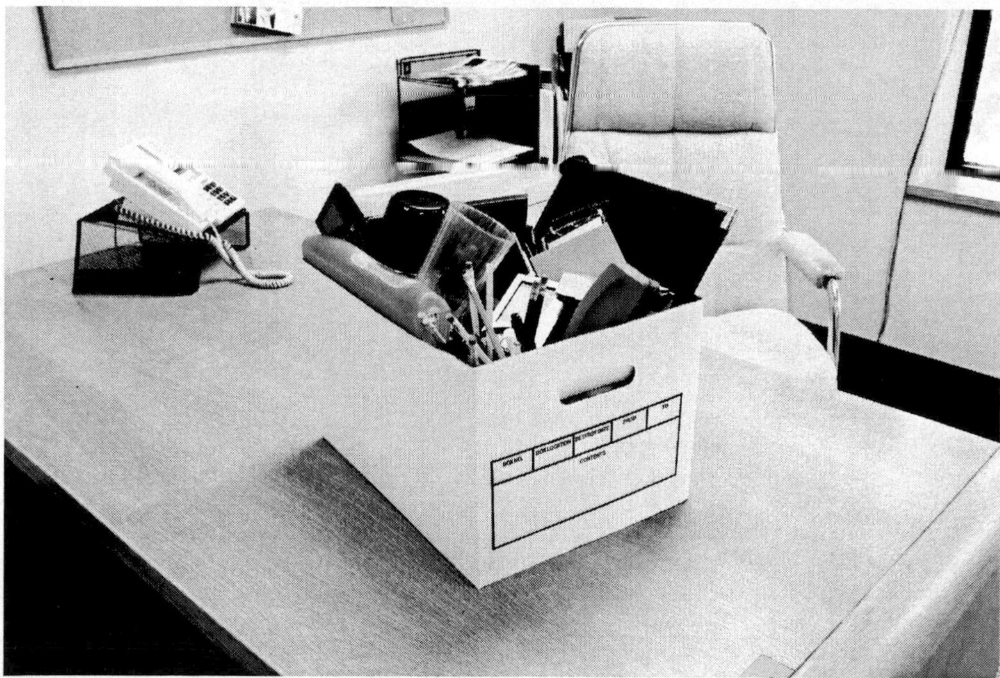

© 2010 Jupiterimages Corporation

No one likes to receive bad news, and few like to give it. In what is heralded as one of the biggest human resources blunders in business, one company found a way around the discomfort of firing someone face-to-face. A total of 400 employees at the Fort Worth, Texas headquarters of Radio Shack Corporation got the ultimate e-mail message early one Tuesday morning. The message simply said, "The work force reduction notification is currently in progress. Unfortunately, your position is one that has been eliminated." Company officials argued that using electronic notification was faster and allowed more privacy than breaking the news in person, and additionally, employees received generous severance packages. Organizational consultant Ken Siegel disagrees, proclaiming, "The bottom line is this: To almost everyone who observes or reads this, it represents a stupefying new low in the annals of management practice." It's unclear what, if any, the long-term effect will be for Radio Shack. Many wonder if this will hurt Radio Shack's ability to recruit and retain talent in the future. It isn't just Radio Shack that finds it challenging to deal with letting employees go. Terminating employees can be a painful job for many managers. The communication that takes place requires careful preparation and substantial levels of skill. Some organizations are even outsourcing the job to "terminators" to handle this difficult task for them.

Using language that softens the blow of a termination has also grown in popularity. Here are just a few ways to say you're about to lose your job without saying you've been fired:

- Career alternative enhancement program
- Career-change opportunity
- Dehiring staff
- Derecruiting resources
- Downsizing employment
- Employee reduction activities
- Implementing a skills mix adjustment
- Negative employee retention
- Optimizing outplacement potential
- Rectification of a workforce imbalance
- Redundancy elimination
- Right-sizing employment
- Selecting out manpower
- Vocation relocation policy

So if anyone ever uses one of these phrases to fire you, take heart, you're not unemployed. You're simply "in an orderly transition between career changes while undergoing a period of non-waged involuntary leisure during your temporary outplacement."[1]

Sources: Adapted from information in Joyce, A. (2006, September 10). Fired via e-mail, and other tales of poor exits. Washington Post, p. F01. Retrieved July 1, 2008, from http://www.washingtonpost.com/wp-dyn/content/article/2006/09/09/AR2006090900103.html; Hollon, J. (2006, September 11). You've been deleted: Firing by e-mail. Workforce Management, p. 42.

1. UNDERSTANDING COMMUNICATION

LEARNING OBJECTIVES

1. **Define communication.**
2. **Understand the communication process.**

communication

The process by which information is exchanged between individuals through a common system of symbols, signs, or behavior.

Communication is vital to organizations—it's how we coordinate actions and achieve goals. It is defined in Webster's dictionary as a process by which information is exchanged between individuals through a common system of symbols, signs, or behavior. We know that 50% to 90% of a manager's time is spent communicating,[2] and communication ability is related to a manager's performance.[3] In most work environments, a miscommunication is an annoyance—it can interrupt workflow by causing delays and interpersonal strife. But, in some work arenas, like operating rooms and airplane cockpits, communication can be a matter of life and death.

So, just how prevalent is miscommunication in the workplace? You may not be surprised to learn that the relationship between miscommunication and negative outcomes is very strong. Data suggest that deficient interpersonal communication was a causal factor in approximately 70% to 80% of all accidents over the last 20 years.[4]

Poor communication can also lead to lawsuits. For example, you might think that malpractice suits are filed against doctors based on the outcome of their treatments alone. But a 1997 study of malpractice suits found that a primary influence on whether or not a doctor is sued is the doctor's communication style. While the combination of a bad outcome and patient unhappiness can quickly lead to litigation, a warm, personal communication style leads to greater patient satisfaction. Simply put, satisfied patients are less likely to sue.[5]

In business, poor communication costs money and wastes time. One study found that 14% of each workweek is wasted on poor communication.[6] In contrast, effective communication is an asset for organizations and individuals alike. Effective communication skills, for example, are an asset for job seekers. A recent study of recruiters at 85 business schools ranked communication and interpersonal skills as the highest skills they were looking for, with 89% of the recruiters saying they were important.[7] On the flip side, good communication can help a company retain its star employees. Surveys find that when employees think their organizations do a good job of keeping them informed about matters that affect them and when they have access to the information they need to do their jobs, they are more satisfied with their employers.[8] So can good communication increase a company's market value? The answer seems to be yes. "When you foster ongoing communications internally, you will have more satisfied employees who will be better equipped to effectively communicate with your customers," says Susan Meisinger, president and CEO of the Society for Human Resource Management. Research finds that organizations that are able to improve their communication integrity also increase their market value by as much as 7%.[9] We will explore the definition and benefits of effective communication in our next section.

FIGURE 8.2

At NASA, success depends on strong communication.

Source: http://en.wikipedia.org/wiki/Image:Orion_briefing_model.jpg.

1.1 The Communication Process

Communication fulfills three main functions within an organization, including coordination, transmission of information, and sharing emotions and feelings. All these functions are vital to a successful organization. The coordination of effort within an organization helps people work toward the same goals. Transmitting information is a vital part of this process. Sharing emotions and feelings bonds teams and unites people in times of celebration and crisis. Effective communication helps people grasp issues, build rapport with coworkers, and achieve consensus. So, how can we communicate effectively? The first step is to understand the communication process.

We all exchange information with others countless times each day by phone, e-mail, printed word, and of course, in person. Let us take a moment to see how a typical communication works using this as a guide.

FIGURE 8.3

Lee Iacocca, past president and CEO of Chrysler until his retirement in 1992, said, "You can have brilliant ideas, but if you can't get them across, your ideas won't get you anywhere."

Source: http://en.wikipedia.org/wiki/Lee_Iacocca.

FIGURE 8.4 Process Model of Communication

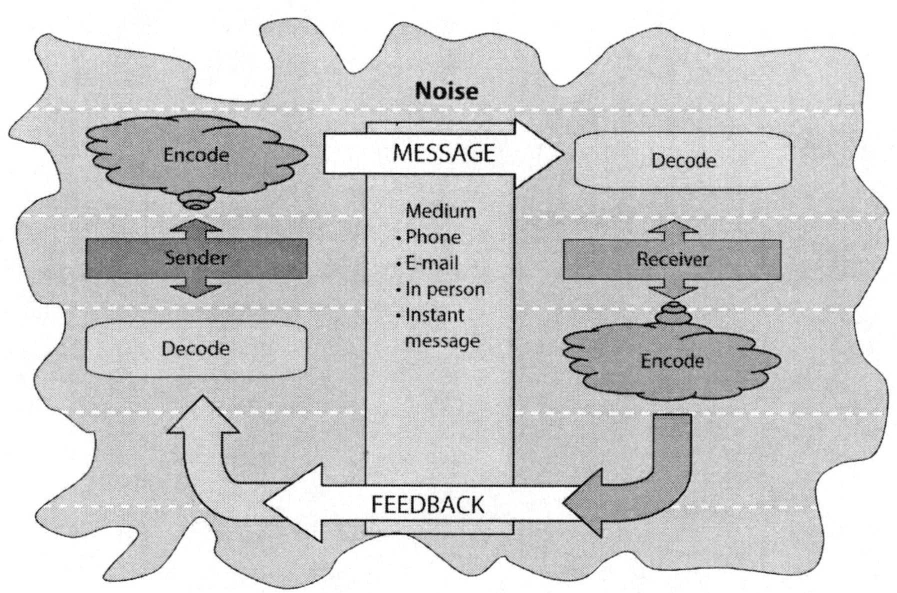

A **sender**, such as a boss, coworker, or customer, originates the message with a thought. For example, the boss's thought could be: *"Get more printer toner cartridges!"*

The sender **encodes** the message, translating the idea into words.

The boss may communicate this thought by saying, *"Hey you guys, let's order more printer toner cartridges."*

The **medium** of this encoded message may be spoken words, written words, or signs.

The **receiver** is the person who receives the message.

The receiver **decodes** the message by assigning meaning to the words.

In this example, our receiver, Bill, has a to-do list a mile long. *"The boss must know how much work I already have,"* the receiver thinks. Bill's mind translates his boss's message as, *"Could you order some printer toner cartridges, in addition to everything else I asked you to do this week...if you can find the time?"*

The meaning that the receiver assigns may not be the meaning that the sender intended, because of factors such as noise. **Noise** is anything that interferes with or distorts the message being transformed. Noise can be external in the environment (such as distractions) or it can be within the receiver. For example, the receiver may be extremely nervous and unable to pay attention to the message. Noise can even occur within the sender: The sender may be unwilling to take the time to convey an accurate message, or the words that are chosen can be ambiguous and prone to misinterpretation.

Picture the next scene. The place: a staff meeting. The time: a few days later. Bill's boss believes the message about printer toner has been received.

"Are the printer toner cartridges here yet?" Bill's boss asks.

"You never said it was a rush job!" Bill protests.

"But!"

"But!"

Miscommunications like these happen in the workplace every day. We've seen that miscommunication does occur in the workplace, but how does a miscommunication happen? It helps to think of the communication process. The series of arrows pointing the way from the sender to the receiver and back again can, and often do, fall short of their target.

sender

The person initiating a communication.

encode

The translation of ideas into words.

medium

The way that a sender's message is conveyed.

receiver

The person who a message is intended to reach.

decode

The process of assigning meaning to a received message.

noise

Anything that interferes with or distorts the message being transformed.

KEY TAKEAWAY

Communication is vital to organizations. Poor communication is prevalent between senders and receivers. Communication fulfills three functions within organizations, including coordination, the transmission of information, and sharing emotions and feelings. Noise can disrupt or distort communication.

EXERCISES

1. Where have you seen the communication process break down at work? At school? At home?
2. Explain how miscommunication might be related to an accident at work.
3. Give an example of noise during the communication process.

2. COMMUNICATION BARRIERS

LEARNING OBJECTIVES

1. Understand different ways that the communication process can be sidetracked.
2. Understand the role poor listening plays in communication problems.
3. Understand what active listening is.
4. Learn strategies to become a more effective listener.

2.1 Barriers to Effective Communication

The biggest single problem in communication is the illusion that it has taken place.
- *George Bernard Shaw*

Filtering

Filtering is the distortion or withholding of information to manage a person's reactions. Some examples of filtering include a manager's keeping a division's negative sales figures from a superior, in this case, the vice president. The old saying, "Don't shoot the messenger!" illustrates the tendency of receivers to vent their negative response to unwanted messages to the sender. A gatekeeper (the vice president's assistant, perhaps) who doesn't pass along a complete message is also filtering. Additionally, the vice president may delete the e-mail announcing the quarter's sales figures before reading it, blocking the message before it arrives.

filtering

The distortion or withholding of information to manage a person's reactions.

As you can see, filtering prevents members of an organization from getting the complete picture of a situation. To maximize your chances of sending and receiving effective communications, it's helpful to deliver a message in multiple ways and to seek information from multiple sources. In this way, the impact of any one person's filtering will be diminished.

Since people tend to filter bad news more during upward communication, it is also helpful to remember that those below you in an organization may be wary of sharing bad news. One way to defuse this tendency to filter is to reward employees who clearly convey information upward, regardless of whether the news is good or bad.

Here are some of the criteria that individuals may use when deciding whether to filter a message or pass it on:

1. *Past experience*: Were previous senders rewarded for passing along news of this kind in the past, or were they criticized?
2. *Knowledge and perception of the speaker*: Has the receiver's direct superior made it clear that "no news is good news?"
3. *Emotional state, involvement with the topic, and level of attention*: Does the sender's fear of failure or criticism prevent the message from being conveyed? Is the topic within the sender's realm of expertise, increasing confidence in the ability to decode the message, or is the sender out of a personal comfort zone when it comes to evaluating the message's significance? Are personal concerns impacting the sender's ability to judge the message's value?

Once again, filtering can lead to miscommunications in business. Listeners translate messages into their own words, each creating a unique version of what was said.[10]

Selective Perception

Small things can command our attention when we're visiting a new place—a new city or a new company. Over time, however, we begin to make assumptions about the environment based on our past experiences. **Selective perception** refers to filtering what we see and hear to suit our own needs. This process is often unconscious. We are bombarded with too much stimuli every day to pay equal attention to everything, so we pick and choose according to our own needs. Selective perception is a time-saver, a necessary tool in a complex culture. But it can also lead to mistakes.

selective perception

The personal filtering of what we see and hear to suit our own needs.

Think back to the example conversation between the person asked to order more toner cartridges and his boss earlier in this chapter. Since Bill found the to-do list from his boss to be unreasonably demanding, he assumed the request could wait. (How else could he do everything else on the list?) The boss, assuming that Bill had heard the urgency in her request, assumed that Bill would place the order before returning to previously stated tasks. Both members of this organization were using selective perception to evaluate the communication. Bill's perception was that the task could wait. The boss's perception was that a time frame was clear, though unstated. When two selective perceptions collide, a misunderstanding occurs.

Information Overload

Messages reach us in countless ways every day. Some messages are societal—advertisements that we may hear or see in the course of our day. Others are professional—e-mails, memos, and voice mails, as well as conversations with our colleagues. Others are personal—messages from and conversations with our loved ones and friends.

information overload

What occurs when the information processing demands on an individual's time to perform interactions and internal calculations exceed the supply or capacity of time available for such processing.

Add these together and it's easy to see how we may be receiving more information than we can take in. This state of imbalance is known as **information overload**, which occurs "when the information processing demands on an individual's time to perform interactions and internal calculations exceed the supply or capacity of time available for such processing."[11] Others note that information overload is "a symptom of the high-tech age, which is too much information for one human being to absorb in an expanding world of people and technology. It comes from all sources including TV, newspapers, and magazines as well as wanted and unwanted regular mail, e-mail and faxes. It has been exacerbated enormously because of the formidable number of results obtained from Web search engines."[12] Other research shows that working in such fragmented fashion significantly impacts efficiency, creativity, and mental acuity.[13]

FIGURE 8.5

A field study found that managers can expect, on average, to do only *3 minutes* of uninterrupted work on any one task before being interrupted by an incoming e-mail, instant message, phone call, coworker, or other distraction.[14]

© 2010 Jupiterimages Corporation

Going back to our example of Bill, let's say he's in his office on the phone with a supplier. While he's talking, he hears the chime of his e-mail alerting him to an important message from his boss. He's scanning through it quickly while still on the phone when a coworker pokes her head into his office saying Bill's late for a staff meeting. The supplier on the other end of the phone line has just given him a choice among the products and delivery dates he requested. Bill realizes he missed hearing the first two options, but he doesn't have time to ask the supplier to repeat them all or to try reconnecting with him at a later time. He chooses the third option—at least he heard that one, he reasons, and it seemed fair. How good was Bill's decision amidst all the information he was processing at the same time?

Emotional Disconnects

An effective communication requires a sender and a receiver who are open to speaking and listening to one another, despite possible differences in opinion or personality. One or both parties may have to put their emotions aside to achieve the goal of communicating clearly. A receiver who is emotionally upset tends to ignore or distort what the sender is saying. A sender who is emotionally upset may be unable to present ideas or feelings effectively.

Lack of Source Familiarity or Credibility

Have you ever told a joke that fell flat? You and the receiver lacked the common context that could have made it funny. (Or yes, it could have just been a lousy joke.) Sarcasm and irony are subtle and, therefore, they are potentially hurtful commodities in business. It's best to keep these types of communications out of the workplace, as their benefits are limited, and their potential dangers are great. Lack of familiarity with the sender can lead to misinterpreting humor, especially in less-rich information channels such as e-mail. For example, an e-mail from Jill that ends with, "Men should be boiled in vats of oil," could be interpreted as antimale if the receiver didn't know that Jill has a penchant for exaggeration and always jokes to let off steam. Similarly, if the sender lacks credibility or is untrustworthy, the message will not get through. Receivers may be suspicious of the sender's motivations (Why is she telling me this?). Likewise, if the sender has communicated erroneous information in the past or has created false emergencies, the current message may be filtered.

Workplace Gossip

grapevine

The informal gossip network within a given organization.

The informal gossip network known as the **grapevine** is a lifeline for many employees seeking information about their company.[15] Researchers agree that the grapevine is an inevitable part of organizational life. Research finds that 70% of all organizational communication occurs at the grapevine level.[16] Employees trust their peers as a source of information, but the grapevine's informal structure can be a barrier to effective communication from the managerial point of view. Its grassroots structure gives it greater credibility in the minds of employees than information delivered through official channels, even when that information is false. Some downsides of the office grapevine are that gossip offers politically minded insiders a powerful tool for disseminating communication (and self-promoting miscommunications) within an organization. In addition, the grapevine lacks a specific sender, which can create a sense of distrust among employees: Who is at the root of the gossip network? When the news is volatile, suspicions may arise as to the person or person behind the message. Managers who understand the grapevine's power can use it to send and receive messages of their own. They can also decrease the grapevine's power by sending official messages quickly and accurately, should big news arise.

Semantics

Words can mean different things to different people, or they might not mean anything to another person. This is called **semantics.** For example, companies often have their own acronyms and buzzwords (called business **jargon**) that are clear to them but impenetrable to outsiders. For example, at IBM, GBS is focusing on BPTS, using expertise acquired from the PwC purchase (which had to be sold to avoid conflicts of interest in light of SOX) to fend off other BPO providers and inroads by the Bangalore tiger. Does this make sense to you? If not, here's the translation: IBM's Global Business Services (GBS) division is focusing on offering companies Business Process Transformation Services (BPTS), using the expertise it acquired from purchasing the management consulting and technology services arm of PricewaterhouseCoopers (PwC), which had to sell the division due to the Sarbanes-Oxley Act (SOX; enacted in response to the major accounting scandals such as Enron). The added management expertise puts it above business process outsourcing (BPO) vendors who focus more on automating processes rather than transforming and improving them. Chief among these BPO competitors is Wipro, often called the "Bangalore tiger" because of its geographic origin and aggressive growth. Given the amount of messages we send and receive everyday, it makes sense that humans would try to find a shortcut—a way to communicate things in code. In business, this code is known as jargon. Jargon is the language of specialized terms used by a group or profession. It is common shorthand among experts and if used sensibly can be a quick and efficient way of communicating. Most jargon consists of unfamiliar terms, abstract words, nonexistent words, acronyms, and abbreviations, with an occasional euphemism thrown in for good measure. Every profession, trade, and organization has its own specialized terms.[17]

semantics

The meaning of a word or phrase.

jargon

A specific set of acronyms or words unique to a specific group or profession.

At first glance, jargon sounds like a good thing—a quicker way to send an effective communication similar to the way text message abbreviations can send common messages in a shorter, yet understandable way. But that's not always how things happen. Jargon can be an obstacle to effective communication, causing listeners to tune out or fostering ill feelings between partners in a conversation. When jargon rules the day, the message can get obscured. A key question to ask yourself before using a phrase of jargon is, "Who is the receiver of my message?" If you are a specialist speaking to another specialist in your area, jargon may be the best way to send a message while forging a professional bond—similar to the way best friends can communicate in code. For example, an IT technician communicating with another IT technician may use jargon as a way of sharing information in a way that reinforces the pair's shared knowledge. But that same conversation should be held in Standard English, free of jargon, when communicating with staff members outside the IT group.

Online Follow-Up

Here is a Web site of twenty-five buzz words in business:

http://www.businessnewsdaily.com/1846-business-buzzwords-2012.html

A discussion of why slang is a problem can be found at the following Web site:

http://sbinfocanada.about.com/od/speakforsuccesscourse/a/speechlesson5.htm

In addition, the OB Toolbox below will help you avoid letting business jargon get in your way at work.

OB Toolbox: Tips for Reducing Miscommunication-by-Jargon

- *Know your audience.* If they weren't sitting beside you in law school, medical school, or in that finance or computer class, then assume they don't know what you are talking about. Speak for the other person and not yourself.
- *Decode your acronyms.* If you use an acronym in verbal or written communication, explain what it means after you use it for the first time. Your audience will filter your message otherwise, as they wonder, "Now what does ROI stand for?" (It stands for "return on investment," btw—by the way.)
- *Limit your jargon use.* Jargon doesn't necessarily make you sound smart or business savvy. It can create communication barriers and obstacles and hurts your ability to build relationships and close deals.

Source: Adapted from ideas in Adubato, S. (2005, March 13). Scrap the jargon…Now! Retrieved July 1, 2008, from The Star-Ledger Web site: http://www.stand-deliver.com/star_ledger/050313.asp.

Gender Differences in Communication

Men and women work together every day, but their different styles of communication can sometimes work against them. Generally speaking, women like to ask questions before starting a project, while men tend to "jump right in." A male manager who's unaware of how most women communicate their readiness to work may misperceive a ready employee as not being prepared.

Another difference that has been noticed is that men often speak in sports metaphors, while many women use their home as a starting place for analogies. Women who believe men are "only talking about the game" may be missing out on a chance to participate in a division's strategy and opportunities for teamwork and "rallying the troops" for success.[18]

"It is important to promote the best possible communication between men and women in the workplace," notes gender policy advisor Dee Norton, who provided the above example. "As we move between the male and female cultures, we sometimes have to change how we behave (speak the language of the other gender) to gain the best results from the situation. Clearly, successful organizations of the future are going to have leaders and team members who understand, respect, and apply the rules of gender culture appropriately."[19]

As we have seen, differences in men's and women's communication styles can lead to misunderstandings in the workplace. Being aware of these differences, however, can be the first step in learning to work with them instead of around them. Keep in mind that men tend to focus more on competition, data, and orders in their communications, while women tend to focus more on cooperation, intuition, and requests. Both styles can be effective in the right situations, but understanding the differences is a first step in avoiding misunderstandings.

Differences in Meaning Between the Sender and Receiver

"Mean what you say, and say what you mean." It's an easy thing to say. But in business, what do those words mean? Simply put, different words mean different things to different people. Age, education, and cultural background are all factors that influence how a person interprets words. The less we consider our audience, the greater our chances of miscommunication will be. Eliminating jargon is one way of ensuring our words will convey real-world concepts to others. Speaking to our audience, as opposed to speaking about ourselves, is another.

Managers who speak about "long-term goals and profits" to a staff that has received scant raises may find their core message ("You're doing a great job—and that benefits the folks in charge!") has infuriated the group they hoped to inspire. Instead, managers who recognize the contributions of their staff and confirm that this work is contributing to company goals in ways "that will benefit the source of our success—our employees as well as executives," will find that their core message ("You're doing a great job—we really value your work.") is received as intended, rather than being misinterpreted.

Biased Language

Words and actions that stereotype others on the basis of personal or group affiliation are examples of bias. Below is a list of words that have the potential to be offensive. The column on the right provides alternative words that can be used instead.[20]

FIGURE 8.6

Avoid	Consider Using
black attorney	attorney
businessman	business person
chairman	chair or chairperson
cleaning lady	cleaner or maintenance worker
male nurse	nurse
manpower	staff or personnel
secretary	assistant or associate

Effective communication is clear, factual, and goal-oriented. It is also respectful. Referring to a person by one adjective (a *brain*, a *diabetic*) reduces the person to that one characteristic. Language that inflames or stereotypes a person poisons the communication process. Language that insults an individual or group based on age, ethnicity, sexual preference, or political beliefs violates public and private standards of decency, ranging from civil rights to corporate regulations.

The effort to create a neutral set of terms to refer to heritage and preferences has resulted in a debate over the nature of "political correctness." Proponents of political correctness see it as a way to defuse the volatile nature of words that stereotyped groups and individuals in the past. Critics of political correctness see its vocabulary as stilted and needlessly cautious.

Many companies offer new employees written guides on standards of speech and conduct. These guides, augmented by common sense and courtesy, are solid starting points for effective, respectful workplace communication.

Tips for appropriate workplace speech include, but are not limited to the following:

- Alternating our use of *he* and *she* when referring to people in general
- Relying on human resources–generated guidelines
- Remembering that terms that feel respectful or comfortable to us may not be comfortable or respectful to others

Poor Listening

The greatest compliment that was ever paid to me was when one asked me what I thought, and attended to my answer.

- *Henry David Thoreau*

A sender may strive to deliver a message clearly. But the receiver's ability to listen effectively is equally vital to successful communication. The average worker spends 55% of their workdays listening. Managers listen up to 70% each day. Unfortunately, listening doesn't lead to understanding in every case.

From a number of different perspectives, listening matters. Former Chrysler CEO Lee Iacocca lamented, "I only wish I could find an institute that teaches people how to listen. After all, a good manager needs to listen at least as much as he needs to talk."[21] Research shows that listening skills were related to promotions.[22]

Listening clearly matters. Listening takes practice, skill, and concentration. Alan Gulick, a Starbucks Corporation spokesperson, believes better listening can improve profits. If every Starbucks employee misheard one $10 order each day, their errors would cost the company a billion dollars annually. To teach its employees to listen, Starbucks created a code that helps employees taking orders hear the size, flavor, and use of milk or decaffeinated coffee. The person making the drink echoes the order aloud.

How Can You Improve Your Listening Skills?

Cicero said, "Silence is one of the great arts of conversation." How often have we been in a conversation with someone else when we are not really listening but itching to convey our portion? This behavior is known as "rehearsing." It suggests the receiver has no intention of considering the sender's message and is actually preparing to respond to an earlier point instead. Effective communication relies on another kind of listening: active listening.

Active listening can be defined as giving full attention to what other people are saying, taking time to understand the points being made, asking questions as needed, and not interrupting at inappropriate times.[23] Active listening creates a real-time relationship between the sender and receiver by acknowledging the content and receipt of a message. As we've seen in the Starbucks example above, repeating and confirming a message's content offers a way to confirm that the correct content is flowing between colleagues. The process creates a bond between coworkers while increasing the flow and accuracy of messaging.

How Can We Listen Actively?

Carl Rogers gave five rules for active listening:

1. Listen for message content.
2. Listen for feelings.
3. Respond to feelings.
4. Note all cues.
5. Paraphrase and restate.

The good news is that listening is a skill that can be learned.[24] The first step is to decide that we want to listen. Casting aside distractions, such as by reducing background or internal noise, is critical. The receiver takes in the sender's message silently, without speaking.

Second, throughout the conversation, show the speaker that you're listening. You can do this nonverbally by nodding your head and keeping your attention focused on the speaker. You can also do it verbally, by saying things like, "Yes," "That's interesting," or other such verbal cues. As you're listening, pay attention to the sender's body language for additional cues about how they're feeling. Interestingly, silence has a role in active listening. During active listening, we are trying to understand what has been said, and in silence we can consider the implications. We can't consider information and object to it at the same time. That's where the power of silence comes into play. Finally, if anything is not clear to you, ask questions. Confirm that you've heard the message accurately, by repeating back a crucial piece like, "Great, I'll see you at 2:00 p.m. in my office." At the end of the conversation, a thank you from both parties is an optional but highly effective way of acknowledging each other's teamwork.

Becoming a More Effective Listener

As we've seen above, active listening creates a more dynamic relationship between a receiver and a sender. It strengthens personal investment in the information being shared. It also forges healthy working relationships among colleagues by making speakers and listeners equally valued members of the communication process.

Many companies offer public speaking courses for their staff, but what about "public listening"? Here are some more ways you can build your listening skills by becoming a more effective listener and banishing communication freezers from your discussions.

OB Toolbox: 10 Ways to Improve Your Listening Habits

1. *Start by stopping.* Take a moment to inhale and exhale quietly before you begin to listen. Your job as a listener is to receive information openly and accurately.
2. *Don't worry about what you'll say when the time comes.* Silence can be a beautiful thing.
3. *Join the sender's team.* When the sender pauses, summarize what you believe has been said. "What I'm hearing is that we need to focus on marketing as well as sales. Is that correct?" Be attentive to physical as well as verbal communications. "I hear you saying that we should focus on marketing, but the way you're shaking your head tells me the idea may not really appeal to you—is that right?"
4. *Don't multitask while listening.* Listening is a full-time job. It's tempting to multitask when you and the sender are in different places, but doing that is counterproductive. The human mind can only focus on one thing at a time. Listening with only part of your brain increases the chances that you'll have questions later, ultimately requiring more of the speaker's time. (And when the speaker is in the same room, multitasking signals a disinterest that is considered rude.)
5. *Try to empathize with the sender's point of view.* You don't have to agree, but can you find common ground?
6. *Confused? Ask questions.* There's nothing wrong with admitting you haven't understood the sender's point. You may even help the sender clarify the message.
7. *Establish eye contact.* Making eye contact with the speaker (if appropriate for the culture) is important.
8. *What is the goal of this communication?* Ask yourself this question at different points during the communication to keep the information flow on track. Be polite. Differences in opinion can be the starting point of consensus.
9. *It's great to be surprised.* Listen with an open mind, not just for what you *want* to hear.
10. *Pay attention to what is not said.* Does the sender's body language seem to contradict the message? If so, clarification may be in order.

Sources: Adapted from information in Barrett, D. J. (2006). Leadership communication. New York: McGraw-Hill/Irwin; Improving verbal skills. (1997). Retrieved July 1, 2008, from the Institute for Management Web site: http://www.itstime.com/aug97.htm; Ten tips: Active listening. (2007, June 4). Retrieved July 1, 2008, from the Communication at Work Web site: http://communication.atwork-network.com/2007/06/04/ten-tips-active-listening/.

Communication Freezers

Communication freezers put an end to effective communication by making the receiver feel judged or defensive. Typical communication stoppers include criticizing, blaming, ordering, judging, or shaming the other person. Some examples of things to avoid saying include the following:

1. Telling the other person what to do:
   - "You must…"
   - "You cannot…"
2. Threatening with "or else" implied:
   - "You had better…"
   - "If you don't…"
3. Making suggestions or telling the other person what they ought to do:
   - "You should…"
   - "It's your responsibility to…"
4. Attempting to educate the other person:
   - "Let me give you the facts."
   - "Experience tells us that…"
5. Judging the other person negatively:
   - "You're not thinking straight."
   - "You're wrong."
6. Giving insincere praise:
   - "You have so much potential."
   - "I know you can do better than this."
7. Psychoanalyzing the other person:
   - "You're jealous."
   - "You have problems with authority."
8. Making light of the other person's problems by generalizing:
   - "Things will get better."
   - "Behind every cloud is a silver lining."
9. Asking excessive or inappropriate questions:
   - "Why did you do that?"
   - "Who has influenced you?"
10. Making light of the problem by kidding:
    - "Think about the positive side."
    - "You think *you've* got problems!"

Sources: Adapted from information in Tramel, M., & Reynolds, H. (1981). Executive leadership. Englewood Cliffs, NJ: Prentice Hall; Saltman, D., & O'Dea, N. Conflict management workshop PowerPoint presentation. Retrieved July 1, 2008, from http://www.nswrdn.com.au/client_images/6806.PDF; Communication stoppers. Retrieved July 1, 2008, from Mental Health Today Web site: http://www.mental-health-today.com/Healing/communicationstop.htm.

KEY TAKEAWAY

Many barriers to effective communication exist. Examples include filtering, selective perception, information overload, emotional disconnects, lack of source credibility, workplace gossip, gender differences, and semantics. The receiver can enhance the probability of effective communication by engaging in active listening.

EXERCISES

1. Most people are poor listeners. Do you agree or disagree with this statement? Please support your position.
2. Please share an example of how differences in shared meaning have affected you.
3. When you see a memo or e-mail full of typos, poor grammar, or incomplete sentences, how do you react? Does it affect your perception of the sender? Why or why not?
4. Give an example of selective perception.
5. Do you use jargon at work or in your classes? If so, do you think it helps or hampers communication? Why or why not?

3. DIFFERENT TYPES OF COMMUNICATION AND CHANNELS

LEARNING OBJECTIVES

1. **Understand different types of communication.**
2. **Understand how communication channels affect communication.**
3. **Recognize different communication directions within organizations.**

3.1 Types of Communication

There are three types of communication, including: verbal communication involving listening to a person to understand the meaning of a message, written communication in which a message is read, and nonverbal communication involving observing a person and inferring meaning. Let's start with verbal communication, which is the most common form of communication.

Verbal Communication

Verbal communications in business take place over the phone or in person. The medium of the message is oral. Let's return to our printer cartridge example. This time, the message is being conveyed from the sender (the manager) to the receiver (an employee named Bill) by telephone. We've already seen how the manager's request to Bill ("Buy more printer toner cartridges!") can go awry. Now let's look at how the same message can travel successfully from sender to receiver.

Manager (speaking on the phone): "Good morning Bill!"

(*By using the employee's name, the manager is establishing a clear, personal link to the receiver.*)

Manager: "Your division's numbers are looking great."

(*The manager's recognition of Bill's role in a winning team further personalizes and emotionalizes the conversation.*)

Manager: "Our next step is to order more printer toner cartridges. Would you place an order for 1,000 printer toner cartridges with Jones Computer Supplies? Our budget for this purchase is $30,000, and the printer toner cartridges need to be here by Wednesday afternoon."

(*The manager breaks down the task into several steps. Each step consists of a specific task, time frame, quantity, or goal.*)

Bill: "Sure thing! I'll call Jones Computer Supplies and order 1,000 more printer toner cartridges, not exceeding a total of $30,000, to be here by Wednesday afternoon."

(*Bill, a model employee, repeats what he has heard. This is the feedback portion of the communication. Feedback helps him recognize any confusion he may have had hearing the manager's message. Feedback also helps the manager hear if she has communicated the message correctly.*)

storytelling

A narrative account of an event or events.

Storytelling has been shown to be an effective form of verbal communication that serves an important organizational function by helping to construct common meanings for individuals within the organization. Stories can help clarify key values and also help demonstrate how certain tasks are performed within an organization. Story frequency, strength, and tone are related to higher organizational commitment.[25] The quality of the stories is related to the ability of entrepreneurs to secure capital for their firms.[26]

While the process may be the same, high stakes communications require more planning, reflection, and skill than normal day-to-day interactions at work. Examples of high stakes communication events include asking for a raise or presenting a business plan to a venture capitalist. In addition to these events, there are also many times in our professional lives when we have **crucial conversations**, which are defined as discussions in which not only are the stakes high, but also the opinions vary and emotions run strong.[27] One of the most consistent recommendations from communications experts is to work toward using *"and"* instead of *"but"* when communicating under these circumstances. In addition, be aware of your communication style and practice being flexible; it is under stressful situations that communication styles can become the most rigid.

crucial conversations

Discussions in which the stakes are high, opinions vary, and emotions run strong.

OB Toolbox: 10 Recommendations for Improving the Quality of Your Conversations

1. *Be the first to say hello.* Use your name in your introduction, in case others have forgotten it.
2. *Think before you speak.* Our impulse is often to imitate movies by offering fast, witty replies in conversation. In the real world, a careful silence can make us sound more intelligent and prevent mistakes.
3. *Be receptive to new ideas.* If you disagree with another person's opinion, saying, "Tell me more," can be a more useful way of moving forward than saying, "That's stupid!"
4. *Repeat someone's name to yourself and then aloud, when being introduced.* The form of the name you use may vary. First names work with peers. Mr. or Ms. is common when meeting superiors in business.
5. *Ask questions.* This establishes your interest in another person.
6. *Listen as much, if not more, than you speak.* This allows you to learn new information.
7. *Use eye contact.* Eye contact shows that you are engaged. Also, be sure to smile and make sure your body language matches your message.
8. *Mirror the other person.* Occasionally repeat what they've said in your own words. "You mean... ?"
9. *Have an exit strategy ready.* Ideal conversations are brief, leaving others wanting more.
10. *Be prepared.* Before beginning a conversation, have three simple facts about yourself and four questions about someone else in mind.

Source: Adapted from information contained in Gabor, D. (1983). How to start a conversation and make friends. New York: Legacy; Post, E. (2005). Emily Post's etiquette advantage in business. New York: Collins Living; Fine, D. (2005). The fine art of small talk. New York: Hyperion.

Written Communication

In contrast to verbal communications, which are oral, written business communications are *printed messages*. Examples of written communications include memos, proposals, e-mails, letters, training manuals, and operating policies. They may be printed on paper or appear on the screen. Written communication is often asynchronous. That is, the sender can write a message that the receiver can read at any time, unlike a conversation that is carried on in real time. A written communication can also be read by many people (such as all employees in a department or all customers). It's a "one-to-many" communication, as opposed to a one-to-one conversation. There are exceptions, of course: A voice mail is an oral message that is asynchronous. Conference calls and speeches are oral one-to-many communications, and e-mails can have only one recipient or many.

Normally, a verbal communication takes place in real time. Written communication, by contrast, can be constructed over a longer period of time. It also can be collaborative. Multiple people can contribute to the content on one document before that document is sent to the intended audience.

Verbal and written communications have different strengths and weaknesses. In business, the decision to communicate verbally or in written form can be a powerful one. As we'll see below, each style of communication has particular strengths and pitfalls. When determining whether to communicate verbally or in writing, ask yourself: *Do I want to convey facts or feelings*? Verbal communications are a better way to convey feelings. Written communications do a better job of conveying facts.

Picture a manager making a speech to a team of twenty employees. The manager is speaking at a normal pace. The employees appear interested. But how much information is being transmitted? Probably not as much as the speaker believes. The fact is that humans listen much faster than they speak. The average public speaker communicates at a speed of about 125 words a minute, and that pace sounds fine to the audience. (In fact, anything faster than that probably would sound unusual. To put that figure in perspective, someone having an excited conversation speaks at about 150 words a minute.) Based on these numbers, we could assume that the audience has more than enough time to take in each word the speaker delivers, which actually creates a problem. The average person in the audience can hear 400 to 500 words a minute.[28] The audience has *more than enough time* to hear. As a result, their minds may wander.

As you can see, oral communication is the most often used form of communication, but it is also an inherently flawed medium for conveying specific facts. Listeners' minds wander. It's nothing personal—in fact, it's a completely normal psychological occurrence. In business, once we understand this fact, we can make more intelligent communication choices based on the kind of information we want to convey.

Most jobs involve some degree of writing. According to the National Commission on Writing, 67% of salaried employees in large American companies and professional state employees have some kind of writing responsibility. Half of responding companies reported that they take writing into consideration when hiring professional employees, and 91% always take writing into account when hiring.[29] Luckily, it is possible to learn to write clearly.

FIGURE 8.7

Communication mediums have come a long way since Alexander Graham Bell's original telephone.

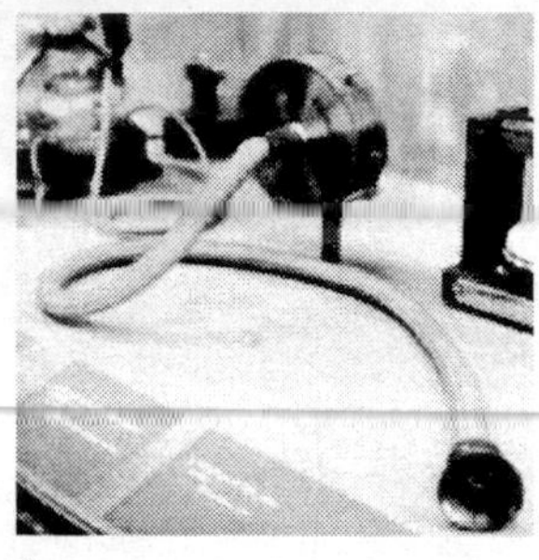

Source: http://wikimediafoundation.org/wiki/File:CNAM-IMG_0564.jpg.

Here are some tips on writing well. Thomas Jefferson summed up the rules of writing well with this idea: "Don't use two words when one will do." Put another way, half the words can have twice the impact. One of the oldest myths in business is that writing more will make us sound more important. The opposite is true. Leaders who can communicate simply and clearly project a stronger image than those who write a lot but say nothing.

Putting Jefferson's Rules Into Action: Five Ways to Communicate More With Fewer Words

1. *Picture the receiver in your mind before you begin to write.* After all, a written communication is a link between people.
2. *Choose simple words.* When in doubt, choose the shorter word ("Automobile or car? Car!")
3. *Be polite and clear.* Your message will make a strong, clear impact.
4. *Make your message brief and direct by trimming redundant words or phrases.* "Having thus explored our first option, I would now like to begin to explore the second option that may be open to us." versus "After considering Option 1, I would like to look at Option 2."
5. *Choose strong, active verbs.* "I suggest…" instead of "It would seem to me that we might…"

Remember, concise writing equals effective communication.

Nonverbal Communication

What you say is a vital part of any communication. Surprisingly, what you *don't say* can be even more important. Research shows that nonverbal cues can also affect whether or not you get a job offer. Judges examining videotapes of actual applicants were able to assess the social skills of job candidates with the sound turned off. They watched the rate of gesturing, time spent talking, and formality of dress to determine which candidates would be the most socially successful on the job.[30] Research also shows that 55% of in-person communication comes from nonverbal cues such as facial expressions, body stance, and tone of voice. According to one study, only 7% of a receiver's comprehension of a message is based on the sender's actual words, 38% is based on paralanguage (the tone, pace, and volume of speech), and 55% is based on *nonverbal cues* (body language).[31] To be effective communicators, our body language, appearance, and tone must align with the words we're trying to convey. Research shows that when individuals are lying, they are more likely to blink more frequently, shift their weight, and shrug.[32]

A different tone can change the perceived meaning of a message. See the table below for how clearly this can be true. If we only read these words, we would be left to wonder, but during a conversation, the tone conveys a great deal of information.

Don't Use That Tone With Me!

Changing your tone can dramatically change your meaning.

Placement of the emphasis	What it means
I did not tell John you were late.	Someone else told John you were late.
I did ***not*** tell John you were late.	This did not happen.
I did not ***tell*** John you were late.	I may have implied it.
I did not tell ***John*** you were late.	But maybe I told Sharon and José.
I did not tell John ***you*** were late.	I was talking about someone else.
I did not tell John you ***were*** late.	I told him you still are late.
I did not tell John you were ***late***.	I told him you were attending another meeting.

Source: Based on ideas in Kiely, M. (October, 1993). When "no" means "yes." Marketing, 7–9.

Now you can see how changing the tone of voice in a conversation can incite or diffuse a misunderstanding. For another example, imagine that you're a customer interested in opening a new bank account. At one bank, the bank officer is dressed neatly. She looks you in the eye when she speaks. Her tone is friendly. Her words are easy to understand, yet professional sounding. "Thank you for considering Bank of the East Coast. We appreciate this opportunity and would love to explore ways that we can work together to help your business grow," she says with a friendly smile. At the second bank, the bank officer's tie is stained. He looks over your head and down at his desk as he speaks. He shifts in his seat and fidgets with his hands. His words say, "Thank you for considering Bank of the West Coast. We appreciate this opportunity and would love to explore ways that we can work together to help you business grow," but he mumbles his words, and his voice conveys no enthusiasm or warmth. Which bank would you choose? The speaker's body language must match his or her words. If a sender's words and body language don't match—if a sender smiles while telling a sad tale, for example—the mismatch between verbal and nonverbal cues can cause a receiver to actively dislike the sender.

Following are a few examples of nonverbal cues that can support or detract from a sender's message.

Body Language

A simple rule of thumb is that simplicity, directness, and warmth conveys sincerity. Sincerity is vital for effective communication. In some cultures, a firm handshake, given with a warm, dry hand, is a great way to establish trust. A weak, clammy handshake might convey a lack of trustworthiness. Gnawing one's lip conveys uncertainty. A direct smile conveys confidence.

FIGURE 8.8

"Say what's on your mind, Harris—the language of dance has always eluded me."

Eye Contact

In business, the style and duration of eye contact varies greatly across cultures. In the United States, looking someone in the eye (for about a second) is considered a sign of trustworthiness.

Facial Expressions

The human face can produce thousands of different expressions. These expressions have been decoded by experts as corresponding to hundreds of different emotional states.[33] Our faces convey basic information to the outside world. Happiness is associated with an upturned mouth and slightly closed eyes; fear with an open mouth and wide-eyed stare. Shifty eyes and pursed lips convey a lack of trustworthiness. The impact of facial expressions in conversation is instantaneous. Our brains may register them as "a feeling" about someone's character. For this reason, it is important to consider how we appear in business as well as what we say. The muscles of our faces convey our emotions. We can send a silent message without saying a word. A change in facial expression can change our emotional state. Before an interview, for example, if we focus on feeling confident, our face will convey that confidence to an interviewer. Adopting a smile (even if we're feeling stressed) can reduce the body's stress levels.

Posture

The position of our body relative to a chair or other person is another powerful silent messenger that conveys interest, aloofness, professionalism, or lack thereof. Head up, back straight (but not rigid) implies an upright character. In interview situations, experts advise mirroring an interviewer's tendency to lean in and settle back in a seat. The subtle repetition of the other person's posture conveys that we are listening and responding.

Touch

The meaning of a simple touch differs between individuals, genders, and cultures. In Mexico, when doing business, men may find themselves being grasped on the arm by another man. To pull away is seen as rude. In Indonesia, to touch anyone on the head or to touch anything with one's foot is considered highly offensive. In the Far East and some parts of Asia, according to business etiquette writer Nazir Daud, "It is considered impolite for a woman to shake a man's hand."[34] Americans, as we have noted above, place great value in a firm handshake. But handshaking as a competitive sport ("the bone-crusher") can come off as needlessly aggressive both at home and abroad.

Space

Anthropologist Edward T. Hall coined the term *proxemics* to denote the different kinds of distance that occur between people. These distances vary among cultures. The chart below outlines the basic proxemics of everyday life and their associated meaning.[35]

FIGURE 8.9

Distance between speakers is partially determined by their intimacy level.

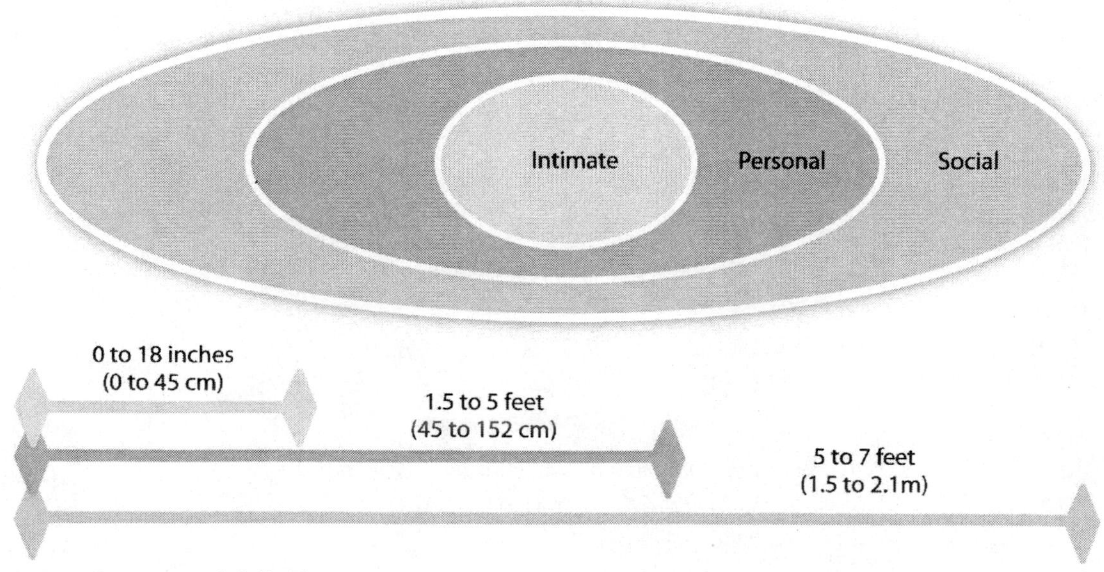

Source: Hall, E. T. (1966). The hidden dimension. New York: Doubleday.

Standing too far away from a colleague (public speaking distance) or too close to a colleague (intimate distance for embracing) can thwart an effective verbal communication in business.

3.2 Communication Channels

The channel, or medium, used to communicate a message affects how accurately the message will be received. Channels vary in their "information-richness." Information-rich channels convey more nonverbal information. Research shows that effective managers tend to use more information-rich communication channels than less effective managers.[36] The figure below illustrates the information richness of different channels.

FIGURE 8.10

Information channels differ in their richness.

Information Channel	Information Richness
Face-to-face conversation	High
Videoconferencing	High
Telephone conversation	High
E-mails	Medium
Handheld devices	Medium
Blogs	Medium
Written letters and memos	Medium
Formal written documents	Low
Spreadsheets	Low

Sources: Adapted from information in Daft, R. L., & Lenge, R. H. (1984). Information richness: A new approach to managerial behavior and organizational design. In B. Staw & L. Cummings (Eds.), Research in organizational behavior, vol. 6 (pp. 191–233). Greenwich, CT: JAI Press; Lengel, R. H., & Daft, D. L. (1988). The selection of communication media as an executive skill. Academy of Management Executive, 11, 225–232.

The key to effective communication is to match the communication channel with the goal of the message.[37] For example, written media may be a better choice when the sender wants a record of the content, has less urgency for a response, is physically separated from the receiver, and doesn't require a lot of feedback from the receiver, or when the message is complicated and may take some time to understand.

Oral communication, on the other hand, makes more sense when the sender is conveying a sensitive or emotional message, needs feedback immediately, and does not need a permanent record of the conversation.

FIGURE 8.11 Guide for When to Use Written versus Verbal Communication

Use Written Communication When:	Use Verbal Communication When:
conveying facts	conveying emotion and feelings
the message needs to become part of a permanent file	the message does not need to be permanent
there is little time urgency	there is time urgency
you do not need immediate feedback	you need immediate feedback
the ideas are complicated	the ideas are simple or can be made simple with explanations

FIGURE 8.12

Make sure to match the medium to the task. Trying to accomplish a visual task such as choosing colors is more challenging on the phone versus in person.

© 2010 Jupiterimages Corporation

Like face-to-face and telephone conversations, videoconferencing has high information richness, because receivers and senders can see or hear beyond just the words that are used—they can see the sender's body language or hear the tone of their voice. Handheld devices, blogs, and written letters and memos offer medium-rich channels, because they convey words and pictures or photos. Formal written documents, such as legal documents and budget spreadsheets, convey the least richness, because the format is often rigid and standardized. As a result, the tone of the message is often lost.

The growth of e-mail has been spectacular, but it has also created challenges in managing information and increasing the speed of doing businesses. Over 100 million adults in the United States use e-mail at least once a day.[38] Internet users around the world send an estimated 60 billion e-mails each day, and a large portion of these are spam or scam attempts.[39] That makes e-mail the second most popular medium of communication worldwide, second only to voice. Less than 1% of all written human communications even reaches paper these days.[40] To combat the overuse of e-mail, companies such as Intel have even instituted "no e-mail Fridays." During these times, all communication is done via other communication channels. Learning to be more effective in your e-mail communications is an important skill. To learn more, check out the OB Toolbox on business e-mail do's and don'ts.

OB Toolbox: Business E-mail Do's and Don'ts

1. DON'T send or forward chain e-mails.
2. DON'T put anything in an e-mail that you don't want the world to see.
3. DON'T write a message in capital letters—this is the equivalent of SHOUTING.
4. DON'T routinely CC everyone. Reducing inbox clutter is a great way to increase communication.
5. DON'T hit send until you've spell-checked your e-mail.
6. DO use a subject line that summarizes your message, adjusting it as the message changes over time.
7. DO make your request in the first line of your e-mail. (And if that's all you need to say, stop there!)
8. DO end your e-mail with a brief sign-off such as, "Thank you," followed by your name and contact information.
9. DO think of a work e-mail as a binding communication.
10. DO let others know if you've received an e-mail in error.

Sources: Adapted from information in Leland, K., & Bailey, K. (2000). Customer service for dummies. New York: Wiley; Information Technology Services. (1997). Top 10 email dos and top ten email don'ts. Retrieved July 1, 2008, from the University of Illinois at Chicago Medical Center Web site: http://www.uic.edu/hsc/uicmc/its/customers/email-tips.htm; Kawasaki, G. (2006, February 3). The effective emailer. Retrieved July 1, 2008, from How to Change the World Web site: http://blog.guykawasaki.com/2006/02/the_effective_e.html.

An important although often ignored rule when communicating emotional information is that e-mail's lack of richness can be your loss. As we saw in the chart above, e-mail is a medium-rich channel. It can convey facts quickly. But when it comes to emotion, e-mail's flaws make it a far less desirable choice than oral communication—the 55% of nonverbal cues that make a conversation comprehensible to a listener are missing. Researchers also note that e-mail readers don't pick up on sarcasm and other tonal aspects of writing as much as the writer believes they will.[41]

The sender may believe that certain emotional signifiers have been included in a message. But, with written words alone, those signifiers are not there. This gap between the form and content of e-mail inspired the rise of emoticons—symbols that offer clues to the emotional side of the words in each message. Generally speaking, however, emoticons are not considered professional in business communication.

You might feel uncomfortable conveying an emotionally laden message verbally, especially when the message contains unwanted news. Sending an e-mail to your staff that there will be no bonuses this year may seem easier than breaking the bad news face-to-face, but that doesn't mean that e-mail is an effective or appropriate way to break this kind of news. When the message is emotional, the sender should use verbal communication. Indeed, a good rule of thumb is that more emotionally laden messages require more thought in the choice of channel and how they are communicated.

Career Advice

Communication can occur without you even realizing it. Consider the following: Is your e-mail name professional? The typical convention for business e-mail contains some form of your name. While an e-mail name like "LazyGirl" or "DeathMonkey" may be fine for chatting online with your friends, they may send the wrong signal to individuals you e-mail such as professors and prospective employers.

Is your outgoing voice mail greeting professional? If not, change it. Faculty and prospective recruiters will draw certain conclusions if, upon calling you, they get a message that screams, "Party, party, party!"

Do you have a "private" social networking Web site on MySpace.com, Facebook.com, or Xanga.com? If so, consider what it says about you to employers or clients. If it is information you wouldn't share at work, it probably shouldn't be there.

Googled yourself lately? If not, you probably should. Potential employers have begun searching the Web as part of background checking, and you should be aware of what's out there about you.

3.3 Direction of Communication Within Organizations

Information can move horizontally, from a sender to a receiver, as we've seen. It can also move vertically, down from top management, or up from the front line. Information can also move diagonally between and among levels of an organization, such as a message from a customer service rep to a manager in the manufacturing department or a message from the chief financial officer sent down to all department heads.

FIGURE 8.13

Organizational communication travels in many different directions.

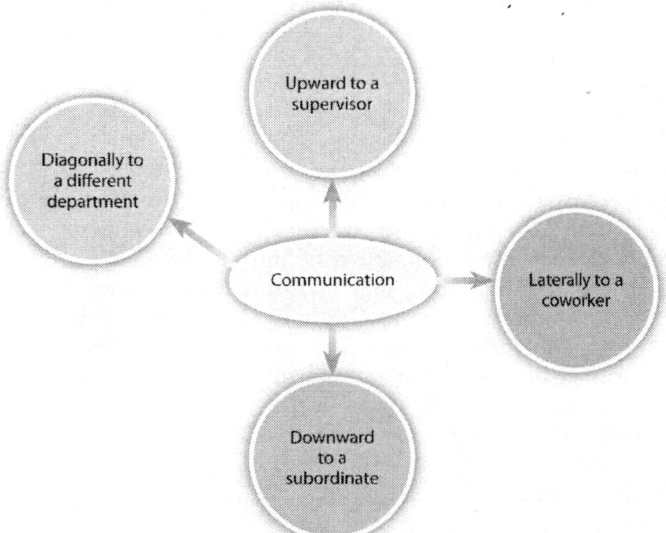

There is a chance for these arrows to go awry, of course. As Mihaly Csikszentmihalyi, author of best-selling books such as *Flow*, has noted, "In large organizations the dilution of information as it passes up and down the hierarchy, and horizontally across departments, can undermine the effort to focus on common goals."[42]

The organizational status of the sender can impact the receiver's attentiveness to the message. For example, consider the following: A senior manager sends a memo to a production supervisor. The supervisor, who has a lower status within the organization, is likely to pay close attention to the message. The same information conveyed in the opposite direction, however, might not get the attention it deserves. The message would be filtered by the senior manager's perception of priorities and urgencies.

Requests are just one kind of communication in business. Other communications, either verbal or written, may seek, give, or exchange information. Research shows that frequent communications with one's supervisor is related to better job performance ratings and overall organizational performance.[43] Research also shows that lateral communication done between peers can influence important organizational outcomes such as turnover.[44]

FIGURE 8.14 How Managers Spend Time Communicating at Work

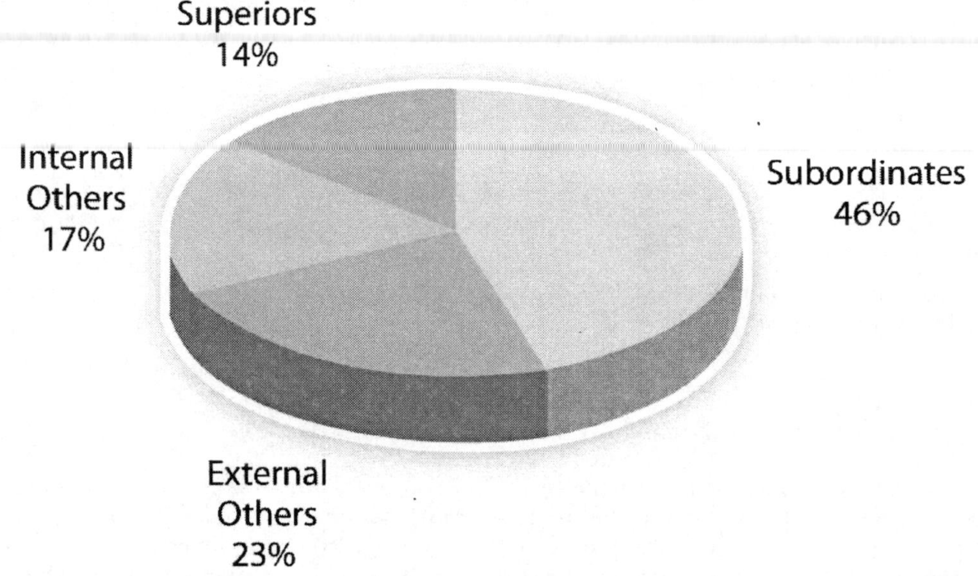

Source: Adapted from information in Luthans, F., & Larsen, J. K. (1986). How managers really communicate. Human Relations, 39, 161–178.

3.4 External Communications

External communications deliver specific businesses messages to individuals outside an organization. They may announce changes in staff or strategy, earnings, and more. The goal of an external communication is to create a specific message that the receiver will understand and share with others. Examples of external communications include the following.

Press Releases

public relations

Professionals who create external communications about a client's product, services, or practices for specific receivers.

Public relations professionals create external communications about a client's product, services, or practices for specific receivers. These receivers, it is hoped, will share the message with others. In time, as the message is passed along, it should *appear* to be independent of the sender, creating the illusion of an independently generated consumer trend, public opinion, and so on.

The message of a public relations effort may be *b2b* (business to business), *b2c* (business to consumer), or media related. The message can take different forms. Press releases try to convey a newsworthy message, real or manufactured. It may be constructed like a news item, inviting editors or reporters to reprint the message in part or as a whole, with or without acknowledgement of the sender's identity. Public relations campaigns create messages over time through contests, special events, trade shows, and media interviews in addition to press releases.

Ads

Advertising places external business messages before target receivers through media buys. A media buy is a fee that is paid to a television network, Web site, magazine, and so on by an advertiser to insert an advertisement. The fee is based on the perceived value of the audience who watches, reads, listens to, or frequents the space where the ad will appear.

In recent years, receivers have begun to filter advertiser's messages. This phenomenon is perceived to be a result of the large amount of ads the average person sees each day and a growing level of consumer wariness of paid messaging. Advertisers, in turn, are trying to create alternative forms of advertising that receivers won't filter. The *advertorial* is one example of an external communication that combines the look of an article with the focused message of an ad. Product placements in videos, movies, and games are other ways that advertisers strive to reach receivers with commercial messages.

Web Pages

A Web page's external communication can combine elements of public relations, advertising, and editorial content, reaching receivers on multiple levels and in multiple ways. Banner ads, blogs, and advertiser-driven "click-through" areas are just a few of the elements that allow a business to deliver a message to a receiver online. The perceived flexibility of online communications can impart a less formal (and therefore, more believable) quality to an external communication. A message relayed in a daily blog post, for example, will reach a receiver differently than if it is delivered in an annual report. The popularity and power of blogs is growing, with 11% of Fortune 500 companies having official blogs (up from 4% in 2005). In fact, blogs have become so important to companies such as Coca-Cola Company, Eastman Kodak Company, and Marriott International Inc. that they have created official positions within their organizations titled "chief blogging officer."[45] The "real-time" quality of Web communications may appeal to receivers who might filter out traditional ads and public relations messages because of their prefab quality. Despite a spontaneous feel, many online pages can be revisited many times in a single day. For this reason, clear and accurate external communications are as vital for online use as they are in traditional media.

Customer Communications

Customer communications can include letters, catalogs, direct mail, e-mails, text messages, and telemarketing messages. Some receivers automatically filter these types of bulk messages. Others will be receptive. The key to a successful external communication to customers is to convey a business message in a personally compelling way—dramatic news, a money-saving coupon, and so forth.

KEY TAKEAWAY

Types of communication include verbal, written, and nonverbal. Surprisingly, 55% of face-to-face communication comes from nonverbal cues such as tone or body language. Different communication channels are more or less effective at transmitting different kinds of information. In addition, communication flows in different directions within organizations.

EXERCISES

1. How aware are you of your own body language? Has your body language ever gotten you in trouble while communicating with someone?
2. In your experience, how is silence used in communication?
3. If the meaning behind verbal communication is only 7% words, what does this imply for written communication?
4. How could you use your knowledge of communication richness to be more effective in your own communications?
5. What are the three biggest advantages and disadvantages you see regarding technology and communications?

4. THE ROLE OF ETHICS AND NATIONAL CULTURE

LEARNING OBJECTIVES

1. Consider the role of ethics in communication.
2. Consider the role of national culture on communication.

4.1 Ethics and Communication

"People aren't happy when the unexpected happens, but they are even unhappier if they find out you tried to hide it," says Bruce Patton, a partner at Boston-based Vantage Partners LLC.[46] To speak or not to speak? One of the most challenging areas of effective business communication occurs in moments of crisis management. But in an age of instant information, the burden on business to speak out quickly and clearly in times of crisis has never been greater.

The alternative to a clear message is seen as a communication blocker, in addition to being guilty of the misdeed, disaster, or infraction at hand. The Exxon Valdez disaster is a classic example of ineffective crisis management and communication. When millions of barrels of oil spilled into Prince William Sound, the company's poor response only added to the damage. Exxon Mobil Corporation executives refused to acknowledge the extent of the problem and declined to comment on the accident for almost a week. Exxon also sent a succession of lower level spokespeople to deal with the media.[47]

Instead, a more effective method of crisis communication is to have the company's highest ranking official become the spokesperson who communicates the situation. This is the approach that James Burke, the chairman of Johnson & Johnson Services, Inc., took when tampering was discovered with Tylenol bottles. He became the face of the crisis, communicating with the public and explaining what J & J would do. His forthrightness built trust and allayed customer fears.

Ethical, forthright communication applies inside the company as well as externally with the public. "When the truth is missing, people feel demoralized, less confident, and ultimately are less loyal," write leadership experts Beverly Kaye and Sharon Jordan-Evans. "Research overwhelmingly supports the notion that engaged employees are 'in the know.' They want to be trusted with the truth about the business, including its challenges and downturns."[48]

4.2 Cross-Cultural Communication

Culture is a shared set of beliefs and experiences common to people in a specific setting. The setting that creates a culture can be geographic, religious, or professional. As you might guess, the same individual can be a member of many cultures, all of which may play a part in the interpretation of certain words.

The different and often "multicultural" identity of individuals in the same organization can lead to some unexpected and potentially large miscommunications. For example, during the Cold War, Soviet leader Nikita Khruschev told the American delegation at the United Nations, "We will bury you!" His words were interpreted as a threat of nuclear annihilation. However, a more accurate reading of Khruschev's words would have been, "We will overtake you!" meaning economic superiority. The words, as well as the fear and suspicion that the West had of the Soviet Union at the time, led to the more alarmist and sinister interpretation.[49]

Miscommunications can arise between individuals of the same culture as well. Many words in the English language mean different things to different people. Words can be misunderstood if the sender and receiver do not share common experiences. A sender's words cannot communicate the desired meaning if the receiver has not had some experience with the objects or concepts the words describe.[50]

It is particularly important to keep this fact in mind when you are communicating with individuals who may not speak English as a first language. For example, when speaking with nonnative English-speaking colleagues, avoid "isn't it?" questions. This sentence construction does not exist in many other languages and can be confusing for nonnative English speakers. For example, to the question, "You are coming, aren't you?" they may answer, "Yes" (I am coming) or "No" (I am coming), depending on how they interpret the question.[51]

Cultures also vary in terms of the desired amount of situational context related to interpreting situations. People in very high context cultures put a high value on establishing relationships prior to working with others and tend to take longer to negotiate deals. Examples of high context cultures include China, Korea, and Japan. Conversely, people in low context cultures "get down to business" and tend to negotiate quickly. Examples of low context cultures include Germany, Scandinavia, and the United States.[52]

Finally, don't forget the role of nonverbal communication. As we learned in the nonverbal communication section, in the United States, looking someone in the eye when talking is considered a sign of trustworthiness. In China, by contrast, a lack of eye contact conveys respect. A recruiting agency that places English teachers warns prospective teachers that something that works well in one culture can offend in another: "In Western countries, one expects to maintain eye contact when we talk with people. This is a norm we consider basic and essential. This is not the case among the Chinese. On the contrary, because of the more authoritarian nature of the Chinese society, steady eye contact is viewed as inappropriate, especially when subordinates talk with their superiors."[53]

FIGURE 8.15 Gestures Around the Globe

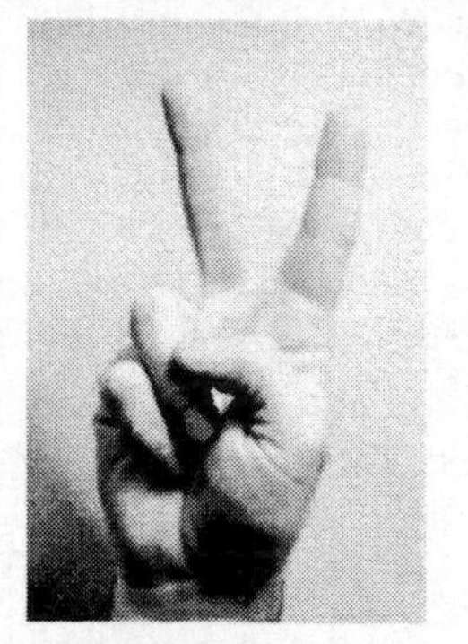	*"V" for victory*. Use this gesture with caution! While in North America it signs victory or peace, in England and Australia it means something closer to "take this!"
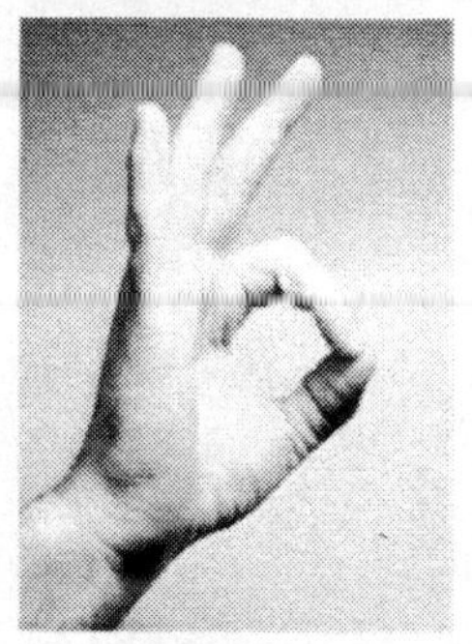	*The "OK" gesture*. While in North America it means things are going well, in France it means a person is thought to be worthless, in Japan it refers to money, and in Brazil, Russia, and Germany it means something really not appropriate for the workplace.
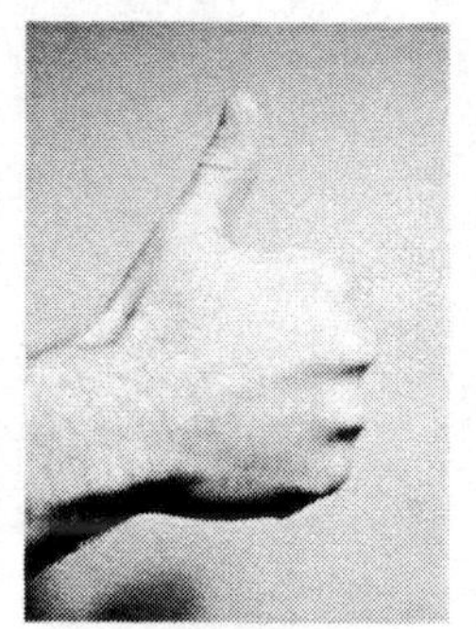	The *"thumbs up"* means one in Germany, five in Japan, but good job in North America. This can lead to confusion.
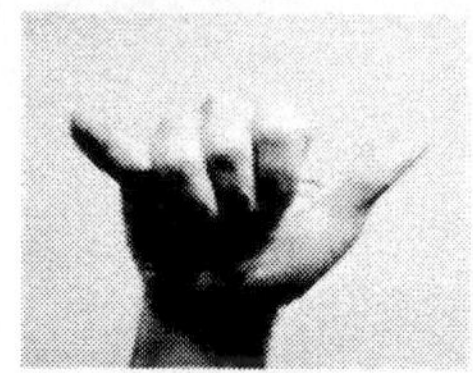	*"Hook 'em horns."* In Texas this is the University of Texas rallying call because it looks like the horns of a bull. However, in Italy it means you are being tricked, while in Brazil and Venezuela it means you are warding off evil.
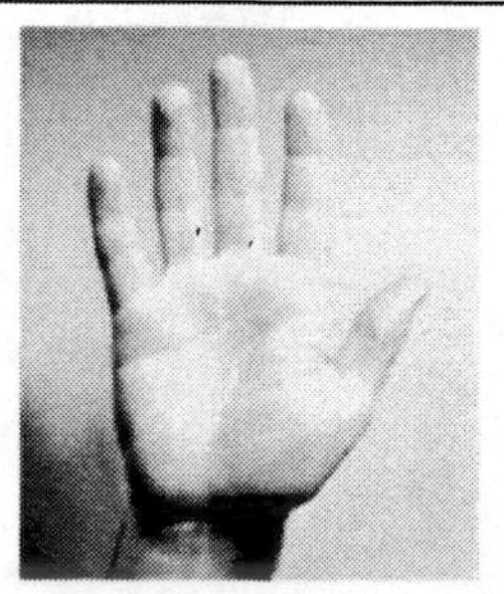	*Waving your hand.* In much of Europe waving your hand indicates a disagreement. However, in North America it is routinely used as a way to signal greetings or to get someone's attention.

Adapted from information in Axtell, R. E. (1998). Gestures: The do's and taboos of body language around the world. New York: John Wiley.

It's easy to see how meaning could become confused, depending on how and when these signals are used. When in doubt, experts recommend that you ask someone around you to help you interpret the meaning of different gestures, that you be sensitive, and that you remain observant when dealing with a culture different from your own.

KEY TAKEAWAY

Ethical, forthright communication applies inside a company as well as externally with the public. Trying to cover up or ignore problems has been the downfall of many organizational members. There are differences in word meanings and nonverbal communication. For example, in North America, the nonverbal V means victory or peace, but in Australia means something closer to "take this," which could still fit if your team wins a championship but probably isn't exactly what was meant.

EXERCISES

1. How can you assess if you are engaging in ethical communication?
2. What experiences have you had with cross-cultural communications? Please share at least one experience when this has gone well and one when it has not gone well.
3. What advice would you give to someone who will be managing a new division of a company in another culture in terms of communication?

5. CONCLUSION

In this chapter we have reviewed why effective communication matters to organizations. Communication may break down as a result of many communication barriers that may be attributed to the sender or receiver. Therefore, effective communication requires familiarity with the barriers. Choosing the right channel for communication is also important, because choosing the wrong medium undermines the message. When communication occurs in the cross-cultural context, extra caution is needed, given that different cultures have different norms regarding nonverbal communication, and different words will be interpreted differently across cultures. By being sensitive to the errors outlined in this chapter and adopting active listening skills, you may increase your communication effectiveness.

6. EXERCISES

ETHICAL DILEMMA

How far would you go to find out who is talking to whom?[54]

In 2006, Hewlett-Packard Development Company LP became embroiled in a controversy over methods used to investigate media leaks from its board. HP Chairperson Patricia Dunn could have simply asked the directors who was the source cited in the story, sought an apology, and gone from there. With some direct face-to-face communication, the story would likely have ended quickly. It did not. "Not only did investigators impersonate board members, employees and journalists to obtain their phone records, but according to multiple reports, they also surveilled an HP director and a reporter for CNet Networks Inc. They sent monitoring spyware in an e-mail to that reporter by concocting a phony tip. They even snooped on the phone records of former CEO and Chairperson Carly Fiorina, who had launched the quest to identify media sources in the first place." The situation continued to escalate. For example, the *New York Times* reported that HP consultants even considered planting clerical or custodial workers at CNet and the *Wall Street Journal* to learn who was leaking information to them. Following this, Patricia Dunn, as well as three executives, left the company. A congressional hearing and several federal investigations later, executives were charged with felonies, and HP paid $14.5 million to settle civil charges related to the scandal. HP is not the only company to use such methods; recent admissions by the investigation firms involved suggest that the use of ethically questionable investigative tactics by large companies is quite common. "It betrays a type of corporate culture that is so self-obsessed, (that) really considers itself not only above the law, but above, I think, ethical decency, that you have to ask yourself, where did the shame come in?" said Charles King, an analyst with Pund-IT Inc.

Consider this situation from a multiple stakeholder perspective. Imagine you are…

- *a CEO* faced with leaks regarding your strategic vision. What would you do to determine who was sharing the information? What would be the advantages and disadvantages of these approaches?
- *a shareholder* with HP stock. What would you want to see done to protect your investment in the company?
- *a board member who was spied upon*. What would your reaction be to learning that you were investigated?
- *an investigator hired by HP*. What role do you have to uphold ethical standards?

As several observers have noted, HP spent a lot of time establishing whether or not their activities were technically legal but little time considering whether or not their actions were ethical.

GROUP EXERCISE

You Know What I Mean, Right?

Purpose

This exercise illustrates how words we commonly take for granted are not universal in their meaning.

Time

Approximately 20 minutes.

1. Write down the number that comes to mind for each of the following questions. Remember that there are no right or wrong answers—just go with your first response. Do not discuss your answers with anyone in the class until instructed to do so.
    - My neighbor just bought an expensive car. How much did it cost? _____
    - Several people were in line for the movie. How many people were in line? _____
    - The ballot measure was approved overwhelmingly. What percentage of votes did the measure receive? _____
    - My boss is an older man. How old is he? _____
    - I recently saw an article in the paper. How long ago did I see it? _____
2. Your instructor will summarize the responses from the class.
3. Discuss the following questions (either as a class or in small groups).
    - Do you agree that words mean different things to different people?
    - How large was the range of responses for each of the questions? Why was this?
    - Did this surprise you? Why or why not?

What can you apply from this exercise to make you a better communicator?

ENDNOTES

1. Wright, N. (n.d.). *Keep it jargon-free*. Retrieved from the Plain Language Action and Information Network Web site: http://www.plainlanguage.gov/howto/wordsuggestions/jargonfree.cfm.
2. Schnake, M. E., Dumler, M. P., Cochran, D. S., & Barnett, T. R. (1990). Effects of differences in subordinate perceptions of superiors' communication practices. *Journal of Business Communication, 27*, 37–50.
3. Penley, L. E., Alexander, E. R., Jernigan, I. E., & Henwood, C. I. (1991). Communication abilities of managers: The relationship of performance. *Journal of Management, 17*, 57–76.
4. NASA study cited by Baron, R. (n.d.). Barriers to effective communication: Implications for the cockpit. Retrieved July 3, 2008, from AirlineSafety.com: http://www.airlinesafety.com/editorials/BarriersToCommunication.htm.
5. Communications skills cut malpractice risk—study reveals most important reason that patients decide to file malpractice suits is because of poor communication by physicians and not medical errors. (1997, October). *USA Today*.
6. Armour, S. (1998, September 30). Failure to communicate costly for companies. *USA Today*, p. 1A.
7. Alsop, R. (2006, September 20). The top business schools: Recruiters' M.B.A. picks. *Wall Street Journal Online*. Retrieved September 20, 2006, from http://online.wsj.com/article/SB115860376846766495.html?mod=2_1245_1.
8. [illegible] *ance Report*. Retrieved July 1, 2008, from http://www.mercerHR.com.
9. Meisinger, S. (2003, February). Enhancing communications—Ours and yours. *HR Magazine*. Retrieved July 1, 2008, from http://www.shrm.org/hrmagazine/archive/0203toc.asp.
10. Alessandra, T. (1993). *Communicating at work*. New York: Fireside.
11. Schick, A. G., Gordon, L. A., & Haka, S. (1990). Information overload: A temporal approach. *Accounting, Organizations, and Society, 15*, 199–220.
12. Retrieved July 1, 2008, from PC Magazine encyclopedia Web site: http://www.pcmag.com/encyclopedia_term/0,2542,t=information+overload&i=44950,00.asp and reinforced by information in Dawley, D. D., & Anthony, W. P. (2003). User perceptions of e-mail at work. *Journal of Business and Technical Communication, 17*, 170–200.
13. Based on Overholt, A. (2001, February). Intel's got (too much) mail. *Fast Company*. Retrieved July 2, 2008, from http://www.fastcompany.com/online/44/intel.html and http://blogs.intel.com/it/2006/10/information_overload.php.
14. González, V. M., & Gloria, M. (2004). Constant, constant, multi-tasking craziness. *CHI 2004*. Retrieved July 2, 2008, from http://www.interruptions.net/literature/Gonzalez-CHI04-p113-gonzalez.pdf.
15. Kurland, N. B., & Pelled, L. H. (2000). Passing the word: Toward a model of gossip and power in the workplace. *Academy of Management Review, 25*, 428–438.
16. Crampton, S. M. (1998). The informal communication network: Factors influencing grapevine activity. *Public Personnel Management*. Retrieved July 2, 2008, from http://www.allbusiness.com/management/735210-1.html.
17. Wright, N. (n.d.). Keep it jargon-free. Retrieved July 2, 2008, from the Plain Language Action and Information Network Web site: http://www.plainlanguage.gov/howto/wordsuggestions/jargonfree.cfm.
18. Krotz, J. L. (n.d.). 6 tips for bridging the communication gap. Retrieved from the Microsoft Small Business Center Web site: http://www.microsoft.com/smallbusiness/resources/management/leadership-training/women-vs-men-6-tips-for-bridging-the-communication-gap.aspx.
19. CDR Dee Norton. (n.d.). *Gender and communication—finding common ground*. Retrieved July 2, 2008, from http://www.uscg.mil/leadership/gender.htm.
20. Adapted from information in Ashcraft, K., & Mumby, D. K. (2003). *Reworking gender*. Thousand Oaks, CA: Sage; Miller, C., & Swift, K. (1980). *The handbook of nonsexist writing*. New York: Lippincott & Crowell; Procter, M. (2007, September 11). *Unbiased language*. (n.d.). Retrieved July 2, 2008, from http://www.utoronto.ca/writing/unbias.html.
21. Iacocca, L., & Novak, W. (1984). *Iacocca: An autobiography*. New York: Bantam Press.
22. Sypher, B. D., Bostrom, R. N., & Seibert, J. H. (1989). Listening, communication abilities, and success at work. *Journal of Business Communication, 26*, 293–303.
23. O*NET Resource Center, the nation's primary source of occupational information accessed at http://online.onetcenter.org/skills/.
24. Brownell, J. (1990). Perceptions of effective listeners: A management study. *Journal of Business Communications, 27*, 401–415.
25. McCarthy, J. F. (2008). Short stories at work: Storytelling as an indicator of organizational commitment. *Group & Organization Management, 33*, 163–193.
26. Martens, M. L., Jennings, J. E., & Devereaux, J. P. (2007). Do the stories they tell get them the money they need? The role of entrepreneurial narratives in resource acquisition. *Academy of Management Journal, 50*, 1107–1132.
27. Patterson, K., Grenny, J., McMillan, R., & Switzler, A. (2002). *Crucial conversations: Tools for talking when stakes are high*. New York: McGraw-Hill.
28. Lee, D., & Hatesohl, D. *Listening: Our most used communication skill*. Retrieved July 2, 2008, from the University of Missouri Web site: http://extension.missouri.edu/explore/comm/cm0150.htm.
29. Flink, H. (2007, March). Tell it like it is: Essential communication skills for engineers. *Industrial Engineer, 39*, 44–49.
30. Gifford, R., Ng, C. F., & Wilkinson, M. (1985). Nonverbal cues in the employment interview: Links between applicant qualities and interviewer judgments. *Journal of Applied Psychology, 70*, 729–736.
31. Mehrabian, A. (1981). *Silent messages*. New York: Wadsworth.
32. Siegman, A. W. (1985). *Multichannel integrations of nonverbal behavior*. Hillsdale, NJ: L. Erlbaum Associates.
33. Ekman, P., Friesen, W. V., & Hager, J. C. The facial action coding system (FACS). Retrieved July 2, 2008, from http://face-and-emotion.com/dataface/facs/manual.
34. Daud, N. (n.d.). Business etiquette. Retrieved July 2, 2008, from http://ezinearticles.com/?Business-Etiquette---Shaking-Hands-around-the-World&id=746227.
35. Hall, E. T. (1966). *The hidden dimension*. New York: Doubleday.
36. Allen, D. G., & Griffeth, R. W. (1997). Vertical and lateral information processing; Fulk, J., & Boyd, B. (1991). Emerging theories of communication in organizations. *Journal of Management, 17*, 407–446; Yates, J., & Orlikowski, W. J. (1992). Genres of organizational communication: A structurational approach to studying communication and media. *Academy of Management Review, 17*, 299–326.
37. Barry, B., & Fulmer, I. S. (2004). The medium and the message: The adaptive use of communication media in dyadic influence. *Academy of Management Review, 29*, [illegible]
38. Taylor, C. (2002, June 10). 12 steps for email addicts. *Time.com*. Retrieved July 2, 2008, from http://www.time.com/time/magazine/article/0,9171,1002621,00.html.
39. 60 Billion emails sent daily worldwide. (2006, April 26). Retrieved July 2, 2008, from CNET.UK: http://www.cnet.co.uk/misc/print/0,39030763,49265163,00.htm.
40. Isom, D. K. (updated October 19, 2005). Electronic discovery: New power, new risks. Retrieved July 2, 2008, from the Utah State Bar Web site: http://utahbar.org/barjournal2000/html/november_2003_2.html.
41. Kruger, J. (2005). Egocentrism over email: Can we communicate as well as we think? *Journal of Personality and Social Psychology, 89*, 925–936.
42. Quotation listed on Inspirational Business Quotes. Retrieved July 1, 2008, from http://www.woopidoo.com/business_quotes/effort-quotes.htm.
43. Snyder, R. A., & Morris, J. H. (1984). Organizational communication and performance. *Journal of Applied Psychology, 69*, 461–465; Kacmar, K. M., Witt, L. A., Zivnuska, S., & Gully, S. M. (2003). The interactive effect of leader-member exchange and communication frequency on performance ratings. *Journal of Applied Psychology, 88*, 764–772.
44. Krackhardt, D., & Porter, L. W. (1986). The snowball effect: Turnover embedded in communication networks. *Journal of Applied Psychology, 71*, 50–55.
45. Chief blogging officer title catching on with corporations. (2008, May 1). *Workforce Management*. Retrieved July 2, 2008, from http://www.workforce.com/section/00/article/25/50/77.html.
46. Michelman, P. (2004, December 13). Sharing news that *might* be bad. Harvard Business School Working Knowledge Web site. Retrieved July 2, 2008, from http://hbswk.hbs.edu/item/4538.html.
47. Holusha, J. (1989, April 4). Exxon's public-relations problem. *New York Times*. Retrieved July 2, 2008, from http://query.nytimes.com/gst/fullpage.html?res=950DE1DA1031F932A15757C0A96F948260.
48. Kaye, B., & Jordan-Evans, S. (2008, September 11). Tell them the truth. *Fast Company*. Retrieved January 27, 2009, from http://www.fastcompany.com/resources/talent/bksje/092107-tellthemthetruth.html.
49. Garner, E. (2007, December 3). Seven barriers to great communication. Retrieved July 2, 2008, from Hodu.com: http://www.hodu.com/barriers.shtml.
50. Effective communication. (2004, May 31). Retrieved July 2, 2008, from DynamicFlight.com: http://www.dynamicflight.com/avcfibook/communication.
51. Lifland, S. (2006). Multicultural communication tips. *American Management Association*. Retrieved July 2, 2008, from http://www.amanet.org/movingahead/editorial.cfm?Ed=37&BNKNAVID=24&display=1.
52. This section draws on work by Hall, E. (1976). *Beyond culture*. Garden City, NY: Doubleday; and ideas in Munter, M. (1993). Cross-cultural communication for managers. *Business Horizons, 36*, 69–78.
53. Chinese culture—differences and taboos. (n.d.). Retrieved January 27, 2009, from the Footprints Recruiting Inc. Web site: http://www.footprintsrecruiting.com/content_321.php?abarcar_Session=2284f8a72fa606078aed24b8218f08b9.
54. Based on information in Bergstein, B. (2006, September 20). HP spy scandal hits new weirdness level. Retrieved July 1, 2008, from the *BusinessWeek.com Web site*: http://www.businessweek.com/ap/tech/D8K8QTHO0.htm?chan=search; Allison, K. (2006, September 30). Spy methods used in other companies. Retrieved July 1, 2008, from *FT.com*: http://www.msnbc.msn.com/id/15067438/; Fried, I. (2006, December 7). HP settles with California in spy scandal. Retrieved July 1, 2008, from *cNET news.com*: http://www.news.com/HP-settles-with-California-in-spy-scandal/2100-1014_3-6141814.html.

CHAPTER 9
Managing Groups and Teams

LEARNING OBJECTIVES

After reading this chapter, you should be able to do the following:

1. Recognize and understand group dynamics and development.
2. Understand the difference between groups and teams.
3. Compare and contrast different types of teams.
4. Understand how to design effective teams.
5. Explore ideas around teams and ethics.
6. Understand cross-cultural influences on teams.

Teamwork at General Electric

Teamwork can make something as complex as an airplane engine possible.

© 2010 Jupiterimages Corporation

In Durham, North Carolina, Robert Henderson was opening a factory for General Electric Company (GE). The goal of the factory was to manufacture the largest commercial jet engine in the world. Henderson's opportunity was great and so were his challenges. GE hadn't designed a jet engine from the ground up for over two decades. Developing the jet engine project had already cost GE $1.5 billion. That was a huge sum of money to invest—and an unacceptable sum to lose should things go wrong in the manufacturing stage.

How could one person fulfill such a vital corporate mission? The answer, Henderson decided, was that one person couldn't fulfill the mission. Even Jack Welch, GE's CEO at the time said, "We now know where productivity comes from. It comes from challenged, empowered, excited, rewarded teams of people."

Empowering factory workers to contribute to GE's success sounded great in theory. But how to accomplish these goals in real life was a more challenging question. Factory floors, traditionally, are unempowered workplaces where workers are more like cogs in a vast machine than self-determining team members.

In the name of teamwork and profitability, Henderson traveled to other factories looking for places where worker autonomy was high. He implemented his favorite ideas at the factory at Durham. Instead of hiring generic "mechanics," for example, Henderson hired staffers with FAA mechanic's licenses. This superior training created a team capable of making vital decisions with minimal oversight, a fact that upped the factory's output and his workers' feelings of worth.

Henderson's "self-managing" factory functioned beautifully. And it looked different, too. Plant manager Jack Fish described Henderson's radical factory, saying Henderson "didn't want to see supervisors, he didn't want to see forklifts running all over the place, he didn't even want it to look traditional. There's clutter in most plants, racks of parts and so on. He didn't want that."

Henderson also contracted out non-job-related chores, such as bathroom cleaning, that might have been assigned to workers in traditional factories. His insistence that his workers should contribute their highest talents to the team showed how much he valued them. And his team valued their jobs in turn.

Six years later, a *Fast Company* reporter visiting the plant noted, "GE/Durham team members take such pride in the engines they make that they routinely take brooms in hand to sweep out the beds of the 18-wheelers that transport those engines—just to make sure that no damage occurs in transit." For his part, Henderson, who remained at GE beyond the project, noted, "I was just constantly amazed by what was accomplished there."

GE's bottom line showed the benefits of teamwork, too. From the early 1980s, when Welch became CEO, until 2000, when he retired, GE generated more wealth than any organization in the history of the world.

Sources: Fishman, C. (1999, September). How teamwork took flight. Fast Company. Retrieved August 1, 2008, from http://www.fastcompany.com/node/38322/print; Lear, R. (1998, July–August). Jack Welch speaks: Wisdom from the world's greatest business leader, Chief Executive; Guttman, H. (2008, January–February). Leading high-performance teams: Horizontal, high-performance teams with real decision-making clout and accountability for results can transform a company. Chief Executive, 231, 33.

1. GROUP DYNAMICS

LEARNING OBJECTIVES

1. **Understand the difference between informal and formal groups.**
2. **Learn the stages of group development.**
3. **Identify examples of the punctuated equilibrium model.**
4. **Learn how group cohesion affects groups.**
5. **Learn how social loafing affects groups.**
6. **Learn how collective efficacy affects groups.**

1.1 Types of Groups: Formal and Informal

group

A collection of individuals who interact with each other such that one person's actions have an impact on the others.

What is a **group**? A group is a collection of individuals who interact with each other such that one person's actions have an impact on the others. In organizations, most work is done within groups. How groups function has important implications for organizational productivity. Groups where people get along, feel the desire to contribute to the team, and are capable of coordinating their efforts may have high performance levels, whereas teams characterized by extreme levels of conflict or hostility may demoralize members of the workforce.

In organizations, you may encounter different types of groups. **Informal work groups** are made up of two or more individuals who are associated with one another in ways not prescribed by the formal organization. For example, a few people in the company who get together to play tennis on the weekend would be considered an informal group. A **formal work group** is made up of managers, subordinates, or both with close associations among group members that influence the behavior of individuals in the group. We will discuss many different types of formal work groups later on in this chapter.

informal work groups

Two or more individuals who are associated with one another in ways not prescribed by the formal organization.

formal work group

Is made up of managers, subordinates, or both with close associations among group members that influence the behavior of individuals in the group.

1.2 Stages of Group Development

Forming, Storming, Norming, and Performing

American organizational psychologist Bruce Tuckman presented a robust model in 1965 that is still widely used today. Based on his observations of group behavior in a variety of settings, he proposed a four-stage map of group evolution, also known as the **forming-storming-norming-performing model**.[1] Later he enhanced the model by adding a fifth and final stage, the **adjourning phase**. Interestingly enough, just as an individual moves through developmental stages such as childhood, adolescence, and adulthood, so does a group, although in a much shorter period of time. According to this theory, in order to successfully facilitate a group, the leader needs to move through various leadership styles over time. Generally, this is accomplished by first being more directive, eventually serving as a coach, and later, once the group is able to assume more power and responsibility for itself, shifting to a delegator. While research has not confirmed that this is descriptive of how groups progress, knowing and following these steps can help groups be more effective. For example, groups that do not go through the storming phase early on will often return to this stage toward the end of the group process to address unresolved issues. Another example of the validity of the group development model involves groups that take the time to get to know each other socially in the forming stage. When this occurs, groups tend to handle future challenges better because the individuals have an understanding of each other's needs.

forming-storming-norming-performing model

Proposed by Bruce Tuckman in 1965 and involved a four-stage map of group evolution.

adjourning phase

The fifth and final stage later added to the Tuckman model.

FIGURE 9.2 Stages of the Group Development Model

Forming

In the **forming** stage, the group comes together for the first time. The members may already know each other or they may be total strangers. In either case, there is a level of formality, some anxiety, and a degree of guardedness as group members are not sure what is going to happen next. "Will I be accepted? What will my role be? Who has the power here?" These are some of the questions participants think about during this stage of group formation. Because of the large amount of uncertainty, members tend to be polite, conflict avoidant, and observant. They are trying to figure out the "rules of the game" without being too vulnerable. At this point, they may also be quite excited and optimistic about the task at hand, perhaps experiencing a level of pride at being chosen to join a particular group. Group members are trying to achieve several goals at this stage, although this may not necessarily be done consciously. First, they are trying to get to know each other. Often this can be accomplished by finding some common ground. Members also begin to explore group boundaries to determine what will be considered acceptable behavior. "Can I interrupt? Can I leave when I feel like it?" This trial phase may also involve testing the appointed leader or seeing if a leader emerges from the group. At this point, group members are also discovering how the group will work in terms of what needs to be done and who will be responsible for each task. This stage is often characterized by abstract discussions about issues to be addressed by the group; those who like to get moving can become impatient with this part of the process. This phase is usually short in duration, perhaps a meeting or two.

forming

Stage when the group comes together for the first time.

Storming

storming

Stage when participants focus less on keeping their guard up as they shed social facades, becoming more authentic and more argumentative.

Once group members feel sufficiently safe and included, they tend to enter the **storming** phase. Participants focus less on keeping their guard up as they shed social facades, becoming more authentic and more argumentative. Group members begin to explore their power and influence, and they often stake out their territory by differentiating themselves from the other group members rather than seeking common ground. Discussions can become heated as participants raise contending points of view and values, or argue over how tasks should be done and who is assigned to them. It is not unusual for group members to become defensive, competitive, or jealous. They may even take sides or begin to form cliques within the group. Questioning and resisting direction from the leader is also quite common. "Why should I have to do this? Who designed this project in the first place? Why do I have to listen to you?" Although little seems to get accomplished at this stage, group members are becoming more authentic as they express their deeper thoughts and feelings. What they are really exploring is "Can I truly be me, have power, and be accepted?" During this chaotic stage, a great deal of creative energy that was previously buried is released and available for use, but it takes skill to move the group from storming to norming. In many cases, the group gets stuck in the storming phase.

OB Toolbox: Avoid Getting Stuck in the Storming Phase!

There are several steps you can take to avoid getting stuck in the storming phase of group development. Try the following if you feel the group process you are involved in is not progressing:

- *Normalize conflict.* Let members know this is a natural phase in the group-formation process.
- *Be inclusive.* Continue to make all members feel included and invite all views into the room. Mention how diverse ideas and opinions help foster creativity and innovation.
- *Make sure everyone is heard.* Facilitate heated discussions and help participants understand each other.
- *Support all group members.* This is especially important for those who feel more insecure.
- *Remain positive.* This is a key point to remember about the group's ability to accomplish its goal.
- *Don't rush the group's development.* Remember that working through the storming stage can take several meetings.

Once group members discover that they can be authentic and that the group is capable of handling differences without dissolving, they are ready to enter the next stage, norming.

Norming

norming

Stage when participants find it easy to establish their own ground rules (or *norms*) and define their operating procedures and goals.

"We survived!" is the common sentiment at the **norming** stage. Group members often feel elated at this point, and they are much more committed to each other and the group's goal. Feeling energized by knowing they can handle the "tough stuff," group members are now ready to get to work. Finding themselves more cohesive and cooperative, participants find it easy to establish their own ground rules (or *norms*) and define their operating procedures and goals. The group tends to make big decisions, while subgroups or individuals handle the smaller decisions. Hopefully, at this point the group is more open and respectful toward each other, and members ask each other for both help and feedback. They may even begin to form friendships and share more personal information with each other. At this point, the leader should become more of a facilitator by stepping back and letting the group assume more responsibility for its goal. Since the group's energy is running high, this is an ideal time to host a social or team-building event.

Performing

performing

Stage when participants are not only getting the work done, but they also pay greater attention to *how* they are doing it.

Galvanized by a sense of shared vision and a feeling of unity, the group is ready to go into high gear. Members are more interdependent, individuality and differences are respected, and group members feel themselves to be part of a greater entity. At the **performing** stage, participants are not only getting the work done, but they also pay greater attention to *how* they are doing it. They ask questions like, "Do our operating procedures best support productivity and quality assurance? Do we have suitable means for addressing differences that arise so we can preempt destructive conflicts? Are we relating to and communicating with each other in ways that enhance group dynamics and help us achieve our goals? How can I further develop as a person to become more effective?" By now, the group has matured, becoming more competent, autonomous, and insightful. Group leaders can finally move into coaching roles and help members grow in skill and leadership.

Adjourning

Just as groups form, so do they end. For example, many groups or teams formed in a business context are project oriented and therefore are temporary in nature. Alternatively, a working group may dissolve due to an organizational restructuring. Just as when we graduate from school or leave home for the first time, these endings can be bittersweet, with group members feeling a combination of victory, grief, and insecurity about what is coming next. For those who like routine and bond closely with fellow group members, this transition can be particularly challenging. Group leaders and members alike should be sensitive to handling these endings respectfully and compassionately. An ideal way to close a group is to set aside time to debrief ("How did it all go? What did we learn?"), acknowledge each other, and celebrate a job well done.

1.3 The Punctuated-Equilibrium Model

As you may have noted, the five-stage model we have just reviewed is a linear process. According to the model, a group progresses to the performing stage, at which point it finds itself in an ongoing, smooth-sailing situation until the group dissolves. In reality, subsequent researchers, most notably Joy H. Karriker, have found that the life of a group is much more dynamic and cyclical in nature.[2] For example, a group may operate in the performing stage for several months. Then, because of a disruption, such as a competing emerging technology that changes the rules of the game or the introduction of a new CEO, the group may move back into the storming phase before returning to performing. Ideally, any regression in the linear group progression will ultimately result in a higher level of functioning. Proponents of this cyclical model draw from behavioral scientist Connie Gersick's study of **punctuated equilibrium**.[3]

punctuated equilibrium

The theory that change within groups occurs in rapid, radical spurts rather than gradually over time.

The concept of punctuated equilibrium was first proposed in 1972 by paleontologists Niles Eldredge and Stephen Jay Gould, who both believed that evolution occurred in rapid, radical spurts rather than gradually over time. Identifying numerous examples of this pattern in social behavior, Gersick found that the concept applied to organizational change. She proposed that groups remain fairly static, maintaining a certain equilibrium for long periods of time. Change during these periods is incremental, largely due to the resistance to change that arises when systems take root and processes become institutionalized. In this model, revolutionary change occurs in brief, punctuated bursts, generally catalyzed by a crisis or problem that breaks through the systemic inertia and shakes up the deep organizational structures in place. At this point, the organization or group has the opportunity to learn and create new structures that are better aligned with current realities. Whether the group does this is not guaranteed. In sum, in Gersick's model, groups can repeatedly cycle through the storming and performing stages, with revolutionary change taking place during short transitional windows. For organizations and groups who understand that disruption, conflict, and chaos are inevitable in the life of a social system, these disruptions represent opportunities for innovation and creativity.

FIGURE 9.3 The Punctuated Equilibrium Model

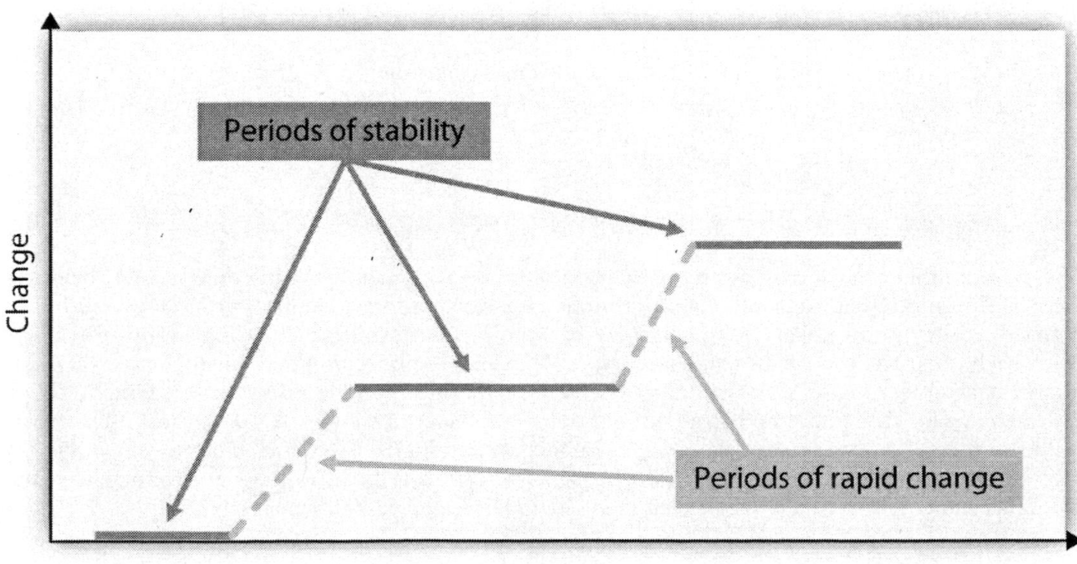

1.4 Cohesion

cohesion

The degree of camaraderie within the group.

Cohesion can be thought of as a kind of social glue. It refers to the degree of camaraderie within the group. Cohesive groups are those in which members are attached to each other and act as one unit. Generally speaking, the more cohesive a group is, the more productive it will be and the more rewarding the experience will be for the group's members.[4] Members of cohesive groups tend to have the following characteristics: They have a collective identity; they experience a moral bond and a desire to remain part of the group; they share a sense of purpose, working together on a meaningful task or cause; and they establish a structured pattern of communication.

The fundamental factors affecting group cohesion include the following:

- *Similarity.* The more similar group members are in terms of age, sex, education, skills, attitudes, values, and beliefs, the more likely the group will bond.
- *Stability.* The longer a group stays together, the more cohesive it becomes.
- *Size.* Smaller groups tend to have higher levels of cohesion.
- *Support.* When group members receive coaching and are encouraged to support their fellow team members, group identity strengthens.
- *Satisfaction.* Cohesion is correlated with how pleased group members are with each other's performance, behavior, and conformity to group norms.

As you might imagine, there are many benefits in creating a cohesive group. Members are generally more personally satisfied and feel greater self-confidence and self-esteem when in a group where they feel they belong. For many, membership in such a group can be a buffer against stress, which can improve mental and physical well-being. Because members are invested in the group and its work, they are more likely to regularly attend and actively participate in the group, taking more responsibility for the group's functioning. In addition, members can draw on the strength of the group to persevere through challenging situations that might otherwise be too hard to tackle alone.

OB Toolbox: Steps to Creating and Maintaining a Cohesive Team

- *Align the group with the greater organization.* Establish common objectives in which members can get involved.
- *Let members have choices in setting their own goals.* Include them in decision making at the organizational level.
- *Define clear roles.* Demonstrate how each person's contribution furthers the group goal—everyone is responsible for a special piece of the puzzle.
- *Situate group members in close proximity to each other.* This builds familiarity.
- *Give frequent praise.* Both individuals and groups benefit from praise. Also encourage them to praise each other. This builds individual self-confidence, reaffirms positive behavior, and creates an overall positive atmosphere.
- *Treat all members with dignity and respect.* This demonstrates that there are no favorites and everyone is valued.
- *Celebrate differences.* This highlights each individual's contribution while also making diversity a norm.
- *Establish common rituals.* Thursday morning coffee, monthly potlucks—these reaffirm group identity and create shared experiences.

Can a Group Have Too Much Cohesion?

Keep in mind that groups can have too much cohesion. Because members can come to value belonging over all else, an internal pressure to conform may arise, causing some members to modify their behavior to adhere to group norms. Members may become conflict avoidant, focusing more on trying to please each other so as not to be ostracized. In some cases, members might censor themselves to maintain the party line. As such, there is a superficial sense of harmony and less diversity of thought. Having less tolerance for deviants, who threaten the group's static identity, cohesive groups will often excommunicate members who dare to disagree. Members attempting to make a change may even be criticized or undermined by other members, who perceive this as a threat to the status quo. The painful possibility of being marginalized can keep many members in line with the majority.

The more strongly members identify with the group, the easier it is to see outsiders as inferior, or enemies in extreme cases, which can lead to increased insularity. This form of prejudice can have a downward spiral effect. Not only is the group not getting corrective feedback from within its own confines, it is also closing itself off from input and a cross-fertilization of ideas from the outside. In such an environment, groups can easily adopt extreme ideas that will not be challenged. Denial increases as problems are ignored and failures are blamed on external factors. With limited, often biased, information and no internal or external opposition, groups like these can make disastrous decisions. **Groupthink** is a group pressure phenomenon that increases the risk of the group making flawed decisions by allowing reductions in mental efficiency, reality testing, and moral judgment. Groupthink is most common in highly cohesive groups.[5]

groupthink

A tendency to avoid a critical evaluation of ideas the group favors.

Cohesive groups can go awry in much milder ways. For example, group members can value their social interactions so much that they have fun together but spend little time on accomplishing their assigned task. Or a group's goal may begin to diverge from the larger organization's goal and those trying to uphold the organization's goal may be ostracized (e.g., teasing the class "brain" for doing well in school).

In addition, research shows that cohesion leads to acceptance of group norms.[6] Groups with high task commitment do well, but imagine a group where the norms are to work as little as possible? As you might imagine, these groups get little accomplished and can actually work together against the organization's goals.

FIGURE 9.4

Groups with high cohesion and high task commitment tend to be the most effective.

	Low task commitment	High task commitment
Low group cohesion	Low performance	Performance ranges depending on a number of factors
High group cohesion	Low performance	High performance

1.5 Social Loafing

Social loafing refers to the tendency of individuals to put in less effort when working in a group context. This phenomenon, also known as the Ringelmann effect, was first noted by French agricultural engineer Max Ringelmann in 1913. In one study, he had people pull on a rope individually and in groups. He found that as the number of people pulling increased, the group's total pulling force was less than the individual efforts had been when measured alone.[7]

social loafing

The tendency of individuals to put in less effort when working in a group context.

Why do people work less hard when they are working with other people? Observations show that as the size of the group grows, this effect becomes larger as well.[8] The social loafing tendency is less a matter of being lazy and more a matter of perceiving that one will receive neither one's fair share of rewards if the group is successful nor blame if the group fails. Rationales for this behavior include, "My own effort will have little effect on the outcome," "Others aren't pulling their weight, so why should I?" or "I don't have much to contribute, but no one will notice anyway." This is a consistent effect across a great number of group tasks and countries.[9] Research also shows that perceptions of fairness are related to less social loafing.[10] Therefore, teams that are deemed as more fair should also see less social loafing.

OB Toolbox: Tips for Preventing Social Loafing in Your Group

When designing a group project, here are some considerations to keep in mind:

- *Carefully choose the number of individuals you need to get the task done.* The likelihood of social loafing increases as group size increases (especially if the group consists of 10 or more people), because it is easier for people to feel unneeded or inadequate, and it is easier for them to "hide" in a larger group.

- *Clearly define each member's tasks in front of the entire group.* If you assign a task to the entire group, social loafing is more likely. For example, instead of stating, "By Monday, let's find several articles on the topic of stress," you can set the goal of "By Monday, each of us will be responsible for finding five articles on the topic of stress." When individuals have specific goals, they become more accountable for their performance.
- *Design and communicate to the entire group a system for evaluating each person's contribution.* You may have a midterm feedback session in which each member gives feedback to every other member. This would increase the sense of accountability individuals have. You may even want to discuss the principle of social loafing in order to discourage it.
- *Build a cohesive group.* When group members develop strong relational bonds, they are more committed to each other and the success of the group, and they are therefore more likely to pull their own weight.
- *Assign tasks that are highly engaging and inherently rewarding.* Design challenging, unique, and varied activities that will have a significant impact on the individuals themselves, the organization, or the external environment. For example, one group member may be responsible for crafting a new incentive-pay system through which employees can direct some of their bonus to their favorite nonprofits.
- *Make sure individuals feel that they are needed.* If the group ignores a member's contributions because these contributions do not meet the group's performance standards, members will feel discouraged and are unlikely to contribute in the future. Make sure that everyone feels included and needed by the group.

1.6 Collective Efficacy

collective efficacy

A group's perception of its ability to successfully perform well.

Collective efficacy refers to a group's perception of its ability to successfully perform well.[11] Collective efficacy is influenced by a number of factors, including watching others ("that group did it and we're better than them"), verbal persuasion ("we can do this"), and how a person feels ("this is a good group"). Research shows that a group's collective efficacy is related to its performance.[12] In addition, this relationship is higher when task interdependence (the degree an individual's task is linked to someone else's work) is high rather than low.

KEY TAKEAWAY

Groups may be either formal or informal. Groups go through developmental stages much like individuals do. The forming-storming-norming-performing-adjourning model is useful in prescribing stages that groups should pay attention to as they develop. The punctuated-equilibrium model of group development argues that groups often move forward during bursts of change after long periods without change. Groups that are similar, stable, small, supportive, and satisfied tend to be more cohesive than groups that are not. Cohesion can help support group performance if the group values task completion. Too much cohesion can also be a concern for groups. Social loafing increases as groups become larger. When collective efficacy is high, groups tend to perform better.

EXERCISES

1. If you believe the punctuated-equilibrium model is true about groups, how can you use this knowledge to help your own group?
2. Think about the most cohesive group you have ever been in. How did it compare in terms of similarity, stability, size, support, and satisfaction?
3. Why do you think social loafing occurs within groups?
4. What can be done to combat social loafing?
5. Have you seen instances of collective efficacy helping or hurting a team? Please explain your answer.

2. UNDERSTANDING TEAM DESIGN CHARACTERISTICS

LEARNING OBJECTIVES

1. Understand the difference between groups and teams.
2. Understand the factors leading to the rise in the use of teams.
3. Understand how tasks and roles affect teams.
4. Identify different types of teams.
5. Identify team design considerations.

Effective teams give companies a significant competitive advantage. In a high-functioning team, the sum is truly greater than the parts. Team members not only benefit from each other's diverse experiences and perspectives but also stimulate each other's creativity. Plus, for many people, working in a team can be more fun than working alone.

2.1 Differences Between Groups and Teams

Organizations consist of groups of people. What exactly is the difference between a group and a team? A group is a collection of individuals. Within an organization, groups might consist of project-related groups such as a product group or division, or they can encompass an entire store or branch of a company. The performance of a group consists of the inputs of the group minus any process losses, such as the quality of a product, ramp-up time to production, or the sales for a given month. **Process loss** is any aspect of group interaction that inhibits group functioning.

process loss

Any aspect of group interaction that inhibits group functioning.

Why do we say *group* instead of *team*? A collection of people is not a team, though they may learn to function in that way. A **team** is a cohesive coalition of people working together to achieve mutual goals. Being on a team does not equate to a total suppression of personal agendas, but it does require a commitment to the vision and involves each individual working toward accomplishing the team's objective. Teams differ from other types of groups in that members are focused on a joint goal or product, such as a presentation, discussing a topic, writing a report, creating a new design or prototype, or winning a team Olympic medal. Moreover, teams also tend to be defined by their relatively smaller size. For example, according to one definition, "A team is a *small* number of people with complementary skills who are committed to a common purpose, performance goals, and approach for which they are mutually accountable."[13]

team

A cohesive coalition of people working together to achieve mutual goals.

The purpose of assembling a team is to accomplish larger, more complex goals than what would be possible for an individual working alone or even the simple sum of several individuals' working independently. Teamwork is also needed in cases in which multiple skills are tapped or where buy-in is required from several individuals. Teams can, but do not always, provide improved performance. Working together to further a team agenda seems to increase mutual cooperation between what are often competing factions. The aim and purpose of a team is to perform, get results, and achieve victory in the workplace. The best managers are those who can gather together a group of individuals and mold them into an effective team.

The key properties of a true team include collaborative action in which, along with a common goal, teams have collaborative tasks. Conversely, in a group, individuals are responsible only for their own area. They also share the rewards of strong team performance with their compensation based on shared outcomes. Compensation of individuals must be based primarily on a shared outcome, not individual performance. Members are also willing to sacrifice for the common good, in which individuals give up scarce resources for the common good instead of competing for those resources. For example, in soccer and basketball teams, the individuals actively help each other, forgo their own chance to score by passing the ball, and win or lose collectively as a team.

The early 1990s saw a dramatic rise in the use of teams within organizations, along with dramatic results such as the Miller Brewing Company increasing productivity 30% in the plants that used self-directed teams compared to those that used the traditional organization. This same method allowed Texas Instruments Inc. in Malaysia to reduce defects from 100 parts per million to 20 parts per million. In addition, Westinghouse Electric Corporation reduced its cycle time from 12 to 2 weeks and Harris Corporation was able to achieve an 18% reduction in costs.[14] The team method has served countless companies over the years through both quantifiable improvements and more subtle individual worker-related benefits.

Companies like Schneider Electric, maker of Square D circuit breakers, switched to self-directed teams and found that overtime on machines such as the punch-press dropped 70%. Productivity increased because the set-up operators themselves were able to manipulate the work in much more effective ways than a supervisor could dictate.[15] In 2001, clothing retailer Chico's Retailer Services Inc. was looking to grow its business. The company hired Scott Edmonds as president, and 2 years later revenues had almost doubled from $378 million to $760 million. By 2006, revenues were $1.6 billion and Chico's had 9 years of double-digit same-store sales growth. What did Edmonds do to get these results? He created a horizontal organization with high-performance teams that were empowered with decision-making ability and accountability for results.

The use of teams also began to increase because advances in technology have resulted in more complex systems that require contributions from multiple people across the organization. Overall, team-based organizations have more motivation and involvement, and teams can often accomplish more than individuals.[16] It is no wonder organizations are relying on teams more and more.

It is important to keep in mind that teams are not a cure-all for organizations. To determine whether a team is needed, organizations should consider whether a variety of knowledge, skills, and abilities are needed, whether ideas and feedback are needed from different groups within the organization, how interdependent the tasks are, if wide cooperation is needed to get things done, and whether the organization would benefit from shared goals.[17] If the answer to these questions is yes, then a team or teams might make sense. For example, research shows that the more team members perceive that outcomes are interdependent, the better they share information and the better they perform.[18] Let's take a closer look at the different team characteristics, types of teams companies use, and how to design effective teams.

FIGURE 9.5

Teams are only as good as their weakest link. While Michael Phelps has been dubbed "the world's greatest swimmer" and received a great deal of personal attention, he could not have achieved his record eight gold medals in one Olympic games without the help of his teammates Aaron Peirsol, Brendan Hansen, and Jason Lezak.

Source: http://simple.wikipedia.org/wiki/Image:Michael_Phelps_with_President_Bush_-_20080811.jpeg.

2.2 Team Tasks

Teams differ in terms of the tasks they are trying to accomplish. Richard Hackman identified three major classes of tasks: production tasks, idea-generation tasks, and problem-solving tasks.[19] **Production tasks** include actually making something, such as a building, product, or a marketing plan. **Idea-generation tasks** deal with creative tasks, such as brainstorming a new direction or creating a new process. **Problem-solving tasks** refer to coming up with plans for actions and making decisions. For example, a team may be charged with coming up with a new marketing slogan, which is an idea-generation task, while another team might be asked to manage an entire line of products, including making decisions about products to produce, managing the production of the product lines, marketing them, and staffing their division. The second team has all three types of tasks to accomplish at different points in time.

production tasks

Tasks that include actually making something such as a building, product, or a marketing plan.

idea-generation tasks

Creative tasks such as brainstorming a new direction or creating a new process.

problem-solving tasks

Refers to coming up with plans for actions and making decisions.

Another key to understanding how tasks are related to teams is to understand their level of task interdependence. **Task interdependence** refers to the degree that team members are dependent on one another to get information, support, or materials from other team members to be effective. Research shows that self-managing teams are most effective when their tasks are highly interdependent.[20] There are three types of task interdependence. **Pooled interdependence** exists when team members may work independently and simply combine their efforts to create the team's output. For example, when students meet to divide the section of a research paper and one person simply puts all the sections together to create one paper, the team is using the pooled interdependence model. However, they might decide that it makes more sense to start with one person writing the introduction of their research paper, then the second person reads what was written by the first person and, drawing from this section, writes about the findings within the paper. Using the findings section, the third person writes the conclusions. If one person's output becomes another person's input, the team would be experiencing **sequential interdependence**. And finally, if the student team decided that in order to create a top-notch research paper they should work together on each phase of the research paper so that their best ideas would be captured at each stage, they would be undertaking **reciprocal interdependence**. Another important type of interdependence that is not specific to the task itself is **outcome interdependence**, in which the rewards that an individual receives depend on the performance of others.

task interdependence

The degree that team members are dependent upon one another to get information, support, or materials from other team members to be effective.

pooled interdependence

When team members may work independently and simply combine their efforts to create the team's output.

sequential interdependence

In a team, when one person's output becomes another person's input.

reciprocal interdependence

Team members working on each task simultaneously.

outcome interdependence

When the rewards that an individual receives depend on the performance of others.

2.3 Team Roles

Robert Sutton points out that the success of U.S. Airways Flight 1549 to land with no fatalities when it crashed into the Hudson River in New York City is a good example of an effective work team.[21] For example, reports show that Captain Chesley Sullenberger took over flying from copilot Jeff Skiles, who had handled the takeoff, but had less experience in the Airbus.[22] This is consistent with the research findings that effective teams divide up tasks so the best people are in the best positions.

Studies show that individuals who are more aware of team roles and the behavior required for each role perform better than individuals who do not. This fact remains true for both student project teams as well as work teams, even after accounting for intelligence and personality.[23] Early research found that teams tend to have two categories of roles consisting of those related to the tasks at hand and those related to the team's functioning. For example, teams that focus only on production at all costs may be successful in the short run, but if they pay no attention to how team members feel about working 70 hours a week, they are likely to experience high turnover.

Based on decades of research on teams, 10 key roles have been identified.[24] Team leadership is effective when leaders are able to adapt the roles they are contributing or asking others to contribute to fit what the team needs given its stage and the tasks at hand.[25] Ineffective leaders might always engage in the same task role behaviors, when what they really need is to focus on social roles, put disagreements aside, and get back to work. While these behaviors can be effective from time to time, if the team doesn't modify its role behaviors as things change, they most likely will not be effective.

FIGURE 9.6

Production tasks include actually making something, such as a team of construction workers creating a new building.

FIGURE 9.7

Teams are based on many roles being carried out, as summarized by the Team Role Typology. These 10 roles include task roles (green), social roles (yellow), and boundary-spanning roles (orange).

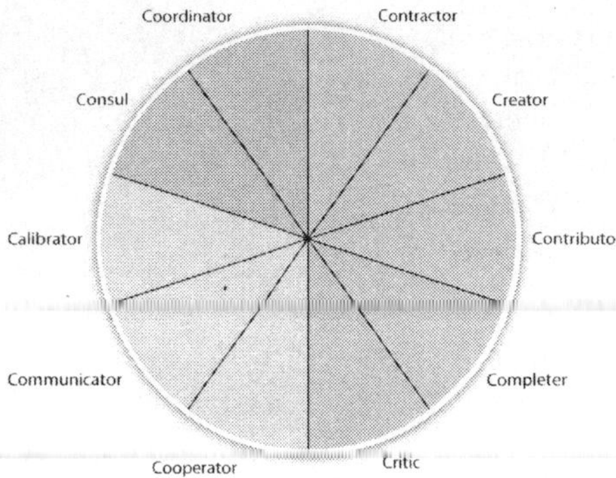

Source: Mumford, T. V., Van Iddekinge, C., Morgeson, F. P., & Campion, M. A. (2008). The team role test: Development and validation of a team role knowledge situational judgment test. Journal of Applied Psychology, 93, 250–267; Mumford, T. V., Campion, M. A., & Morgeson, F. P. (2006). Situational judgments in work teams: A team role typology. In J. A. Weekley and R. E. Ployhart (Eds.), Situational judgment tests: Theory, measurement, and application (pp. 319–344). Mahwah, NJ: Erlbaum.

Task Roles

Five roles make up the task portion of the typology. The contractor role includes behaviors that serve to organize the team's work, including creating team timelines, production schedules, and task sequencing. The creator role deals more with changes in the team's task process structure. For example, reframing the team goals and looking at the context of goals would fall under this role. The contributor role is important, because it brings information and expertise to the team. This role is characterized by sharing knowledge and training with those who have less expertise to strengthen the team. Research shows that teams with highly intelligent members and evenly distributed workloads are more effective than those with uneven workloads.[26] The completer role is also important, as it transforms ideas into action. Behaviors associated with this role include following up on tasks, such as gathering needed background information or summarizing the team's ideas into reports. Finally, the critic role includes "devil's advocate" behaviors that go against the assumptions being made by the team.

Social Roles

Social roles serve to keep the team operating effectively. When the social roles are filled, team members feel more cohesive, and the group is less prone to suffer process losses or biases such as social loafing, groupthink, or a lack of participation from all members. Three roles fall under the umbrella of social roles. The cooperator role includes supporting those with expertise toward the team's goals. This is a proactive role. The communicator role includes behaviors that are targeted at collaboration, such as practicing good listening skills and appropriately using humor to diffuse tense situations. Having a good communicator helps the team to feel more open to sharing ideas. The calibrator role is an important one that serves to keep the team on track in terms of suggesting any needed changes to the team's process. This role includes initiating discussions about potential team problems such as power struggles or other tensions. Similarly, this role may involve settling disagreements or pointing out what is working and what is not in terms of team process.

Boundary-Spanning Roles

The final two goals are related to activities outside the team that help to connect the team to the larger organization.[27] Teams that engage in a greater level of boundary-spanning behaviors increase their team effectiveness.[28] The consul role includes gathering information from the larger organization and informing those within the organization about team activities, goals, and successes. Often the consul role is filled by team managers or leaders. The coordinator role includes interfacing with others within the organization so that the team's efforts are in line with other individuals and teams within the organization.

2.4 Types of Teams

There are several types of temporary teams. In fact, one-third of all teams in the United States are temporary in nature.[29] An example of a temporary team is a **task force** that is asked to address a specific issue or problem until it is resolved. Other teams may be temporary or ongoing, such as **product development teams**. In addition, matrix organizations have **cross-functional teams** in which individuals from different parts of the organization staff the team, which may be temporary or long-standing in nature.

Virtual teams are teams in which members are not located in the same physical place. They may be in different cities, states, or even different countries. Some virtual teams are formed by necessity, such as to take advantage of lower labor costs in different countries with upwards of 8.4 million individuals working virtually in at least one team.[30] Often, virtual teams are formed to take advantage of distributed expertise or time—the needed experts may be living in different cities. A company that sells products around the world, for example, may need technologists who can solve customer problems at any hour of the day or night. It may be difficult to find the caliber of people needed who would be willing to work at 2:00 a.m. on a Saturday, for example. So companies organize virtual technical support teams. BakBone Software Inc., for example, has a 13-member technical support team. All members have degrees in computer science and are divided among offices in California, Maryland, England, and Tokyo. BakBone believes it has been able to hire stronger candidates by drawing from a diverse talent pool and hiring in different geographic regions rather than being limited to one region or time zone.[31]

task force

A type of temporary team which is asked to address a specific issue or problem until it is resolved.

product development teams

Other teams that may be temporary or ongoing.

cross-functional teams

Teams that involve individuals from different parts of the organization staff.

virtual teams

Teams where members are not located in the same physical place.

Despite potential benefits, virtual teams present special management challenges. Managers often think that they have to see team members working in order to believe that work is being done. Because this kind of oversight is impossible in virtual team situations, it is important to devise evaluation schemes that focus on deliverables. Are team members delivering what they said they would? In self-managed teams, are team members producing the results the team decided to measure itself on?

Another special challenge of virtual teams is building trust. Will team members deliver results just as they would in face-to-face teams? Can members trust each other to do what they said they would do? Companies often invest in bringing a virtual team together at least once so members can get to know each other and build trust.[32] In manager-led virtual teams, managers should be held accountable for their team's results and evaluated on their ability as a team leader.

Finally, communication is especially important in virtual teams, be it through e-mail, phone calls, conference calls, or project management tools that help organize work. If individuals in a virtual team are not fully engaged and tend to avoid conflict, team performance can suffer.[33] A wiki is an Internet-based method for many people to collaborate and contribute to a document or discussion. Essentially, the document remains available for team members to access and amend at any time. The most famous example is Wikipedia, which is gaining traction as a way to structure project work globally and get information into the hands of those that need it. Empowered organizations put information into everyone's hands.[34] Research shows that empowered teams are more effective than those that are not empowered.[35]

Top management teams are appointed by the chief executive officer (CEO) and, ideally, reflect the skills and areas that the CEO considers vital for the company. There are no formal rules about top management team design or structure. The top team often includes representatives from functional areas, such as finance, human resources, and marketing, or key geographic areas, such as Europe, Asia, and North America. Depending on the company, other areas may be represented, such as legal counsel or the company's chief technologist. Typical top management team member titles include chief operating officer (COO), chief financial officer (CFO), chief marketing officer (CMO), or chief technology officer (CTO). Because CEOs spend an increasing amount of time outside their companies (e.g., with suppliers, customers, and regulators), the role of the COO has taken on a much higher level of internal operating responsibilities. In most American companies, the CEO also serves as chairman of the board and can have the additional title of president. Companies have top teams to help set the company's vision and strategic direction. Top teams make decisions on new markets, expansions, acquisitions, or divestitures. The top team is also important for its symbolic role: How the top team behaves dictates the organization's culture and priorities by allocating resources and by modeling behaviors that will likely be emulated lower down in the organization. Importantly, the top team is most effective when team composition is diverse—functionally and demographically—and when it can truly operate as a *team*, not just as a *group* of individual executives.[36]

top management teams

Teams appointed by the chief executive officer (CEO) and, ideally, reflect the skills and areas that the CEO considers vital for the company.

Chapter 1 began with the quote that the people make the place, and this holds especially true for members of the top management team. In a study of 15 firms that demonstrated excellence, defined as sustained performance over a 15-year period, leadership researcher Jim Collins noted that those firms attended to people first and strategy second. "They got the right people on the bus, moved the wrong people off the bus, ushered the right people to the right seats—then they figured out where to drive it."[37] The best teams plan for turnover. Succession planning is the process of identifying future members of the top management team. Effective succession planning allows the best top teams to achieve high performance today and create a legacy of high performance for the future.

2.5 Team Leadership and Autonomy

Teams also vary in terms of how they are led. **Traditional manager-led teams** are teams in which the manager serves as the team leader. The manager assigns work to other team members. These types of teams are the most natural to form, with managers having the power to hire and fire team members and being held accountable for the team's results.

traditional manager-led teams

Teams where the manager serves as the team leader.

Self-managed teams are a new form of team that rose in popularity with the Total Quality Movement in the 1980s. Unlike manager-led teams, these teams manage themselves and do not report directly to a supervisor. Instead, team members select their own leader, and they may even take turns in the leadership role. Self-managed teams also have the power to select new team members. As a whole, the team shares responsibility for a significant task, such as assembly of an entire car. The task is ongoing rather than a temporary task such as a charity fund drive for a given year.

self-managed teams

Teams that manage themselves and do not report directly to a supervisor. Instead, team members select their own leader, and they may even take turns in the leadership role.

Organizations began to use self-managed teams as a way to reduce hierarchy by allowing team members to complete tasks and solve problems on their own. The benefits of self-managed teams extend much further. Research has shown that employees in self-managed teams have higher job satisfaction, increased self-esteem, and grow more on the job. The benefits to the organization include increased productivity, increased flexibility, and lower turnover. Self-managed teams can be found at all levels of the organization, and they bring particular benefits to lower level employees by giving them a sense of ownership of their jobs that they may not otherwise have. The increased satisfaction can also reduce absenteeism, because employees do not want to let their team members down.

Typical team goals are improving quality, reducing costs, and meeting deadlines. Teams also have a "stretch" goal—a goal that is difficult to reach but important to the business unit. Many teams also have special project goals. Texas Instruments (TI), a company that makes semiconductors, used self-directed teams to make improvements in work processes.[38] Teams were allowed to set their own goals in conjunction with managers and other teams. TI also added an individual component to the typical team compensation system. This individual component rewarded team members for learning new skills that added to their knowledge. These "knowledge blocks" include topics such as leadership, administration, and problem solving. The team decides what additional skills people might need to help the team meet its objectives. Team members would then take classes and/or otherwise demonstrate their proficiency in that new skill on the job in order to get certification for mastery of the skill. Individuals could then be evaluated based on their contribution to the team and how they are building skills to support the team.

empowered teams

Teams that have the *responsibility* as well as the *authority* to achieve their goals.

self-directed teams

A special form of self-managed teams where members determine who will lead them with no external oversight.

Self-managed teams are **empowered teams**, which means that they have the *responsibility* as well as the *authority* to achieve their goals. Team members have the power to control tasks and processes and to make decisions. Research shows that self-managed teams may be at a higher risk of suffering from negative outcomes due to conflict, so it is important that they are supported with training to help them deal with conflict effectively.[39] Self-managed teams may still have a leader who helps them coordinate with the larger organization.[40] For a product team composed of engineering, production, and marketing employees, being empowered means that the team can decide everything about a product's appearance, production, and cost without having to get permission or sign-off from higher management. As a result, empowered teams can more effectively meet tighter deadlines. At AT&T Inc., for example, the model-4200 phone team cut development time in half while lowering costs and improving quality by using the empowered team approach.[41] A special form of self-managed teams are **self-directed teams**, which also determine who will lead them with no external oversight.

FIGURE 9.8

Team leadership is a major determinant of how autonomous a team can be.

Traditionally managed teams	Self-managed teams	Self-directed team
• Leader resides outside the team	• The team manages itself but still has a team leader	• The team makes all decisions internally about leadership and how work is done
• Potential for low autonomy	• Potential for low, medium, or high autonomy	• Potential for high autonomy

2.6 Designing Effective Teams

Designing an effective team means making decisions about team composition (who should be on the team), team size (the optimal number of people on the team), and team diversity (should team members be of similar background, such as all engineers, or of different backgrounds). Answering these questions will depend, to a large extent, on the type of task that the team will be performing. Teams can be charged with a variety of tasks, from problem solving to generating creative and innovative ideas to managing the daily operations of a manufacturing plant.

Who Are the Best Individuals for the Team?

A key consideration when forming a team is to ensure that all the team members are qualified for the roles they will fill for the team. This process often entails understanding the knowledge, skills, and abilities (KSAs) of team members as well as the personality traits needed before starting the selection process.[42] When talking to potential team members, be sure to communicate the job requirements and norms of the team. To the degree that this is not possible, such as when already existing groups are utilized, think of ways to train the team members as much as possible to help ensure success. In addition to task knowledge, research has shown that individuals who understand the concepts covered in this chapter and in this book, such as conflict resolution, motivation, planning, and leadership, actually perform better on their jobs. This finding holds for a variety of jobs, including being an officer in the U.S. Air Force, an employee at a pulp mill, or a team member at a box manufacturing plant.[43]

How Large Should My Team Be?

Interestingly, research has shown that regardless of team size, the most active team member speaks 43% of the time. The difference is that the team member who participates the least in a 3-person team is still active 23% of the time versus only 3% in a 10-person team.[44] When deciding team size, a good rule of thumb is a size of two to twenty members. Research shows that groups with more than 20 members have less cooperation.[45] The majority of teams have 10 members or less, because the larger the team, the harder it is to coordinate and interact as a team. With fewer individuals, team members are more able to work through differences and agree on a common plan of action. They have a clearer understanding of others' roles and greater accountability to fulfill their roles (remember social loafing?). Some tasks, however, require larger team sizes because of the need for diverse skills or because of the complexity of the task. In those cases, the best solution is to create subteams in which one member from each subteam is a member of a larger coordinating team. The relationship between team size and performance seems to greatly depend on the level of task interdependence, with some studies finding larger teams outproducing smaller teams and other studies finding just the opposite.[46] The bottom line is that team size should be matched to the goals of the team.

FIGURE 9.9

The ideal size for a team depends on the task at hand. Groups larger than 10 members tend to be harder to coordinate and often break into subteams to accomplish the work at hand.

© 2010 Jupiterimages Corporation

How Diverse Should My Team Be?

Team composition and team diversity often go hand in hand. Teams whose members have complementary skills are often more successful, because members can see each other's blind spots. One team member's strengths can compensate for another's weaknesses.[47] For example, consider the challenge that companies face when trying to forecast future sales of a given product. Workers who are educated as forecasters have the analytic skills needed for forecasting, but these workers often lack critical information about customers. Salespeople, in contrast, regularly communicate with customers, which means they're in the know about upcoming customer decisions. But salespeople often lack the analytic skills, discipline, or desire to enter this knowledge into spreadsheets and software that will help a company forecast future sales. Putting forecasters and salespeople together on a team tasked with determining the most accurate product forecast each quarter makes the best use of each member's skills and expertise.

Diversity in team composition can help teams come up with more creative and effective solutions. Research shows that teams that believe in the value of diversity performed better than teams that do not.[48] The more diverse a team is in terms of expertise, gender, age, and background, the more ability the group has to avoid the problems of groupthink.[49] For example, different educational levels for team members were related to more creativity in R&D teams and faster time to market for new products.[50] Members will be more inclined to make different kinds of mistakes, which means that they'll be able to catch and correct those mistakes.

KEY TAKEAWAY

Groups and teams are not the same thing. Organizations have moved toward the extensive use of teams within organizations. The tasks a team is charged with accomplishing affect how they perform. In general, task interdependence works well for self-managing teams. Team roles consist of task, social, and boundary-spanning roles. Different types of teams include task forces, product development teams, cross-functional teams, and top management teams. Team leadership and autonomy varies, depending on whether the team is traditionally managed, self-managed, or self-directed. Teams are most effective when they comprise members with the right skills for the tasks at hand, are not too large, and contain diversity across team members.

EXERCISES

1. Think of the last team you were in. Did the task you were asked to do affect the team? Why or why not?
2. Which of the 10 work roles do you normally take in a team? How difficult or easy do you think it would be for you to take on a different role?
3. Have you ever worked in a virtual team? If so, what were the challenges and advantages of working virtually?
4. How large do you think teams should be and why?

3. MANAGEMENT OF TEAMS

LEARNING OBJECTIVES

1. **Understand how to create team norms, roles, and expectations.**
2. **Identify keys to running effective team meetings.**

3.1 Establishing Team Norms

Team Norms

norms

Shared expectations about how things operate within a group or team.

Norms are shared expectations about how things operate within a group or team. Just as new employees learn to understand and share the assumptions, norms, and values that are part of an organization's culture, they also must learn the norms of their immediate team. This understanding helps teams be more cohesive and perform better. Norms are a powerful way of ensuring coordination within a team. For example, is it acceptable to be late to meetings? How prepared are you supposed to be at the meetings? Is it acceptable to criticize someone else's work? These norms are shaped early during the life of a team and affect whether the team is productive, cohesive, and successful.

Square Wheels Exercise and Group Discussion

Sometimes it can be challenging to start a conversation around team ground rules and performance. The following exercise can be used to get individuals talking about what works and what doesn't work in teams they've worked in and how your team can be designed most effectively.

Used with permission. © Performance Management Company, 1992–2004. Square Wheels® is a registered servicemark of PMC.

What is happening in this picture represents how many organizations seem to operate. On a piece of paper have everyone in your team write on this form and identify as many of the key issues and opportunities for improvement as you can. Following this, have a conversation around what this illustration might mean for your own team.

Team Contracts

Scientific research, as well as experience working with thousands of teams, show that teams that are able to articulate and agree on established ground rules, goals, and roles and develop a **team contract** around these standards are better equipped to face challenges that may arise within the team.[51] Having a team contract does not necessarily mean that the team will be successful, but it can serve as a road map when the team veers off course. The following questions can help to create a meaningful team contract:

team contract

Agreements on established ground rules, goals, and roles.

- *Team Values and Goals*
    - What are our shared team values?
    - What is our team goal?
- *Team Roles and Leadership*
    - Who does what within this team? (Who takes notes at the meeting? Who sets the agenda? Who assigns tasks? Who runs the meetings?)
    - Does the team have a formal leader?
    - If so, what are his or her roles?
- *Team Decision Making*
    - How are minor decisions made?
    - How are major decisions made?
- *Team Communication*
    - Who do you contact if you cannot make a meeting?
    - Who communicates with whom?
    - How often will the team meet?
- *Team Performance*
    - What constitutes good team performance?
    - What if a team member tries hard but does not seem to be producing quality work?
    - How will poor attendance/work quality be dealt with?

3.2 Team Meetings

Anyone who has been involved in a team knows it involves team meetings. While few individuals relish the idea of team meetings, they serve an important function in terms of information sharing and decision making. They also serve an important social function and can help to build team cohesion and a task function in terms of coordination. Unfortunately, we've all attended meetings that were a waste of time and little happened that couldn't have been accomplished by reading an e-mail in 5 minutes. To run effective meetings, it helps to think of meetings in terms of three sequential steps.[52]

Before the Meeting

Much of the effectiveness of a meeting is determined before the team gathers. There are three key things you can do to ensure the team members get the most out of their meeting.

Is a meeting needed? Leaders should do a number of things prior to the meeting to help make it effective. The first thing is to be sure a meeting is even needed. If the meeting is primarily informational in nature, ask yourself if it is imperative that the group fully understands the information and if future decisions will be built upon this information. If so, a meeting may be needed. If not, perhaps simply communicating with everyone in a written format will save valuable time. Similarly, decision-making meetings make the most sense when the problem is complex and important, there are questions of fairness to be resolved, and commitment is needed moving forward.

Create and distribute an agenda. An agenda is important in helping to inform those invited about the purpose of the meeting. It also helps organize the flow of the meeting and keep the team on track.

Send a reminder prior to the meeting. Reminding everyone of the purpose, time, and location of the meeting helps everyone prepare themselves. Anyone who has attended a team meeting only to find there is no reason to meet because members haven't completed their agreed-upon tasks knows that, as a result, team performance or morale can be negatively impacted. Follow up to make sure everyone is prepared. As a team member, inform others immediately if you will not be ready with your tasks so that they can determine whether the meeting should be postponed.

During the Meeting

During the meeting there are several things you can do to make sure the team starts and keeps on track.

Start the meeting on time. Waiting for members who are running late only punishes those who are on time and reinforces the idea that it's OK to be late. Starting the meeting promptly sends an important signal that you are respectful of everyone's time.

Follow the meeting agenda. Veering off agenda communicates to members that the agenda is not important. It also makes it difficult for others to keep track of where you are in the meeting.

Manage group dynamics for full participation. As you've seen in this chapter, a number of group dynamics can limit a team's functioning. Be on the lookout for full participation and engagement from all team members, as well as any potential problems such as social loafing, group conflict, or groupthink.

FIGURE 9.11

Summarize the meeting with action items. Be sure to clarify team member roles moving forward. If individuals' tasks are not clear, chances are that role confusion will arise later. There should be clear notes from the meeting regarding who is responsible for each action item and the time frames associated with next steps.

End the meeting on time. This is vitality important, as it shows that you respect everyone's time and are organized. If another meeting is needed to follow up, schedule it later, but don't let the meeting run over.

After the Meeting

Follow up on action items. During the meeting, participants probably generated several action items. It is likely that you'll need to follow up on the action items of others.

FIGURE 9.12

Conducting meetings standing up saves time yet keeps information flowing across the team.[53] This technique is used by Johnson & Johnson Services Inc., Ritz-Carlton Company LLC, ThoughtWorks Inc., Agile Software, and Corning Inc.

Source: Photo used by permission of Jason Yip.

KEY TAKEAWAY

Much like group development, team socialization takes place over the life of the team. The stages move from evaluation to commitment to role transition. Team norms are important for the team process and help to establish who is doing what for the team and how the team will function. Creating a team contract helps with this process. Keys to address in a team contract are team values and goals, team roles and leadership, team decision making, team communication expectations, and how team performance is characterized. Team meetings can help a team coordinate and share information. Effective meetings include preparation, management during the meeting, and follow-up on action items generated in the meeting.

EXERCISES

1. Have the norms for most of the teams you have belonged to been formal or informal? How do you think that has affected these teams?
2. Have you ever been involved in creating a team contract? Explain how you think that may have influenced how the team functioned.
3. Should the person requesting a meeting always prepare a meeting agenda? Why or why not?
4. Do you think conducting team meetings standing up is a good idea? Why or why not?

4. BARRIERS TO EFFECTIVE TEAMS

LEARNING OBJECTIVES

1. **Recognize common barriers to effective teams.**
2. **Learn how to address some of the most common barriers and maintain group effectiveness.**

Problems can arise in any team that will hurt the team's effectiveness. Here are some common problems faced by teams and how to deal with them.

4.1 Common Problems Faced by Teams

Challenges of Knowing Where to Begin

At the start of a project, team members may be at a loss as to how to begin. Also, they may have reached the end of a task but are unable to move on to the next step or put the task to rest. Floundering often results from a lack of clear goals, so the remedy is to go back to the team's mission or plan and make sure that it is clear to everyone. Team leaders can help move the team past floundering by asking, "What is holding us up? Do we need more data? Do we need assurances or support? Does anyone feel that we've missed something important?"

Dominating Team Members

Some team members may have a dominating personality that encroaches on the participation or air time of others. This overbearing behavior may hurt the team morale or the momentum of the team. A good way to overcome this barrier is to design a team evaluation to include a "balance of participation" in meetings. Knowing that fair and equitable participation by all will affect the team's performance evaluation will help team members limit domination by one member and encourage participation from all members, even shy or reluctant ones. Team members can say, "We've heard from Mary on this issue, so let's hear from others about their ideas."

Poor Performance of Team Members

Research shows that teams deal with poor performers in different ways, depending on members' perceptions of the reasons for poor performance.[54] In situations in which the poor performer is perceived as lacking in ability, teams are more likely to train the member. When members perceive the individual as simply being low on motivation, they are more likely to try to motivate or reject the poor performer. Keep in mind that justice is an important part of keeping individuals working hard for the team.[55] Be sure that poor performers are dealt with in a way that is deemed fair by all the team members.

Poorly Managed Team Conflict

Disagreements among team members are normal and should be expected. Healthy teams raise issues and discuss differing points of view, because that will ultimately help the team reach stronger, more well-reasoned decisions. Unfortunately, sometimes disagreements arise owing to personality issues or feuds that predated a team's formation. Ideally, teams should be designed to avoid bringing adversaries together on the same team. If that is not possible, the next best solution is to have adversaries discuss their issues privately, so the team's progress is not disrupted. The team leader or other team member can offer to facilitate the discussion. One way to make a discussion between conflicting parties meaningful is to form a behavioral contract between the two parties. That is, if one party agrees to do X, then the other will agree to do Y.[56]

KEY TAKEAWAY

Barriers to effective teams include the challenges of knowing where to begin, dominating team members, the poor performance of team members, and poorly managed team conflict.

EXERCISES

1. How could some of the things discussed in "Understanding Team Design Characteristics" help to avoid the common barriers to team effectiveness?
2. Have you ever been involved in a team where dominating team members hurt the team's performance? Share what happened and how the team dealt with this.

5. THE ROLE OF ETHICS AND NATIONAL CULTURE

LEARNING OBJECTIVES

1. Consider the role of ethics and teams.
2. Consider teams around the globe.

5.1 Ethics and Teams

The use of teams, especially self-managing teams, has been seen as a way to overcome the negatives of bureaucracy and hierarchical control. Giving teams the authority and responsibility to make their own decisions seems to empower individuals and the team alike by distributing power more equitably. Interestingly, research by James Barker shows that sometimes replacing a hierarchy with self-managing teams can actually increase control over individual workers and constrain members more powerfully than a hierarchical system.[57] Studying a small manufacturing company that switched to self-managing teams, Barker interviewed team members and found an unexpected result. Team members felt more closely watched under self-managing teams than under the old system. Ronald, a technical worker, said, "I don't have to sit there and look for the boss to be around; and if the boss is not around, I can sit there and talk to my neighbor or do what I want. Now the whole team is around me and the whole team is observing what I'm doing." Ronald said that while his old supervisor might tolerate someone coming in a few minutes late, his team had adopted a "no tolerance" policy on tardiness, and members carefully monitored their own behaviors.

Team pressure can harm a company as well. Consider a sales team whose motto of "sales above all" hurts the ability of the company to gain loyal customers.[58] The sales team feels pressure to lie to customers to make sales. Their misrepresentations and unethical behavior gets them the quick sale but curtails their ability to get future sales from repeat customers.

5.2 Teams Around the Globe

People from different cultures often have different beliefs, norms, and ways of viewing the world. These kinds of country-by-country differences have been studied by the GLOBE Project, in which 170 researchers collected and analyzed data on cultural values, practices, and leadership attributes from over 17,000 managers in 62 societal cultures.[59] GLOBE identified nine dimensions of culture. One of the identified dimensions is a measure called **collectivism**. Collectivism focuses on the degree to which the society reinforces collective over individual achievement. Collectivist societies value interpersonal relationships over individual achievement. Societies that rank high on collectivism show more close ties between individuals. The United States and Australia rank low on the collectivism dimension, whereas countries such as Mexico and Taiwan rank high on that dimension. High collectivism manifests itself in close, long-term commitment to the member group. In a collectivist culture, loyalty is paramount and overrides most other societal rules and regulations. The society fosters strong relationships in which everyone takes responsibility for fellow members of their group.

Harrison, McKinnon, Wu, and Chow explored the cultural factors that may influence how well employees adapt to fluid work groups.[60] The researchers studied groups in Taiwan and Australia. Taiwan ranks high on collectivism, while Australia ranks low. The results: Australian managers reported that employees adapted more readily to working in different teams, working under different leaders, and taking on leadership of project teams than the middle managers in Taiwan reported. The two samples were matched in terms of the functional background of the managers, size and industries of the firms, and local firms. These additional controls provided greater confidence in attributing the observed differences to cultural values.

In other research, researchers analyzed the evaluation of team member behavior by part-time MBA students in the United States and Mexico.[61] The United States ranks low on collectivism while Mexico ranks high. They found that collectivism (measured at the individual level) had a positive relationship to the evaluation of a teammate. Furthermore, the evaluation was higher for in-group members among the Mexican respondents than among the U.S. respondents.

Power distance is another culture dimension. People in high power distance countries expect unequal power distribution and greater stratification, whether that stratification is economic, social, or political. An individual in a position of authority in these countries expects (and receives) obedience. Decision making is hierarchical, with limited participation and communication. Countries with a low power distance rating, such as Australia, value cooperative interaction across power levels. Individuals stress equality and opportunity for everyone.

Another study by researchers compared national differences in teamwork metaphors used by employees in six multinational corporations in four countries: the United States, France, Puerto Rico, and the Philippines.[62] They identified five metaphors: military, family, sports, associates, and community. Results showed national variation in the use of the five metaphors. Specifically, countries high in individualism (United States and France) tended to use the sports or associates metaphors, while countries high in power distance (Philippines and Puerto Rico) tended to use the military or family metaphors. Further, power distance and collectivistic values were negatively associated with the use of teamwork metaphors that emphasized clear roles and broad scope. These results suggest that the meaning of teamwork may differ across cultures and, in turn, imply potential differences in team norms and team-member behaviors.

KEY TAKEAWAY

Self managing teams shift the role of control from management to the team itself. This can be highly effective, but if team members put too much pressure on one another, problems can arise. It is also important to make sure teams work toward organizational goals as well as specific team-level goals. Teams around the globe vary in terms of collectivism and power distance. These differences can affect how teams operate in countries around the world.

EXERCISES

1. Have you ever felt pressure from team members to do something you didn't want to do? If so, how did you handle it?
2. In what ways do you think culture can affect a team?

6. CONCLUSION

Research shows that group formation is a beneficial but highly dynamic process. The life cycle of teams can often closely resemble various stages in individual development. In order to maintain group effectiveness, individuals should be aware of key stages as well as methods to avoid becoming stuck along the way. Good leadership skills combined with knowledge of group development will help any group perform at its peak level. Teams, though similar, are different from groups in both scope and composition. Groups are often small collections of individuals with various skill sets that combine to address a specific issue, whereas teams can be much larger and often consist of people with overlapping abilities working toward a common goal.

Many issues that can plague groups can also hinder the efficacy of a team. Problems such as social loafing or groupthink can be avoided by paying careful attention to team member differences and providing clear definitions for roles, expectancy, measurement, and rewards. Because many tasks in today's world have become so complex, groups and teams have become an essential component of an organization's success. The success of the team/group rests within the successful management of its members and making sure all aspects of work are fair for each member.

7. EXERCISES

ETHICAL DILEMMA

Imagine you work at an ad agency and your team is charged with coming up with the name for BeautyBees's latest perfume. You have been with the company for 6 months. The branding team has been brainstorming for the last 2 hours, filling up pages and pages of the flipchart with innovative, imaginative names. Feeling daunted by how loudly, quickly, and assertively branding team members are shouting out suggestions, you decide to sit this one out, even though you have some ideas. You are uncomfortable shouting over everyone else and you reason that the group would discount your input anyway. Plus, everyone else is generating so many good names that the group is bound to succeed regardless of your input.

What Do You Think?

1. Is your lack of participation ethical? Why or why not?
2. What are the implications of speaking up or not speaking up?
3. Would you change your answer if you'd been with the company for 10 years instead of 6 months?

ENDNOTES

1. Tuckman, B. (1965). Developmental sequence in small groups. *Psychological Bulletin, 63*, 384–399.
2. Karriker, J. H. (2005). Cyclical group development and interaction-based leadership emergence in autonomous teams: An integrated model. *Journal of Leadership & Organizational Studies, 11*, 54–64.
3. Gersick, C. J. G. (1991). Revolutionary change theories: A multilevel exploration of the punctuated equilibrium paradigm. *Academy of Management Review, 16*, 10–36.
4. Beal, D. J., Cohen, R. R., Burke, M. J., & McLendon, C. L. (2003). Cohesion and performance in groups: A meta-analytic clarification of construct relations. *Journal of Applied Psychology, 88*, 989–1004; Evans, C. R., & Dion, K. L. (1991). Group cohesion and performance: A meta-analysis. *Small Group Research, 22*, 175–186.
5. Janis, I. L. (1972). *Victims of Groupthink*. New York: Houghton Mifflin.
6. Goodman, P. S., Ravlin, E., & Schminke, M. (1987). Understanding groups in organizations. *Research in Organizational Behavior, 9*, 121–173.
7. Karau, S. J., & Williams, K. D. (1993). Social loafing: A meta-analytic review and theoretical integration. *Journal of Personality and Social Psychology, 65*, 681–706.
8. Karau, S. J., & Williams, K. D. (1993). Social loafing: A meta-analytic review and theoretical integration. *Journal of Personality and Social Psychology, 65*, 681–706.
9. Gabrenya, W. L., Latane, B., & Wang, Y. (1983). Social loafing in cross-cultural perspective. *Journal of Cross-Cultural Perspective, 14*, 368–384; Harkins, S., & Petty, R. E. (1982). Effects of task difficulty and task uniqueness on social loafing. *Journal of Personality and Social Psychology, 43*, 1214–1229; Taylor, D. W., & Faust, W. L. (1952). Twenty questions: Efficiency of problem-solving as a function of the size of the group. *Journal of Experimental Psychology, 44*, 360–363; Ziller, R. C. (1957). Four techniques of group decision-making under uncertainty. *Journal of Applied Psychology, 41*, 384–388.
10. Price, K. H., Harrison, D. A., & Gavin, J. H. (2006). Withholding inputs in team contexts: Member composition, interaction processes, evaluation structure, and social loafing. *Journal of Applied Psychology, 91*, 1375–1384.
11. Bandura, A. (1997). *Self-efficacy: The exercise of control*. San Francisco: Jossey-Bass.
12. Gully, S. M., Incalcaterra, K. A., Joshi, A., & Beaubien, J. M. (2002). A meta-analysis of team-efficacy, potency, and performance: Interdependence and level of analysis as moderators of observed relationships. *Journal of Applied Psychology, 87*, 819–832; Porter, C. O. L. H. (2005). Goal orientation: Effects on backing up behavior, performance, efficacy, and commitment in teams. *Journal of Applied Psychology, 90*, 811–818; Tasa, K., Taggar, S., & Seijts, G. H. (2007). The development of collective efficacy in teams: A multilevel and longitudinal perspective. *Journal of Applied Psychology, 92*, 17–27.
13. Katzenbach, J. R., & Smith, D. K. (1993). *The wisdom of teams: Creating the high-performance organization*. Boston: Harvard Business School.
14. Welins, R., Byham, W., & Dixon, G. (1994). *Inside teams*. San Francisco: Jossey-Bass.
15. Moskal, B. (1988, June 20). Supervisors, begone! *Industry Week Newsletter*.
16. Cannon-Bowers, J. A., & Salas, E. (2001, February). Team effectiveness and competencies. In W. Karwowski (Ed.), *International encyclopedia of ergonomics and human factors* (p. 1383). Boca Raton, FL: CRC Press.
17. Rees, F. (1997). *Teamwork from start to finish*. San Francisco: Jossey-Bass.
18. De Dreu, C. K. W. (2007). Cooperative outcome interdependence, task reflexivity, and team effectiveness: A motivated information processing perspective. *Journal of Applied Psychology, 92*, 628–638.
19. Hackman, J. R. (1976). Group influences on individuals. In M. D. Dunnette (Ed.), *Handbook of industrial and organizational psychology*. Chicago, IL: Rand-McNally.
20. Langfred, C. W. (2005). Autonomy and performance in teams: The multilevel moderating effect of task interdependence. *Journal of Management, 31*, 513–529; Liden, R. C., Wayne, S. J., & Bradway, L. K. (1997). Task interdependence as a moderator of the relation between group control and performance. *Human Relations, 50*, 169–181.
21. Sutton, R. (2009, January 18). Miracle on the Hudson: The group dynamics angle. *Work matters*. Retrieved January 19, 2009, from http://bobsutton.typepad.com/my_weblog/2009/01/miracle-on-the-hudson-the-group-dynamics-angle.html.
22. Caruso, D. B. (2009, January 18). 5 white-knuckled minutes aboard Flight 1549. *Yahoo! News*. Retrieved January 19, 2009, from http://news.yahoo.com/s/ap/20090118/ap_on_re_us/plane_splashdown_cockpit_drama.
23. Mumford, T. V., Van Iddekinge, C. H., Morgeson, F. P., & Campion, M. A. (2008). The Team Role Test: Development and validation of a team role knowledge situational judgment test. *Journal of Applied Psychology, 93*, 250–267.
24. Bales, R. F. (1950). *Interaction process analysis: A method for the study of small groups*. Cambridge, MA: Addison-Wesley; Benne, K. D., & Sheats, P. (1948). Functional roles of group members. *Journal of Social Issues, 4*, 41–49; Belbin, R. M. (1993). *Management teams: Why they succeed or fail*. Oxford, England: Butterworth-Heinemann.
25. Kozlowski, S. W. J., Gully, S. M., McHugh, P. P., Salas, E., & Cannon-Bowers, J. A. (1996). A dynamic theory of leadership and team effectiveness: Developmental and task contingent roles. In G. Ferris (Ed.), *Research in personnel and human resource management, 14* (pp. 253–305). Greenwich, CT: JAI Press; Kozlowski, S. W. J., Gully, S. M., Salas, E., & Cannon-Bowers, J. A. (1996). Team leadership and development: Theory, principles, and guidelines for training leaders and teams. In M. M. Beyerlein, D. A. Johnson, & S. T. Beyerlein (Eds.), *Advances in interdisciplinary studies of work teams, vol. 3* (pp. 253–291). Greenwich, CT: JAI Press.
26. Ellis, A. P. J., Hollenbeck, J. R., Ilgen, D. R., Porter, C. O. L. H., West, B. J., & Moon, H. (2003). Team learning: Collectively connecting the dots. *Journal of Applied Psychology, 88*, 821–835.
27. Anacona, D. G. (1990). Outward bound: Strategies for team survival in an organization. *Academy of Management Journal, 33*, 334–365; Anacona, D. G. (1992). Bridging the boundary: External activity and performance in organizational teams. *Administrative Science Quarterly, 37*, 634–665; Druskat, V. U., & Wheeler, J. V. (2003). Managing from the boundary: The effective leadership of self-managing work teams. *Academy of Management Journal, 46*, 435–457.
28. Marrone, J. A., Tesluk, P. E., & Carson, J. B. (2007). A multi-level investigation of antecedents and consequences of team member boundary-spanning behavior. *Academy of Management Journal, 50*, 1423–1439.
29. Gordon, J. (1992). Work teams: How far have they come? *Training, 29*, 59–62.
30. Ahuja, M., & Galvin, J. (2003). Socialization in virtual group. *Journal of Management, 29*, 161–185.
31. Alexander, S. (2000, November 10). Virtual teams going global. *Infoworld*. Retrieved August 1, 2008, from http://www.infoworld.com/articles/ca/xml/00/11/13/001113cavirtual.html.
32. Kirkman, B. L., Rosen, B., Gibson, C. B., Tesluk, P. E., & McPherson, S. O. (2002). Five challenges to virtual team success: Lessons from Sabre, Inc. *Academy of Management Executive, 16*, 67–79.
33. Montoya-Weiss, M. M., Massey, A. P., & Song, M. (2001). Getting it together: Temporal coordination and conflict management in global virtual teams. *Academy of Management Journal, 44*, 1251–1262.
34. Kirkman, B. L., & Rosen, B. (2000). Powering up teams. *Organizational Dynamics*, 48–66.
35. Mathieu, J. E., Gilson, L. L., & Ruddy, T. M. (2006). Empowerment and team effectiveness: An empirical test of an integrated model. *Journal of Applied Psychology, 91*, 97–108.
36. Carpenter, M. A., Geletkanycz, M. A., & Sanders, W. G. (2004). The upper echelons revisited: The antecedents, elements, and consequences of TMT composition. *Journal of Management, 30*, 749–778.
37. Collins, J. (2001, July–August). Level leadership. *Harvard Business Review*, 66–76.
38. Welins, R., Byham, W., & Dixon, G. (1994). *Inside teams*. San Francisco: Jossey-Bass.
39. Alper, S., Tjosvold, D., & Law, K. S. (2000). Conflict management, efficacy, and performance in organizational teams. *Personnel Psychology, 53*, 625–642; Langfred, C. W. (2007). The downside of self-management: A longitudinal study of the effects of conflict on trust, autonomy, and task interdependence in self-managing teams. *Academy of Management Journal, 50*, 885–900.
40. Morgeson, F. P. (2005). The external leadership of self-managing teams: Intervening in the context of novel and disruptive events. *Journal of Applied Psychology, 90*, 497–508.
41. Parker, G. (1994). *Crossfunctional teams*. San Francisco: Jossey-Bass.
42. Humphrey, S. E., Hollenbeck, J. R., Meyer, C. J., & Ilgen, D. R. (2007). Trait configurations in self-managed teams: A conceptual examination of the use of seeding for maximizing and minimizing trait variance in teams. *Journal of Applied Psychology, 92*, 885–892.
43. Hirschfeld, R. R., Jordan, M. H., Field, H. S., Giles, W. F., & Armenakis, A. A. (2006). Becoming team players: Team members' mastery of teamwork knowledge as a predictor of team task proficiency and observed teamwork effectiveness. *Journal of Applied Psychology, 91*, 467–474; Stevens, M. J., & Campion, M. A. (1999). Staffing work teams: Development and validation of a selection test for teamwork settings. *Journal of Management, 25*, 207–228.
44. McGrath, J. E. (1984). *Groups: Interaction and performance*. Englewood Cliffs, NJ: Prentice Hall; Solomon, H. (1960). *Mathematical thinking in the measurement of behavior*. Glencoe, IL: Free Press.
45. Gratton, L., & Erickson, T. J. (2007, November). 8 ways to build collaborative teams. *Harvard Business Review*, 101–109.
46. Campion, M. A., Medsker, G. J., & Higgs, A. C. (1993). Relations between work group characteristics and effectiveness: Implications for designing effective work groups. *Personnel Psychology, 46*, 823–850; Magjuka, R. J., & Baldwin, T. T. (1991). Team-based employee involvement programs: Effects of design and administration. *Personnel Psychology, 44*, 793–812; Vinokur-Kaplan, D. (1995). Treatment teams that work (and those that don't): An application of Hackman's group effectiveness model to interdisciplinary teams in psychiatric hospitals. *Journal of Applied Behavioral Science, 31*, 303–327.
47. Jackson, S. E., Joshi, A., & Erhardt, N. L. (2003). Recent research on team and organizational diversity: SWOT analysis and implications. *Journal of Management, 29*, 801–830; van Knippenberg, D., De Dreu, C. K. W., & Homan, A. C. (2004). Work group diversity and group performance: An integrative model and research agenda. *Journal of Applied Psychology, 89*, 1008–1022.
48. Homan, A. C., van Knippenberg, D., Van Kleef, G. A., & De Dreu, C. K. W. (2007). Bridging faultlines by valuing diversity: Diversity beliefs, information elaboration, and performance in diverse work groups. *Journal of Applied Psychology, 92*, 1189–1199.
49. Surowiecki, J. (2005). *The wisdom of crowds*. New York: Anchor Books.
50. Eisenhardt, K. M., & Tabrizi, B. N. (1995). Accelerating adaptive processes: Product innovation in the global computer industry. *Science Quarterly, 4*, 84–110; Shin, S. J., & Zhou, J. (2007). When is educational specialization heterogeneity related to creativity in research and development teams? Transformational leadership as a moderator. *Journal of Applied Psychology, 92*, 1709–1721.
51. Katzenback, J. R., & Smith, D. K. (1993). *The wisdom of teams*. Boston, MA: Harvard Business School; Porter, T. W., & Lilly, B. S. (1996). The effects of conflict, trust, and task commitment on project team performance. *International Journal of Conflict Management, 7*, 361–376.
52. Haynes, M. E. (1997). *Effective meeting skills*. Menlo Park, CA: Crisp.

53. Bluedorn, A. C., Turban, D. B., & Love, M. S. (1999). The effects of stand-up and sit-down meeting formats on meeting outcomes. *Journal of Applied Psychology, 84,* 277–285.

54. Jackson, C. L., & LePine, J. A. (2003). Peer responses to a team's weakest link: A test and extension of LePine and Van Dyne's model. *Journal of Applied Psychology, 88,* 459–475.

55. Colquitt, J. A. (2004). Does the justice of the one interact with the justice of the many? Reactions to procedural justice in teams. *Journal of Applied Psychology, 89,* 633–646.

56. Scholtes, P. (1988). *The team handbook.* Madison, WI: Joiner Associates.

57. Barker, J. R. (1993, September). Tightening the iron cage: Concertive control in self-managing teams. *Administrative Science Quarterly, 38,* 408–437.

58. DiModica. P. (2008, March 13). Managing sales team ethics and sales morality. *Value Forward Group.* Retrieved August 1, 2008, from http://www.valueforward.com/20080313.html.

59. Javidan, M., Dorfman, P., Sully de Luque, M., & House, R. (2006, February). In the eye of the beholder: Cross cultural lessons in leadership from Project GLOBE. *Academy of Management Perspectives, 20,* 67–90.

60. Harrison, G. L., McKinnon, J. L., Wu, A., & Chow, C. W. (2000). Cultural influences on adaptation to fluid workgroups and teams. *Journal of International Business Studies, 31*(3), 489–505.

61. Gomez, C., Kirkman, B. L., & Shapiro, D. L. (2000). The impact of collectivism and in-group/out-group membership on the evaluation generosity of team members. *Academy of Management Journal, 43*(6), 1097–1106.

62. Gibson, C. B., & Zellmer-Bruhn, M. E. (2001). Metaphors and meaning: An intercultural analysis of the concept of teamwork. *Administrative Science Quarterly, 46*(2), 274–303.

CHAPTER 10
Conflict and Negotiations

LEARNING OBJECTIVES

After reading this chapter, you should be able to do the following:

1. Understand the different types of conflict.
2. Understand the causes of conflict.
3. Understand the consequences of conflict.
4. Understand how to manage conflict effectively.
5. Understand the stages of the negotiation process.
6. Understand how to avoid common negotiation mistakes.
7. Engage in conflict management and negotiation ethically.
8. Understand cross-cultural differences in conflict and negotiation.

Negotiation Failure: The Case of PointCast

Many "dot-com" start-ups of the 1990s consisted of little more than a few employees and a room full of servers.

In 1997, a company called PointCast Network Inc. was the hottest start-up in Silicon Valley. Its founder and CEO, Christopher Hassett, was "the most famous guy on the Internet," said Hassett's former attorney, Allen Morgan. Hassett was named CNet's newsmaker of the year—an honor previously bestowed on giants such as Bill Gates of Microsoft and Larry Ellison of Oracle. The "push technology" that PointCast pioneered was making headlines as well as being featured on the cover of *Wired* as "The Radical Future of the Media beyond the Web."

All the attention around PointCast motivated one of the world's largest communications companies—Rupert Murdoch's News Corporation—to make them an offer of $450 million. Negotiations were intense and lasted weeks. With media speculation that PointCast—a company with almost no revenue—deserved to be valued at $750 million, some people say Hassett started believing the hype and with the support of his board asked for more money. "People involved in the company thought they'd be the next Netscape. They hung out for more," Murdoch said. The Murdochs, instead, lowered their initial offer to $400 million, but added incentive clauses that brought the offer close to the original $450 million if PointCast met its financial projections.

PointCast also rejected that offer and News Corp walked away from the bargaining table. The timing couldn't have been worse for PointCast, as "push" technology became old news thanks to the maturing of alternatives such as Yahoo. By the time PointCast decided to go public in 1998, the company was valued at half of News Corp's last offer. Worse, the process of filing an initial public offering (IPO) requires the company to disclose all potential dangers to investors. PointCast's disclosures—such as news that customers had left because of poor performance—scared off so many investors that PointCast ultimately withdrew its IPO. By that time Hassett had been forced out by the board, but the company never fully recovered. In the end, PointCast was acquired in 1999 by Idealab for $7 million. In this case, stalled negotiations cost the firm a steep price of $443 million.

Referring to the missed opportunity, an industry expert said, "It may go down as one of the biggest mistakes in Internet history." According to Steve Lippin, writing in the *Wall Street Journal*, "Merger professionals point to these euphemistically called 'social issues'—ego and corporate pride, that is—as among the most difficult aspects of negotiating multibillion-dollar mergers these days. Although financial issues can be vexing too, these social issues can be deal-breakers."

In a similar and more recent situation in 2008, Yahoo CEO Jerry Yang was ousted by the Board of Directors following failed deals with Microsoft and Google. Yang's behavior during negotiations indicated that he wasn't interested in bargaining as much as playing "hard to get." He "kept saying we should get more money, we should get more money, and [he was] not realizing how precarious their position was," says high-tech analyst Rob Enderle. In other words, even deals that look great financially can fall apart if participants fail to pay attention to organizational behavior issues such as perception, groupthink, and power and influence.

Sources: Arnoldy, B. (2008, November 19). Why Yahoo's Jerry Yang stepped down. Retrieved January 20, 2009, from the Christian Science Monitor Web site: http://www.csmonitor.com/2008/1119/p02s01-usec.html; Auletta, K. (1998, November 19). The last sure thing. New Yorker; Lipin, S. (1996, August 22). In many merger deals, ego and pride play big roles in which way talks go. Wall Street Journal, Eastern edition, p. C1; Wired News Report. (1999, May 11). PointCast fire sale. Wired. Retrieved November 14, 2008, from http://www.wired.com/techbiz/media/news/1999/05/19618.

1. UNDERSTANDING CONFLICT

LEARNING OBJECTIVES

1. **Define conflict.**
2. **Understand different types of conflict.**
3. **Address whether conflict is always negative.**

Let's take a closer look at these social issues such as conflict to understand how they can derail companies and individuals alike—and what to do to prevent such consequences from happening to you. In this chapter, you'll see that managing conflict and engaging in effective negotiation are both key for effective organizational behavior within organizations as well as daily life. Conflicts range from minor annoyances to outright violence. For example, one million workers (18,000 people per week) are assaulted on the job in the United States alone.[1] One of the major ways to avoid conflicts escalating to these levels is through understanding the causes of conflict and developing methods for managing potential negative outcomes. Negotiation is one of the most effective ways to decrease conflict and will also be examined in depth in this chapter.

Similar to how conflicts can range from minor to major, negotiations vary in terms of their consequences. A high-stakes negotiation at work might mean the difference between a company's survival and its demise. On the other end of the spectrum, we deal with minor negotiations on a regular basis, such as negotiating with a coworker about which movie to see. Maybe you make a concession: "OK, we'll watch what you want but I get to pick where we eat." Maybe you hold tough: "I don't want to watch anything except a comedy." Perhaps you even look for a third option that would mutually satisfy both parties. Regardless of the level, conflict management and negotiation tactics are important skills that can be learned. First, let's take a deeper look at conflict.

Conflict is a process that involves people disagreeing. Researchers have noted that conflict is like the common cold. Everyone knows what it is, but understanding its causes and how to treat it is much more challenging.[2] As we noted earlier, conflict can range from minor disagreements to workplace violence. In addition, there are three types of conflict that can arise within organizations. Let's take a look at each of them in turn.

conflict

A process that involves people disagreeing.

1.1 Types of Conflict

Intrapersonal Conflict

Intrapersonal conflict arises within a person. For example, when you're uncertain about what is expected or wanted, or you have a sense of being inadequate to perform a task, you are experiencing intrapersonal conflict. Intrapersonal conflict can arise because of differences in roles. A manager may want to oversee a subordinate's work, believing that such oversight is a necessary part of the job. The subordinate, on the other hand, may consider such extensive oversight to be micromanagement or evidence of a lack of trust. Role conflict, another type of intrapersonal conflict, includes having two different job descriptions that seem mutually exclusive. This type of conflict can arise if you're the head of one team but also a member of another team. A third type of intrapersonal conflict involves role ambiguity. Perhaps you've been given the task of finding a trainer for a company's business writing training program. You may feel unsure about what kind of person to hire—a well-known but expensive trainer or a local, unknown but low-priced trainer. If you haven't been given guidelines about what's expected, you may be wrestling with several options.

intrapersonal conflict

Conflict that arises within a person.

Interpersonal Conflict

Interpersonal conflict is among individuals such as coworkers, a manager and an employee, or CEOs and their staff. For example, in 2006 the CEO of Airbus S.A.S., Christian Streiff, resigned because of his conflict with the board of directors over issues such as how to restructure the company.[3] This example may reflect a well-known trend among CEOs. According to one estimate, 31.9% of CEOs resigned from their jobs because they had conflict with the board of directors.[4] CEOs of competing companies might also have public conflicts. In 1997, Michael Dell was asked what he would do about Apple Computer. "What would I do? I'd shut it down and give the money back to shareholders." Ten years later, Steve Jobs, the CEO of Apple Inc., indicated he had clearly held a grudge as he shot back at Dell in an e-mail to his employees, stating, "Team, it turned out Michael Dell wasn't perfect in predicting the future. Based on today's stock market close, Apple is worth more than Dell."[5] In part, their long-time disagreements stem from their differences. Interpersonal conflict often arises because of competition, as the Dell/Apple example shows, or because of personality or values differences. For example, one person's style may be to "go with the gut" on decisions, while another person wants to make decisions based on facts. Those differences will lead to conflict if the individuals reach different conclusions. Many companies suffer because of interpersonal conflicts. Keeping conflicts centered around ideas rather than individual differences is important in avoiding a conflict escalation.

FIGURE 10.2

Of the conflict between Michael Dell (shown here) and Steve Jobs, David Yoffie, a professor at the Harvard Business School who closely follows the computer industry, notes that the conflict may stem from their differences in terms of being from different generations and having different management styles.

Source: http://en.wikipedia.org/wiki/Image:Michael_Dell,_square_crop.jpg.

interpersonal conflict

A type of conflict between two people.

Intergroup Conflict

FIGURE 10.3

Conflicts such as the Air Canada pilot strike can have ripple effects. For example, Air Canada's parent company threatened to cancel a $6.1 billion contract with Boeing for new planes if they were unable to negotiate an agreement with the pilots who would fly them. Conflict consequences such as these could affect those working at this Boeing Factory in Seattle, Washington.

Source: http://commons.wikimedia.org/wiki/Image:Boeing_Factory_2002.jpg.

intergroup conflict

Conflict that takes place among different groups, such as different departments or divisions in a company, or between union and management, or between companies, such as companies who supply the same customer.

Intergroup conflict is conflict that takes place among different groups. Types of groups may include different departments or divisions in a company, and employee union and management, or competing companies that supply the same customers. Departments may conflict over budget allocations; unions and management may disagree over work rules; suppliers may conflict with each other on the quality of parts. Merging two groups together can lead to friction between the groups—especially if there are scarce resources to be divided among the group. For example, in what has been called "the most difficult and hard-fought labor issue in an airline merger," Canadian Air and Air Canada pilots were locked into years of personal and legal conflict when the two airlines' seniority lists were combined following the merger.[6] Seniority is a valuable and scarce resource for pilots, because it helps to determine who flies the newest and biggest planes, who receives the best flight routes, and who is paid the most. In response to the loss of seniority, former Canadian Air pilots picketed at shareholder meetings, threatened to call in sick, and had ongoing conflicts with pilots from Air Canada. The conflicts with pilots continue to this day. The history of past conflicts among organizations and employees makes new deals challenging.

1.2 Is Conflict Always Bad?

Most people are uncomfortable with conflict, but is conflict always bad? Conflict can be dysfunctional if it paralyzes an organization, leads to less than optimal performance, or, in the worst case, leads to workplace violence. Surprisingly, a moderate amount of conflict can actually be a healthy (and necessary) part of organizational life.[7] To understand how to get to a positive level of conflict, we need to understand its root causes, consequences, and tools to help manage it. The impact of too much or too little conflict can disrupt performance. If conflict is too low, then performance is low. If conflict is too high, then performance also tends to be low. The goal is to hold conflict levels in the middle of this range. While it might seem strange to want a particular level of conflict, a medium level of task-related conflict is often viewed as optimal, because it represents a situation in which a healthy debate of ideas takes place.

FIGURE 10.4 The Inverted U Relationship Between Performance and Conflict

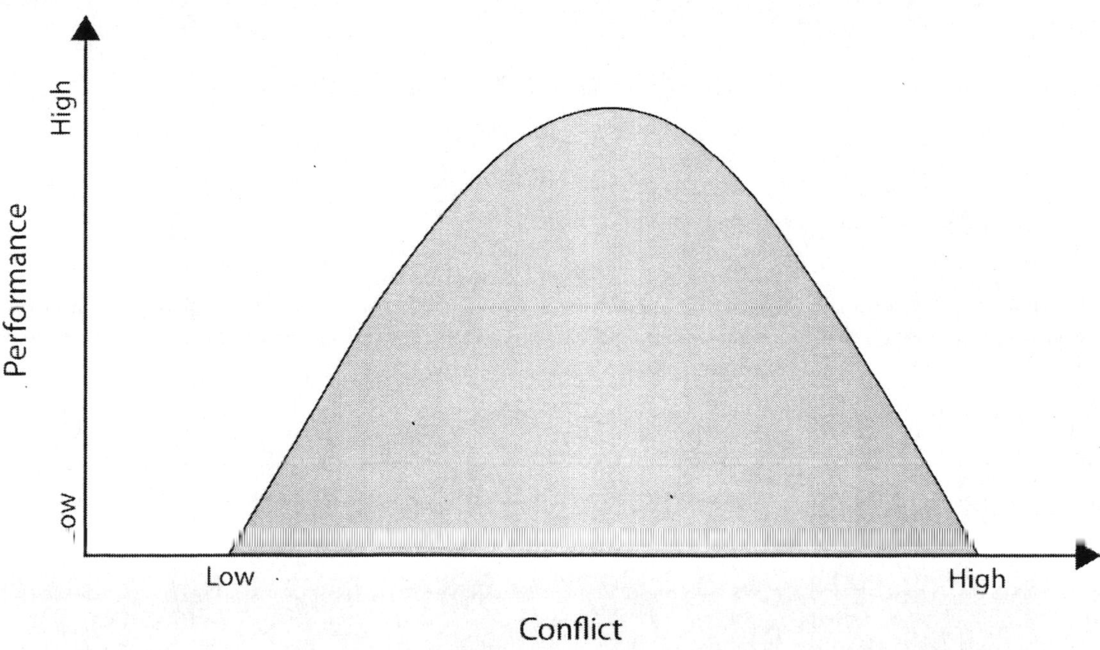

Task conflict can be good in certain circumstances, such as in the early stages of decision making, because it stimulates creativity. However, it can interfere with complex tasks in the long run.[8] Personal conflicts, such as personal attacks, are never healthy because they cause stress and distress, which undermines performance. The worst cases of personal conflicts can lead to workplace bullying. At Intel Corporation, all new employees go through a 4-hour training module to learn "constructive confrontation." The content of the training program includes dealing with others in a positive manner, using facts rather than opinion to persuade others, and focusing on the problem at hand rather than the people involved. "We don't spend time being defensive or taking things personally. We cut through all of that and get to the issues," notes a trainer from Intel University.[9] The success of the training remains unclear, but the presence of this program indicates that Intel understands the potentially positive effect of a moderate level of conflict. Research focusing on effective teams across time found that they were characterized by low but increasing levels of process conflict (how do we get things done?), low levels of relationship conflict with a rise toward the end of the project (personal disagreements among team members), and moderate levels of task conflict in the middle of the task time line.[10]

KEY TAKEAWAY

Conflict can be a problem for individuals and organizations. There are several different types of conflict, including intrapersonal, interpersonal, and intergroup conflict. Moderate conflict can be a healthy and necessary part of organizational life.

EXERCISES

1. What are the types of conflicts that individuals may have at work? Which type have you experienced the most?
2. What are some primary causes of conflict at work?
3. Explain how miscommunication might be related to a conflict at work.

2. CAUSES AND OUTCOMES OF CONFLICT

LEARNING OBJECTIVES

1. Understand different causes of conflict.
2. Understand jobs at risk for conflict.
3. Learn the outcomes of conflict.

There are many potential root causes of conflict at work. We'll go over six of them here. Remember, anything that leads to a disagreement can be a cause of conflict. Although conflict is common to organizations, some organizations have more than others.

FIGURE 10.5 Potential Causes of Conflict

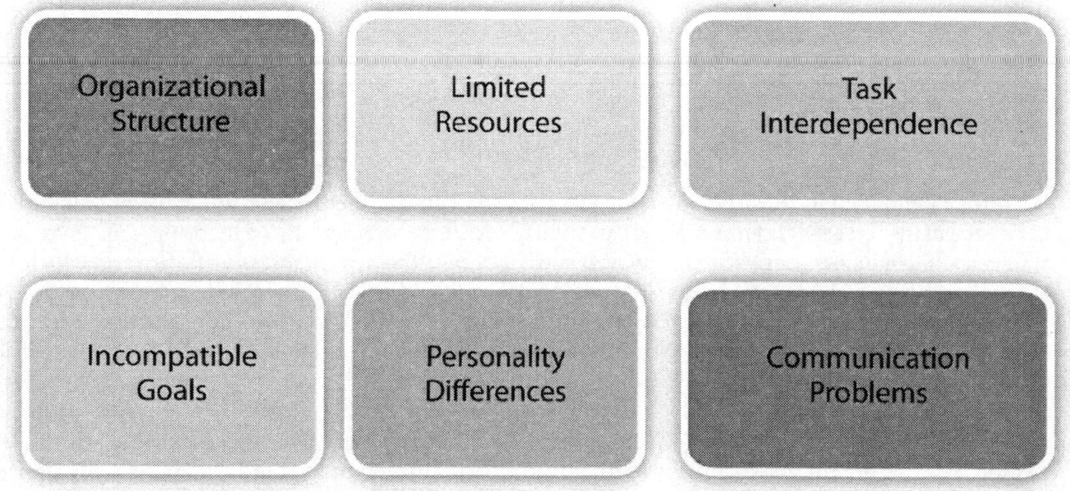

2.1 Causes of Conflict

Organizational Structure

Conflict tends to take different forms, depending upon the organizational structure.[11] For example, if a company uses a matrix structure as its organizational form, it will have decisional conflict built in, because the structure specifies that each manager report to two bosses. For example, global company ABB Inc. is organized around a matrix structure based on the dimensions of country and industry. This structure can lead to confusion as the company is divided geographically into 1,200 different units and by industry into 50 different units.[12]

Limited Resources

Resources such as money, time, and equipment are often scarce. Competition among people or departments for limited resources is a frequent cause for conflict. For example, cutting-edge laptops and gadgets such as a BlackBerry or iPhone are expensive resources that may be allocated to employees on a need-to-have basis in some companies. When a group of employees have access to such resources while others do not, conflict may arise among employees or between employees and management. While technical employees may feel that these devices are crucial to their productivity, employees with customer contact such as sales representatives may make the point that these devices are important for them to make a good impression to clients. Because important resources are often limited, this is one source of conflict many companies have to live with.

Task Interdependence

Another cause of conflict is task interdependence; that is, when accomplishment of your goal requires reliance on others to perform their tasks. For example, if you're tasked with creating advertising for your product, you're dependent on the creative team to design the words and layout, the photographer or videographer to create the visuals, the media buyer to purchase the advertising space, and so on. The completion of your goal (airing or publishing your ad) is dependent on others.

Incompatible Goals

Sometimes conflict arises when two parties think that their goals are mutually exclusive. Within an organization, incompatible goals often arise because of the different ways department managers are compensated. For example, a sales manager's bonus may be tied to how many sales are made for the company. As a result, the individual might be tempted to offer customers "freebies" such as expedited delivery in order to make the sale. In contrast, a transportation manager's compensation may be based on how much money the company saves on transit. In this case, the goal might be to eliminate expedited delivery because it adds expense. The two will butt heads until the company resolves the conflict by changing the compensation scheme. For example, if the company assigns the bonus based on profitability of a sale, not just the dollar amount, the cost of the expediting would be subtracted from the value of the sale. It might still make sense to expedite the order if the sale is large enough, in which case both parties would support it. On the other hand, if the expediting negates the value of the sale, neither party would be in favor of the added expense.

Personality Differences

Personality differences among coworkers are common. By understanding some fundamental differences among the way people think and act, we can better understand how others see the world. Knowing that these differences are natural and normal lets us anticipate and mitigate interpersonal conflict—it's often not about "you" but simply a different way of seeing and behaving. For example, Type A individuals have been found to have more conflicts with their coworkers than Type B individuals.[13]

Communication Problems

Sometimes conflict arises simply out of a small, unintentional communication problem, such as lost e-mails or dealing with people who don't return phone calls. Giving feedback is also a case in which the best intentions can quickly escalate into a conflict situation. When communicating, be sure to focus on behavior and its effects, not on the person. For example, say that Jeff always arrives late to all your meetings. You think he has a bad attitude, but you don't really know what Jeff's attitude is. You do know, however, the effect that Jeff's behavior has on you. You could say, "Jeff, when you come late to the meeting, I feel like my time is wasted." Jeff can't argue with that statement, because it is a fact of the impact of his behavior on you. It's indisputable, because it is your reality. What Jeff can say is that he did not intend such an effect, and then you can have a discussion regarding the behavior.

In another example, the Hershey Company was engaged in talks behind closed doors with Cadbury Schweppes about a possible merger. No information about this deal was shared with Hershey's major stakeholder, the Hershey Trust. When Robert Vowler, CEO of the Hershey Trust, discovered that talks were underway without anyone consulting the Trust, tensions between the major stakeholders began to rise. As Hershey's continued to underperform, steps were taken in what is now called the "Sunday night massacre," in which several board members were forced to resign and Richard Lenny, Hershey's then current CEO, retired.[14] This example shows how a lack of communication can lead to an escalation of conflict. Time will tell what the lasting effects of this conflict will be, but in the short term, effective communication will be the key. Now, let's turn our attention to the outcomes of conflict.

2.2 Outcomes of Conflict

One of the most common outcomes of conflict is that it upsets parties in the short run.[15] However, conflict can have both positive and negative outcomes. On the positive side, conflict can result in greater creativity or better decisions. For example, as a result of a disagreement over a policy, a manager may learn from an employee that newer technologies help solve problems in an unanticipated new way.

Positive outcomes include the following:

- Consideration of a broader range of ideas, resulting in a better, stronger idea
- Surfacing of assumptions that may be inaccurate
- Increased participation and creativity
- Clarification of individual views that build learning

On the other hand, conflict can be dysfunctional if it is excessive or involves personal attacks or underhanded tactics.

Examples of negative outcomes include the following:

- Increased stress and anxiety among individuals, which decreases productivity and satisfaction
- Feelings of being defeated and demeaned, which lowers individuals' morale and may increase turnover
- A climate of mistrust, which hinders the teamwork and cooperation necessary to get work done

Is Your Job at Risk for Workplace Violence?

You may be at increased risk for workplace violence if your job involves the following:

- Dealing With People
  - *Caring for others either emotionally or physically*, such as at a nursing home.
  - *Interacting with frustrated customers*, such as with retail sales.
  - *Supervising others*, such as being a manager.
  - *Denying requests others make of you*, such as with customer service.
- Being in High-Risk Situations
  - *Dealing with valuables or exchanging money*, such as in banking.
  - *Handling weapons*, such as in law enforcement.
  - *Working with drugs, alcohol, or those under the influence of them*, such as bartending.
  - *Working nights or weekends*, such as gas station attendants.

Sources: Adapted from information in LeBlanc, M. M., & Kelloway, E. K. (2002). Predictors and outcomes of workplace violence and aggression. Journal of Applied Psychology, 87, 444–453; National Institute for Occupational Safety and Health. (1997). Violence in the workplace. Retrieved November 12, 2008, from http://www.cdc.gov/niosh/violfs.html; National Institute for Occupational Safety and Health. (2006). Workplace prevention strategies and research needs. Retrieved November 12, 2008, from http://www.cdc.gov/niosh/docs/2006-144/.

Given these negative outcomes, how can conflict be managed so that it does not become dysfunctional or even dangerous? We'll explore this in the next section.

KEY TAKEAWAY

Conflict has many causes, including organizational structures, limitations on resources, task interdependence, goal incompatibility, personality differences, and communication challenges. Outcomes of well-managed conflict include increased participation and creativity, while negatives of poorly managed conflict include increased stress and anxiety. Jobs that deal with people are at higher risk for conflict.

EXERCISES

1. What are some primary causes of conflict at work?
2. What are the outcomes of workplace conflict? Which types of job are the most at risk for workplace violence? Why do you think that is?
3. What outcomes have you observed from conflict?

3. CONFLICT MANAGEMENT

LEARNING OBJECTIVES

1. **Understand different ways to manage conflict.**
2. **Understand your own communication style.**
3. **Learn to stimulate conflict if needed.**

There are a number of different ways of managing organizational conflict, which are highlighted in this section. **Conflict management** refers to resolving disagreements effectively.

conflict management

Resolving disagreements effectively.

3.1 Ways to Manage Conflict

Change the Structure

When structure is a cause of dysfunctional conflict, structural change can be the solution to resolving the conflict. Consider this situation. Vanessa, the lead engineer in charge of new product development, has submitted her components list to Tom, the procurement officer, for purchasing. Tom, as usual, has rejected two of the key components, refusing the expenditure on the purchase. Vanessa is furious, saying, "Every time I give you a request to buy a new part, you fight me on it. Why can't you ever trust my judgment and honor my request?"

Tom counters, "You're always choosing the newest, leading-edge parts—they're hard to find and expensive to purchase. I'm supposed to keep costs down, and your requests always break my budget."

"But when you don't order the parts we need for a new product, you delay the whole project," Vanessa says.

Sharon, the business unit's vice president, hits upon a structural solution by stating, "From now on, both of you will be evaluated on the total cost and the overall performance of the product. You need to work together to keep component costs low while minimizing quality issues later on." If the conflict is at an intergroup level, such as between two departments, a structural solution could be to have those two departments report to the same executive, who could align their previously incompatible goals.

Change the Composition of the Team

If the conflict is between team members, the easiest solution may be to change the composition of the team, separating the personalities that were at odds. In instances in which conflict is attributed to the widely different styles, values, and preferences of a small number of members, replacing some of these members may resolve the problem. If that's not possible because everyone's skills are needed on the team and substitutes aren't available, consider a physical layout solution. Research has shown that when known antagonists are seated directly across from each other, the amount of conflict increases. However, when they are seated side by side, the conflict tends to decrease.[16]

Create a Common Opposing Force

Group conflict within an organization can be mitigated by focusing attention on a common enemy such as the competition. For example, two software groups may be vying against each other for marketing dollars, each wanting to maximize advertising money devoted to their product. But, by focusing attention on a competitor company, the groups may decide to work together to enhance the marketing effectiveness for the company as a whole. The "enemy" need not be another company—it could be a concept, such as a recession, that unites previously warring departments to save jobs during a downturn.

Consider Majority Rule

Sometimes a group conflict can be resolved through majority rule. That is, group members take a vote, and the idea with the most votes is the one that gets implemented. The majority rule approach can work if the participants feel that the procedure is fair. It is important to keep in mind that this strategy will become ineffective if used repeatedly with the same members typically winning. Moreover, the approach should be used sparingly. It should follow a healthy discussion of the issues and points of contention, not be a substitute for that discussion.

Problem Solve

Problem solving is a common approach to resolving conflict. In problem-solving mode, the individuals or groups in conflict are asked to focus on the problem, not on each other, and to uncover the root cause of the problem. This approach recognizes the rarity of one side being completely right and the other being completely wrong.

3.2 Conflict-Handling Styles

Individuals vary in the way that they handle conflicts. There are five common styles of handling conflicts. These styles can be mapped onto a grid that shows the varying degree of cooperation and assertiveness each style entails. Let us look at each in turn.

FIGURE 10.6 Conflict-Handling Styles

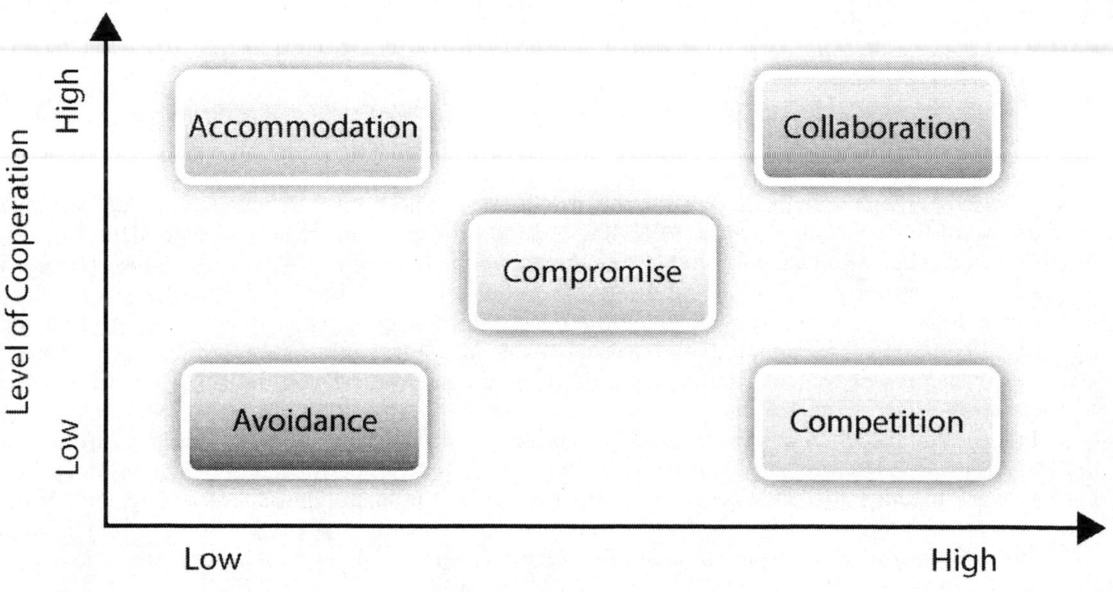

Avoidance

avoiding

An uncooperative and unassertive conflict-handling style.

The **avoiding** style is uncooperative and unassertive. People exhibiting this style seek to avoid conflict altogether by denying that it is there. They are prone to postponing any decisions in which a conflict may arise. People using this style may say things such as, "I don't really care if we work this out," or "I don't think there's any problem. I feel fine about how things are." Conflict avoidance may be habitual to some people because of personality traits such as the need for affiliation. While conflict avoidance may not be a significant problem if the issue at hand is trivial, it becomes a problem when individuals avoid confronting important issues because of a dislike for conflict or a perceived inability to handle the other party's reactions.

Accommodation

accommodating

A cooperative and unassertive conflict-handling style.

The **accommodating** style is cooperative and unassertive. In this style, the person gives in to what the other side wants, even if it means giving up one's personal goals. People who use this style may fear speaking up for themselves or they may place a higher value on the relationship, believing that disagreeing with an idea might be hurtful to the other person. They will say things such as, "Let's do it your way" or "If it's important to you, I can go along with it." Accommodation may be an effective strategy if the issue at hand is more important to others compared to oneself. However, if a person perpetually uses this style, that individual may start to see that personal interests and well-being are neglected.

Compromise

The **compromising** style is a middle-ground style, in which individuals have some desire to express their own concerns and get their way but still respect the other person's goals. The compromiser may say things such as, "Perhaps I ought to reconsider my initial position" or "Maybe we can both agree to give in a little." In a compromise, each person sacrifices something valuable to them. For example, in 2005 the luxurious Lanesborough Hotel in London advertised incorrect nightly rates for £35, as opposed to £350. When the hotel received a large number of online bookings at this rate, the initial reaction was to insist that customers cancel their reservations and book at the correct rate. The situation was about to lead to a public relations crisis. As a result, they agreed to book the rooms at the advertised price for a maximum of three nights, thereby limiting the damage to the hotel's bottom line as well as its reputation.[17]

compromising

A middle-ground conflict-handling style, in which a person has some desire to express their own concerns and get their way but still respects the other person's goals as well.

Competition

People exhibiting a **competing** style want to reach their goal or get their solution adopted regardless of what others say or how they feel. They are more interested in getting the outcome they want as opposed to keeping the other party happy, and they push for the deal they are interested in making. Competition may lead to poor relationships with others if one is always seeking to maximize their own outcomes at the expense of others' well-being. This approach may be effective if one has strong moral objections to the alternatives or if the alternatives one is opposing are unethical or harmful.

FIGURE 10.7

Body language can fuel a conflict.

© 2010 Jupiterimages Corporation

Collaboration

The **collaborating** style is high on both assertiveness and cooperation. This is a strategy to use for achieving the best outcome from conflict—both sides argue for their position, supporting it with facts and rationale while listening attentively to the other side. The objective is to find a win–win solution to the problem in which both parties get what they want. They'll challenge points but not each other. They'll emphasize problem solving and integration of each other's goals. For example, an employee who wants to complete an MBA program may have a conflict with management when he wants to reduce his work hours. Instead of taking opposing positions in which the employee defends his need to pursue his career goals while the manager emphasizes the company's need for the employee, both parties may review alternatives to find an integrative solution. In the end, the employee may decide to pursue the degree while taking online classes, and the company may realize that paying for the employee's tuition is a worthwhile investment. This may be a win–win solution to the problem in which no one gives up what is personally important, and every party gains something from the exchange.

competing

A conflict-handling style that is highly assertive but low on cooperation.

collaborating

A conflict-handling style that is high on both assertiveness and cooperation.

Which Style Is Best?

Like much of organizational behavior, there is no one "right way" to deal with conflict. Much of the time it will depend on the situation. However, the collaborative style has the potential to be highly effective in many different situations.

We do know that most individuals have a dominant style that they tend to use most frequently. Think of your friend who is always looking for a fight or your coworker who always backs down from a disagreement. Successful individuals are able to match their style to the situation. There are times when avoiding a conflict can be a great choice. For example, if a driver cuts you off in traffic, ignoring it and going on with your day is a good alternative to "road rage." However, if a colleague keeps claiming ownership of your ideas, it may be time for a confrontation. Allowing such intellectual plagiarism to continue could easily be more destructive to your career than confronting the individual. Research also shows that when it comes to dealing with conflict, managers prefer forcing, while their subordinates are more likely to engage in avoiding, accommodating, or compromising.[18] It is also likely that individuals will respond similarly to the person engaging in conflict. For example, if one person is forcing, others are likely to respond with a forcing tactic as well.

3.3 What If You Don't Have Enough Conflict Over Ideas?

Part of effective conflict management is knowing when proper stimulation is necessary. Many people think that conflict is inherently bad—that it undermines goals or shows that a group or meeting is not running smoothly. In fact, if there is no conflict, it may mean that people are silencing themselves and withholding their opinions. The reality is that within meaningful group discussions there are usually varying opinions about the best course of action. If people are suppressing their opinions, the final result may not be the best solution. During healthy debates, people point out difficulties or weaknesses in a proposed alternative and can work together to solve them. The key to keeping the disagreement healthy is to keep the discussion focused on the task, not the personalities. For example, a comment such as "Jack's ideas have never worked before. I doubt his current idea will be any better" is not constructive. Instead, a comment such as "This production step uses a degreaser that's considered a hazardous material. Can we think of an alternative degreaser that's nontoxic?" is more productive. It challenges the group to improve upon the existing idea.

Traditionally, Hewlett-Packard Development Company LP was known as a "nice" organization. Throughout its history, HP viewed itself as a scientific organization, and their culture valued teamwork and respect. But over time, HP learned that you can be "nice to death." In fact, in the 1990s, HP found it difficult to partner with other organizations because of their culture differences. During role plays created to help HP managers be more dynamic, the trainers had to modify several role-plays, because participants simply said, "That would never happen at HP," over the smallest conflict. All this probably played a role in the discomfort many felt with Carly Fiorina's style as CEO and the merge she orchestrated with Compaq Computer Corporation, which ultimately caused the board of directors to fire Fiorina. On the other hand, no one is calling HP "too nice" anymore.

OB Toolbox: How Can You Stimulate Conflict?

- *Encourage people to raise issues and disagree with you or the status quo without fear of reprisal.* An issue festering beneath the surface, when brought out into the open, may turn out to be a minor issue that can be easily addressed and resolved.
- *Assign a devil's advocate to stimulate alternative viewpoints.* If a business unit is getting stagnant, bring in new people to "shake things up."
- *Create a competition among teams, offering a bonus to the team that comes up with the best solution to a problem.* For example, have two product development teams compete on designing a new product. Or, reward the team that has the fewest customer complaints or achieves the highest customer satisfaction rating.
- *Build some ambiguity into the process.* When individuals are free to come up with their own ideas about how to complete a task, the outcome may be surprising, and it allows for more healthy disagreements along the way.

KEY TAKEAWAY

Conflict management techniques include changing organizational structures to avoid built-in conflict, changing team members, creating a common "enemy," using majority rules, and problem solving. Conflict management styles include accommodating others, avoiding the conflict, collaborating, competing, and compromising. People tend to have a dominant style. At times it makes sense to build in some conflict over ideas if none exists.

EXERCISES

1. List three ways to decrease a conflict situation. What are some pros and cons of each of these approaches?
2. Do you deal with conflict differently with friends and family than you do at work? If so, why do you think that is?
3. What is your usual conflict-handling style at work? Do you see it as effective or ineffective?
4. Describe a situation in which not having enough conflict can be a problem.

4. NEGOTIATIONS

LEARNING OBJECTIVES

1. Learn the five phases of negotiation.
2. Learn negotiation strategies.
3. Avoid common mistakes in negotiations.
4. Learn about third-party negotiations.

A common way that parties deal with conflict is via negotiation. **Negotiation** is a process whereby two or more parties work toward an agreement. There are five phases of negotiation, which are described below.

negotiation

A process whereby two or more parties work toward an agreement.

4.1 The Five Phases of Negotiation

Phase 1: Investigation

The first step in negotiation is the **investigation**, or information gathering stage. This is a key stage that is often ignored. Surprisingly, the first place to begin is with yourself: What are your goals for the negotiation? What do you want to achieve? What would you concede? What would you absolutely not concede? Leigh Steinberg, the most powerful agent in sports (he was the role model for Tom Cruise's character in *Jerry Maguire*), puts it this way: "You need the clearest possible view of your goals. And you need to be brutally honest with yourself about your priorities."[19]

During the negotiation, you'll inevitably be faced with making choices. It's best to know what you want, so that in the heat of the moment you're able to make the best decision. For example, if you'll be negotiating for a new job, ask yourself, "What do I value most? Is it the salary level? Working with coworkers whom I like? Working at a prestigious company? Working in a certain geographic area? Do I want a company that will groom me for future positions or do I want to change jobs often in pursuit of new challenges?"

FIGURE 10.8 The Five Phases of Negotiation

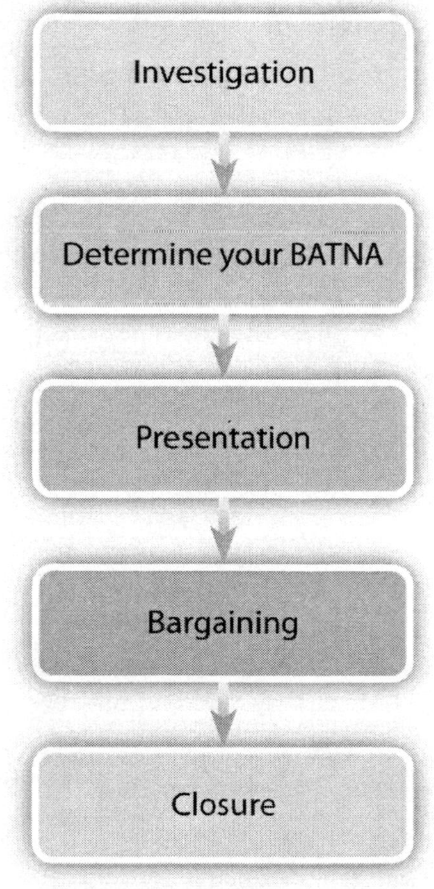

investigation

The first step in negotiation in which information is gathered.

Phase 2: Determine Your BATNA

If you don't know where you're going, you will probably end up somewhere else.
- *Lawrence J. Peter*

BATNA

Stands for the "best alternative to a negotiated agreement." Determining your BATNA is one important part of the investigation and planning phase in negotiation.

One important part of the investigation and planning phase is to determine your **BATNA**, which is an acronym that stands for the "best alternative to a negotiated agreement." Roger Fisher and William Ury coined this phrase in their book *Getting to Yes: Negotiating without Giving In*.

Thinking through your BATNA is important to helping you decide whether to accept an offer you receive during the negotiation. You need to know what your alternatives are. If you have various alternatives, you can look at the proposed deal more critically. Could you get a better outcome than the proposed deal? Your BATNA will help you reject an unfavorable deal. On the other hand, if the deal is better than another outcome you could get (that is, better than your BATNA), then you should accept it.

Think about it in common sense terms: When you know your opponent is desperate for a deal, you can demand much more. If it looks like they have a lot of other options outside the negotiation, you'll be more likely to make concessions.

As Fisher and Ury said, "The reason you negotiate is to produce something better than the results you can obtain without negotiating. What are those results? What is that alternative? What is your BATNA—your Best Alternative To a Negotiated Agreement? That is the standard against which any proposed agreement should be measured."[20]

The party with the best BATNA has the best negotiating position, so try to improve your BATNA whenever possible by exploring possible alternatives.[21]

Going back to the example of your new job negotiation, consider your options to the offer you receive. If your pay is lower than what you want, what alternatives do you have? A job with another company? Looking for another job? Going back to school? While you're thinking about your BATNA, take some time to think about the other party's BATNA. Do they have an employee who could readily replace you?

Once you've gotten a clear understanding of your own goals, investigate the person you'll be negotiating with. What does that person (or company) want? Put yourself in the other party's shoes. What alternatives could they have? For example, in the job negotiations, the other side wants a good employee at a fair price. That may lead you to do research on salary levels: What is the pay rate for the position you're seeking? What is the culture of the company?

Greenpeace's goals are to safeguard the environment by getting large companies and organizations to adopt more environmentally friendly practices such as using fewer plastic components. Part of the background research Greenpeace engages in involves uncovering facts. For instance, medical device makers are using harmful PVCs as a tubing material because PVCs are inexpensive. But are there alternatives to PVCs that are also cost-effective? Greenpeace's research found that yes, there are.[22] Knowing this lets Greenpeace counter those arguments and puts Greenpeace in a stronger position to achieve its goals.

OB Toolbox: BATNA Best Practices

1. Brainstorm a list of alternatives that you might conceivably take if the negotiation doesn't lead to a favorable outcome for you.
2. Improve on some of the more promising ideas and convert them into actionable alternatives.
3. Identify the most beneficial alternative to be kept in reserve as a fall-back during the negotiation.
4. Remember that your BATNA may evolve over time, so keep revising it to make sure it is still accurate.
5. Don't reveal your BATNA to the other party. If your BATNA turns out to be worse than what the other party expected, their offer may go down, as PointCast learned in the opening case.

Sources: Adapted from information in Spangler, B. (2003, June). Best Alternative to a Negotiated Agreement (BATNA). Retrieved November 12, 2008, from http://www.beyondintractability.org/essay/batna/; Conflict Research Consortium, University of Colorado. (1998). Limits to agreement: Better alternatives. Retrieved November 12, 2008, from http://www.colorado.edu/conflict/peace/problem/batna.htm; Venter, D. (2003). What is a BATNA? Retrieved January 14, 2008, from http://www.negotiationeurope.com/articles/batna.html.

Phase 3: Presentation

The third phase of negotiation is **presentation**. In this phase, you assemble the information you've gathered in a way that supports your position. In a job hiring or salary negotiation situation, for instance, you can present facts that show what you've contributed to the organization in the past (or in a previous position), which in turn demonstrates your value. Perhaps you created a blog that brought attention to your company or got donations or funding for a charity. Perhaps you're a team player who brings out the best in a group.

FIGURE 10.9

All phases of the negotiation process are important. The presentation is the one that normally receives the most attention, but the work done before that point is equally important.

© 2010 Jupiterimages Corporation

Phase 4: Bargaining

During the **bargaining** phase, each party discusses their goals and seeks to get an agreement. A natural part of this process is making **concessions**, namely, giving up one thing to get something else in return. Making a concession is not a sign of weakness—parties expect to give up some of their goals. Rather, concessions demonstrate cooperativeness and help move the negotiation toward its conclusion. Making concessions is particularly important in tense union-management disputes, which can get bogged down by old issues. Making a concession shows forward movement and process, and it allays concerns about rigidity or closed-mindedness. What would a typical concession be? Concessions are often in the areas of money, time, resources, responsibilities, or autonomy. When negotiating for the purchase of products, for example, you might agree to pay a higher price in exchange for getting the products sooner. Alternatively, you could ask to pay a lower price in exchange for giving the manufacturer more time or flexibility in when they deliver the product.

presentation

The third phase of negotiation.

bargaining

The fourth phase of negotiation.

concessions

Giving up one thing to get something else in return.

One key to the bargaining phase is to ask questions. Don't simply take a statement such as "we can't do that" at face value. Rather, try to find out why the party has that constraint. Let's take a look at an example. Say that you're a retailer and you want to buy patio furniture from a manufacturer. You want to have the sets in time for spring sales. During the negotiations, your goal is to get the lowest price with the earliest delivery date. The manufacturer, of course, wants to get the highest price with the longest lead time before delivery. As negotiations stall, you evaluate your options to decide what's more important: a slightly lower price or a slightly longer delivery date? You do a quick calculation. The manufacturer has offered to deliver the products by April 30, but you know that some of your customers make their patio furniture selection early in the spring, and missing those early sales could cost you $1 million. So, you suggest that you can accept the April 30 delivery date if the manufacturer will agree to drop the price by $1 million.

"I appreciate the offer," the manufacturer replies, "but I can't accommodate such a large price cut." Instead of leaving it at that, you ask, "I'm surprised that a 2-month delivery would be so costly to you. Tell me more about your manufacturing process so that I can understand why you can't manufacture the products in that time frame."

"*Manufacturing* the products in that time frame is not the problem," the manufacturer replies, "but getting them *shipped* from Asia is what's expensive for us."

When you hear that, a light bulb goes off. You know that your firm has favorable contracts with shipping companies because of the high volume of business the firm gives them. You make the following counteroffer: "Why don't we agree that my company will arrange and pay for the shipper, and you agree to have the products ready to ship on March 30 for $10.5 million instead of $11 million?" The manufacturer accepts the offer—the biggest expense and constraint (the shipping) has been lifted. You, in turn, have saved money as well.[23]

Phase 5: Closure

Closure is an important part of negotiations. At the close of a negotiation, you and the other party have either come to an agreement on the terms, or one party has decided that the final offer is unacceptable and therefore must be walked away from. Most negotiators assume that if their best offer has been rejected, there's nothing left to do. You made your best offer and that's the best you can do. The savviest of negotiators, however, see the rejection as an opportunity to learn. "What would it have taken for us to reach an agreement?"

closure

The last part of negotiation in which you and the other party have either come to an agreement on the terms, or one party has decided that the final offer is unacceptable and therefore must be walked away from.

Recently, a CEO had been in negotiations with a customer. After learning the customer decided to go with the competition, the CEO decided to inquire as to why negotiations had fallen through. With nothing left to lose, the CEO placed a call to the prospect's vice president and asked why the offer had been rejected, explaining that the answer would help improve future offerings. Surprisingly, the VP explained the deal was given to the competitor because, despite charging more, the competitor offered after-sales service on the product. The CEO was taken by surprise, originally assuming that the VP was most interested in obtaining the lowest price possible. In order accommodate a very low price, various extras such as after-sales service had been cut from the offer. Having learned that the VP was seeking service, not the lowest cost, the CEO said, "Knowing what I know now, I'm confident that I could have beaten the competitor's bid. Would you accept a revised offer?" The VP agreed, and a week later the CEO had a signed contract.[24]

Sometimes at the end of negotiations, it's clear why a deal was not reached. But if you're confused about why a deal did not happen, consider making a follow-up call. Even though you may not win the deal back in the end, you might learn something that's useful for future negotiations. What's more, the other party may be more willing to disclose the information if they don't think you're in a "selling" mode.

Should You Negotiate for a Higher Salary?

Yes! According to a survey conducted by CareerBuilder.com, 58% of hiring managers say they leave some negotiating room when extending initial job offers. The survey also found that many of the hiring managers agree to a candidate's request for a higher salary. "Salary negotiation has become a growing opportunity in the job acquisition process," says Bill Hawkins, president and CEO of The Hawkins Company, a full-service executive search firm with offices in Los Angeles and Atlanta. "Candidates who fail to make a counteroffer could forfeit significant income."

Source: Adapted from information in Reed-Woodard, M. (2007, April). Taking money off the table. Black Enterprise, 37(9), 60–61.

4.2 Negotiation Strategies

Distributive Approach

distributive view

The traditional fixed-pie approach in which negotiators see the situation as a pie that they have to divide between them.

The **distributive view** of negotiation is the traditional fixed-pie approach. That is, negotiators see the situation as a pie that they have to divide between them. Each tries to get more of the pie and "win." For example, managers may compete over shares of a budget. If marketing gets a 10% increase in its budget, another department such as R&D will need to decrease its budget by 10% to offset the marketing increase. Focusing on a fixed pie is a common mistake in negotiation, because this view limits the creative solutions possible.

Integrative Approach

integrative approach

An approach to negotiation in which both parties look for ways to integrate their goals under a larger umbrella.

A newer, more creative approach to negotiation is called the **integrative approach**. In this approach, both parties look for ways to integrate their goals under a larger umbrella. That is, they look for ways to *expand* the pie, so that each party gets more. This is also called a win–win approach. The first step of the integrative approach is to enter the negotiation from a cooperative rather than an adversarial stance. The second step is all about listening. Listening develops trust as each party learns what the other wants and everyone involved arrives at a mutual understanding. Then, all parties can explore ways to achieve the individual goals. The general idea is, "If we put our heads together, we can find a solution that addresses everybody's needs." Unfortunately, integrative outcomes are not the norm. A summary of 32 experiments on negotiations found that although they could have resulted in integrated outcomes, only 20% did so.[25] One key factor related to finding integrated solutions is the experience of the negotiators who were able to reach them.[26]

OB Toolbox: Seven Steps to Negotiating a Higher Salary

- Step 1: *Overcome your fear.*
    - The first step is to overcome your fears. Many people don't even begin a salary negotiation. We may be afraid of angering the boss or think that because we are doing a good job, we'll automatically be rewarded. But, just because you're doing a good job doesn't mean you'll automatically get a raise. Why? If you don't ask for one, the boss may believe you're satisfied with what you're getting. So why should he pay you more? Imagine going into a car dealership and being absolutely delighted with a car choice. The sticker price is $19,000. Would you pay the dealer $23,000 just because you really like the car? Of course not. You probably wouldn't even offer $19,000. If the car was up for auction, however, and another bidder offered $20,000, you'd likely increase your offer, too.
    - That's what salary negotiation is like. Your boss may be thrilled with you but at the same time is running a business. There's no reason to pay an employee more if you seem satisfied with your current salary.

- Step 2: *Get the facts.*
    - Before you enter into the negotiation, do some background research. What are other companies paying people in your position? Check sites such as Payscale.com, salary.com, and salaryexpert.com to get a feel for the market. Look at surveys conducted by your professional organization.
- Step 3: *Build your case.*
    - How important are you to the organization? How have you contributed? Perhaps you contributed by increasing sales, winning over angry customers, getting feuding team members to cooperate, and so on. Make a list of your contributions. Be sure to focus on the contributions that your boss values most. Is it getting recognition for the department? Easing workload? If another employer has shown interest in you, mention that as a fact. However, don't use this as a threat unless you're prepared to take the other offer. Mentioning interest from another employer gets the boss to think, "If I don't give this raise, I may lose the employee." (By the way, if you don't feel you have a strong case for your raise, perhaps this isn't the time to ask for one.)
- Step 4: *Know what you want.*
    - Set your target salary goal based on your research and the norms of what your organization will pay. Now ask yourself if you don't get this figure, would you quit? If not, are there other alternatives besides a salary increase that you'd consider? For example, would you accept a higher title? More vacation time? Paid training to learn a new skill? Flexible hours?
- Step 5: *Begin assertively.*
    - Start the discussion on a strong but friendly tone. "I think I'm worth more than I'm being paid." List the ways you've contributed to the company.
- Step 6: *Don't make the first offer.*
    - Let your boss name the figure. You can do this by asking, "How much of a raise could you approve?" However, if the boss insists that you name a figure, ask for the most that you can reasonably expect to get. You want to be reasonable, but you need to allow room to make a concession. Your boss will assume your opening number was high and will offer you less, so asking for the actual figure you want may leave you feeling disappointed.
    - If the boss opens with, "The salary range for this position is $66,000 to 78,000," ask for the high end. If your goal was higher than that range, challenge the range by explaining how you are an exception and why you deserve more.
- Step 7: *Listen more than talk.*
    - You'll learn more by listening rather than talking. The more you listen, the better the boss will feel about you—people tend to like and trust people who listen to them.
    - If you can't get a raise now, get your boss to agree to one in a few months if you meet agreed-upon objectives.

Sources: Adapted from information in Brodow, E. (2006). Negotiation boot camp. New York: Currency/Doubleday; Nemko, M. (2007, December 31). The general way to get a raise. U.S. News & World Report, 57.

4.3 Avoiding Common Mistakes in Negotiations

Failing to Negotiate/Accepting the First Offer

You may have heard that women typically make less money than men. Researchers have established that about one-third of the gender differences observed in the salaries of men and women can be traced back to differences in starting salaries, with women making less, on average, when they start their jobs.[27] Some people are taught to feel that negotiation is a conflict situation, and these individuals may tend to avoid negotiations to avoid conflict. Research shows that this negotiation avoidance is especially prevalent among women. For example, one study looked at students from Carnegie-Mellon who were getting their first job after earning a master's degree. The study found that only 7% of the women negotiated their offer, while men negotiated 57% of the time.[28] The result had profound consequences. Researchers calculate that people who routinely negotiate salary increases will earn over $1 million more by retirement than people who accept an initial offer every time without asking for more.[29] The good news is that it appears that it is possible to increase negotiation efforts and confidence by training people to use effective negotiation skills.[30]

Letting Your Ego Get in the Way

Thinking only about yourself is a common mistake, as we saw in the opening case. People from the United States tend to fall into a self-serving bias in which they overinflate their own worth and discount the worth of others. This can be a disadvantage during negotiations. Instead, think about why the other person would want to accept the deal. People aren't likely to accept a deal that doesn't offer any benefit to them. Help them meet their own goals while you achieve yours. Integrative outcomes depend on having good listening skills, and if you are thinking only about your own needs, you may miss out on important opportunities. Remember that a good business relationship can only be created and maintained if both parties get a fair deal.

Having Unrealistic Expectations

Susan Podziba, a professor of mediation at Harvard and MIT, plays broker for some of the toughest negotiations around, from public policy to marital disputes. She takes an integrative approach in the negotiations, identifying goals that are large enough to encompass both sides. As she puts it, "We are never going to be able to sit at a table with the goal of creating peace and harmony between fishermen and conservationists. But we can establish goals big enough to include the key interests of each party and resolve the specific impasse we are currently facing. Setting reasonable goals at the outset that address each party's concerns will decrease the tension in the room, and will improve the chances of reaching an agreement."[31] Those who set unreasonable expectations are more likely to fail.

Getting Overly Emotional

Negotiations, by their very nature, are emotional. The findings regarding the outcomes of expressing anger during negotiations are mixed. Some researchers have found that those who express anger negotiate worse deals than those who do not,[32] and that during online negotiations, those parties who encountered anger were more likely to compete than those who did not.[33] In a study of online negotiations, words such as *despise*, *disgusted*, *furious*, and *hate* were related to a reduced chance of reaching an agreement.[34] However, this finding may depend on individual personalities. Research has also shown that those with more power may be more effective when displaying anger. The weaker party may perceive the anger as potentially signaling that the deal is falling apart and may concede items to help move things along.[35] This holds for online negotiations as well. In a study of 355 eBay disputes in which mediation was requested by one or both of the parties, similar results were found. Overall, anger hurts the mediation process unless one of the parties was perceived as much more powerful than the other party, in which case anger hastened a deal.[36] Another aspect of getting overly emotional is forgetting that facial expressions are universal across cultures, and when your words and facial expressions don't match, you are less likely to be trusted.[37]

Letting Past Negative Outcomes Affect the Present Ones

Research shows that negotiators who had previously experienced ineffective negotiations were more likely to have failed negotiations in the future. Those who were unable to negotiate some type of deal in previous negotiation situations tended to have lower outcomes than those who had successfully negotiated deals in the past.[38] The key to remember is that there is a tendency to let the past repeat itself. Being aware of this tendency allows you to overcome it. Be vigilant to examine the issues at hand and not to be overly swayed by past experiences, especially while you are starting out as a negotiator and have limited experiences.

Tips for Negotiation Success

- *Focus on agreement first.* If you reach an impasse during negotiations, sometimes the best recourse is to agree that you disagree on those topics and then focus only on the ones that you can reach an agreement on. Summarize what you've agreed on, so that everyone feels like they're agreeing, and leave out the points you don't agree on. Then take up those issues again in a different context, such as over dinner or coffee. Dealing with those issues separately may help the negotiation process.
- *Be patient.* If you don't have a deadline by which an agreement needs to be reached, use that flexibility to your advantage. The other party may be forced by circumstances to agree to your terms, so if you can be patient you may be able to get the best deal.
- *Whose reality?* During negotiations, each side is presenting their case—their version of reality. Whose version of reality will prevail? Leigh Steinberg offers this example from the NFL, when he was negotiating the salary of Warren Moon. Moon was 41 years old. That was a fact. Did that mean he was hanging on by a thread and lucky to be employed in the first place? "Should he be grateful for any

money that the team pays him?" Steinberg posed, "Or is he a quarterback who was among the league leaders in completions and attempts last year? Is he a team leader who took a previously moribund group of players, united them, and helped them have the best record that they've had in recent years?" All those facts are true, and negotiation brings the relevant facts to the forefront and argues their merit.

- *Deadlines.* Research shows that negotiators are more likely to strike a deal by making more concessions and thinking more creatively as deadlines loom than at any other time in the negotiation process.
- *Be comfortable with silence.* After you have made an offer, allow the other party to respond. Many people become uncomfortable with silence and feel they need to say something. Wait and listen instead.

Sources: Adapted from information in Stuhlmacher, A. F., Gillespie, T. L., & Champagne, M. V. (1998). The impact of time pressure in negotiation: A meta-analysis. International Journal of Conflict Management, 9, 97–116; Webber, A. (1998, October). How to get them to show you the money. Fast Company. Retrieved November 13, 2008 from http://www.fastcompany.com/magazine/19/showmoney.html.

4.4 When All Else Fails: Third-Party Negotiations

Alternative Dispute Resolution

Alternative Dispute Resolution (ADR) includes mediation, arbitration, and other ways of resolving conflicts with the help of a specially trained, neutral third party without the need for a formal trial or hearing.[39] Many companies find this effective in dealing with challenging problems. For example, Eastman Kodak Company added an alternative dispute resolution panel of internal employees to help them handle cases of perceived discrimination and hopefully stop a conflict from escalating.[40]

Alternative Dispute Resolution (ADR)

Includes mediation, arbitration, and other ways of resolving conflicts with the help of a specially trained, neutral third party without the need for a formal trial or hearing.

Mediation

In **mediation**, an outside third party (the mediator) enters the situation with the goal of assisting the parties in reaching an agreement. The mediator can facilitate, suggest, and recommend. The mediator works with both parties to reach a solution but does not represent either side. Rather, the mediator's role is to help the parties share feelings, air and verify facts, exchange perceptions, and work toward agreements. Susan Podziba, a mediation expert, has helped get groups that sometimes have a hard time seeing the other side's point of view to open up and talk to one another. Her work includes such groups as pro-choice and pro-life advocates, individuals from Israel and Palestine, as well as fishermen and environmentalists. According to the U.S. Equal Employment Opportunity Commission, "Mediation gives the parties the opportunity to discuss the issues raised in the charge, clear up misunderstandings, determine the underlying interests or concerns, find areas of agreement and, ultimately, to incorporate those areas of agreements into resolutions. A mediator does not resolve the charge or impose a decision on the parties. Instead, the mediator helps the parties to agree on a mutually acceptable resolution. The mediation process is strictly confidential."[41] One of the advantages of mediation is that the mediator helps the parties design their own solutions, including resolving issues that are important to both parties, not just the ones under specific dispute. Interestingly, sometimes mediation solves a conflict even if no resolution is reached. Here's a quote from Avis Ridley-Thomas, the founder and administrator of the Los Angeles City Attorney's Dispute Resolution Program, who explains, "Even if there is no agreement reached in mediation, people are happy that they engaged in the process. It often opens up the possibility for resolution in ways that people had not anticipated."[42] An independent survey showed 96% of all respondents and 91% of all charging parties who used mediation would use it again if offered.[43]

mediation

A process in which an outside third party (the mediator) enters the situation with the goal of assisting the parties to reach an agreement.

You Know It's Time for a Mediator When...

- *The parties are unable to find a solution themselves.*
- *Personal differences are standing in the way of a successful solution.*
- *The parties have stopped talking with one another.*
- *Obtaining a quick resolution is important.*

Sources: Adapted from information in Crawley, J. (1994). Constructive conflict management. San Diego: Pfeiffer; Mache, K. (1990). Handbook of dispute resolution: Alternative dispute resolution in action. London: Routledge.

Arbitration

arbitration

A process that involves bringing in a third party, the arbitrator, who has the authority to act as a judge and make a binding decision to which both parties must adhere.

In contrast to mediation, in which parties work with the mediator to arrive at a solution, in **arbitration** the parties submit the dispute to the third-party arbitrator. It is the arbitrator who makes the final decision. The arbitrator is a neutral third party, but the decision made by the arbitrator is final (the decision is called the "award"). Awards are made in writing and are binding to the parties involved in the case.[44] Arbitration is often used in union-management grievance conflicts.

Arbitration-Mediation

FIGURE 10.10

As a last resort, judges resolve conflicts.

Source: http://upload.wikimedia.org/wikipedia/commons/4/44/Supreme_Court_Front_Dusk.jpg.

It is common to see mediation followed by arbitration. An alternative technique is to follow the arbitration with mediation. The format of this conflict resolution approach is to have both sides formally make their cases before an arbitrator. The arbitrator then makes a decision and places it in a sealed envelope. Following this, the two parties work through mediation. If they are unable to reach an agreement on their own, the arbitration decisions become binding. Researchers using this technique found that it led to voluntary agreements between the two parties 71% of the time versus 50% for mediation followed by arbitration.[45]

KEY TAKEAWAY

Negotiation consists of five phases that include investigation, determining your BATNA, presentation, bargaining, and closure. Different negotiation strategies include the distributive approach (fixed-pie approach) and the integrative approach (expanding-the-pie approach). Research shows that some common mistakes made during negotiations include accepting the first offer made, letting egos get in the way, having unrealistic expectations, getting overly emotional, and letting past negative outcomes affect the present ones. Third-party negotiators are sometimes needed when two sides cannot agree.

EXERCISES

1. What are the negotiation phases and what goes on during each of them?
2. When negotiating, is establishing a BATNA important? Why or why not?
3. What are the third-party conflict resolution options available?

5. THE ROLE OF ETHICS AND NATIONAL CULTURE

LEARNING OBJECTIVES

1. Consider the role of ethics in negotiation.
2. Consider the role of national culture in negotiation.

5.1 Ethics and Negotiations

Are hardball tactics OK to use? Sometimes a course of action is legal, but is questionable in terms of ethics. A good rule of thumb is that hardball tactics should not be used because the negotiation is likely not to be the last time you will interact with the other party. Therefore, finding a way to make a deal that works for both sides is preferable. Otherwise, if you have the complete upper hand and use it to "destroy" the other party, it's likely that at a future date the other party will have the upper hand and will use it to retaliate mercilessly against you. What's more, your reputation as a negotiator will suffer. As J. Paul Getty said, "My father said: 'You must never try to make all the money that's in a deal. Let the other fellow make some money too, because if you have a reputation for always making all the money, you won't have many deals.'"[46]

Ethics establish a way of doing what is right, fair, and honest. If your counterpart feels you are being unfair or dishonest, he or she is less likely to make any concessions—or even to negotiate with you in the first place.

Here are some tips for ethical negotiations:

- Be honest.
- Keep your promises.
- Follow the Platinum Rule. The Golden Rule tells us to treat others the way we want to be treated. Author Tony Alessandra goes a step further with the Platinum Rule: "Treat people the way they want to be treated." Caring about others enough to treat them the way they want to be treated helps build long-term relationships based on ethics and trust.[47]

5.2 Negotiation Around the Globe

Not understanding cultural differences is another common mistake. Some cultures have a higher or lower threshold for conflict. For example, in countries such as Japan or Korea, the preference is for harmony (called *wa* in Japan) rather than overt conflict.[48] Americans and Germans have a much higher tolerance for conflict as a way of working through issues. In a study of Japanese, German, and American cultures, it was found that almost half of the preference for different conflict management styles was related to the country in which participants were raised.[49]

In Japan, much like Pakistan, the tendency is not to trust what is heard from the other party until a strong relationship is formed. Similarly, in China, conversations start out with innocuous topics to set a mood of friendliness.[50] This differs a great deal from American negotiators who tend to like to "get down to business" and heavily weigh first offers as reference points that anchor the process as both sides make demands and later offers.

There are also differences in how individuals from different cultures use information and offers during the negotiation process. Observations show that Japanese negotiators tend to use offers as an information exchange process.[51] Research has found that American negotiators tend to reveal more information than their Japanese counterparts.[52] Japanese negotiators might learn little from a single offer, but patterns of offers over time are interpreted and factored into their negotiations. Since Japan is a high-context culture, information is learned from what is not said as well as from what is said.

Even the way that negotiations are viewed can differ across cultures. For example, the Western cultures tend to think of negotiations as a business activity rather than a social activity, but in other cultures, the first step in negotiations is to develop a trusting relationship. Negotiators in Brazil, for example, seriously damaged relationships when they tried to push negotiations to continue during the Carnival festival. "The local guys took that as a disrespectful action," said Oscar Lopez, commercial director for Hexaprint, S.A. De C.V. in Mexico. "It took several weeks to restore confidence and move on."[53]

Also keep in mind what agreement means in different cultures. For example, in China, nodding of the head does not mean that the Chinese counterpart is agreeing to what you are proposing, merely that they are listening and following what you are saying. "Culturally, Chinese companies and workers do not like to say no," says a buyer at a manufacturer based in the United States. Here's how to overcome the problem. Instead of phrasing a question as, "Can you do this for us?" which would put the Chinese official in an uncomfortable position of saying no (which they likely would not do), rephrase the question as, "How will you do this for us and when will it be done?"[54]

KEY TAKEAWAY

Being honest during negotiations, keeping your promises, and treating others as you would like to be treated all help you negotiate ethically. Not understanding the culture of a person or group of people you are negotiating with can be a major mistake. Try to learn as much as you can about the culture of others involved and be sure to clarify key points along the way. Also, keep in mind that agreement (e.g., nodding one's head up and down or saying "yes, yes") may not mean the same thing in all cultures.

EXERCISES

1. Is the goal of negotiation to maximize your economic outcome at all costs? Why or why not? Is it ethical to do so?
2. What are some similarities and differences in conflict management preference and negotiation practices among different countries around the globe? Have you had any experiences with individuals from other cultures? If so, how did it go? How might it have gone better?

6. CONCLUSION

Conflict can run the gamut from minor annoyances to physically violent situations. At the same time, conflict can increase creativity and innovation, or it can bring organizations to a grinding halt. There are many different types of conflict, including interpersonal, intrapersonal, and intergroup. Within organizations, there are many common situations that can spur conflict. Certain organizational structures, such as a matrix structure, can cause any given employee to have multiple bosses and conflicting or overwhelming demands. A scarcity of resources for employees to complete tasks is another common cause of organizational conflict, particularly if groups within the organization compete over those resources. Of course, simple personality clashes can create intrapersonal conflict in any situation. Communication problems are also a very common source of conflict even when no actual problem would exist otherwise. When conflict arises, it can be handled by any number of methods, each with varying degrees of cooperation and competitiveness. Different situations require different conflict handling methods, and no one method is best.

Negotiations occur during many important processes, and possessing astute negation skills can be an incredible tool. A key component to negotiations involves having a BATNA, or "best alternative to a negotiated agreement." Negotiations typically move through five phases, including investigation, determining your BATNA, presentation, bargaining, and closure. During a negotiation, it is important not to make any number of common mistakes. These mistakes can include accepting the first offer, letting ego get in the way, having unrealistic expectations of the outcome of the negotiation, becoming too emotional during the process, or being weighed down by previous failures and letting the past repeat itself. It is important to keep in mind that many cultures have preferential methods for handling conflict and negotiation. Individuals should understand the cultural background of others to better navigate what could otherwise become a messy situation.

7. EXERCISES

ETHICAL DILEMMA

Imagine that you are part of a bargaining team that has been engaged in negotiations for 6 long months. One night, as you are getting ready to leave and are gathering your things, you notice a piece of green paper on the ground near where Devin, a member of the opposite negotiation team, was sitting just a few minutes earlier. When you pick it up, you realize that it is a list of the ideal outcome for the other team.

At first you are ecstatic—this is the information you need to end these negotiations! Then you begin to recall your organizational behavior course and all those ethical dilemmas that seemed so easy back then. What should you do? Should you use the information for your team? I mean, why not, they were careless enough to leave it behind? On the other hand, would that be ethical?

Thinking back to that OB course, you recall some key questions you should ask yourself during negotiations:

- Would this be honest?
- Would this involve keeping my promises?
- Would I be following the Platinum Rule and be "treating people the way they want to be treated?"

As you are pondering these questions, you also realize that this is a key decision. There are some additional questions you should ask yourself around making ethical decisions if you plan on using this information to help your team:

- Is this decision fair?
- Will I feel better or worse about myself after I make this decision?
- Does this decision break any organizational rules?
- Does this decision break any laws?
- How would I feel if this decision were broadcast on the news?

Just as you think you've made your decision, Devin from the opposing team walks back in and asks you if you've seen a green piece of paper.

- What would you do?
- What are the ethical dilemmas involved?
- How would you justify your choice?
- What would be the consequences of your choice?

INDIVIDUAL EXERCISE

A Case of Listening: When Silence Is Golden[55]

Listening can be an effective tool during negotiations. William Devine was representing a client on a land purchase. "The owner and I spent 2 hours on the phone horse-trading contract issues, then turned to the price," Devine explained. "We were $100,000 apart." The owner then said, "The price your client proposes will leave us well short of our projections. That makes it very tough on us." The line went silent.

"My impulse was to say something in response to the silence, and I started to speak, then stopped. As I hesitated, I sensed that if I said, 'My client can pay all cash,' or 'It's still a good deal for you,' then the owner would take my comment as an invitation to joust, we would battle over the hundred grand, and my client would end up having to pay some or all of that sum. The owner had not asked a question or proposed a compromise, so no response was required from me at that moment. I decided to remain silent. After what felt like days but was probably less than 30 seconds, I heard, 'But I guess it's good for us [i.e., his company] to just get this deal done, so we'll do it.'"

Devine saved his client $100,000 by staying silent.

Questions to Think About

1. What does this case suggest about the role of silence in negotiations?
2. Have you ever had a similar experience when saying nothing paid off?
3. Are there times when silence is a bad idea? Explain your answer.

GROUP EXERCISE

Salary Negotiations

Thinking about negotiations is a lot easier than actually engaging in them. In order to give you some practice with the information in this chapter, you will engage in a salary negotiation.

1. To make this more meaningful, the exercise will be based on a job that you are actually interested in. Think of a job you would like to have (either now or in the future). Imagine you have been offered this job. The salary is OK. It is about 15% below the market rate for this type of job, but you really want the job.
2. What will you do?
    - Will you negotiate for a higher salary?
    - What are the pros and cons of this choice?
3. If you've decided to negotiate (and we strongly suggest you do), work through the next six steps in the OB Toolbox "Seven Steps to Negotiating a Higher Salary." Once you are up to step 5, let your instructor know you are ready to begin the negotiation process.

ENDNOTES

1. National Institute for Occupational Safety and Health. (1997). Violence in the workplace. Retrieved November 14, 2008, from http://www.cdc.gov/niosh/violfs.html.
2. Wall, J. A., & Callister, R. R. (1995). Conflict and its management. *Journal of Management, 21*, 515–558.
3. Michaels, D., Power, S., & Gauthier-Villars, D. (2006, October 10). Airbus CEO's resignation reflects company's deep structural woes. *Wall Street Journal*, pp. A1–A10.
4. Whitehouse, K. (2008, January 14). Why CEOs need to be honest with their boards. *Wall Street Journal*, Eastern edition, pp. R1–R3.
5. Haddad, C. (2001, April 18). Why Jobs and Dell are always sparring. *Business Week Online*. Retrieved May 1, 2008, from http://www.businessweek.com/bwdaily/dnflash/apr2001/nf20010418_461.htm; Markoff, J. (2006, January 16). Michael Dell should eat his words, Apple chief suggests. *New York Times*. Retrieved January 19, 2007, from http://www.nytimes.com/2006/01/16/technology/16apple.html.
6. Stoykewych, R. E. (2003, March 7). A note on the seniority resolutions arising out of the merger of Air Canada and Canadian Airlines. Paper presented at the American Bar Association Midwinter Meeting, Laguna Beach, CA.
7. Amason, A. C. (1996). Distinguishing the effects of functional and dysfunctional conflict on strategic decision making: Resolving a paradox for top management teams. *Academy of Management Journal, 39*, 123–148.
8. De Dreu, C. K. W., & Weingart, L. R. (2003). Task versus relationship conflict: Team performance, and team member satisfaction: A meta-analysis. *Journal of Applied Psychology, 88*, 741–749.
9. Dahle, C. (2001, June). Is the Internet second nature? *Fast Company, 48*, 144.
10. Jehn, K. A., & Mannix, E. A. (2001). The dynamic nature of conflict: A longitudinal study of intergroup conflict and group performance. *Academy of Management Journal, 44*, 238–251.
11. Jaffe, D. (2000). *Organizational theory: Tension and change*. New York: McGraw Hill.
12. Taylor, W. (1991, March–April). The logic of global business: An interview with ABB's Percy Barnevik. *Harvard Business Review, 69*, 90–105.
13. Baron, R. A. (1989). Personality and organizational conflict: Type A behavior pattern and self-monitoring. *Organizational Behavior and Human Decision Processes, 44*, 281–297.
14. Jargon, J., Karnitschnig, M., & Lublin, J. S. (2008, February 23). How Hershey went sour. *Wall Street Journal*, pp. B1, B5.
15. Bergman, T. J., & Volkema, R. J. (1989). Understanding and managing interpersonal conflict at work: Its issues, interactive processes and consequences. In D. M. Kolb & J. M. Kolb (Eds.), *Hidden conflict in organizations* (pp. 7–19). Newbury Park, CA: Sage.
16. Gordon, J., Mondy, R. W., Sharplin, A., & Premeaux, S. R. (1990). *Management and organizational behavior*. New York: Simon & Schuster, p. 540.
17. Horowitz, A., Jacobson, D., Lasswell, M., & Thomas, O. (2006, January–February). 101 dumbest moments in business. *Business 2.0, 7*(1), 98–136.
18. Howat, G., & London, M. (1980). Attributions of conflict management strategies in supervisor-subordinate dyads. *Journal of Applied Psychology, 65*, 172–175.
19. Webber, A. (1998, October). How to get them to show you the money. *Fast Company*, 198. Retrieved November 14, 2008, from http://www.fastcompany.com/magazine/19/showmoney.html.
20. Fisher, R., & Ury, W. (1981). *Getting to yes: Negotiating agreement without giving in*. New York: Penguin Books.
21. Pinkley, R. L. (1995). Impact of knowledge regarding alternatives to settlement in dyadic negotiations: Whose knowledge counts? *Journal of Applied Psychology, 80*, 403–417.
22. Layne, A. (1999, November). Conflict resolution at Greenpeace? *Fast Company*. Retrieved November 14, 2008, from http://www.fastcompany.com/articles/1999/12/rick_hind.html.
23. Adapted from Malhotra, D., & Bazerman, M. H. (2007, September). Investigative negotiation. *Harvard Business Review, 85*, 72.
24. Malhotra, D., & Bazerman, M. H. (2007, September). Investigative negotiation. *Harvard Business Review, 85*, 72.
25. Thompson, L., & Hrebec, D. (1996). Lose-lose agreements in interdependent decision making. *Psychological Bulletin, 120*, 396–409.
26. Thompson, L. (1990). Negotiation behavior and outcomes: Empirical evidence and theoretical issues. *Psychological Bulletin, 108*, 515–532.
27. Gerhart, B. (1990). Gender differences in current and starting salaries: The role of performance, college major, and job title. *Industrial and Labor Relations Review, 43*, 418–433.
28. CNN. (2003, August 21). Interview with Linda Babcock. Retrieved November 14, 2008, from http://transcripts.cnn.com/TRANSCRIPTS/0308/21/se.04.html.
29. Babcock, L., & Lascheve, S. (2003). *Women don't ask: Negotiation and the gender divide*. Princeton, NJ: Princeton University Press.
30. Stevens, C. K., Bavetta, A. G., & Gist, M. E. (1993). Gender differences in the acquisition of salary negotiation skills: The role of goals, self-efficacy, and perceived control. *Journal of Applied Psychology, 78*, 723–735.
31. Rothenberger, C. (2008, September 11). Negotiation 201: Refine your skills. *Fast Company*. Retrieved January 11, 2008, from http://www.fastcompany.com/articles/team/prob_podziba.html.
32. Kopelman, S., Rosette, A. S., & Thompson, L. (2006). The three faces of Eve: An examination of the strategic display of positive, negative, and neutral emotions in negotiations. *Organizational behavior and human decision processes, 99*, 81–101.
33. Friedman, R., Anderson, C., Brett, J., Olekalns, M., Goates, N., & Lisco, C. C. (2004). The positive and negative effects of anger on dispute resolution: Evidence from electronically mediated disputes. *Journal of Applied Psychology, 89*, 369–376.
34. Brett, J. M., Olekalns, M., Friedman, R., Goates, N., Anderson, C., & Lisco, C. C. (2007). Sticks and stones: Language, face, and online dispute resolution. *Academy of Management Journal, 50*, 85–99.
35. Van Kleef, G. A., & Cote, S. (2007). Expressing anger in conflict: When it helps and when it hurts. *Journal of Applied Psychology, 92*, 1557–1569.
36. Friedman, R., Anderson, C., Brett, J., Olekalns, M., Goates, N., & Lisco, C. C. (2004). The positive and negative effects of anger on dispute resolution: Evidence from electronically mediated disputes. *Journal of Applied Psychology, 89*, 369–376.
37. [illegible] Professional; Holloway, L. (2007, December). Mixed signals: Are you saying one thing, while your face says otherwise? *Entrepreneur, 35*, 49.
38. O'Connor, K. M., Arnold, J. A., & Burris, E. R. (2005). Negotiators' bargaining histories and their effects on future negotiation performance. *Journal of Applied Psychology, 90*, 350–362.
39. New York State Unified Court System. (2008, October 28). Alternative dispute resolution. Retrieved November 14, 2008, from http://www.courts.state.ny.us/ip/adr/index.shtml.
40. Deutsch, C. H. (2004, August 24). Race remains a difficult issue for many workers at Kodak. *New York Times*.
41. The U.S. Equal Employment Opportunity Commission. (2007, December 4). *Mediation*. Retrieved November 13, 2008, from http://www.eeoc.gov/mediate/index.html.
42. Layne, A. (1999, November). Conflict resolution at Greenpeace? *Fast Company*. Retrieved November 11, 2008, from http://www.fastcompany.com/articles/1999/12/rick_hind.html.
43. Layne, A. (1999, November). Conflict resolution at Greenpeace? *Fast Company*. Retrieved November 11, 2008, from http://www.fastcompany.com/articles/1999/12/rick_hind.html.
44. American Arbitration Association. (2007). Arbitration and mediation. Retrieved November 11, 2008, from http://www.adr.org/arb_med.
45. Conlon, D. E., Moon, H., & Ng, K. Y. (2002). Putting the cart before the horse: The benefits of arbitrating before mediating. *Journal of Applied Psychology, 87*, 978–984.
46. Quote retrieved January 29, 2009, from http://www.saidwhat.co.uk/keywordquotes/money.
47. Stark, P. B., & Flaherty, J. (2003). Ethical negotiations: 10 tips to ensure win–win outcomes. *Negotiator · Magazine*. Retrieved November 11, 2008, from http://www.negotiatormagazine.com/showarticle.php?file=article106&page=1.
48. Lebra, T. S. (1976). *Japanese patterns of behavior*. Honolulu, HI: University Press of Hawaii.
49. Tinsley, C. (1998). Models of conflict resolution in Japanese, German, and American cultures. *Journal of Applied Psychology, 83*, 316–323.
50. U.S. Commerce Department. (2007). Retrieved November 11, 2008, from http://www.Buyusa.gov.
51. Adair, W. L., Weingart, L., & Brett, J. (2007). The timing and function of offers in the U.S. and Japanese negotiations. *Journal of Applied Psychology, 92*, 1056–1068.
52. Adair, W. L., Okumua, T., & Brett, J. M. (2001). Negotiation behavior when cultures collide: The United States and Japan. *Journal of Applied Psychology, 86*, 371–385.
53. Teague, P. E. (2006, August 17). Collaboration trumps negotiations. *Purchasing, 135*(11), 58.
54. Hannon, D. (2006, May 18). DO's and DON'Ts of doing business in China. *Purchasing, 135*(8), 52.
55. Devine, W. (2002, September 30). Anatomy of a deal-maker. *California Real Estate Journal*. Retrieved November 14, 2008 from http://www.wdesquire.com/pages/dealmaker.html.

CHAPTER 11
Making Decisions

LEARNING OBJECTIVES

After reading this chapter, you should be able to do the following:

1. Understand what is involved in decision making.
2. Compare and contrast different decision-making models.
3. Compare and contrast individual and group decision making.
4. Understand potential decision-making traps and how to avoid them.
5. Understand the pros and cons of different decision-making aids.
6. Engage in ethical decision making.
7. Understand cross-cultural differences in decision making.

Empowered Decision Making: The Case of Ingar Skaug

Ingar Skaug, CEO of Wilh. Wilhelmsen Lines, ASA, saw changing the decision-making climate of the company as one of the first changes needed when he took over in 1989.

Source: http://www.wilhelmsen.com/about/invest/corporate/Management/Pages/IngarSkaug.aspx.

"If you always do what you always did, you always get what you always got," according to Ingar Skaug—and he should know. Skaug is president and CEO of Wilh. Wilhelmsen, ASA, a leading global maritime industry company based in Norway with 23,000 employees and 516 offices worldwide. He faced major challenges when he began his job at Wilhelmsen Lines in 1989. The entire top management team of the company had been killed in an airplane crash while returning from a ship dedication ceremony. As you can imagine, employees were mourning the loss of their friends and leadership team. While Skaug knew that changes needed to be made within the organization, he also knew that he had to proceed slowly and carefully in implementing any changes. The biggest challenge he saw was the decision-making style within the company.

Skaug recalls this dilemma as follows. "I found myself in a situation in Wilhelmsen Lines where everyone was coming to my office in the morning and they expected me to take all the decisions. I said to people, 'Those are not my decisions. I don't want to take those decisions. You take those decisions.' So for half a year they were screaming about that I was very afraid of making decisions. So I had a little bit of a struggle with the organization, with the people there at the time. They thought I was a very poor manager because I didn't dare to make decisions. I had to teach them. I had to force the people to make their own decisions."

His lessons paid off over the years. The company has now invented a cargo ship capable of transporting 10,000 vehicles while running exclusively on renewable energy via the power of the sun, wind, and water. He and others within the company cite the freedom that employees feel to make decisions and mistakes on their way to making discoveries in improved methods as a major factor in their success in revolutionizing the shipping industry one innovation at a time.

Sources: McCathy, J. F., O'Connell, D. J., & Hall, D. T. (2005). Leading beyond tragedy: The balance of personal identity and adaptability. Leadership & Organizational Development Journal, 26, 458–475; Skaug, I. (2007, July). Breaking free in turbulent times: The intersection of turbulence, innovation and leadership: Unleashing creativity and driving positive change. Business Leadership Review, 4, 1–7; Furness, V. (2005). Interview with Ingar Skaug. European Business Forum. Retrieved April 4, 2008, from http://www.ebfonline.com/article.aspx?extraid=30; Norwegian executive Ingar Skaug named chairman of Center for Creative Leadership (2006). Retrieved April 4, 2008, from http://www.ccl.org/leadership/news/2006/skaug.aspx.

1. UNDERSTANDING DECISION MAKING

LEARNING OBJECTIVES

1. **Define decision making.**
2. **Understand different types of decisions.**

decision making

Making choices among alternative courses of action, including inaction.

Decision making refers to making choices among alternative courses of action—which may also include inaction. While it can be argued that management is decision making, half of the decisions made by managers within organizations ultimately fail.[1] Therefore, increasing effectiveness in decision making is an important part of maximizing your effectiveness at work. This chapter will help you understand how to make decisions alone or in a group while avoiding common decision-making pitfalls.

Individuals throughout organizations use the information they gather to make a wide range of decisions. These decisions may affect the lives of others and change the course of an organization. For example, the decisions made by executives and consulting firms for Enron ultimately resulted in a $60 billion loss for investors, thousands of employees without jobs, and the loss of all employee retirement funds. But Sherron Watkins, a former Enron employee and now-famous whistleblower, uncovered the accounting problems and tried to enact change. Similarly, the decision made by firms to trade in mortgage-backed securities is having negative consequences for the entire economy in the United States. All parties involved in such outcomes made a decision, and everyone is now living with the consequences of those decisions.

FIGURE 11.2

It is important to remember that decisions have consequences.

"The dip in sales seems to coincide with the decision to eliminate the sales staff."

1.1 Types of Decisions

Most discussions of decision making assume that only senior executives make decisions or that only senior executives' decisions matter. This is a dangerous mistake.

- *Peter Drucker*

Despite the far-reaching nature of the decisions in the previous example, not all decisions have major consequences or even require a lot of thought. For example, before you come to class, you make simple and habitual decisions such as what to wear, what to eat, and which route to take as you go to and from home and school. You probably do not spend much time on these mundane decisions. These types of straightforward decisions are termed **programmed decisions**, or decisions that occur frequently enough that we develop an automated response to them. The automated response we use to make these decisions is called the **decision rule**. For example, many restaurants face customer complaints as a routine part of doing business. Because complaints are a recurring problem, responding to them may become a programmed decision. The restaurant might enact a policy stating that every time they receive a valid customer complaint, the customer should receive a free dessert, which represents a decision rule.

On the other hand, unique and important decisions require conscious thinking, information gathering, and careful consideration of alternatives. These are called **nonprogrammed decisions**. For example, in 2005 McDonald's Corporation became aware of the need to respond to growing customer concerns regarding the unhealthy aspects (high in fat and calories) of the food they sell. This is a nonprogrammed decision, because for several decades, customers of fast-food restaurants were more concerned with the taste and price of the food, rather than its healthiness. In response to this problem, McDonald's decided to offer healthier alternatives such as the choice to substitute French fries in Happy Meals with apple slices and in 2007 they banned the use of trans fat at their restaurants.

programmed decisions

Decisions that occur frequently enough that we develop an automated response to them.

decision rule

Automated response to problems that occur routinely.

nonprogrammed decisions

Unique, nonroutine, and important. These decisions require conscious thinking, information gathering, and careful consideration of alternatives.

A crisis situation also constitutes a nonprogrammed decision for companies. For example, the leadership of Nutrorim was facing a tough decision. They had recently introduced a new product, ChargeUp with Lipitrene, an improved version of their popular sports drink powder, ChargeUp. At some point, a phone call came from a state health department to inform them of 11 cases of gastrointestinal distress that might be related to their product, which led to a decision to recall ChargeUp. The decision was made without an investigation of the information. While this decision was conservative, it was made without a process that weighed the information. Two weeks later it became clear that the reported health problems were unrelated to Nutrorim's product. In fact, all the cases were traced back to a contaminated health club juice bar. However, the damage to the brand and to the balance sheets was already done. This unfortunate decision caused Nutrorim to rethink the way decisions were made when under pressure. The company now gathers information to make informed choices even when time is of the essence.[2]

FIGURE 11.3

In order to ensure consistency around the globe such as at this St. Petersburg, Russia, location, McDonald's Corporation trains all restaurant managers at Hamburger University where they take the equivalent to 2 years of college courses and learn how to make decisions on the job. The curriculum is taught in 28 languages.

Source: http://upload.wikimedia.org/wikipedia/commons/a/a2/McDonalds_in_St_Petersburg_2004.JPG.

Decisions can be classified into three categories based on the level at which they occur. **Strategic decisions** set the course of an organization. **Tactical decisions** are decisions about how things will get done. Finally, **operational decisions** refer to decisions that employees make each day to make the organization run. For example, think about the restaurant that routinely offers a free dessert when a customer complaint is received. The owner of the restaurant made a strategic decision to have great customer service. The manager of the restaurant implemented the free dessert policy as a way to handle customer complaints, which is a tactical decision. Finally, the servers at the restaurant are making individual decisions each day by evaluating whether each customer complaint received is legitimate and warrants a free dessert.

strategic decisions

Decisions that are made to set the course of an organization.

tactical decisions

Decisions about how things will get done.

operational decisions

Decisions employees make each day to make the organization function.

FIGURE 11.4 Examples of Decisions Commonly Made Within Organizations

Level of Decision	*Examples of Decision*	*Who Typically Makes Decisions*
Strategic Decisions	Should we merge with another company? Should we pursue a new product line? Should we downsize our organization?	Top Management Teams, CEOs, and Boards of Directors
Tactical Decisions	What should we do to help facilitate employees from the two companies working together? How should we market the new product line? Who should be let go when we downsize?	Managers
Operational Decisions	How often should I communicate with my new coworkers? What should I say to customers about our new product? How will I balance my new work demands?	Employees throughout the organization

In this chapter we are going to discuss different decision-making models designed to understand and evaluate the effectiveness of nonprogrammed decisions. We will cover four decision-making approaches, starting with the rational decision-making model, moving to the bounded rationality decision-making model, the intuitive decision-making model, and ending with the creative decision-making model.

1.2 Making Rational Decisions

The **rational decision-making model** describes a series of steps that decision makers should consider if their goal is to maximize the quality of their outcomes. In other words, if you want to make sure that you make the best choice, going through the formal steps of the rational decision-making model may make sense.

rational decision-making model

A series of steps that decision makers should consider if their goal is to maximize their outcome and make the best choice.

Let's imagine that your old, clunky car has broken down, and you have enough money saved for a substantial down payment on a new car. It will be the first major purchase of your life, and you want to make the right choice. The first step, therefore, has already been completed—we know that you want to buy a new car. Next, in step 2, you'll need to decide which factors are important to you. How many passengers do you want to accommodate? How important is fuel economy to you? Is safety a major concern? You only have a certain amount of money saved, and you don't want to take on too much debt, so price range is an important factor as well. If you know you want to have room for at least five adults, get at least 20 miles per gallon, drive a car with a strong safety rating, not spend more than $22,000 on the purchase, and like how it looks, you have identified the **decision criteria**. All the potential options for purchasing your car will be evaluated against these criteria. Before we can move too much further, you need to decide how important each factor is to your decision in step 3. If each is equally important, then there is no need to weigh them, but if you know that price and mpg are key factors, you might weigh them heavily and keep the other criteria with medium importance. Step 4 requires you to generate all **alternatives** about your options. Then, in step 5, you need to use this information to evaluate each alternative against the criteria you have established. You choose the best alternative (step 6), and then you would go out and buy your new car (step 7).

decision criteria

A set of parameters against which all of the potential options in decision making will be evaluated.

alternatives

Other possible solutions to a problem in a decision-making process.

Of course, the outcome of this decision will influence the next decision made. That is where step 8 comes in. For example, if you purchase a car and have nothing but problems with it, you will be less likely to consider the same make and model when purchasing a car the next time.

FIGURE 11.5 Steps in the Rational Decision-Making Model

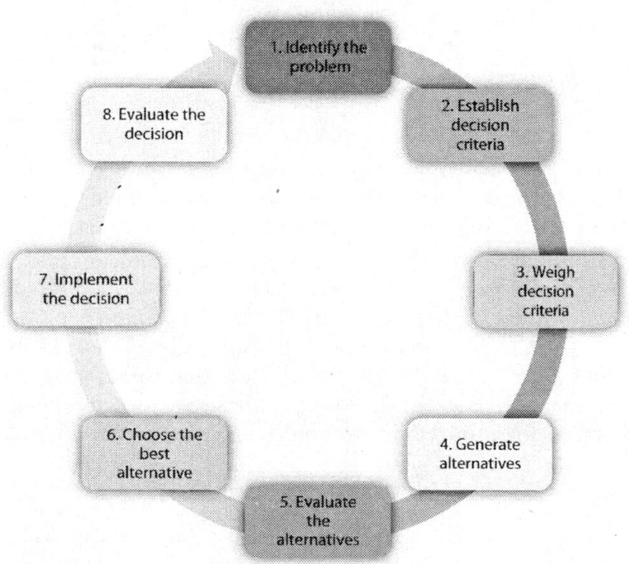

While decision makers can get off track during any of these steps, research shows that searching for alternatives in the fourth step can be the most challenging and often leads to failure. In fact, one researcher found that no alternative generation occurred in 85% of the decisions he studied.[3] Conversely, successful managers know what they want at the outset of the decision-making process, set objectives for others to respond to, carry out an unrestricted search for solutions, get key people to participate, and avoid using their power to push their perspective.[4]

The rational decision-making model has important lessons for decision makers. First, when making a decision, you may want to make sure that you establish your decision criteria before you search for alternatives. This would prevent you from liking one option too much and setting your criteria accordingly. For example, let's say you started browsing cars online before you generated your decision criteria. You may come across a car that you feel reflects your sense of style and you develop an emotional bond with the car. Then, because of your love for the particular car, you may say to yourself that the fuel economy of the car and the innovative braking system are the most important criteria. After purchasing it, you may realize that the car is too small for your friends to ride in the back seat, which was something you should have thought about. Setting criteria before you search for alternatives may prevent you from making such mistakes. Another advantage of the rational model is that it urges decision makers to generate all alternatives instead of only a few. By generating a large number of alternatives that cover a wide range of possibilities, you are unlikely to make a more effective decision that does not require sacrificing one criterion for the sake of another.

Despite all its benefits, you may have noticed that this decision-making model involves a number of unrealistic assumptions as well. It assumes that people completely understand the decision to be made, that they know all their available choices, that they have no perceptual biases, and that they want to make optimal decisions. Nobel Prize winning economist Herbert Simon observed that while the rational decision-making model may be a helpful device in aiding decision makers when working through problems, it doesn't represent how decisions are frequently made within organizations. In fact, Simon argued that it didn't even come close.

analysis paralysis

A decision-making process in which more and more time is spent on gathering information and thinking about it, but no decisions actually get made.

Think about how you make important decisions in your life. It is likely that you rarely sit down and complete all 8 of the steps in the rational decision-making model. For example, this model proposed that we should search for all possible alternatives before making a decision, but that process is time consuming, and individuals are often under time pressure to make decisions. Moreover, even if we had access to all the information that was available, it could be challenging to compare the pros and cons of each alternative and rank them according to our preferences. Anyone who has recently purchased a new laptop computer or cell phone can attest to the challenge of sorting through the different strengths and limitations of each brand and model and arriving at the solution that best meets particular needs. In fact, the availability of too much information can lead to **analysis paralysis**, in which more and more time is spent on gathering information and thinking about it, but no decisions actually get made. A senior executive at Hewlett-Packard Development Company LP admits that his company suffered from this spiral of analyzing things for too long to the point where data gathering led to "not making decisions, instead of us making decisions."[5] Moreover, you may not always be interested in reaching an optimal decision. For example, if you are looking to purchase a house, you may be willing and able to invest a great deal of time and energy to find your dream house, but if you are only looking for an apartment to rent for the academic year, you may be willing to take the first one that meets your criteria of being clean, close to campus, and within your price range.

1.3 Making "Good Enough" Decisions

bounded rationality model

According to this model, individuals knowingly limit their options to a manageable set and choose the first acceptable alternative without conducting an exhaustive search for alternatives.

satisfice

To accept the first alternative that meets minimum criteria.

The **bounded rationality model** of decision making recognizes the limitations of our decision-making processes. According to this model, individuals knowingly limit their options to a manageable set and choose the first acceptable alternative without conducting an exhaustive search for alternatives. An important part of the bounded rationality approach is the tendency to **satisfice** (a term coined by Herbert Simon from *satisfy* and *suffice*), which refers to accepting the first alternative that meets your minimum criteria. For example, many college graduates do not conduct a national or international search for potential job openings. Instead, they focus their search on a limited geographic area, and they tend to accept the first offer in their chosen area, even if it may not be the ideal job situation. Satisficing is similar to rational decision making. The main difference is that rather than choosing the best option and maximizing the potential outcome, the decision maker saves cognitive time and effort by accepting the first alternative that meets the minimum threshold.

1.4 Making Intuitive Decisions

intuitive decision-making model

Arriving at decisions without conscious reasoning. The model argues that in a given situation, experts making decisions scan the environment for cues to recognize patterns.

The **intuitive decision-making model** has emerged as an alternative to other decision making processes. This model refers to arriving at decisions without conscious reasoning. A total of 89% of managers surveyed admitted to using intuition to make decisions at least sometimes and 59% said they used intuition often.[6] Managers make decisions under challenging circumstances, including time pressures, constraints, a great deal of uncertainty, changing conditions, and highly visible and high-stakes outcomes. Thus, it makes sense that they would not have the time to use the rational decision-making model. Yet when CEOs, financial analysts, and health care workers are asked about the critical decisions they make, seldom do they attribute success to luck. To an outside observer, it may seem like they are making guesses as to the course of action to take, but it turns out that experts systematically make decisions using a different model than was earlier suspected. Research on life-or-death decisions made by fire chiefs, pilots, and nurses finds that experts do not choose among a list of well thought out alternatives. They don't decide between two or three options and choose the best one. Instead, they consider only one option at a time. The intuitive decision-making model argues that in a given situation, experts making decisions scan the environment for cues to recognize patterns.[7] Once a pattern is recognized, they can play a potential course of action through to its outcome based on their prior experience. Thanks to training, experience, and knowledge, these decision makers have an idea of how well a given solution may work. If they run through the mental model and find that the solution will not work, they alter the solution before setting it into action. If it still is not deemed a workable solution, it is discarded as an option, and a new idea is tested until a workable solution is found. Once a viable course of action is identified, the decision maker puts the solution into motion. The key point is that only one choice is considered at a time. Novices are not able to make effective decisions this way, because they do not have enough prior experience to draw upon.

1.5 Making Creative Decisions

In addition to the rational decision making, bounded rationality, and intuitive decision-making models, creative decision making is a vital part of being an effective decision maker. **Creativity** is the generation of new, imaginative ideas. With the flattening of organizations and intense competition among companies, individuals and organizations are driven to be creative in decisions ranging from cutting costs to generating new ways of doing business. Please note that, while creativity is the first step in the innovation process, creativity and innovation are not the same thing. Innovation begins with creative ideas, but it also involves realistic planning and follow-through. Innovations such as 3M's Clearview Window Tinting grow out of a creative decision-making process about what may or may not work to solve real-world problems.

creativity

The generation of new ideas that are original, fluent, and flexible.

The five steps to creative decision making are similar to the previous decision-making models in some keys ways. All the models include problem identification, which is the step in which the need for problem solving becomes apparent. If you do not recognize that you have a problem, it is impossible to solve it. Immersion is the step in which the decision maker consciously thinks about the problem and gathers information. A key to success in creative decision making is having or acquiring expertise in the area being studied. Then, incubation occurs. During incubation, the individual sets the problem aside and does not think about it for a while. At this time, the brain is actually working on the problem unconsciously. Then comes illumination, or the insight moment when the solution to the problem becomes apparent to the person, sometimes when it is least expected. This sudden insight is the "eureka" moment, similar to what happened to the ancient Greek inventor Archimedes, who found a solution to the problem he was working on while taking a bath. Finally, the verification and application stage happens when the decision maker consciously verifies the feasibility of the solution and implements the decision.

FIGURE 11.6 The Creative Decision-Making Process

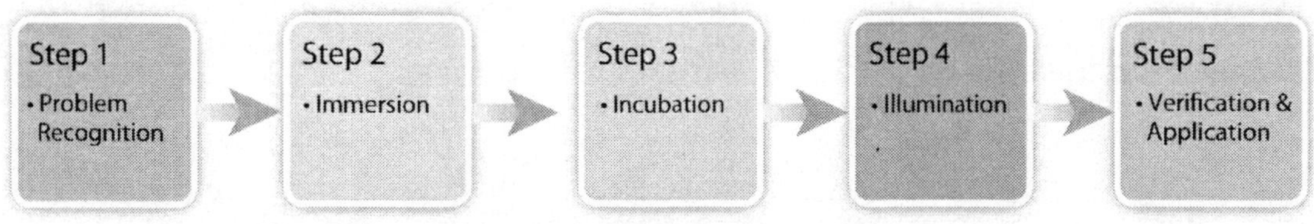

A NASA scientist describes his decision-making process leading to a creative outcome as follows: He had been trying to figure out a better way to de-ice planes to make the process faster and safer. After recognizing the problem, he immersed himself in the literature to understand all the options, and he worked on the problem for months trying to figure out a solution. It was not until he was sitting outside a McDonald's restaurant with his grandchildren that it dawned on him. The golden arches of the M of the McDonald's logo inspired his solution—he would design the de-icer as a series of Ms.[8] This represented the illumination stage. After he tested and verified his creative solution, he was done with that problem, except to reflect on the outcome and process.

How Do You Know If Your Decision-Making Process Is Creative?

fluency

The number of ideas a person is able to generate.

flexibility

How different the ideas are from each other. If individuals are able to generate several unique solutions to a problem, they are high on flexibility.

originality

How unique a person's ideas are.

Researchers focus on three factors to evaluate the level of creativity in the decision-making process. **Fluency** refers to the number of ideas a person is able to generate. **Flexibility** refers to how different the ideas are from one another. If you are able to generate several distinct solutions to a problem, your decision-making process is high on flexibility. **Originality** refers to how unique a person's ideas are. You might say that Reed Hastings, founder and CEO of Netflix Inc. is a pretty creative person. His decision-making process shows at least two elements of creativity. We do not know exactly how many ideas he had over the course of his career, but his ideas are fairly different from each other. After teaching math in Africa with the Peace Corps, Hastings was accepted at Stanford, where he earned a master's degree in computer science. Soon after starting work at a software company, he invented a successful debugging tool, which led to his founding of the computer troubleshooting company Pure Software LLC in 1991. After a merger and the subsequent sale of the resulting company in 1997, Hastings founded Netflix, which revolutionized the DVD rental business with online rentals delivered through the mail with no late fees. In 2007, Hastings was elected to Microsoft's board of directors. As you can see, his ideas are high in originality and flexibility.[9]

FIGURE 11.7 Dimensions of Creativity

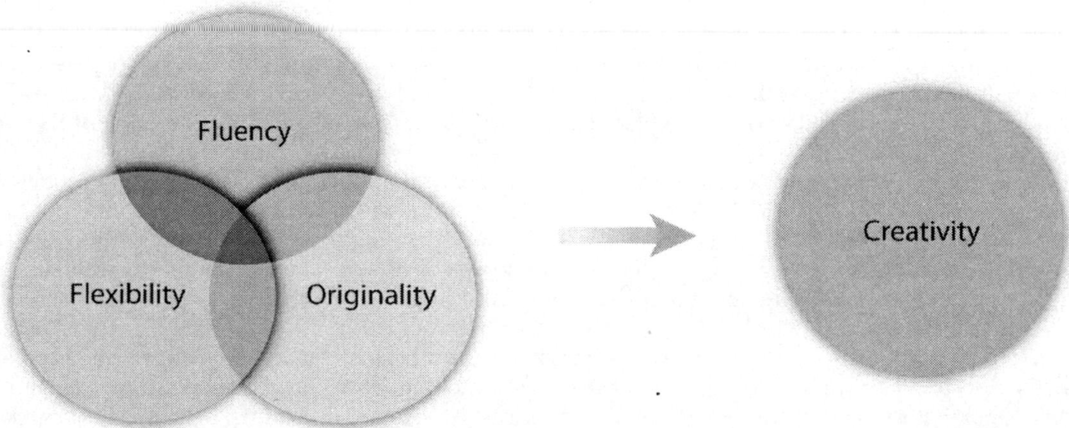

Some experts have proposed that creativity occurs as an interaction among three factors: people's personality traits (openness to experience, risk taking), their attributes (expertise, imagination, motivation), and the situational context (encouragement from others, time pressure, physical structures).[10] For example, research shows that individuals who are open to experience, less conscientious, more self-accepting, and more impulsive tend to be more creative.[11]

OB Toolbox: Ideas for Enhancing Organizational Creativity

- Team Composition
  - *Diversify your team* to give them more inputs to build on and more opportunities to create functional conflict while avoiding personal conflict.
  - *Change group membership* to stimulate new ideas and new interaction patterns.
  - *Leaderless teams* can allow teams freedom to create without trying to please anyone up front.
- Team Process
  - *Engage in brainstorming* to generate ideas. Remember to set a high goal for the number of ideas the group should come up with, encourage wild ideas, and take brainwriting breaks.
  - *Use the nominal group technique (see* Tools and Techniques for Making Better Decisions *below) in person or electronically* to avoid some common group process pitfalls. Consider anonymous feedback as well.
  - *Use analogies* to envision problems and solutions.
- Leadership
  - *Challenge teams* so that they are engaged but not overwhelmed.
  - *Let people decide how to achieve goals*, rather than telling them what goals to achieve.

- *Support and celebrate creativity* even when it leads to a mistake. Be sure to set up processes to learn from mistakes as well.
- *Role model* creative behavior.

- Culture
    - *Institute organizational memory* so that individuals do not spend time on routine tasks.
    - *Build a physical space conducive to creativity* that is playful and humorous—this is a place where ideas can thrive.
    - *Incorporate creative behavior* into the performance appraisal process.

Sources: Adapted from ideas in Amabile, T. M. (1998). How to kill creativity. Harvard Business Review, 76, 76–87; Gundry, L. K., Kickul, J. R., & Prather, C. W. (1994). Building the creative organization. Organizational Dynamics, 22, 22–37; Keith, N., & Frese, M. (2008). Effectiveness of error management training: A meta-analysis. Journal of Applied Psychology, 93, 59–69. Pearsall, M. J., Ellis, A. P. J., & Evans, J. M. (2008). Unlocking the effects of gender faultlines on team creativity: Is activation the key? Journal of Applied Psychology, 93, 225–234. Thompson, L. (2003). Improving the creativity of organizational work groups. Academy of Management Executive, 17, 96–109.

There are many techniques available that enhance and improve creativity. Linus Pauling, the Nobel Prize winner who popularized the idea that vitamin C could help strengthen the immune system, said, "The best way to have a good idea is to have a lot of ideas."[12] One popular method of generating ideas is to use brainstorming. **Brainstorming** is a group process of generating ideas that follow a set of guidelines, including no criticism of ideas during the brainstorming process, the idea that no suggestion is too crazy, and building on other ideas (piggybacking). Research shows that the quantity of ideas actually leads to better idea quality in the end, so setting high **idea quotas**, in which the group must reach a set number of ideas before they are done, is recommended to avoid process loss and maximize the effectiveness of brainstorming. Another unique aspect of brainstorming is that since the variety of backgrounds and approaches give the group more to draw upon, the more people are included in the process, the better the decision outcome will be. A variation of brainstorming is **wildstorming**, in which the group focuses on ideas that are impossible and then imagines what would need to happen to make them possible.[13]

brainstorming

A process of generating ideas that follows a set of guidelines, including not criticizing ideas during the process, the idea that no suggestion is too crazy, and building on other ideas (piggybacking).

idea quotas

A set number of ideas a group must reach before they are done with brainstorming.

wildstorming

A variation of brainstorming in which the group focuses on ideas that are impossible and then imagines what would need to happen to make them possible.

FIGURE 11.8

Which decision-making model should I use?

Decision Making Model	*Use This Model When:*
Rational	• Information on alternatives can be gathered and quantified. • The decision is important. • You are trying to maximize your outcome.
Bounded Rationality	• The minimum criteria are clear. • You do not have or you are not willing to invest much time to make the decision. • You are not trying to maximize your outcome.
Intuitive	• Goals are unclear. • There is time pressure and analysis paralysis would be costly. • You have experience with the problem.
Creative	• Solutions to the problem are not clear. • New solutions need to be generated. • You have time to immerse yourself in the issues.

KEY TAKEAWAY

Decision making is choosing among alternative courses of action, including inaction. There are different types of decisions ranging from automatic, programmed decisions to more intensive nonprogrammed decisions. Structured decision-making processes include rational, bounded rationality, intuitive, and creative decision making. Each of these can be useful, depending on the circumstances and the problem that needs to be solved.

EXERCISES

1. What do you see as the main difference between a successful and an unsuccessful decision? How much does luck versus skill have to do with it? How much time needs to pass to know if a decision is successful or not?
2. Research has shown that over half of the decisions made within organizations fail. Does this surprise you? Why or why not?
3. Have you used the rational decision-making model to make a decision? What was the context? How well did the model work?
4. Share an example of a decision in which you used satisficing. Were you happy with the outcome? Why or why not? When would you be most likely to engage in satisficing?
5. Do you think intuition is respected as a decision-making style? Do you think it should be? Why or why not?

2. FAULTY DECISION MAKING

LEARNING OBJECTIVES

1. **Understand overconfidence bias and how to avoid it.**
2. **Understand hindsight bias and how to avoid it.**
3. **Understand anchoring and how to avoid it.**
4. **Understand framing bias and how to avoid it.**
5. **Understand escalation of commitment and how to avoid it.**

2.1 Avoiding Decision-Making Traps

No matter which model you use, it is important to know and avoid the decision-making traps that exist. Daniel Kahnemann (another Nobel Prize winner) and Amos Tversky spent decades studying how people make decisions. They found that individuals are influenced by overconfidence bias, hindsight bias, anchoring bias, framing bias, and escalation of commitment.

overconfidence bias

What occurs when individuals overestimate their ability to predict future events.

Overconfidence bias occurs when individuals overestimate their ability to predict future events. Many people exhibit signs of overconfidence. For example, 82% of the drivers surveyed feel they are in the top 30% of safe drivers, 86% of students at the Harvard Business School say they are better looking than their peers, and doctors consistently overestimate their ability to detect problems.[14] Much like friends that are 100% sure they can pick the winners of this week's football games despite evidence to the contrary, these individuals are suffering from overconfidence bias. Similarly, in 2008, the French bank Société Générale lost over $7 billion as a result of the rogue actions of a single trader. Jérôme Kerviel, a junior trader in the bank, had extensive knowledge of the bank's control mechanisms and used this knowledge to beat the system. Interestingly, he did not make any money from these transactions himself, and his sole motive was to be successful. He secretly started making risky moves while hiding the evidence. He made a lot of profit for the company early on and became overly confident in his abilities to make even more. In his defense, he was merely able to say that he got "carried away."[15] People who purchase lottery tickets as a way to make money are probably suffering from overconfidence bias. It is three times more likely for a person driving ten miles to buy a lottery ticket to be killed in a car accident than to win the jackpot.[16] Further, research shows that overconfidence leads to less successful negotiations.[17] To avoid this bias, take the time to stop and ask yourself if you are being realistic in your judgments.

Hindsight bias is the opposite of overconfidence bias, as it occurs when looking backward in time and mistakes seem obvious after they have already occurred. In other words, after a surprising event occurred, many individuals are likely to think that they already knew the event was going to happen. This bias may occur because they are selectively reconstructing the events. Hindsight bias tends to become a problem when judging someone else's decisions. For example, let's say a company driver hears the engine making unusual sounds before starting the morning routine. Being familiar with this car in particular, the driver may conclude that the probability of a serious problem is small and continues to drive the car. During the day, the car malfunctions and stops miles away from the office. It would be easy to criticize the decision to continue to drive the car because in hindsight, the noises heard in the morning would make us believe that the driver should have known something was wrong and taken the car in for service. However, the driver in question may have heard similar sounds before with no consequences, so based on the information available at the time, continuing with the regular routine may have been a reasonable choice. Therefore, it is important for decision makers to remember this bias before passing judgments on other people's actions.

FIGURE 11.9

Source: Short, J., Bauer, T. N., Simon, L., & Ketchen, D. (2009). Atlas Black, managing to succeed. New York: Flat World Knowledge. Reprinted by permission.

Anchoring refers to the tendency for individuals to rely too heavily on a single piece of information. Job seekers often fall into this trap by focusing on a desired salary while ignoring other aspects of the job offer such as additional benefits, fit with the job, and working environment. Similarly, but more dramatically, lives were lost in the Great Bear Wilderness Disaster when the coroner, within 5 minutes of arriving at the accident scene, declared all five passengers of a small plane dead, which halted the search effort for potential survivors. The next day two survivors who had been declared dead walked out of the forest. How could a mistake like this have been made? One theory is that decision biases played a large role in this serious error, and anchoring on the fact that the plane had been consumed by flames led the coroner to call off the search for any possible survivors.[18]

Framing bias is another concern for decision makers. Framing bias refers to the tendency of decision makers to be influenced by the way that a situation or problem is presented. For example, when making a purchase, customers find it easier to let go of a discount as opposed to accepting a surcharge, even though they both might cost the person the same amount of money. Similarly, customers tend to prefer a statement such as "85% lean beef" as opposed to "15% fat."[19] It is important to be aware of this tendency, because depending on how a problem is presented to us, we might choose an alternative that is disadvantageous simply because of the way it is framed.

Escalation of commitment occurs when individuals continue on a failing course of action after information reveals it may be a poor path to follow. It is sometimes called the "sunken costs fallacy," because continuation is often based on the idea that one has already invested in the course of action. For example, imagine a person who purchases a used car, which turns out to need something repaired every few weeks. An effective way of dealing with this situation might be to sell the car without incurring further losses, donate the car, or use it until it falls apart. However, many people would spend hours of their time and hundreds, even thousands of dollars repairing the car in the hopes that they might recover their initial investment. Thus, rather than cutting their losses, they waste time and energy while trying to justify their purchase of the car.

A classic example of escalation of commitment from the corporate world is Motorola Inc.'s Iridium project. In the 1980s, phone coverage around the world was weak. For example, it could take hours of dealing with a chain of telephone operators in several different countries to get a call through from Cleveland to Calcutta. There was a real need within the business community to improve phone access around the world. Motorola envisioned solving this problem using 66 low-orbiting satellites, enabling users to place a direct call to any location around the world. At the time of idea development, the project was technologically advanced, sophisticated, and made financial sense. Motorola spun off Iridium as a separate company in 1991. It took researchers a total of 15 years to develop the product from idea to market release. However, in the 1990s, the landscape for cell phone technology was dramatically different from that in the 1980s, and the widespread cell phone coverage around the world eliminated most of the projected customer base for Iridium. Had they been paying attention to these developments, the decision makers could have abandoned the project at some point in the early 1990s. Instead, they released the Iridium phone to the market in 1998. The phone cost $3,000, and it was literally the size of a brick. Moreover, it was not possible to use the phone in moving cars or inside buildings. Not surprisingly, the launch was a failure, and Iridium filed for bankruptcy in 1999.[20] In the end, the company was purchased for $25 million by a group of investors (whereas it cost the company $5 billion to develop its product), scaled down its operations, and modified it for use by the Department of Defense to connect soldiers in remote areas not served by land lines or cell phones.

Why does escalation of commitment occur? There may be many reasons, but two are particularly important. First, decision makers may not want to admit that they were wrong. This may be because of

hindsight bias

The opposite of overconfidence bias, as it occurs when looking backward in time and mistakes seem obvious after they have already occurred.

anchoring

The tendency for individuals to rely too heavily on a single piece of information.

framing bias

The tendency of decision makers to be influenced by the way problems are presented.

escalation of commitment

When individuals continue on a failing course of action after information reveals it may be a poor path to follow.

personal pride or being afraid of the consequences of such an admission. Second, decision makers may incorrectly believe that spending more time and energy might somehow help them recover their losses. Effective decision makers avoid escalation of commitment by distinguishing between when persistence may actually pay off versus when it might mean escalation of commitment. To avoid escalation of commitment, you might consider having strict turning back points. For example, you might determine up front that you will not spend more than $500 trying to repair the car and will sell it when you reach that point. You might also consider assigning separate decision makers for the initial buying and subsequent selling decisions. Periodic evaluations of an initially sound decision to see whether the decision still makes sense is also another way of preventing escalation of commitment. This type of review becomes particularly important in projects such as the Iridium phone, in which the initial decision is not immediately implemented but instead needs to go through a lengthy development process. In such cases, it becomes important to periodically assess the soundness of the initial decision in the face of changing market conditions. Finally, creating an organizational climate in which individuals do not fear admitting that their initial decision no longer makes economic sense would go a long way in preventing escalation of commitment, as it could lower the regret the decision maker may experience.[21]

FIGURE 11.10

Motorola released the Iridium phone to the market in 1998. The phone cost $3,000 and it was literally the size of a brick.

Source: http://upload.wikimedia.org/wikipedia/commons/b/b0/Iridium_phone.jpg.

So far we have focused on how individuals make decisions and how to avoid decision traps. Next we shift our focus to the group level. There are many similarities as well as many differences between individual and group decision making. There are many factors that influence group dynamics and also affect the group decision-making process. We will discuss some of them in the following section.

KEY TAKEAWAY

Understanding decision-making traps can help you avoid and manage them. Overconfidence bias can cause you to ignore obvious information. Hindsight bias can similarly cause a person to incorrectly believe in their ability to predict events. Anchoring and framing biases show the importance of the way problems or alternatives are presented in influencing one's decision. Escalation of commitment demonstrates how individuals' desire to be consistent or avoid admitting a mistake can cause them to continue to invest in a decision that is no longer prudent.

EXERCISES

1. Describe a time when you fell into one of the decision-making traps. How did you come to realize that you had made a poor decision?
2. How can you avoid escalation of commitment?
3. Share an example of anchoring.
4. Which of the traps seems the most dangerous for decision makers and why?

3. DECISION MAKING IN GROUPS

LEARNING OBJECTIVES

1. Understand the pros and cons of individual and group decision making.
2. Learn to recognize the signs of groupthink.
3. Recognize different tools and techniques for making better decisions.

3.1 When It Comes to Decision Making, Are Two Heads Better Than One?

The answer to this question depends on several factors. Group decision making has the advantage of drawing from the experiences and perspectives of a larger number of individuals. Hence, a group may have the potential to be more creative and lead to more effective decisions. In fact, groups may sometimes achieve results beyond what they could have done as individuals. Groups may also make the task more enjoyable for the members. Finally, when the decision is made by a group rather than a single individual, implementation of the decision will be easier, because group members will be more invested in the decision. If the group is diverse, better decisions may be made, because different group members may have different ideas based on their backgrounds and experiences. Research shows that for top management teams, diverse groups that debate issues make decisions that are more comprehensive and better for the bottom line.[22]

Despite its popularity within organizations, group decision making suffers from a number of disadvantages. We know that groups rarely outperform their best member.[23] While groups have the potential to arrive at an effective decision, they often suffer from process losses. For example, groups may suffer from coordination problems. Anyone who has worked with a team of individuals on a project can attest to the difficulty of coordinating members' work or even coordinating everyone's presence in a team meeting. Furthermore, groups can suffer from groupthink. Finally, group decision making takes more time compared to individual decision making, because all members need to discuss their thoughts regarding different alternatives.

Thus, whether an individual or a group decision is preferable will depend on the specifics of the situation. For example, if there is an emergency and a decision needs to be made quickly, individual decision making might be preferred. Individual decision making may also be appropriate if the individual in question has all the information needed to make the decision and if implementation problems are not expected. On the other hand, if one person does not have all the information and skills needed to make a decision, if implementing the decision will be difficult without the involvement of those who will be affected by the decision, and if time urgency is more modest, then decision making by a group may be more effective.

FIGURE 11.11 Advantages and Disadvantages of Different Levels of Decision Making

Individual Decision Making		***Group Decision Making***	
Pros	***Cons***	***Pros***	***Cons***
Typically faster than group decision making	Fewer ideas	Diversity of ideas and can piggyback on others' ideas	Takes longer
Best individual in a group usually outperforms the group	Identifying the best individual can be challenging	Greater commitment to ideas	Group dynamics such as groupthink can occur
Accountability is easier to determine	Possible to put off making decisions if left alone to do it	Interaction can be fun and serves as a teambuilding task	Social loafing—harder to identify responsibility for decisions

3.2 Groupthink

FIGURE 11.12

In January 1986, the space shuttle *Challenger* exploded 73 seconds after liftoff, killing all seven astronauts aboard. The decision to launch *Challenger* that day, despite problems with mechanical components of the vehicle and unfavorable weather conditions, is cited as an example of groupthink.[24]

Source: http://en.wikipedia.org/wiki/Image:Challenger_flight_51-l_crew.jpg.

groupthink

A tendency to avoid a critical evaluation of ideas the group favors.

Have you ever been in a decision-making group that you felt was heading in the wrong direction but you didn't speak up and say so? If so, you have already been a victim of groupthink. **Groupthink** is a tendency to avoid a critical evaluation of ideas the group favors. Iriving Janis, author of a book called *Victims of Groupthink*, explained that groupthink is characterized by eight symptoms:[25]

1. **Illusion of invulnerability** is shared by most or all of the group members, which creates excessive optimism and encourages them to take extreme risks.
2. **Collective rationalizations** occur, in which members downplay negative information or warnings that might cause them to reconsider their assumptions.
3. **An unquestioned belief in the group's inherent morality** occurs, which may incline members to ignore ethical or moral consequences of their actions.
4. **Stereotyped views of outgroups** are seen when groups discount rivals' abilities to make effective responses.
5. **Direct pressure** is exerted on any members who express strong arguments against any of the group's stereotypes, illusions, or commitments.
6. **Self-censorship** occurs when members of the group minimize their own doubts and counterarguments.
7. **Illusions of unanimity** occur, based on self-censorship and direct pressure on the group. The lack of dissent is viewed as unanimity.
8. **The emergence of self-appointed mindguards** happens when one or more members protect the group from information that runs counter to the group's assumptions and course of action.

OB Toolbox: Recommendations for Avoiding Groupthink

- Groups should do the following:
  - Discuss the symptoms of groupthink and how to avoid them.
  - Assign a rotating devil's advocate to every meeting.
  - Invite experts or qualified colleagues who are not part of the core decision-making group to attend meetings and get reactions from outsiders on a regular basis and share these with the group.
  - Encourage a culture of difference where different ideas are valued.
  - Debate the ethical implications of the decisions and potential solutions being considered.
- Individuals should do the following:
  - Monitor personal behavior for signs of groupthink and modify behavior if needed.

- Check for self-censorship.
- Carefully avoid mindguard behaviors.
- Avoid putting pressure on other group members to conform.
- Remind members of the ground rules for avoiding groupthink if they get off track.

- Group leaders should do the following:
  - Break the group into two subgroups from time to time.
  - Have more than one group work on the same problem if time and resources allow it. This makes sense for highly critical decisions.
  - Remain impartial and refrain from stating preferences at the outset of decisions.
  - Set a tone of encouraging critical evaluations throughout deliberations.
  - Create an anonymous feedback channel through which all group members can contribute if desired.

Sources: Adapted and expanded from Janis, I. L. (1972). Victims of groupthink. New York: Houghton Mifflin; Whyte, G. (1991). Decision failures: Why they occur and how to prevent them. Academy of Management Executive, 5, 23–31.

3.3 Tools and Techniques for Making Better Decisions

Nominal Group Technique (NGT) was developed to help with group decision making by ensuring that all members participate fully. NGT is not a technique to be used routinely at all meetings. Rather, it is used to structure group meetings when members are grappling with problem solving or idea generation. It follows four steps.[26] First, each member of the group begins by independently and silently writing down ideas. Second, the group goes in order around the room to gather all the ideas that were generated. This process continues until all the ideas are shared. Third, a discussion takes place around each idea, and members ask for and give clarification and make evaluative statements. Finally, group members vote for their favorite ideas by using ranking or rating techniques. Following the four-step NGT helps to ensure that all members participate fully, and it avoids group decision-making problems such as groupthink.

Nominal Group Technique (NGT)

A technique designed to help with group decision making by ensuring that all members participate fully.

Delphi Technique is unique because it is a group process using written responses to a series of questionnaires instead of physically bringing individuals together to make a decision. The first questionnaire asks individuals to respond to a broad question such as stating the problem, outlining objectives, or proposing solutions. Each subsequent questionnaire is built from the information gathered in the previous one. The process ends when the group reaches a consensus. Facilitators can decide whether to keep responses anonymous. This process is often used to generate best practices from experts. For example, Purdue University Professor Michael Campion used this process when he was editor of the research journal *Personnel Psychology* and wanted to determine the qualities that distinguished a good research article. Using the Delphi technique, he was able to gather responses from hundreds of top researchers from around the world and distill them into a checklist of criteria that he could use to evaluate articles submitted to his journal, all without ever having to leave his office.[27]

Delphi Technique

A group process that utilizes written responses to a series of questionnaires instead of physically bringing individuals together to make a decision.

Majority rule refers to a decision-making rule in which each member of the group is given a single vote and the option receiving the greatest number of votes is selected. This technique has remained popular, perhaps due to its simplicity, speed, ease of use, and representational fairness. Research also supports majority rule as an effective decision-making technique.[28] However, those who did not vote in favor of the decision will be less likely to support it.

majority rule

A decision-making rule in which each member of the group is given a single vote, and the option receiving the greatest number of votes is selected.

Consensus is another decision-making rule that groups may use when the goal is to gain support for an idea or plan of action. While consensus tends to require more time, it may make sense when support is needed to enact the plan. The process works by discussing the issues at hand, generating a proposal, calling for consensus, and discussing any concerns. If concerns still exist, the proposal is modified to accommodate them. These steps are repeated until consensus is reached. Thus, this decision-making rule is inclusive, participatory, cooperative, and democratic. Research shows that consensus can lead to better accuracy,[29] and it helps members feel greater satisfaction with decisions.[30] However, groups take longer with this approach, and if consensus cannot be reached, members tend to become frustrated.[31]

FIGURE 11.13

Communicating is a key aspect of making decisions in a group. In order to generate potential alternatives, brainstorming and critical thinking are needed to avoid groupthink.

consensus

A decision-making rule that groups may use when the goal is to gain support for an idea or plan of action. This decision-making rule is inclusive, participatory, cooperative, and democratic.

premortem

A way to imagine what might go wrong and avoid it before spending a cent or having to change course along the way.

OB Toolbox: Perform a Project "Premortem"

Doctors routinely perform postmortems to understand what went wrong with a patient who has died. The idea is for everyone to learn from the unfortunate outcome so that future patients will not meet a similar fate. But what if you could avoid a horrible outcome before it happened by proactively identifying project risks? Research has shown that the simple exercise of imagining what could go wrong with a given decision can increase people's ability to correctly identify reasons for future successes or failures by 30%.[32] A "**premortem**" is a way to imagine what might go wrong and avoid it before spending a cent or having to change course along the way. Gary Klein, an expert on decision making in fast-paced, uncertain, complex, and critical environments, recommends that decision makers follow a five-step process to increase their chances of success.

1. A planning team comes up with an outline of a plan, such as the launching of a new product.
2. Either the existing group or a unique group is then told to imagine looking into a crystal ball and seeing that the new product failed miserably. They then write down all the reasons they can imagine that might have led to this failure. Each team member shares items from their list until all the potential problems have been identified.
3. The list is reviewed for additional ideas.
4. The issues are sorted into categories in the search for themes.
5. The plan should then be revised to correct the flaws and avoid these potential problems.

This technique allows groups to truly delve into "what if" scenarios. For example, in a premortem session at a Fortune 500 company, an executive imagined that a potential billion-dollar environmental sustainability project might fail because the CEO had retired.

Sources: Breen, B. (2000, August). What's your intuition? Fast Company, 290; Klein, G. (2007, September). Performing a project premortem. Harvard Business Review, 85, 18–19; Klein, G. (2003). The power of intuition: How to use your gut feelings to make better decisions at work. New York: Random House; Pliske, R., McCloskey, M., & Klein, G. (2001). Decision skills training: Facilitating learning from experience. In E. Salas & G. Klein (Eds.), Linking expertise and naturalistic decision making (pp. 37–53). Mahwah, NJ: Lawrence Erlbaum Associates.

Group Decision Support Systems (GDSS) are interactive computer-based systems that are able to combine communication and decision technologies to help groups make better decisions. Research shows that a GDSS can actually improve the output of groups' collaborative work through higher information sharing.[33] Organizations know that having effective **knowledge management systems** to share information is important, and their spending reflects this reality. Businesses invested $2.7 billion into new systems in 2002, and projections were for this number to double every 5 years. As the popularity of these systems grows, they risk becoming counterproductive. Humans can only process so many ideas and information at one time. As virtual meetings grow larger, it is reasonable to assume that information overload can occur and good ideas will fall through the cracks, essentially recreating a problem that the GDSS was intended to solve, which is to make sure every idea is heard. Another problem is the system possibly becoming too complicated. If the systems evolve to a point of uncomfortable complexity, it has recreated the problem. Those who understand the interface will control the narrative of the discussion, while those who are less savvy will only be along for the ride.[34] Lastly, many of these programs fail to take into account the factor of human psychology. These systems could make employees more reluctant to share information because of lack of control, lack of immediate feedback, or the fear of online "flames."

Group Decision Support Systems (GDSS)

Interactive computer-based systems that are able to combine communication and decision technologies to help groups make better decisions.

knowledge management systems

Systems for managing knowledge in organizations, supporting creation, capture, storage, and dissemination of information.

Decision trees are diagrams in which answers to yes or no questions lead decision makers to address additional questions until they reach the end of the tree. Decision trees are helpful in avoiding er- [illegible].[35] Decision trees tend to be helpful in guiding the decision maker to a predetermined alternative and ensuring consistency of decision making—that is, every time certain conditions are present, the decision maker will follow one course of action as opposed to others if the decision is made using a decision tree.

decision trees

Diagrams where answers to [illegible] decision makers to address additional questions until they reach the end of the tree.

FIGURE 11.14

Utilizing decision trees can improve investment decisions by optimizing them for maximum payoff. A decision tree consists of three types of nodes. Decision nodes are commonly represented by squares. Chance nodes are represented by circles. End nodes are represented by triangles.

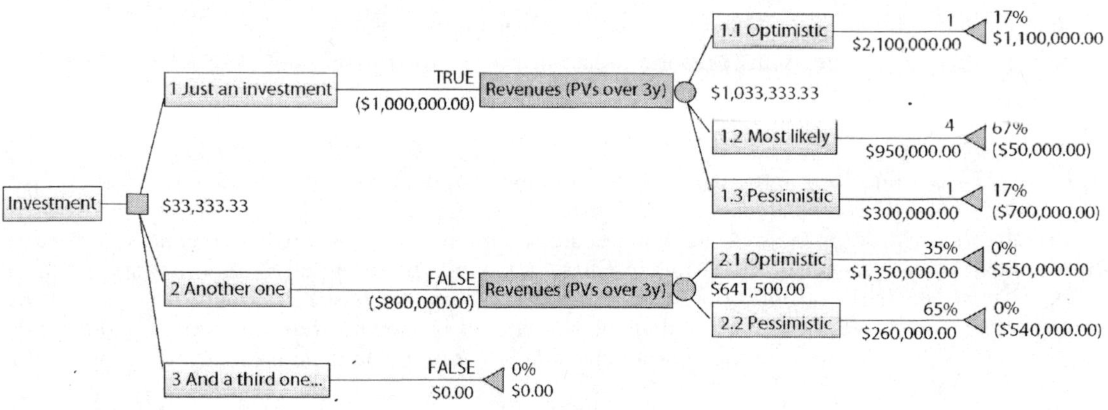

Source: http://upload.wikimedia.org/wikipedia/en/9/93/Investment_decision_Insight.png.

KEY TAKEAWAY

There are trade-offs between making decisions alone and within a group. Groups have a greater diversity of experiences and ideas than individuals, but they also have potential process losses such as groupthink. Groupthink can be avoided by recognizing the eight symptoms discussed. Finally, there are a variety of tools and techniques available for helping to make more effective decisions in groups, including the nominal group technique, Delphi technique, majority rule, consensus, GDSS, and decision trees.

EXERCISES

1. Do you prefer to make decisions in a group or alone? What are the main reasons for your preference?
2. Have you been in a group that used the brainstorming technique? Was it an effective tool for coming up with creative ideas? Please share examples.
3. Have you been in a group that experienced groupthink? If so, how did you deal with it?
4. Which of the decision-making tools discussed in this chapter (NGT, Delphi, and so on) have you used? How effective were they?

4. THE ROLE OF ETHICS AND NATIONAL CULTURE

LEARNING OBJECTIVES

1. **Consider the role of ethical behavior on decision making.**
2. **Consider the role of national culture on decision making.**

4.1 Ethics and Decision Making

Because many decisions involve an ethical component, one of the most important considerations in management is whether the decisions you are making as an employee or manager are ethical. Here are some basic questions you can ask yourself to assess the ethics of a decision.[36]

- Is this decision fair?
- Will I feel better or worse about myself after I make this decision?
- Does this decision break any organizational rules?
- Does this decision break any laws?
- How would I feel if this decision were broadcast on the news?

The current economic crisis in the United States and many other parts of the world is a perfect example of legal yet unethical decisions resulting in disaster. Many experts agree that one of the driving forces behind the sliding economy was the lending practices of many banks (of which several no longer exist). In March of 2008, a memo from JPMorgan Chase & Co. was leaked to an Oregon newspaper called "Zippy Cheats & Tricks" (Zippy is Chase's automated, computer-based loan approval system). Although Chase executives firmly stated that the contents of the memo were not company policy, the contents clearly indicate some of the questionable ethics involved with the risky loans now clogging the financial system.

In the memo, several steps were outlined to help a broker push a client's approval through the system, including, "In the income section of your 1003, make sure you input all income in base income. DO NOT break it down by overtime, commissions or bonus. NO GIFT FUNDS! If your borrower is getting a gift, add it to a bank account along with the rest of the assets. Be sure to remove any mention of gift funds on the rest of your 1003. If you do not get Stated/Stated, try resubmitting with slightly higher income. Inch it up $500 to see if you can get the findings you want. Do the same for assets."[37]

While it is not possible to determine how widely circulated the memo was, the mentality it captures was clearly present during the lending boom that precipitated the current meltdown. While some actions during this period were distinctly illegal, many people worked well within the law and simply made unethical decisions. Imagine a real estate agent that knows a potential buyer's income. The buyer wants to purchase a home priced at $400,000, and the agent knows the individual cannot afford to make payments on a mortgage of that size. Instead of advising the buyer accordingly and losing a large commission, the agent finds a bank willing to lend money to an unqualified borrower, collects the commission for the sale, and moves on to the next client. It is clear how these types of unethical yet legal decisions can have dramatic consequences.

Suppose you are the CEO of a small company that needs to cut operational costs or face bankruptcy. You have decided that you will not be issuing the yearly bonus that employees have come to expect. The first thing you think about after coming to this decision is whether or not it is fair. It seems logical to you that since the alternative would be the failure of the company and everyone's losing their jobs, not receiving a bonus is preferable to being out of work. Additionally, you will not be collecting a bonus yourself, so that the decision will affect everyone equally. After deciding that the decision seems fair, you try to assess how you will feel about yourself after informing employees that there will not be a bonus this year. Although you do not like the idea of not being able to issue the yearly bonus, you are the CEO, and CEOs often have to make tough decisions. Since your ultimate priority is to save the company from bankruptcy, you decide it is better to withhold bonuses rather than issuing them, knowing the company cannot afford it. Despite the fact that bonuses have been issued every year since the company was founded, there are no organizational policies or laws requiring that employees receive a bonus; it has simply been a company tradition. The last thing you think about is how you would feel if your decision were broadcast on the news. Because of the dire nature of the situation, and because the fate of the business is at stake, you feel confident that this course of action is preferable to laying off loyal employees. As long as the facts of the situation were reported correctly, you feel the public would understand why the decision was made.

4.2 Decision Making Around the Globe

Decision-making styles and approaches tend to differ depending on the context, and one important contextual factor to keep in mind is the culture in which decisions are being made. Research on Japanese and Dutch decision makers show that while both cultures are consensus-oriented, Japanese managers tend to seek consensus much more than Dutch managers.[38] Additionally, American managers tend to value quick decision making, while Chinese managers are more reflective and take their time to make important decisions—especially when they involve some sort of potential conflict.

Another example of how decision-making styles may differ across cultures is the style used in Japan called *nemawashi*. Nemawashi refers to building consensus within a group before a decision is made. Japanese decision makers talk to parties whose support is needed beforehand, explain the subject, address their concerns, and build their support. Using this method clearly takes time and may lead to slower decision making. However, because all parties important to the decision will give their stamp of approval before the decision is made, this technique leads to a quicker implementation of the final decision once it is decided.

KEY TAKEAWAY

Asking yourself some key questions can help you determine if a decision you are considering is ethical. A decision being legal does not automatically make it ethical. Unethical decisions can lead to business failures for a variety of reasons. Different cultures have different styles of decision making. In countries with a collectivist orientation, a high value is placed on building consensus. Some national cultures value quick decision making, whereas others believe in taking time to arrive at a decision. Taking national culture into account is important in effective cross-cultural business interactions.

EXERCISES

1. How can you assess if you are making ethical decisions or not?
2. Have you seen examples of ethical or unethical decisions being made? Describe what you observed.
3. Have you seen examples of national culture affecting decision making?
4. What advice surrounding decision making would you give to someone who will be managing a new division of a company in another culture?
5. What can go wrong when cultural factors are ignored?

5. CONCLUSION

Decision making is a critical component of business. Some decisions are obvious and can be made quickly, without investing much time and effort in the decision-making process. Others, however, require substantial consideration of the circumstances surrounding the decision, available alternatives, and potential outcomes. Fortunately, there are several methods that can be used when making a difficult decision, depending on various environmental factors. Some decisions are best made by groups. Group decision-making processes also have multiple models to follow, depending on the situation. Even when specific models are followed, groups and individuals can often fall into potential decision-making pitfalls. If too little information is available, decisions might be made based on a feeling. On the other hand, if too much information is presented, people can suffer from analysis paralysis, in which no decision is reached because of the overwhelming number of alternatives.

Ethics and culture both play a part in decision making. From time to time, a decision can be legal but not ethical. These gray areas that surround decision making can further complicate the process, but following basic guidelines can help people ensure that the decisions they make are ethical and fair. Additionally, different cultures can have different styles of decision making. In some countries such as the United States, it may be customary to come to a simple majority when making a decision. Conversely, a country such as Japan will often take the time to reach consensus when making decisions. Being aware of the various methods for making decisions as well as potential problems that may arise can help people become effective decision makers in any situation.

6. EXERCISES

ETHICAL DILEMMA

Herb's Concoction (and Martha's Dilemma): The Case of the Deadly Fertilizer[39]

Martha Wang worked in the Consumer Affairs Department of a company called Herb's Garden Products. Martha was a relatively new employee and had only worked there 6 months, while most employees at Herb's had been with the company since its beginning back in 1958. She enjoyed her job and hoped to be promoted at her next performance appraisal. One especially exciting part of working at Herb's was that they had made a public commitment to protecting the environment. There were regular meetings at work about the choice to brand the organization in this way, sell their products at "green" markets, and capture some of the growing consumer market for natural products. Martha's values were closely aligned with this mentality, so she really loved her new job at Herb's Garden Products. How quickly things change.

One day, Martha received a call from a dissatisfied customer who complained that Herb's Special Fertilizer Mix killed her dog, an expensive and beloved toy poodle. Martha knew that the fertilizer was made mostly of fish byproducts and chicken manure, but she had also heard there was a "secret ingredient" that had only been revealed to long-time employees. The company had advertised the product as "safe enough to eat for breakfast" and "able to work wonders on any plant." However, Martha had used the product only once herself. Shortly after applying the fertilizer, Martha found several dead birds near the garden where she had spread the most fertilizer. At the time, she convinced herself this was just a coincidence. Listening now to this customer describing the death of her small dog after lying on the soil near the fertilizer, Martha began to wonder if those birds had perished for the same reason. Martha took the customer's name and number and went immediately to her boss.

Martha's boss was Herb's nephew, Mac. Once Martha explained her story about her own experience with the fertilizer and the customer's claim that it killed her dog, Mac began to smile. "Some people will complain about the littlest things," Mac said. Martha protested that it was her job as a consumer affairs officer to address the serious concerns of this customer and follow company procedure to ensure the safety of future customers and their pets. Mac laughed and said, "You really believe that something is wrong with our product? We've been selling this fertilizer for 35 years. People love it! Now and again someone whines about finding dead animals, but that's just their imagination. After all, we use all-natural ingredients!" Martha thanked Mac for his help and slowly headed back toward her cubicle. She felt extremely confused and torn about her role at this point. What should she tell the customer when she called her back? Was the fertilizer safe? Should she worry about working in a place with potentially dangerous products? What about quality issues for the company's products in general? Were Herb's other products unsafe or of poor quality? What might be the environmental impact of this product as it runs off into lakes and streams? As her head began to spin with the difficulty of the task ahead of her, the phone suddenly rang. It was Herb himself, the owner and founder of the company. "Martha," the voice on the other line whispered, "Herb's Special Fertilizer is our best seller! Don't let us down."

NOW It Is Your Turn

- What kind of decision does Martha face? What are some of her decision-making challenges?
- What recommendations do you have for a company facing this situation? What should they do to deal with this customer complaint? From the perspective of the management at Herb's Garden Products, what are some next steps that could be taken?

INDIVIDUAL EXERCISE

The Nine Dots Problem

Instructions: Using only four straight lines, intersect all the dots without ever lifting up your pen or pencil.

GROUP EXERCISE

Moon Walk and Talk[40]

Warning: *Do not discuss this exercise with other members of your class until instructed to do so.*

You are a member of the moon space crew originally scheduled to rendezvous with a mother ship on the lighted surface of the moon. Due to mechanical difficulties, however, your ship was forced to land at a spot some 200 miles (320 km) from the rendezvous point. During reentry and landing, much of the equipment aboard was damaged, and because survival depends on reaching the mother ship, the most critical items available must be chosen for the 200-mile (320 km) trip. Please see the list of the 15 items left intact and undamaged after landing. Your task is to rank the items in terms of their importance for your crew to reach the rendezvous point. Place the number 1 by the most important, 2 by the next most important, and so on, with 15 being the least important.

Undamaged items	My ranking	Group ranking	NASA ranking	My difference	Group difference
Box of matches					
Food concentrates					
50 feet of nylon					
Parachute silk					
Portable heating unit					
Two 45-caliber pistols					
One case dehydrated milk					
Two 100 lb. tanks oxygen					
Stellar map (of moon's constellations)					
Life raft					
Magnetic compass					
5 gallons of water					
Signal flares					
First aid kit containing injection needles					
Solar powered FM receiver–transmitter					

ENDNOTES

1. Ireland, R. D., & Miller, C. C. (2004). Decision making and firm success. *Academy of Management Executive, 18,* 8–12; Nutt, P. C. (2002). *Why decisions fail.* San Francisco: Berrett-Koehler; Nutt, P. C. (1999). Surprising but true: Half the decisions in organizations fail. *Academy of Management Executive, 13,* 75–90.
2. Garvin, D. A. (2006, January). All the wrong moves. *Harvard Business Review, 84,* 18–23.
3. Nutt, P. C. (1994). Types of organizational decision processes. *Administrative Science Quarterly, 29,* 414–550.
4. Nutt, P. C. (1998). Surprising but true: Half the decisions in organizations fail. *Academy of Management Executive, 13,* 75–90.
5. Zell, D. M., Glassman, A. M., & Duron, S. A. (2007). Strategic management in turbulent times: The short and glorious history of accelerated decision making at Hewlett-Packard. *Organizational Dynamics, 36,* 93–104.
6. Burke, L. A., & Miller, M. K. (1999). Taking the mystery out of intuitive decision making. *Academy of Management Executive, 13,* 91–98.
7. Breen, B. (2000, August). What's your intuition? *Fast Company,* 290; Klein, G. (2003). *Intuition at work.* New York: Doubleday; Salas, E., & Klein, G. (2001). *Linking expertise and naturalistic decision making.* Mahwah, NJ: Lawrence Erlbaum Associates.
8. In person interview conducted by author Talya Bauer at Ames Research Center, Mountain View, CA, 1990.
9. Conlin, M. (2007, September [illegible]). [illegible] *Business Week Online.* Retrieved March 1, 2008, from http://www.businessweek.com/managing/content/sep2007/ca20070913_564868.htm?campaign_id=rss_null.
10. Amabile, T. M. (1988). A model of creativity and innovation in organizations. In B. M. Staw & L. L. Cummings (Eds.), *Research in organizational behavior, vol. 10* (pp. 123–167) Greenwich, CT: JAI Press; Amabile, T. M., Conti, R., Coon, H., Lazenby, J., & Herron, M. (1996). Assessing the work environment for creativity. *Academy of Management Journal, 39,* 1154–1184; Ford, C. M., & Gioia, D. A. (2000). Factors influencing creativity in the domain of managerial decision making. *Journal of Management, 26,* 705–732; Tierney, P., Farmer, S. M., & Graen, G. B. (1999). An examination of leadership and employee creativity: The relevance of traits and relationships. *Personnel Psychology, 52,* 591–620; Woodman, R. W., Sawyer, J. E., & Griffin, R. W. (1993). Toward a theory of organizational creativity. *Academy of Management Review, 18,* 293–321.
11. Feist, G. J. (1998). A meta-analysis of personality in scientific and artistic creativity. *Personality and Social Psychology Review, 2,* 290–309.
12. Quote retrieved May 1, 2008, from http://www.whatquote.com/quotes/linus-pauling/250801-the-best-way-to-have.htm.
13. Scott, G., Leritz, L. E., & Mumford, M. D. (2004). The effectiveness of creativity training: A quantitative review. *Creativity Research Journal, 16,* 361–388.
14. Tilson, W. (1999, September 20). The perils of investor overconfidence. Retrieved March 1, 2008, from http://www.fool.com/BoringPort/1999/BoringPort990920.htm.
15. The rogue rebuttal. (2008, February 9). *Economist, 386,* 82.
16. Orkin, M. (1991). *Can you win? The real odds for casino gambling, sports betting and lotteries.* New York: W. H. Freeman.
17. Neale, M. A., & Bazerman, M. H. (1985). The effects of framing and negotiator overconfidence on bargaining behaviors and outcomes. *Academy of Management Journal, 28,* 34–49.
18. Becker, W. S. (2007). Missed opportunities: The Great Bear Wilderness Disaster. *Organizational Dynamics, 36,* 363–376.
19. Li, S., Sun, Y., & Wang, Y. (2007). 50% off or buy one get one free? Frame preference as a function of consumable nature in dairy products. *Journal of Social Psychology, 147,* 413–421.
20. Finkelstein, S., & Sanford, S. H. (2000, November). Learning from corporate mistakes: The rise and fall of Iridium. *Organizational Dynamics, 29*(2), 138–148.
21. Wong, K. F. E., & Kwong, J. Y. Y. (2007). The role of anticipated regret in escalation of commitment. *Journal of Applied Psychology, 92,* 545–554.
22. Simons, T., Pelled, L. H., & Smith, K. A. (1999). Making use of difference: Diversity, debate, decision comprehensiveness in top management teams. *Academy of Management Journal, 42,* 662–673.
23. Miner, F. C. (1984). Group versus individual decision making: An investigation of performance measures, decision strategies, and process losses/gains. *Organizational Behavior and Human Performance, 33,* 112–124.
24. Esser, J. K., & Lindoerfer, J. L. (1989). Groupthink and the space shuttle *Challenger* accident: Toward a quantitative case analysis. *Journal of Behavioral Decision Making, 2,* 167–177; Moorhead, G., Ference, R., & Neck, C. P. (1991). Group decision fiascoes continue: Space shuttle *Challenger* and a revised groupthink framework. *Human Relations, 44,* 539–550.
25. Janis, I. L. (1972). *Victims of groupthink.* New York: Houghton Mifflin.
26. Delbecq, A. L., Van de Ven, A. H., & Gustafson, D. H. (1975). *Group techniques for program planning: A guide to nominal group and Delphi processes.* Glenview, IL: Scott Foresman.
27. Campion, M. A. (1993). Article review checklist: A criterion checklist for reviewing research articles in applied psychology. *Personnel Psychology, 46,* 705–718.
28. Hastie, R., & Kameda, T. (2005). The robust beauty of majority rules in group decisions. *Psychological Review, 112,* 494–508.
29. Roch, S. G. (2007). Why convene rater teams: An investigation of the benefits of anticipated discussion, consensus, and [illegible] *man Decision Processes, 104,* 14–29.
30. Mohammed, S., & Ringseis, E. (2001). Cognitive diversity and consensus in group decision making: The role of inputs, processes, and outcomes. *Organizational Behavior and Human Decision Processes, 85,* 310–335.
31. Peterson, R. (1999). Can you have too much of a good thing? The limits of voice for improving satisfaction with leaders. *Personality and Social Psychology, 25,* 313–324.
32. Mitchell, D. J., Russo, J., & Pennington, N. (1989). Back to the future: Temporal perspective in the explanation of events. *Journal of Behaviorial Decision Making, 2,* 25–38.
33. Lam, S. S. K., & Schaubroeck, J. (2000). Improving group decisions by better pooling information: A comparative advantage of group decision support systems. *Journal of Applied Psychology, 85,* 565–573.
34. Nunamaker, J. F., Jr., Dennis, A. R., Valacich, J. S., Vogel, D. R., & George, J. F. (1991, July). Electronic meetings to support group work. *Communications of the ACM, 34*(7), 40–61.
35. Wright, G., & Goodwin, P. (2002). Eliminating a framing bias by using simple instructions to "think harder" and respondents with managerial experience: Comment on "breaking the frame." *Strategic Management Journal, 23,* 1059–1067.
36. Adapted from ideas contained in Kenneth Blanchard and Norman Vincent Peale (1988). *The power of ethical management.* New York: William Morrow.
37. Manning, J. (2008, March 27). Chase mortgage memo pushes "Cheats & Tricks." *The Oregonian.* Retrieved November 1, 2008, from http://www.oregonlive.com/business/index.ssf/2008/03/chase_memo_pushes_che.html.
38. Noorderhaven, N. G. (2007). Comprehensiveness versus pragmatism: Consensus at the Japanese-Dutch interface. *Journal of Management Studies, 44,* 1349–1370.
39. Jeanne Enders, Portland State University. Used by permission of the author.
40. NASA educational materials. Retrieved March 2, 2008, from http://www.nasa.gov/audience/foreducators/topnav/materials/listbytype/Survival_Lesson.html.

CHAPTER 12
Leading People Within Organizations

LEARNING OBJECTIVES

After reading this chapter, you should be able to do the following:

1. Define what leadership is and identify traits of effective leaders.
2. Describe behaviors that effective leaders demonstrate.
3. Specify the contexts in which various leadership styles are effective.
4. Explain the concepts of transformational, transactional, charismatic, servant, and authentic leadership.

Opening Case: Indra Nooyi Takes the Pepsi Challenge

The CEO of PepsiCo, Indra Nooyi, is a leader who demonstrates passion for her vision and energizes those around her toward her vision for the company.

Source: http://en.wikipedia.org/wiki/Image:Indra_Nooyi_-_World_Economic_Forum_Annual_Meeting_Davos_2008.jpg.

She is among the Top 100 most influential people in *Time* magazine's 2008 list. She is also number 5 in *Forbes*'s (2007) most influential women in the world, number 1 in *Fortune*'s 50 most powerful women (2006), and number 22 in *Fortune*'s 25 most powerful people in business (2007). The lists go on and on. To those familiar with her work and style, this should come as no surprise: Even before she became the CEO of PepsiCo Inc. in 2006, she was one of the most powerful executives at Pepsi and one of the two candidates being groomed for the coveted CEO position. Born in Chennai, India, Nooyi graduated from Yale's School of Management and worked in companies such as the Boston Consulting Group Inc., Motorola Inc., and ABB Inc. She also led an all-girls rock band in high school, but that is a different story.

What makes her one of the top leaders in the business world today? To start with, she has a clear vision for Pepsi, which seems to be the right vision for the company at this point in time. Her vision is framed under the term "performance with purpose", which is based on two key ideas: tackling the obesity epidemic by improving the nutritional status of PepsiCo products and making PepsiCo an environmentally sustainable company. She is an inspirational speaker and rallies people around her vision for the company. She has the track record to show that she means what she says. She was instrumental in Pepsi's acquisition of the food conglomerate Quaker Oats Company and the juice maker Tropicana Products Inc., both of which have healthy product lines. She is bent on reducing Pepsi's reliance on high-sugar, high-calorie beverages, and she made sure that Pepsi removed trans fats from all its products before its competitors. On the environmental side, she is striving for a net zero impact on the environment. Among her priorities are plans to reduce the plastic used in beverage bottles and find biodegradable packaging solutions for PepsiCo products. Her vision is long-term and could be risky for short-term earnings, but it is also timely and important.

Those who work with her feel challenged by her high performance standards and expectation of excellence. She is not afraid to give people negative feedback, and with humor too. She pushes people until they come up with a solution to a problem and does not take "I don't know" for an answer. For example, she insisted that her team find an alternative to the expensive palm oil and did not stop urging them forward until the alternative arrived: rice bran oil.

Nooyi is well liked and respected because she listens to those around her, even when they disagree with her. Her background cuts across national boundaries, which gives her a true appreciation for diversity, and she expects those around her to bring their values to work. In fact, when she graduated from college, she wore a sari to a job interview at Boston Consulting, where she got the job. She is an unusually collaborative person in the top suite of a Fortune 500 company, and she seeks help and information when she needs it. She has friendships with three ex-CEOs of PepsiCo who serve as her informal advisors, and when she was selected to the top position at PepsiCo, she made sure that her rival for the position got a pay raise and was given influence in the company so she did not lose him. She says that the best advice she received was from her father, who taught her to assume that people have good intentions. She says that expecting people to have good intentions helps her prevent misunderstandings and show empathy for them. It seems that she is a role model to other business leaders around the world, and PepsiCo is well positioned to tackle the challenges the future may bring.

Sources: Adapted from information in Birger, J., Chandler, C., Fortt, J., Gimbel, B., Gumbel, P., et al. (2008, May 12). The best advice I ever got. Fortune, 157(10), 70–80; Brady, D. (2007, June 11). Keeping cool in hot water. Business Week, 4038, 49; Compton, J. (2007, October 15). Performance with purpose. Beverage World, 126(10), 32; McKay, B. (2008, May 6). Pepsi to cut plastic used in bottles. Wall Street Journal, Eastern edition, B2; Morris, B., & Neering, P. A. (2008, May 3). The Pepsi challenge: Can this snack and soda giant go healthy? CEO Indra Nooyi says yes but cola wars and corn prices will test her leadership. Fortune, 157(4), 54–66; Schultz, H. (2008, May 12). Indra Nooyi. Time, 171(19), 116–117; Seldman, M. (2008, June). Elevating aspirations at PepsiCo. T+D, 62(6), 36–38; The Pepsi challenge (2006, August 19). Economist, 380(8491), 51–52.

leadership

The act of influencing others toward a goal.

formal leaders

Those who hold a position of authority and may utilize the power that comes from their position, as well as their personal power to influence others.

informal leaders

Those without a formal position of authority within the organization but demonstrate leadership by influencing those around them through personal forms of power.

Leadership may be defined as the act of influencing others to work toward a goal. Leaders exist at all levels of an organization. Some leaders hold a position of authority and may utilize the power that comes from their position, as well as their personal power to influence others. They are called **formal leaders**. In contrast, **informal leaders** are without a formal position of authority within the organization but demonstrate leadership by influencing others through personal forms of power. One caveat is important here: Leaders do not rely on the use of force to influence people. Instead, people willingly adopt the leader's goal as their own goal. If a person is relying on force and punishment, the person is a dictator, not a leader.

What makes leaders effective? What distinguishes people who are perceived as leaders from those who are not perceived as leaders? More importantly, how do we train future leaders and improve our own leadership ability? These are important questions that have attracted scholarly attention in the past several decades. In this chapter, we will review the history of leadership studies and summarize the major findings relating to these important questions. Around the world, we view leaders as at least partly responsible for their team or company's success and failure. Company CEOs are paid millions of dollars in salaries and stock options with the assumption that they hold their company's future in their hands. In politics, education, sports, profit and nonprofit sectors, the influence of leaders over the behaviors of individuals and organizations is rarely questioned. When people and organizations fail, managers and CEOs are often viewed as responsible. Some people criticize the assumption that leadership always matters and call this belief "the romance of leadership." However, research evidence pointing to the importance of leaders for organizational success is accumulating.[1]

1. WHO IS A LEADER? TRAIT APPROACHES TO LEADERSHIP

LEARNING OBJECTIVES

1. Learn the position of trait approaches in the history of leadership studies.
2. Explain the traits that are associated with leadership.
3. Discuss the limitations of trait approaches to leadership.

The earliest approach to the study of leadership sought to identify a set of traits that distinguished leaders from nonleaders. What were the personality characteristics and the physical and psychological attributes of people who are viewed as leaders? Because of the problems in measurement of personality traits at the time, different studies used different measures. By 1940, researchers concluded that the search for leadership-defining traits was futile. In recent years, though, after the advances in personality literature such as the development of the Big Five personality framework, researchers have had more success in identifying traits that predict leadership.[2] Most importantly, charismatic leadership, which is among the contemporary approaches to leadership, may be viewed as an example of a trait approach.

The traits that show relatively strong relations with leadership are discussed below.[3]

1.1 Intelligence

General mental ability, which psychologists refer to as "g" and which is often called "IQ" in everyday language, has been related to a person's emerging as a leader within a group. Specifically, people who have high mental abilities are more likely to be viewed as leaders in their environment.[5] We should caution, though, that intelligence is a positive but modest predictor of leadership, and when actual intelligence is measured with paper-and-pencil tests, its relationship to leadership is a bit weaker compared to when intelligence is defined as the perceived intelligence of a leader.[6] In addition to having a high IQ, effective leaders tend to have high emotional intelligence (EQ). People with high EQ demonstrate a high level of self awareness, motivation, empathy, and social skills. The psychologist who coined the term *emotional intelligence*, Daniel Goleman, believes that IQ is a threshold quality: It matters for entry- to high-level management jobs, but once you get there, it no longer helps leaders, because most leaders already have a high IQ. According to Goleman, what differentiates effective leaders from ineffective ones becomes their ability to control their own emotions and understand other people's emotions, their internal motivation, and their social skills.[7]

FIGURE 12.2

Many observers believe that Carly Fiorina, the ousted CEO of HP, demonstrated high levels of intelligence but low levels of empathy for the people around her, which led to an overreliance on numbers while ignoring the human cost of her decisions.[4]

Source: http://commons.wikimedia.org/wiki/Image:CarlyFiorina49416.jpeg.

1.2 Big 5 Personality Traits

Psychologists have proposed various systems for categorizing the characteristics that make up an individual's unique personality; one of the most widely accepted is the "Big Five" model, which rates an individual according to Openness to experience, Conscientiousness, Extraversion, Agreeableness, and Neuroticism. Several of the Big Five personality traits have been related to leadership emergence (whether someone is viewed as a leader by others) and effectiveness.[8]

FIGURE 12.3 Big Five Personality Traits

Trait	Description
Openness	Being curious, original, intellectual, creative, and open to new ideas.
Conscientiousness	Being organized, systematic, punctual, achievement-oriented, and dependable.
Extraversion	Being outgoing, talkative, sociable, and enjoying social situations.
Agreeableness	Being affable, tolerant, sensitive, trusting, kind, and warm.
Neuroticism	Being anxious, irritable, temperamental, and moody.

FIGURE 12.4

Steve Ballmer, CEO of Microsoft Corporation, is an extraverted leader. For example, to celebrate Microsoft's 25th anniversary, Ballmer enthusiastically popped out of the anniversary cake to surprise the audience.

Source: http://en.wikipedia.org/wiki/Image:Steve_ballmer_2007_outdoors 2.jpg.

For example, extraversion is related to leadership. *Extraverts* are sociable, assertive, and energetic people. They enjoy interacting with others in their environment and demonstrate self-confidence. Because they are both dominant and sociable in their environment, they emerge as leaders in a wide variety of situations. Out of all personality traits, extraversion has the strongest relationship with both leader emergence and leader effectiveness. This is not to say that all effective leaders are extraverts, but you are more likely to find extraverts in leadership positions. An example of an introverted leader is Jim Buckmaster, the CEO of Craigslist. He is known as an introvert, and he admits to not having meetings because he does not like them.[9] Research shows that another personality trait related to leadership is *conscientiousness*. Conscientious people are organized, take initiative, and demonstrate persistence in their endeavors. Conscientious people are more likely to emerge as leaders and be effective in that role. Finally, people who have *openness to experience*—those who demonstrate originality, creativity, and are open to trying new things—tend to emerge as leaders and also be quite effective.

1.3 Self-Esteem

Self-esteem is not one of the Big Five personality traits, but it is an important aspect of one's personality. The degree to which a person is at peace with oneself and has an overall positive assessment of one's self worth and capabilities seem to be relevant to whether someone is viewed as a leader. Leaders with high self-esteem support their subordinates more and, when punishment is administered, they punish more effectively.[10] It is possible that those with high self-esteem have greater levels of self-confidence and this affects their image in the eyes of their followers. Self-esteem may also explain the relationship between some physical attributes and leader emergence. For example, research shows a strong relationship between being tall and being viewed as a leader (as well as one's career success over life). It is proposed that self-esteem may be the key mechanism linking height to being viewed as a leader, because people who are taller are also found to have higher self-esteem and therefore may project greater levels of charisma as well as confidence to their followers.[11]

1.4 Integrity

Research also shows that people who are effective as leaders tend to have a moral compass and demonstrate honesty and integrity.[12] Leaders whose integrity is questioned lose their trustworthiness, and they hurt their company's business along the way. For example, when it was revealed that Whole Foods Market CEO John Mackey was using a pseudonym to make negative comments online about the company's rival Wild Oats Markets Inc., his actions were heavily criticized, his leadership was questioned, and the company's reputation was affected.[13]

FIGURE 12.5 Key Traits Associated With Leadership

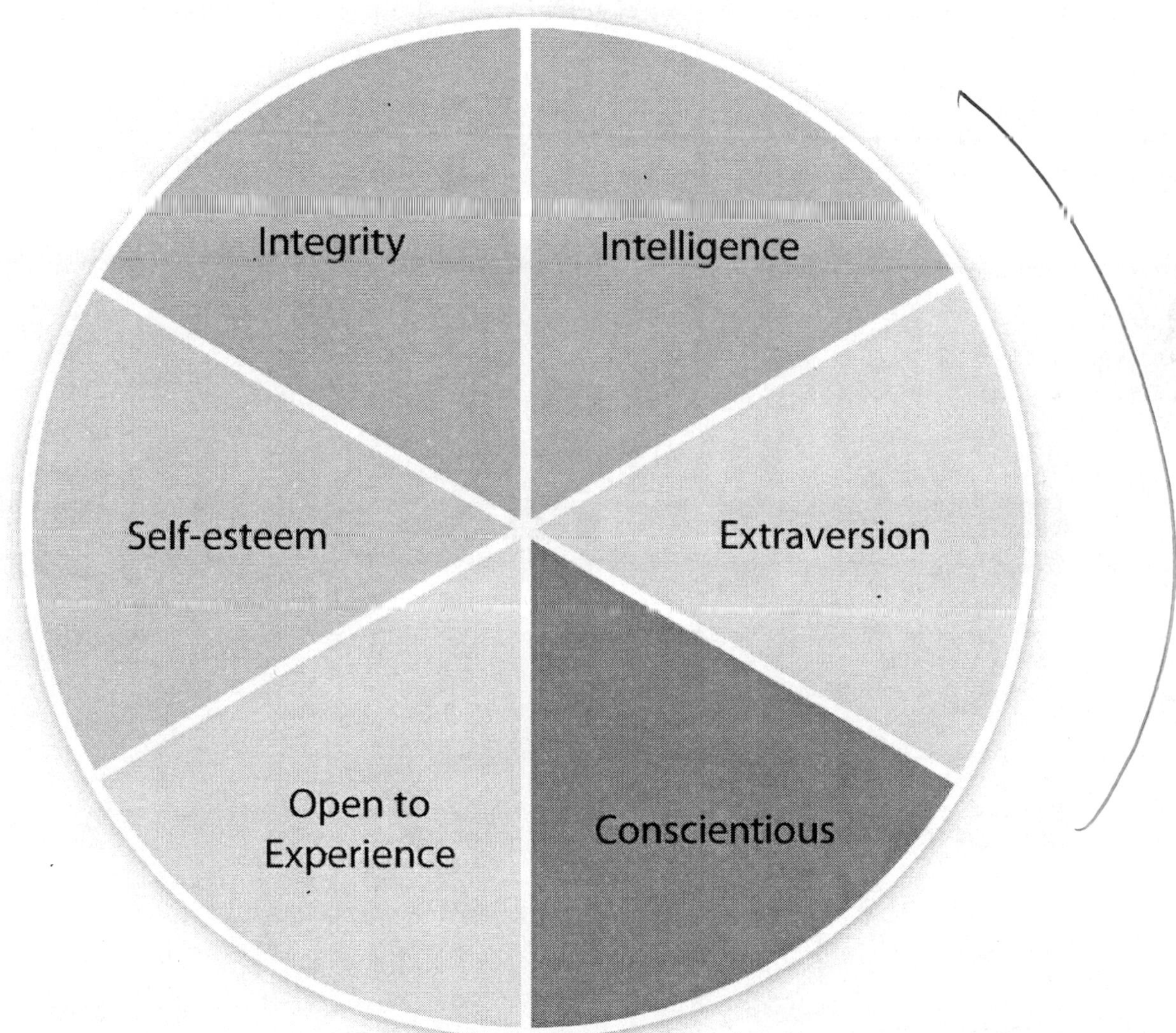

There are also some traits that are negatively related to leader emergence and being successful in that position. For example, agreeable people who are modest, good natured, and avoid conflict are less likely to be perceived as leaders.[14]

Despite problems in trait approaches, these findings can still be useful to managers and companies. For example, knowing about leader traits helps organizations select the right people into positions of responsibility. The key to benefiting from the findings of trait researchers is to be aware that not all traits are equally effective in predicting leadership potential across all circumstances. Some organizational situations allow leader traits to make a greater difference.[15] For example, in small, entrepreneurial organizations where leaders have a lot of leeway to determine their own behavior, the type of traits leaders have may make a difference in leadership potential. In large, bureaucratic, and rule-bound organizations such as the government and the military, a leader's traits may have less to do with how the person behaves and whether the person is a successful leader.[16] Moreover, some traits become relevant in specific circumstances. For example, bravery is likely to be a key characteristic in military leaders, but not necessarily in business leaders. Scholars now conclude that instead of trying to identify a few traits that distinguish leaders from nonleaders, it is important to identify the conditions under which different traits affect a leader's performance, as well as whether a person emerges as a leader.[17]

FIGURE 12.6

Condoleezza Rice had different responsibilities as the provost of Stanford University compared to her role as secretary of state for the United States. Do you think these differences affected her behavior as a leader?

Source: http://en.wikipedia.org/wiki/Image:Condoleezza_Rice_cropped.jpg.

KEY TAKEAWAY

Many studies searched for a limited set of personal attributes, or traits, which would make someone be viewed as a leader and be successful as a leader. Some traits that are consistently related to leadership include intelligence (both mental ability and emotional intelligence), personality (extraversion, conscientiousness, openness to experience, self-esteem), and integrity. The main limitation of the trait approach was that it ignored the situation in which leadership occurred. Therefore, it is more useful to specify the conditions under which different traits are needed.

EXERCISES

1. Think of a leader you admire. What traits does this person have? Are they consistent with the traits discussed in this chapter? If not, why is this person effective despite the presence of different traits?
2. Can the findings of traits approaches be used to train potential leaders? Which traits seem easier to teach? Which are more stable?
3. How can organizations identify future leaders with a given set of traits? Which methods would be useful for this purpose?
4. What other traits can you think of that would be relevant to leadership?

2. WHAT DO LEADERS DO? BEHAVIORAL APPROACHES TO LEADERSHIP

LEARNING OBJECTIVES

1. Explain the behaviors that are associated with leadership.
2. Identify the three alternative decision-making styles leaders use and the conditions under which they are more effective.
3. Discuss the limitations of behavioral approaches to leadership.

2.1 Leader Behaviors

When trait researchers became disillusioned in the 1940s, their attention turned to studying leader behaviors. What did effective leaders actually do? Which behaviors made them perceived as leaders? Which behaviors increased their success? To answer these questions, researchers at Ohio State University and the University of Michigan used many different techniques, such as observing leaders in laboratory settings as well as surveying them. This research stream led to the discovery of two broad categories of behaviors: task-oriented behaviors (sometimes called **initiating structure**) and people-oriented behaviors (also called **consideration**). **Task-oriented leader behaviors** involve structuring the roles of subordinates, providing them with instructions, and behaving in ways that will increase the performance of the group. Task-oriented behaviors are directives given to employees to get things done and to ensure that organizational goals are met. **People-oriented leader behaviors** include showing concern for employee feelings and treating employees with respect. People-oriented leaders genuinely care about the well-being of their employees, and they demonstrate their concern in their actions and decisions. At the time, researchers thought that these two categories of behaviors were the keys to the puzzle of leadership.[18] However, research did not support the argument that demonstrating both of these behaviors would necessarily make leaders effective.[19]

task-oriented leader behaviors

Structuring the roles of subordinates, providing them with instructions, and behaving in ways that will increase the performance of the group (also called initiating structure).

people-oriented leader behaviors

Showing concern for employee feelings and treating employees with respect (also called consideration).

When we look at the overall findings regarding these leader behaviors, it seems that both types of behaviors, in the aggregate, are beneficial to organizations, but for different purposes. For example, when leaders demonstrate people-oriented behaviors, employees tend to be more satisfied and react more positively. However, when leaders are task oriented, productivity tends to be a bit higher.[20] Moreover, the situation in which these behaviors are demonstrated seems to matter. In small companies, task-oriented behaviors were found to be more effective than in large companies.[21] There is also some evidence that very high levels of leader task-oriented behaviors may cause burnout with employees.[22]

FIGURE 12.7

Behavioral approaches to leadership showed that task-oriented and people-oriented behaviors are two key aspects of leadership.

2.2 Leader Decision Making

Another question behavioral researchers focused on involved how leaders actually make decisions and the influence of decision-making styles on leader effectiveness and employee reactions. Three types of decision-making styles were studied. In **authoritarian decision making**, leaders make the decision alone without necessarily involving employees in the decision-making process. When leaders use **democratic decision making**, employees participate in the making of the decision. Finally, leaders using **laissez-faire decision making** leave employees alone to make the decision. The leader provides minimum guidance and involvement in the decision.

authoritarian decision making

What occurs when leaders make the decision alone without necessarily involving employees in the decision-making process.

democratic decision making

What occurs when leaders and employees participate in the making of the decision.

laissez-faire decision making

What occurs when leaders leave employees alone to make the decision. The leader provides minimum guidance and involvement in the decision.

As with other lines of research on leadership, research did not identify one decision-making style as the best. It seems that the effectiveness of the style the leader is using depends on the circumstances. A review of the literature shows that when leaders use more democratic or participative decision-making styles, employees tend to be more satisfied; however, the effects on decision quality or employee productivity are weaker. Moreover, instead of expecting to be involved in every single decision, employees seem to care more about the overall participativeness of the organizational climate.[23] Different types of employees may also expect different levels of involvement. In a research organization, scientists viewed democratic leadership most favorably and authoritarian leadership least favorably,[24] but employees working in large groups where opportunities for member interaction was limited preferred authoritarian leader decision making.[25] Finally, the effectiveness of each style seems to depend on who is using it. There are examples of effective leaders using both authoritarian and democratic styles. At Hyundai Motor America, high-level managers use authoritarian decision-making styles, and the company is performing very well.[26]

FIGURE 12.8

Google cofounders Larry Page and Sergey Brin (shown here) are known for their democratic decision-making styles.

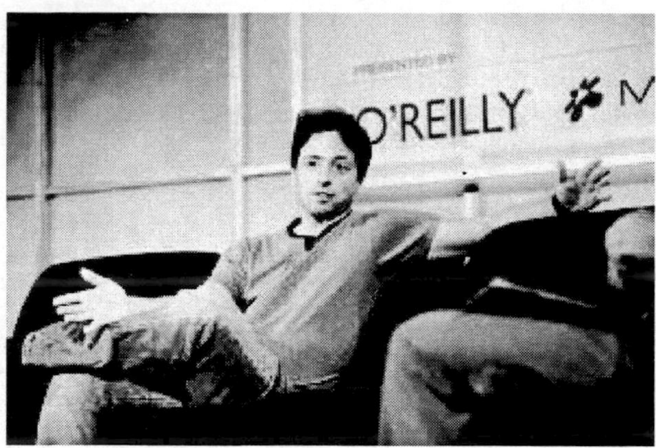

Source: http://commons.wikimedia.org/wiki/ Image:Sergey_Brin,_Web_2.0_Conference.jpg.

The track record of the laissez-faire decision-making style is more problematic. Research shows that this style is negatively related to employee satisfaction with leaders and leader effectiveness.[27] Laissez-faire leaders create high levels of ambiguity about job expectations on the part of employees, and employees also engage in higher levels of conflict when leaders are using the laissez-faire style.[28]

Leadership Assumptions about Human Nature

Why do some managers believe that the only way to manage employees is to force and coerce them to work while others adopt a more humane approach? Douglas McGregor, an MIT Sloan School of Management professor, believed that a manager's actions toward employees were dictated by having one of two basic sets of assumptions about employee attitudes. His two contrasting categories, outlined in his 1960 book, *The Human Side of Enterprise*, are known as Theory X and Theory Y.

Theory X

A theory of human nature which assumes that employees are lazy, do not enjoy working, and will avoid expending energy on work whenever possible.

Theory Y

A theory of human nature which assumes that employees are not lazy, can enjoy work, and will put effort into furthering organizational goals.

According to McGregor, some managers subscribe to **Theory X**. The main assumptions of Theory X managers are that employees are lazy, do not enjoy working, and will avoid expending energy on work whenever possible. For a manager, this theory suggests employees need to be forced to work through any number of control mechanisms ranging from threats to actual punishments. Because of the assumptions they make about human nature, Theory X managers end up establishing rigid work environments. Theory X also assumes employees completely lack ambition. As a result, managers must take full responsibility for their subordinates' actions, as these employees will never take initiative outside of regular job duties to accomplish tasks.

In contrast, **Theory Y** paints a much more positive view of employees' attitudes and behaviors. Under Theory Y employees are not lazy, can enjoy work, and will put effort into furthering organizational goals. Because these managers can assume that employees will act in the best interests of the organization given the chance, Theory Y managers allow employees autonomy and help them become committed to particular goals. They tend to adopt a more supportive role, often focusing on maintaining a work environment in which employees can be innovative and prosperous within their roles.

One way of improving our leadership style would be to become conscious about our theories of human nature, and question the validity of our implicit theories.

Source: McGregor, D. (1960). Human side of enterprise. New York: McGraw Hill.

2.3 Limitations of Behavioral Approaches

Behavioral approaches, similar to trait approaches, fell out of favor because they neglected the environment in which behaviors are demonstrated. The hope of the researchers was that the identified behaviors would predict leadership under all circumstances, but it may be unrealistic to expect that a given set of behaviors would work under all circumstances. What makes a high school principal effective on the job may be very different from what makes a military leader effective, which would be different from behaviors creating success in small or large business enterprises. It turns out that specifying the conditions under which these behaviors are more effective may be a better approach.

KEY TAKEAWAY

When researchers failed to identify a set of traits that would distinguish effective from ineffective leaders, research attention turned to the study of leader behaviors. Leaders may demonstrate task-oriented and people-oriented behaviors. Both seem to be related to important outcomes, with task-oriented behaviors more strongly relating to leader effectiveness and people-oriented behaviors leading to employee satisfaction. Leaders can also make decisions using authoritarian, democratic, or laissez-faire styles. While laissez-faire has certain downsides, there is no best style, and the effectiveness of each style seems to vary across situations. Because of the inconsistency of results, researchers realized the importance of the context in which leadership occurs, which paved the way to contingency theories of leadership.

EXERCISES

1. Give an example of a leader you admire whose behavior is primarily task oriented, and one whose behavior is primarily people oriented.
2. What are the limitations of authoritarian decision making? Under which conditions do you think authoritarian style would be more effective?
3. What are the limitations of democratic decision making? Under which conditions do you think democratic style would be more effective?
4. What are the limitations of laissez-faire decision making? Under which conditions do you think laissez-faire style would be more effective?
5. Examine your own leadership style. Which behaviors are you more likely to demonstrate? Which decision-making style are you more likely to use?

3. WHAT IS THE ROLE OF THE CONTEXT? CONTINGENCY APPROACHES TO LEADERSHIP

LEARNING OBJECTIVES

1. Learn about the major situational conditions that determine the effectiveness of different leadership styles.
2. Identify the conditions under which highly task-oriented and highly people-oriented leaders can be successful based on Fiedler's contingency theory.
3. Describe the Path-Goal theory of leadership.
4. Describe a method by which leaders can decide how democratic or authoritarian their decision making should be.

What is the best leadership style? By now, you must have realized that this may not be the right question to ask. Instead, a better question might be: Under which conditions are certain leadership styles more effective? After the disappointing results of trait and behavioral approaches, several scholars developed leadership theories that specifically incorporated the role of the environment. Specifically, researchers started following a contingency approach to leadership—rather than trying to identify traits or behaviors that would be effective under all conditions, the attention moved toward specifying the situations under which different styles would be effective.

3.1 Fiedler's Contingency Theory

The earliest and one of the most influential contingency theories was developed by Frederick Fiedler.[29] According to the theory, a leader's style is measured by a scale called Least Preferred Coworker scale (LPC). People who are filling out this survey are asked to think of a person who is their least preferred coworker. Then, they rate this person in terms of how friendly, nice, and cooperative this person is. Imagine someone you did not enjoy working with. Can you describe this person in positive terms? In other words, if you can say that the person you hated working with was still a nice person, you would have a high LPC score. This means that you have a people-oriented personality, and you can separate your liking of a person from your ability to work with that person. On the other hand, if you think that the person you hated working with was also someone you did not like on a personal level, you would have a low LPC score. To you, being unable to work with someone would mean that you also dislike that person. In other words, you are a task-oriented person.

According to Fiedler's theory, different people can be effective in different situations. The LPC score is akin to a personality trait and is not likely to change. Instead, placing the right people in the right situation or changing the situation to suit an individual is important to increase a leader's effectiveness. The theory predicts that in "favorable" and "unfavorable" situations, a low LPC leader—one who has feelings of dislike for coworkers who are difficult to work with—would be successful. When situational favorableness is medium, a high LPC leader—one who is able to personally like coworkers who are difficult to work with—is more likely to succeed.

How does Fiedler determine whether a situation is "favorable," "medium," or "unfavorable"? There are three conditions creating situational favorableness: leader-subordinate relations, position power, and task structure. If the leader has a good relationship with most people and has high position power, and the task at hand is structured, the situation is very favorable. When the leader has low-quality relations with employees and has low position power, and the task at hand it relatively unstructured, the situation is very unfavorable.

FIGURE 12.9 Situational Favorableness

Situational favorableness	Leader-subordinate relations	Position Power	Task structure	Best Style
Favorable	Good	High	High	Low LPC Leader
	Good	High	Low	
	Good	Low	High	
Medium	Good	Low	Low	High LPC Leader
	Poor	High	High	
	Poor	High	Low	
	Poor	Low	High	
Unfavorable	Poor	Low	Low	Low LPC leader

Sources: Based on information in Fiedler, F. E. (1967). A theory of leadership effectiveness. New York: McGraw-Hill; Fiedler, F. E. (1964). A contingency model of leader effectiveness. In L. Berkowitz (Ed.), Advances in experimental social psychology, vol. 1 (pp. 149–190). New York: Academic Press.

Research partially supports the predictions of Fiedler's contingency theory.[30] Specifically, there is more support for the theory's predictions about when low LPC leadership should be used, but the part about when high LPC leadership would be more effective received less support. Even though the theory was not supported in its entirety, it is a useful framework to think about when task- versus people-oriented leadership may be more effective. Moreover, the theory is important because of its explicit recognition of the importance of the context of leadership.

3.2 Situational Leadership

Another contingency approach to leadership is Kenneth Blanchard and Paul Hersey's Situational Leadership Theory (SLT) which argues that leaders must use different leadership styles depending on their followers' development level.[31] According to this model, employee readiness (defined as a combination of their competence and commitment levels) is the key factor determining the proper leadership style. This approach has been highly popular with 14 million managers across 42 countries undergoing SLT training and 70% of Fortune 500 companies employing its use.[32]

The model summarizes the level of directive and supportive behaviors that leaders may exhibit. The model argues that to be effective, leaders must use the right style of behaviors at the right time in each employee's development. It is recognized that followers are key to a leader's success. Employees who are at the earliest stages of developing are seen as being highly committed but with low competence for the tasks. Thus, leaders should be highly directive and less supportive. As the employee becomes more competent, the leader should engage in more coaching behaviors. Supportive behaviors are recommended once the employee is at moderate to high levels of competence. And finally, delegating is the recommended approach for leaders dealing with employees who are both highly committed and highly competent. While the SLT is popular with managers, relatively easy to understand and use, and has endured for decades, research has been mixed in its support of the basic assumptions of the model.[33] Therefore, while it can be a useful way to think about matching behaviors to situations, overreliance on this model, at the exclusion of other models, is premature.

TABLE 12.1

Situational Leadership Theory helps leaders match their style to follower readiness levels.

Follower Readiness Level	Competence (Low)	Competence (Low)	Competence (Moderate to High)	Competence (High)
	Commitment (High)	Commitment (Low)	Commitment (Variable)	Commitment (High)
Recommended Leader Style	Directing Behavior	Coaching Behavior	Supporting Behavior	Delegating Behavior

3.3 Path-Goal Theory of Leadership

Robert House's path-goal theory of leadership is based on the expectancy theory of motivation.[34] The expectancy theory of motivation suggests that employees are motivated when they believe—or expect—that (a) their effort will lead to high performance, (b) their high performance will be rewarded, and (c) the rewards they will receive are valuable to them. According to the path-goal theory of leadership, the leader's main job is to make sure that all three of these conditions exist. Thus, leaders will create satisfied and high-performing employees by making sure that employee effort leads to performance, and their performance is rewarded by desired rewards. The leader removes roadblocks along the way and creates an environment that subordinates find motivational.

The theory also makes specific predictions about what type of leader behavior will be effective under which circumstances.[35] The theory identifies four leadership styles. Each of these styles can be effective, depending on the characteristics of employees (such as their ability level, preferences, locus of control, and achievement motivation) and characteristics of the work environment (such as the level of role ambiguity, the degree of stress present in the environment, and the degree to which the tasks are unpleasant).

Four Leadership Styles

directive leaders

Leaders who provide specific directions to their employees. They lead employees by clarifying role expectations, setting schedules, and making sure that employees know what to do on a given work day.

Directive leaders provide specific directions to their employees. They lead employees by clarifying role expectations, setting schedules, and making sure that employees know what to do on a given work day. The theory predicts that the directive style will work well when employees are experiencing role ambiguity on the job. If people are unclear about how to go about doing their jobs, giving them specific directions will motivate them. On the other hand, if employees already have role clarity, and if they are performing boring, routine, and highly structured jobs, giving them direction does not help. In fact, it may hurt them by creating an even more restricting atmosphere. Directive leadership is also thought to be less effective when employees have high levels of ability. When managing professional employees with high levels of expertise and job-specific knowledge, telling them what to do may create a low-empowerment environment, which impairs motivation.

supportive leaders

Leaders who provide emotional support to employees. They treat employees well, care about them on a personal level, and they are encouraging.

Supportive leaders provide emotional support to employees. They treat employees well, care about them on a personal level, and they are encouraging. Supportive leadership is predicted to be effective when employees are under a lot of stress or performing boring, repetitive jobs. When employees know exactly how to perform their jobs but their jobs are unpleasant, supportive leadership may be more effective.

participative leaders

Those who make sure that employees are involved in the making of important decisions.

Participative leaders make sure that employees are involved in the making of important decisions. Participative leadership may be more effective when employees have high levels of ability, and when the decisions to be made are personally relevant to them. For employees with a high internal locus of control (those who believe that they control their own destiny), participative leadership is a way of indirectly controlling organizational decisions, which is likely to be appreciated.

achievement-oriented leaders

Those who set goals for employees and encourage them to reach their goals.

Achievement-oriented leaders set goals for employees and encourage them to reach their goals. Their style challenges employees and focuses their attention on work-related goals. This style is likely to be effective when employees have both high levels of ability and high levels of achievement motivation.

The path-goal theory of leadership has received partial but encouraging levels of support from researchers. Because the theory is highly complicated, it has not been fully and adequately tested.[36] The theory's biggest contribution may be that it highlights the importance of a leader's ability to change styles depending on the circumstances. Unlike Fiedler's contingency theory, in which the leader's style is assumed to be fixed and only the environment can be changed, House's path-goal theory underlines the importance of varying one's style depending on the situation.

FIGURE 12.10 Predictions of the Path-Goal Theory Approach to Leadership

Situation	Appropriate Leadership Style
• When employees have high role ambiguity • When employees have low abilities • When employees have external locus of control	Directive
• When tasks are boring and repetitive • When tasks are stressful	Supportive
• When employees have high abilities • When the decision is relevant to employees • When employees have high internal locus of control	Participative
• When employees have high abilities • When employees have high achievement motivation	Achievement-oriented

Sources: Based on information presented in House, R. J. (1996). Path-goal theory of leadership: Lessons, legacy, and a reformulated theory. Leadership Quarterly, 7, 323–352; House, R. J., & Mitchell, T. R. (1974). Path-goal theory of leadership. Journal of Contemporary Business, 3, 81–97.

3.4 Vroom and Yetton's Normative Decision Model

Yale School of Management Professor Victor Vroom and his colleagues Philip Yetton and Arthur Jago developed a decision-making tool to help leaders determine how much involvement they should seek when making decisions.[37] The model starts by having leaders answer several key questions and working their way through a decision tree based on their responses. Let's try it. Imagine that you want to help your employees lower their stress so that you can minimize employee absenteeism. There are a number of approaches you could take to reduce employee stress, such as offering gym memberships, providing employee assistance programs, a nap room, and so forth.

Let's refer to the model and start with the first question. As you answer each question as high (H) or low (L), follow the corresponding path down the funnel.

1. *Decision Significance.* The decision has high significance, because the approach chosen needs to be effective at reducing employee stress for the insurance premiums to be lowered. In other words, there is a quality requirement to the decision. Follow the path through H.
2. *Importance of Commitment.* Does the leader need employee cooperation to implement the decision? In our example, the answer is high, because employees may simply ignore the resources if they do not like them. Follow the path through H.
3. *Leader expertise.* Does the leader have all the information needed to make a high quality decision? In our example, leader expertise is low. You do not have information regarding what your employees need or what kinds of stress reduction resources they would prefer. Follow the path through L.
4. *Likelihood of commitment.* If the leader makes the decision alone, what is the likelihood that the employees would accept it? Let's assume that the answer is low. Based on the leader's experience with this group, they would likely ignore the decision if the leader makes it alone. Follow the path from L.
5. *Goal alignment.* Are the employee goals aligned with organizational goals? In this instance, employee and organizational goals may be aligned because you both want to ensure that employees are healthier. So let's say the alignment is high, and follow H.
6. *Group expertise.* Does the group have expertise in this decision-making area? The group in question has little information about which alternatives are costlier, or more user friendly. We'll say group expertise is low. Follow the path from L.
7. *Team competence.* What is the ability of this particular team to solve the problem? Let's imagine that this is a new team that just got together and they have little demonstrated expertise to work together effectively. We will answer this as low or L.

Based on the answers to the questions we gave, the normative approach recommends consulting employees as a group. In other words, the leader may make the decision alone after gathering information from employees and is not advised to delegate the decision to the team or to make the decision alone.

FIGURE 12.11

Vroom and Yetton's leadership decision tree shows leaders which styles will be most effective in different situations.

	Decision Significance	Importance of Commitment	Leader Expertise	Likelihood of Commitment	Goal Alignment	Group Expertise	Team Competance	
PROBLEM STATEMENT	H	H	H	H	-	-	-	Decide
				L	H	H	H	Facilitate
							L	Consult (Group)
						L	-	
					L	-	-	
			L	H	H	H	H	Delegate
							L	Consult (Individually)
						L	-	
					L	-	-	
				L	H	H	H	Facilitate
							L	Consult (Group)
						L	-	
					L	-	-	
		L	H	-	-	-	-	Decide
			L	-	H	H	H	Facilitate
							L	Consult (Individually)
						L	-	
					L	-	-	
	L	H	-	H	-	-	-	Decide
				L	-	-	H	Delegate
							L	Facilitate
		L	-	-	-	-	-	Decide

Source: Used by permission from Victor H. Vroom.

Decision-Making Styles

- *Decide*. The leader makes the decision alone using available information.
- *Consult Individually*. The leader obtains additional information from group members before making the decision alone.
- *Consult as a group*. The leader shares the problem with group members individually and makes the final decision alone.
- *Facilitate*. The leader shares information about the problem with group members collectively, and acts as a facilitator. The leader sets the parameters of the decision.
- *Delegate*. The leader lets the team make the decision.

Vroom and Yetton's normative model is somewhat complicated, but research results support the validity of the model. On average, leaders using the style recommended by the model tend to make more effective decisions compared to leaders using a style not recommended by the model.[38]

KEY TAKEAWAY

The contingency approaches to leadership describe the role the situation would have in choosing the most effective leadership style. Fiedler's contingency theory argued that task oriented leaders would be most effective when the situation was the most and the least favorable, whereas people-oriented leaders would be effective when situational favorableness was moderate. Situational Leadership Theory takes the maturity level of followers into account. House's path-goal theory states that the leader's job is to ensure that employees view their effort as leading to performance, and to increase the belief that performance would be rewarded. For this purpose, leaders would use directive-, supportive-, participative-, and achievement-oriented leadership styles depending on what employees needed to feel motivated. Vroom and Yetton's normative model is a guide leaders can use to decide how participative they should be given decision environment characteristics.

EXERCISES

1. Do you believe that the least preferred coworker technique is a valid method of measuring someone's leadership style? Why or why not?
2. Do you believe that leaders can vary their style to demonstrate directive-, supportive-, achievement-, and participative-oriented styles with respect to different employees? Or does each leader tend to have a personal style that he or she regularly uses toward all employees?
3. What do you see as the limitations of the Vroom-Yetton leadership decision-making approach?
4. Which of the leadership theories covered in this section do you think are most useful and least useful to practicing managers? Why?

4. WHAT'S NEW? CONTEMPORARY APPROACHES TO LEADERSHIP

LEARNING OBJECTIVES

1. Learn about the difference between transformational and transactional leaders.
2. Find out about the relationship between charismatic leadership and how it relates to leader performance.
3. Learn how to be charismatic.
4. Describe how high-quality leader-subordinate relationships develop.
5. Define servant leadership and evaluate its potential for leadership effectiveness.
6. Define authentic leadership and evaluate its potential for leadership effectiveness.

What are the leadership theories that have the greatest contributions to offer to today's business environment? In this section, we will review the most recent developments in the field of leadership.

4.1 Transformational Leadership

transformational leaders

Those who lead employees by aligning employee goals with the leader's goals. These leaders use their charisma, inspirational motivation, intellectual stimulation, and individualized consideration to influence their followers.

transactional leaders

Those who ensure that employees demonstrate the right behaviors and provide resources in exchange. These leaders provide contingent rewards and manage by exception.

Transformational leadership theory is a recent addition to the literature, but more research has been conducted on this theory than all the contingency theories combined. The theory distinguishes transformational and transactional leaders. **Transformational leaders** lead employees by aligning employee goals with the leader's goals. Thus, employees working for transformational leaders start focusing on the company's well-being rather than on what is best for them as individual employees. On the other hand, **transactional leaders** ensure that employees demonstrate the right behaviors and provide resources in exchange.[39]

Transformational leaders have four tools in their possession, which they use to influence employees and create commitment to the company goals.[40] First, transformational leaders are charismatic. **Charisma** refers to behaviors leaders demonstrate that create confidence in, commitment to, and admiration for the leader.[41] Charismatic individuals have a “magnetic” personality that is appealing to followers. Second, transformational leaders use **inspirational motivation**, or come up with a vision that is inspiring to others. Third is the use of **intellectual stimulation**, which means that they challenge organizational norms and status quo, and they encourage employees to think creatively and work harder. Finally, they use **individualized consideration**, which means that they show personal care and concern for the well-being of their followers. Examples of transformational leaders include Steve Jobs of Apple Inc.; Lee Iaccoca, who transformed Chrysler Motors LLC in the 1980s; and Jack Welch, who was the CEO of General Electric Company for 20 years. Each of these leaders is charismatic and is held responsible for the turnarounds of their companies.

While transformational leaders rely on their charisma, persuasiveness, and personal appeal to change and inspire their companies, transactional leaders use three different methods. **Contingent rewards** mean rewarding employees for their accomplishments. **Active management by exception** involves leaving employees to do their jobs without interference, but at the same time proactively predicting potential problems and preventing them from occurring. **Passive management by exception** is similar in that it involves leaving employees alone, but in this method the manager waits until something goes wrong before coming to the rescue.

Which leadership style do you think is more effective, transformational or transactional? Research shows that transformational leadership is a very powerful influence over leader effectiveness as well as employee satisfaction.[42] In fact, transformational leaders increase the intrinsic motivation of their followers, build more effective relationships with employees, increase performance and creativity of their followers, increase team performance, and create higher levels of commitment to organizational change efforts.[43] However, except for passive management by exception, the transactional leadership styles are also effective, and they also have positive influences over leader performance as well as employee attitudes.[44] To maximize their effectiveness, leaders are encouraged to demonstrate both transformational and transactional styles. They should also monitor themselves to avoid demonstrating passive management by exception, or leaving employees to their own devices until problems arise.

Why is transformational leadership effective? The key factor may be **trust**. Trust is the belief that the leader will show integrity, fairness, and predictability in his or her dealings with others. Research shows that when leaders demonstrate transformational leadership behaviors, followers are more likely to trust the leader. The tendency to trust in transactional leaders is substantially lower. Because transformational leaders express greater levels of concern for people’s well-being and appeal to people’s values, followers are more likely to believe that the leader has a trustworthy character.[45]

Is transformational leadership genetic? Some people assume that charisma is something people are born with. You either have charisma, or you don’t. However, research does not support this idea. We must acknowledge that there is a connection between some personality traits and charisma. Specifically, people who have a neurotic personality tend to demonstrate lower levels of charisma, and people who are extraverted tend to have higher levels of charisma. However, personality explains only around 10% of the variance in charisma.[46] A large body of research has shown that it is possible to train people to increase their charisma and increase their transformational leadership.[47]

charisma

Behaviors leaders demonstrate that create confidence in, commitment to, and admiration for the leader.

inspirational motivation

When leaders come up with a vision that is inspiring to others.

intellectual stimulation

When leaders challenge organizational norms and status quo, and encourage employees to think creatively and work harder.

individualized consideration

When leaders show personal care and concern for the well-being of their followers.

contingent rewards

Rewarding employees for their accomplishments.

active management by exception

Leaving employees alone but at the same time proactively predicting potential problems and preventing them from occurring.

passive management by exception

Leaving employees alone but then coming to the rescue if anything goes wrong.

trust

The belief that the other party will show integrity, fairness, and predictability in one’s actions toward the other.

Even if charisma can be learned, a more fundamental question remains: Is it really needed? Charisma is only one element of transformational leadership, and leaders can be effective without charisma. In fact, charisma has a dark side. For every charismatic hero such as Lee Iaccoca, Steve Jobs, and Virgin Atlantic Airways Ltd.'s Sir Richard Branson, there are charismatic personalities who harmed their organizations or nations, such as Adoph Hitler of Germany and Jeff Skilling of Enron Corporation. Leadership experts warn that when organizations are in a crisis, a board of directors or hiring manager may turn to heroes who they hope will save the organization, and sometimes hire people who have no particular qualifications other than being perceived as charismatic.[48]

An interesting study shows that when companies have performed well, their CEOs are perceived as charismatic, but CEO charisma has no relation to the future performance of a company.[49] So, what we view as someone's charisma may be largely because of their association with a successful company, and the success of a company depends on a large set of factors, including industry effects and historical performance. While it is true that charismatic leaders may sometimes achieve great results, the search for charismatic leaders under all circumstances may be irrational.

FIGURE 12.12

Mustafa Kemal Ataturk, the founder of the Turkish Republic and its first president, is known as a charismatic leader. He is widely admired and respected in Turkey and around the world. His picture appears in all schools, state buildings, all denominations of Turkish lira, and in many people's homes in Turkey.

Source: http://commons.wikimedia.org/wiki/Image:Ataturk_and_flag_of_Turkey.jpg.

OB Toolbox: Be Charismatic!

- *Have a vision around which people can gather.* When framing requests or addressing others, instead of emphasizing short-term goals, stress the importance of the long-term vision. When giving a message, think about the overarching purpose. What is the ultimate goal? Why should people care? What are you trying to achieve?
- *Tie the vision to history.* In addition to stressing the ideal future, charismatic leaders also bring up the history and how the shared history ties to the future.
- *Watch your body language.* Charismatic leaders are energetic and passionate about their ideas. This involves truly believing in your own ideas. When talking to others, be confident, look them in the eye, and express your belief in your ideas.
- *Make sure that employees have confidence in themselves.* You can achieve this by showing that you believe in them and trust in their abilities. If they have real reason to doubt their abilities, make sure that you address the underlying issue, such as training and mentoring.
- *Challenge the status quo.* Charismatic leaders solve current problems by radically rethinking the way things are done and suggesting alternatives that are risky, novel, and unconventional.

Sources: Adapted from ideas in Frese, M., Beimel, S., & Schoenborg, S. (2003). Action training for charismatic leadership: Two evaluations of studies of a commercial training module on inspirational communication of a vision. Personnel Psychology, 56, 671–697; Shamir, B., House, R. J., & Arthur, M. B. (1993). The motivational effects of charismatic leadership: A self-concept based theory. Organization Science, 4, 577–594.

4.2 Leader-Member Exchange (LMX) Theory

Leader-member exchange (LMX) theory proposes that the type of relationship leaders have with their followers (members of the organization) is the key to understanding how leaders influence employees. Leaders form different types of relationships with their employees. In **high-quality LMX relationships**, the leader forms a trust-based relationship with the member. The leader and member like each other, help each other when needed, and respect each other. In these relationships, the leader and the member are each ready to go above and beyond their job descriptions to promote the other's ability to succeed. In contrast, in **low-quality LMX relationships**, the leader and the member have lower levels of trust, liking, and respect toward each other. These relationships do not have to involve actively disliking each other, but the leader and member do not go beyond their formal job descriptions in their exchanges. In other words, the member does his job, the leader provides rewards and punishments, and the relationship does not involve high levels of loyalty or obligation toward each other.[50]

high-quality LMX relationships

A high-quality, trust-based relationship between a leader and a follower.

low-quality LMX relationships

A situation in which the leader and the employee have lower levels of trust, liking, and respect toward each other.

FIGURE 12.13 Antecedents and Consequences of Leader Member Exchange

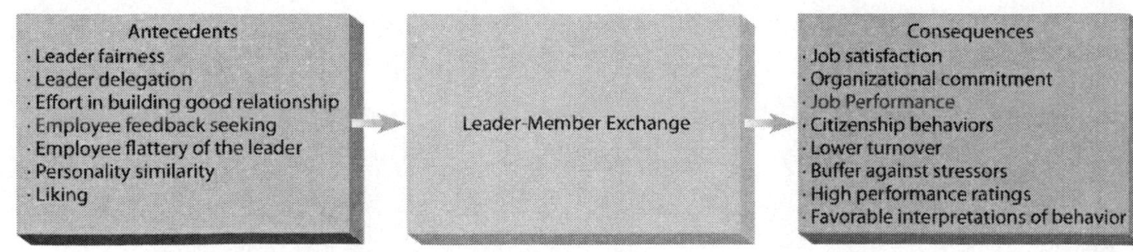

If you have work experience, you may have witnessed the different types of relationships managers form with their employees. In fact, many leaders end up developing differentiated relationships with their followers. Within the same work group, they may have in-group members who are close to them, and out-group members who are more distant. If you have ever been in a high LMX relationship with your manager, you may attest to the advantages of the relationship. Research shows that high LMX members are more satisfied with their jobs, more committed to their companies, have higher levels of clarity about what is expected of them, and perform at a higher level.[51] Employees' high levels of performance may not be a surprise, since they receive higher levels of resources and help from their managers as well as more information and guidance. If they have questions, these employees feel more comfortable seeking feedback or information.[52] Because of all the help, support, and guidance they receive, employees who have a good relationship with the manager are in a better position to perform well. Given all they receive, these employees are motivated to reciprocate to the manager, and therefore they demonstrate higher levels of citizenship behaviors such as helping the leader and coworkers.[53] Being in a high LMX relationship is also advantageous because a high-quality relationship is a buffer against many stressors, such as being a misfit in a company, having personality traits that do not match job demands, and having unmet expectations.[54] The list of the benefits high LMX employees receive is long, and it is not surprising that these employees are less likely to leave their jobs.[55]

The problem, of course, is that not all employees have a high-quality relationship with their leader, and those who are in the leader's out-group may suffer as a result. But how do you develop a high-quality relationship with your leader? It seems that this depends on many factors. Managers can help develop such a meaningful and trust-based relationship by treating their employees in a fair and dignified manner.[56] They can also test to see if the employee is trustworthy by delegating certain tasks when the employee first starts working with the manager.[57] Employees also have an active role in developing the relationship. Employees can put forth effort into developing a good relationship by seeking feedback to improve their performance, being open to learning new things on the job, and engaging in political behaviors such as the use of flattery.[58] Interestingly, high performance does not seem to be enough to develop a high-quality exchange. Instead, interpersonal factors such as the similarity of personalities and a mutual liking and respect are more powerful influences over how the relationship develops.[59] Finally, the relationship develops differently in different types of companies, and corporate culture matters in how leaders develop these relationships. In performance-oriented cultures, the relevant factor seems to be how the leader distributes rewards, whereas in people-oriented cultures, the leader treating people with dignity is more important.[60]

Self-Assessment: Rate Your LMX

Answer the following questions using 1 = not at all, 2 = somewhat, 3 = fully agree.

1. _____ I like my supervisor very much as a person.
2. _____ My supervisor is the kind of person one would like to have as a friend.
3. _____ My supervisor is a lot of fun to work with.
4. _____ My supervisor defends my work actions to a superior, even without complete knowledge of the issue in question.
5. _____ My supervisor would come to my defense if I were "attacked" by others.
6. _____ My supervisor would defend me to others in the organization if I made an honest mistake.
7. _____ I do work for my supervisor that goes beyond what is specified in my job description.
8. _____ I am willing to apply extra efforts, beyond those normally required, to further the interests of my work group.
9. _____ I do not mind working my hardest for my supervisor.
10. _____ I am impressed with my supervisor's knowledge of his or her job.
11. _____ I respect my supervisor's knowledge of and competence on the job.
12. _____ I admire my supervisor's professional skills.

Scoring:

Add your score for 1, 2, 3 = _____. This is your score on the *Liking* factor of LMX.

A score of 3 to 4 indicates a low LMX in terms of liking. A score of 5 to 6 indicates an average LMX in terms of liking. A score of 7+ indicates a high LMX in terms of liking.

Add your score for 4, 5, 6 = _____. This is your score on the *Loyalty* factor of LMX.

A score of 3 to 4 indicates a low LMX in terms of loyalty. A score of 5 to 6 indicates an average LMX in terms of loyalty. A score of 7+ indicates a high LMX in terms of loyalty.

Add your score for 7, 8, 9 = _____. This is your score on the *Contribution* factor of LMX.

A score of 3 to 4 indicates a low LMX in terms of contribution. A score of 5 to 6 indicates an average LMX in terms of contribution. A score of 7+ indicates a high LMX in terms of contribution.

Add your score for 10, 11, 12 = _____. This is your score on the *Professional Respect* factor of LMX.

A score of 3 to 4 indicates a low LMX in terms of professional respect. A score of 5 to 6 indicates an average LMX in terms of professional respect. A score of 7+ indicates a high LMX in terms of professional respect.

Source: Adapted from Liden, R. C., & Maslyn, J. M. (1998). Multidimensionality of leader-member exchange: An empirical assessment through scale development. Journal of Management, 24, 43–72. Used by permission of Sage Publications.

Should you worry if you do not have a high-quality relationship with your manager? One problem in a low-quality exchange is that employees may not have access to the positive work environment available to high LMX members. Secondly, low LMX employees may feel that their situation is unfair. Even when their objective performance does not warrant it, those who have a good relationship with the leader tend to have positive performance appraisals.[61] Moreover, they are more likely to be given the benefit of the doubt. For example, when high LMX employees succeed, the manager is more likely to think that they succeeded because they put forth a lot of effort and had high abilities, whereas for low LMX members who perform objectively well, the manager is less likely to make the same attribution.[62] In other words, the leader may interpret the same situation differently, depending on which employee is involved, and may reward low LMX employees less despite equivalent performance. In short, those with a low-quality relationship with their leader may experience a work environment that may not be supportive or fair.

Despite its negative consequences, we cannot say that all employees want to have a high-quality relationship with their leader. Some employees may genuinely dislike the leader and may not value the rewards in the leader's possession. If the leader is not well liked in the company and is known as abusive or unethical, being close to such a person may imply guilt by association. For employees who have no interest in advancing their careers in the current company (such as a student employee who is working in retail but has no interest in retail as a career), having a low-quality exchange may afford the opportunity to just do one's job without having to go above and beyond the job requirements. Finally, not all leaders are equally capable of influencing their employees by having a good relationship with them: It also depends on the power and influence of the leader in the company as a whole and how the leader is treated within the organization. Leaders who are more powerful will have more to share with their employees.[63]

What LMX theory implies for leaders is that one way of influencing employees is through the types of relationships leaders form with their subordinates. These relationships develop naturally through the work-related and personal interactions between the manager and the employee. Because they occur naturally, some leaders may not be aware of the power that lies in them. These relationships have an important influence over employee attitudes and behaviors. In the worst case, they have the potential to create an environment characterized by favoritism and unfairness. Therefore, managers are advised to be aware of how they build these relationships: Put forth effort in cultivating these relationships consciously, be open to forming good relationships with people from all backgrounds regardless of characteristics such as sex, race, age, or disability status, and prevent these relationships from leading to an unfair work environment.

OB Toolbox: Ideas for Improving Your Relationship With Your Manager

Having a good relationship with your manager [illegible] ability to communicate with your manager, and help you be successful in your job. Here are some tips to developing a high-quality exchange.

- *Create interaction opportunities with your manager.* One way of doing this would be seeking feedback from your manager with the intention of improving your performance. Be careful though: If the manager believes that you are seeking feedback for a different purpose, it will not help.
- *People are more attracted to those who are similar to them.* So find out where your similarities lie. What does your manager like that you also like? Do you have similar working styles? Do you have any mutual experiences? Bringing up your commonalities in conversations may help.
- *Utilize impression management tactics, but be tactful.* If there are work-related areas in which you can sincerely compliment your manager, do so. For example, if your manager made a decision that you agree with, you may share your support. Most people, including managers, appreciate positive feedback. However, flattering your manager in non-work-related areas (such as appearance) or using flattery in an insincere way (praising an action you do not agree with) will only backfire and cause you to be labeled as a flatterer.
- *Be a reliable employee.* Managers need people they can trust. By performing at a high level, demonstrating predictable and consistent behavior, and by volunteering for challenging assignments, you can prove your worth.
- *Be aware that relationships develop early* (as early as the first week of your working together). So be careful how you behave during the interview and your very first days. If you rub your manager the wrong way early on, it will be harder to recover the relationship.

Sources: Based on information presented in Colella, A., & Varma, A. (2001). The impact of subordinate disability on leader-member exchange relationships. Academy of Management Journal, 44, 304–315; Liden, R. C., Wayne, S. J., & Stilwell, D. (1993). A longitudinal study on the early development of leader-member exchanges. Journal of Applied Psychology, 78, 662–674; Maslyn, J. M., & Uhl-Bien, M. (2001). Leader-member exchange and its dimensions: Effects of self-effort and other's effort on relationship quality. Journal of Applied Psychology, 86, 697–708; Wing, L., Xu, H., & Snape, E. (2007). Feedback-seeking behavior and leader-member exchange: Do supervisor-attributed motives matter? Academy of Management Journal, 50, 348–363.

4.3 Servant Leadership

The early 21st century has been marked by a series of highly publicized corporate ethics scandals: Between 2000 and 2003 we witnessed the scandals of Enron, WorldCom, Arthur Andersen LLP, Qwest Communications International Inc., and Global Crossing Ltd. As corporate ethics scandals shake investor confidence in corporations and leaders, the importance of ethical leadership and keeping long-term interests of stakeholders in mind is becoming more widely acknowledged.

Servant leadership is a leadership approach that defines the leader's role as serving the needs of others. According to this approach, the primary mission of the leader is to develop employees and help them reach their goals. Servant leaders put their employees first, understand their personal needs and desires, empower them, and help them develop in their careers. Unlike mainstream management approaches, the overriding objective in servant leadership is not limited to getting employees to contribute to organizational goals. Instead, servant leaders feel an obligation to their employees, customers, and the external community. Employee happiness is seen as an end in itself, and servant leaders sometimes sacrifice their own well-being to help employees succeed. In addition to a clear focus on having a

servant leadership

A leadership approach that defines the leader's role as serving the needs of others.

moral compass, servant leaders are also interested in serving the community. In other words, their efforts to help others are not restricted to company insiders, and they are genuinely concerned about the broader community surrounding their organization.[64] According to historian Doris Kearns Goodwin, Abraham Lincoln was a servant leader because of his balance of social conscience, empathy, and generosity.[65]

Even though servant leadership has some overlap with other leadership approaches such as transformational leadership, its explicit focus on ethics, community development, and self-sacrifice are distinct characteristics of this leadership style. Research shows that servant leadership has a positive impact on employee commitment, employee citizenship behaviors toward the community (such as participating in community volunteering), and job performance.[66] Leaders who follow the servant leadership approach create a climate of fairness in their departments, which leads to higher levels of interpersonal helping behavior.[67]

Servant leadership is a tough transition for many managers who are socialized to put their own needs first, be driven by success, and tell people what to do. In fact, many of today's corporate leaders are not known for their humility! However, leaders who have adopted this approach attest to its effectiveness. David Wolfskehl, of Action Fast Print in New Jersey, founded his printing company when he was 24 years old. He marks the day he started asking employees what he can do for them as the beginning of his company's new culture. In the next 2 years, his company increased its productivity by 30%.[68]

OB Toolbox: Be a Servant Leader

One of the influential leadership paradigms involves leaders putting others first. This could be a hard transition for an achievement-oriented and success-driven manager who rises to high levels. Here are some tips to achieve servant leadership.

- *Don't ask what your employees can do for you.* Think of what you can do for them. Your job as a leader is to be of service to them. How can you relieve their stress? Protect them from undue pressure? Pitch in to help them? Think about creative ways of helping ease their lives.
- *One of your key priorities should be to help employees reach their goals.* This involves getting to know them. Learn about who they are and what their values and priorities are.
- *Be humble.* You are not supposed to have all the answers and dictate others. One way of achieving this humbleness may be to do volunteer work.
- *Be open with your employees.* Ask them questions. Give them information so that they understand what is going on in the company.
- *Find ways of helping the external community.* Giving employees opportunities to be involved in community volunteer projects or even thinking and strategizing about making a positive impact on the greater community would help.

Sources: Based on information presented in Buchanan, L. (2007, May). In praise of selflessness: Why the best leaders are servants. Inc, 29(5), 33–35; Douglas, M. E. (2005, March). Service to others. Supervision, 66(3), 6–9; Ramsey, R. D. (2005, October). The new buzz word. Supervision, 66(10), 3–5.

4.4 Authentic Leadership

authentic leadership approach

A leadership approach advising leaders to stay true to their own values.

Leaders have to be a lot of things to a lot of people. They operate within different structures, work with different types of people, and they have to be adaptable. At times, it may seem that a leader's smartest strategy would be to act as a social chameleon, changing his or her style whenever doing so seems advantageous. But this would lose sight of the fact that effective leaders have to stay true to themselves. The **authentic leadership approach** embraces this value: Its key advice is "be yourself." Think about it: We all have different backgrounds, different life experiences, and different role models. These trigger events over the course of our lifetime that shape our values, preferences, and priorities. Instead of trying to fit into societal expectations about what a leader should be, act like, or look like, authentic leaders derive their strength from their own past experiences. Thus, one key characteristic of authentic leaders is that they are self aware. They are introspective, understand where they are coming from, and have a thorough understanding of their own values and priorities. Secondly, they are not afraid to act the way they are. In other words, they have high levels of personal integrity. They say what they think. They behave in a way consistent with their values. As a result, they remain true to themselves. Instead of trying to imitate other great leaders, they find their own style in their personality and life experiences.[69]

One example of an authentic leader is Howard Schultz, the founder of Starbucks Corporation coffeehouses. As a child, Schultz witnessed the job-related difficulties his father experienced as a result of medical problems. Even though he had no idea he would have his own business one day, the desire to protect people was shaped in those years and became one of his foremost values. When he founded Starbucks, he became an industry pioneer by providing health insurance and retirement coverage to part-time as well as full-time employees.[70]

Authentic leadership requires understanding oneself. Therefore, in addition to self reflection, feedback from others is needed to gain a true understanding of one's behavior and its impact on others. Authentic leadership is viewed as a potentially influential style, because employees are more likely to trust such a leader. Moreover, working for an authentic leader is likely to lead to greater levels of satisfaction, performance, and overall well-being on the part of employees.[71]

FIGURE 12.14

An example of an authentic leader is Howard Schultz, the founder of Starbucks coffeehouses. Witnessing his father losing jobs because of medical problems, he became passionate about a company's need to care for its employees.

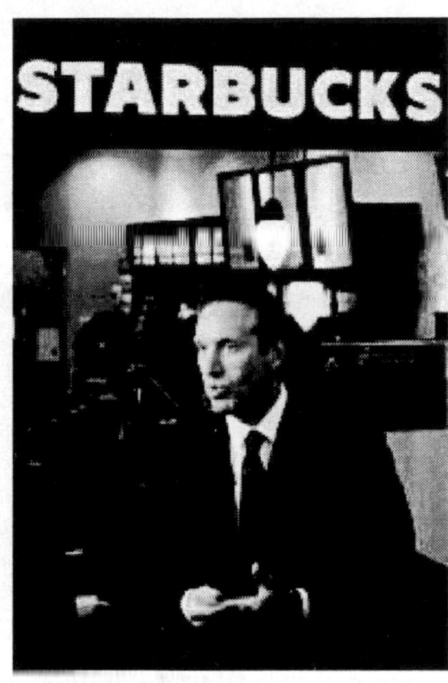

Source: http://upload.wikimedia.org/wikipedia/commons/archive/a/ae/20081006001508!Howard-Schultz-Starbucks.jpg.

KEY TAKEAWAY

Contemporary approaches to leadership include transformational leadership, leader-member exchange, servant leadership, and authentic leadership. The transformational leadership approach highlights the importance of leader charisma, inspirational motivation, intellectual stimulation, and individualized consideration as methods of influence. Its counterpart is the transactional leadership approach, in which the leader focuses on getting employees to achieve organizational goals. According to the leader-member exchange (LMX) approach, the unique, trust-based relationships leaders develop with employees are the key to leadership effectiveness. Recently, leadership scholars started to emphasize the importance of serving others and adopting a customer-oriented view of leadership; another recent focus is on the importance of being true to oneself as a leader. While each leadership approach focuses on a different element of leadership, effective leaders will need to change their style based on the demands of the situation, as well as utilizing their own values and moral compass.

EXERCISES

1. What are the characteristics of transformational leaders? Are transformational leaders more effective than transactional leaders?
2. What is charisma? What are the advantages and disadvantages of charismatic leadership? Should organizations look for charismatic leaders when selecting managers?
3. What are the differences (if any) between a leader having a high-quality exchange with employees and being friends with employees?
4. What does it mean to be a servant leader? Do you know any leaders whose style resembles servant leaders? What are the advantages of adopting such a leadership style?
5. What does it mean to be an authentic leader? How would such a style be developed?

5. THE ROLE OF ETHICS AND NATIONAL CULTURE

LEARNING OBJECTIVES

1. **Consider the role of leadership for ethical behavior.**
2. **Consider the role of national culture on leadership.**

5.1 Leadership and Ethics

As some organizations suffer the consequences of ethical crises that put them out of business or damage their reputations, the role of leadership as a driver of ethical behavior is receiving a lot of scholarly attention as well as acknowledgement in the popular press. Ethical decisions are complex and, even to people who are motivated to do the right thing, the moral component of a decision may not be obvious. Therefore, employees often look to role models, influential people, and their managers for guidance in how to behave. Unfortunately, research shows that people tend to follow leaders or other authority figures even when doing so can put others at risk. The famous Milgram experiments support this point. Milgram conducted experiments in which experimental subjects were greeted by someone in a lab coat and asked to administer electric shocks to other people who gave the wrong answer in a learning task. In fact, the shocks were not real and the learners were actors who expressed pain when shocks were administered. Around two-thirds of the experimental subjects went along with the requests and administered the shocks even after they reached what the subjects thought were dangerous levels. In other words, people in positions of authority are influential in driving others to ethical or unethical behaviors.[72]

It seems that when evaluating whether someone is an effective leader, subordinates pay attention to the level of ethical behaviors the leader demonstrates. In fact, one study indicated that the perception of being ethical explained 10% of the variance in whether an individual was also perceived as a leader. The level of ethical leadership was related to job satisfaction, dedication to the leader, and a willingness to report job-related problems to the leader.[73]

Leaders influence the level of ethical behaviors demonstrated in a company by setting the tone of the organizational climate. Leaders who have high levels of moral development create a more ethical organizational climate.[74] By acting as a role model for ethical behavior, rewarding ethical behaviors, publicly punishing unethical behaviors, and setting high expectations for the level of ethics, leaders play a key role in encouraging ethical behaviors in the workplace.

The more contemporary leadership approaches are more explicit in their recognition that ethics is an important part of effective leadership. Servant leadership emphasizes the importance of a large group of stakeholders, including the external community surrounding a business. On the other hand, authentic leaders have a moral compass, they know what is right and what is wrong, and they have the courage to follow their convictions. Research shows that transformational leaders tend to have higher levels of moral reasoning, even though it is not part of the transformational leadership theory.[75] It seems that ethical behavior is more likely to happen when (a) leaders are ethical themselves, and (b) they create an organizational climate in which employees understand that ethical behaviors are desired, valued, and expected.

5.2 Leadership Around the Globe

Is leadership universal? This is a critical question given the amount of international activity in the world. Companies that have branches in different countries often send expatriates to manage the operations. These expatriates are people who have demonstrated leadership skills at home, but will these same skills work in the host country? Unfortunately, this question has not yet been fully answered. All the leadership theories that we describe in this chapter are U.S.-based. Moreover, around 98% of all leadership research has been conducted in the United States and other western nations. Thus, these leadership theories may have underlying cultural assumptions. The United States is an individualistic, performance-oriented culture, and the leadership theories suitable for this culture may not necessarily be suitable to other cultures.

People who are perceived as leaders in one society may have different traits compared to people perceived as leaders in a different culture, because each society has a concept of ideal leader prototypes. When we see certain characteristics in a person, we make the attribution that this person is a leader. For example, someone who is confident, caring, and charismatic may be viewed as a leader because we feel that these characteristics are related to being a leader. These leadership prototypes are societally driven and may have a lot to do with a country's history and its heroes.

Recently, a large group of researchers from 62 countries came together to form a project group called Global Leadership and Organizational Behavior Effectiveness or GLOBE.[76] This group is one of the first to examine leadership differences around the world. Their results are encouraging, because, in addition to identifying differences, they found similarities in leadership styles as well. Specifically, certain leader traits seem to be universal. Around the world, people feel that honesty, decisiveness, being trustworthy, and being fair are related to leadership effectiveness. There is also universal agreement in characteristics viewed as undesirable in leaders: being irritable, egocentric, and a loner.[77] Visionary and charismatic leaders were found to be the most influential leaders around the world, followed by team-oriented and participative leaders. In other words, there seems to be a substantial generalizability in some leadership styles.

Even though certain leader behaviors such as charismatic or supportive leadership appear to be universal, what makes someone charismatic or supportive may vary across nations. For example, when leaders fit the leadership prototype, they tend to be viewed as charismatic, but in Turkey, if they are successful but did not fit the prototype, they were still viewed as charismatic.[78] In Western and Latin cultures, people who speak in an emotional and excited manner may be viewed as charismatic. In Asian cultures such as China and Japan, speaking in a monotonous voice may be more impressive because it shows that the leader can control emotions. Similarly, how leaders build relationships or act supportively is culturally determined. In collectivist cultures such as Turkey or Mexico, a manager is expected to show personal interest in employees' lives. Visiting an employee's sick mother at the hospital may be a good way of showing concern. Such behavior would be viewed as intrusive or strange in the United States or the Netherlands. Instead, managers may show concern verbally or by lightening the workload of the employee.[79]

There were also many leader characteristics that vary across cultures.[80] Traits such as being autonomous, conflict avoidant, status conscious, and ambitious were culturally dependent. For example, in France, employees do not expect their leaders to demonstrate empathy. Leaders demonstrating self-sacrifice are also viewed negatively, suggesting that servant leadership would be an improper style there. In Middle Eastern cultures such as Egypt, leaders are expected to be superior to lay people. They are supposed to have all the answers, be confident, and authoritarian. In fact, leading like a benevolent autocrat (someone who cares about people but acts alone) may be an appropriate style.[81] Even within the same geography, researchers identified substantial cultural differences. For example, in Europe, there were five clusters of cultures. Directness in interpersonal relationships was viewed positively in Nordic cultures such as Finland, but negatively in Near Eastern cultures such as Turkey. Similarly, leaders who are autonomous were viewed positively in Germanic cultures such as Austria, but negatively in Latin European cultures such as Portugal.[82] Finally, in some cultures, good leaders are paternalistic. These leaders act like a parent to employees, give advice, care for them, and get obedience and loyalty in return.[83]

Given all these differences, effective leaders should develop a sensitivity to cultural differences and adapt their style when they work in different societies or with people from different cultural backgrounds. It seems that flexibility is an important trait for global leaders.

KEY TAKEAWAY

People get their cues for ethical behaviors from leaders. Therefore, leadership characteristics and style will influence the level of ethical behaviors employees demonstrate. Being ethical is related to being perceived as a leader, and ethical leaders create a more satisfied workforce. More contemporary approaches such as servant leadership and authentic leadership explicitly recognize the importance of ethics for leadership effectiveness. Some leadership traits seem to be universal. Visionary, team-oriented, and to a lesser extent participative leadership seem to be the preferred styles around the world. However, traits such as how confident leaders should be and whether they should sacrifice themselves for the good of employees and many others are culturally dependent. Even for universal styles such as charismatic and supportive leadership, how leaders achieve charisma and supportiveness seems to be culturally dependent.

EXERCISES

1. What is the connection between leadership and ethical behaviors?
2. Do you believe that ethical leaders are more successful in organizations?
3. Which of the leadership theories seem to be most applicable to other cultures? Which ones are culturally dependent?

6. CONCLUSION

In this chapter we have reviewed the most influential leadership theories. Trait approaches identify the characteristics required to be perceived as a leader and to be successful in the role. Intelligence, extraversion, conscientiousness, openness to experience, and integrity seem to be leadership traits. Behavioral approaches identify the types of behaviors leaders demonstrate. Both trait and behavioral approaches suffered from a failure to pay attention to the context in which leadership occurs, which led to the development of contingency approaches. Recently, ethics became an explicit focus of leadership theories such as servant leadership and authentic leadership. It seems that being conscious of one's style and making sure that leaders demonstrate the behaviors that address employee, organizational, and stakeholder needs are important and require flexibility on the part of leaders.

7. EXERCISES

ETHICAL DILEMMA

You are currently a department manager and Jim is your "trusted assistant." You have very similar working styles, and you went to the same college and worked in the insurance industry for several years. Before working in this company, you both worked at a different company and you have this shared history with him. You can trust him to come to your aid, support you in your decisions, and be loyal to you. Because of your trust in him, you do not supervise his work closely, and you give him a lot of leeway in how he structures his work. He sometimes chooses to work from home, and he has flexibility in his work hours, which is unusual in the department.

Now you decided to promote him to be the assistant department manager. However, when you shared this opinion with someone else in the department, you realized that this could be a problem. Apparently, Jim is not liked by his colleagues in the department and is known as an "impression manager." Others view him as a slacker when you are not around, and the fact that he gets the first pick in schedules and gets the choice assignments causes a lot of frustration on the part of others. They feel that you are playing favorites.

Discussion Questions:

1. What would you do?
2. Would you still promote him?
3. How would you address this unpleasant situation within your department?

INDIVIDUAL EXERCISE

Ideas for Developing Yourself as an Authentic Leader

Authentic leaders have high levels of self-awareness, and their behavior is driven by their core personal values. This leadership approach recognizes the importance of self-reflection and understanding one's life history. Answer the following questions while you are alone to gain a better understanding of your own core values and authentic leadership style.

- Understand Your History
    - *Review your life history.* What are the major events in your life? How did these events make you the person you are right now?
    - *Think about your role models.* Who were your role models as you were growing up? What did you learn from your role models?
- Take Stock of Who You Are Now
    - *Describe your personality.* How does your personality affect your life?
    - *Know your strengths and weaknesses.* What are they and how can you continue to improve yourself?
- Reflect on Your Successes and Challenges
    - *Keep a journal.* Research shows that journaling is an effective tool for self reflection. Write down challenges you face and solutions you used to check your progress.
- Make Integrity a Priority
    - *Understand your core values.* What are your core values? Name three of your most important values.
    - *Do an ethics check.* Are you being consistent with your core values? If not, how can you get back on track?
- Understand the Power of Words
    - *Words shape reality.* Keep in mind that the words you use to describe people and situations matter. For example, how might the daily reality be different if you refer to those you manage as associates or team members rather than employees or subordinates?

In view of your answers to the questions above, what kind of a leader would you be if you truly acted out your values? How would people working with you respond to such a leadership style?

GROUP EXERCISE

You are charged with hiring a manager for a fast-food restaurant. The operations within the store are highly standardized, and employees have very specific job descriptions. The person will be in charge of managing around 30 employees. There is a high degree of turnover among employees, so retention will be an important priority. Most employees who work in the restaurant are young with low levels of work experience, and few of them view the restaurant business as a full-time career. The atmosphere in the restaurant has a fast pace. In this company, managers are often promoted from within, and this position is an exception. Therefore, the incoming manager may not expect a warm welcome from employees who were passed over for a promotion, as well as their colleagues. Finally, the position power of the manager will be somewhat limited because employees are unionized. Therefore, the manager will have limited opportunities for distributing pay raises or bonuses.

Discussion Questions

1. Identify the leadership traits and behaviors that are desirable for this position.
2. Design an approach to selecting this person. Which methods of employee selection would you use? Why?
3. Develop interview questions to be used in hiring this manager. Your questions should be aimed at predicting the leadership capabilities of the person in question.

ENDNOTES

1. Hogan, R., Curphy, G. J., & Hogan, J. (1994). What we know about leadership: Effectiveness and personality. *American Psychologist, 49*, 493–504.

2. House, R. J., & Aditya, R. N. (1997). The social scientific study of leadership: Quo Vadis? *Journal of Management, 23*, 409–473.

3. Judge, T. A., Bono, J. E., Ilies, R., & Gerhardt, M. W. (2002). Personality and leadership: A qualitative and quantitative review. *Journal of Applied Psychology, 87*, 765–780.

4. Karlgaard, R. (2002, February 18). Vote Carly. *Forbes, 169*(4), 37.

5. House, R. J., & Aditya, R. N. (1997). The social scientific study of leadership: Quo Vadis? *Journal of Management, 23*, 409–473; Ilies, R., Gerhardt, M. W., & Huy, L. (2004). Individual differences in leadership emergence: Integrating meta-analytic findings and behavioral genetics estimates. *International Journal of Selection and Assessment, 12*, 207–219; Lord, R. G., De Vader, C. L., & Alliger, G. M. (1986). A meta-analysis of the relation between personality traits and leadership perceptions: An application of validity generalization procedures. *Journal of Applied Psychology, 71*, 402–410; Taggar, S., Hackett, R., & Saha, S. (1999). Leadership emergence in autonomous work teams: Antecedents and outcomes. *Personnel Psychology, 52*, 899–926.

6. Judge, T. A., Colbert, A. E., & Ilies, R. (2004). Intelligence and leadership: A quantitative review and test of theoretical propositions. *Journal of Applied Psychology, 89*, 542–552.

7. Goleman, D. (January, 2004). What makes a leader? *Harvard Business Review, 82*(1), 82–91.

8. Judge, T. A., Bono, J. E., Ilies, R., & Gerhardt, M. W. (2002). Personality and leadership: A qualitative and quantitative review. *Journal of Applied Psychology, 87*, 765–780.

9. Buckmaster, J. (2008, May). How does he manage? Classified website boss. *Management Today*, 15.

10. Atwater, L. E., Dionne, S. D., Camobreco, J. F., Avolio, B. J., & Lau, A. (1998). Individual attributes and leadership style: Predicting the use of punishment and its effects. *Journal of Organizational Behavior, 19*, 559–576; Niebuhr, R. E., & Davis, K. R. (1984). Self-esteem: Relationship with leader behavior perceptions as moderated by the duration of the superior-subordinate dyad association. *Personality and Social Psychology Bulletin, 10*, 51–59.

11. Judge, T. A., & Cable, D. M. (2004). The effect of physical height on workplace success and income: Preliminary test of a theoretical model. *Journal of Applied Psychology, 89*, 428–441.

12. Reave, L. (2005). Spiritual values and practices related to leadership effectiveness. *Leadership Quarterly, 16*, 655–687.

13. Farrell, G., & Davidson, P. (2007, July 13). Whole Foods' CEO was busy guy online. *USA Today*, Money section, p. 04B.

14. Judge, T. A., Bono, J. E., Ilies, R., & Gerhardt, M. W. (2002). Personality and leadership: A qualitative and quantitative review. *Journal of Applied Psychology, 87*, 765–780.

15. House, R. J., & Aditya, R. N. (1997). The social scientific study of leadership: Quo Vadis? *Journal of Management, 23*, 409–473.

16. Judge, T. A., Bono, J. E., Ilies, R., & Gerhardt, M. W. (2002). Personality and leadership: A qualitative and quantitative review. *Journal of Applied Psychology, 87*, 765–780.

17. Hackman, J. R., & Wageman, R. (2007). Asking the right questions about leadership: Discussion and conclusions. *American Psychologist, 62*, 43–47.

18. See House, R. J., & Aditya, R. N. (1997). The social scientific study of leadership: Quo Vadis? *Journal of Management, 23*, 409–473.

19. Nystrom, P. C. (1978). Managers and the hi-hi leader myth. *Academy of Management Journal, 21*, 325–331.

20. Judge, T. A., Piccolo, R. F., & Ilies, R. (2004). The forgotten ones? The validity of consideration and initiating structure in leadership research. *Journal of Applied Psychology, 89*, 36–51.

21. Miles, R. H., & Petty, M. M. (1977). Leader effectiveness in small bureaucracies. *Academy of Management Journal, 20*, 238–250.

22. Seltzer, J., & Numerof, R. E. (1988). Supervisory leadership and subordinate burnout. *Academy of Management Journal, 31*, 439–446.

23. Miller, K. I., & Monge, P. R. (1986). Participation, satisfaction, and productivity: A meta-analytic review. *Academy of Management Journal, 29*, 727–753.

24. Baumgartel, H. (1957). Leadership style as a variable in research administration. *Administrative Science Quarterly, 2*, 344–360.

25. Vroom, V. H., & Mann, F. C. (1960). Leader authoritarianism and employee attitudes. *Personnel Psychology, 13*, 125–140.

26. Deutschman, A. (2004, September). Googling for courage. *Fast Company, 86*, 58–59; Welch, D., Kiley, D., Ihlwan, M. (2008, March 17). My way or the highway at Hyundai. *Business Week, 4075*, 48–51.

27. Judge, T. A., & Piccolo, R. F. (2004). Transformational and transactional leadership: A meta-analytic test of their relative validity. *Journal of Applied Psychology, 89*, 755–768.

28. Skogstad, A., Einarsen, S., Torsheim, T., Aasland, M. S., & Hetland, H. (2007). The destructiveness of laissez-faire leadership behavior. *Journal of Occupational Health Psychology, 12*, 80–92.

29. Fiedler, F. (1967). *A theory of leadership effectiveness*. New York: McGraw-Hill; Fiedler, F. E. (1964). A contingency model of leader effectiveness. In L. Berkowitz (Ed.), *Advances in experimental social psychology, vol. 1* (pp. 149–190). New York: Academic Press.

30. Peters, L. H., Hartke, D. D., & Pohlmann, J. T. (1985). Fiedler's contingency theory of leadership: An application of the meta-analysis procedures of Schmidt and Hunter. *Psychological Bulletin, 97*, 274–285; Strube, M. J., & Garcia, J. E. (1981). A meta-analytic investigation of Fiedler's contingency model of leadership effectiveness. *Psychological Bulletin, 90*, 307–321; Vecchio, R. P. (1983). Assessing the validity of Fiedler's contingency model of leadership effectiveness: A closer look at Strube and Garcia. *Psychological Bulletin, 93*, 404–408.

31. Hersey, P.H., Blanchard, K.H., ' Johnson, D.E. (2007). *Management of Organizational Behavior: Leadership human resources*. Upper Saddle River, NJ: Prentice Hall.

32. http://www.situational.com/Views/SituationalLeadership/RightHereRightNow.aspx

33. Blank, W.,'Green, S.G., ' Weitzel, J.R. (1990). A test of the situational leadership theory. *Personnel Psychology, 43*, 579–597; Graeff, C. L. (1983). The situational leadership theory: A critical review. *Academy of Management Review, 8*, 285–291; Fernandez, C.F., ' Vecchio, R.P. (2002). Situational leadership theory revisited: A test of an across-jobs perspective. *Leadership Quarterly, 8*, 67–84.

34. House, R. J. (1971). A path goal theory of leader effectiveness. *Administrative Science Quarterly, 16*(3), 321–338.

35. House, R. J. (1996). Path-goal theory of leadership: Lessons, legacy, and a reformulated theory. *Leadership Quarterly, 7*, 323–352; House, R. J., & Mitchell, T. R. (1974). Path-goal theory of leadership. *Journal of Contemporary Business, 3*, 81–97.

36. House, R. J., & Aditya, R. N. (1997). The social scientific study of leadership: Quo Vadis? *Journal of Management, 23*, 409–473; Stinson, J. E., & Johnson, T. W. (1975). The path-goal theory of leadership: A partial test and suggested refinement. *Academy of Management Journal, 18*, 242–252; Wofford, J. C., & Liska, L. Z. (1993). Path-goal theories of leadership: A meta-analysis. *Journal of Management, 19*, 857–876.

37. Vroom, V. H. (2000). Leadership and the decision making process. *Organizational Dynamics, 68*, 82–94; Vroom, V. H., & Yetton, P. W. (1973). *Leadership and decision-making*. Pittsburg: University of Pittsburg Press; Jago, A., & Vroom, V. H. (1980). An evaluation of two alternatives to the Vroom/Yetton Normative Model. *Academy of Management Journal, 23*, 347–355; Vroom, V. H., & Jago, A. G. 1988. *The new leadership: managing participation in organizations*. Englewood Cliffs, NJ: Prentice Hall.

38. Vroom, V. H., & Jago, G. (1978). On the validity of the Vroom Yetton model. *Journal of Applied Psychology, 63*, 151–162.

39. Bass, B. M. (1985). *Leadership and performance beyond expectations*. New York: Free Press; Burns, J. M. (1978). *Leadership*. New York: Harper & Row.

40. Bass, B. M. (1985). *Leadership and performance beyond expectations*. New York: Free Press; Burns, J. M. (1978). *Leadership*. New York: Harper & Row; Bycio, P., Hackett, R. D., & Allen, J. S. (1995). Further assessment of Bass's (1985) conceptualization of transactional and transformational leadership. *Journal of Applied Psychology, 80*, 468–478; Judge, T. A., & Piccolo, R. F. (2004). Transformational and transactional leadership: A meta-analytic test of their relative validity. *Journal of Applied Psychology, 89*, 755–768.

41. Shamir, B., House, R. J., & Arthur, M. B. (1993). The motivational effects of charismatic leadership: A self-concept based theory. *Organization Science, 4*, 577–594.

42. Judge, T. A., & Piccolo, R. F. (2004). Transformational and transactional leadership: A meta-analytic test of their relative validity. *Journal of Applied Psychology, 89*, 755–768.

43. Herold, D. M., Fedor, D. B., Caldwell, S., & Liu, Y. (2008). The effects of transformational and change leadership on employees' commitment to a change: A multilevel study. *Journal of Applied Psychology, 93*, 346–357; Piccolo, R. F., & Colquitt, J. A. (2006). Transformational leadership and job behaviors: The mediating role of core job characteristics. *Academy of Management Journal, 49*, 327–340; Schaubroeck, J., Lam, S. K., & Cha, S. E. (2007). Embracing transformational leadership: Team values and the impact of leader behavior on team performance. *Journal of Applied Psychology, 92*, 1020–1030; Shin, S. J., & Zhou, J. (2003). Transformational leadership, conservation, and creativity: Evidence from Korea. *Academy of Management Journal, 46*, 703–714; Wang, H., Law, K. S., Hackett, R. D., Duanxu, W., & Zhen, X. C. (2005). Leader-member exchange as a mediator of the relationship between transformational leadership and followers' performance and organizational citizenship behavior. *Academy of Management Journal, 48*, 420–432.

44. Judge, T. A., & Piccolo, R. F. (2004). Transformational and transactional leadership: A meta-analytic test of their relative validity. *Journal of Applied Psychology, 89*, 755–768.

45. Dirks, K. T., & Ferrin, D. L. (2002). Trust in leadership: Meta-analytic findings and implications for research and practice. *Journal of Applied Psychology, 87*, 611–628.

46. Bono, J. E., & Judge, T. A. (2004). Personality and transformational and transactional leadership: A meta-analysis. *Journal of Applied Psychology, 89*, 901–910.

47. Barling, J., Weber, T., & Kelloway, E. K. (1996). Effects of transformational leadership training on attitudinal and financial outcomes: A field experiment. *Journal of Applied Psychology, 81*, 827–832; Dvir, T., Eden, D., Avolio, B. J., & Shamir, B. (2002). Impact of transformational leadership on follower development and performance: A field experiment. *Academy of Management Journal, 45*, 735–744; Frese, M., Beimel, S., & Schoenborg, S. (2003). Action training for charismatic leadership: Two evaluations of studies of a commercial training module on inspirational communication of a vision. *Personnel Psychology, 56*, 671–697.

48. Khurana, R. (2002, September). The curse of the superstar CEO. *Harvard Business Review, 80*(9), 60–66.

49. Agle, B. R., Nagarajan, N. J., Sonnenfeld, J. A., & Srinivasan, D. (2006). Does CEO charisma matter? An empirical analysis of the relationships among organizational performance, environmental uncertainty, and top management team perceptions of CEO charisma. *Academy of Management Journal, 49*, 161–174.

50. Dansereau, F., Jr., Graen, G., & Haga, W. J. (1975). A vertical dyad linkage approach to leadership within formal organizations: A longitudinal investigation of the role making process. *Organizational Behavior & Human Performance, 13*(1), 46–78; Erdogan, B., & Liden, R. C. (2002). Social exchanges in the workplace: A review of recent developments and future research directions in leader-member exchange theory. In L. L. Neider & C. A. Schriesheim (Eds.), *Leadership* (pp. 65–114), Greenwich, CT: Information Age Press; Gerstner, C. R., & Day, D. V. (1997). Meta-analytic review of leader-member exchange theory: Correlates and construct issues. *Journal of Applied Psychology, 82*, 827–844; Graen, G. B., & Uhl-Bien, M. (1995). Relationship-based approach to

leadership: Development of leader-member exchange (LMX) theory over 25 years: Applying a multi-level multi-domain perspective. *Leadership Quarterly, 6*(2), 219–247; Liden, R. C., & Maslyn, J. M. (1998). Multidimensionality of leader-member exchange: An empirical assessment through scale development. *Journal of Management, 24*, 43–72.

51. Gerstner, C. R., & Day, D. V. (1997). Meta-analytic review of leader-member exchange theory: Correlates and construct issues. *Journal of Applied Psychology, 82*, 827–844; Hui, C., Law, K. S., & Chen, Z. X. (1999). A structural equation model of the effects of negative affectivity, leader-member exchange, and perceived job mobility on in-role and extra-role performance: A Chinese case. *Organizational Behavior and Human Decision Processes, 77*, 3–21; Kraimer, M. L., Wayne, S. J., & Jaworski, R. A. (2001). Sources of support and expatriate performance: The mediating role of expatriate adjustment. *Personnel Psychology, 54*, 71–99; Liden, R. C., Wayne, S. J., & Sparrowe, R. T. (2000). An examination of the mediating role of psychological empowerment on the relations between the job, interpersonal relationships, and work outcomes. *Journal of Applied Psychology, 85*, 407–416; Settoon, R. P., Bennett, N., & Liden, R. C. (1996). Social exchange in organizations: Perceived organizational support, leader-member exchange, and employee reciprocity. *Journal of Applied Psychology, 81*, 219–227; Tierney, P., Farmer, S. M., & Graen, G. B. (1999). An examination of leadership and employee creativity: The relevance of traits and relationships. *Personnel Psychology, 52*, 591–620; Wayne, S. J., Shore, L. M., & Liden. R. C. (1997). Perceived organizational support and leader-member exchange: A social exchange perspective. *Academy of Management Journal, 40*, 82–111.

52. Chen, Z., Lam, W., & Zhong, J. A. (2007). Leader-member exchange and member performance: A new look at individual-level negative feedback seeking behavior and team-level empowerment climate. *Journal of Applied Psychology, 92*, 202–212.

53. Ilies, R., Nahrgang, J. D., & Morgeson, F. P. (2007). Leader-member exchange and citizenship behaviors: A meta-analysis. *Journal of Applied Psychology, 92*, 269–277.

54. [illegible] moderating role of extraversion: Leader-member exchange, performance, and turnover during new executive development. *Journal of Applied Psychology, 91*, 298–310; Erdogan, B., Kraimer, M. L., & Liden, R. C. (2004). Work value congruence and intrinsic career success. *Personnel Psychology, 57*, 305–332; Major, D. A., Kozlowski, S. W., Chao, G. T., & Gardner, P. D. (1995). A longitudinal investigation of newcomer expectations, early socialization outcomes, and the moderating effects of role development factors. *Journal of Applied Psychology, 80*, 418–431.

55. Ferris, G. R. (1985). Role of leadership in the employee withdrawal process: A constructive replication. *Journal of Applied Psychology, 70*, 777–781; Graen, G. B., Liden, R. C., & Hoel, W. (1982). Role of leadership in the employee withdrawal process. *Journal of Applied Psychology, 67*, 868–872.

56. Masterson, S. S., Lewis, K., Goldman, B. M., & Taylor, M. S. (2000). Integrating justice and social exchange: The differing effects of fair procedures and treatment on work relationships. *Academy of Management Journal, 43*, 738–748.

57. Bauer, T. N., & Green, S. G. (1996). Development of a leader-member exchange: A longitudinal test. *Academy of Management Journal, 39*, 1538–1567.

58. Colella, A., & Varma, A. (2001). The impact of subordinate disability on leader-member exchange relationships. *Academy of Management Journal, 44*, 304–315; Maslyn, J. M., & Uhl Bien, M. (2001). Leader member exchange and its dimensions: Effects of self-effort and other's effort on relationship quality. *Journal of Applied Psychology, 86*, 697–708; Janssen, O., & Van Yperen, N. W. (2004). Employees' goal orientations, the quality of leader-member exchange, and the outcomes of job performance and job satisfaction. *Academy of Management Journal, 47*, 368–384; Wing, L., Xu, H., & Snape, E. (2007). Feedback-seeking behavior and leader-member exchange: Do supervisor-attributed motives matter? *Academy of Management Journal, 50*, 348–363.

59. Engle, E. M., & Lord, R. G. (1997). Implicit theories, self-schemas, and leader-member exchange. *Academy of Management Journal, 40*, 988–1010; Liden, R. C., Wayne, S. J., & Stilwell, D. (1993). A longitudinal study on the early development of leader-member exchanges. *Journal of Applied Psychology, 78*, 662–674; Wayne, S. J., Shore, L. M., & Liden. R. C. (1997). Perceived organizational support and leader-member exchange: A social exchange perspective. *Academy of Management Journal, 40*, 82–111.

60. Erdogan, B., Liden, R. C., & Kraimer, M. L. (2006). Justice and leader-member exchange: The moderating role of organizational culture. *Academy of Management Journal, 49*, 395–406.

61. Duarte, N. T., Goodson, J. R., & Klich, N. R. (1994). Effects of dyadic quality and duration on performance appraisal. *Academy of Management Journal, 37*, 499–521.

62. Heneman, R. L., Greenberger, D. B., & Anonyuo, C. (1989). Attributions and exchanges: The effects of interpersonal factors on the diagnosis of employee performance. *Academy of Management Journal, 32*, 466–476.

63. Erdogan, B., & Enders, J. (2007). Support from the top: Supervisors' perceived organizational support as a moderator of leader-member exchange to satisfaction and performance relationships. *Journal of Applied Psychology, 92*, 321–330; Sparrowe, R. T., & Liden, R. C. (2005). Two routes to influence: Integrating leader-member exchange and social network perspectives. *Administrative Science Quarterly, 50*, 505–535; Tangirala, S., Green, S. G., & Ramanujam, R. (2007). In the shadow of the boss's boss: Effects of supervisors' upward exchange relationships on employees. *Journal of Applied Psychology, 92*, 309–320.

64. Greenleaf, R. K. (1977). *Servant Leadership: A journey into the nature of legitimate power and greatness*. Mahwah, NJ: Paulist Press; Liden, R. C., Wayne, S., J., Zhao, H., & Henderson, D. (2008). Servant leadership: Development of a multidimensional measure and multi-level assessment. *Leadership Quarterly, 19*, 161–177.

65. Goodwin, D. K. (2005, June 26). The master of the game. *Time*. Retrieved November 20, 2008, from http://www.time.com/time/printout/0,8816,1077300,00.html.

66. Liden, R. C., Wayne, S., J., Zhao, H., & Henderson, D. (2008). Servant leadership: Development of a multidimensional measure and multi-level assessment. *Leadership Quarterly, 19*, 161–177.

67. Ehrhart, M. G. (2004). Leadership and procedural justice climate as antecedents of unit-level organizational citizenship behavior. *Personnel Psychology, 57*, 61–94.

68. Buchanan, L. (2007, May). In praise of selflessness: Why the best leaders are servants. *Inc., 29*(5), 33–35.

69. Avolio, B. J., & Gardner, W. L. (2005). Authentic leadership development: Getting to the root of positive forms of leadership. *Leadership Quarterly, 16*, 315–338; Gardner, W. L., Avolio, B. J., Luthans, F., May, D. R., & Walumbwa, F. (2005). "Can you see the real me?" A self-based model of authentic leader and follower development. *Leadership Quarterly, 16*, 343–372; George, B. (2007). Authentic leaders: They inspire and empower others. *Leadership Excellence, 24*(9), 16–17; Ilies, R., Morgeson, F. P., & Nahrgang, J. D. (2005). Authentic leadership and eudaemonic well-being: Understanding leader-follower outcomes. *Leadership Quarterly, 16*, 373–394; Sparrowe, R. T. (2005). Authentic leadership and the narrative self. *Leadership Quarterly, 16*, 419–439.

70. Shamir, B., & Eilam, G. (2005). What's your story? A life-stories approach to authentic leadership development. *Leadership Quarterly, 16*, 395–417.

71. Walumbwa, F. O., Avolio, B. J., Gardner, W. L., Wernsing, T. S., & Peterson, S. J. (2008). Authentic leadership: Development and validation of a theory-based measure. *Journ-* [illegible]

72. Milgram, S. (1974). *Obedience to authority; an experimental view*. New York: Harper & Row; Trevino, L. K., & Brown, M. E. (2004). Managing to be ethical: Debunking five business ethics myths. *Academy of Management Executive, 18*(2), 69–81.

73. Brown, M. E., Trevino, L. K., & Harrison, D. A. (2005). Ethical leadership: A social learning perspective for construct development and testing. *Organizational Behavior and Human Decision Processes, 97*, 117–134; Morgan, R. B. (1993). Self- and co-worker perceptions of ethics and their relationships to leadership and salary. *Academy of Management Journal, 36*, 200–214.

74. Schminke, M., Ambrose, M. L., & Neubaum, D. O. (2005). The effect of leader moral development on ethical climate and employee attitudes. *Organizational Behavior and Human Decision Processes, 97*, 135–151.

75. Turner, N., Barling, J., Epitropaki, O., Butcher, V., & Milner, C. (2002). Transformational leadership and moral reasoning. *Journal of Applied Psychology, 87*, 304–311.

76. House, R. J., Hanges, P. J., Javidan, M., Dorfman, P., & Gupta, V. (2004). *Culture, leadership, and organizations: The Globe Study of 62 societies*. Thousand Oaks, CA: Sage.

77. Den Hartog, D. N., House, R. J., Hanges, P. J., Ruiz-Quintanilla, S. A., & Dorfman, P. W. (1999). Culture specific and cross-culturally generalized implicit leadership theories: Are attributes of charismatic/transformational leadership universally endorsed? *Leadership Quarterly, 10*(2), 219–256; Javidan, M., Dorfman, P. W., De Luque, M. S., & House, R. J. (2006). In the eye of the beholder: Cross cultural lessons in leadership from project GLOBE. *Academy of Management Perspectives, 20*(1), 67–90.

78. Ensari, N., & Murphy, S. E. (2003). Cross-cultural variations in leadership perceptions and attribution of charisma to the leader. *Organizational Behavior and Human Decision Processes, 92*, 52–66.

79. Brodbeck, F. C., Frese, M., Akerblom, S., & Audia, G. (2000). Cultural variation of leadership prototypes across 22 European countries. *Journal of Occupational and Organizational Psychology, 31*, 1–29; Den Hartog, D. N., House, R. J., Hanges, P. J., Ruis-Quintanilla, S. A., & Dorfman, P. W. (1999). Culture specific and cross-culturally generalized implicit leadership theories: Are attributes of charismatic/transformational leadership universally endorsed? *Leadership Quarterly, 10*, 219–256.

80. Dorfman, P. W., Howell, J. P., Hibino, J. P., Lee, J. K., Tate, U., & Bautista, A. (1997). Leadership in Western and Asian countries: Commonalities and differences in effective leadership processes across cultures. *Leadership Quarterly, 8*, 233–274; Gerstner, C. R., & Day, D. V. (1994). Cross-cultural comparison of leadership prototypes. *Leadership Quarterly, 5*, 121–134.

81. Javidan, M., Dorfman, P. W., De Luque, M. S., & House, R. J. (2006). In the eye of the beholder: Cross cultural lessons in leadership from project GLOBE. *Academy of Management Perspectives, 20*(1), 67–90.

82. Brodbeck, F. C., Frese, M., Akerblom, S., & Audia, G. (2000). Cultural variation of leadership prototypes across 22 European countries. *Journal of Occupational and Organizational Psychology, 31*, 1–29.

83. Aycan, Z., Kanungo, R. N., Mendonca, M., Yu, K., Deller, J., Stahl, G., et al. (2000). Impact of culture on human resource management practices: A 10-country comparison. *Applied Psychology: An International Review, 49*, 192–221; Pellegrini, E. K., & Scandura, T. A. (2008). Paternalistic leadership: A review and agenda for future research. *Journal of Management, 34*, 556–593.

CHAPTER 13

Power and Politics

LEARNING OBJECTIVES

After reading this chapter, you should be able to do the following:

1. Understand the meaning of power.
2. Recognize the positive and negative aspects of power and influence.
3. Recognize the sources of power.
4. Understand and recognize influence tactics and impression management.
5. Learn the definition of a social network and how to analyze your own network.
6. Understand the antecedents and consequences of organizational politics.
7. Understand how ethics affect power.
8. Understand cross-cultural influences on power use.

Focus on Power—The Case of Steve Jobs

Source: http://www.flickr.com/photos/51035629850@N01/522131312.

On November 27, 2007, *Fortune* named Steve Jobs the most powerful person in business. The CEO of Apple Inc. has transformed no fewer than five different industries: computers, Hollywood movies, music, retailing, and wireless phones. His Apple II ushered in the personal computer era in 1977, and the graphical interface of the Macintosh in 1984 set the standard that all other PCs emulated. His company Pixar defined the computer-animated feature film. The iPod, iTunes, and iPhone revolutionized how we listen to music, how we pay for and receive all types of digital content, and what we expect of a mobile phone.

How has Jobs done it? As we'll see in this chapter, Jobs draws on all six types of power: expert, legitimate, reward, referent, information, and coercive. His vision and sheer force of will helped him succeed as a young unknown. But the same determination that helps him succeed has a darker side—an autocracy and drive for perfection that can make him tyrannical. Forcefulness is helpful when tackling large, intractable problems, says Stanford social psychologist Roderick Kramer, who calls Jobs one of the "great intimidators." Jobs has been known to berate people to the point of tears, but at the same time, "He inspires astounding effort and creativity from his people."

Employee Andy Herzfeld, the lead designer of the original Mac operating system, says Jobs imbues employees with a "messianic zeal" and can make them feel that they're working on the greatest product in the world. But at the same time, Jobs is very hard to please, so Apple employees work hard to win his approval. "He has the ability to pull the best out of people," says Cordell Ratzlaff, who worked closely with Jobs on OS X for 18 months. "I learned a tremendous amount from him." Jobs's ability to persuade and influence has come to be called a "reality distortion field." As Bud Tribble put it, "In his presence, reality is malleable. He can convince anyone of practically anything." Hertzfeld describes his style as "a confounding mélange of a charismatic rhetorical style, an indomitable will, and an eagerness to bend any fact to fit the purpose at hand."

The influence works even when you're aware of it, and it works even on "enemies": "No other high-tech impresario could walk into the annual sales meeting of one of his fiercest rivals and get a standing ovation," which is what Jobs got in 2002 from Intel Corporation (the ally of Apple archrival Microsoft in the partnership known as Wintel: Windows + Intel).

Jobs's power is not infallible—he was ousted from his own company in 1987 by the man he hired to help him run it—but he was brought back in 1997. The only years that Apple was unprofitable were the years during Jobs's absence. Many are watching to see how Apple runs without Jobs who took a 6-month leave of absence in early 2009.

Sources: Schlender, B. (2007, November 27). The power of Steve Jobs. Fortune, 117–118; Sutton, R. (2007). The no asshole rule. New York: Warner Business Books; Kahney, L. (2008, March 18). How Apple got everything right by doing everything wrong. Wired. Retrieved January 4, 2008, from http://www.wired.com/techbiz/it/magazine/16-04/bz_apple; Hertzfeld, A. (1981, February). Reality distortion field. Retrieved January 4, 2008, from http://folklore.org/StoryView.py?story=Reality_Distortion_Field.txt.

Video Connection

If you are interested in learning more about Steve Jobs as he describes pivotal moments in his life, view Steve Jobs's commencement speech at Stanford in 2005, available at the following Web site: http://www.youtube.com/watch?v=UF8uR6Z6KLc

1. THE BASICS OF POWER

LEARNING OBJECTIVES

1. **Learn the meaning of *power*.**
2. **Understand how power can have both positive and negative consequences.**
3. **Learn about different sources of power.**
4. **Understand the relationship between dependency and power.**

1.1 What Is Power?

power

The ability to influence the behavior of others to get what you want.

We'll look at the aspects and nuances of power in more detail in this chapter, but simply put, **power** is the ability to influence the behavior of others to get what you want. Gerald Salancik and Jeffery Pfeffer concur, noting, "Power is simply the ability to get things done the way one wants them to be done."[1] If you want a larger budget to open a new store in a large city and you get the budget increase, you have used your power to influence the decision.

Power distribution is usually visible within organizations. For example, Salancik and Pfeffer gathered information from a company with 21 department managers and asked 10 of those department heads to rank all the managers according to the influence each person had in the organization. Although ranking 21 managers might seem like a difficult task, all the managers were immediately able to create that list. When Salancik and Pfeffer compared the rankings, they found virtually no disagreement in how the top 5 and bottom 5 managers were ranked. The only slight differences came from individuals ranking themselves higher than their colleagues ranked them. The same findings held true for factories, banks, and universities.

1.2 Positive and Negative Consequences of Power

The fact that we can see and succumb to power means that power has both positive and negative consequences. On one hand, powerful CEOs can align an entire organization to move together to achieve goals. Amazing philanthropists such as Paul Farmer, a doctor who brought hospitals, medicine, and doctors to remote Haiti, and Greg Mortenson, a mountaineer who founded the Central Asia Institute and built schools across Pakistan, draw on their own power to organize others toward lofty goals; they have changed the lives of thousands of individuals in countries around the world for the better.[2] On the other hand, autocracy can destroy companies and countries alike. The phrase, "Power tends to corrupt, and absolute power corrupts absolutely" was first said by English historian John Emerich Edward

Dalberg, who warned that power was inherently evil and its holders were not to be trusted. History shows that power can be intoxicating and can be devastating when abused, as seen in high-profile cases such as those involving Enron Corporation and government leaders such as the impeached Illinois Governor Rod Blagojevich in 2009. One reason that power can be so easily abused is because individuals are often quick to conform. To understand this relationship better, we will examine three famous researchers who studied conformity in a variety of contexts.

Conformity

Conformity refers to people's tendencies to behave consistently with social norms. Conformity can refer to small things such as how people tend to face forward in an elevator. There's no rule listed in the elevator saying which way to face, yet it is expected that everyone will face forward. To test this, the next time you're in an elevator with strangers, simply stand facing the back of the elevator without saying anything. You may notice that those around you become uncomfortable. Conformity can result in engaging in unethical behaviors, because you are led by someone you admire and respect who has power over you. Guards at Abu Ghraib said they were just following orders when they tortured prisoners.[3] People conform because they want to fit in with and please those around them. There is also a tendency to look to others in ambiguous situations, which can lead to conformity. The response to "Why did you do that?" being "Because everyone else was doing it" sums up this tendency.

conformity

People's tendencies to behave consistently with social norms.

So, does conformity occur only in rare or extreme circumstances? Actually, this is not the case. Three classic sets of studies illustrate how important it is to create checks and balances to help individuals resist the tendency to conform or to abuse authority. To illustrate this, we will examine findings from the Milgram, Asch, and Zimbardo studies.

The Milgram Studies

Stanley Milgram, a psychologist at Yale in the 1960s, set out to study conformity to authority. His work tested how far individuals would go in hurting another individual when told to do so by a researcher. A key factor in the Milgram study and others that will be discussed is the use of confederates, or people who seem to be participants but are actually paid by the researchers to take on a certain role. Participants believed that they were engaged in an experiment on learning. The participant (teacher) would ask a series of questions to another "participant" (learner). The teachers were instructed to shock the learners whenever an incorrect answer was given. The learner was not a participant at all but actually a confederate who would pretend to be hurt by the shocks and yell out in pain when the button was pushed. Starting at 15 volts of power, the participants were asked to increase the intensity of the shocks over time. Some expressed concern when the voltage was at 135 volts, but few stopped once they were told by the researcher that they would not personally be held responsible for the outcome of the experiment and that their help was needed to complete the experiment. In the end, all the participants were willing to go up to 300 volts, and a shocking 65% were willing to administer the maximum of 450 volts even as they heard screams of pain from the learner.[4]

FIGURE 13.2

This is an illustration of the setup of a Milgram experiment. The experimenter (E) convinces the subject ("Teacher" T) to give what are believed to be painful electric shocks to another subject, who is actually an actor ("Learner" L). Many subjects continued to give shocks despite pleas of mercy from the actors.

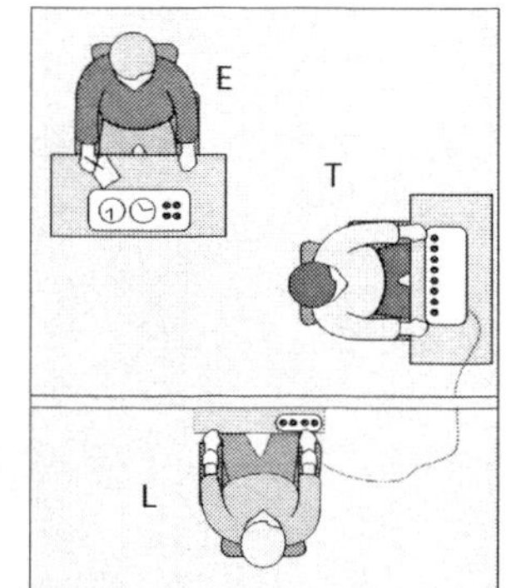

Source: http://en.wikipedia.org/wiki/Image:Milgram_Experiment_v2.png.

The Asch Studies

Another researcher, Solomon Asch, found that individuals could be influenced to say that two lines were the same length when one was clearly shorter than the other. This effect was established using groups of four or more participants who were told they were in experiments of visual perception. However, only one person in the group was actually in the experiment. The rest were confederates, and the researchers had predetermined whether or not they gave accurate answers. Groups were shown a focal line and a choice of three other lines of varying length, with one being the same length as the focal line. Most of the time the confederates would correctly state which choice matched the focal line, but occasionally they would give an obviously wrong answer. For example, looking at the following lines, the confederates might say that choice C matches the length of the focal line. When this happened, the actual research participant would go along with the wrong answer 37% of the time. When asked why they went along with the group, participants said they assumed that the rest of the group, for whatever reason, had more information regarding the correct choice. It only took three other individuals saying the wrong answer for the participant to routinely agree with the group. However, this effect was decreased by 75% if just one of the insiders gave the correct answer, even if the rest of the group gave the incorrect answer. This finding illustrates the power that even a small dissenting minority can have. Additionally, it holds even if the dissenting confederate gives a different incorrect answer. As long as one confederate gave an answer that was different from the majority, participants were more likely to give the correct answer themselves.[5] A meta-analysis of 133 studies using Asch's research design revealed two interesting patterns. First, within the United States, the level of conformity has been decreasing since the 1950s. Second, studies done in collectivistic countries such as Japan showed more conformity than those done in more individualistic countries such as Great Britain.[6]

FIGURE 13.3

Participants were asked one by one to say which of the lines on the right matched the line on the focal line on the left. While A is an exact match, many participants conformed when others unanimously chose B or C.

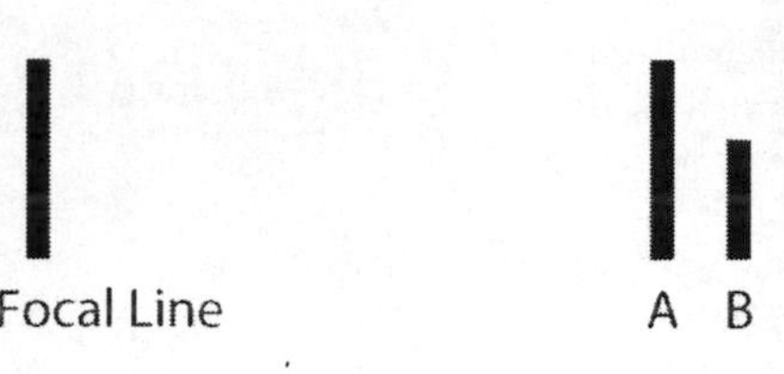

The Zimbardo Study

Philip Zimbardo, a researcher at Stanford University, conducted a famous experiment in the 1970s.[7] While this experiment would probably not make it past the human subjects committee of schools today, at the time, he was authorized to place an ad in the paper that asked for male volunteers to help understand prison management. After excluding any volunteers with psychological or medical problems or with any history of crime or drug abuse, he identified 24 volunteers to participate in his study. Researchers randomly assigned 18 individuals to the role of prisoner or guard. Those assigned the role of "prisoners" were surprised when they were picked up by actual police officers and then transferred to a prison that had been created in the basement of the Stanford psychology building. The guards in the experiment were told to keep order but received no training. Zimbardo was shocked with how quickly the expected roles emerged. Prisoners began to feel depressed and helpless. Guards began to be aggressive and abusive. The original experiment was scheduled to last 2 weeks, but Zimbardo ended it after only 6 days upon seeing how deeply entrenched in their roles everyone, including himself, had become. Next we will examine the relationship between dependency and power.

The Relationship Between Dependency and Power

Dependency

dependency

Directly related to power. The more that a person or unit is dependent on you, the more power you have.

Dependency is directly related to power. The more that a person or unit is dependent on you, the more power you have. The strategic contingencies model provides a good description of how dependency works. According to the model, dependency is power that a person or unit gains from their ability to handle actual or potential problems facing the organization.[8] You know how dependent you are on someone when you answer three key questions that are addressed in the following sections.

Scarcity

scarcity

In the context of dependency, refers to the uniqueness of a resource.

In the context of dependency, **scarcity** refers to the uniqueness of a resource. The more difficult something is to obtain, the more valuable it tends to be. Effective persuaders exploit this reality by making an opportunity or offer seem more attractive because it is limited or exclusive. They might convince you to take on a project because "it's rare to get a chance to work on a new project like this," or "You have to sign on today because if you don't, I have to offer it to someone else."

Importance

importance

The value of the resource.

Importance refers to the value of the resource. The key question here is "How important is this?" If the resources or skills you control are vital to the organization, you will gain some power. The more vital the resources that you control are, the more power you will have. For example, if Kecia is the only person who knows how to fill out reimbursement forms, it is important that you are able to work with her, because getting paid back for business trips and expenses is important to most of us.

Substitutability

substitutability

One's ability to find another option that works as well as the one offered.

Finally, **substitutability** refers to one's ability to find another option that works as well as the one offered. The question around whether something is substitutable is "How difficult would it be for me to find another way to this?" The harder it is to find a substitute, the more dependent the person becomes and the more power someone else has over them. If you are the only person who knows how to make a piece of equipment work, you will be very powerful in the organization. This is true unless another piece of equipment is brought in to serve the same function. At that point, your power would diminish. Similarly, countries with large supplies of crude oil have traditionally had power to the extent that other countries need oil to function. As the price of oil climbs, alternative energy sources such as wind, solar, and hydropower become more attractive to investors and governments. For example, in response to soaring fuel costs and environmental concerns, in 2009 Japan Airlines successfully tested a blend of aircraft fuel made from a mix of camelina, jatropha, and algae on the engine of a Boeing 747-300 aircraft.[9]

FIGURE 13.4

Possessing any of the three aspects of a resource could make others depend on you, two would make you extremely needed, and having all three could make you indispensable.

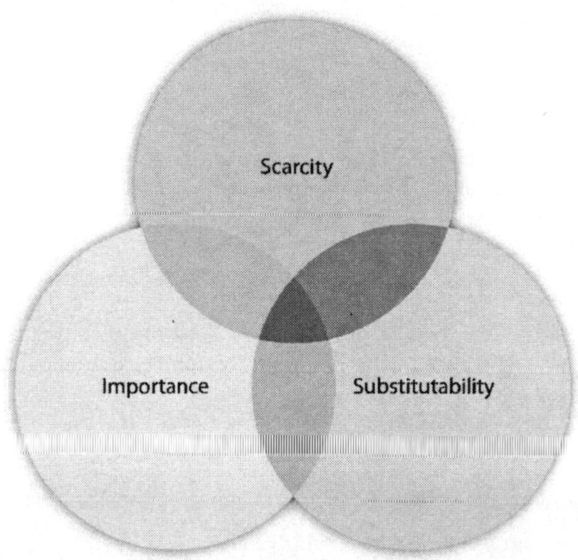

KEY TAKEAWAY

Power is the ability to influence the behavior of others to get what you want. It is often visible to others within organizations. Conformity manifests itself in several ways, and research shows that individuals will defer to a group even when they may know that what they are doing is inaccurate or unethical. Having just one person dissent helps to buffer this effect. The more dependent someone is on you, the more power you have over them. Dependency is increased when you possess something that is considered scarce, important, and non-substitutable by others.

EXERCISES

1. What does the phrase "Power corrupts and absolute power corrupts absolutely" refer to? What experiences have you had that confirm or refute this assumption?
2. Thinking about the Milgram and Zimbardo studies, do you think you would behave the same or differently in those situations? Why or why not?
3. What lessons can be learned from the past studies of conformity to help avoid abuses of power in the future?
4. Give an example of someone who you are dependent upon. Think about how scarcity, importance, and substitutability affect this dependency.

2. THE POWER TO INFLUENCE

LEARNING OBJECTIVES

1. Identify the five sources of power.
2. Understand influence tactics.
3. Learn about impression management.
4. Examine the impact of the direction of influence attempts.

2.1 Bases of Power

Having power and using power are two different things. For example, imagine a manager who has the power to reward or punish employees. When the manager makes a request, he or she will probably be obeyed even though the manager does not actually reward the employee. The fact that the manager has the ability to give rewards and punishments will be enough for employees to follow the request. What are the sources of one's power over others? Researchers identified six sources of power, which include legitimate, reward, coercive, expert, information, and referent.[10] You might earn power from one source or all six depending on the situation. Let us take a look at each of these in turn, and continue with Steve Jobs from the opening case as our example.

FIGURE 13.5

People who have legitimate power should be aware of how their choices and behaviors affect others.

"I was just going to say, 'Well, I don't make the rules.' But, of course, I do make the rules."

Legitimate Power

Legitimate power is power that comes from one's organizational role or position. For example, a boss can assign projects, a policeman can arrest a citizen, and a teacher assigns grades. Others comply with the requests these individuals make because they accept the legitimacy of the position, whether they like or agree with the request or not. Steve Jobs has enjoyed legitimate power as the CEO of Apple. He could set deadlines and employees comply even if they think the deadlines were overly ambitious. Start-up organizations often have founders who use their legitimate power to influence individuals to work long hours week after week in order to help the company survive.

legitimate power

Power that comes from one's organizational role or position.

Reward Power

Reward power is the ability to grant a reward, such as an increase in pay, a perk, or an attractive job assignment. Reward power tends to accompany legitimate power and is highest when the reward is scarce. Anyone can wield reward power, however, in the form of public praise or giving someone something in exchange for their compliance. When Steve Jobs ran Apple, he had reward power in the form of raises and promotions. Another example of reward power comes from Bill Gross, founder of Idealab, who has the power to launch new companies or not. He created his company with the idea of launching other new companies as soon as they could develop viable ideas. If members could convince him that their ideas were viable, he gave the company a maximum of $250,000 in seed money, and gave the management team and employees a 30% stake in the company and the CEO 10% of the company. That way, everyone had a stake in the company. The CEO's salary was capped at $75,000 to maintain the sense of equity. When one of the companies, Citysearch, went public, all employees benefited from the $270 million valuation.

reward power

The ability to grant a reward, such as an increase in pay, a perk, or an attractive job assignment.

Coercive Power

In contrast, **coercive power** is the ability to take something away or punish someone for noncompliance. Coercive power often works through fear, and it forces people to do something that ordinarily they would not choose to do. The most extreme example of coercion is government dictators who threaten physical harm for noncompliance. Parents may also use coercion such as grounding their child as punishment for noncompliance. Steve Jobs has been known to use coercion—yelling at employees and threatening to fire them. When John Wiley & Sons Inc. published an unauthorized biography of Jobs, Jobs's response was to prohibit sales of all books from that publisher in any Apple retail store.[11] In other examples, John D. Rockefeller was ruthless when running Standard Oil Company. He not only undercut his competitors through pricing, but he used his coercive power to get railroads to refuse to transport his competitor's products. American presidents have been known to use coercion power. President Lyndon Baines Johnson once told a White House staffer, "Just you remember this. There's only two kinds at the White house. There's elephants and there's ants. And I'm the only elephant."[12]

coercive power

The ability to take something away or punish someone for noncompliance.

Expert Power

Expert power comes from knowledge and skill. Steve Jobs has expert power from his ability to know what customers want—even before they can articulate it. Others who have expert power in an organization include long-time employees, such as a steelworker who knows the temperature combinations and length of time to get the best yields. Technology companies are often characterized by expert, rather than legitimate power. Many of these firms utilize a flat or matrix structure in which clear lines of legitimate power become blurred as everyone communicates with everyone else regardless of position.

expert power

Power that comes from knowledge and skill.

Information Power

Information power is similar to expert power but differs in its source. Experts tend to have a vast amount of knowledge or skill, whereas information power is distinguished by *access* to specific information. For example, knowing price information gives a person information power during negotiations. Within organizations, a person's social network can either isolate them from information power or serve to create it. As we will see later in this chapter, those who are able to span boundaries and serve to connect different parts of the organizations often have a great deal of information power. In the TV show *Mad Men*, which is set in the 1960s, it is clear that the switchboard operators have a great deal of information power as they place all calls and are able to listen in on all the phone conversations within the advertising firm.

information power

Power that comes from access to specific information.

Referent Power

Referent power stems from the personal characteristics of the person such as the degree to which we like, respect, and want to be like them. Referent power is often called **charisma**—the ability to attract others, win their admiration, and hold them spellbound. Steve Jobs's influence as described in the opening case is an example of this charisma.

FIGURE 13.6

As the 44th elected president of the United States, Barack Obama has legitimate power. As commander-in-chief of the U.S. Armed Forces, he also has coercive power. His ability to appoint individuals to cabinet positions affords him reward power. Individuals differ on the degree to which they feel he has expert and referent power, as he received 52% of the popular vote in the 2008 election. Shortly after the election, he began to be briefed on national security issues, providing him with substantial information power as well.

Source: http://en.wikipedia.org/wiki/Image:ObamaSouthCarolina.jpg.

referent power

Power that stems from the personal characteristics of the person such as the degree to which we like, respect, and want to be like them.

charisma

The ability to attract others, win their admiration, and hold them spellbound.

2.2 What Is Influence?

Starting at infancy, we all try to get others to do what we want. We learn early what works in getting us to our goals. Instead of crying and throwing a tantrum, we may figure out that smiling and using language causes everyone less stress and brings us the rewards we seek.

By the time you hit the workplace, you have had vast experience with influence techniques. You have probably picked out a few that you use most often. To be effective in a wide number of situations, however, it's best to expand your repertoire of skills and become competent in several techniques, knowing how and when to use them as well as understanding when they are being used on you. If you watch someone who is good at influencing others, you will most probably observe that person switching tactics depending on the context. The more tactics you have at your disposal, the more likely it is that you will achieve your influence goals.

Al Gore and many others have spent years trying to influence us to think about the changes in the environment and the implications of global warming. They speak, write, network, and lobby to get others to pay attention. But Gore, for example, does not stop there. He also works to persuade us with direct, action-based suggestions such as asking everyone to switch the kind of light bulbs they use, turn off appliances when not in use, drive vehicles with better fuel economy, and even take shorter showers. Ironically, Gore has more influence now as a private citizen regarding these issues than he was able to exert as a congressman, senator, and vice president of the United States.

OB Toolbox: Self-Assessment

Do You Have the Characteristics of Powerful Influencers?

People who are considered to be skilled influencers share the following attributes.

How often do you engage in them? 0 = never, 1= sometimes, 2 = always.

- present information that can be checked for accuracy
- provide a consistent message that does not change from situation to situation
- display authority and enthusiasm (often described as charisma)
- offer something in return for compliance
- act likable
- show empathy through listening
- show you are aware of circumstances, others, and yourself
- plan ahead

If you scored 0–6: You do not engage in much effective influencing behavior. Think of ways to enhance this skill. A great place to start is to recognize the items on the list above and think about ways to enhance them for yourself.

If you scored 7–12: You engage in some influencing behavior. Consider the context of each of these influence attempts to see if you should be using more or less of it depending on your overall goals.

If you scored 13–16: You have a great deal of influence potential. Be careful that you are not manipulating others and that you are using your influence when it is important rather than just to get your own way.

2.3 Commonly Used Influence Tactics

FIGURE 13.7 Influence Tactics Use and Outcomes[13]

	Frequency of Use	Resistance	Compliance	Commitment
Rational persuasion	54%	47%	30%	23%
Legitimating	13%	44%	56%	0%
Personal appeals	7%	25%	33%	42%
Exchange	7%	24%	41%	35%
Ingratiation	6%	41%	28%	31%
Pressure	6%	56%	41%	3%
Coalitions	3%	53%	44%	3%
Inspirational appeals	2%	0%	10%	90%
Consultation	2%	18%	27%	55%

Source: Adapted from information in Falbe, C. M., & Yukl, G. (1992). Consequences for managers of using single influence tactics and combinations of tactics. Academy of Management Journal, 35, 638–652.

Researchers have identified distinct influence tactics and discovered that there are few differences between the way bosses, subordinates, and peers use them, which we will discuss at greater depth later on in this chapter. We will focus on nine influence tactics. Responses to influence attempts include resistance, compliance, or commitment. **Resistance** occurs when the influence target does not wish to comply with the request and either passively or actively repels the influence attempt. **Compliance** occurs when the target does not necessarily want to obey, but they do. **Commitment** occurs when the target not only agrees to the request but also actively supports it as well. Within organizations, commitment helps to get things done, because others can help to keep initiatives alive long after compliant changes have been made or resistance has been overcome.

resistance

Occurs when the influence target does not wish to comply with the request and either passively or actively repels the influence attempt.

compliance

Occurs when the target does not necessarily want to obey, but they do.

commitment

Occurs when the target not only agrees to the request but also actively supports it as well.

rational persuasion

Includes using facts, data, and logical arguments to try to convince others that your point of view is the best alternative.

inspirational appeals

Those that seek to tap into our values, emotions, and beliefs to gain support for a request or course of action.

consultation

The influence agent's asking others for help in directly influencing or planning to influence another person or group.

ingratiation

Different forms of making others feel good about themselves.

personal appeal

Helping another person because you like them and they asked for your help.

exchange

Give-and-take in which someone does something for you and you do something for them in return.

coalition tactics

A group of individuals working together toward a common goal to influence others.

pressure

Exerting undue influence on someone to do what you want, or else something undesirable will occur.

legitimating tactics

Those that occur when the appeal is based on legitimate or position power.

1. **Rational persuasion** includes using facts, data, and logical arguments to try to convince others that your point of view is the best alternative. This is the most commonly applied influence tactic. One experiment illustrates the power of reason. People were lined up at a copy machine and another person, after joining the line asked, "May I go to the head of the line?" Amazingly, 63% of the people in the line agreed to let the requester jump ahead. When the line jumper makes a slight change in the request by asking, "May I go to the head of the line because I have copies to make?" the number of people who agreed jumped to over 90%. The word *because* was the only difference. Effective rational persuasion includes the presentation of factual information that is clear and specific, relevant, and timely. Across studies summarized in a meta-analysis, rationality was related to positive work outcomes.[14]
2. **Inspirational appeals** seek to tap into our values, emotions, and beliefs to gain support for a request or course of action. When President John F. Kennedy said, "Ask not what your country can do for you, ask what you can do for your country," he appealed to the higher selves of an entire nation. Effective inspirational appeals are authentic, personal, big-thinking, and enthusiastic.
3. **Consultation** refers to the influence agent's asking others for help in directly influencing or planning to influence another person or group. Consultation is most effective in organizations and cultures that value democratic decision making.
4. **Ingratiation** refers to different forms of making others feel good about themselves. Ingratiation includes any form of flattery done either before or during the influence attempt. Research shows that ingratiation can affect individuals. For example, in a study of résumés, those résumés that were accompanied with a cover letter containing ingratiating information were rated higher than résumés without this information. Other than the cover letter accompanying them, the résumés were identical.[15] Effective ingratiation is honest, infrequent, and well intended.
5. **Personal appeal** refers to helping another person because you like them and they asked for your help. We enjoy saying yes to people we know and like. A famous psychological experiment showed that in dorms, the most well-liked people were those who lived by the stairwell—they were the most often seen by others who entered and left the hallway. The repeated contact brought a level of familiarity and comfort. Therefore, personal appeals are most effective with people who know and like you.
6. **Exchange** refers to give-and-take in which someone does something for you, and you do something for them in return. The rule of reciprocation says that "we should try to repay, in kind, what another person has provided us."[16] The application of the rule obliges us and makes us indebted to the giver. One experiment illustrates how a small initial gift can open people to a substantially larger request at a later time. One group of subjects was given a bottle of Coke. Later, all subjects were asked to buy raffle tickets. On the average, people who had been given the drink bought twice as many raffle tickets as those who had not been given the unsolicited drinks.
7. **Coalition tactics** refer to a group of individuals working together toward a common goal to influence others. Common examples of coalitions within organizations are unions that may threaten to strike if their demands are not met. Coalitions also take advantage of peer pressure. The influencer tries to build a case by bringing in the unseen as allies to convince someone to think, feel, or do something. A well-known psychology experiment draws upon this tactic. The experimenters stare at the top of a building in the middle of a busy street. Within moments, people who were walking by in a hurry stop and also look at the top of the building, trying to figure out what the others are looking at. When the experimenters leave, the pattern continues, often for hours. This tactic is also extremely popular among advertisers and businesses that use client lists to promote their goods and services. The fact that a client bought from the company is a silent testimonial.
8. **Pressure** refers to exerting undue influence on someone to do what you want or else something undesirable will occur. This often includes threats and frequent interactions until the target agrees. Research shows that managers with low referent power tend to use pressure tactics more frequently than those with higher referent power.[17] Pressure tactics are most effective when used in a crisis situation and when they come from someone who has the other's best interests in mind, such as getting an employee to an employee assistance program to deal with a substance abuse problem.
9. **Legitimating tactics** occur when the appeal is based on legitimate or position power. "By the power vested in me…": This tactic relies upon compliance with rules, laws, and regulations. It is not intended to motivate people but to align them behind a direction. Obedience to authority is filled with both positive and negative images. Position, title, knowledge, experience, and demeanor grant authority, and it is easy to see how it can be abused. If someone hides behind

people's rightful authority to assert themselves, it can seem heavy-handed and without choice. You must come across as an authority figure by the way you act, speak, and look. Think about the number of commercials with doctors, lawyers, and other professionals who look and sound the part, even if they are actors. People want to be convinced that the person is an authority worth heeding. Authority is often used as a last resort. If it does not work, you will not have much else to draw from in your goal to persuade someone.

From the Best-Seller's List: Making OB Connections

You can make more friends in two months by becoming interested in other people than you can in two years by trying to get other people interested in you.

- Dale Carnegie

Source: http://en.wikipedia.org/wiki/File:Picturecarnegie.jpg.

How to Make Friends and Influence People was written by Dale Carnegie in 1936 and has sold millions of copies worldwide. While this book first appeared over 70 years ago, the recommendations still make a great deal of sense regarding power and influence in modern-day organizations. For example, he recommends that in order to get others to like you, you should remember six things:

1. Become genuinely interested in other people.
2. Smile.
3. Remember that a person's name is to that person the sweetest and most important sound in any language.
4. Be a good listener. Encourage others to talk about themselves.
5. Talk in terms of the other person's interests.
6. Make the other person feel important—and do it sincerely.

This book relates to power and politics in a number of important ways. Carnegie specifically deals with enhancing referent power. Referent power grows if others like, respect, and admire you. Referent power is more effective than formal power bases and is positively related to employees' satisfaction with supervision, organizational commitment, and performance. One of the keys to these recommendations is to engage in them in a genuine manner. This can be the difference between being seen as political versus understanding politics.

2.4 Impression Management

Impression management means actively shaping the way you are perceived by others. You can do this through your choice of clothing, the avatars or photos you use to represent yourself online, the descriptions of yourself on a résumé or in an online profile, and so forth. By using impression management strategies, you control information that make others see you in the way you want to be seen. Consider when you are "being yourself" with your friends or with your family—you probably act differently around your best friend than around your mother.[18]

impression management

Actively shaping the way you are perceived by others.

On the job, the most effective approach to impression management is to do two things at once—build credibility and maintain authenticity. As Harvard Business School Professor Laura Morgan Roberts puts it, "When you present yourself in a manner that is both true to self and valued and believed by others, impression management can yield a host of favorable outcomes for you, your team, and your organization."[19]

There may be aspects of your "true self" that you choose not to disclose at work, although you would disclose them to your close friends. That kind of impression management may help to achieve group cohesiveness and meet professional expectations. But if you try to win social approval at work by being too different from your true self—contradicting your personal values—you might feel psychological distress.

It's important to keep in mind that whether you're actively managing your professional image or not, your coworkers are forming impressions of you. They watch your behavior and draw conclusions about the kind of person you are, whether you'll keep your word, whether you'll stay to finish a task, and how you'll react in a difficult situation.

Since people are forming these theories about you no matter what, you should take charge of managing their impressions of you. To do this, ask yourself how you want to be seen. What qualities or character traits do you want to convey? Perhaps it's a can-do attitude, an ability to mediate, an ability to make a decision, or an ability to dig into details to thoroughly understand and solve a problem.

Then, ask yourself what the professional expectations are of you and what aspects of your social identity you want to emphasize or minimize in your interactions with others. If you want to be seen as a leader, you might disclose how you organized an event. If you want to be seen as a caring person in whom people can confide, you might disclose that you're a volunteer on a crisis helpline. You can use a variety of impression management strategies to accomplish the outcomes you want.

Here are the three main categories of strategies and examples of each:

nonverbal impression management

Includes the clothes you choose to wear, body language, and your demeanor.

verbal impression management

Includes your tone of voice, rate of speech, what you choose to say and how you say it.

behavior impression management

Includes how you perform on the job and how you interact with others.

- **Nonverbal impression management** includes the clothes you choose to wear and your demeanor. An example of a nonverbal signal is body art, including piercings and tattoos. While the number of people in the United States who have body art has risen from 1% in 1976 to 24% in 2006, it can hold you back at work. Vault.com did a survey and found that 58% of the managers they surveyed said they would be less likely to hire someone with visible body art, and over 75% of respondents felt body art was unprofessional. Given these numbers, it should not be surprising that 67% of employees say they conceal body art while they are at work.[20]
- **Verbal impression management** includes your tone of voice, rate of speech, what you choose to say and how you say it. We know that 38% of the comprehension of verbal communication comes from these cues. Managing how you project yourself in this way can alter the impression that others have of you. For example, if your voice has a high pitch and it is shaky, others may assume that you are nervous or unsure of yourself.
- **Behavior impression management** includes how you perform on the job and how you interact with others. Complimenting your boss is an example of a behavior that would indicate impression management. Other impression management behaviors include conforming, making excuses, apologizing, promoting your skills, doing favors, and making desirable associations known. Impression management has been shown to be related to higher performance ratings by increasing liking, perceived similarity, and network centrality.[21]

FIGURE 13.9

Impression management includes how a person dresses, how they stand, and the way they behave at work.

© 2010 *Jupiterimages Corporation*

Research shows that impression management occurs throughout the workplace. It is especially salient when it comes to job interviews and promotional contexts. Research shows that structured interviews suffer from less impression management bias than unstructured interviews, and that longer interviews lead to a lessening of the effects as well.[22]

2.5 Direction of Influence

The type of influence tactic used tends to vary based on the target. For example, you would probably use different influence tactics with your boss than you would with a peer or with employees working under you.

Upward Influence

upward influence

The ability to influence your boss and others in positions higher than yours.

Upward influence, as its name implies, is the ability to influence your boss and others in positions higher than yours. Upward influence may include appealing to a higher authority or citing the firm's goals as an overarching reason for others to follow your cause. Upward influence can also take the form of an alliance with a higher status person (or with the perception that there is such an alliance).[23] As complexity grows, the need for this upward influence grows as well—the ability of one person at the top to know enough to make all the decisions becomes less likely. Moreover, even if someone did know enough, the sheer ability to make all the needed decisions fast enough is no longer possible. This limitation means that individuals at all levels of the organization need to be able to make and influence decisions. By helping higher-ups be more effective, employees can gain more power for themselves and their unit as well. On the flip side, allowing yourself to be influenced by those reporting to you may build your credibility and power as a leader who listens. Then, during a time when you do need to take unilateral, decisive action, others will be more likely to give you the benefit of the doubt and follow. Both Asian American and Caucasian

American managers report using different tactics with superiors than those used with their subordinates.[24] Managers reported using coalitions and rationality with managers and assertiveness with subordinates. Other research establishes that subordinates' use of rationality, assertiveness, and reciprocal exchange was related to more favorable outcomes such as promotions and raises, while self-promotion led to more negative outcomes.[25]

Influence takes place even before employees are hired. For example, ingratiation and rationality were used frequently by fire fighters during interviews.[26] Extraverts tend to engage in a greater use of self-promotion tactics while interviewing, and research shows that extraverts are more likely to use inspirational appeal and ingratiation as influence tactics.[27] Research shows that ingratiation was positively related to perceived fit with the organization and recruiters' hiring recommendations.[28]

Downward Influence

Downward influence is the ability to influence employees lower than you. This is best achieved through an inspiring vision. By articulating a clear vision, you help people see the end goal and move toward it. You often don't need to specify exactly what needs to be done to get there—people will be able to figure it out on their own. An inspiring vision builds buy-in and gets people moving in the same direction. Research conducted within large savings banks shows that managers can learn to be more effective at influence attempts. The experimental group of managers received a feedback report and went through a workshop to help them become more effective in their influence attempts. The control group of managers received no feedback on their prior influence attempts. When subordinates were asked 3 months later to evaluate potential changes in their managers' behavior, the experimental group had much higher ratings of the appropriate use of influence.[29] Research also shows that the better the quality of the relationship between the subordinate and their supervisor, the more positively resistance to influence attempts are seen.[30] In other words, bosses who like their employees are less likely to interpret resistance as a problem.

downward influence

The ability to influence those in positions lower than yours.

Peer Influence

Peer influence occurs all the time. But, to be effective within organizations, peers need to be willing to influence each other without being destructively competitive.[31] There are times to support each other and times to challenge—the end goal is to create better decisions and results for the organization and to hold each other accountable. Executives spend a great deal of their time working to influence other executives to support their initiatives. Research shows that across all functional groups of executives, finance or human resources as an example, rational persuasion is the most frequently used influence tactic.[32]

OB Toolbox: Getting Comfortable With Power

Now that you've learned a great deal about power and influence within organizations, consider asking yourself how comfortable you are with the three statements below:

- Are you comfortable saying, "I want to be powerful" to yourself? Why or why not?
- Are you comfortable saying, "I want to be powerful" to someone else? Why or why not?
- Are you comfortable having someone say, "You are powerful" to you? Why or why not?

Discomfort with power reduces your power. Experts know that leaders need to feel comfortable with power. Those who feel uncomfortable with power send those signals out unconsciously. If you feel uncomfortable with power, consider putting the statement in a shared positive light by saying, "I want to be powerful so that we can accomplish this goal."

KEY TAKEAWAY

Individuals have six potential sources of power, including legitimate, reward, coercive, expert, information, and referent power. Influence tactics are the way that individuals attempt to influence one another in organizations. Rational persuasion is the most frequently used influence tactic, although it is frequently met with resistance. Inspirational appeals result in commitment 90% of the time, but the tactic is utilized only 2% of the time. The other tactics include legitimizing, personal appeals, exchanges, ingratiation, pressure, forming coalitions, and consultation. Impression management behaviors include conforming, making excuses, apologizing, promoting your skills, doing favors, and making associations with desirable others known. Influence attempts may be upward, downward, or lateral in nature.

EXERCISES

1. Which of the six bases of power do you usually draw upon? Which do you use the least of at this time?
2. Distinguish between coercive and reward power.
3. Which tactics seem to be the most effective? Explain your answer.
4. Why do you think rational persuasion is the most frequently utilized influence tactic?
5. Give an example of someone you've tried to influence lately. Was it an upward, downward, or lateral influence attempt?

3. ORGANIZATIONAL POLITICS

LEARNING OBJECTIVES

1. **Understand what organizational politics are.**
2. **Examine political behavior within organizations.**

3.1 Organizational Politics

Organizational politics are informal, unofficial, and sometimes behind-the-scenes efforts to sell ideas, influence an organization, increase power, or achieve other targeted objectives.[33] Politics has been around for millennia. Aristotle wrote that politics stems from a diversity of interests, and those competing interests must be resolved in some way. "Rational" decision making alone may not work when interests are fundamentally incongruent, so political behaviors and influence tactics arise.

Today, work in organizations requires skill in handling conflicting agendas and shifting power bases. Effective politics isn't about winning at all costs but about maintaining relationships while achieving results. Although often portrayed negatively, organizational politics are not inherently bad. Instead, it's important to be aware of the potentially destructive aspects of organizational politics in order to minimize their negative effect. Of course, individuals within organizations can waste time overly engaging in political behavior. Research reported in *HR Magazine* found that managers waste 20% of their time managing politics. However, as John Kotter wrote in *Power and Influence*, "Without political awareness and skill, we face the inevitable prospect of becoming immersed in bureaucratic infighting, parochial politics and destructive power struggles, which greatly retard organizational initiative, innovation, morale, and performance."[34]

In our discussion about power, we saw that power issues often arise around scarce resources. Organizations typically have limited resources that must be allocated in some way. Individuals and groups within the organization may disagree about how those resources should be allocated, so they may naturally seek to gain those resources for themselves or for their interest groups, which gives rise to organizational politics. Simply put, with organizational politics, individuals ally themselves with like-minded others in an attempt to win the scarce resources. They'll engage in behavior typically seen in government organizations, such as bargaining, negotiating, alliance building, and resolving conflicting interests.

Politics are a part of organizational life, because organizations are made up of different interests that need to be aligned. In fact, 93% of managers surveyed reported that workplace politics exist in their organization, and 70% felt that in order to be successful, a person has to engage in politics.[35] In the negative light, saying that someone is "political" generally stirs up images of back-room dealing, manipulation, or hidden agendas for personal gain. A person engaging in these types of political behaviors is said to be engaging in self-serving behavior that is not sanctioned by the organization.[36]

Examples of these self-serving behaviors include bypassing the chain of command to get approval for a special project, going through improper channels to obtain special favors, or lobbying high-level managers just before they make a promotion decision. These types of actions undermine fairness in the organization, because not everyone engages in politicking to meet their own objectives. Those who follow proper procedures often feel jealous and resentful because they perceive unfair distributions of the organization's resources, including rewards and recognition.[37]

Researchers have found that if employees think their organization is overly driven by politics, the employees are less committed to the organization,[38] have lower job satisfaction,[39] perform worse on the job,[40] have higher levels of job anxiety,[41] and have a higher incidence of depressed mood.[42]

The negative side of organizational politics is more likely to flare up in times of organizational change or when there are difficult decisions to be made and a scarcity of resources that breeds competition among organizational groups. To minimize overly political behavior, company leaders can provide equal access to information, model collaborative behavior, and demonstrate that political maneuvering will not be rewarded or tolerated. Furthermore, leaders should encourage managers throughout the organization to provide high levels of feedback to employees about their performance. High levels of feedback reduce the perception of organizational politics and improve employee morale and work performance.[43] Remember that politics can be a healthy way to get things done within organizations.

3.2 Antecedents of Political Behavior

Individual Antecedents

There are a number of potential individual antecedents of political behavior. We will start off by understanding the role that personality has in shaping whether someone will engage in political behavior.

Political skill refers to peoples' interpersonal style, including their ability to relate well to others, self-monitor, alter their reactions depending upon the situation they are in, and inspire confidence and trust.[44] Researchers have found that individuals who are high on political skill are more effective at their jobs or at least in influencing their supervisors' performance ratings of them.[45] Individuals who are high in *internal locus of control* believe that they can make a difference in organizational outcomes. They do not leave things to fate. Therefore, we would expect those high in internal locus of control to engage in more political behavior. Research shows that these individuals perceive politics around them to a greater degree.[46] *Investment in the organization* is also related to political behavior. If a person is highly invested in an organization either financially or emotionally, they will be more likely to engage in political behavior because they care deeply about the fate of the organization. Finally, *expectations of success* also matter. When a person expects that they will be successful in changing an outcome, they are more likely to engage in political behavior. Think about it: If you know there is no chance that you can influence an outcome, why would you spend your valuable time and resources working to effect change? You wouldn't. Over time you'd learn to live with the outcomes rather than trying to change them.[47]

political skill

Peoples' interpersonal style, including their ability to relate well to others, self-monitor, alter their reactions depending upon the situation they are in, and inspire confidence and trust.

FIGURE 13.10

Individual and organizational antecedents can both lead to political behavior.

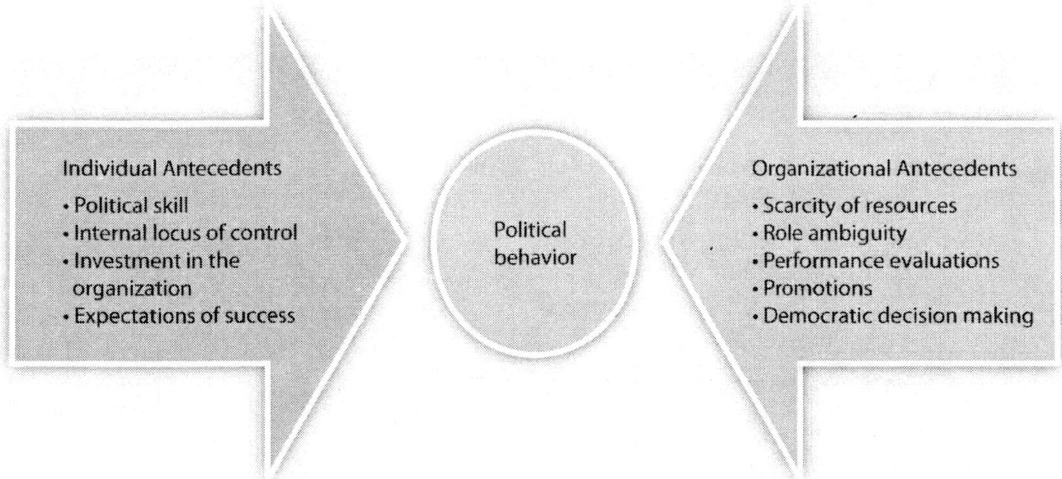

Organizational Antecedents

Scarcity of resources breeds politics. When resources such as monetary incentives or promotions are limited, people see the organization as more political. Any type of ambiguity can relate to greater organizational politics. For example, *role ambiguity* allows individuals to negotiate and redefine their roles. This freedom can become a political process. Research shows that when people do not feel clear about their job responsibilities, they perceive the organization as more political.[48] Ambiguity also exists around *performance evaluations* and *promotions*. These human resource practices can lead to greater political behavior, such as impression management, throughout the organization. As you might imagine, *democratic decision making* leads to more political behavior. Since many people have a say in the process of making decisions, there are more people available to be influenced.

turf wars

Members of the organization are engaged in turf wars when they are more concerned about their own area of operations than doing what's best for the entire organization in the long run.

OB Toolbox: Overcoming Ineffective Politics

Author and consultant Patrick Lencioni recommends the following four steps for overcoming ineffective politics due to turf wars. When members of the organization are more concerned about their own area of operations than doing what's best for the entire organization, in the long run you may have a problem with **turf wars**. Taking these four steps can help overcome this situation:

1. *Create a thematic goal.* The goal should be something that everyone in the organization can believe in, such as, for a hospital, giving the best care to all patients. This goal should be a single goal, qualitative, time-bound, and shared.
2. *Create a set of defining objectives.* This step should include objectives that everyone agrees will help bring the thematic goal to fruition.
3. *Create a set of ongoing standard operating objectives.* This process should be done within each area so that the best operating standards are developed. These objectives should also be shared across the organization so everyone is aware of them.
4. *Create metrics to measure them.* Measuring whether the standard operating objectives get done is a vital step in the process. Rather than someone else pointing out what isn't working, all the people within the department will have the information necessary to come to this conclusion and correct the problem, because ultimately, everyone in the organization cares about achieving the thematic goal.

Source: Adapted from information in Lencioni, P. M. (2006). Silos, politics and turf wars: A leadership fable about destroying the barriers that turn colleagues into competitors. New York: Jossey-Bass.

KEY TAKEAWAY

Organizational politics is a natural part of organizational life. Organizations that are driven by unhealthy levels of political behavior suffer from lowered employee organizational commitment, job satisfaction, and performance as well as higher levels of job anxiety and depression. Individual antecedents of political behavior include political skill, internal locus of control, high investment in the organization, and expectations of success. Organizational antecedents include scarcity of resources, role ambiguity, frequent performance evaluations and promotions, and democratic decision making.

EXERCISES

1. Do you think politics are a positive or negative thing for organizations? Why?
2. Describe an example of a negative outcome due to politics.
3. Describe an example of a positive outcome due to politics.
4. Can you think of additional individual or organizational antecedents of political behavior?
5. What political behaviors have you observed within school groups or your workplace? Were they successful? Why or why not?

4. UNDERSTANDING SOCIAL NETWORKS

LEARNING OBJECTIVES

1. Learn what social networks are.
2. Understand social network analysis.

4.1 Social Networks

We've seen that power comes from many sources. One major source relates to who you know and how much access you have to information within your organization. **Social networks** are visual maps of relationships between individuals. They are vital parts of organizational life as well as important when you are first looking for a job. For example, if you are interested in being hired by Proctor & Gamble, you might call upon your social network—the network of people you know—to find the people who can help you accomplish this task. You might ask your network if they know anyone at Proctor & Gamble. If you did so, the people you'd call on aren't just your friends and family—they're part of your informal network. In fact, research finds that 75% to 95% of all jobs are never formally advertised but are filled through such social networks.[49]

social networks

A map of the relationships between individuals.

Much of the work that gets done in organizations is done through informal networks as well. Networks serve three important functions. First, they deliver private information. Second, they allow individuals to gain access to diverse skills sets. Third, they can help create power.

Organizations can conduct a **social network analysis (SNA)**, a systematic effort to examine the structure of social relationships in a group. Their purpose is to uncover the informal connections between people. SNA dates back to 1934 when Joseph Moreno introduced the tools of sociometry. More recently, the advent of computers has made SNA possible on large networks. In the past decade, SNA has become widely used across fields.

social network analysis (SNA)

A systematic effort to examine the structure of social relationships in a group.

Conducting SNA

SNA can be conducted either directly or indirectly. The indirect way is to analyze e-mails between people. For example, which employees e-mail each other? How often? Who replies to whom? Another technique is to observe a group in action to see which employees talk to each other and who approaches whom for what. Additional, nonintrusive options are to look at project structures of billable hours such as determining which individuals regularly work together. Direct approaches to SNA involve doing a survey that asks questions directly.[50] For example, the survey might ask individuals, "Who would you go to for technical information? Who can you rely on to give you the pulse of the company? Who do you trust to keep your best interests in mind?" SNA can reveal who is trusted, important in decision making (that is, to whom do people turn for advice before making an important decision?), and innovative ("With whom are you most likely to discuss a new idea?"). The direct approach is likely to be more targeted, but some people may see it as an unwanted intrusion.

Analyzing Network Ties and Key Network Roles

Once the data is collected, SNA software is used to create the maps for analysis. The maps draw incoming and outgoing arrows between people to show the number of ties coming into a person (contacts that the person receives) and the number of ties outgoing (contacts that the person initiates). There are three key roles in a network. **Central connectors** are people linked to the greatest number of people. **Boundary spanners** are people who connect one network to another within the company or even across organizations. **Peripheral specialists** have special expertise that can be drawn upon even though they often work independently of the group.

central connectors

People linked to the greatest number of people.

boundary spanners

People who connect one network to another within the company or even across organizations.

peripheral specialists

People with special expertise that can be drawn upon even though they often work independently of the group.

Analysis: Strong and Weak Ties

strong ties

Ties that often indicate emotional support, not just informational support between people.

weak ties

Ties characterized by less frequent interaction and often do not have as much emotional attachment, but they are also easier to maintain, and therefore people can have more of them.

You can recognize the strength of ties between people by counting the frequency of ties. The more interactions people have, the stronger the ties those individuals have with each other. **Strong ties** often indicate emotional support, not just informational support between people. Ties that are reciprocated tend to be stronger as well. **Weak ties** are characterized by less frequent interaction and often do not have as much emotional attachment, but they are also easier to maintain, and therefore people can have more of them. Weak ties are particularly useful for innovation, because people who are good friends tend to see the same information, whereas people who are merely acquaintances are likely to be exposed to different information. Thus, a casual encounter may spark that creative idea. Social networks tend to be informal, but by doing an SNA, the company can harness their power to help improve communication throughout the company (such as by making sure people have the information to share) and to help generate and spread innovation (by giving information to the boundary-spanning people who will pass it on beyond their work group). Social networks serve to promote collaboration, improve new product development, and respond to emergencies or unusual circumstances quickly.[51]

Social networks connect people with others. Consider networking Web sites such as Facebook or LinkedIn, where being connected with many people makes you more visible. This is becoming more and more salient as 80% of 12- to 17-year-olds use MySpace at least weekly, and over 40,000 MySpace groups are devoted to companies and colleagues.[52] In business, the more central you are, the more power you will have. The closer you are to more people, the more powerful you are.[53] If you are the person who many people link to and you serve as a node between people, you have brokering power—you can introduce people to each other. People high on this "betweenness" are also in a position to withhold information from one person to the next, which can happen during power plays. You also have a greater number of people to call on when you need something, which makes you less dependent on any one person. The more ties you have that are incoming (toward you), the more trusted you are.

Social network analysis shows who communicates with whom, who knows whom, and where gaps in communication or collaboration may exist. After conducting a network analysis, organizations can take actions to modify people's roles or responsibilities in ways that improve communication or diffuse innovation throughout the organization more effectively by putting people or departments in touch with each other.

FIGURE 13.11

Mark Zuckerberg, cofounder of Facebook, helped to bring social networking to thousands of individuals.

Source: http://commons.wikimedia.org/wiki/Image:Zuckerberg2.jpg.

Building Your Own Network

There are several simple steps you can take to help build your own social network. For example, you can go to lunch with someone new. You can also try to do more to encourage, help, and share with others. You can seek information outside your own class or work group. You can spend time with people from work outside work. All these suggestions are effective ways to naturally build your social network.

FIGURE 13.12

Doing social things such as playing golf or tennis outside work is one way to help build your social network.

KEY TAKEAWAY

Social networks make up a key part of organizations. A social network analysis (SNA) involves tracing who interacts with whom. Central connectors have a large number of contacts. Boundary spanners connect to several networks of people. Peripheral specialists often work independently. Strong and weak ties can both be helpful for gathering information and building one's network.

EXERCISES

1. Have you ever thought about your own social network before? What do you think about it now?
2. Do you think the direct or indirect approach to doing a social network analysis is the most accurate?
3. Do you think it is ethical to play golf or tennis with coworkers to build your social network? Why or why not?
4. How have computers influenced social networking?

5. THE ROLE OF ETHICS AND NATIONAL CULTURE

LEARNING OBJECTIVES

1. **Consider the role of ethics and power.**
2. **Consider the role of national culture on power.**

5.1 Ethics and Power

Power brings a special need for ethics, because the circumstances of power make it easy for misuse to occur. As we have seen, a company president wields at least three sources of power: legitimate from the position they hold, coercive from the ability to fire employees, and reward such as the ability to give raises and perks. Expert power and referent power often enter the mix as well. Now take the example of setting the CEO's pay. In a public company, the CEO presumably has to answer to the board of directors and the shareholders. But what if the CEO appoints many of the people on the board? What if the board and the CEO are friends? Consider the case of Richard Grasso, former chairman of the New York Stock Exchange (NYSE), whose compensation was $140 million plus another $48 million in retirement benefits. At that time, the average starting salary of a trader on the NYSE was $90,000, so Grasso was being paid 1,555 times more than a starting employee. The NYSE Board of Directors approved Grasso's payment package, but many of the board members had been appointed to their positions by Grasso himself. What's more, the NYSE's function is to regulate publicly traded companies. As Hartman and Desjardins noted, "The companies being regulated by the NYSE were the very same companies that were paying Grasso."[54] Grasso ultimately resigned amid public criticism but kept the $140 million. Other CEOs have not faced the same outcry, even though average CEO pay increased 200% to 400% during the same time period that average worker pay increased only 4.3%.[55] Some CEOs have earned a great deal of respect by limiting what they are paid. For example, Japan Airlines CEO Haruka Nishimatsu earns the equivalent to $90,000 per year while running the 10th largest airline in the world. In addition, he rides the bus to work and eats in the company cafeteria with everyone else.[56]

Video Connection: Haruka Nishimatsu

If you are interested in learning more about CEO Haruka Nishimatsu, view this CBS News video segment, available at the following Web site:

http://www.cbsnews.com/video/watch/?id=4761187n

FIGURE 13.13

CEOs like James Sinegal of Costco Wholesale Corporation note that compensation is not the main motivation for their work. Consistent with this sentiment, by choice, Sinegal remains one of the lowest paid CEOs of a Standard & Poor's 500 company, and he has not received a raise in 7 consecutive years.

Source: Used with permission. Photo by France Freeman, Costco Wholesale.

5.2 Power Around the Globe

Power also has a cultural dimension. In some countries, power is centralized in the hands of a few. This type of distribution makes up high power distance countries. Within organizations in these countries, the structure is hierarchical, and compensation is based on your position in the hierarchy. People in high power distance countries expect unequal distribution of power, such as large differences in pay and status.[57] People in positions of authority in these countries expect (and receive) obedience. In Brazil, for example, there are formal relationships between the leader and followers, and it's clear who has the most power in any given work environment. Important decisions, including decisions on hiring and raises, are made by the person in charge, and decisions are often based on loyalty rather than on formal review mechanisms. Japan is also a higher power distant country and has unequal power and wealth among its citizens. But, people do not perceive this inequity as inherently wrong; rather, they accept it as their cultural heritage. Other examples of high power distance countries include the Arab nations, the Philippines, Venezuela, and Spain.

Countries with a low power distance rating, such as Australia, the Netherlands, and Sweden, value cooperative interaction across power levels. They emphasize equality and opportunity for everyone. For example, Australians want their leaders to be achievement-oriented, visionary, and inspirational, but they don't want their leaders to stand out too much. Leaders need to be seen as "one of us."[58] Organizational structures in low power distance countries are flatter with higher worker involvement. Status is based on achievement rather than class distinction or birth. People in power cannot arbitrarily hire their relatives or reward those loyal to them. There are formal review mechanisms in place to give everyone a fair chance at pay raises, and the difference in pay between high-level and lower level jobs is smaller.

These differences in perceptions of power become especially important in international ventures in which people of different countries work together. For example, in a joint venture between an American and a Mexican company, American managers were continually frustrated with what they perceived to be slow decision making by Mexican managers. Even the e-mails sent to the Mexican subsidiary were taking a long time to be answered. Mexico ranks higher on the power distance dimension than the United States—company structures are more hierarchical, and decisions are made only by top managers; therefore, lower level managers in Mexico could not make decisions on behalf of their bosses. In the case of e-mails, employees were consulting with their managers before answering each e-mail, taking a long time to answer them.

In addition to differing perceptions of power, how people influence each other seems to be determined by culture. Cross-cultural research shows that the more task-oriented influence tactics, such as rational persuasion, are seen as more effective in the United States than in China, and that Chinese managers rated tactics involving relationships such as coalitions as more effective than did the American managers.[59]

KEY TAKEAWAY

Power can be easily abused. This is especially the case of CEOs who are rewarded by a board of directors that is often staffed by trusted friends and colleagues of the CEO. It is not hard to imagine that this might become a conflict of interest. Countries differ in terms of power distance. Some countries such as Brazil see a formal relationship between leaders and followers based on a rigid hierarchy.

EXERCISES

1. What could be done to make sure that CEOs are paid fairly for their work rather than as a favor from their friends?
2. What is some advice about power that you would give to a colleague who was leaving to China to set up a new business?

6. CONCLUSION

Power and politics in organizations are common. In most cases, each concept is necessary and executed with skill and precision. Unfortunately, power can lead to conformity from those around us, and this occurring conformity can breed corruption. The amount of power you have has strong ties to how much others depend on you. If you are deemed a valuable resource within an organization, then you are able to wield that dependability to make demands and get others to do what you want. Besides having an innate or acquired control over particular resources, there are several social aspects of power to draw on.

Methods for obtaining more power in an organization can often lead to political behaviors. As one person seeks to influence another to support an idea, politics begins to play out. Though necessary in some instances, many people that follow the rules see the politics of an organization as resulting in an unfair distribution of resources. Still others, despite understanding the politics of a given organization, see it as an unnecessary time consumer.

Politics, influence, and power can often reside within your social network. When an individual is core to a social structure, they will often have some degree of control over others. Social networks can also help you acquire jobs, make beneficial connections, and generally make like easier. It is often a good idea to analyze your social network and determine if it needs to be strengthened or tailored.

7. EXERCISES

ETHICAL DILEMMA

It is two days before your performance appraisal. Your performance this quarter has been less than desirable. You came close to reaching your sales targets, but you did not meet them, and you are hoping to still get the merit pay raise to be determined as a result of your performance appraisal. You do not really like your manager, but you are hoping to advance in this company, and being on your manager's good side may be a good idea both for your current performance appraisal and for your future in this company.

- You are now at a meeting with your manager and a group of employees. Your manager is giving financial information to all employees about different markets. Yet, some of this information is inaccurate, which could lead to wrong pricing decisions and loss of money by the company. If you correct him, though, he would most likely get upset with you because he does not like being corrected. Would you correct him? How and when?
- Today is also the day on which your manager's boss is collecting information about your manager's leadership style, so that they can give him a 360-degree appraisal. They assure you that your comments about your manager will remain confidential, but the nature of your thoughts is such that he probably would guess you are the person who made those comments. Specifically, you think that your manager takes offense easily, has a bad temper, and could be more effective in time management. Would you share your thoughts with your manager's manager?
- You are now at the coffee shop and grabbing a cup of coffee and some pastries. You notice that they have almond coffee cake, which is your manager's favorite. Would you pick some up for your manager?

INDIVIDUAL EXERCISE

Map Your Social Network[60]

- Step 1: Think of a specific objective you have at work or school that involves other people. Once you have thought of an objective, jot it down.
- Step 2: Use Figure 13.14 to list 5 to 15 people at your school or in your professional network who you have regular contact with and who are relevant to the objective you identified.
- Step 3: Rate how tightly connected you are with the people in your network by placing a check in the corresponding column (barely connected, loosely connected, somewhat connected, or tightly connected) on the right-hand side of their name.
- Step 4: Circle the name of anyone who has introduced you to 4 or more new people since you have known them.
- Step 5: In Figure 13.15, place a check mark in the intersecting box of people that know each other. For example, if person 1 knows person 2, put a check mark under the 2 at the top of the table. Continue to do this throughout the grid (grayed boxes should be left blank).
- Step 6: Analyze your network using the guidelines on the following calculations.
- Step 7: Consider ways to strengthen your network.

	Name	Barely Connected	Loosely Connected	Somewhat Connected	Tightly Connected
1					
2					
3					
4					
5					
6					
7					
8					
9					
10					
11					
12					
13					
14					
15					

	2	3	4	5	6	7	8	9	10	11	12	13	14	15
1														
2														
3														
4														
5														
6														
7														
8														
9														
10														
11														
12														
13														
14														
15														

Let's see how your social network adds up:

Calculating Network Size

The number of people you listed in your own network for this situation

N = _____

Calculating Network Density

It is important to understand what the maximum density of your network is. This refers to how dense it would be if ***everyone*** in your network knew each other.

(N * (N – 1)/2 = M) or (_____ * (_____ – 1)/2 = M)

M = _____

Total number of checkmarks in Figure 13.15, which represents number of relationships among people in your network.

C = _____

Density of your network (will range between 0 and 1)

C / M = D

_____/_____ = D

D = _____

Network Size

N = number of people in your network. The more people in your network, the greater the amount of information and possibly access to greater resources you have. We stopped at 15 people but many individuals have more people in their network than 15.

Network Strength

The strength of your network is also important. You can talk about this in terms of percentages of your relationships. What percentage are very tightly connected? Close? Somewhat connected? Or barely connected?

- ___% Tightly Connected
- ___% Somewhat Connected

- ___% Loosely Connected
- ___% Barely Connected

For most people, it would be hard to manage a huge network where all the ties are very close, just by virtue of the amount of time and energy it takes to satisfy the conditions for closeness.

Identifying Central Connectors

Count how many names you circled in step 4. Each of these individuals plays a special role in your network as they are central connectors who serve to expand your network by introducing you to new people. If you are also a central connector, this can be a benefit to assessing information as long as you are able to keep the network from distracting you from your work.

Network Density

Network density is important. When a person's network density is 1.0 that indicates that everyone in the network knows everyone else. Whether this is good or bad depends on a few things. For example, if everyone in your network has additional networks they belong to as well, you would be playing a central role in their networks and you would be a boundary spanner. But, if they also have high network density, the odds are that no new information is getting introduced into your group. You are basically a closed loop in which the same people interact with one another, and it is challenging to assess changes in the environment or to be innovative.

Social networks change over time depending on your tenure in an industry or company. The longer you have been in a given industry, the more likely it is that you will see your network size begin to shrink and become more dense.

Consider factors relating to power and influence and how you might go about strengthening and increasing the size of your network.

What are the pros and cons of doing so?

GROUP EXERCISE

In a group, analyze the following individuals in terms of their potential power bases. The first step is to discuss which types of power a person with the job listed on the left-hand column could have. If you can think of an example of them having a type of power, write the example in that column.

	Legitimate power	Reward power	Coercive power	Information power	Referent power
Flight attendant					
Computer programmer					
Executive assistant					
Manager					
Mailroom person					
Customer service representative					
CEO					

ENDNOTES

1. Salancik, G., & Pfeffer, J. (1989). Who gets power. In M. Thushman, C. O'Reily, & D. Nadler (Eds.), *Management of organizations*. New York: Harper & Row.

2. Kidder, T. (2004). *Mountains beyond mountains: The quest of Dr. Paul Farmer, a man who would cure the world.* New York: Random House; Mortenson, G., & Relin, D. O. (2006). *Three cups of tea: One man's mission to promote peace…One school at a time.* New York: Viking.

3. CNN.com. (2005, January 15). Graner sentenced to 10 years for abuses. Retrieved November 4, 2008, from http://www.cnn.com/2005/LAW/01/15/graner.court.martial/.

4. Milgram, S. (1974). *Obedience to authority*. New York: Harper & Row.

5. Asch, S. E. (1952b). *Social psychology*. Englewood Cliffs, NJ: Prentice Hall; Asch, S. E. (1956). Studies of independence and conformity. A minority of one against a unanimous majority. *Psychological Monographs, 70*(9), Whole No. 416.

6. Bond, R., & Smith, P. B. (1996). Culture and conformity: A meta-analysis of studies using Asch's (1952b, 1956) line judgment task. *Psychological Bulletin, 119*, 111–137.

7. Zimbardo, P. G. Stanford prison experiment. Retrieved January 30, 2009, from http://www.prisonexp.org/.

8. Saunders, C. (1990, January). The strategic contingencies theory of power: Multiple perspectives. *Journal of Management Studies, 21*(1), 1–18.

9. Krauss, C. (2009, January 30). Japan Airlines joins the biofuels race. *New York Times.* Retrieved January 30, 2009, from [illegible] japan-airlines-joins-the-biofuels-race/.

10. French, J. P. R., Jr., & Raven, B. (1960). The bases of social power. In D. Cartwright & A. Zander (Eds.), *Group dynamics* (pp. 607–623). New York: Harper and Row.

11. Hafner, K. (2005, April 30). Steve Jobs' review of his biography: Ban it. *New York Times*. Retrieved January 5, 2008, from http://www.nytimes.com/2005/04/30/technology/30apple.html?ei=5090&en=7cc0ad54117bc197&ex=1272513600&partner=rssuserland&emc=rss.

12. Hughes, R., Ginnet, R., & Curphy, G. (1995). Power, influence and influence tactics. In J. T. Wren (Ed.), *The leaders companion* (p. 345). New York: Free Press.

13. Kipnis, D., Schmidt, S. M., & Wilkinson, J. (1980). Interorganizational influence tactics: Explorations in getting one's way. *Journal of Applied Psychology, 65*, 440–452; Schriescheim, C. A., & Hinkin, T. R. (1990). Influence tactics used by subordinates: A theoretical and empirical analysis and refinement of Kipnis, Schmidt, and Wilkinson subscales. *Journal of Applied Psychology, 75*, 132–140; Yukl, G., & Falbe, C. M. (1991). The Importance of different power sources in downward and lateral relations. *Journal of Applied Psychology, 76*, 416–423.

14. Higgins, C. A., Judge, T. A., & Ferris, G. R. (2003). Influence tactics and work outcomes: A meta-analysis. *Journal of Organizational Behavior, 24*, 89–106.

15. Varma, A., Toh, S. M., & Pichler, S. (2006). Ingratiation in job applications: Impact on selection decisions. *Journal of Managerial Psychology, 21*, 200–210.

16. Cialdini, R. (2000). *Influence: Science and practice*. Boston: Allyn & Bacon, p. 20.

17. Yukl, G., Kim, H., & Falbe, C. M. (1996). Antecedents of influence outcomes. *Journal of Applied Psychology, 81*, 309–317.

18. Dunn, E., & Forrin, N. (2005). *Impression management.* Retrieved July 8, 2008, from http://www.psych.ubc.ca/~dunnlab/publications/Dunn_Forrin_2005.pdf.

19. Stark, M. (2005, June 20). Creating a positive professional image. Q&A with Laura Morgan Roberts. Retrieved July 8, 2008, from the Harvard Business School Web site: http://hbswk.hbs.edu/item/4860.html.

20. Society for Industrial and Organizational Psychology Inc. (SIOP). (2008, February 6). Body art on the rise but not so trendy at work. Retrieved February 8, 2008, from the SIOP Web site: http://www.siop.org.

21. Barsness, Z. I., Diekmann, K. A., & Seidel, M. L. (2005). Motivation and opportunity: The role of remote work, demographic dissimilarity, and social network centrality in impression management. *Academy of Management Journal, 48*, 401–419; Wayne, S. J., & Liden, R. C. (1995). Effects of impression management on performance ratings: A longitudinal study. *Academy of Management Journal, 38*, 232–260.

22. Tsai, W., Chen, C., & Chiu, S. (2005). Exploring boundaries of the effects of applicant impression management tactics in job interviews. *Journal of Management, 31*, 108–125.

23. Farmer, S. M., & Maslyn, J. M. (1999). Why are styles of upward influence neglected? Making the case for a configurational approach to influences. *Journal of Management, 25*, 653–682; Farmer, S. M., Maslyn, J. M., Fedor, D. B., & Goodman, J. S. (1997). Putting upward influence strategies in context. *Journal of Organizational Behavior, 18*, 17–42.

24. Xin, K. R., & Tsui, A. S. (1996). Different folks for different folks? Influence tactics by Asian-American and Caucasian-American managers. *Leadership Quarterly, 7*, 109–132.

25. Orpen, C. (1996). The effects of ingratiation and self promotion tactics on employee career success. *Social Behavior and Personality, 24*, 213–214; Wayne, S. J., Liden, R. C., Graf, I. K., & Ferris, G. R. (1997). The role of upward influence tactics in human resource decisions. *Personnel Psychology, 50*, 979–1006.

26. McFarland, L. A., Ryan, A. M., & Kriska, S. D. (2002). Field study investigation of applicant use of influence tactics in a selection interview. *Journal of Psychology, 136*, 383–398.

27. Cable, D. M., & Judge, T. A. (2003). Managers' upward influence tactic strategies: The role of manager personality and supervisor leadership style. *Journal of Organizational Behavior, 24*, 197–214; Kristof-Brown, A., Barrick, M. R., & Franke, M. (2002). Applicant impression management: Dispositional influences and consequences for recruiter perceptions of fit and similarity. *Journal of Management, 53*, 925–954.

28. Higgins, C. A., & Judge, T. A. (2004). The effect of applicant influence tactics on recruiter perceptions of fit and hiring recommendations: A field study. *Journal of Applied Psychology, 89*, 622–632.

29. Seifer, C. F., Yukl, G., & McDonald, R. A. (2003). Effects of multisource feedback and a feedback facilitator on the influence behavior of managers toward subordinates. *Journal of Applied Psychology, 88*, 561–569.

30. Tepper, B. J., Uhl-Bien, M., Kohut, G. F., Rogelberg, S. G., Lockhart, D. E., & Ensley, M. D. (2006). Subordinates' resistance and managers' evaluations of subordinates' performance. *Journal of Management, 32*, 185–208.

31. Cohen, A., & Bradford, D. (2002). Power and influence in the 21st century. In S. Chowdhurt (Ed.), *Organizations of the 21st century*. London: Financial Times-Prentice Hall.

32. Enns, H. G., & McFarlin, D. B. (2003). When executives influence peers: Does function matter? *Human Resource Management, 42*, 125–142.

33. Brandon, R., & Seldman, M. (2004). *Survival of the savvy: High-integrity political tactics for career and company success*. New York: Free Press; Hochwarter, W. A., Witt, L. A., & Kacmar, K. M. (2000). Perceptions of organizational politics as a moderator of the relationship between conscientiousness and job performance. *Journal of Applied Psychology, 85*, 472–478.

34. Kotter, J. (1985). *Power and influence*. New York: Free Press.

35. Gandz, J., & Murray, V. V. (1980). The experience of workplace politics. *Academy of Management Journal, 23*, 237–251.

36. [illegible] Perceptions of organizational politics: Prediction, stress-related implications, and outcomes, *Human Relations, 49*, 233–266; Valle, M., & Perrewe, P. L. (2000). Do politics perceptions relate to political behaviors? Tests of an implicit assumption and expanded model. *Human Relations, 53*, 359–386; Harris, K. J., James, M., & Boonthanom, R. (2005). Perceptions of organizational politics and cooperation as moderators of the relationship between job strains and intent to turnover. *Journal of Managerial Issues, 17*, 26–42; Randall, M. L., Cropanzano, R., Bormann, C. A., & Birjulin, A. (1999). Organizational politics and organizational support as predictors of work attitudes, job performance, and organizational citizenship behavior. *Journal of Organizational Behavior, 20*, 159–174.

37. Parker, C. P., Dipboye, R. L., & Jackson, S. L. (1995). Perceptions of organizational politics: An investigation of antecedents and consequences. *Journal of Management, 21*, 891–912.

38. Maslyn, J. M., & Fedor, D. B. (1998). Perceptions of politics: Does measuring different loci matter? *Journal of Applied Psychology, 84*, 645–653; Nye, L. G., & Wit, L. A. (1993). Dimensionality and construct validity of the perceptions of politics scale (POPS). *Educational and Psychological Measurement, 53*, 821–829.

39. Ferris, G. R., Frink, D. D., Bhawuk, D. P., Zhou, J., & Gilmore, D. C. (1996). Reactions of diverse groups to politics in the workplace. *Journal of Management, 22*, 23–44; Hochwarter, W. A., Ferris, G. R., Laird, M. D., Treadway, D. C., & Gallagher, V. C. (in press). Nonlinear politics perceptions—work outcomes relationships: A three-study, five-sample investigation. *Journal of Management*; Kacmar, K. L., Bozeman, D. P., Carlson, D. S., & Anthony, W. P. (1999). An examination of the perceptions of organizational politics model: Replication and extension. *Human Relations, 52*, 383–416.

40. Anderson, T. P. (1994). Creating measures of dysfunctional office and organizational politics: The DOOP and short-form DOOP scales psychology. *Journal of Human Behavior, 31*, 24–34.

41. Ferris, G. R., Frink, D. D., Bhawuk, D. P., Zhou, J., & Gilmore, D. C. (1996). Reactions of diverse groups to politics in the workplace. *Journal of Management, 22*, 23–44; Kacmar, K. M., & Ferris, G. R. (1989). Theoretical and methodological considerations in the age-job satisfaction relationship. *Journal of Applied Psychology, 74*, 201–207.

42. Byrne, Z. S., Kacmar, C., Stoner, J., & Hochwarter, W. A. (2005). The relationship between perceptions of politics and depressed mood at work: Unique moderators across three levels. *Journal of Occupational Health Psychology, 10*(4), 330–343.

43. Rosen, C., Levy, P., & Hall, R. (2006, January). Placing perceptions of politics in the context of the feedback environment, employee attitudes, and job performance. *Journal of Applied Psychology, 91*(10), 21.

44. Ferris, G. R., Perrewé, P. L., Anthony, W. P., & Gilmore, D. C. (2000). Political skill at work. *Organizational Dynamics, 28*, 25–37.

45. Ferris, G. R., Fedor, D. B., & King, T. R. (1994). A political conceptualization of managerial behavior. *Human Resource Management Review, 4*, 1–34; Kilduff, M., & Day, D. (1994). Do chameleons get ahead? The effects of self-monitoring on managerial careers. *Academy of Management Journal, 37*, 1047–1060.

46. Valle, M., & Perrewe, P. L. (2000). Do politics perceptions relate to political behaviors? Test of an implicit assumption and expanded model. *Human Relations, 53*, 359–386.

47. Bandura, A. (1996). *Self-efficacy: The exercise of control*. New York: Worth Publishers.

48. Muhammad, A. H. (2007, Fall). Antecedents of organizational politic perceptions in Kuwait business organizations. *Competitiveness Review, 17*(14), 234.

49. Hansen, K. (2008). *A foot in the door: Networking your way into the hidden job market.* Berkeley, CA: Ten Speed Press.

50. Cross, R., Parker, A., Prusak, L., & Borgatti, S. P. (2001). Knowing what we know: Supporting knowledge creation and sharing in social networks. *Organizational Dynamics 30*(2), 100–120.

51. Cross, R., Liedtka, J., & Weiss, L. (2005). *A practical guide to social networks. Harvard Business Review, 83*(3), 124–132.

52. Frauenheim, E. (2007). Social revolution: A wired workforce community. *Workforce Management.* Retrieved November 27, 2007, from http://www.workforce.com/section/10/feature/25/20/77/index.html.

53. Cross, R. L., Parker, A., & Cross, R. (2004). *The hidden power of social networks: Understanding how work really gets done in organizations.* Harvard, MA: Harvard Business Publishing.

54. Hartman, L., & Desjardins, J. (2008). *Business ethics.* New York: McGraw-Hill, p. 43.

55. CEO paycharts. (2005). Retrieved January 4, 2008, from the *Fair Economy* Web site: http://www.faireconomy.org/issues/ceo_pay.

56. Petersen, B. (2009, January 28). Japan Airline boss sets exec example. *CBS Evening News.* Retrieved January 28, 2009, from http://www.cbsnews.com/stories/2009/01/28/eveningnews/main4761136.shtml.

57. Javidan, M. Dorfman, P., Sully de Luque, M., & House, R. (2006, February). In the eye of the beholder: Cross cultural lessons in leadership from project GLOBE. *Academy of Management Perspectives, 20,* 67–90.

58. Ashkanasy, N. (1998, August). What matters most in leadership: A 60 nation study—implications of GLOBE country-specific empirical findings for organizational behavior and management. Presentation at Academy of Management Conference, San Diego, CA.

59. Fu, P. P., & Yukl, G. (2000). Perceived effectiveness of influence tactics in the United States and China. *Leadership Quarterly, 11,* 251–266; Yukl, G., Fu, P. P., & McDonald, R. (2003). Cross-cultural differences in perceived effectiveness of influence tactics for initiating or resisting change. *Applied Psychology: An International Review, 52,* 68–82.

60. Adapted from information in Carpenter, M.A., & Sanders, W.M. (2007). *Strategic Management.* Upper Saddle River, NJ: Pearson Education; Wasserman, S., & Faust, K. (1994). Social network analysis: Methods and applications. NY: Cambridge University Press; Watt, D.J. (2003). *Six degrees: The science of the connected age.* NY: W.W. Norton & Company Ltd.

CHAPTER 14

Organizational Structure and Change

LEARNING OBJECTIVES

After reading this chapter, you should be able to do the following:

1. Define organizational structure.
2. Identify the basic elements of structure.
3. Explain the difference between mechanistic and organic structures and describe factors shaping an organization's structure.
4. Describe matrix, boundaryless, and learning organizations.
5. Understand how structure affects ethics.
6. Understand cross-cultural influences on structure and change.

Success at Toyota

Toyota's unique production system, its emphasis on continuous learning and improvement, and matrix structure are among the reasons for the company's leadership in the automotive industry.

Source: http://commons.wikimedia.org/wiki/Image:Toyota_Headquarter_Toyota_City.jpg.

In the first quarter of 2007, Toyota Motor Company overtook General Motors Corporation in sales for the first time as the top automotive manufacturer in the world. Thus, the largest automotive manufacturer of Japan became the top manufacturer of cars in the world. In terms of productivity, efficiency, and profitability, Toyota was already at the top. Analysts and observers are eager to explain Toyota's success, and one frequently cited reason for this accomplishment is Toyota's unique lean manufacturing system.

What is lean manufacturing? Toyota Production System (TPS) is built on the principles of "just-in-time" production. In other words, raw materials and supplies are delivered to the assembly line exactly at the time they are to be used. This system has little room for slack resources, emphasizes the importance of efficiency on the part of employees, and minimizes wasted resources. TPS also gives power to the employees on the front lines. Assembly line workers are empowered to pull a cord and stop the manufacturing line when they see a problem. In a system based on just-in-time delivery, assembly line stoppages might have been viewed as costly, but Toyota employees would find it unthinkable to let a flaw pass through the system.

Toyota enacts its production system with the help of its human resource strategies, culture, and structure. From the human resource perspective, they have employment stability, high investment in training and development, and internal promotions, all promoting a sense of employee ownership of the process. On the culture side, an emphasis on learning and modesty when it comes to evaluating past successes differentiates them from competitors, yet their structure is also a key reason for their ability to put TPS into action.

TPS requires all employees to be an expert in what they do, which encourages specialization. Thus, Toyota is a functional organization. Each employee reports to a functional manager. At the same time, they understand the importance of a focus on the final product. As a result, a matrix organization is created where each employee also reports to a chief engineer who represents the interests of the customer. Meetings are conducted every two days to coordinate the relations between chief engineers and functional managers. Toyota's structure also has other formal mechanisms facilitating communication among functions, such as module development teams, which are cross-functional teams that bring together product and production engineers. Through this structure, Toyota strikes a balance between being highly traditional and bureaucratic while at the same time agile and innovative.

Toyota culture and structure facilitate constant learning and continuous improvement. Employees at all levels are expected to analyze the gap between actual and expected performance and understand the causes of all problems. Without such understanding, they believe, improvements are not likely. Their culture emphasizes rethinking of how things are done, and sayings such as "never be satisfied" and "there's gotta be a better way" are part of their daily life. For example, if a car comes down the assembly line with a defect, fixing the defect is not the priority. Instead, the emphasis is on understanding the cause of the defect so it is not repeated. Management encourages experimentation and views failures as the key to learning. One way in which they learn from mistakes is to hold "reflection" meetings to recount what went wrong and how things can be improved in the future. In addition to facilitating learning at the individual and team levels, they take steps to make sure that what is learned is shared with the rest of the organization. This is achieved by putting implied knowledge into writing.

Just-in-time production requires harmonious relations with suppliers, because suppliers are responsible for ensuring timely delivery of quality components. In fact, around 75% of each Toyota car is produced by suppliers. Toyota managed to create strategic alliances that eliminate some of the boundaries that exist between typical manufacturers and suppliers. Unlike GM or Ford Motor Company, Toyota does not go to the lowest bidding supplier, pit suppliers against each other, or threaten them. In fact, while GM and Ford are known as having poor relations with their suppliers, Toyota manages to build highly effective and long-term relations with the exact same suppliers, becoming their best customer and partner in the process despite cross-cultural differences. Toyota invests in its suppliers by sending engineers to observe and improve production processes and provides guest engineers to introduce suppliers to Toyota's own production methods. Toyota even shares critical information with supply companies to help them be successful. In fact, Toyota and its suppliers are called the "Toyota group" in Japan. The level of cooperation Toyota has with its suppliers blurs the lines between organizations and moves them one step closer to becoming a boundaryless organization.

Sources: Based on information from Dyer, J. H., & Nobeoka, K. (2000). Creating and managing a high-performance knowledge-sharing network: The Toyota case. Strategic Management Journal, 21, 345–367; Liker, J. K., & Choi, T. Y. (2004, December). Building deep supplier relationships. Harvard Business Review, 82(12), 104–113; Liker, J. K., & Morgan, J. M. (2006). The Toyota way in services: The case of lean product development. Academy of Management Perspectives, 20(2), 5–20; Spear, S. J. (2004, May). Learning to lead at Toyota. Harvard Business Review, 82(5), 78–86; Takeuchi, H., Osono, E., & Shimizu, N. (2008, June). The contradictions that drive Toyota's success. Harvard Business Review, 86(6), 96–104.

organizational structure

How individual and teamwork within an organization is coordinated.

As much as individual and team level factors influence work attitudes and behaviors, the organization's structure can be an even more powerful influence over employee actions. **Organizational structure** refers to how the work of individuals and teams within an organization is coordinated. In order to achieve organizational goals and objectives, individual work needs to be coordinated and managed. Structure is a valuable tool in achieving coordination, as it specifies reporting relationships (who reports to whom), delineates formal communication channels, and describes how separate actions of individuals are linked together.

1. ORGANIZATIONAL STRUCTURE

LEARNING OBJECTIVES

1. Explain the role of formalization, centralization, levels in the hierarchy, and departmentalization for employee attitudes and behaviors.
2. Describe how the elements of organizational structure can be combined to create mechanistic and organic structures.
3. Understand the advantages and disadvantages of mechanistic and organic structures for organizations.
4. Explain what a matrix structure is, and the challenges of working in a structure such as this.
5. Define boundaryless organizations.
6. Define learning organizations and list the steps organizations can take to become learning organizations.

1.1 Building Blocks of Structure

What exactly do we mean by organizational structure? In other words, which elements of a company's structure make a difference in how we behave and how work is coordinated? We will review four aspects of structure that have been frequently studied in the literature. We view these four elements as the building blocks, or elements, making up a company's structure. Then we will examine how these building blocks come together to form two different configurations of structures.

Centralization

Centralization is the degree to which decision making authority is concentrated at higher levels in an organization. In centralized companies, many important decisions are made at higher levels of the hierarchy, whereas in decentralized companies, decisions are made and problems are solved at lower levels by employees who are closer to the problem in question.

centralization

The degree to which decision making authority is concentrated at higher levels in an organization.

As an employee, where would you feel more comfortable and productive? If your answer is "decentralized," you are not alone. Decentralized companies give more authority to lower level employees, resulting in a sense of empowerment. Decisions are often faster, and employees believe that decentralized companies provide greater levels of procedural fairness to employees. Job candidates are more likely to be attracted to decentralized organizations. Because centralized organizations assign decision making responsibility to higher level managers, there are greater demands on the mental and physical capabilities of CEOs and other high-level managers. Despite many perceived disadvantages, centralization may lead to more efficient operations, particularly if the company is operating in a stable environment.[1]

Many companies find that the centralization of operations leads to inefficiencies in decision making. For example, in the 1980s, Caterpillar Inc. suffered the consequences of centralized decision making. At the time, all pricing decisions were made in the corporate headquarters in Peoria, Illinois. This meant that when a sales representative working in Africa wanted to give a discount on a product, they needed to check with headquarters. Headquarters did not always have accurate or timely information about the subsidiary markets to make an effective decision. The dramatic reorganization of the company sought to avoid problems such as these.[2] At the other end of the spectrum, organizations can suffer from extreme decentralization. For example, some analysts believe that the Federal Bureau of Investigation (FBI) experiences some problems because all its structure and systems are based on the assumption that crime needs to be caught *after* it happens. Over time, this assumption led to a situation in which, instead of following an overarching strategy, each unit is completely decentralized, and field agents determine how investigations should be pursued. It has been argued that due to the change in the nature of crimes, the FBI's need to gather accurate intelligence *before* a crime is committed requires more centralized decision making and strategy development.[3]

FIGURE 14.2

Changing their decision-making approach to a more decentralized style has helped Caterpillar Inc. compete at the global level.

Source: http://commons.wikimedia.org/wiki/Image:Bauma_2007_Bulldozer_Caterpillar_2.jpg.

Hitting the right balance between decentralization and centralization is a challenge for many organizations. At the Home Depot Inc., the retail giant with over 2,000 stores across the United States, Canada, Mexico, and China, one of the major changes their former CEO Robert Nardelli did was to centralize most of its operations. Before the transition, Home Depot store managers made a number of decisions autonomously and each store had an entrepreneurial culture. Nardelli's changes initially saved the company a lot of money. For example, for a company of that size, centralizing purchasing operations led to big cost savings, because the company could negotiate significant discounts from suppliers. At the same time, many analysts think that the centralization went too far, leading to the loss of the service-oriented culture at the stores.[4]

Formalization

formalization

The extent to which policies, procedures, job descriptions, and rules are written and explicitly articulated.

Formalization is the extent to which policies, procedures, job descriptions, and rules are written and explicitly articulated. In other words, formalized structures are those in which there are many written rules and regulations. These structures control employee behavior using written rules, and employees have little autonomy to make decisions on a case-by-case basis. Formalization makes employee behavior more predictable. Whenever a problem at work arises, employees know to turn to a handbook or a procedure guideline. Therefore, employees respond to problems in a similar way across the organization, which leads to consistency of behavior.

While formalization reduces ambiguity and provides direction to employees, it is not without disadvantages. A high degree of formalization may actually lead to reduced innovativeness, because employees are used to behaving in a certain manner. In fact, strategic decision making in such organizations often occurs only when there is a crisis. A formalized structure is associated with reduced motivation and job satisfaction as well as a slower pace of decision making.[5] The service industry is particularly susceptible to problems associated with high levels of formalization. Sometimes employees who are listening to a customer's problems may need to take action, but the answer may not be specified in any procedural guidelines or rulebook. For example, while a handful of airlines such as Southwest Airlines Company do a good job of empowering their employees to handle complaints, in many airlines lower level employees have limited power to resolve a customer problem and are constrained by stringent rules that outline a limited number of acceptable responses.

Hierarchical Levels

tall structures

An organization where there are several layers of management between frontline employees and the top level.

flat structures

An organization with few layers, often with large numbers of employees reporting to a single manager.

span of control

The number of employees reporting to a single manager.

Another important element of a company's structure is the number of levels it has in the hierarchy. Keeping the size of the organization constant, **tall structures** have several layers of management between frontline employees and the top level, while **flat structures** consist of few layers. A closely related concept is **span of control**, or the number of employees reporting to a single manager. In tall structures, span of control tends to be smaller, resulting in greater opportunities for managers to supervise and monitor employee activities. In contrast, flat structures involve a wider span of control. In such a structure, managers will be relatively unable to provide close supervision, leading to greater levels of freedom of action for each employee. Research indicates that flat organizations provide greater need satisfaction for employees, and greater levels of self-actualization.[6] Companies such as the IKEA Group, the Swedish furniture manufacturer and retailer, are successfully using flat structures to build an employee mentality of job involvement and ownership. At the same time, there may be some challenges associated with flat structures. In flat structures, employees will not have many opportunities to receive supervision and guidance from the manager, making it necessary for employees to be self-reliant. In fact, research shows that when managers supervise a large number of employees, which is more likely to happen in flat structures, employees experience greater levels of role ambiguity.[7] This may be a disadvantage for employees who need closer guidance from their managers. Moreover, in a flat structure, advancement opportunities will be more limited, because there are fewer management layers. Finally, while employees report that flat structures are better at satisfying their higher order needs such as self-actualization, they also report that tall structures are better at satisfying security needs of employees.[8] Because tall structures are typical of large and well-established companies, it is possible that when working in such organizations, employees feel a greater sense of job security.

Departmentalization

Organizational structures differ in terms of departmentalization. Organizations using **functional structures** group jobs based on similarity in functions. Such structures may have departments such as marketing, manufacturing, finance, accounting, human resources, and information technology. In these structures, each person serves a specialized role and handles large volumes of transactions. For example, a marketing employee working in a functional structure may serve as an event planner, planning promotional events for all the products of the company. In organizations using **divisional structures**, departments represent the unique products, services, customers, or geographic locations the company is serving. In other words, each unique product or service the company is producing will have its own department. Within each department, functions such as marketing, manufacturing, and other roles are replicated. In these structures, employees act like generalists as opposed to specialists. Instead of performing specialized tasks, employees will be in charge of performing many different tasks in the service of the product. For example, a marketing employee working in this structure may be in charge of planning promotions, coordinating relations with advertising agencies, and planning and conducting marketing research.

In reality, many structures are a hybrid of functional and divisional forms. For example, if the company has multiple product lines, departmentalizing by product may increase innovation and reduce response times. Each of these departments may have dedicated marketing, manufacturing, and customer service employees serving the specific product, yet the company may also find that centralizing some operations and retaining the functional structure makes sense and is more cost effective for roles such as human resources management and information technology. The same organization may also create geographic departments, if it is serving different countries.

FIGURE 14.3

Companies such as IKEA, the Swedish furniture manufacturer and retailer, are successfully using flat structures within stores to build an employee attitude of job involvement and ownership.

Source: http://commons.wikimedia.org/wiki/Image:Ikea_almhult.jpg.

functional structures

Grouping of jobs based on similarity in functions.

divisional structures

Grouping of jobs based on the products, services, customers, or geographic locations the company is serving.

FIGURE 14.4 An Example of a Pharmaceutical Company With Functional Departments

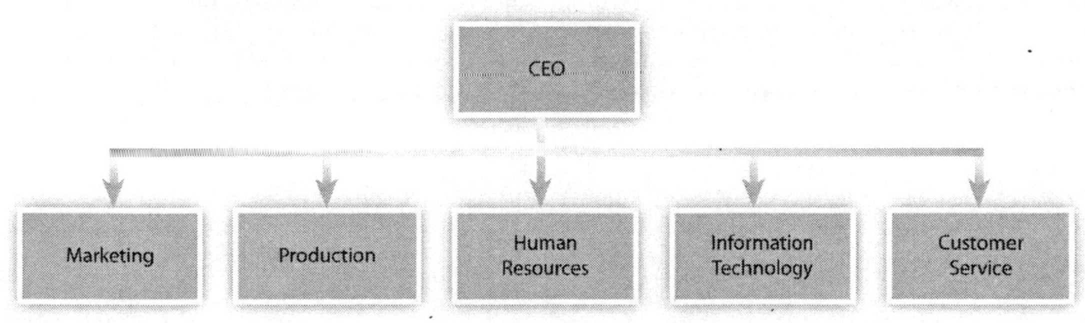

FIGURE 14.5 An Example of a Pharmaceutical Company With Product Departments

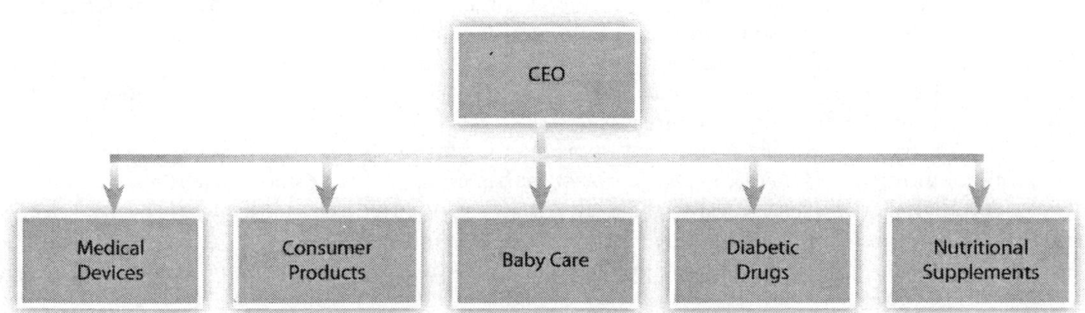

Functional structures tend to be effective when an organization does not have a large number of products and services requiring special attention. When a company has a diverse product line, each product will have unique demands, deeming traditional structures less useful for promptly addressing customer demands and anticipating market changes. Functional structures are also more effective in stable environments that are slower to change. In contrast, organizations using product departments are more agile and can perform better in turbulent environments. The type of employee who will succeed under each structure is also different. Research shows that when employees work in product departments in turbulent environments, because activities are diverse and complex, their performance depends on their general mental abilities.[9]

Two Configurations: Mechanistic and Organic Structures

The different elements making up organizational structures in the form of formalization, centralization, number of levels in the hierarchy, and departmentalization often coexist. As a result, we can talk about two configurations of organizational structures, depending on how these elements are arranged.

mechanistic structures

Structures that resemble a bureaucracy and are highly formalized and centralized.

Mechanistic structures are similar to bureaucracies, as they are highly formalized and centralized. Communication tends to follow formal channels, and employees are given specific job descriptions delineating their roles and responsibilities. Mechanistic organizations are often rigid and resist change, making them unsuitable for being innovative and taking quick action. These forms have the downside of inhibiting entrepreneurial action and discouraging the use of individual initiative on the part of employees. Not only do mechanistic structures have disadvantages for innovativeness, they also limit individual autonomy and self-determination, which will likely lead to lower levels of intrinsic motivation on the job.[10] Despite these downsides, mechanistic structures have advantages when the environment is more stable. The main advantage of a mechanistic structure is its efficiency. Therefore, in organizations that are trying to maximize efficiency and minimize costs, mechanistic structures provide advantages. For example, McDonald's Corporation has a famously bureaucratic structure in which employee jobs are highly formalized, with clear lines of communication and very specific job descriptions. This structure is an advantage for them, because it allows McDonald's to produce a uniform product around the world at minimum cost. Moreover, mechanistic structures tend to be advantageous for new ventures. New businesses often suffer from a lack of structure, role ambiguity, and uncertainty. The presence of a mechanistic structure has been shown to be related to firm performance in new ventures.[11]

organic structures

Flexible and decentralized structures with low levels of formalization where communication lines are more fluid and flexible.

Organic structures are flexible, decentralized structures with low levels of formalization. Communication lines are more fluid and flexible. Employee job descriptions are broader, and employees are asked to perform duties based on the specific needs of the organization at the time as well as their own expertise levels. Organic structures tend to be related to higher levels of job satisfaction on the part of employees. These structures are conducive to entrepreneurial behavior and innovativeness.[12] An example of a company that has an organic structure is 3M. The company is strongly committed to decentralization. At 3M, there are close to 100 profit centers, with each division feeling like a small company. Each division manager acts autonomously and is accountable for his or her actions. As operations within each division get too big and a product created by a division becomes profitable, the operation is spun off to create a separate business unit. This is done to protect the agility of the company and the small-company atmosphere.[13]

1.2 Contemporary Forms of Organizational Structures

Matrix Organizations

matrix organizations

A cross between a traditional functional structure with a product structure. Specifically, employees reporting to department managers are also pooled together to form project or product teams.

Matrix organizations cross a traditional functional structure with a product structure. Specifically, employees reporting to department managers are also pooled together to form project or product teams. As a result, each person reports to a department manager as well as a project or product manager. In this structure, product managers have control and say over product-related matters. Matrix structures are created in response to uncertainty and dynamism of the environment and the need to give particular attention to specific products or projects. Instead of completely switching from a product-based structure, a company may utilize a matrix structure to balance the benefits of product-based and traditional functional structures.

Using the matrix structure as opposed to product departments may increase communication and cooperation among departments, because project managers will need to coordinate their actions with department managers. In fact, research shows that matrix structure increases the frequency of informal and formal communication within the organization.[14] Matrix structures also have the benefit of providing quick responses to technical problems and customer demands. The existence of a project manager keeps the focus on the product or service that is being provided.

unity of command

A situation where each person reports to a single manager. Traditional organizations are based on the principle of unity of command, while matrix organizations do not follow this principle.

Despite these potential benefits, matrix structures are not without costs. In a matrix, each employee reports to at least two or more managers. In other words, the matrix organization violates the **unity of command** principle that is often prevalent in traditional organizations. In organizations with unity of command, each person reports to a single manager. As a result, communication flows through predictable lines and coordination is easier. Because matrix organizations do not follow unity of command, this is a situation ripe with conflict. Because multiple managers are in charge of guiding the behaviors of each employee, there may be power struggles or turf wars among managers. The managers are more interdependent compared to a traditional or product-based structure, and they will need to spend more effort coordinating their work. From the employee's perspective, there is potential for interpersonal conflict with team members as well as with leaders. The presence of multiple leaders may create role conflict. The necessity to work with a team consisting of employees with different functional backgrounds increases the potential for task conflict at work.[15] Solving these problems will require a great deal of patience and proactivity on the part of the employee.

FIGURE 14.6

An example of a matrix structure at a software development company. Business analysts, developers, and testers each report to a functional department manager and to a project manager simultaneously.

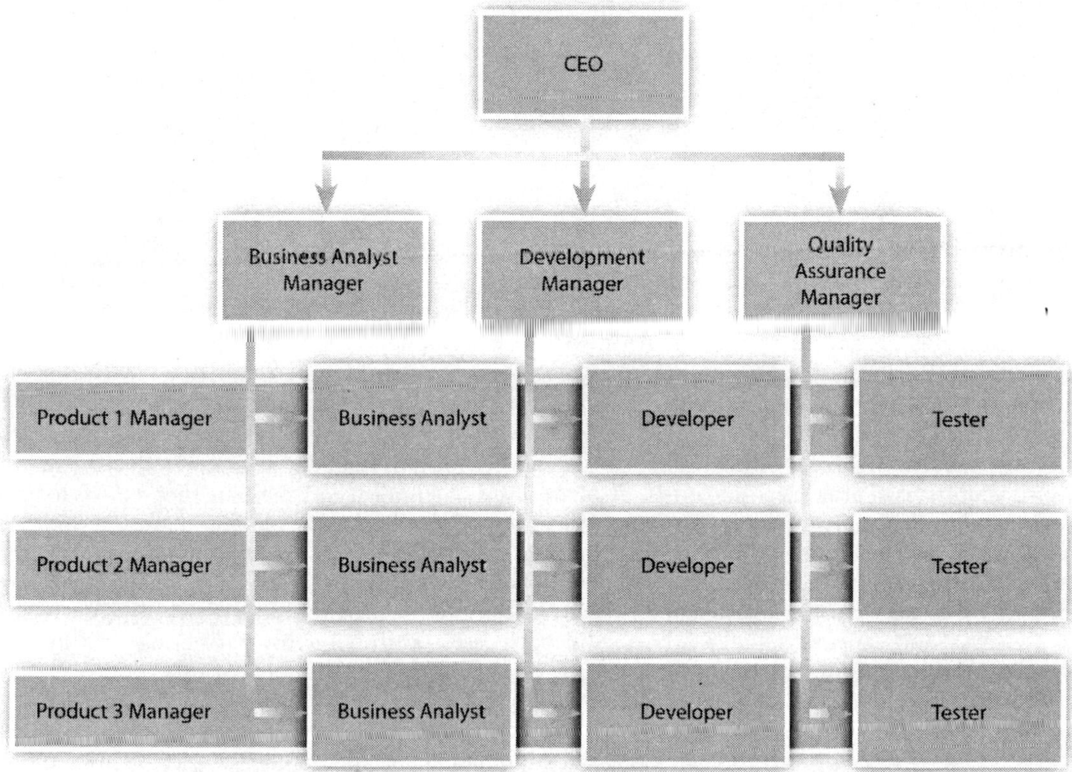

The matrix structure is used in many information technology companies engaged in software development. See the example of a matrix structure for an IT company presented in the following figure. Nike Inc. is another company that utilizes the matrix organization successfully. New product introduction is a task shared by regional managers and product managers. While product managers are in charge of deciding how to launch a product, regional managers are allowed to make modifications based on the region.[16]

OB Toolbox: Managed by a Crowd

Due to the widespread use of matrix structures and similar organizational forms, you may find that you are reporting to multiple bosses as opposed to just one. Here is what you can do to make this situation work more smoothly for everyone involved:

- *Do not assume that having multiple bosses is necessarily a bad thing!* Yes, there are more opportunities for role overload and role conflict, but there are also more chances of learning from several senior people. This may turn out to be a great learning experience.
- *Make sure that all your managers are familiar with your overall work load.* One challenge of having multiple bosses is that you may end up with too much work, because they may place expectations on you without checking with each other. For example, you may post your "to do" list on a Web board or on a whiteboard in your office for them to keep track of.
- *Make conflicts known to managers.* Another challenge is the potential for role conflict. If the managers are not coordinating with each other, they may place contradictory expectations on you. Also, keep good records of all e-mails and CC all relevant managers in conversations that are pertinent to them.
- *Do not be afraid to request a meeting with all your managers, and potentially with their own managers if you reach an impasse.* This structure places serious communication and coordination challenges on all those involved, and having meetings may clear the air.

- *Make an effort to establish an effective relation with each manager.* When you have multiple bosses, you will need to manage good relations with each of them.
- *You need to understand the styles of each manager and vary your style with each.* Some may appreciate frequent updates on all you are doing, while others may judge you based solely on ultimate results. Make an effort to understand their styles and do not assume that something that works with one will work with the other.
- *Be cognizant of the relationships among those managers as well.* Never complain about one to the other. Also, be aware that if two managers truly dislike each other, being too friendly with one in the presence of the other may affect your relations with the other.

Sources: Adapted from information in Frings, C. S. (2002, August). Management Q & A: Answering your questions on multiple bosses and not following standard operating procedure. Medical Laboratory Observer, 34(8), 24–25; Hymowitz, C. (2003, August 12). Managers suddenly have to answer to a crowd of bosses. Wall Street Journal, B1; McCune, J. (2006, August–September). Multiple bosses multiple directions. Office Pro, 66(6), 10–14.

Boundaryless Organizations

Boundaryless organization is a term coined by Jack Welch of General Electric Company and refers to an organization that eliminates traditional barriers between departments, as well as barriers between the organization and the external environment. Many different types of boundaryless organizations exist. One form is the **modular organization** where all the nonessential functions are outsourced. The idea behind this format is to retain only the value-generating and strategic functions in-house, while the rest of the operations are outsourced to many suppliers. An example of a company doing this is Toyota. By managing relationships with hundreds of suppliers, Toyota achieves efficiency and quality in its operations. **Strategic alliances** constitute another form of boundaryless design. Here, similar to a joint venture, two or more companies find an area of collaboration and combine their efforts to create a partnership that is beneficial for both parties. In this form, the traditional boundaries between two competitors may be broken. As an example, Starbucks Corporation formed a highly successful partnership with PepsiCo Inc. to market its Frappuchino cold drinks. Starbucks has immediate brand name recognition in this cold coffee drink, but its desire to capture shelf space in supermarkets required marketing savvy and experience that Starbucks did not possess at the time. By partnering with PepsiCo, Starbucks gained an important head start in the marketing and distribution of this product. Finally, boundaryless organizations may involve eliminating the barriers separating employees, such as traditional management layers or walls between different departments. Structures such as self-managing teams create an environment where employees coordinate their efforts and change their own roles to suit the demands of the situation, as opposed to insisting that something is "not my job."[17]

boundaryless organization

A term coined by Jack Welch of GE and refers to an organization that eliminates traditional barriers between departments as well as barriers between the organization and the external environment.

modular organization

An organization where all the nonessential functions are outsourced.

strategic alliances

A form of boundaryless design where two or more companies find an area of collaboration and combine their efforts to create a partnership that is beneficial for both parties.

Learning Organizations

A **learning organization** is one where acquiring knowledge and changing behavior as a result of the newly gained knowledge are part of an organization's design. In these structures, experimenting, learning new things, and reflecting on new knowledge are the norms. At the same time, there are many procedures and systems in place that facilitate learning at the organizational level.

learning organization

An organization where acquiring knowledge and changing behavior as a result of the newly acquired knowledge is part of an organization's design.

In learning organizations, experimentation and testing potentially better operational methods are encouraged. This is true not only in response to environmental threats, but also as a way of identifying future opportunities. 3M is one company that institutionalized experimenting with new ideas in the form of allowing each engineer to spend one day a week working on a personal project. At IBM Corporation, this is achieved by taking highly successful business managers and putting them in charge of emerging business opportunities (EBOs). IBM is a company that has no difficulty coming up with new ideas, as evidenced by the number of patents it holds. Yet commercializing these ideas has been a problem in the past, owing to an emphasis on short-term results. To change this situation, the company began experimenting with the idea of EBOs. By setting up a structure in which failure is tolerated and risk taking is encouraged, the company took a big step toward becoming a learning organization.[18]

Learning organizations are also good at learning from experience, be it their own or a competitors'. In order to learn from past mistakes, companies conduct a thorough analysis of them. Some companies choose to conduct formal retrospective meetings to analyze the challenges encountered and areas for improvement. In order to learn from others, these companies vigorously study competitors, market leaders in different industries, clients, and customers. By benchmarking against industry best practices, they constantly look for ways of improving their own operations. Learning organizations are also good at studying customer habits to generate ideas. For example, Xerox Corporation uses anthropologists to understand and gain insights into how customers are actually using their office products.[19] By using these techniques, learning organizations facilitate innovativeness and make it easier to achieve organizational change.

KEY TAKEAWAY

The degree to which a company is centralized and formalized, the number of levels in the company hierarchy, and the type of departmentalization the company uses are key elements of a company's structure. These elements of structure affect the degree to which the company is effective and innovative as well as employee attitudes and behaviors at work. These elements come together to create mechanistic and organic structures. Rigid and bureaucratic, mechanistic structures help companies achieve efficiency, while organic structures, which are decentralized and flexible, aid companies in achieving innovativeness. The changing environment of organizations creates the need for newer forms of organizing. Matrix structures are a cross between functional and product-based divisional structures. They facilitate information flow and reduce response time to customers but have challenges, because each employee reports to multiple managers. Boundaryless organizations blur the boundaries between departments or the boundaries between the focal organization and others in the environment. These organizations may take the form of a modular organization, strategic alliance, or self-managing teams. Learning organizations institutionalize experimentation and benchmarking.

EXERCISES

1. What are the advantages and disadvantages of decentralization?
2. All else being equal, would you prefer to work in a tall or flat organization? Why?
3. What are the advantages of departmentalization by product?
4. Have you ever reported to more than one manager? What were the challenges of such a situation?
5. What do you think are the advantages and disadvantages of being employed by a boundaryless organization?
6. What can organizations do to institutionalize organizational learning? What practices and policies would aid in knowledge acquisition and retention?

2. ORGANIZATIONAL CHANGE

LEARNING OBJECTIVES

1. **Identify the external forces creating change on the part of organizations.**
2. **Understand how organizations respond to changes in the external environment.**
3. **Understand why people resist change.**

2.1 Why Do Organizations Change?

Organizational change is the movement of an organization from one state of affairs to another. Organizational change can take many forms. It may involve a change in a company's structure, strategy, policies, procedures, technology, or culture. The change may be planned years in advance or may be forced upon an organization because of a shift in the environment. Organizational change can be radical and alter the way an organization operates, or it may be incremental and slowly change the way things are done. In any case, regardless of the type, change involves letting go of the old ways in which work is done and adjusting to the new ways. Therefore, fundamentally, it is a process that involves effective people management.

organizational change

The movement of an organization from one state of affairs to another.

Workforce Demographics

FIGURE 14.7

Organizations change in response to changes in their environment. One of the current changes is in the demographics of the workforce.

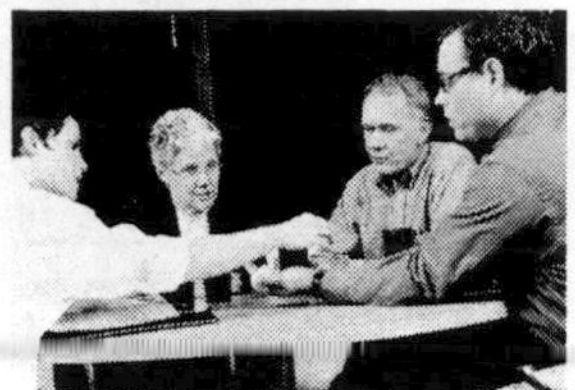

Organizational change is often a response to changes in the environment. For example, both the United States Department of Labor and Organization for Economic Co-operation and Development (OECD) estimate that the age of the workforce is on the rise.[20] What does this mean for companies? Organizations may realize that as the workforce gets older the types of benefits they prefer may change. Work arrangements such as flexible work hours and job sharing may become more popular as employees remain in the workforce even after retirement. As the workforce rapidly ages, it also becomes possible that employees who are unhappy with their current work situation will choose to retire, resulting in a sudden loss of valuable knowledge and expertise on the part of organizations. Therefore, organizations will have to devise strategies to retain these employees and plan for their retirement. Finally, a critical issue is finding ways of dealing with age-related stereotypes, which act as barriers in the retention of these employees.

Technology

Sometimes change is motivated by rapid developments in *technology*. Moore's law (a prediction by Gordon Moore, cofounder of Intel Corporation) dictates that the overall complexity of computer circuits will double every 18 months with no increase in cost.[21] Such change is motivating corporations to rapidly change their technology. Sometimes technology produces such profound developments that companies struggle to adapt. A recent example is from the music industry. When CDs were first introduced in the 1980s, they were substantially more appealing than the traditional LPs. Record companies were easily able to double the prices, even though producing CDs cost a fraction of what it cost to produce LPs. For decades, record producing companies benefited from this status quo. Yet when peer-to-peer file sharing through software such as Napster and Kazaa threatened the core of their business, companies in the music industry found themselves completely unprepared for such disruptive technological changes. Their first response was to sue the users of file-sharing software, sometimes even underage kids. They also kept looking for a technology that would make it impossible to copy a CD or DVD, which has yet to emerge. Until Apple Inc.'s iTunes came up with a new way to sell music online, it was doubtful that consumers would ever be willing to pay for music that was otherwise available for free (albeit illegally so). Only time will tell if the industry will be able to adapt itself to the changes forced upon it.[22]

FIGURE 14.8

Ray Kurzweil expanded Moore's law from integrated circuits to earlier transistors, vacuum tubes, relays, and electromechanical computers to show that his trend holds there as well.

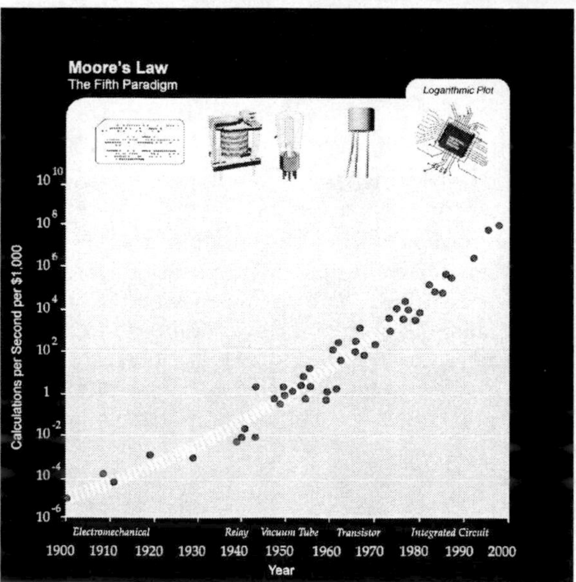

Source: http://upload.wikimedia.org/wikipedia/commons/c/c5/PPTMooresLawai.jpg.

Globalization

Globalization is another threat and opportunity for organizations, depending on their ability to adapt to it. Organizations are finding that it is often cheaper to produce goods and deliver services in some countries compared to others. This led many companies to utilize manufacturing facilities overseas, with China as a popular destination. For a while, knowledge work was thought to be safe from outsourcing, but now we are also seeing many service operations moved to places with cheaper wages. For example, many companies have outsourced software development to India, with Indian companies such as Wipro Ltd. and Infosys Technologies Ltd. emerging as global giants. Given these changes, understanding how to manage a global workforce is a necessity. Many companies realize that outsourcing forces them to operate in an institutional environment that is radically different from what they are used to at home. Dealing with employee stress resulting from jobs being moved overseas, retraining the workforce, and learning to compete with a global workforce on a global scale are changes companies are trying to come to grips with.

Market Conditions

Changes in the market conditions may also create changes as companies struggle to adjust. For example, as of this writing, the airline industry in the United States is undergoing serious changes. Demand for air travel was affected after the September 11 terrorist attacks. Also, the widespread use of the Internet to book plane travels made it possible to compare airline prices much more efficiently and easily, encouraging airlines to compete primarily based on cost. This strategy seems to have backfired when coupled with the dramatic increases in the cost of fuel. As a result, airlines are cutting back on amenities that were taken for granted for decades, such as the price of a ticket including meals, beverages, and checking luggage. Some airlines, such as Delta Air Lines Inc. and Northwest Airlines Inc., have merged to deal with this climate, and talks involving other mergers in this industry continue.

How does a change in the environment create change within an organization? Note that environmental change does not automatically change how business is done. Whether or not the organization changes in response to environmental challenges and threats depends on the decision makers' reactions to what is happening in the environment.

Organizational Growth

It is natural for once small start-up companies to grow if they are successful. An example of this growth is the evolution of the Widmer Brothers Brewing Company, which started as two brothers brewing beer in their garage to become the 11th largest brewery in the United States. This growth happened over time as the popularity of their key product—Hefeweizen—grew in popularity; the company had to expand to meet demand, growing from the 2 founders to 400 employees in 2008 after Widmer Brothers merged with Redhook Ale Brewery to become Craft Brewers Alliance Inc. The newly formed company has five main departments, including Operations, Sales, Marketing, Finance, and Retail, who report to the CEO. Anheuser-Busch Companies Inc. continues to have a minority stake in both beer companies. So, while 50% of all new small businesses fail in their first year,[23] those that succeed often evolve into large, complex organizations over time.

FIGURE 14.9

In 1984, brothers Kurt (on the left) and Rob Widmer founded Widmer Brothers, which is now the 11th largest brewery in the United States.

Source: Permission granted by Widmer Brothers Brewing Co.

Poor Performance

Change is more likely to happen if the company is performing poorly and if there is a perceived threat from the environment. In fact, poorly performing companies often find it easier to change compared to successful companies. Why? High performance actually leads to overconfidence and inertia. As a result, successful companies often keep doing what made them a success in the first place. When it comes to the relationship between company performance and organizational change, the saying "nothing fails like success" may be fitting. For example, Polaroid Corporation was the number one producer of instant films and cameras in 1994. The company filed for bankruptcy in less than a decade, unable to adapt to the rapid advances in the 1-hour photo development and digital photography technologies. Successful companies that manage to change have special practices in place to keep the organization open to changes. As a case in point, Nokia finds that it is important to periodically change the perspective of key decision makers. For this purpose, they rotate heads of businesses to different posts to give them a fresh perspective. In addition to the success of a business, change in a company's upper level management is a motivator for change at the organization level. Research shows that long-tenured CEOs are unlikely to change their formula for success. Instead, new CEOs and new top management teams create change in a company's culture and structure.[24]

2.2 Resistance to Change

Changing an organization is often essential for a company to remain competitive. Failure to change may influence the ability of a company to survive. Yet, employees do not always welcome changes in methods. According to a 2007 survey conducted by the Society for Human Resource Management (SHRM), resistance to change is one of the top two reasons why change efforts fail. In fact, reactions to organizational change may range from resistance to compliance to being an enthusiastic supporter of the change, with the latter being the exception rather than the norm.[25]

FIGURE 14.10

Reactions to change may take many forms.

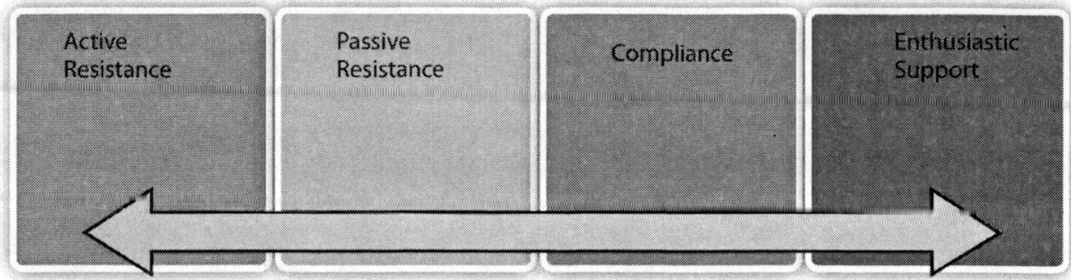

active resistance

The most negative reaction to a proposed change attempt.

passive resistance

Being disturbed by changes without necessarily voicing these opinions.

compliance

Going along with proposed changes with little enthusiasm.

enthusiastic support

Defenders of the new way and actually encourage others around them to give support to the change effort as well.

Active resistance is the most negative reaction to a proposed change attempt. Those who engage in active resistance may sabotage the change effort and be outspoken objectors to the new procedures. In contrast, **passive resistance** involves being disturbed by changes without necessarily voicing these opinions. Instead, passive resisters may quietly dislike the change, feel stressed and unhappy, and even look for an alternative job without necessarily bringing their point to the attention of decision makers. **Compliance**, on the other hand, involves going along with proposed changes with little enthusiasm. Finally, those who show **enthusiastic support** are defenders of the new way and actually encourage others around them to give support to the change effort as well.

Any change attempt will have to overcome the resistance on the part of people to be successful. Otherwise, the result will be loss of time and energy as well as an inability on the part of the organization to adapt to the changes in the environment and make its operations more efficient. Resistance to change also has negative consequences for the people in question. Research shows that when people negatively react to organizational change, they experience negative emotions, use sick time more often, and are more likely to voluntarily leave the company.[26]

The following is a dramatic example of how resistance to change may prevent improving the status quo. Have you ever wondered why the letters on keyboards are laid out the way they are? The QWERTY keyboard, named after the first six letters in the top row, was actually engineered to slow us down. The first prototypes of the typewriter keyboard would jam if the keys right next to each other were hit at the same time. Therefore, it was important for manufacturers to slow typers down. They achieved this by putting the most commonly used letters to the left-hand side, and scattering the most frequently used letters all over the keyboard. Later, the issue of letters being stuck was resolved. In fact, an alternative to the QWERTY named the Dvorak keyboard provides a much more efficient design and allows individuals to double traditional typing speeds. Yet the shift never occurred. The reasons? Large numbers of people resisted the change. Teachers and typists resisted, because they would lose their specialized knowledge. Manufacturers resisted because of costs inherent in making the switch and the initial inefficiencies in the learning curve.[27] In short, the best idea does not necessarily win, and changing people requires understanding why they resist.

FIGURE 14.11

The Dvorak keyboard is a more efficient design compared to the QWERTY keyboard. Due to resistance from typists, manufacturers, and teachers, it never gained widespread adoption.

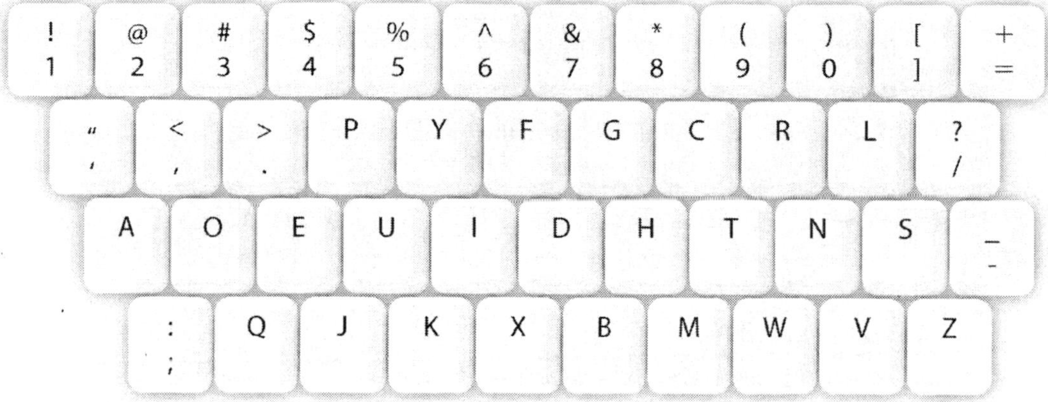

Why Do People Resist Change?

Disrupted Habits

People often resist change for the simple reason that change disrupts our habits. Do you think about how you are driving when you drive? Most of the time probably not, because driving generally becomes an automated activity after a while. You may sometimes even realize that you have reached your destination without noticing the roads you used or having consciously thought about any of your body movements. Now imagine you drive for a living, and even though you are used to driving an automatic car, you are now forced to use a stick shift. You can most likely figure out how to drive a stick, but it will take time, and until you figure it out, you cannot drive on auto pilot. You will have to reconfigure your body movements and practice shifting until you become good at it. You may find that for this simple reason, people sometimes are surprisingly outspoken when confronted with simple changes such as updating to a newer version of a particular software or a change in their voice mail system.

Personality

Some people are more resistant to change than others. Research shows that people who have a positive self-concept are better at coping with change, probably because those who have high self-esteem may feel that whatever the changes are, they are likely to adjust to it well and be successful in the new system. People with a more positive self-concept and those who are more optimistic may also view change as an opportunity to shine as opposed to a threat that is overwhelming. Finally, risk tolerance is another predictor of how resistant someone will be to stress. For people who are risk avoidant, the possibility of a change in technology or structure may be more threatening.[28]

Feelings of Uncertainty

Change inevitably brings feelings of uncertainty. You have just heard that your company is merging with another. What would be your reaction? Such change is often turbulent, and it is often unclear what is going to happen to each individual. Some positions may be eliminated. Some people may see a change in their job duties. Things can get better—or they may get worse. The feeling that the future is unclear is enough to create stress for people, because it leads to a sense of lost control.[29]

Fear of Failure

FIGURE 14.12

One common reason employees resist change is the fear of failure under the new system.

© 2010 Jupiterimages Corporation

People also resist change when they feel that their performance may be affected under the new system. People who are experts in their jobs may be less than welcoming of the changes, because they may be unsure whether their success would last under the new system. Studies show that people who feel that they can perform well under the new system are more likely to be committed to the proposed change, while those who have lower confidence in their ability to perform after changes are less committed.[30]

Personal Impact of Change

It would be too simplistic to argue that people resist all change, regardless of its form. In fact, people tend to be more welcoming of change that is favorable to them on a personal level (such as giving them more power over others, or change that improves quality of life such as bigger and nicer offices). Research also shows that commitment to change is highest when proposed changes affect the work unit with a low impact on how individual jobs are performed.[31]

Prevalence of Change

Any change effort should be considered within the context of all the other changes that are introduced in a company. Does the company have a history of making short-lived changes? If the company structure went from functional to product-based to geographic to matrix within the past five years, and the top management is in the process of going back to a functional structure again, a certain level of resistance is to be expected because people are likely to be fatigued as a result of the constant changes. Moreover, the lack of a history of successful changes may cause people to feel skeptical toward the newly planned changes. Therefore, considering the history of changes in the company is important to understanding why people resist. Also, how big is the planned change? If the company is considering a simple switch to a new computer program, such as introducing Microsoft Access for database management, the change may not be as extensive or stressful compared to a switch to an enterprise resource planning (ERP) system such as SAP or PeopleSoft, which require a significant time commitment and can fundamentally affect how business is conducted.[32]

Perceived Loss of Power

One other reason why people may resist change is that change may affect their power and influence in the organization. Imagine that your company moved to a more team-based structure, turning supervisors into team leaders. In the old structure, supervisors were in charge of hiring and firing all those reporting to them. Under the new system, this power is given to the team itself. Instead of monitoring the progress the team is making toward goals, the job of a team leader is to provide support and mentoring to the team in general and ensure that the team has access to all resources to be effective. Given the loss in prestige and status in the new structure, some supervisors may resist the proposed changes even if it is better for the organization to operate around teams.

In summary, there are many reasons individuals resist change, which may prevent an organization from making important changes.

Is All Resistance Bad?

Resistance to change may be a positive force in some instances. In fact, resistance to change is a valuable feedback tool that should not be ignored. Why are people resisting the proposed changes? Do they feel that the new system will not work? If so, why not? By listening to people and incorporating their suggestions into the change effort, it is possible to make a more effective change. Some of a company's most committed employees may be the most vocal opponents of a change effort. They may fear that the organization they feel such a strong attachment to is being threatened by the planned change effort and the change will ultimately hurt the company. In contrast, people who have less loyalty to the organization may comply with the proposed changes simply because they do not care enough about the fate of the company to oppose the changes. As a result, when dealing with those who resist change, it is important to avoid blaming them for a lack of loyalty.[33]

OB Toolbox: Life After Being Downsized

Organizational change sometimes means reducing the number of people working in the company to make operations more efficient. Sometime in your career, you may find that you go through this painful, sometimes traumatic experience. What do you do to recover in the aftermath of a downsizing?

- *Be calm.* This is easier said than done, but it happens to the best of us. Remember that it was not your fault. Many companies lay off employees during downsizing despite their stellar performance, so do not take it personally.
- *Do not get angry.* When you hear the news, make sure that you do not express your disappointment in a way that would burn your bridges. In fact, many companies rehire workers they lay off or bring them in as external consultants. Do not say or do something in anger that closes all doors. Remember, during downsizing companies are often forced to let go of employees they *want* to keep.
- *Know your rights.* Are you getting a severance package afterward? Are you going to have continued access to some benefits? Does the company provide assistance to those who are laid off? Find out what is being offered. You may also want to ask for a letter of recommendation from your former boss to help with your job hunt.
- *Think about your ideal job situation.* Are you in the right field? Do you have all the skills and education you need to work in the right field? Some people will look at a layoff as a time to settle for any job that comes along, but this may not be an effective long-term strategy. Instead, imagine your ideal situation and find out what you need to do to get there.
- *Get help.* There are many organizations and career coaches offering career support, advice, and networking opportunities. Surround yourself with positive people who are supportive. Getting assistance may help you make yourself more marketable or simply provide you with necessary emotional support.
- *Polish your resume and job hunting skills.* You may benefit from someone else proofreading your resume and practicing interviews with you.
- *Do not give up!* You found a job once, you will find it again. Stay positive, be patient, and do not lose hope.

Sources: Based on information in How to maximize your take when you get laid off. (2008, November). Money, 37(11), 132; Kamberg, M. L. (2000, May–June). Surviving the ups & downs of corporate restructuring. Women in Business, 52(3). Palmer, K. (2008, March 24). Re-energizing your career. U.S. News & World Report, 144(9). Weinstein, B. (2008, September 29). Downsizing 102: When it happens to you. Business Week Online. Retrieved on October 25, 2008, from http://www.businessweek.com/managing/content/sep2008/ca20080926_140228.htm.

2.3 Planning and Executing Change Effectively

FIGURE 14.13

Lewin's three-stage process of change emphasizes the importance of preparation or unfreezing before change, and reinforcement of change afterward or refreezing.

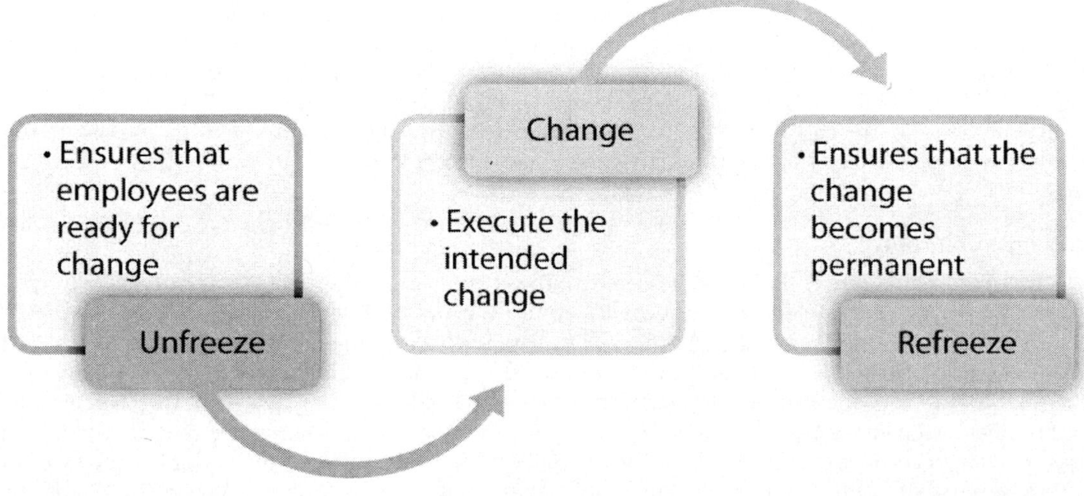

unfreezing

Or making sure that organizational members are ready for and receptive to change, is the first step in Lewin's suggested change model.

change

Or executing the planned changes, is the second phase of Lewin's change model.

refreezing

The final stage of Lewin's change model, involves ensuring that change becomes permanent and the new habits, rules, or procedures become the norm.

How do you plan, organize, and execute change effectively? One of the most useful frameworks in this area is Kurt Lewin's three-stage model of planned change.[34] The assumption is that change will encounter resistance. Therefore, executing change without prior preparation is likely to lead to failure. Instead, organizations should start with **unfreezing**, or making sure that organizational members are ready for and receptive to change. This is followed by **change**, or executing the planned changes. Finally, **refreezing** involves ensuring that change becomes permanent and the new habits, rules, or procedures become the norm. John Kotter, a Harvard University professor, wrote a book in 1996 titled *Leading Change* in which he discussed eight steps to changing an organization.[35] In the next section, we integrate the two models with more recent work in the area to present a roadmap to how organizations may want to approach change.

Unfreezing Prior to Change

Many change efforts fail because people are insufficiently prepared for change. When employees are not prepared, they are more likely to resist the change effort and less likely to effectively function under the new system. What can organizations do prior to change to prepare employees? There are a number of things that are important at this stage.

Create a Vision for Change

In successful change efforts, the leader has an overall vision for the change.[36] When this vision is exciting and paints a picture of a future that employees would be proud to be a part of, people are likely to be more committed to change. For example, Toyota is a master of *kaizen*, or continuous improvement. They also follow the philosophy of **kakushin**, or revolutionary change, as needed. Regardless of the nature of the particular change, there is an overall vision for the company that justifies and explains why change is necessary "to build the dream car of the future."[37]

Communicating a Plan for Change

Do people know what the change entails, or are they hearing about the planned changes through the grapevine or office gossip? When employees know what is going to happen, and when and why, they may conquer their discomfort with change. Research shows that those who have more complete information about upcoming changes are more committed to a change effort.[38]

Ensuring that top management communicates with employees about the upcoming changes also has symbolic value.[39] In any organization, many changes are done on a daily basis, with some taking root and some disappearing after a short while. When top management and the company CEO discuss the importance of the changes in meetings, employees are provided with a reason to trust that this change is a strategic initiative. For example, while changing the employee performance appraisal system, the CEO of Kimberly-Clark Corporation made sure to mention the new system in all meetings with employees, indicating that the change was supported by the CEO.

Develop a Sense of Urgency

People are more likely to accept change if they feel that there is a need for it. If employees feel their company is doing well, the perceived need for change will be smaller. Those who plan the change will need to make the case that there is an external or internal threat to the organization's competitiveness, reputation, or sometimes even its survival, and failure to act will have dire consequences. For example, Lou Gerstner, the former CEO of IBM, executed a successful transformation of the company. In his biography *Elephants Can Dance*, he highlights how he achieved cooperation as follows: "Our greatest ally in shaking loose the past was IBM's eminent collapse. Rather than go with the usual impulse to put on a happy face, I decided to keep the crisis front and center. I didn't want to lose the sense of urgency."[40]

Building a Coalition

In order to convince people that change is needed, the change leader does not necessarily have to convince every person individually. In fact, people's opinions toward change are affected by opinion leaders, or those people who have a strong influence over the behaviors and attitudes of others.[41] Instead of trying to get everyone on board at the same time, it may be more useful to convince and prepare the opinion leaders. Once these individuals agree that change is needed and will be useful, they will become helpful allies in ensuring that the rest of the organization is ready for change.[42] For example, Paul Pressler, after becoming the CEO of Gap Inc. in 2002, initiated a culture change effort in the hope of creating a sense of identity among the company's many brands such as Banana Republic, Old Navy, and Gap. For this purpose, management segmented the employees into groups instead of trying to reach out to all employees at the same time. Gap Inc. started by training the 2,000 senior managers in Leadership Summits, who in turn were instrumental in ensuring the cooperation of the remaining 150,000 employees of the company.[43]

Provide Support

Employees should feel that their needs are not ignored. Therefore, management may prepare employees for change by providing emotional and instrumental support. Emotional support may be in the form of frequently discussing the changes, encouraging employees to voice their concerns, and simply expressing confidence in employees' ability to perform effectively under the new system. Instrumental support may be in the form of providing a training program to employees so they know how to function under the new system.

Allow Employees to Participate

Studies show that employees who participate in planning change efforts tend to have more positive opinions about the change. Why? They will have the opportunity to voice their concerns. They can shape the change effort so that their concerns are addressed. They will be more knowledgeable about the reasons for change, alternatives to the proposed changes, and why the chosen alternative was better than the others. Finally, they will feel a sense of ownership of the planned change and are more likely to be on board.[44] Participation may be more useful if it starts at earlier stages, preferably while the problem is still being diagnosed. For example, assume that a company suspects there are problems with manufacturing quality. One way of convincing employees that there is a problem that needs to be solved would be to ask them to take customer calls about the product quality. Once employees experience the problem firsthand, they will be more motivated to solve the problem.

Executing Change

The second stage of Lewin's three-step change model is executing change. At this stage, the organization implements the planned changes on technology, structure, culture, or procedures. The specifics of how change should be executed will depend on the type of change. However, there are some tips that may facilitate the success of a change effort.

Continue to Provide Support

As the change is underway, employees may experience high amounts of stress. They may make mistakes more often or experience uncertainty about their new responsibilities or job descriptions. Management has an important role in helping employees cope with this stress by displaying support, patience, and continuing to provide support to employees even after the change is complete.

Create Small Wins

During a change effort, if the organization can create a history of small wins, change acceptance will be more likely.[45] If the change is large in scope and the payoff is a long time away, employees may not realize change is occurring during the transformation period. On the other hand, if people see changes, improvements, and successes along the way, they will be inspired and motivated to continue the change effort. For this reason, breaking up the proposed change into phases may be a good idea, because it creates smaller targets. Small wins are also important for planners of change to make the point that their idea is on the right track. Early success gives change planners more credibility, while early failures may be a setback.[46]

Eliminate Obstacles

When the change effort is in place, many obstacles may crop up along the way. There may be key people who publicly support the change effort while silently undermining the planned changes. There may be obstacles rooted in a company's structure, existing processes, or culture. It is the management's job to identify, understand, and remove these obstacles.[47] Ideally, these obstacles would have been eliminated before implementing the change, but sometimes unexpected roadblocks emerge as change is underway.

Kotter's Eight-stage Process for Change

Harvard Business School professor John P. Kotter proposed that companies should follow eight stages when instituting change. Here is a summary of his suggested steps.

1. Create a sense of urgency when introducing the change effort.
2. Build a coalition.
3. Create a vision for change and make change a part of the vision.
4. Communicate a plan for change
5. Eliminate obstacles to change

6. Create small wins
7. Build on change
8. Make change a part of culture.

Source: Kotter, J. P. (1996). Leading change. Boston, MA: Harvard Business. School Press.

Refreezing

After the change is implemented, the long-term success of a change effort depends on whether change becomes part of the company's culture. In other words, the revised ways of thinking, behaving, and performing should become routine. For this reason, there are a number of things management can do.

Publicize Success

In order to make change permanent, the organization may benefit from sharing the results of the change effort with employees. What was gained from the implemented changes? How much money did the company save? How much did the company's reputation improve? What was the reduction in accidents after new procedures were put in place? Sharing concrete results with employees increases their confidence that the implemented change was a right decision.

Build on Prior Change

Once results start coming, it is important to benefit from the momentum created by these early successes by pushing for even more change. Following the philosophy of continuous improvement may be a good idea here. Instead of declaring victory early, the company is advised to make continuous improvements to how business is conducted.

Reward Change Adoption

In order to ensure that change becomes permanent, organizations may benefit from rewarding those who embrace the change effort. The rewards do not necessarily have to be financial. The simple act of recognizing those who are giving support to the change effort in front of their peers may encourage others to get on board. When the new behaviors employees are expected to demonstrate (such as using a new computer program, filling out a new form, or simply greeting customers once they enter the store) are made part of an organization's reward system, those behaviors are more likely to be taken seriously and repeated, making the change effort successful.[48]

Make Change a Part of Organizational Culture

If the change effort has been successful, change will have become a part of corporate culture. In other words, in addition to the changes in procedures, processes, or technology, the mindset of people will also have changed. If change occurs only in superficial elements, it would be misleading to declare change a success. For example, if a company institutes a wellness program emphasizing healthy habits, rewarding employees for adopting healthy choices and providing resources to maximize health, this change effort would be deemed a true success if valuing employee health and well-being also becomes a part of the organization's culture. Creating a Web site, and printing booklets and distributing them are all tools leading to this goal, but achieving the true goal also necessitates a change in ingrained assumptions of management and employees putting work before employee health and well-being.

OB Toolbox: Overcome Resistance to Your Proposals

You feel that change is needed. You have a great idea. But people around you do not seem convinced. They are resisting your great idea. How do you make change happen?

- *Listen to naysayers.* You may think that your idea is great, but listening to those who resist may give you valuable ideas about why it may not work and how to design it more effectively.
- *Is your change revolutionary?* If you are trying to dramatically change the way things are done, you will find that resistance is greater. If your proposal involves incrementally making things better, you may have better luck.
- *Involve those around you in planning the change.* Instead of providing the solutions, make them part of the solution. If they admit that there is a problem and participate in planning a way out, you would have to do less convincing when it is time to implement the change.

- *Do you have credibility?* When trying to persuade people to change their ways, it helps if you have a history of suggesting implementable changes. Otherwise, you may be ignored or met with suspicion. This means you need to establish trust and a history of keeping promises over time before you propose a major change.
- *Present data to your audience.* Be prepared to defend the technical aspects of your ideas and provide evidence that your proposal is likely to work.
- *Appeal to your audience's ideals.* Frame your proposal around the big picture. Are you going to create happier clients? Is this going to lead to a better reputation for the company? Identify the long-term goals you are hoping to accomplish that people would be proud to be a part of.
- *Understand the reasons for resistance.* Is your audience resisting because they fear change? Does the change you propose mean more work for them? Does it impact them in a negative way? Understanding the consequences of your proposal for the parties involved may help you tailor your pitch to your audience.

Sources: McGoon, C. (1995, March). Secrets of building influence. Communication World, 12(3), 16; Michelman, P. (2007, July). Overcoming resistance to change. Harvard Management Update, 12(7), 3–4; Stanley, T. L. (2002, January). Change: A common-sense approach. Supervision, 63(1), 7–10.

KEY TAKEAWAY

Organizations change in response to changes in the environment and in response to the way decision makers interpret these changes. When it comes to organizational change, one of the biggest obstacles is resistance to change. People resist change because change disrupts habits, conflicts with certain personality types, causes a fear of failure, can have potentially negative impacts, can result in a potential for loss of power, and, when done too frequently, can exhaust employees. Change effort can be conceptualized as a three-step process in which employees are first prepared for change, then change is implemented, and finally, the new behavioral patterns become permanent.

EXERCISES

1. Can you think of an organizational or personal change that you had to go through? Have you encountered any resistance to this change? What were the reasons?
2. How would you deal with employees who are resisting change because their habits are threatened? How would you deal with them if they are resisting because of a fear of failure?
3. What are the benefits of employee participation in change management?
4. Imagine that you are introducing a new system to college students in which they would have to use a special ID number the university creates for them for activities such as logging onto campus computers or using library resources. How would you plan and implement the change? Explain using Lewin's three-step framework.
5. Why are successful companies less likely to change? What should companies do in order to make organizational change part of their culture?

3. THE ROLE OF ETHICS AND NATIONAL CULTURE

LEARNING OBJECTIVES

1. **Consider the role of organizational structure and change in ethical behavior.**
2. **Consider the role of national culture for organizational structure and change.**

3.1 Organizational Structure, Change, and Ethics

Is there a relationship between how a company is structured and the degree of ethical behavior displayed within an organization? Research indicates that such a link exists. Specifically, when corporate culture is too rigid and hierarchical, employees have fewer opportunities to develop their moral intelligence. Understanding what is ethical or not requires employees to be regularly confronted with ethical dilemmas. When employees do not have any autonomy to make decisions, and when such decisions are usually referred to a higher level, they do not find the opportunity to experience moral development, which may have implications for the degree of ethical behaviors demonstrated by employees.[49]

Organizational change is a time when managers are expected to behave ethically, because many moral dilemmas are likely to emerge when an organization is faced with change. One of the common issues occurs when organizational change takes the form of downsizing or rightsizing. Many organizations realize the human impact of downsizing on employees and prefer to deal with the rising cost of human resources in other ways. Retraining employees in different areas, early retirement programs, hiring freezes, and job sharing are all alternatives to downsizing. There are also ethical issues that arise when the decision to terminate some employees is made, such as whether employees are going to be given advance notice regarding the layoffs, if they will be allowed to return to their work stations and say good-bye to their colleagues, or if they will be escorted to the door by security. If the company takes precautions to soften the blow of layoffs, such downsizing is likely to be perceived as more ethical.

3.2 Organizational Structure and Change Around the Globe

ringi system

Involves proposals at lower levels being signed and passed along to higher level management in an effort to build consensus.

Organizations around the globe are not uniform in terms of organizational structure. In fact, there seem to be systematic differences in how companies are structured based on the country of origin. For example, one study compared Japanese, Swedish, and British organizations and found significant differences in the degree of centralization and formalization of these structures. Japanese organizations were much more centralized, as evidenced by a decision making system named ringi. The **ringi system** involves proposals at lower levels being signed and passed along to higher level management in an effort to build consensus.[50] In another study, organizations in the United States and Australia were found to be characterized by higher levels of decentralization, whereas organizations in Singapore and Hong Kong emphasized group-centered decision making and higher levels of centralization. These differences can be traced to the degree of individualism inherent in the national culture. Individualistic cultures attach greater importance to autonomy and personal freedom. Therefore, in these cultures, structures giving responsibility to lower level employees will be more common.[51]

How change is instituted depends at least partly on national culture. Cultures differ in the degree to which they are open to change. Cultures that are uncertainty avoidant (such as Germany and France) are relatively uncomfortable with change and prefer structured situations that reduce ambiguity, whereas cultures low in uncertainty avoidance (such as the United States and China) are more comfortable with change.

Additionally, the way in which change is introduced to an organization is likely to differ across cultures. Research shows that in the United States, change agents are more likely to use inspirational appeals and rational persuasion (such as "This change will ensure that we will remain competitive in the marketplace."). On the other hand, in China a more effective influence strategy seems to be asking for the help of a higher level person to ensure the success of the change process. The change agent may visit the higher status individual outside the work environment (such as going to the person's home to discuss the issue), and then the cooperation of this person becomes instrumental in achieving change.[52]

KEY TAKEAWAY

Structure has implications for the degree of ethical behaviors that may be found in an organization. Moreover, organizational change involves events during which a company's ethics may be put to test. National culture is one reason companies are structured in a certain way, and individualistic societies may have a greater frequency of organizations that are decentralized. National culture affects the extent to which organizations are open to change and how change is executed within an organization.

EXERCISES

1. What is an ethical way of conducting layoffs?
2. Do you believe that it is an organization's ethical obligation to share all information about the planned changes with employees? Why or why not?
3. What is the relationship between organizational change and national culture?

4. CONCLUSION

Organizations can function within a number of different structures, each possessing distinct advantages and disadvantages. Although any structure that is not properly managed will be plagued with issues, some organizational models are better equipped for particular environments and tasks. A change in the environment often requires change within the organization operating within that environment.

Change in almost any aspect of a company's operations can be met with resistance, and different cultures can have different reactions to both the change and the means to promote the change. In order to better facilitate necessary changes, several steps can be taken that have been proven to lower the anxiety of employees and ease the transformation process. Often, the simple act of including employees in the change process can drastically reduce opposition to new methods. In some organizations this level of inclusion is not possible, and instead organizations can recruit a small number of opinion leaders to promote the benefits of coming changes.

Some types of change, such as mergers, often come with job losses. In these situations, it is important to remain fair and ethical while laying off employees. Once change has occurred, it is vital to take any steps necessary to reinforce the new system. Employees can often require continued support well after an organizational change.

5. EXERCISES

ETHICAL DILEMMA

Imagine that you are a manager at a consumer products company. Your company is in negotiations for a merger. If and when the two companies merge, it seems probable that some jobs will be lost, but you have no idea how many or who will be gone. You have five subordinates. One is in the process of buying a house while undertaking a large debt. The second just received a relatively lucrative job offer and asked for your opinion as his mentor. You feel that knowing about the possibility of this merger is important to them in making these life choices. At the same time, you fear that once you let them know, everyone in the company will find out and the negotiations are not complete yet. You may end up losing some of your best employees, and the merger may not even happen. What do you do? Do you have an ethical obligation to share this piece of news with your employees? How would you handle a situation such as this?

INDIVIDUAL EXERCISE

Planning for a Change in Organizational Structure

Imagine that your company is switching to a matrix structure. Before, you were working in a functional structure. Now, every employee is going to report to a team leader as well as a department manager.

- Draw a hypothetical organizational chart for the previous and new structures.
- Create a list of things that need to be done before the change occurs.
- Create a list of things that need to be done after the change occurs.
- What are the sources of resistance you foresee for a change such as this? What is your plan of action to overcome this potential resistance?

GROUP EXERCISE

Organizational Change Role Play

Get your assigned role from your instructor.

Discussion Questions

1. Was the manager successful in securing the cooperation of the employee? Why or why not?
2. What could the manager have done differently to secure the employee's cooperation?
3. Why was the employee resisting change?

ENDNOTES

1. Ambrose, M. L., & Cropanzano, R. S. (2000). The effect of organizational structure on perceptions of procedural fairness. *Journal of Applied Psychology, 85*, 294–304; Miller, D., Droge, C., & Toulouse, J. (1988). Strategic process and content as mediators between organizational context and structure. *Academy of Management Journal, 31*, 544–569; Oldham, G. R., & Hackman, R. J. (1981). Relationships between organizational structure and employee reactions: Comparing alternative frameworks. *Administrative Science Quarterly, 26*, 66–83; Pierce, J. L., & Delbecq, A. L. (1977). Organization Structure, individual attitudes and innovation. *Academy of Management Review, 2*, 27–37; Schminke, M., Ambrose, M. L., & Cropanzano, R. S. (2000). The effect of organizational structure on perceptions of procedural fairness. *Journal of Applied Psychology, 85*, 294–304; Turban, D. B., & Keon, T. L. (1993). Organizational attractiveness: An interactionist perspective. *Journal of Applied Psychology, 78*, 184–193; Wally, S., & Baum, J. R. (1994). Personal and structural determinants of the pace of strategic decision making. *Academy of Management Journal, 37*, 932–956.

2. Nelson, G. L., & Pasternack, B. A. (2005). *Results: Keep what's good, fix what's wrong, and unlock great performance*. New York: Crown Business.

3. Brazil, J. J. (2007, April). Mission: Impossible? *Fast Company, 114*, 92–109.

4. Charan, R. (2006, April). Home Depot's blueprint for culture change. *Harvard Business Review, 84*(4), 60–70; Marquez, J. (2007, January 15). Big bucks at door for Depot HR leader. *Workforce Management, 86*(1).

5. Fredrickson, J. W. (1986). The strategic decision process and organizational structure. *Academy of Management Review, 11*, 280–297; Oldham, G. R., & Hackman, R. J. (1981). Relationships between organizational structure and employee reactions: Comparing alternative frameworks. *Administrative Science Quarterly, 26*, 66–83; Pierce, J. L., & Delbecq, A. L. (1977). Organization structure, individual attitudes and innovation. *Academy of Management Review, 2*, 27–37; Wally, S., & Baum, J. R. (1994). Strategic decision speed and firm performance. *Strategic Management Journal, 24*, 1107–1129.

6. Ghiselli, E. E., & Johnson, D. A. (1970). Need satisfaction, managerial success, and organizational structure. *Personnel Psychology, 23*, 569–576; Porter, L. W., & Siegel, J. (2006). Relationships of tall and flat organization structures to the satisfactions of foreign managers. *Personnel Psychology, 18*, 379–392.

7. Chonko, L. B. (1982). The relationship of span of control to sales representatives' experienced role conflict and role ambiguity. *Academy of Management Journal, 25*, 452–456.

8. Porter, L. W., & Lawler, E. E. (1964). The effects of tall versus flat organization structures on managerial job satisfaction. *Personnel Psychology, 17*, 135–148.

9. Hollenbeck, J. R., Moon, H., Ellis, A. P. J., West, B. J., & Ilgen, D. R (2002). Structural contingency theory and individual differences: Examination of external and internal person-team fit. *Journal of Applied Psychology, 87*, 599–606.

10. Burns, T., & Stalker, M. G. (1961). *The management of innovation*. London: Tavistock; Covin, J. G., & Slevin, D. P. (1988). The influence of organizational structure. *Journal of Management Studies, 25*, 217–234; Schollhammer, H. (1982). *Internal corporate entrepreneurship*. Englewood, NJ: Prentice Hall; Sherman, J. D., & Smith, H. L. (1984). The influence of organizational structure on intrinsic versus extrinsic motivation. *Academy of Management Journal, 27*, 877–885; Slevin, D. P., & Covin, J. G. (1990). Juggling entrepreneurial style and organizational structure—how to get your act together. *Sloan Management Review, 31*(2), 43–53.

11. Sine, W. D., Mitsuhashi, H., & Kirsch, D. A. (2006). Revisiting Burns and Stalker: Formal structure and new venture performance in emerging economic sectors. *Academy of Management Journal, 49*, 121–132.

12. Burns, T., & Stalker, M. G. (1961). *The management of innovation*. London: Tavistock; Covin, J. G., & Slevin, D. P. (1988). The influence of organizational structure. *Journal of Management Studies, 25*, 217–234.

13. Adair, J. (2007). *Leadership for innovation: How to organize team creativity and harvest ideas*. London: Kogan Page.

14. Joyce, W. F. (1986). Matrix organization: A social experiment. *Academy of Management Journal, 29*, 536–561.

15. Ford, R. C., & Randolph, W. A. (1992). Cross-functional structures: A review and integration of matrix organization and project management. *Journal of Management, 18*, 267–294.

16. Anand, N., & Daft, R. L. (2007). What is the right organization design? *Organizational Dynamics, 36*(4), 329–344.

17. Dess, G. G., Rasheed, A. M. A., McLaughlin, K. J., & Priem, R. L. (1995). The new corporate architecture. *Academy of Management Executive, 9*(3), 7–18; Rosenbloom, B. (2003). Multi-channel marketing and the retail value chain. *Thexis, 3*, 23–26.

18. Deutschman, A. (2005, March). Building a better skunk works. *Fast Company, 92*, 68–73.

19. Garvin, D. A. (1993, July–August). Building a learning organization. *Harvard Business Review, 71*(4), 78–91.

20. Lerman, R. I., & Schmidt, S. R. (2006). Trends and challenges for work in the 21st century. Retrieved September 10, 2008, from U.S. Department of Labor Web site: http://www.dol.gov/oasam/programs/history/herman/reports/futurework/conference/trends/trendsI.htm.

21. Moore's Law. Retrieved September 5, 2008, from Answers.com Web site: http://www.answers.com/topic/moore-s-law.

22. Lasica, J. D. (2005). *Darknet: Hollywood's war against the digital generation*. Hoboken, NJ: Wiley.

23. Get ready. United States Small Business Association. Retrieved November 21, 2008, from http://www.sba.gov/smallbusinessplanner/plan/getready/SERV_SBPLANNER_ISENTFORU.html.

24. Barnett, W. P., & Carroll, G. R. (1995). Modeling internal organizational change. *Annual Review of Sociology, 21*, 217–236; Boeker, W. (1997). Strategic change: The influence of managerial characteristics and organizational growth. *Academy of Management Journal, 40*, 152–170; Deutschman, A. (2005, March). Building a better skunk works. *Fast Company, 92*, 68–73.

25. Change management: The HR strategic imperative as a business partner. (2007, December). *HR Magazine, 52*(12); Huy, Q. N. (1999). Emotional capability, emotional intelligence, and radical change. *Academy of Management Review, 24*, 325–345.

26. Fugate, M., Kinicki, A. J., & Prussia, G. E. (2008). Employee coping with organizational change: An examination of alternative theoretical perspectives and models. *Personnel Psychology, 61*, 1–36.

27. Diamond, J. (2005). *Guns, germs and steel: The fates of human societies*. New York: W. W. Norton.

28. Judge, T. A., Thoresen, C. J., Pucik, V., & Welbourne, T. M. (1999). Managerial coping with organizational change. *Journal of Applied Psychology, 84*, 107–122; Wanberg, C. R., & Banas, J. T. (2000). Predictors and outcomes of openness to changes in a reorganizing workplace. *Journal of Applied Psychology, 85*, 132–142.

29. Ashford, S. J., Lee, C. L., & Bobko, P. (1989). Content, causes, and consequences of job insecurity: A theory-based measure and substantive test. *Academy of Management Journal, 32*, 803–829; Fugate, M., Kinicki, A. J., & Prussia, G. E. (2008). Employee coping with organizational change: An examination of alternative theoretical perspectives and models. *Personnel Psychology, 61*, 1–36.

30. Herold D. M., Fedor D. B., & Caldwell, S. (2007). Beyond change management: A multilevel investigation of contextual and personal influences on employees' commitment to change. *Journal of Applied Psychology, 92*, 942–951.

31. Fedor, D. M., Caldwell, S., & Herold, D. M. (2006). The effects of organizational changes on employee commitment: A multilevel investigation. *Personnel Psychology, 59*, 1–29.

32. Labianca, G., Gray, B., & Brass D. J. (2000). A grounded model of organizational schema change during empowerment. *Organization Science, 11*, 235–257; Rafferty, A. E., & Griffin, M. A. (2006). Perceptions of organizational change: A stress and coping perspective. *Journal of Applied Psychology, 91*, 1154–1162.

33. Ford, J. D., Ford, L. W., & D'Amelio, A. (2008). Resistance to change: The rest of the story. *Academy of Management Review, 33*, 362–377.

34. Lewin K. (1951). *Field theory in social science*. New York: Harper & Row.

35. Kotter, J. P. (1996). *Leading change*. Boston, MA: Harvard Business School Press.

36. Herold D. M., Fedor D. B., Caldwell, S., & Liu, Y. (2008). The effects of transformational and change leadership on employees' commitment to a change: A multilevel study. *Journal of Applied Psychology, 93*, 346–357.

37. Stewart, T. A., & Raman, A. P. (2007, July–August). Lessons from Toyota's long drive. *Harvard Business Review, 85*(7/8), 74–83.

38. Wanberg, C. R., & Banas, J. T. (2000). Predictors and outcomes of openness to changes in a reorganizing workplace. *Journal of Applied Psychology, 85*, 132–142.

39. Armenakis, A. A., Harris, S. G., & Mossholder, K. W. (1993). Creating readiness for organizational change. *Human Relations, 46*, 681–703.

40. Gerstner, L. V. (2002). *Who says elephants can't dance? Inside IBM's historic turnaround*. New York: Harper-Collins; Kotter, J. P. (1996). *Leading change*. Boston: Harvard Business School Press.

41. Burkhardt, M. E. (1994). Social interaction effects following a technological change: A longitudinal investigation. *Academy of Management Journal, 37*, 869–898; Kotter, J. P. (1995, March-April). Leading change: Why transformations fail. *Harvard Business Review, 73*(2), 59–67.

42. Armenakis, A. A., Harris, S. G., & Mossholder, K. W. (1993). Creating readiness for organizational change. *Human Relations, 46*, 681–703.

43. Nash, J. A. (2005, November–December). Comprehensive campaign helps Gap employees embrace cultural change. *Communication World, 22*(6).

44. Wanberg, C. R., & Banas, J. T. (2000). Predictors and outcomes of openness to changes in a reorganizing workplace. *Journal of Applied Psychology, 85*, 132–142.

45. Kotter, J. P. (1996). *Leading change*. Boston, MA: Harvard Business School Press; Reay, T., Golden-Biddle, K., & Germann, K. (2006). Legitimizing a new role: Small wins and microprocesses of change. *Academy of Management Journal, 49*, 977–998.

46. Hamel, G. (2000, July–August). Waking up IBM. *Harvard Business Review, 78*(4), 137–146.

47. Kotter, J. P. (1995, March–April). Leading change: Why transformations fail. *Harvard Business Review, 73*(2), 59–67.

48. Gale, S. F. (2003). Incentives and the art of changing behavior. *Workforce Management, 82*(11), 48–54.

49. White, R. D. (1999). Organizational design and ethics: The effects of rigid hierarchy on moral reasoning. *International Journal of Organization Theory & Behavior, 2*, 431–457.

50. Lincoln, J. R., Hanada, M., & McBride, K. (1986). Organizational structures in Japanese and U.S. manufacturing. *Administrative Science Quarterly, 31*, 338–364.

51. Harrison, G. L., McKinnon, J. L., Panchapakesan, S., & Leung, M. (1994). The influence of culture on organizational design and planning and control in Australia and the United States compared with Singapore and Hong Kong. *Journal of International Financial Management & Accounting, 5*, 242–261.

52. Yukl, G., Fu, P. P., & McDonald, R. (2003). Cross-cultural differences in perceived effectiveness of influence tactics for initiating or resisting change. *Journal of Applied Psychology, 52*, 68–82.

CHAPTER 15

Organizational Culture

LEARNING OBJECTIVES

After reading this chapter, you should be able to do the following:

1. Describe organizational culture and why it is important for an organization.
2. Understand the dimensions that make up a company's culture.
3. Distinguish between weak and strong cultures.
4. Understand factors that create culture.
5. Understand how to change culture.
6. Understand how organizational culture and ethics relate.
7. Understand cross-cultural differences in organizational culture.

Customer Service Culture: The Case of Nordstrom

Nordstrom's unique customer service culture distinguishes it from its competitors.

Source: http://commons.wikimedia.org/wiki/image: nordstrom.jpg.

Nordstrom Inc. is a Seattle-based department store rivaling the likes of Saks Fifth Avenue, Neiman Marcus, and Bloomingdale's. Nordstrom is a Hall of Fame member of *Fortune Magazine*'s "100 Best Companies to Work for" list, including being ranked 34th in 2008. Nordstrom is known for its quality apparel, upscale environment, and generous employee rewards. However, what Nordstrom is most famous for is its delivery of customer service above and beyond the norms of the retail industry. Stories about Nordstrom service abound. For example, according to one story the company confirms, in 1975 Nordstrom moved into a new location that had formerly been a tire store. A customer brought a set of tires into the store to return them. Without a word about the mix-up, the tires were accepted and the customer was fully refunded the purchase price. In a different story, a customer tried on several pairs of shoes but failed to find the right combination of size and color. As she was about to leave, the clerk called other Nordstrom stores, but could only locate the right pair at Macy's, a nearby competitor. The clerk had Macy's ship the shoes to the customer's home at Nordstrom's expense. In a third story, a customer describes wandering into a Portland, Oregon Nordstrom looking for an Armani tuxedo for his daughter's wedding. The sales associate took his measurements just in case one was found. The next day, the customer got a phone call, informing him that the tux was available. When pressed, she revealed that using her connections she found one in New York, had it put on a truck destined to Chicago, and dispatched someone to meet the truck in Chicago at a rest stop. The next day she shipped the tux to the customer's address, and the customer found that the tux had already been altered for his measurements and was ready to wear. What is even more impressive about this story is that Nordstrom does not sell Armani tuxedos.

How does Nordstrom persist in creating these stories? If you guessed that they have a large number of rules and regulations designed to emphasize quality in customer service, you'd be wrong. In fact, the company gives employees a 5½-inch by 7½-inch card as the employee handbook. On one side of the card, the company welcomes employees to Nordstrom, states that their number one goal is to provide outstanding customer service, and for this they have only one rule. On the other side of the card, the single rule is stated: "Use good judgment in all situations." By leaving it in the hands of Nordstrom associates, the company seems to have managed to empower employees who deliver customer service heroics every day.

Sources: Adapted from information in Chatman, J. A., & Eunyoung Cha, S. (2003). Leading by leveraging culture. California Management Review, 45, 19–34; McCarthy, P. D., & Spector, R. (2005). The Nordstrom way to customer service excellence: A handbook for implementing great service in your organization. Hoboken, NJ: John Wiley; Pfeffer, J. (2005). Producing sustainable competitive advantage through the effective management of people. Academy of Management Executive, 19, 95–106.

Just like individuals, you can think of organizations as having their own personalities, more typically known as organizational cultures. The opening case illustrates that Nordstrom is a retailer with the foremost value of making customers happy. At Nordstrom, when a customer is unhappy, employees are expected to identify what would make the person satisfied, and then act on it, without necessarily checking with a superior or consulting a lengthy policy book. If they do not, they receive peer pressure and may be made to feel that they let the company down. In other words, this organization seems to have successfully created a service culture. Understanding how culture is created, communicated, and changed will help you be more effective in your organizational life. But first, let's define organizational culture.

1. UNDERSTANDING ORGANIZATIONAL CULTURE

LEARNING OBJECTIVES

1. **Define organizational culture.**
2. **Understand why organizational culture is important.**
3. **Understand the different levels of organizational culture.**

1.1 What Is Organizational Culture?

organizational culture

A system of shared assumptions, values, and beliefs showing people what is appropriate and inappropriate behavior.

Organizational culture refers to a system of shared assumptions, values, and beliefs that show employees what is appropriate and inappropriate behavior.[1] These values have a strong influence on employee behavior as well as organizational performance. In fact, the term *organizational culture* was made popular in the 1980s when Peters and Waterman's best-selling book *In Search of Excellence* made the argument that company success could be attributed to an organizational culture that was decisive, customer oriented, empowering, and people oriented. Since then, organizational culture has become the subject of numerous research studies, books, and articles. However, organizational culture is still a relatively new concept. In contrast to a topic such as leadership, which has a history spanning several centuries, organizational culture is a young but fast-growing area within organizational behavior.

Culture is by and large invisible to individuals. Even though it affects all employee behaviors, thinking, and behavioral patterns, individuals tend to become more aware of their organization's culture when they have the opportunity to compare it to other organizations. If you have worked in multiple organizations, you can attest to this. Maybe the first organization you worked was a place where employees dressed formally. It was completely inappropriate to question your boss in a meeting; such behaviors would only be acceptable in private. It was important to check your e-mail at night as well as during weekends or else you would face questions on Monday about where you were and whether you were sick. Contrast this company to a second organization where employees dress more casually. You are encouraged to raise issues and question your boss or peers, even in front of clients. What is more important is not to maintain impressions but to arrive at the best solution to any problem. It is widely known that family life is very important, so it is acceptable to leave work a bit early to go to a family event. Additionally, you are not expected to do work at night or over the weekends unless there is a deadline. These two hypothetical organizations illustrate that organizations have different cultures, and culture dictates what is right and what is acceptable behavior as well as what is wrong and unacceptable.

1.2 Why Does Organizational Culture Matter?

An organization's culture may be one of its strongest assets, as well as its biggest liability. In fact, it has been argued that organizations that have a rare and hard-to-imitate organizational culture benefit from it as a competitive advantage.[2] In a survey conducted by the management consulting firm Bain & Company in 2007, worldwide business leaders identified corporate culture as important as corporate strategy for business success.[3] This comes as no surprise to many leaders of successful businesses, who are quick to attribute their company's success to their organization's culture.

Culture, or shared values within the organization, may be related to increased performance. Researchers found a relationship between organizational cultures and company performance, with respect to success indicators such as revenues, sales volume, market share, and stock prices.[4] At the same time, it is important to have a culture that fits with the demands of the company's environment. To the extent shared values are proper for the company in question, company performance may benefit from culture.[5] For example, if a company is in the high-tech industry, having a culture that encourages innovativeness and adaptability will support its performance. However, if a company in the same industry has a culture characterized by stability, a high respect for tradition, and a strong preference for upholding rules and procedures, the company may suffer as a result of its culture. In other words, just as having the "right" culture may be a competitive advantage for an organization, having the "wrong" culture may lead to performance difficulties, may be responsible for organizational failure, and may act as a barrier preventing the company from changing and taking risks.

In addition to having implications for organizational performance, *organizational culture is an effective control mechanism for dictating employee behavior.* Culture is in fact a more powerful way of controlling and managing employee behaviors than organizational rules and regulations. When problems are unique, rules tend to be less helpful. Instead, creating a culture of customer service achieves the same result by encouraging employees to think like customers, knowing that the company priorities in this case are clear: Keeping the customer happy is preferable to other concerns such as saving the cost of a refund.

FIGURE 15.2

"I don't know how it started, either. All I know is that it's part of our corporate culture."

1.3 Levels of Organizational Culture

Organizational culture consists of some aspects that are relatively more visible, as well as aspects that may lie below one's conscious awareness. Organizational culture can be thought of as consisting of three interrelated levels.[6]

FIGURE 15.3

Organizational culture consists of three levels.

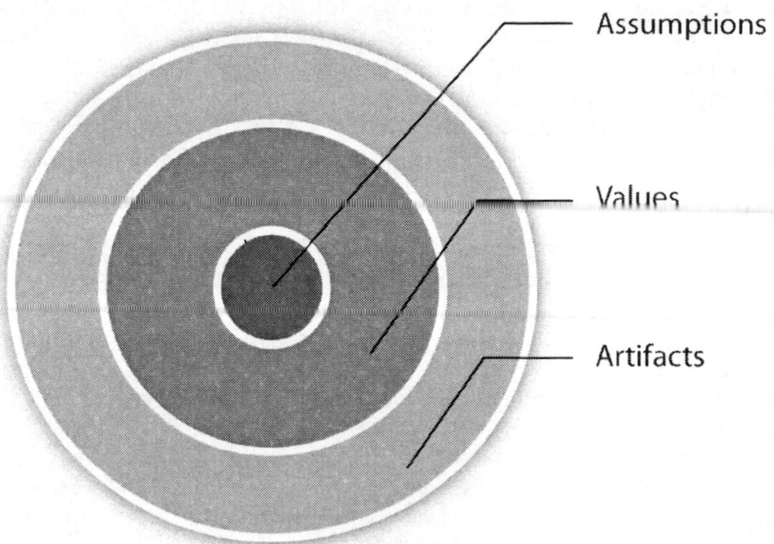

Source: Adapted from Schein, E. H. (1992). Organizational culture and leadership. San Francisco: Jossey-Bass.

assumptions

Taken for granted beliefs about human nature and reality.

values

Shared principles, standards, and goals.

artifacts

The visible and tangible elements of culture.

At the deepest level, below our awareness lie basic **assumptions**. Assumptions are taken for granted, and they reflect beliefs about human nature and reality. At the second level, **values** exist. Values are shared principles, standards, and goals. Finally, at the surface we have **artifacts**, or visible, tangible aspects of organizational culture. For example, in an organization one of the basic assumptions employees and managers share might be that happy employees benefit their organizations. This assumption could translate into values such as social equality, high quality relationships, and having fun. The artifacts reflecting such values might be an executive "open door" policy, an office layout that includes open spaces and gathering areas equipped with pool tables, and frequent company picnics in the workplace. For example, Alcoa Inc. designed their headquarters to reflect the values of making people more visible and accessible, and to promote collaboration.[7] In other words, understanding the organization's culture may start from observing its artifacts: the physical environment, employee interactions, company policies, reward systems, and other observable characteristics. When you are interviewing for a position, observing the physical environment, how people dress, where they relax, and how they talk to others is definitely a good start to understanding the company's culture. However, simply looking at these tangible aspects is unlikely to give a full picture of the organization. An important chunk of what makes up culture exists below one's degree of awareness. The values and, at a deeper level, the assumptions that shape the organization's culture can be uncovered by observing how employees interact and the choices they make, as well as by inquiring about their beliefs and perceptions regarding what is right and appropriate behavior.

KEY TAKEAWAY

Organizational culture is a system of shared assumptions, values, and beliefs that help individuals within an organization understand which behaviors are and are not appropriate within an organization. Cultures can be a source of competitive advantage for organizations. Strong organizational cultures can be an organizing as well as a controlling mechanism for organizations. And finally, organizational culture consists of three levels: assumptions, which are below the surface, values, and artifacts.

EXERCISES

1. Why do companies need culture?
2. Give an example of an aspect of company culture that is a strength and one that is a weakness.
3. In what ways does culture serve as a controlling mechanism?
4. If assumptions are below the surface, why do they matter?
5. Share examples of artifacts you have noticed at different organizations.

2. CHARACTERISTICS OF ORGANIZATIONAL CULTURE

LEARNING OBJECTIVES

1. Understand different dimensions of organizational culture.
2. Understand the role of culture strength.
3. Explore subcultures within organizations

2.1 Dimensions of Culture

Which values characterize an organization's culture? Even though culture may not be immediately observable, identifying a set of values that might be used to describe an organization's culture helps us identify, measure, and manage culture more effectively. For this purpose, several researchers have proposed various culture typologies. One typology that has received a lot of research attention is the *organizational culture profile* (OCP), in which culture is represented by seven distinct values.[8] We will describe the OCP as well as two additional dimensions of organizational culture that are not represented in that framework but are important dimensions to consider: service culture and safety culture.

FIGURE 15.4 Dimensions of Organizational Culture Profile (OCP)

Source: Adapted from information in O'Reilly, C. A., III, Chatman, J. A., & Caldwell, D. F. (1991). People and organizational culture: A profile comparison approach to assessing person-organization fit. Academy of Management Journal, 34, 487–516.

Innovative Cultures

innovative cultures

Cultures that are flexible, adaptable, and experiment with new ideas.

According to the OCP framework, companies that have **innovative cultures** are flexible and adaptable, and experiment with new ideas. These companies are characterized by a flat hierarchy in which titles and other status distinctions tend to be downplayed. For example, W. L. Gore & Associates Inc. is a company with innovative products such as GORE-TEX® (the breathable fabric that is windproof and waterproof), Glide dental floss, and Elixir guitar strings, earning the company the distinction of being elected as the most innovative company in the United States by *Fast Company* magazine in 2004. W. L. Gore consistently manages to innovate and capture the majority of market share in a wide variety of industries, in large part due to its unique culture. In this company, employees do not have bosses in the traditional sense, and risk taking is encouraged by celebrating failures as well as successes.[9] Companies such as W. L. Gore, Genentech Inc., and Google also encourage their employees to take risks by allowing engineers to devote 20% of their time to projects of their own choosing.[10]

Aggressive Cultures

FIGURE 15.5

Microsoft, the company that Bill Gates cofounded, has been described as having an aggressive culture.

Source: http://simple.wikipedia.org/wiki/Image:Bill_Gates_in_Poland_cropped.jpg.

aggressive cultures

Cultures that value competitiveness and outperforming competitors.

Companies with **aggressive cultures** value competitiveness and outperforming competitors: By emphasizing this, they may fall short in the area of corporate social responsibility. For example, Microsoft Corporation is often identified as a company with an aggressive culture. The company has faced a number of antitrust lawsuits and disputes with competitors over the years. In aggressive companies, people may use language such as "We will kill our competition." In the past, Microsoft executives often made statements such as "We are going to cut off Netscape's air supply....Everything they are selling, we are going to give away." Its aggressive culture is cited as a reason for getting into new legal troubles before old ones are resolved.[11] Recently, Microsoft founder Bill Gates established the Bill & Melinda Gates foundation and is planning to devote his time to reducing poverty around the world.[12] It will be interesting to see whether he will bring the same competitive approach to the world of philanthropy.

Outcome-Oriented Cultures

outcome-oriented cultures

Cultures that emphasize achievement, results, and action as important values.

The OCP framework describes **outcome-oriented cultures** as those that emphasize achievement, results, and action as important values. A good example of an outcome-oriented culture may be Best Buy Co. Inc. Having a culture emphasizing sales performance, Best Buy tallies revenues and other relevant figures daily by department. Employees are trained and mentored to sell company products effectively, and they learn how much money their department made every day.[13] In 2005, the company implemented a results oriented work environment (ROWE) program that allows employees to work anywhere and anytime; they are evaluated based on results and fulfillment of clearly outlined objectives.[14] Outcome-oriented cultures hold employees as well as managers accountable for success and utilize systems that reward employee and group output. In these companies, it is more common to see rewards tied to performance indicators as opposed to seniority or loyalty. Research indicates that organizations that have a performance-oriented culture tend to outperform companies that are lacking such a culture.[15] At the same time, some outcome-oriented companies may have such a high drive for outcomes and measurable performance objectives that they may suffer negative consequences. Companies overrewarding employee performance such as Enron Corporation and WorldCom experienced well-publicized business and ethical failures. When performance pressures lead to a culture where unethical behaviors become the norm, individuals see their peers as rivals and short-term results are rewarded; the resulting unhealthy work environment serves as a liability.[16]

Stable Cultures

stable cultures

Cultures that are predictable, rule oriented, and bureaucratic.

Stable cultures are predictable, rule-oriented, and bureaucratic. These organizations aim to coordinate and align individual effort for greatest levels of efficiency. When the environment is stable and certain, these cultures may help the organization be effective by providing stable and constant levels of output.[17] These cultures prevent quick action, and as a result may be a misfit to a changing and dynamic environment. Public sector institutions may be viewed as stable cultures. In the private sector, Kraft Foods Inc. is an example of a company with centralized decision making and rule orientation that suffered as a result of the culture-environment mismatch.[18] Its bureaucratic culture is blamed for killing good ideas in early stages and preventing the company from innovating. When the company started a change program to increase the agility of its culture, one of their first actions was to fight bureaucracy with more bureaucracy: They created the new position of VP of business process simplification, which was later eliminated.[19]

People-Oriented Cultures

People-oriented cultures value fairness, supportiveness, and respect for individual rights. These organizations truly live the mantra that "people are their greatest asset." In addition to having fair procedures and management styles, these companies create an atmosphere where work is fun and employees do not feel required to choose between work and other aspects of their lives. In these organizations, there is a greater emphasis on and expectation of treating people with respect and dignity.[20] One study of new employees in accounting companies found that employees, on average, stayed 14 months longer in companies with people-oriented cultures.[21] Starbucks Corporation is an example of a people-oriented culture. The company pays employees above minimum wage, offers health care and tuition reimbursement benefits to its part-time as well as full-time employees, and has creative perks such as weekly free coffee for all associates. As a result of these policies, the company benefits from a turnover rate lower than the industry average.[22] The company is routinely ranked as one of the best places to work by *Fortune* magazine.

people-oriented cultures

Cultures that value fairness, supportiveness, and respecting individual rights.

Team-Oriented Cultures

Companies with **team-oriented cultures** are collaborative and emphasize cooperation among employees. For example, Southwest Airlines Company facilitates a team-oriented culture by cross-training its employees so that they are capable of helping each other when needed. The company also places emphasis on training intact work teams.[23] Employees participate in twice daily meetings named "morning overview meetings" (MOM) and daily afternoon discussions (DAD) where they collaborate to understand sources of problems and determine future courses of action. In Southwest's selection system, applicants who are not viewed as team players are not hired as employees.[24] In team-oriented organizations, members tend to have more positive relationships with their coworkers and particularly with their managers.[25]

team-oriented cultures

Cultures that are collaborative and emphasize cooperation among employees.

Detail-Oriented Cultures

Organizations with **detail-oriented cultures** are characterized in the OCP framework as emphasizing precision and paying attention to details. Such a culture gives a competitive advantage to companies in the hospitality industry by helping them differentiate themselves from others. For example, Four Seasons Hotels Ltd. and the Ritz-Carlton Company LLC are among hotels who keep records of all customer requests, such as which newspaper the guest prefers or what type of pillow the customer uses. This information is put into a computer system and used to provide better service to returning customers. Any requests hotel employees receive, as well as overhear, might be entered into the database to serve customers better. Recent guests to Four Seasons Paris who were celebrating their 21st anniversary were greeted with a bouquet of 21 roses on their bed. Such clear attention to detail is an effective way of impressing customers and ensuring repeat visits. McDonald's Corporation is another company that specifies in detail how employees should perform their jobs by including photos of exactly how French fries and hamburgers should look when prepared properly.[26]

detail-oriented cultures

Cultures that emphasize precision and paying attention to details.

Service Culture

Service culture is not one of the dimensions of OCP, but given the importance of the retail industry in the overall economy, having a service culture can make or break an organization. Some of the organizations we have illustrated in this section, such as Nordstrom, Southwest Airlines, Ritz-Carlton, and Four Seasons are also famous for their service culture. In these organizations, employees are trained to serve the customer well, and cross-training is the norm. Employees are empowered to resolve customer problems in ways they see fit. Because employees with direct customer contact are in the best position to resolve any issues, employee empowerment is truly valued in these companies. For example, Umpqua Bank, operating in the northwestern United States, is known for its service culture. All employees are trained in all tasks to enable any employee to help customers when needed. Branch employees may come up with unique ways in which they serve customers better, such as opening their lobby for community events or keeping bowls full of water for customers' pets. The branches feature coffee for customers, Internet kiosks, and withdrawn funds are given on a tray along with a piece of chocolate. They also reward employee service performance through bonuses and incentives.[27]

service culture

A culture that emphasizes high quality service.

What differentiates companies with service culture from those without such a culture may be the desire to solve customer-related problems proactively. In other words, in these cultures employees are engaged in their jobs and personally invested in improving customer experience such that they identify issues and come up with solutions without necessarily being told what to do. For example, a British Airways baggage handler noticed that first-class passengers were waiting a long time for their baggage, whereas stand-by passengers often received their luggage first. Noticing this tendency, a baggage handler notified his superiors about this problem, along with the suggestion to load first-class passenger luggage last.[28] This solution was successful in cutting down the wait time by half. Such proactive behavior on the part of employees who share company values is likely to emerge frequently in companies with a service culture.

FIGURE 15.6

The growth in the number of passengers flying with Southwest Airlines from 1973 until 2007. In 2007, Southwest surpassed American Airlines as the most flown domestic airline. While price has played a role in this, their emphasis on service has been a key piece of their culture and competitive advantage.

Source: Adapted from http://upload.wikimedia.org/wikipedia/commons/6/69/Southwest-airlines-passengers.jpg.

Safety Culture

safety culture

A culture that emphasizes safety as a strong workplace norm.

Some jobs are safety sensitive. For example, logger, aircraft pilot, fishing worker, steel worker, and roofer are among the top ten most dangerous jobs in the United States.[29] In organizations where safety-sensitive jobs are performed, creating and maintaining a **safety culture** provides a competitive advantage, because the organization can reduce accidents, maintain high levels of morale and employee retention, and increase profitability by cutting workers' compensation insurance costs. Some companies suffer severe consequences when they are unable to develop such a culture. For example, British Petroleum experienced an explosion in their Texas City, Texas, refinery in 2005, which led to the death of 15 workers while injuring 170. In December 2007, the company announced that it had already depleted the $1.6-billion fund to be used in claims for this explosion.[30] A safety review panel concluded that the development of a safety culture was essential to avoid such occurrences in the future.[31] In companies that have a safety culture, there is a strong commitment to safety starting at management level and trickling down to lower levels. M. B. Herzog Electric Inc. of California, selected as one of America's safest companies by *Occupational Hazards* magazine in 2007, had a zero accident rate for the past 3 years. The company uses safety training programs tailored to specific jobs within the company, and all employees are encouraged to identify all safety hazards they come across when they are performing their jobs. They are also asked to play the role of an OSHA (Occupational Safety and Health Administration) inspector for a day to become more aware of the hidden dangers in the workplace. Managers play a key role in increasing the level of safe behaviors in the workplace, because they can motivate employees day-to-day to demonstrate safe behaviors and act as safety role models. A recent study has shown that in organizations with a safety culture, leaders encourage employees to demonstrate behaviors such as volunteering for safety committees, making recommendations to increase safety, protecting coworkers from hazards, whistleblowing, and in general trying to make their jobs safer.[32]

Strength of Culture

strong culture

A culture that is shared by organizational members.

A **strong culture** is one that is shared by organizational members.[33] In other words, if most employees in the organization show consensus regarding the values of the company, it is possible to talk about the existence of a strong culture. A culture's content is more likely to affect the way employees think and behave when the culture in question is strong. For example, cultural values emphasizing customer service will lead to higher quality customer service if there is widespread agreement among employees on the importance of customer service-related values.[34]

It is important to realize that a strong culture may act as an asset or liability for the organization, depending on the types of values that are shared. For example, imagine a company with a culture that is strongly outcome oriented. If this value system matches the organizational environment, the company outperforms its competitors. On the other hand, a strong outcome-oriented culture coupled with unethical behaviors and an obsession with quantitative performance indicators may be detrimental to an organization's effectiveness. An extreme example of this dysfunctional type of strong culture is Enron.

A strong culture may sometimes outperform a weak culture because of the consistency of expectations. In a strong culture, members know what is expected of them, and the culture serves as an effective control mechanism on member behaviors. Research shows that strong cultures lead to more stable corporate performance in stable environments. However, in volatile environments, the advantages of culture strength disappear.[35]

One limitation of a strong culture is the difficulty of changing a strong culture. If an organization with widely shared beliefs decides to adopt a different set of values, unlearning the old values and learning the new ones will be a challenge, because employees will need to adopt new ways of thinking, behaving, and responding to critical events. For example, the Home Depot Inc. had a decentralized, autonomous culture where many business decisions were made using "gut feeling" while ignoring the available data. When Robert Nardelli became CEO of the company in 2000, he decided to change its culture, starting with centralizing many of the decisions that were previously left to individual stores. This initiative met with substantial resistance, and many high-level employees left during his first year. Despite getting financial results such as doubling the sales of the company, many of the changes he made were criticized. He left the company in January 2007.[36]

A strong culture may also be a liability during a merger. During mergers and acquisitions, companies inevitably experience a clash of cultures, as well as a clash of structures and operating systems. Culture clash becomes more problematic if both parties have unique and strong cultures. For example, during the merger of Daimler AG with Chrysler Motors LLC to create DaimlerChrysler AG, the differing strong cultures of each company acted as a barrier to effective integration. Daimler had a strong engineering culture that was more hierarchical and emphasized routinely working long hours. Daimler employees were used to being part of an elite organization, evidenced by flying first class on all business trips. On the other hand, Chrysler had a sales culture where employees and managers were used to autonomy, working shorter hours, and adhering to budget limits that meant only the elite flew first class. The different ways of thinking and behaving in these two companies introduced a number of unanticipated problems during the integration process.[37] Differences in culture may be part of the reason that, in the end, the merger didn't work out

FIGURE 15.7

Walt Disney created a strong culture at his company, which has evolved since the company's founding in 1923.

Source: http://en.wikipedia.org/wiki/Image:Walt_disney_portrait.jpg.

2.2 Do Organizations Have a Single Culture?

So far, we have assumed that a company has a single culture that is shared throughout the organization. However, you may have realized that this is an oversimplification. In reality there might be multiple cultures within any given organization. For example, people working on the sales floor may experience a different culture from that experienced by people working in the warehouse. A culture that emerges within different departments, branches, or geographic locations is called a **subculture**. Subcultures may arise from the personal characteristics of employees and managers, as well as the different conditions under which work is performed. Within the same organization, marketing and manufacturing departments often have different cultures such that the marketing department may emphasize innovativeness, whereas the manufacturing department may have a shared emphasis on detail orientation. In an interesting study, researchers uncovered five different subcultures within a single police organization. These subcultures differed depending on the level of danger involved and the type of background experience the individuals held, including "crime-fighting street professionals" who did what their job required without rigidly following protocol and "anti-military social workers" who felt that most problems could be resolved by talking to the parties involved.[38] Research has shown that employee perceptions regarding subcultures were related to employee commitment to the organization.[39] Therefore, in addition to understanding the broader organization's values, managers will need to make an effort to understand subculture values to see its impact on workforce behavior and attitudes. Moreover, as an employee, you need to understand the type of subculture in the department where you will work in addition to understanding the company's overall culture.

subculture

A set of values unique to a limited cross-section of the organization.

Sometimes, a subculture may take the form of a **counterculture**. Defined as shared values and beliefs that are in direct opposition to the values of the broader organizational culture,[40] countercultures are often shaped around a charismatic leader. For example, within a largely bureaucratic organization, an enclave of innovativeness and risk taking may emerge within a single department. A counterculture may be tolerated by the organization as long as it is bringing in results and contributing positively to the effectiveness of the organization. However, its existence may be perceived as a threat to the broader

counterculture

Shared values and beliefs that are in direct opposition to the values of the broader organizational culture.

organizational culture. In some cases this may lead to actions that would take away the autonomy of the managers and eliminate the counterculture.

KEY TAKEAWAY

Culture can be understood in terms of seven different culture dimensions, depending on what is most emphasized within the organization. For example, innovative cultures are flexible and adaptable, and they experiment with new ideas, while stable cultures are predictable, rule-oriented, and bureaucratic. Strong cultures can be an asset or a liability for an organization but can be challenging to change. Organizations may have subcultures and countercultures, which can be challenging to manage.

EXERCISES

1. Think about an organization you are familiar with. Based on the dimensions of OCP, how would you characterize its culture?
2. Out of the culture dimensions described, which dimension do you think would lead to higher levels of employee satisfaction and retention? Which one would be related to company performance?
3. What are the pros and cons of an outcome-oriented culture?
4. When bureaucracies were first invented they were considered quite innovative. Do you think that different cultures are more or less effective at different points in time and in different industries? Why or why not?
5. Can you imagine an effective use of subcultures within an organization?

3. CREATING AND MAINTAINING ORGANIZATIONAL CULTURE

LEARNING OBJECTIVES

1. **Understand how cultures are created.**
2. **Learn how to maintain a culture.**
3. **Recognize organizational culture signs.**

3.1 How Are Cultures Created?

Where do cultures come from? Understanding this question is important so that you know how they can be changed. An organization's culture is shaped as the organization faces external and internal challenges and learns how to deal with them. When the organization's way of doing business provides a successful adaptation to environmental challenges and ensures success, those values are retained. These values and ways of doing business are taught to new members as *the* way to do business.[41]

FIGURE 15.8 Culture Creation and Maintenance

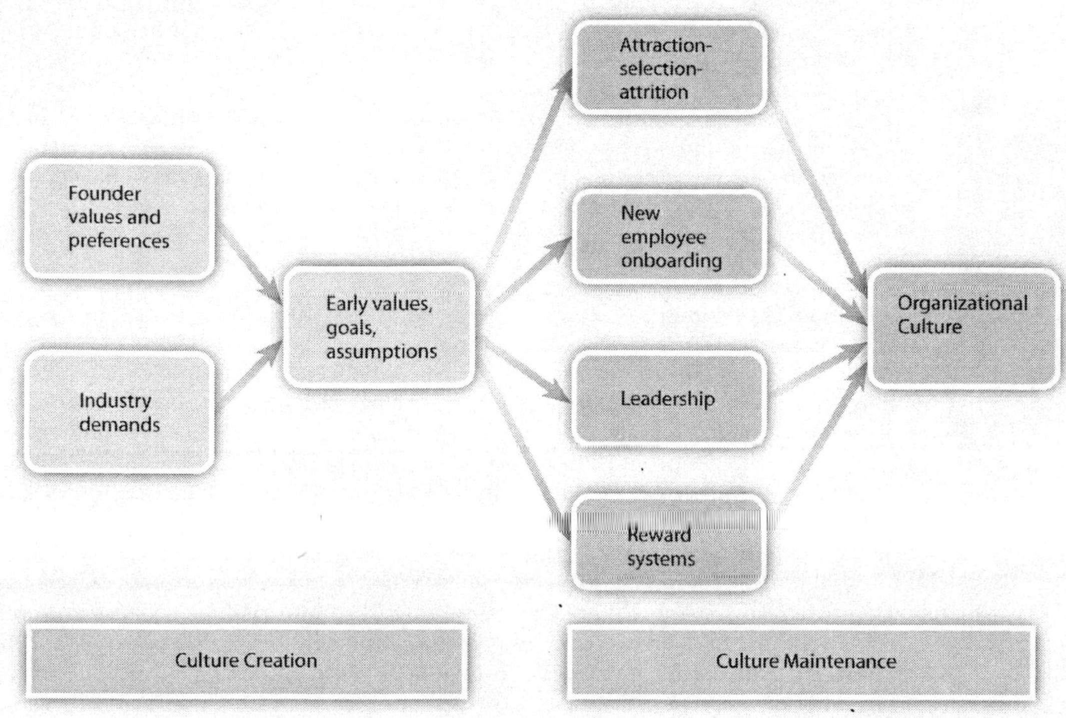

The factors that are most important in the creation of an organization's culture include founders' values, preferences, and industry demands.

Founder's Values

A company's culture, particularly during its early years, is inevitably tied to the personality, background, and values of its founder or founders, as well as their vision for the future of the organization. This explains one reason why culture is so hard to change: It is shaped in the early days of a company's history. When entrepreneurs establish their own businesses, the way they want to do business determines the organization's rules, the structure set-up in the company, and the people they hire to work with them. As a case in point, some of the existing corporate values of the ice cream company Ben & Jerry's Homemade Holdings Inc. can easily be traced to the personalities of its founders Ben Cohen and Jerry Greenfield. In 1978, the two ex-hippie high school friends opened up their first ice-cream shop in a renovated gas station in Burlington, Vermont. Their strong social convictions led them to buy only from the local farmers and devote a certain percentage of their profits to charities. The core values they instilled in their business can still be observed in the current company's devotion to social activism and sustainability, its continuous contributions to charities, use of environmentally friendly materials, and dedication to creating jobs in low-income areas. Even though the company was acquired by Unilever PLC in 2000, the social activism component remains unchanged and Unilever has expressed its commitment to maintaining it.[42] There are many other examples of founders' instilling their own strongly held beliefs or personalities to the businesses they found. For example, as mentioned earlier, Microsoft's aggressive nature is often traced back to Bill Gates and his competitiveness. According to one anecdote, his competitive nature even extends to his personal life such that one of his pastimes is to compete with his wife in solving identical jigsaw puzzles to see who can finish faster.[43] Similarly, Joseph Pratt, a history and management professor, notes, "There definitely is an Exxon way. This is John D. Rockefeller's company, this is Standard Oil of New Jersey, this is the one that is most closely shaped by Rockefeller's traditions. Their values are very clear. They are deeply embedded. They have roots in 100 years of corporate history."[44]

FIGURE 15.9

Ben & Jerry's has locations around the world, including this store in Singapore.

Source: http://commons.wikimedia.org/wiki/Image:BenJerry-UnitedSquare.jpg.

Founder values become part of the corporate culture to the degree they help the company be successful. For example, the social activism of Ben & Jerry's was instilled in the company because founders strongly believed in these issues. However, these values probably would not be surviving three decades later if they had not helped the company in its initial stages. In the case of Ben & Jerry's, these charitable values helped distinguish their brand from larger corporate brands and attracted a loyal customer base. Thus, by providing a competitive advantage, these values were retained as part of the corporate culture and were taught to new members as the right way to do business. Similarly, the early success of Microsoft may be attributed to its relatively aggressive corporate culture, which provided a source of competitive advantage.

Industry Demands

While founders undoubtedly exert a powerful influence over corporate cultures, the industry characteristics also play a role. Industry characteristics and demands act as a force to create similarities among organizational cultures. For example, despite some differences, many companies in the insurance and banking industries are stable and rule oriented, many companies in the high-tech industry have innovative cultures, and companies in the nonprofit industry tend to be people oriented. If the industry is one with a large number of regulatory requirements—for example, banking, health care, and nuclear power plant industries—then we might expect the presence of a large number of rules and regulations, a bureaucratic company structure, and a stable culture. Similarly, the high-tech industry requires agility, taking quick action, and low concern for rules and authority, which may create a relatively more innovative culture.[45] The industry influence over culture is also important to know, because this shows that it may not be possible to imitate the culture of a company in a different industry, even though it may seem admirable to outsiders.

3.2 How Are Cultures Maintained?

As a company matures, its cultural values are refined and strengthened. The early values of a company's culture exert influence over its future values. It is possible to think of organizational culture as an organism that protects itself from external forces. Organizational culture determines what types of people are hired by an organization and what types are left out. Moreover, once new employees are hired, the company assimilates new employees and teaches them the way things are done in the organization. We call these processes *attraction-selection-attrition* and *onboarding* processes. We will also examine the role of *leaders* and *reward systems* in shaping and maintaining an organization's culture. It is important to remember two points: The process of culture creation is in fact more complex and less clean than the name implies. Additionally, the influence of each factor on culture creation is reciprocal. For example, just as leaders may influence what type of values the company has, the culture may also determine what types of behaviors leaders demonstrate.

Attraction-Selection-Attrition (ASA)

Organizational culture is maintained through a process known as attraction-selection-attrition. First, employees are *attracted* to organizations where they will fit in. In other words, different job applicants will find different cultures to be attractive. Someone who has a competitive nature may feel comfortable and prefer to work in a company where interpersonal competition is the norm. Others may prefer to work in a team-oriented workplace. Research shows that employees with different personality traits find different cultures attractive. For example, out of the Big Five personality traits, employees who demonstrate neurotic personalities were less likely to be attracted to innovative cultures, whereas those who had openness to experience were more likely to be attracted to innovative cultures.[46] As a result, individuals will self-select the companies they work for and may stay away from companies that have core values that are radically different from their own.

Of course this process is imperfect, and value similarity is only one reason a candidate might be attracted to a company. There may be other, more powerful attractions such as good benefits. For example, candidates who are potential misfits may still be attracted to Google because of the cool perks associated with being a Google employee. At this point in the process, the second component of the ASA framework prevents them from getting in: *Selection*. Just as candidates are looking for places where they will fit in, companies are also looking for people who will fit into their current corporate culture. Many companies are hiring people for fit with their culture, as opposed to fit with a certain job. For example, Southwest Airlines prides itself for hiring employees based on personality and attitude rather than specific job-related skills, which are learned after being hired. This is important for job applicants to know, because in addition to highlighting your job-relevant skills, you will need to discuss why your personality and values match those of the company. Companies use different techniques to weed out candidates who do not fit with corporate values. For example, Google relies on multiple interviews with future peers. By introducing the candidate to several future coworkers and learning what these coworkers think of the candidate, it becomes easier to assess the level of fit. The Container Store Inc. ensures culture fit by hiring among their customers.[47] This way, they can make sure that job candidates are already interested in organizing their lives and understand the company's commitment to helping customers organize theirs. Companies may also use employee referrals in their recruitment process. By using their current employees as a source of future employees, companies may make sure that the newly hired employees go through a screening process to avoid potential person-culture mismatch.

Even after a company selects people for person-organization fit, there may be new employees who do not fit in. Some candidates may be skillful in impressing recruiters and signal high levels of culture fit even though they do not necessarily share the company's values. Moreover, recruiters may suffer from perceptual biases and hire some candidates thinking that they fit with the culture even though the actual fit is low. In any event, the organization is going to eventually eliminate candidates who do not fit in through *attrition*. Attrition refers to the natural process in which the candidates who do not fit in will leave the company. Research indicates that person-organization misfit is one of the important reasons for employee turnover.[48]

Click and Learn More

Texas Instruments Inc. includes a Workplace and Values Check on its Web page for potential applicants to see if they fit Texas Instrument's culture.

To view this Web site, go to http://focus.ti.com/careers/docs/fitchecktool.tsp?sectionId=152&tabId=1678

As a result of the ASA process, the company attracts, selects, and retains people who share its core values. On the other hand, those people who are different in core values will be excluded from the organization either during the hiring process or later on through naturally occurring turnover. Thus, organizational culture will act as a self-defending organism where intrusive elements are kept out. Supporting the existence of such self-protective mechanisms, research shows that organizations demonstrate a certain level of homogeneity regarding personalities and values of organizational members.[49]

New Employee Onboarding

Another way in which an organization's values, norms, and behavioral patterns are transmitted to employees is through **onboarding** (also referred to as the **organizational socialization** process). Onboarding refers to the process through which new employees learn the attitudes, knowledge, skills, and behaviors required to function effectively within an organization. If an organization can successfully socialize new employees into becoming organizational insiders, new employees feel confident regarding their ability to perform, sense that they will feel accepted by their peers, and understand and share the assumptions, norms, and values that are part of the organization's culture. This understanding and confidence in turn translate into more effective new employees who perform better and have higher job satisfaction, stronger organizational commitment, and longer tenure within the company.[50]

onboarding

The process through which new employees learn the attitudes, knowledge, skills, and behaviors required to function effectively within an organization.

There are many factors that play a role in the successful adjustment of new employees. New employees can engage in several activities to help increase their own chances of success at a new organization. Organizations also engage in different activities, such as implementing orientation programs or matching new employees with mentors, which may facilitate onboarding.

What Can Employees Do During Onboarding?

New employees who are proactive, seek feedback, and build strong relationships tend to be more successful than those who do not.[51] for example, *feedback seeking* helps new employees. Especially on a first job, a new employee can make mistakes or gaffes and may find it hard to understand and interpret the ambiguous reactions of coworkers. New hires may not know whether they are performing up to standards, whether it was a good idea to mention a company mistake in front of a client, or why other employees are asking if they were sick over the weekend because of not responding to work-related e-mails. By actively seeking feedback, new employees may find out sooner rather than later any behaviors that need to be changed and gain a better understanding of whether their behavior fits with the company culture and expectations. Several studies show the benefits of feedback seeking for new employee adjustment.

Relationship building, or *networking*, is another important behavior new employees may demonstrate. Particularly when a company does not have a systematic approach to onboarding, it becomes more important for new employees to facilitate their own onboarding by actively building relationships. According to one estimate, 35% of managers who start a new job fail in the new job and either voluntarily leave or are fired within 1.5 years. Of these, over 60% report not being able to form effective relationships with colleagues as the primary reason for their failure.[52] New employees may take an active role in building relations by seeking opportunities to have a conversation with their new colleagues, arranging lunches or coffee with them, participating in company functions, and making the effort to build a relationship with their new supervisor.[53]

OB Toolbox: You've Got a New Job! Now How Do You Get on Board?

- *Gather information.* Try to find as much about the company and the job as you can before your first day. After you start working, be a good observer, gather information, and read as much as you can to understand your job and the company. Examine how people are interacting, how they dress, and how they act to avoid behaviors that might indicate to others that you are a misfit.
- *Manage your first impression.* First impressions may endure, so make sure that you dress appropriately, are friendly, and communicate your excitement to be a part of the team. Be on your best behavior!
- *Invest in relationship development.* The relationships you develop with your manager and with coworkers will be essential for you to adjust to your new job. Take the time to strike up conversations with them. If there are work functions during your early days, make sure not to miss them!
- *Seek feedback.* Ask your manager or coworkers how well you are doing and whether you are meeting expectations. Listen to what they are telling you and also listen to what they are not saying. Then, make sure to act upon any suggestions for improvement. Be aware that after seeking feedback, you may create a negative impression if you consistently ignore the feedback you receive.
- *Show success early on.* In order to gain the trust of your new manager and colleagues, you may want to establish a history of success early. Volunteer for high-profile projects where you will be able to demonstrate your skills. Alternatively, volunteer for projects that may serve as learning opportunities or that may put you in touch with the key people in the company.

Sources: Adapted from ideas in Couzins, M., & Beagrie, S. (2005, March 1). How to…survive the first six months of a new job. Personnel Today, 27; Wahlgreen, E. (2002, December 5). Getting up to speed at a new job. Business Week Online. Retrieved January 29, 2009, from http://www.businessweek.com/careers/content/dec2002/ca2002123_2774.htm.

What Can Organizations Do During Onboarding?

Many organizations, including Microsoft, Kellogg Company, and Bank of America, take a more structured and systematic approach to new employee onboarding, while others follow a "sink or swim" approach in which new employees struggle to figure out what is expected of them and what the norms are.

formal orientation program

Program that indoctrinates new employees to the company culture, and introduces them to their new jobs and colleagues.

A **formal orientation program** indoctrinates new employees to the company culture, as well as introduces them to their new jobs and colleagues. An orientation program is important, because it has a role in making new employees feel welcome in addition to imparting information that may help new employees be successful on their new jobs. Many large organizations have formal orientation programs consisting of lectures, videotapes, and written material, while some may follow more unusual approaches. According to one estimate, most orientations last anywhere from one to five days, and some companies are currently switching to a computer-based orientation. Ritz-Carlton, the company ranked number 1 in *Training* magazine's 2007 top 125 list, uses a very systematic approach to employee orientation and views orientation as the key to retention. In the two-day classroom orientation, employees spend time with management, dine in the hotel's finest restaurant, and witness the attention to customer service detail firsthand. For example, they receive hand-written welcome notes and their favorite snacks during the break. During these two days, they are introduced to the company's intensive service standards, team orientation, and its own language. Later, on their 21st day, they are tested on the company's service standards and are certified.[54] Research shows that formal orientation programs are helpful in teaching employees about the goals and history of the company, as well as communicating the power structure. Moreover, these programs may also help with a new employee's integration into the team. However, these benefits may not be realized to the same extent in computer-based orientations. In fact, compared to those taking part in a regular, face-to-face orientation, individuals undergoing a computer-based orientation were shown to have lower understanding of their job and the company, indicating that different formats of orientations may not substitute for each other.[55]

What Can Organizational Insiders Do During Onboarding?

mentors

Trusted people who provide employees with advice and support regarding career-related matters.

One of the most important ways in which organizations can help new employees adjust to a company and a new job is through *organizational insiders*—namely supervisors, coworkers, and mentors. Research shows that leaders have a key influence over onboarding, and the information and support leaders provide determine how quickly employees learn about the company politics and culture. Coworker influence determines the degree to which employees adjust to their teams. **Mentors** can be crucial to helping new employees adjust by teaching them the ins and outs of their jobs and how the company really operates. A mentor is a trusted person who provides an employee with advice and support regarding career-related matters. Although a mentor can be any employee or manager who has insights that are valuable to the new employee, mentors tend to be relatively more experienced than their protégés. Mentoring can occur naturally between two interested individuals, or organizations can facilitate this process by having formal mentoring programs. These programs may successfully bring together mentors and protégés who would not come together otherwise. Research indicates that the existence of these programs does not guarantee their success, and there are certain program characteristics that may make these programs more effective. For example, when mentors and protégés feel that they had input in the mentor-protégé matching process, they tend to be more satisfied with the arrangement. Moreover, when mentors receive training beforehand, the outcomes of the program tend to be more positive.[56] Because mentors may help new employees interpret and understand the company's culture, organizations may benefit from selecting mentors who personify the company's values. Thus, organizations may need to design these programs carefully to increase their chance of success.

Leadership

Leaders are instrumental in creating and changing an organization's culture. There is a direct correspondence between a leader's style and an organization's culture. For example, when leaders motivate employees through inspiration, corporate culture tends to be more supportive and people oriented. When leaders motivate by making rewards contingent on performance, the corporate culture tends to be more performance oriented and competitive.[57] In these and many other ways, what leaders do directly influences the cultures their organizations have.

Part of the leader's influence over culture is through role modeling. Many studies have suggested that leader behavior, the consistency between organizational policy and leader actions, and leader role modeling determine the degree to which the organization's culture emphasizes ethics.[58] The leader's own behaviors will signal to employees what is acceptable behavior and what is unacceptable. In an organization in which high-level managers make the effort to involve others in decision making and seek opinions of others, a team-oriented culture is more likely to evolve. By acting as role models, leaders send signals to the organization about the norms and values that are expected to guide the actions of organizational members.

Leaders also shape culture by their reactions to the actions of others around them. For example, do they praise a job well done, or do they praise a favored employee regardless of what was accomplished? How do they react when someone admits to making an honest mistake? What are their priorities? In meetings, what types of questions do they ask? Do they want to know what caused accidents so that they can be prevented, or do they seem more concerned about how much money was lost as a result of an accident? Do they seem outraged when an employee is disrespectful to a coworker, or does their reaction depend on whether they like the harasser? Through their day-to-day actions, leaders shape and maintain an organization's culture.

Reward Systems

Finally, the company culture is shaped by the type of reward systems used in the organization, and the kinds of behaviors and outcomes it chooses to reward and punish. One relevant element of the reward system is whether the organization rewards behaviors or results. Some companies have reward systems that emphasize intangible elements of performance as well as more easily observable metrics. In these companies, supervisors and peers may evaluate an employee's performance by assessing the person's behaviors as well as the results. In such companies, we may expect a culture that is relatively people or team oriented, and employees act as part of a family.[59] On the other hand, in companies that purely reward goal achievement, there is a focus on measuring only the results without much regard to the process. In these companies, we might observe outcome-oriented and competitive cultures. Another categorization of reward systems might be whether the organization uses rankings or ratings. In a company where the reward system pits members against one another, where employees are ranked against each other and the lower performers receive long-term or short-term punishments, it would be hard to develop a culture of people orientation and may lead to a competitive culture. On the other hand, evaluation systems that reward employee behavior by comparing them to absolute standards as opposed to comparing employees to each other may pave the way to a team-oriented culture. Whether the organization rewards performance or seniority would also make a difference in culture. When promotions are based on seniority, it would be difficult to establish a culture of outcome orientation. Finally, the types of behaviors that are rewarded or ignored set the tone for the culture. Service-oriented cultures reward, recognize, and publicize exceptional service on the part of their employees. In safety cultures, safety metrics are emphasized and the organization is proud of its low accident ratings. What behaviors are rewarded, which ones are punished, and which are ignored will determine how a company's culture evolves.

OB Toolbox: Best Practices

How to Maximize Onboarding Success

Onboarding plans should have the following characteristics:

- *Written down.* If your organization does not have a formal plan, write one yourself. It may not make sense to share it with others, but at least you will have a roadmap. If your organization does have one, refer to it on a monthly basis.
- *Participatory.* The power of onboarding programs is in the interaction. Try to get participation from others to the extent possible and engage in onboarding activities offered to you by the organization.
- *Tracked over time.* Keep in mind that research shows onboarding has a rhythm of 30-, 60-, 90-, and 180-day milestones. Be sure to track your progress.
- *Clear on objectives, timeline, roles, and responsibilities.* This will help ensure that role conflict and ambiguity doesn't detour your onboarding process.
- *Clear on scheduled key stakeholder meetings with managers and mentors.* Include a plan for
    1. going over strengths and development areas;
    2. hearing about potential problems and critical advice to help you be successful.
- Be sure to include a list of your key questions and things you need to help you do your job better.

Source: Adapted from Bauer, T. N., & Elder, E. (2006). *Onboarding newcomers into an organization.* 58th Annual Society for Human Resource Management (SHRM) Conference & Exposition. Washington, DC.

3.3 Visual Elements of Organizational Culture

How do you find out about a company's culture? We emphasized earlier that culture influences the way members of the organization think, behave, and interact with one another. Thus, one way of finding out about a company's culture is by observing employees or interviewing them. At the same time, culture manifests itself in some visible aspects of the organization's environment. In this section, we discuss five ways in which culture shows itself to observers and employees.

Mission Statement

mission statement

A statement of purpose, describing who the company is and what it does.

A **mission statement** is a statement of purpose, describing who the company is and what it does. Many companies have mission statements, but they do not always reflect the company's values and its purpose. An effective mission statement is well known by employees, is transmitted to all employees starting from their first day at work, and influences employee behavior.

Not all mission statements are effective, because some are written by public relations specialists and can be found in a company's Web site, but it does not affect how employees act or behave. In fact, some mission statements reflect who the company wants to be as opposed to who they actually are. If the mission statement does not affect employee behavior on a day-to-day basis, it has little usefulness as a tool for understanding the company's culture. An oft-cited example of a mission statement that had little impact on how a company operates belongs to Enron. Their missions and values statement began, "As a partner in the communities in which we operate, Enron believes it has a responsibility to conduct itself according to certain basic principles." Their values statement included such ironic declarations as "We do not tolerate abusive or disrespectful treatment. Ruthlessness, callousness and arrogance don't belong here."[60]

A mission statement that is taken seriously and widely communicated may provide insights into the corporate culture. For example, the Mayo Clinic's mission statement is "The needs of the patient come first." This mission statement evolved from the founders who are quoted as saying, "The best interest of the patient is the only interest to be considered." Mayo Clinics have a corporate culture that puts patients first. For example, no incentives are given to physicians based on the number of patients they see. Because doctors are salaried, they have no interest in retaining a patient for themselves and they refer the patient to other doctors when needed.[61] Wal-Mart Stores Inc. may be another example of a company who lives its mission statement, and therefore its mission statement may give hints about its culture: "Saving people money so they can live better."[62] In fact, their culture emphasizes thrift and cost control in everything they do. For example, even though most CEOs of large companies in the United States have lavish salaries and showy offices, Wal-Mart's CEO Michael Duke and other high-level corporate officers work out of modest offices in the company's headquarters.

FIGURE 15.10 Visual Elements of Culture

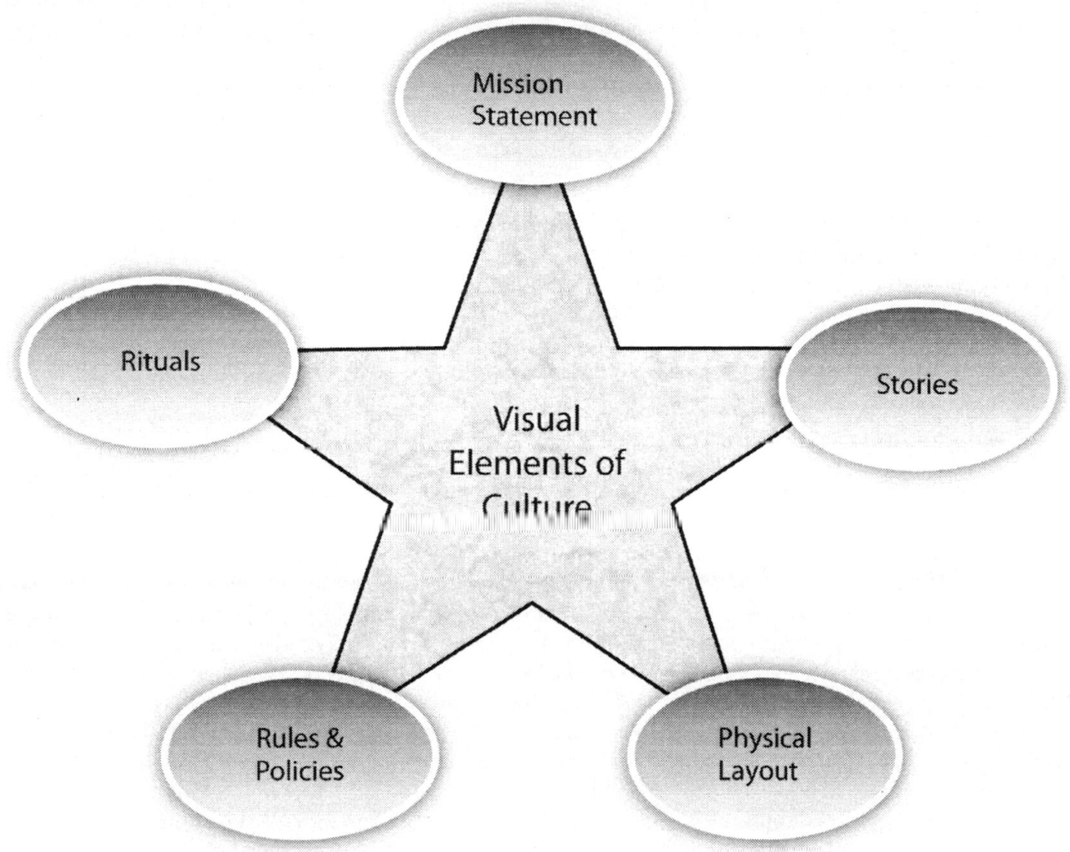

Rituals

Rituals refer to repetitive activities within an organization that have symbolic meaning.[63] Usually rituals have their roots in the history of a company's culture. They create camaraderie and a sense of belonging among employees. They also serve to teach employees corporate values and create identification with the organization. For example, at the cosmetics firm Mary Kay Inc., employees attend award ceremonies recognizing their top salespeople with an award of a new car—traditionally a pink Cadillac. These ceremonies are conducted in large auditoriums where participants wear elaborate evening gowns and sing company songs that create emotional excitement. During this ritual, employees feel a connection to the company culture and its values, such as self-determination, will power, and enthusiasm.[64] Another example of rituals is the Saturday morning meetings of Wal-Mart. This ritual was first created by the company founder Sam Walton, who used these meetings to discuss which products and practices were doing well and which required adjustment. He was able to use this information to make changes in Wal-Mart's stores before the start of the week, which gave him a competitive advantage over rival stores who would make their adjustments based on weekly sales figures during the middle of the following week. Today, hundreds of Wal-Mart associates attend the Saturday morning meetings in the Bentonville, Arkansas, headquarters. The meetings, which run from 7:00 to 9:30 a.m., start and end with the Wal-Mart cheer; the agenda includes a discussion of weekly sales figures and merchandising tactics. As a ritual, the meetings help maintain a small-company atmosphere, ensure employee involvement and accountability, communicate a performance orientation, and demonstrate taking quick action.[65]

FIGURE 15.11

Tradition is important at Wal-Mart. Sam Walton's original Walton's Five and Dime is now the Wal-Mart Visitor's Center in Bentonville, Arkansas.

Source: http://commons.wikimedia.org/wiki/Image:09-02-06-OriginalWaltons.jpg.

rituals

Repetitive activities within an organization that have symbolic meaning.

Rules and Policies

Another way in which an observer may find out about a company's culture is to examine its rules and policies. Companies create rules to determine acceptable and unacceptable behavior, and thus the rules that exist in a company will signal the type of values it has. Policies about issues such as decision making, human resources, and employee privacy reveal what the company values and emphasizes. For example, a company that has a policy such as "all pricing decisions of merchandise will be made at corporate headquarters" is likely to have a centralized culture that is hierarchical, as opposed to decentralized and empowering. Similarly, a company that extends benefits to both part-time and full-time employees, as well as to spouses and domestic partners, signals to employees and observers that it cares about its employees and shows concern for their well-being. By offering employees flexible work hours, sabbaticals, and telecommuting opportunities, a company may communicate its emphasis on work-life balance. The presence or absence of policies on sensitive issues such as English-only rules, bullying or unfair treatment of others, workplace surveillance, open-door policies, sexual harassment, workplace romances, and corporate social responsibility all provide pieces of the puzzle that make up a company's culture.

Physical Layout

A company's building, including the layout of employee offices and other work spaces, communicates important messages about a company's culture. The building architecture may indicate the core values of an organization's culture. For example, visitors walking into the Nike Inc. campus in Beaverton, Oregon, can witness firsthand some of the distinguishing characteristics of the company's culture. The campus is set on 74 acres and boasts an artificial lake, walking trails, soccer fields, and cutting-edge fitness centers. The campus functions as a symbol of Nike's values such as energy, physical fitness, an emphasis on quality, and a competitive orientation. In addition, at fitness centers on the Nike headquarters, only those wearing Nike shoes and apparel are allowed in. This sends a strong signal that loyalty is expected. The company's devotion to athletes and their winning spirits is manifested in campus buildings named after famous athletes, photos of athletes hanging on the walls, and honorary statues dotting the campus.[66] A very different tone awaits visitors to Wal-Mart headquarters, where managers have gray and windowless offices.[67] By putting its managers in small offices and avoiding outward signs of flashiness, Wal-Mart does a good job of highlighting its values of economy.

The layout of the office space also is a strong indicator of a company's culture. A company that has an open layout where high-level managers interact with employees may have a culture of team orientation and egalitarianism, whereas a company where high-level managers have their own floor may indicate a higher level of hierarchy. Microsoft employees tend to have offices with walls and a door, because the culture emphasizes solitude, concentration, and privacy. In contrast, Intel Corporation is famous for its standard cubicles, which reflect its culture of equality. The same value can also be observed in its avoidance of private and reserved parking spots.[68] The degree to which playfulness, humor, and fun is part of a company's culture may be indicated in the office environment. For example, Jive Software boasts a colorful, modern, and comfortable office design. Their break room is equipped with a keg of beer, free snacks and sodas, an XBOX 360, and Nintendo Wii. A casual observation of their work environment sends the message that employees who work there see their work as fun.[69]

Stories

Perhaps the most colorful and effective way in which organizations communicate their culture to new employees and organizational members is through the skillful use of stories. A story can highlight a critical event an organization faced and the collective response to it, or can emphasize a heroic effort of a single employee illustrating the company's values. The stories usually engage employee emotions and generate employee identification with the company or the heroes of the tale. A compelling story may be a key mechanism through which managers motivate employees by giving their behavior direction and energizing them toward a certain goal.[70] Moreover, stories shared with new employees communicate the company's history, its values and priorities, and serve the purpose of creating a bond between the new employee and the organization. For example, you may already be familiar with the story of how a scientist at 3M invented Post-it notes. Arthur Fry, a 3M scientist, was using slips of paper to mark the pages of hymns in his church choir, but they kept falling off. He remembered a super-weak adhesive that had been invented in 3M's labs, and he coated the markers with this adhesive. Thus, the Post-it notes were born. However, marketing surveys for the interest in such a product were weak, and the distributors were not convinced that it had a market. Instead of giving up, Fry distributed samples of the small yellow sticky notes to secretaries throughout his company. Once they tried them, people loved them and asked for more. Word spread, and this led to the ultimate success of the product. As you can see, this story does a great job of describing the core values of a 3M employee: Being innovative by finding unexpected uses for objects, persevering, and being proactive in the face of negative feedback.[71]

OB Toolbox: As a Job Candidate, How Would You Find Out If You Are a Good Fit?

- *Do your research.* Talking to friends and family members who are familiar with the company, doing an online search for news articles about the company, browsing the company's Web site, and reading their mission statement would be a good start.

- *Observe the physical environment.* Do people work in cubicles or in offices? What is the dress code? What is the building structure? Do employees look happy, tired, or stressed? The answers to these questions are all pieces of the puzzle.
- *Read between the lines.* For example, the absence of a lengthy employee handbook or detailed procedures might mean that the company is more flexible and less bureaucratic.
- *How are you treated?* The recruitment process is your first connection to the company. Were you treated with respect? Do they maintain contact with you, or are you being ignored for long stretches at a time?
- *Ask questions.* What happened to the previous incumbent of this job? What does it take to be successful in this firm? What would their ideal candidate for the job look like? The answers to these questions will reveal a lot about the way they do business.
- *Listen to your gut.* Your feelings about the place in general, and your future manager and coworkers in particular, are important signs that you should not ignore.

Sources: Adapted from ideas in Daniel, L., & Brandon, C. (2006). Finding the right job fit. HR Magazine, 51, 62–67; Sacks, D. (2005). Cracking your next company's culture. Fast Company, 99, 85–87.

KEY TAKEAWAY

Organization cultures are created by a variety of factors, including founders' values and preferences, industry demands, and early values, goals, and assumptions. Culture is maintained through attraction-selection-attrition, new employee onboarding, leadership, and organizational reward systems. Signs of a company's culture include the organization's mission statement, stories, physical layout, rules and policies, and rituals.

EXERCISES

1. Do you think it is a good idea for companies to emphasize person-organization fit when hiring new employees? What advantages and disadvantages do you see when hiring people who fit with company values?
2. What is the influence of company founders on company culture? Give examples based on your personal knowledge.
3. What are the methods companies use to aid with employee onboarding? What is the importance of onboarding for organizations?
4. What type of a company do you feel would be a good fit for you? What type of a culture would be a misfit for you? In your past work experience, were there any moments when you felt that you did not fit with the organization? Why?
5. What is the role of physical layout as an indicator of company culture? What type of a physical layout would you expect from a company that is people oriented? Team oriented? Stable?

4. CREATING CULTURE CHANGE

LEARNING OBJECTIVES

1. **Explain why culture change may be necessary.**
2. **Understand the process of culture change.**

4.1 How Do Cultures Change?

Culture is part of a company's DNA and is resistant to change efforts. Unfortunately, many organizations may not even realize that their current culture constitutes a barrier against organizational productivity and performance. Changing company culture may be the key to the company turnaround when there is a mismatch between an organization's values and the demands of its environment.

Certain conditions may help with culture change. For example, if an organization is *experiencing failure* in the short run or is under threat of bankruptcy or an imminent loss of market share, it would be easier to convince managers and employees that culture change is necessary. A company can use such downturns to generate employee commitment to the change effort. However, if the organization has been successful in the past, and if employees do not perceive an urgency necessitating culture change, the change effort will be more challenging. Sometimes the external environment may force an organization to undergo culture change. *Mergers and acquisitions* are another example of an event that changes a company's culture. In fact, the ability of the two merging companies to harmonize their corporate cultures is often what makes or breaks a merger effort. When Ben & Jerry's was acquired by Unilever, Ben & Jerry's had to change parts of its culture while attempting to retain some of its unique aspects. Corporate social responsibility, creativity, and fun remained as parts of the culture. In fact, when Unilever appointed a veteran French executive as the CEO of Ben & Jerry's in 2000, he was greeted by an Eiffel tower made out of ice cream pints, Edith Piaf songs, and employees wearing berets and dark glasses. At the same time, the company had to become more performance oriented in response to the acquisition. All employees had to keep an eye on the bottom line. For this purpose, they took an accounting and finance course for which they had to operate a lemonade stand.[72] Achieving culture change is challenging, and many companies ultimately fail in this mission. Research and case studies of companies that successfully changed their culture indicate that the following six steps increase the chances of success.[73]

FIGURE 15.12 Six Steps to Culture Change

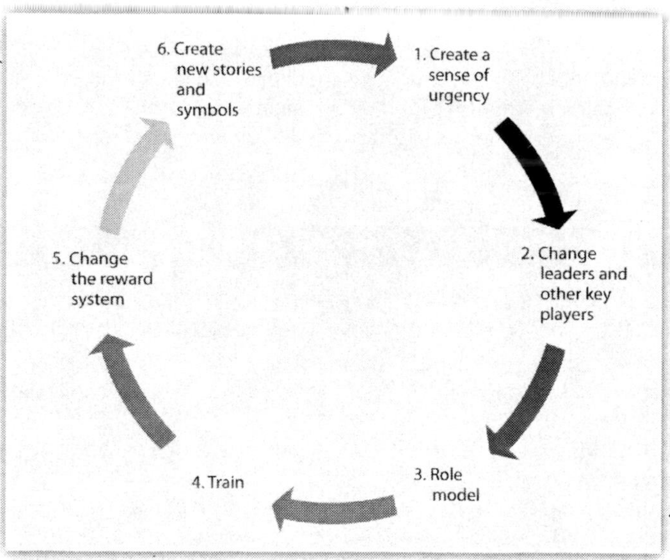

Creating a Sense of Urgency

In order for the change effort to be successful, it is important to communicate the need for change to employees. One way of doing this is to create a sense of urgency on the part of employees and explain to them why changing the fundamental way in which business is done is so important. In successful culture change efforts, leaders communicate with employees and present a case for culture change as the essential element that will lead the company to eventual success. As an example, consider the situation at IBM Corporation in 1993 when Lou Gerstner was brought in as CEO and chairman. After decades of dominating the market for mainframe computers, IBM was rapidly losing market share to competitors, and its efforts to sell personal computers—the original "PC"—were seriously undercut by cheaper "clones." In the public's estimation, the name IBM had become associated with obsolescence. Gerstner recalls that the crisis IBM was facing became his ally in changing the organization's culture. Instead of spreading optimism about the company's future, he used the crisis at every opportunity to get buy-in from employees.[74]

Changing Leaders and Other Key Players

A leader's vision is an important factor that influences how things are done in an organization. Thus, culture change often follows changes at the highest levels of the organization. Moreover, in order to implement the change effort quickly and efficiently, a company may find it helpful to remove managers and other powerful employees who are acting as a barrier to change. Because of political reasons, self interest, or habits, managers may create powerful resistance to change efforts. In such cases, replacing these positions with employees and managers giving visible support to the change effort may increase the likelihood that the change effort succeeds. For example, when Robert Iger replaced Michael Eisner as CEO of the Walt Disney Company, one of the first things he did was to abolish the central planning unit, which was staffed by people close to ex-CEO Eisner. This department was viewed as a barrier to creativity at Disney, and its removal from the company was helpful in ensuring the innovativeness of the company culture.[75]

Role Modeling

Role modeling is the process by which employees modify their own beliefs and behaviors to reflect those of the leader.[76] CEOs can model the behaviors that are expected of employees to change the culture. The ultimate goal is that these behaviors will trickle down to lower level employees. For example, when Robert Iger took over Disney, in order to show his commitment to innovation, he personally became involved in the process of game creation, attended summits of developers, and gave feedback to programmers about the games. Thus, he modeled his engagement in the idea creation process. In contrast, modeling of inappropriate behavior from the top will lead to the same behavior trickling down to lower levels. A recent example of this type of role modeling is the scandal involving Hewlett-Packard Development Company LP board members. In 2006, when board members were suspected of leaking confidential company information to the press, the company's top-level executives hired a team of security experts to find the source of the leak. The investigators sought the phone records of board members, linking them to journalists. For this purpose, they posed as board members and called phone companies to obtain the itemized home phone records of board members and journalists. When the investigators' methods came to light, HP's chairman and four other top executives faced criminal and civil charges. When such behavior is modeled at top levels, it is likely to have an adverse impact on the company culture.[77]

Training

Well-crafted training programs may be instrumental in bringing about culture change by teaching employees the new norms and behavioral styles. For example, after the space shuttle Columbia disintegrated upon reentry from a February 2003 mission, NASA decided to change its culture to become more safety sensitive and minimize decision-making errors leading to unsafe behaviors. The change effort included training programs in team processes and cognitive bias awareness. Similarly, when auto repairer Midas International Corporation felt the need to change its culture to be more committed to customers, they developed a training program making employees familiar with customer emotions and helping form better connections with them. Customer reports have been overwhelmingly positive in stores that underwent this training.[78]

Changing the Reward System

The criteria with which employees are rewarded and punished have a powerful role in determining the cultural values in existence. Switching from a commission-based incentive structure to a straight salary system may be instrumental in bringing about customer focus among sales employees. Moreover, by rewarding employees who embrace the company's new values and even promoting these employees, organizations can make sure that changes in culture have a lasting impact. If a company wants to develop a team-oriented culture where employees collaborate with each other, methods such as using individual-based incentives may backfire. Instead, distributing bonuses to intact teams might be more successful in bringing about culture change.

Creating New Symbols and Stories

Finally, the success of the culture change effort may be increased by developing new rituals, symbols, and stories. Continental Airlines Inc. is a company that successfully changed its culture to be less bureaucratic and more team oriented in the 1990s. One of the first things management did to show employees that they really meant to abolish many of the detailed procedures the company had and create a culture of empowerment was to burn the heavy 800-page company policy manual in their parking lot. The new manual was only 80 pages. This action symbolized the upcoming changes in the culture and served as a powerful story that circulated among employees. Another early action was the redecorating of waiting areas and repainting of all their planes, again symbolizing the new order of things.[79] By replacing the old symbols and stories, the new symbols and stories will help enable the culture change and ensure that the new values are communicated.

KEY TAKEAWAY

Organizations need to change their culture to respond to changing conditions in the environment, to remain competitive, and to avoid complacency or stagnation. Culture change often begins by the creation of a sense of urgency. Next, a change of leaders and other key players may enact change and serve as effective role models of new behavior. Training can also be targeted toward fostering these new behaviors. Reward systems are changed within the organization. Finally, the organization creates new stories and symbols.

EXERCISES

1. Can new employees change a company's culture? If so, how?
2. Are there conditions under which change is not possible? If so, what would such conditions be?
3. Have you ever observed a change process at an organization you were involved with? If so, what worked well and what didn't?
4. What recommendations would you have for someone considering a major change of culture within their own organization?

5. THE ROLE OF ETHICS AND NATIONAL CULTURE

LEARNING OBJECTIVES

1. **Consider the role of culture in ethical behavior.**
2. **Consider the role of national culture on organizational culture.**

5.1 Organizational Culture and Ethics

A recent study of 3,000 employees and managers in the United States confirms that the degree to which employees in an organization behave ethically depends on the culture of the organization.[80] Without a culture emphasizing the importance of integrity, honesty, and trust, mandatory ethics training programs are often doomed to fail. Thus, creating such a culture is essential to avoiding the failures of organizations such as WorldCom and Enron. How is such a culture created?

The factors we highlighted in this chapter will play a role in creating an ethical culture. Among all factors affecting ethical culture creation, leadership may be the most influential. Leaders, by demonstrating high levels of honesty and integrity in their actions, can model the behaviors that are demanded in an organization. If their actions contradict their words, establishing a culture of ethics will be extremely difficult. As an example, former chairman and CEO of Enron Kenneth Lay forced all his employees to use his sister's travel agency, even though the agency did not provide high-quality service or better prices.[81] Such behavior at the top is sure to trickle down. Leaders also have a role in creating a culture of ethics, because they establish the reward systems being used in a company. There is a relationship between setting very difficult goals for employees and unethical behavior.[82] When leaders create an extremely performance-oriented culture where only results matter and there is no tolerance for missing one's targets, the culture may start rewarding unethical behaviors. Instead, in organizations such as General Electric Company where managers are evaluated partly based on metrics assessing ethics, behaving in an ethical manner becomes part of the core company values.[83]

5.2 Organizational Culture Around the Globe

The values, norms, and beliefs of a company may also be at least partially imposed by the national culture. When an entrepreneur establishes an organization, the values transmitted to the organization may be because of the cultural values of the founder and the overall society. If the national culture in general emphasizes competitiveness, a large number of the companies operating in this context may also be competitive. In countries emphasizing harmony and conflict resolution, a team-oriented culture may more easily take root. For example, one study comparing universities in Arab countries and Japan found that the Japanese universities were characterized by modesty and frugality, potentially reflecting elements of the Japanese culture. The study also found that the Arab universities had buildings that were designed to impress and had restricted access, which may be a reflection of the relatively high power distance of the Arab cultures. Similarly, another study found that elements of Brazilian culture such as relationships being more important than jobs, tendency toward hierarchy, and flexibility were reflected in organizational culture values such as being hierarchical and emphasizing relational networks.[84] It is important for managers to know the relationship between national culture and company culture, because the relationship explains why it would sometimes be challenging to create the same company culture globally.

KEY TAKEAWAY

Without a culture emphasizing the importance of integrity, honesty, and trust, the mandatory ethics training programs are often doomed to fail. The values, norms, and beliefs of a company may also be at least partially imposed by the national culture.

EXERCISES

1. Have you seen examples of ethical or unethical organizational cultures? Describe what you observed.
2. Have you seen examples of national culture affecting an organization's culture?
3. What advice would you give to someone who was interested in starting a new division of a company in another culture?

6. CONCLUSION

To summarize, in this chapter we have reviewed what defines organizational culture, how it is created, and how it can be changed. Corporate culture may be the greatest strength or a serious limitation for a company, depending on whether the values held are in line with corporate strategy and environmental demands. Even though changing an organization's culture is difficult, success of the organization may require the change. Leaders, through their actions, role modeling, rule making, and story creation, serve as instrumental change agents.

7. EXERCISES

ETHICAL DILEMMA

Your company is in the process of hiring a benefits specialist. As a future peer of the person to be hired, you will be one of the interviewers and will talk to all candidates. The company you are working for is a small organization that was acquired. The job advertisement for the position talks about the high level of autonomy that will be available to the job incumbent. Moreover, your manager wants you to sell the position by highlighting the opportunities that come from being a part of a *Fortune* 500, such as career growth and the opportunity to gain global expertise. The problem is that you do not believe being part of a larger company is such a benefit. In fact, since the company has been acquired by the *Fortune* 500, the way business is being conducted has changed dramatically. Now there are many rules and regulations that prevent employees from making important decisions autonomously. Moreover, no one from this branch was ever considered for a position in the headquarters or for any global openings. In other words, the picture being painted by the hiring managers and the company's HR department in the job advertisements is inflated and not realistic. Your manager feels you should sell the job and the company because your competitors are doing the same thing, and being honest might mean losing great candidates. You know that you and your manager will interview several candidates together.

Is this unethical? Why or why not? What would you do before and during the interview to address this dilemma?

INDIVIDUAL EXERCISE

Impact of HR Practices on Organizational Culture

Below are scenarios of critical decisions you may need to make as a manager. Read each question and select one from each pair of statements. Then, think about the impact your choice would have on the company's culture.

1. You need to lay off 10 people. Would you
   a. lay off the newest 10 people?
   b. lay off the 10 people who have the lowest performance evaluations?
2. You need to establish a dress code. Would you
   a. ask employees to use their best judgment?
   b. create a detailed dress code highlighting what is proper and improper?
3. You need to monitor employees during work hours. Would you
   a. not monitor them because they are professionals and you trust them?
   b. install a program monitoring their Web usage to ensure that they are spending work hours actually doing work?
4. You need to conduct performance appraisals. Would you
   a. evaluate people on the basis of their behaviors?
   b. evaluate people on the basis of their results (numerical sales figures and so on)?
5. You need to promote individuals. Would you promote individuals based on
   a. seniority?
   b. objective performance?

GROUP EXERCISE

Recruiting Employees Who Fit the Culture

You are an employee of a local bookstore. The store currently employs 50 employees and is growing. This is a family-owned business, and employees feel a sense of belonging to this company. Business is conducted in an informal manner, there are not many rules, and people feel like they are part of a family. There are many friendships at work, and employees feel that they have a lot of autonomy regarding how they perform their jobs. Customer service is also very important in this company. Employees on the sales floor often chat with their customers about books and recommend readings they might like. Because the company is growing, they will need to hire several employees over the next months. They want to establish recruitment and selection practices so that they can hire people who have a high degree of fit with the current culture.

Working within groups, discuss the effectiveness of the following recruitment tools. Evaluate each recruitment source. Which ones would yield candidates with a high degree of fit with the company's current culture?

1. Newspaper advertisements
2. Magazine advertisements
3. Radio advertisements
4. Hiring customers
5. Hiring walk-ins
6. Employee referrals
7. Using the state unemployment agency

Next, create interview questions for a person who will work on the sales floor. What types of questions would you ask during the interview to assess person-organization fit? How would you conduct the interview (who would be involved in the interviewing process, where would you conduct the interview, and so on) to maximize the chances of someone with a high person-organization fit?

END OF CHAPTER CASE—GOOGLE

Google is one of the best-known and most admired companies around the world.[85] So much so that *googling* is the term many use to refer to searching information on the Web. Founded in 1998 by two Stanford university graduates, Larry Page and Sergey Brin, Google is responsible for creating the most frequently used Web search engine on the Internet, as well as other innovative applications such as Gmail, Google Earth, Google Maps, and Picasa. The envy of other Silicon Valley companies, Google grew from 10 employees working in a garage in Palo Alto to 10,000 employees operating around the world. What is the formula behind this success? Can it be traced to any single concept such as effective leadership, reward systems, or open communication?

It seems that Google has always operated based on solid principles that may be traced back to its founders. In a world crowded with search engines, they were probably the first company that put users first. Their mission statement summarizes their commitment to end user needs: "To organize the world's information and to make it universally accessible and useful." While other companies were focused on marketing their sites and increasing advertising revenues, Google stripped the search page of all distractions and presented Internet users with a blank page consisting only of a company logo and a search box. Google resisted pop-up advertising, because the company felt that it was annoying to end users. They insisted that all their advertisements would be clearly marked as "sponsored links." Improving user experience and always putting it before making money in the short term seem to have been critical to Google's success.

Keeping employees happy [illegible] take to heart. Google created a unique work environment that attracts, motivates, and retains the best players in the field. Google was ranked as the number 1 place to work for by *Fortune* magazine in 2008. This is no surprise if one looks closer at how Google treats employees. In its Mountain View, California, campus called the "Googleplex," employees are treated to free gourmet food including sushi bars and espresso stations. In fact, many employees complain that once they started working for Google, they gained 10 to 15 pounds. Employees have access to gyms, shower facilities, video games, on-site child care, and doctors. A truly family friendly place, Google offers 12 weeks of maternity or paternity leave with 75% of full pay, and offers $500 for take-out meals for the entire family with a newborn. All these perks and more create a place where employees feel that they are treated well and their needs are taken care of. Moreover, these perks contribute to the feeling that employees are working at a unique, cool place that is different from everywhere else they have ever worked.

In addition to offering many perks to employees, thereby encouraging employees to actually want to spend time at work rather than someplace else, Google encourages employee risk taking and innovativeness. How is this done? When a vice president in charge of the company's advertising system made a mistake that cost the company millions of dollars and apologized for the mistake, she was commended by Larry Page, who congratulated her for making the mistake and noting that he would rather run a company where people are moving quickly and doing too much, as opposed to being too cautious and doing too little. This attitude toward acting fast and accepting the cost of resulting mistakes as a natural consequence of moving fast may explain why the company is outperforming competitors such as Microsoft and Yahoo! Inc. One of the current challenges for Google is to expand into new fields outside their Web search engine business. To promote new ideas, Google encourages all engineers to spend 20% of their time working on individual projects.

Decisions at Google are made in teams. Even the company management is in the hands of a triad: Larry Page and Sergey Brin hired Eric Schmidt to act as the CEO of the company, and they are reportedly leading the company by consensus. In other words, this is not a company where decisions are made by the most senior person and then implemented top down. It is common for several small teams to attack each problem and for employees to try to influence each other using rational persuasion and data. Gut feeling has little impact on how decisions are made. In some meetings, people reportedly are not allowed to say, "I think…" and instead they must say, "The data suggests…" To facilitate teamwork, employees work in open office environments where private offices are assigned only to a select few. Even Kai-Fu Lee, the famous employee whose defection from Microsoft was the target of a lawsuit, did not get his own office and shared a cubicle with two other employees.

How do they maintain these unique values? In a company emphasizing hiring the smartest people, it is very likely that they will attract big egos that are difficult to work with. Google realizes that its strength comes from its small-company values emphasizing risk taking, agility, and cooperation. Therefore, Google employees take their hiring process very seriously. Hiring is extremely competitive and getting to work at Google is not unlike applying to a college. Candidates may be asked to write essays about how they will perform their future jobs. Recently, they targeted potential new employees using billboards featuring brain teasers directing potential candidates to a Web site where they were subjected to more brain teasers. Candidates who figure out the answers to the brain teasers would then be invited to submit resumes. Each candidate may be interviewed by as many as eight people on several occasions. Through this scrutiny, hiring personnel are trying to select "Googley" employees who will share the company's values, perform their jobs well, and be liked by others within the company. By attracting kindred spirits, selecting those who will fit in, and keeping potential misfits out, the company perpetuates its own values that have made it successful.

Will this culture survive in the long run? It may be too early to tell, given that the company is only a little over a decade old. The founders emphasized that becoming a publicly traded company would not change their culture, and they would not introduce more rules or change the way things are done at Google to please Wall Street. But can a public corporation really act like a start-up? Can a global giant facing scrutiny on issues including privacy, copyright, and censorship maintain its culture rooted in its days in a Palo Alto garage? Larry Page is quoted as saying, "We have a mantra: don't be evil, which is to do the best things we know how for our users, for our customers, for everyone. So I think if we were known for that, it would be a wonderful thing." As long as this mantra continues to guide the company's actions, we might expect the company to retain its distinctive personality, regardless of what the future holds.

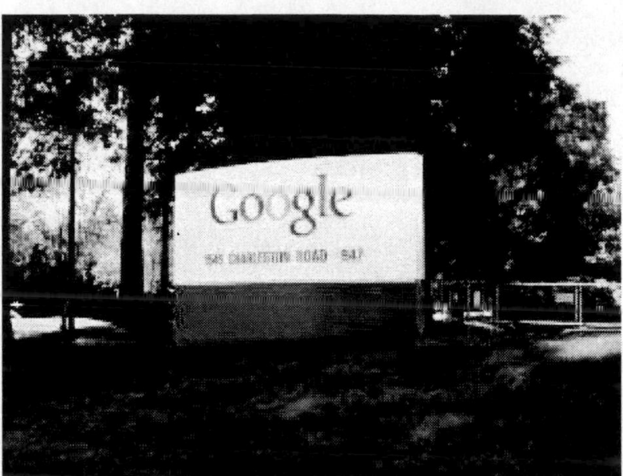

Source: http://en.wikipedia.org/wiki/File:Googleplex_Welcome_Sign.jpg.

Discussion Questions

1. Describe Google's culture using the OCP typology presented in this chapter.
2. What are the factors responsible for the specific culture that exists in Google?
3. Do you think Google's culture is responsible for its performance? Or does Google have this particular culture because it is so successful?
4. How does Google protect its culture?
5. Do you see any challenges Google may face in the future because of its culture?

ENDNOTES

1. Chatman, J. A., & Eunyoung Cha, S. (2003). Leading by leveraging culture. *California Management Review, 45*, 19–34; Kerr, J., & Slocum, J. W., Jr. (2005). Managing corporate culture through reward systems. *Academy of Management Executive, 19*, 130–138.
2. Barney, J. B. (1986). Organizational culture: Can it be a source of sustained competitive advantage? *Academy of Management Review, 11*, 656–665.
3. Why culture can mean life or death for your organization. (2007, September). *HR Focus, 84*, 9.
4. Kotter, J. P., & Heskett, J. L. (1992). *Corporate culture and performance*. New York: Free Press; Marcoulides, G. A., & Heck, R. H. (1993, May). Organizational culture and performance: Proposing and testing a model. *Organizational Science, 4*, 209–225.
5. Arogyaswamy, B., & Byles, C. H. (1987). Organizational culture: Internal and external fits. *Journal of Management, 13*, 647–658.
6. Schein, E. H. (1992). *Organizational culture and leadership*. San Francisco: Jossey-Bass.
7. Stegmeier, D. (2008). *Innovations in office design: The critical influence approach to effective work environments*. Hoboken, NJ: John Wiley.
8. Chatman, J. A., & Jehn, K. A. (1991). Assessing the relationship between industry characteristics and organizational culture: How different can you be? *Academy of Management Journal, 37*, 522–553; O'Reilly, C. A., III, Chatman, J. A., & Caldwell, D. F. (1991). People and organizational culture: A profile comparison approach to assessing person-organization fit. *Academy of Management Journal, 34*, 487–516.
9. Deutschman, A. (2004, December). The fabric of creativity. [illegible]
10. Deutschman, A. (2004, December). The fabric of creativity. *Fast Company, 89*, 54–62; Morris, B., Burke, D., & Neering, P. (2006, January 23). The best place to work now. *Fortune, 153*, 78–86.
11. Greene, J., Reinhardt, A., & Lowry, T. (2004, May 31). Teaching Microsoft to make nice? *Business Week, 3885*, 80–81; Schlender, B. (1998, June 22). Gates' crusade. *Fortune, 137*, 30–32.
12. Schlender, B. (2007, December 10). Bill Gates. *Fortune, 156*, 54.
13. Copeland, M. V. (2004, July). Best Buy's selling machine. *Business 2.0, 5*, 92–102.
14. Thompson, J. (2005, September). The time we waste. *Management Today*, pp. 44–47.
15. Nohria, N., Joyce, W., & Roberson, B. (2003, July). What really works. *Harvard Business Review, 81*, 42–52.
16. Probst, G., & Raisch, S. (2005). Organizational crisis: The logic of failure. *Academy of Management Executive, 19*, 90–105.
17. Westrum, R. (2004, August). Increasing the number of guards at nuclear power plants. *Risk Analysis: An International Journal, 24*, 959–961.
18. Thompson, S. (2006, September 18). Kraft CEO slams company, trims marketing staff. *Advertising Age, 76*, 3–62.
19. Boyle, M. (2004, November 15). Kraft's arrested development. *Fortune, 150*, 144; Thompson, S. (2005, February 28). Kraft simplification strategy anything but. *Advertising Age, 76*, 3–63; Thompson, S. (2006, September 18). Kraft CEO slams company, trims marketing staff. *Advertising Age, 77*, 3–62.
20. Erdogan, B., Liden, R. C., & Kraimer, M. L. (2006). Justice and leader-member exchange: The moderating role of organizational culture. *Academy of Management Journal, 49*, 395–406.
21. Sheridan, J. (1992). Organizational culture and employee retention. *Academy of Management Journal, 35*, 1036–1056.
22. Weber, G. (2005, February). Preserving the counter culture. *Workforce Management, 84*, 28–34; Motivation secrets of the 100 best employers. (2003, October). *HR Focus, 80*, 1–15.
23. Bolino, M. C., & Turnley, W. H. (2003). Going the extra mile: Cultivating and managing employee citizenship behavior. *Academy of Management Executive, 17*, 60–71.
24. Miles, S. J., & Mangold, G. (2005). Positioning Southwest Airlines through employee branding. *Business Horizons, 48*, 535–545.
25. Erdogan, B., Liden, R. C., & Kraimer, M. L. (2006). Justice and leader-member exchange: The moderating role of organizational culture. *Academy of Management Journal, 49*, 395–406.
26. Fitch, S. (2004, May 10). Soft pillows and sharp elbows. *Forbes, 173*, 66–78; ford, R. C., & Heaton, C. P. (2001). Lessons from hospitality that can serve anyone. *Organizational Dynamics, 30*, 30–47; Kolesnikov-Jessop, S. (2005, November). Four Seasons Singapore: Tops in Asia. *Institutional Investor, 39*, 103–104; Markels, A. (2007, April 23). Dishing it out in style. *U.S. News & World Report, 142*, 52–55.
27. Conley, L. (2005, April). Cultural phenomenon. *Fast Company, 93*, 76–77; Kuehner-Herbert, K. (2003, June 20). Unorthodox branch style gets more so at Umpqua. *American Banker, 168*, 5.
28. Ford, R. C., & Heaton, C. P. (2001). Lessons from hospitality that can serve anyone. *Organizational Dynamics, 30*, 30–47.
29. Christie, L. (2005). America's most dangerous jobs. Survey: Loggers and fisherman still take the most risk; roofers record sharp increase in fatalities. CNN/Money. Retrieved from http://money.cnn.com/2005/08/26/pf/jobs_jeopardy/.
30. Tennissen, M. (2007, December 19). Second BP trial ends early with settlement. *Southeast Texas Record*.
31. Hofmann, M. A. (2007, January 22). BP slammed for poor leadership on safety. *Business Insurance, 41*, 3–26.
32. Hofmann, D. A., Morgeson, F. P., & Gerras, S. J. (2003). Climate as a moderator of the relationship between leader-member exchange and content specific citizenship: Safety climate as an exemplar. *Journal of Applied Psychology, 88*, 170–178; Smith, S. (2007, November). Safety is electric at M. B. Herzog. *Occupational Hazards, 69*, 42.
33. Arogyaswamy, B., & Byles, C. M. (1987). Organizational culture: Internal and external fits. *Journal of Management, 13*, 647–658; Chatman, J. A., & Eunyoung Cha, S. (2003). Leading by leveraging culture. *California Management Review, 45*, 20–34.
34. Schneider, B., Salvaggio, A., & Subirats, M. (2002). Climate strength: A new direction for climate research. *Journal of Applied Psychology, 87*, 220–229.
35. Sorensen, J. B. (2002). The strength of corporate culture and the reliability of firm performance. *Administrative Science Quarterly, 47*, 70–91.
36. Charan, R. (2006, April). Home Depot's blueprint for culture change. *Harvard Business Review, 84*, 60–70; Herman, J., & Wernle, B. (2007, August 13). The book on Bob Nardelli: Driven, demanding. *Automotive News, 81*, 42.
37. Badrtalei, J., & Bates, D. L. (2007). Effect of organizational cultures on mergers and acquisitions: The case of DaimlerChrysler. *International Journal of Management, 24*, 303–317; Bower, J. L. (2001). Not all M&As are alike—and that matters. *Harvard Business Review, 79*, 92–101.
38. Jermier, J. M., Slocum, J. W., Jr., Fry, L. W., & Gaines, J. (1991, May). Organizational subcultures in a soft bureaucracy: Resistance behind the myth and facade of an official culture. *Organization Science, 2*, 170–194.
39. Lok, P., Westwood, R., & Crawford, J. (2005). Perceptions of organisational subculture and their significance for organisational commitment. *Applied Psychology: An International Review, 54*, 490–514.
40. Kerr, J., & Slocum, J. W., Jr. (2005). Managing corporate [illegible] *Management Executive, 19*, 130–138.
41. Schein, E. H. (1992). *Organizational culture and leadership*. San Francisco: Jossey-Bass.
42. Kiger, P. J. (April, 2005). Corporate crunch. *Workforce Management, 84*, 32–38; Rubis, L., Fox, A., Pomeroy, A., Leonard, B., Shea, T. F., Moss, D., Kraft, G., & Overman, S. (2005). 50 for history. *HR Magazine, 50*, 13, 10–24; Smalley, S. (2007, December 3). Ben & Jerry's bitter crunch. *Newsweek, 150*, 50.
43. Schlender, B. (1998, June 22). Gates' crusade. *Fortune, 137*, 30–32.
44. Mouawad, J. (2008, November 16). Exxon doesn't plan on ditching oil. *International Herald Tribune*. Retrieved November 16, 2008, from http://www.iht.com/articles/2008/11/16/business/16exxon.php.
45. Chatman, J. A., & Jehn, K. A. (1994). Assessing the relationship between industry characteristics and organizational culture: How different can you be? *Academy of Management Journal, 37*, 522–553; Gordon, G. G. (1991). Industry determinants of organizational culture. *Academy of Management Review, 16*, 396–415.
46. Judge, T. A., & Cable, D. M. (1997). Applicant personality, organizational culture, and organization attraction. *Personnel Psychology, 50*, 359–394.
47. Arnold, J. T. (2007, April). Customers as employees. *HR Magazine*, 77–82.
48. Kristof-Brown, A. L., Zimmerman, R. D., & Johnson, E. C. (2005). Consequences of individuals' fit at work: A meta-analysis of person-job, person-organization, person-group, and person-supervisor fit. *Personnel Psychology, 58*, 281–342; O'Reilly, III, C. A., Chatman, J. A., & Caldwell, D. F. (1991). People and organizational culture: A profile comparison approach to assessing person-organization fit. *Academy of Management Journal, 34*, 487–516.
49. Giberson, T. R., Resick, C. J., & Dickson, M. W. (2005). Embedding leader characteristics: An examination of homogeneity of personality and values in organizations. *Journal of Applied Psychology, 90*, 1002–1010.
50. Bauer, T. N., Bodner, T., Erdogan, B., Truxillo, D. M., & Tucker, J. S. (2007). Newcomer adjustment during organizational socialization: A meta-analytic review of antecedents, outcomes, and methods. *Journal of Applied Psychology, 92*, 707–721.
51. Bauer, T. N., & Green, S. G. (1998). Testing the combined effects of newcomer information seeking and manager behavior on socialization. *Journal of Applied Psychology, 83*, 72–83; Kammeyer-Mueller, J. D., & Wanberg, C. R. (2003). Unwrapping the organizational entry process: Disentangling multiple antecedents and their pathways to adjustment. *Journal of Applied Psychology, 88*, 779–794; Wanberg, C. R., & Kammeyer-Mueller, J. D. (2000). Predictors and outcomes of proactivity in the socialization process. *Journal of Applied Psychology, 85*, 373–385.
52. Fisher, A. (2005, March 7). Starting a new job? Don't blow it. *Fortune, 151*, 48.
53. Kim, T., Cable, D. M., & Kim, S. (2005). Socialization tactics, employee proactivity, and person-organization fit. *Journal of Applied Psychology, 90*, 232–241.
54. Durett, J. (2006, March 1). Technology opens the door to success at Ritz-Carlton. Retrieved January 28, 2009, from http://www.managesmarter.com/msg/search/article_display.jsp?vnu_content_id=1002157749; Elswick, J. (2000, February). Puttin' on the Ritz: Hotel chain touts training to benefit its recruiting and retention. *Employee Benefit News, 14*, 9; The Ritz-Carlton Company: How it became a "legend" in service. (2001, Jan–Feb). *Corporate University Review, 9*, 16.
55. Klein, H. J., & Weaver, N. A. (2000). The effectiveness of an organizational level orientation training program in the socialization of new employees. *Personnel Psychology, 53*, 47–66; Moscato, D. (2005, April). Using technology to get employees on board. *HR Magazine, 50*, 107–109; Wesson, M. J., & Gogus, C. I. (2005). Shaking hands with a computer: An examination of two methods of organizational newcomer orientation. *Journal of Applied Psychology, 90*, 1018–1026.
56. Allen, T. D., Eby, L. T., & Lentz, E. (2006). Mentorship behaviors and mentorship quality associated with formal mentoring programs: Closing the gap between research and practice. *Journal of Applied Psychology, 91*, 567–578.
57. Sarros, J. C., Gray, J., & Densten, I. L. (2002). Leadership and its impact on organizational culture. *International Journal of Business Studies, 10*, 1–26.
58. Driscoll, K., & McKee, M. (2007). Restorying a culture of ethical and spiritual values: A role for leader storytelling. *Journal of Business Ethics, 73*, 205–217.

59. Kerr, J., & Slocum, J. W., Jr. (2005). Managing corporate culture through reward systems. *Academy of Management Executive, 19,* 130–138.

60. Kunen, J. S. (2002, January 19). Enron's vision (and values) thing. *The New York Times,* p. 19.

61. Jarnagin, C., & Slocum, J. W., Jr. (2007). Creating corporate cultures through mythopoetic leadership. *Organizational Dynamics, 36,* 288–302.

62. Wal-Mart Stores Inc. (2008). Investor frequently asked questions. Retrieved November 20, 2008, from http://walmartstores.com/Investors/7614.aspx.

63. Anand, N. (2005). *Blackwell encyclopedic dictionary of organizational behavior.* Cambridge: Wiley.

64. Jarnagin, C., & Slocum, J. W., Jr. (2007). Creating corporate cultures through mythopoetic leadership. *Organizational Dynamics, 36,* 288–302.

65. Schlender, B. (2005, April 18). Wal-Mart's $288 billion meeting. *Fortune, 151,* 90–106; Wal around the world. (2001, December 8). *Economist, 361,* 55–57.

66. Capowski, G. S. (1993, June). Designing a corporate identity. *Management Review, 82,* 37–41; Collins, J., & Porras, J. I. (1996). Building your company's vision. *Harvard Business Review, 74,* 65–77; Labich, K., & Carvell, T. (1995, September 18). Nike vs. Reebok. *Fortune, 132,* 90–114; Mitchell, C. (2002). Selling the brand inside. *Harvard Business Review, 80,* 99–105.

67. Berner, R. (2007, February 12). My Year at Wal-Mart. *Business Week, 4021,* 70–74.

68. Clark, D. (2007, October 15). Why Silicon Valley is rethinking the cubicle office. *Wall Street Journal, 250,* p. B9.

69. Jive Software. (2008). Careers. Retrieved November 20, 2008, from http://www.jivesoftware.com/company.

70. Beslin, R. (2007). Story building: A new tool for engaging employees in setting direction. *Ivey Business Journal, 71,* 1–8.

71. Higgins, J. M., & McAllester, C. (2002). Want innovation? Then use cultural artifacts that support it. *Organizational Dynamics, 31,* 74–84.

72. Kiger, P. J. (2005, April). Corporate crunch. *Workforce Management, 84,* 32–38.

73. Schein, E. H. (1990). Organizational culture. *American Psychologist, 45,* 109–119.

74. Gerstner, L. V. (2002). *Who says elephants can't dance?* New York: Harper-Collins.

75. McGregor, J., McConnon, A., Weintraub, A., Holmes, S., & Grover, R. (2007, May 14). The 25 most innovative companies. *Business Week, 4034,* 52–60.

76. Kark, R., & Van Dijk, D. (2007). Motivation to lead, motivation to follow: The role of the self-regulatory focus in leadership processes. *Academy of Management Review, 32,* 500–528.

77. Barron, J. (2007, January). The HP Way: Fostering an ethical culture in the wake of scandal. *Business Credit, 109,* 8–10.

78. BST to guide culture change effort at NASA. (June, 2004). *Professional Safety, 49,* 16; J. B. (June, 2001). The Midas touch. *Training, 38,* 26.

79. Higgins, J., & McAllester, C. (2004). If you want strategic change, don't forget to change your cultural artifacts. *Journal of Change Management, 4,* 63–73.

80. Gebler, D. (2006, May). Creating an ethical culture. *Strategic Finance, 87,* 28–34.

81. Watkins, S. (2003, November). Former Enron vice president Sherron Watkins on the Enron collapse. *Academy of Management Executive, 17,* 119–125.

82. Schweitzer, M., Ordonez, L., & Douma, B. (2004). The role of goal setting in motivating unethical behavior. *Academy of Management Journal, 47,* 422–432.

83. Heineman, B. W., Jr. (2007, April). Avoiding integrity land mines. *Harvard Business Review, 85,* 100–108.

84. Dedoussis, E. (2004). A cross-cultural comparison of organizational culture: Evidence from universities in the Arab world and Japan. *Cross Cultural Management, 11,* 15–34; Garibaldi de Hilal, A. (2006). Brazilian national culture, organizational culture and cultural agreement: Findings from a multinational company. *International Journal of Cross Cultural Management, 6,* 139–167.

85. Adapted from ideas in Elgin, B., Hof, R. D., & Greene, J. (2005, August 8). Revenge of the nerds—again. *Business Week,* 3946, 28–31; Hardy, Q. (2005, November 14). Google thinks small. *Forbes, 176*(10), 198–202; Lashinky, A. (2006, October 2). Chaos by design. *Fortune, 154*(7), 86–98; Mangalindan, M. (2004, March 29). The grownup at Google: How Eric Schmidt imposed better management tactics but didn't stifle search giant. *Wall Street Journal,* p. B1; Lohr, S. (2005, December 5). At Google, cube culture has new rules. *New York Times,* Section C, Column 6, Business/Financial Desk, 8; Schoeneman, D. (2006, December 31). Can Google come out to play? *New York Times,* Section 9, Column 2, Style Desk, 1; Warner, M. (2004, June). What your company can learn from Google. *Business 2.0, 5*(5), 100–106.

Index

360-degree feedback 123

ability 17-22, 27-30, 42-46, 55-59, 70-71, 79-82, 87-91, 116, 120-122, 128, 133-145, 154-155, 160-172, 192, 196-203, 208-209, 250-252, 256, 266-270, 274-277, 282-285, 295-302, 306-309, 313, 322, 330-337, 355, 362

absenteeism 32, 47, 54-56, 74-88, 104, 112-115, 146, 202, 277

accommodating 33, 224-226

achievement-oriented leaders 276

active management by exception 281

active resistance 332

adequate notice 123-126

adjourning phase 191

affect-driven behavior 152

Affective Events Theory (AET) 151

affirmative action 35-37, 45-48

aggressive cultures 348

agreeableness 55, 60, 267

alarm phase 137

Alternative Dispute Resolution (ADR) 233

alternatives 27-30, 82, 112-113, 118, 128, 216, 225-231, 239, 243-247, 253-260, 277, 282, 292, 337-340

amygdala 137

analysis paralysis 246, 260

anchoring 250-252

arbitration 233-234, 239

artifacts 346-347, 370

assumptions 31, 93, 165, 200, 204, 221, 246, 254, 272-275, 289, 344-347, 355, 361

attitude 58, 71-78, 86, 90, 108, 143, 221, 306, 325, 354, 367

attitude surveys 77

attribution 65-66, 71, 289, 293

auditory learner 13-14

authentic leadership approach 286

authoritarian decision making [illegible]

autonomy 40, 70, 76, 84, 89-90, 114-118, 130-133, 146-148, 153, 190, 201-203, 212, 229, 273, 324-326, 340, 351-352, 365-366

avoiding 70, 103, 143, 148, 156, 168, 217, 224-226, 231, 242, 248-250, 254-257, 360, 364, 370

bargaining 216, 229, 236-239, 263, 308

BATNA 227-228, 234-236

behavior impression management 306

benevolents 98

bonuses 10, 35, 46, 90, 101, 105, 123-129, 134, 179, 259, 291, 349, 363

boundary spanners 311-313

boundaryless organization 322, 328-329

bounded rationality model 246

brainstorming 12, 198, 211, 248-249, 256-258

burnout 152, 159-160, 271, 292

case studies 16-17, 362

causation 17

central connectors 311-313, 318

centralization 323-326, 340

change 4, 9-12, 16-21, 28-34, 40-43, 53-57, 64-70, 86, 96-99, 104, 109, 113-117, 121-127, 134-140, 150-151, 156, 162, 168, 174-179, 193-199, 211-212, 223, 227, 239-242, 248, 256, 260, 274-276, 281, 287, 292-293, 302-304, 309, 318-343, 348-353, 361-370

charisma 160, 268, 280-282, 287-288, 292-293, 302

closure 229, 234-236

coalition tactics 304

coercive power 301-302

cognitive dissonance 153

cohesion 190, 194-196, 205, 212

collaborating 225-226

collective efficacy 160, 190, 196, 212

collectivistic cultures 40, 84

commitment 10, 34-35, 47, 71-88, 100, 112, 117, 121, 127-128, 134, 142, 159, 172, 187, 195-197, 205-212, 250-252, 260 263, 275-277, 281, 286, 292, 303-310, 334, 342, 350-355, 362-363, 367-369

communication 10, 19, 30, 40-43, 55, 93, 123, 159-187, 194, 201, 205-209, 221-223, 257, 282, 292, 306, 312, 322, 326-327, 339-342, 367

competing 130, 193, 197, 217-218, 225-226

compliance 32, 301-304, 332

compromising 20, 225

concessions 228-229, 233-235

conflict 19, 29, 47, 55-57, 76-78, 82-88, 139-140, 147-153, 159-160, 171, 190-194, 201-208, 212-239, 248, 259, 269-272, 289, 314, 326-327, 342, 358, 364

conflict management 171, 212-216, 223-226, 233-239

conformity 40-41, 52, 194, 297-299, 314, 319

conscientiousness 54, 59-60, 76, 134, 268-270, 290, 319

consensus 62-66, 71, 125, 163, 170, 255-263, 340, 350, 367

consistency 16-17, 65, 99, 244, 257, 324, 351, 357

consultation 304-307

contingent rewards 280-281

continuous schedule 104

control group 16, 307

correlation 16-17, 53, 59, 77-80

counterculture 351-352

creativity 9, 27-28, 37-40, 47, 70, 74, 87, 127, 134, 141, 149, 159, 166, 192-193, 197, 203, 212, 219-222, 236, 242, 247-249, 263, 268, 281, 292-295, 342, 362-363, 369

cross-functional teams 200-203, 322

crucial conversations 173, 187

cultural intelligence 42, 48

culture 1, 9-10, 18-26, 35-51, 66-71, 75, 82-85, 105-106, 110, 124, 128-131, 155, 165-170, 182-187, 201-204, 209-210, 226-228, 235-236, 249, 254, 258-260, 283-289, 293, 313-314, 319-324, 329-331, 336-370

data 16-17, 48-50, 59, 63, 73, 145, 162, 168, 208-209, 246, 304, 311, 339, 351, 367

datum 17

decision criteria 245-246

decision making 9-12, 18, 27-30, 41, 45, 66-73, 99, 133, 194, 205, 209, 249, 239-263, 272-274, 292, 304, 308-314, 323-324, 340, 348, 357

decision rule 243

decision trees 257

decode 164-167

deep acting 153, 160

deep-level diversity 29, 47

Delphi Technique 255-257

democratic decision making 272-273, 304, 310

dependency 133, 296-299

detail-oriented cultures 349

directive leaders 276

distinctiveness 65

distributive justice 98-99, 105, 110

distributive view 230

diversity 25-48, 107, 194, 202-203, 212, 257, 263-266, 308

divisional structures 325, 329

downward influence 307

emotion 67, 71, 136, 142-143, 149-155, 160, 178, 187

emotional intelligence 136, 151-156, 160, 267-270

emotional labor 135, 139, 146, 151-156, 160

Employee Assistance Programs (EAPs) 148

employee engagement 18, 23, 87

empowered teams 201-202

empowerment 43, 71, 84, 112, 116-118, 130-133, 212, 293, 323, 342, 349, 363

encode 164

enthusiastic support 332

entitleds 98

environmental 20, 60, 66, 75-76, 91, 136, 256-260, 265, 292, 298, 328-331, 352, 365

equity sensitivity 98, 109

escalation of commitment 250-252, 263

esteem needs 92-93, 106

ethnocentrism 43

exchange 28, 48, 69-70, 76, 87-88, 97, 109-110, 116, 134, 163, 180, 187, 225, 229, 233-235, 280-288, 292-293, 301-307, 313, 369

exhaustion phase 138, 156

existence 38, 91-96, 326, 350-351, 355, 363

exit interview 78, 86

expatriate 38, 69, 293

expectancy 96, 100-112, 210, 276

experimental design 16

expert power 301, 313

external attribution 65-66

external locus of control 58, 66-68, 101

extinction 103

extraversion 54, 60, 67-70, 76, 267-270, 293

fair hearing 123-126

faking 50, 59, 68, 153

false consensus error 62, 66

faultline 29-30

feedback 2, 21, 33, 43-46, 54-58, 76, 86, 90, 95-96, 101, 109-116, 120-125, 130-133, 172, 177, 192-198, 221, 248, 255-257, 266, 283-287, 293, 307-309, 319, 334, 355-356, 360-363

feminine cultures 42

field studies 16-17

filtering 165, 171

first impressions 64, 356

fixed-ratio schedules 104

flat structures 324-325

flexibility 4, 81, 113, 140, 181, 201, 229-232, 248, 289-290, 365

flow 13, 144, 149, 159, 169-170, 179, 205, 329

fluency
248

formal leaders
266

formal orientation program
356

formal work group
191

formalization
323-326, 340

forming
57, 76, 84, 92, 191-196, 202, 285, 306-307, 350

forming-storming-norming -performing model
191, 196

framing bias
250, 251, 257, [illegible]

functional structures
325-326, 342

gainsharing
128-129, 134

General Adaptation Syndrome (GAS)
137, 143

general mental ability
70, 79, 87, 267

generalizability
16, 63, 85, 289

genuine acting
153

glass ceiling.
30-32

goal commitment
71, 121, 134

grapevine
166-167, 187, 336

group
4-5, 10-12, 16, 20-22, 26-40, 44-48, 53, 63, 67-70, 76-77, 81-82, 87-88, 92, 106-109, 119, 126, 131, 136, 145, 155-160, 167-169, 187-213, 218-229, 233-242, 248-267, 271, 277-279, 283-284, 288-289, 297-299, 304-307, 311-325, 340, 348, 369

Group Decision Support Systems (GDSS)
257

groupthink
195, 200-206, 210-212, 216, 253-258, 263

growth
8, 27-28, 49, 73-76, 91-96, 116-117, 133, 148, 167, 178, 198, 331, 342, 350, 365

growth need strength
116

high-quality LMX relationships
282

hindsight bias
250-252

hygiene factors
93-96

hypotheses
15-17, 88

idea quotas
249

idea-generation tasks
198

importance
35, 40-43, 52, 67-70, 79-81, 89-90, 102, 106-107, 112, 121, 126-128, 133, 153, 245, 252, 262, 266, 273-277, 282-291, 298-299, 321-322, 335-336, 340, 349-350, 361-365

impression management
70-71, 285, 295, 300, 305-309, 319

individualistic cultures
40, 84, 340

individualized consideration
280-281, 287

informal leaders
266

informal work groups
191

information overload
139, 159, 166, 171, 187, 257

information power
301

ingratiation
110, 304-307, 319

innovative cultures
348, 352-354

inspirational appeals
304-307, 340

inspirational motivation
280-281, 287

instrumental values
52

instrumentality
100-105, 133

integrative approach
230-234

intellectual stimulation
280-281, 287

interactional justice
98-99, 106, 160

intergroup conflict
218-219, 239

internal attribution
65-66

internal locus of control
58, 70, 87, 309-310

interpersonal conflict
217, 239

intrapersonal conflict
217, 236

intuitive decision-making model
245-247

investigation
64, 71, 87, 133-134, 149, 160, 186, 212, 227 228, 234-236, 244, 263, 292-293, 319, 323, 342

jargon
167-168, 172, 187, 239

job characteristics model
114-118, 133

job enlargement
113-114, 118, 133

job enrichment
114, 118, 133

job performance
10, 47, 51, 58-60, 68-71, 78-90, 100, 113-117, 133, 142, 159, 180, 286, 293, 319

job rotation
113-114, 118, 133

job satisfaction
10, 16-18, 23, 34-37, 47, 51-53, 59, 70-80, 84-88, 109-116, 133-136, 148, 152, 160, 285-288, 308-310, 319, 324-326, 342, 355

job specialization
112-114, 118

journaling
12-13, 22, 125, 291

judgment based on evidence
123-126

kinesthetic learner
13-14

knowledge management systems
257

lab study
16

laissez-faire decision making
272-273

leadership
1, 12, 30-31, 38-44, 48, 54-56, 70-71, 87-88, 95, 109, 115-116, 133-134, 170-171, 182, 187, 191-192, 199-213, 241-244, 248, 263-293, 310, 315, 319-321, 336, 342-346, 357, 361-370

learning organization
328, 342

legitimate power
293, 300-302

legitimating tactics
304

levels of analysis 10-13

low-quality LMX relationships 282

majority rule 223, 255-257

Management by Objectives (MBO) 121

masculine cultures 42

matrix organizations 200, 326

mechanistic structures 320-329

mediation 160, 232-234, 239

medium 19, 77, 124, 148, 164, 172-178, 185-187, 218, 245, 274

mentors 29, 36, 355-358

merit pay 101, 126-129, 315

meta-analysis 16, 47-48, 70-71, 87-88, 105, 109, 133-134, 159-160, 212, 233, 239, 249, 263, 292-293, 297, 304, 319, 369

mission statement 358-361, 367

modular organization 328-329

motivation 9-10, 32, 38, 46, 54, 58, 66, 70-71, 80-83, 89-118, 122-133, 159, 198, 203, 208, 263, 267, 276, 280-281, 287, 314, 319, 342, 369-370

motivators 94-96, 126-127

need for achievement 91-95, 119, 133

need for affiliation 94-95, 224

need for power 94-95

negative affective people 56

negative emotions 136, 150-152, 332

negative reinforcement 103

negotiation 12, 31, 44-48, 215-216, 227-239

neuroticism 55-56, 60, 267

noise 164, 170

Nominal Group Technique (NGT) 255

nonprogrammed decisions 243-245, 250

nonverbal impression management 306

norming 191-192, 196

norms 30, 42-43, 85, 185, 192-195, 203-210, 231, 281, 297, 328, 343, 355-357, 363-365

OB Mod 104-105

offshoring 21, 48

onboarding 1, 354-361

openness 42, 53-54, 60, 67-71, 130, 248, 267-270, 290, 342, 354

operational decisions 244

organic structures 321-329

organizational behavior (OB) 7-9

organizational change 193, 309, 328-335, 339-342

organizational citizenship behaviors (OCB) 80

organizational commitment 34, 74-81, 87-88, 142, 172, 310, 355

organizational culture 1, 48, 70, 293, 338, 343-370

organizational structure 220, 321-342

originality 248, 268

outcome interdependence 199, 212

outcome-oriented cultures 348

outsourcing 21-23, 162, 167, 331

overconfidence bias 250-252

participative leaders 276, 289

passive management by exception 281

passive resistance 332

people-oriented cultures 283, 349

people-oriented leader behaviors 271

perception 26, 32, 48-71, 99-100, 116, 123, 165-166, 171-172, 180, 196, 216, 288, 297, 306-309

performance appraisal 122-127, 131-134, 249, 260, 293, 315, 336

performing 18, 46, 58, 77-84, 90, 96-104, 113-116, 122-123, 127, 134, 191-196, 202, 256, 272, 276, 285, 325, 331, 338, 355

peripheral specialists 311-313

persona 152-154

personal appeal 281, 304

personality 9-10, 48-62, 66-71, 75-88, 98-101, 109-110, 116, 125, 142-143, 152, 159-160, 166, 187, 199-202, 208, 212, 217, 221-224, 236-239, 263, 267-270, 274, 281-286, 291-292, 309, 319, 333, 339, 353-354, 368-369

physiological needs 92

piece rate incentives 127

political skill 309-310, 319

pooled interdependence 199

positive affective people 56

positive emotions 57, 149-153, 160

positive reinforcement 103, 109

power 1, 5, 9, 19, 26, 30, 41-44, 56, 67, 88-96, 106-112, 117-118, 130-134, 138, 167-170, 181, 187, 191-192, 200-202, 209-210, 216, 232, 239-245, 256, 263-266, 274, 285, 291-326, 334, 339, 354-359, 365, 369

power distance 41-43, 67, 88, 106, 110, 130, 134, 209-210, 314, 365

premortem 256

presentation 2, 115, 171, 197, 229, 234-236, 304, 320

pressure 12, 58, 70, 76, 113, 137, 141-145, 156, 194-195, 209-210, 233, 246-248, 254-255, 286, 304-307, 344

proactive personality
57-60, 71

problem-solving tasks
198

procedural justice
47, 99-100, 109-110, 134, 213, 293

process loss
197, 249

product development teams
200-203, 226

production tasks
198-199

profit sharing
112, 128

programmed decisions
243, 250

psychological contract
76-78

psychological contract breach
76

public relations
83, 180-181, 225, 358

punctuated equilibrium
190-193, 212

punishment
103-106, 266-268, 292, 301

rational decision-making model
245-246, 250

rational persuasion
304-308, 314, 340, 367

receiver
164-185, 262

reciprocal interdependence
199

referent
97-98, 105, 295, 300-307, 313, 318

referent power
302-307, 313, 318

refreezing
335-338

relatedness
91-96

relationship management
154

reliability
16-17, 369

resistance
137-138, 143, 193, 303, 307, 319, 332-342, 351, 362, 369

resistance phase
138

reward power
301-302, 308

ringi system
340

rituals
194, 359-363

role ambiguity
76-82, 139, 159, 276, 309-310, 324-326, 342

role conflict
76, 82, 139, 159, 217, 327, 342, 358

role overload
139, 145, 327

sabbaticals
140, 360

safety culture
[illegible]

safety need
92-93

sales commissions
128-129

satisfice
246

scarcity
236, 298-299, 309-310

selective perception
63, 69-71, 165, 171-172

self-actualization need
92-96, 116, 324

self-awareness
154, 291

self-directed teams
198, 202

self-effacement bias
62, 66

self-efficacy
57-60, 70-71, 119, 133, 154, 160, 212, 239, 319

self-enhancement bias
62, 66

self-esteem
57-62, 67-68, 76, 101, 116, 147, 194, 201, 268-270, 292, 333

self-fulfilling prophecy
63

self-managed teams
10, 134, 201-202, 212

self-management
154, 212

self-monitoring
57, 70-71, 239, 319

self-serving bias
65, 232

semantics
167

sender
164-185

sequential interdependence
199

servant leadership
280, 285-293

service culture
343-350

similarity-attraction phenomenon
29

skill variety
114-118

SMART goal
119-122

social awareness
22, 154

social loafing
47, 190, 195-196, 200-206, 210-212

social needs
92-93

social network analysis (SNA)
311-313

social networks
57, 70, 142, 311-320

span of control
324, 342

stable cultures
348, 352

stereotypes
30-32, 37, 45-47, 63-66, 71, 125-126, 169, 254, 330

stock option
129, 134

storming
191-196

storytelling
23, 172, 187, 369

strategic alliances
322, 328

strategic decisions
244

stress
9-12, 28, 32, 41, 48, 55-57, 69, 75-87, 99-100, 109, 113, 124, 133-160, 176, 194-196, 210, 219-222, 276-277, 282, 286, 302, 319, 331-333, 337, 342

stressors
74-76, 82, 87, 135-141, 148, 159-160, 283

strong culture
35, 350-351

strong ties
312-314

structural empowerment
116

subculture
351, 369

substitutability
298-299

supportive leaders
276

surface acting
153-154, 160

surface-level diversity
29

surveys
15-17, 26, 52, 74-78, 86, 163, 231, 360

sustainable business practices
20

tactical decisions
244

tall structures
324

task force
26, 200

task identity
115-118

task interdependence
196-199, 203, 212, 220-222

task significance
115-118, 133

task-oriented leader behaviors
271

team
4-5, 9-10, 27-35, 40, 47-48, 55-56, 60, 69-70, 81-83, 95, 108-111, 121-129, 134-136, 145-154, 168-173, 185, 189-213, 217-233, 237-241, 248-249, 253-256, 266, 277-281, 289-293, 301, 305, 322, 326-327, 334, 341-342, 349, 354-364

team contract
205-207

team-oriented cultures
349

telecommuting
7, 42, 77, 87, 115, 133, 148-149, 159-160, 360

terminal values
52

Thematic Apperception Test (TAT)
94

Theory X
272

Theory Y
272-273

time management
75, 145-148, 157-158, 315

top management teams
201-203, 239, 253, 263, 331

traditional manager-led teams
201

transactional leaders
280-281, 288

transformational leaders
280-281, 288

treatment group
16

triple bottom line
20

trust
76-80, 85-88, 121-122, 134-136, 147, 166, 175-176, 182, 201, 212, 217, 221-223, 230-231, 235, 281-292, 309-311, 336-339, 356, 364-366

turf wars
310, 326

turnover
7, 18, 23, 28-32, 49-50, 54, 59, 70-78, 82-88, 112-115, 119, 133-134, 142, 148, 159-160, 180, 187, 199-201, 222, 291-293, 319, 349, 355

type A personalities
142

type B personalities
142

uncertainty avoidance
41-43, 67, 340

unfreezing
335-336

unity of command
326

upward influence
306, 319

valence
100-105, 133

validity
16-17, 48, 59-60, 70-71, 87, 109, 133, 160, 191, 273, 292, 319

values
4, 15, 21-23, 29, 35-38, 42-45, 49-53, 57-62, 66-71, 76, 84, 99, 109, 140, 172, 192-196, 204-210, 217, 223, 231, 260, 266, 286-287, 291-292, 304-306, 344-370

variable ratio
104, 109

variables
15-17, 133, 159

verbal impression management
306

virtual teams
200-201, 212

visual learner
13

weak ties
312-313

whistleblowers
84

wildstorming
249